Study Guide for
EMERGENCY CARE
IN THE STREETS,
FIFTH EDITION

Study Guide for
EMERGENCY CARE IN THE STREETS, FIFTH EDITION

Nancy L. Caroline, M.D.

Adjunct Professor, Anesthesiology/Critical Care Medicine,
University of Pittsburgh School of Medicine,
Pittsburgh, Pennsylvania

Little, Brown and Company
Boston   New York   Toronto   London

ISBN 0-316-12893-7

Printed in the United States of America

SEM

Editorial: Evan R. Schnittman
Production Editor: Marie A. Salter
Copyeditor: Debra Corman
Production Supervisor: Cate Rickard
Cover Designer: Cate Rickard

In memory of Ron Rozin, M.D.

Contents

Preface

Training to be a paramedic has never been an easy assignment, but today it is more challenging than ever. Today's aspiring paramedic has to master a much larger body of information than his or her predecessor did ten or even five years ago. Accordingly, today's version of *Emergency Care in the Streets* has a lot more material than did *its* predecessors ten or even five years ago. The paramedic student contemplating the bigger, weightier version of *Emergency Care in the Streets* may well wonder, then, "How am I ever going to learn all that stuff?"

The *Study Guide for Emergency Care in the Streets, Fifth Edition,* was compiled to address that question. It is called a study guide because its purpose is just that: to guide the student in his or her study of the textbook material.

Each chapter of *Emergency Care in the Streets* begins with a list of *objectives*, an explicit description of the material the student is expected to have mastered by the conclusion of the chapter. Each one of those objectives is tested in the corresponding chapter of the *Study Guide.*

No two students learn in the same way or at the same pace. Each student will devise the learning strategy most suitable to his or her needs. Here is one approach that works for many students. For each chapter:

- First, read the objectives at the beginning of the chapter in the textbook.
- Next, browse through the questions in the *Study Guide.* See how many of them you can answer already, before you have even read the textbook chapter. That is, use the *Study Guide* chapter first as a **pretest** to assess how much you already know about the subject.
- Now go back and study the chapter in the text-

book until you feel confident you can meet the stated knowledge objectives.
- Return to the corresponding chapter in the *Study Guide* and work through the questions, using the chapter now as a **posttest.**
- Score your results by checking your answers against those in the Answers section of the *Study Guide.* You'll be surprised to see how smart you've become since taking the pretest!
- Finally, if there are questions you had difficulty answering, return to the textbook and go over the relevant material again.

Even proceeding slowly and methodically through the textbook and *Study Guide,* the student may feel overwhelmed every now and then by the sheer volume of new material. For that reason, we have included four Stop and Review sections in the *Study Guide*—opportunities to pause and consolidate what has been learned as well as to chase down some of the items that are slipping from memory.

Throughout the *Study Guide,* two areas of emphasis will become apparent. The first is vocabulary, for learning to speak the medical language is one of the more important skills the paramedic must acquire. There are few things more tedious, however, than memorizing lists of words, so vocabulary exercises have been presented in the form of puzzles, to make the task of learning new words less onerous. The second area of emphasis is clinical decision making under prehospital conditions. Case histories are presented to convey some of the flavor of "street medicine," so that the newly certified paramedic will have fewer surprises when he or she graduates from the classroom to the streets.

N.L.C.

Study Guide for
EMERGENCY CARE
IN THE STREETS,
FIFTH EDITION

QUESTIONS

1
Roles and Responsibilities of the Paramedic

1. Imagine for a moment that someone you care for—one of your parents, for example—has been seriously injured in a road accident. A crowd of bystanders has gathered. There is a lot of noise and confusion. An ambulance arrives at the scene, and two paramedics jump out of the vehicle and hasten over to treat the injured. What kind of people would *you* want treating your loved ones? What personal qualities and abilities should they possess? List 10 personality traits or capabilities you would like these paramedics to have.

   a.

   b.

   c.

   d.

   e.

   f.

   g.

   h.

   i.

   j.

2. Being a paramedic involves taking on a lot of new and serious responsibilities. List five responsibilities of a paramedic.

   a.

   b.

   c.

   d.

   e.

3. The step from EMT-A to EMT-Paramedic is, in some respects, a quantum leap. While many EMT-As are part-time volunteers who may make their living in other fields altogether, the vast majority of EMT-Ps are full-time professionals, for whom emergency care is a career. Accordingly, the training of an EMT-P is much longer and more rigorous than that of an EMT-A. And the EMT-P is therefore permitted to deploy a variety of skills that are not allowed to the EMT-A. List five skills that a certified paramedic, but not an EMT-A, may perform.

a.

b.

c.

d.

e.

4. No paramedic service in the United States may perform advanced life support procedures without medical control. What *is* medical control, and why is it necessary?

_____

_____

_____

_____

_____

_____

_____

_____

_____

_____

_____

_____

_____

_____

5. In fact, medical control consists of several different activities. Give an example of

a. Prospective medical control:

b. Immediate medical control:

c. Retrospective medical control:

6. One of the first things that is going to happen to you after you have finished your paramedic course and slept off the ill effects of your graduation party is this: YOU ARE GOING TO START FORGETTING. Most particularly, you are going to start forgetting the information and the skills that you don't *use* very often. The antidote to forgetting is review and practice. List three strategies you think will be helpful to *you* in fighting skill and knowledge decay.

a.

b.

c.

7. Hidden in the grid below are 25 traits or attributes of the perfect paramedic, written horizontally, vertically, and diagonally. How many of those traits can you find? We've found one of them for you and circled it: NEAT. Circle all the others.

```
S K N O W S H I S L I M I T S R
L I N K C A R I N G R O U S T Y
I C N O N S M O K E R C H I R E
C O L C W H O O R G A N I Z E D
E N G E L L I D A C U T E R E E
N F P R O F E S S I O N A L T C
S I F T O M O D E S T O R I S I
E D W I N I S A G I L E L U M S
D E C F C O U R T E O U S T A I
N N A I L I R E L I A B L E R V
I T L E A D E R C O M B E D T E
C A M D R A W N T I C C L E A N
E N D E D I C A T E D D I E S T
```

Among the words in the grid are words that fit into the blanks in the statements below. Fill in those blanks.

a. A paramedic who has passed the written and practical examinations of the National Registry of Emergency Medical Technicians is said to be

_____.

b. When a paramedic obtains official permission from a state agency to practice as a paramedic in that state, the paramedic is _____.

c. Being a _____ means conforming to the standards of conduct and performance in a given area.

2
EMS Systems

1. An EMS system is just that—a *system*, consisting of many components. If any one of those components is inadequate, the whole system can fail. List the links in the EMS chain.

   a.

   b.

   c.

   d.

   e.

   f.

   g.

   h.

   i.

2. Even the best EMS system will not benefit the average citizen if he does not know how to make use of it. List three things a member of the community needs to know in order to make optimum use of his local emergency medical service.

   a.

   b.

   c.

3. In the bad old days of "swoop-and-scoop" ambulance services, the function of an ambulance was solely to snatch the patient and move him as quickly as possible to the hospital. Today, by contrast, it is considered mandatory for ambulance personnel at least to *begin* stabilizing measures at the scene.

   a. Why is treatment started at the scene? (Give an example.)

   b. Give an example of a situation in which it is not feasible to stabilize a patient completely before transport.

4. Ambulance *transport* itself has also changed enormously since the swoop-and-scoop era. List two ways in which ambulance transport today differs from that 40 years ago.

   a.

   b.

5. You work for the Ambling Ambulance Co. and operate in a region that is served by four hospitals:

   a. Ambling Community Hospital is a 60-bed facility located right in town. It has five full-time doctors (including a general surgeon and an orthopedic surgeon) on the staff, who are usually present in the hospital until around 5 P.M. After hours, they have to be called in from home. The x-ray department and laboratory also operate only from 8 A.M. to 5 P.M., although the technicians can also be called in from home after hours. There are two operating rooms and a recovery room. There are no intensive care facilities. The emergency room is well equipped. After 5 P.M., it is staffed by a nurse and a physician's assistant, with a backup physician on call at home. The nurses' lounge always has coffee and doughnuts for hungry paramedics.

   b. Babcockle County Hospital is about 4 miles out of town. It is larger than the Community Hospital—around 200 beds—and has 24-hour physician coverage only in the emergency room and coronary care unit. X-ray and laboratory facilities operate around the clock.

   c. Doodleberry General Hospital is a 350-bed facility 15 miles from town. It has physicians on call in every department around the clock, although the specialists work only until around 5 P.M.; thereafter they have to be called in from home. Doodleberry General has a fully equipped emergency room, a coronary care unit, a general intensive care unit, and a regional burn center.

   d. University Hospital is an 800-bed teaching hospital affiliated with the medical school 30 miles away. It is a Category I hospital, that is, a comprehensive emergency facility capable of rendering advanced emergency and intensive care. It has a regional trauma center with a helipad on the roof.

In the course of a busy week, you respond to the calls described below. All of them occur right in town. Beside each case, indicate (by filling in the appropriate letter) to which hospital you would transport the patient.

_____ A 20-year-old woman, rescued at 10 A.M. from a house fire, with third-degree burns over 35 percent of her body.

_____ A 42-year-old man involved in a vehicular accident around midnight; he is found unconscious, in shock, with massive trauma to the chest.

_____ A 14-year-old boy who sustained a probable fracture to the forearm while skateboarding to school.

_____ A construction worker who fell 30 feet from a scaffolding and complains that he can't move his legs.

_____ A 51-year-old man who experienced crushing chest pains after supper.

_____ A 12-year-old girl who suffered an acute asthmatic attack during school.

_____ A cardiac arrest victim, with CPR in progress, who had collapsed during a morning meeting in his office.

_____ A 20-year-old man with abdominal pain suspected to be acute appendicitis.

6. According to the dictionary, communication is a process by which information is exchanged. In EMS, information must go back and forth in several different channels. Suppose you had to design the communications network for *your* EMS system. Who needs to be connected to whom? Draw a diagram to show those connections.

7. You have been appointed by the mayor to serve on your local EMS Council, which has just been established for the purpose of planning and implementing a comprehensive EMS system for the county. List five issues you will have to resolve before you can put the first ambulances on the road.

   a.

   b.

   c.

   d.

   e.

8. After one of the regular gripe sessions at your base, you decide to try to study the problems of your ambulance service more systematically and see if you can come up with ways of improving things. Describe a simple project you could undertake to evaluate some aspect of EMS in your area as a first step in improving the service you give the public.

3
Medicolegal and Ethical Issues

1. Hidden in the grid below are 25 words relevant to the material in this chapter, written horizontally, vertically, and diagonally. Find the hidden words and then use them to fill in the blanks in the sentences beneath the grid.

```
A F A M E D I C A L R E C O R D E D
B R A N C A V E T S U I C I D E R O
I M P L I E D C O N S E N T E N T G
D R A I S E D A R E D A P E L A M B
D A M A G E S T T U M M U L U S T I
E P U B L A I R I C I V I L S U I T
L E V I A T E M E A N S P I T R A E
E D M L I T T O P R O T O C O L B Y
G R U I S E T E R R O R E D N A E
A I R T O O N E G L I G E N C E N S
T I D Y Y U C K R O O S T S A Y D O
E V E R Y T U R K Y I S O E R F O R
D A R I N F O R M E D C O N S E N T
G O O D S A M A R I T A N K M O M I
E N L O G O O D C A R E F U L E E E
C E R T I F I C A T I O N E T E N S
H E A V Y B A S C O M P E T E N T T
```

a. The intentional and unjustified detention of a person against his will: _____

b. An action instituted by a private individual against another private individual: _____

c. Official written procedure for diagnosis, triage, treatment, or transport: _____

d. Compensation for injury: _____

e. Assumption on behalf of a person unable to give permission for treatment that he would have done so: _____

f. Act providing limited immunity from liability to persons who stop and help at the scene of an emergency: _____

g. Permission to practice a profession granted by a state agency: _____

h. The process by which a professional organization grants recognition to someone who has met its qualifications:

_____

i. The actions of a paramedic in the field are considered the _____ practice of a physician.

j. A patient's voluntary agreement to be treated, after being told about the risks and benefits of the proposed treatment: _____. In order to give that agreement, a person must be conscious and mentally _____.

k. A finding in civil cases that the balance of evidence shows the defendant was responsible for the plaintiff's injuries:

_____

l. To create in another person a fear of immediate bodily harm: _____

m. Wrongful act that gives rise to a civil action:

_____

n. Abrupt termination of contact with the patient without giving him sufficient opportunity to find another equally qualified health professional to take over his care:

_____

o. Legal obligation of public ambulance services to respond to a call for help in their jurisdiction: _____

p. Any act of touching another person without that person's permission: _____

q. An act of omission or commission that results in injury to a patient: _____

r. Two examples of reportable cases: _____ and _____

s. Two examples of coroner's cases: _____ and _____

t. Permission from the parent or legal guardian is required to treat a _____.

u. The paramedic's best defense against being sued: _____

v. The paramedic's best defense if he does have to go to court as a witness or defendant:

_____

2. If you have a copy of the Good Samaritan statute from your own state, use that statute to answer this question. Otherwise, refer to the Florida statute quoted in your textbook.

a. Who is protected under this act?

b. According to the act, what conditions need to be met for a person not to be held liable for civil damages?

c. What actions are _excluded_, either explicitly or by implication, from protection under the act?

3. If legal action is taken against a paramedic, the charge most likely to be brought is that of professional negligence, or "malpractice." To prove that the paramedic was negligent, the plaintiff must demonstrate four things. List the four elements required to prove negligence.

a.

b.

c.

d.

4. Failure to obtain consent before providing medical treatment may give rise to charges of technical assault and battery. What are the requirements for obtaining consent to treat the following?

   a. A conscious, mentally competent adult:

   b. A child:

5. Described below are six emergency calls. Circle the letter beside those calls in which it is permissible for a paramedic to give treatment without obtaining expressed consent from the patient. In those cases in which you may *not* treat the patient without expressed consent, describe what action you *would* take.

   a. A 12-year-old boy has fallen at school and sprained his ankle. The school authorities have so far been unable to reach the boy's parents.

   b. A middle-aged woman is found in cardiac arrest.

   c. A young man called for an ambulance after his 19-year-old girlfriend swallowed a large number of sleeping pills. She is awake and refuses treatment. She says, "Go away and let me die."

   d. A 20-year-old man has taken PCP (a psychedelic drug that often induces violent behavior) and has tried to gouge out his eyes. He is bleeding profusely from the face and screaming, "Don't come near me."

   e. A 14-year-old boy was knocked from his bicycle and run over by a truck. He is unconscious and bleeding. Both legs appear fractured. Bystanders do not know the boy or his parents.

   f. A 43-year-old man has crushing chest pain. His wife called for the ambulance. The man says he doesn't need an ambulance, he just has indigestion. His face is gray, and he is sweating profusely.

6. You are called to the scene of an accident in which a pedestrian has been struck by a car. The driver of the car says the pedestrian staggered out into the street in front of him. The pedestrian is now sitting on the curb. He has an obvious bruise on his head. He is unkempt and smells strongly of alcohol. He tells you that he doesn't want to go to the hospital. You suspect that the patient may not be competent to make that decision. List three things you can check to assess his mental competence.

   a.

   b.

   c.

7. When legal questions arise regarding the care given to a patient, the paramedic's best protection is a legible, thorough, accurate medical record (trip sheet). That record should include at least the following:

   a.

   b.

   c.

   d.

   e.

   f.

8. List at least four types of cases that paramedics or other health professionals in your state are required to report to the appropriate authorities.

   a.

   b.

   c.

   d.

9. Special precautions need to be observed in coroner's cases, lest you disturb evidence important to law enforcement officials. List four types of cases that are designated as coroner's cases in your state.

   a.

   b.

   c.

   d.

10. Ethics are the rules of right and wrong that we live by. Medical ethics are rules of right and wrong that guide the behavior of health professionals. State in one or two sentences what *you* regard as the guiding principle of your work as a paramedic.

    _____
    _____
    _____
    _____
    _____
    _____
    _____
    _____
    _____
    _____

11. At the end of this question, there is a secret message containing the most important lesson of this chapter. To decode the secret message, first fill in the words defined below. Then use the letters from those words to fill in the blanks in the secret message, according to the number beneath each letter.

a. Termination of contact with the patient before he has time to arrange

   other care ＿ ＿ ＿ ＿ ＿ ＿ ＿ M ＿ ＿ ＿
   　　　　　　 5　8　19　33　1　39　26　　22　40　11

b. Obligation to respond to a call in your jurisdiction ＿ ＿ ＿ ＿　＿ ＿　＿ C ＿
   　　　　　　　　　　　　　　　　　　　　　　27　30　6　28　24　36　25　15

c. Official written procedure for diagnosis, treatment, etc. ＿ ＿ ＿ ＿ ＿ C ＿ L
   　　　　　　　　　　　　　　　　　　　　　　　18　38　2　34　13　29

d. If a patient refuses treatment, he and a ＿ ＿ ＿ ＿ ＿ ＿ ＿ should sign the trip sheet.
   　　　　　　　　　　　　　　　　　　 3　21　20　23　9　7　10

e. Reflex that occurs when you touch the back of someone's throat ＿ A ＿
   　　　　　　　　　　　　　　　　　　　　　　　　　　 35　　41

f. World Health Organization ＿.＿.＿.
   　　　　　　　　　　　　 37　4　32

g. System of blood grouping named after a monkey ＿ ＿
   　　　　　　　　　　　　　　　　　　　　 14　16

h. Opposite of many ＿ ＿ ＿
   　　　　　　　　 12　17　31

Secret Message: ＿ ＿　＿ ＿ ＿ ＿ ＿　＿ ＿ ＿ ＿　＿ ＿ ＿　＿ ＿ ＿
   　　　　　　　 1　2　3　4　5　6　7　8　9　10　11　12　13　14　15　16　17

＿ ＿ ＿ ＿ ＿ ＿ ＿　＿ ＿ ＿　＿ ＿ ＿　＿ ＿ ＿ ＿　＿ ＿　＿ ＿ ＿ ＿ ＿.
18　19　20　21　22　23　24　25　26　27　28　29　30　31　32　33　34　35　36　37　38　39　40　41

4
Stress Management

1. Hidden in the grid below are 30 words or phrases related to what we have studied in Chapter 4. First find the words; then use them to answer questions a–g below. (Some words may be used to answer more than one of the questions.)

```
B A F F L E D A D I S P L A C E M E N T
A C C E P T A N C E L A I D Y M A T C H
R O O T A R N H E L P L E S S N E S S A
G O N N E R G C A L I R O P E N I N G S
A B F M V E E R Y I N G E R I A T O R S
I A U A L E R T I N G R E S P O N S E L
N N S R E G R E S S I O N E S S P A T E
I X I R N U I S A N C C O C H I R R I S
N I O I L O N O I F A T I G U E O I R A
G E N A E V U J J O B L O S S D J N E T
A T A G L E D T R U N K J A M I E S M W
T Y P E P R E S S E D H A B I V C O E O
O V E R R E A C T I O N Y S T O T M N R
R E P E L A T H R O N E I S P R I N T K
A M O U N T H R E E T R E A T C O I L S
D E M O T I O N S L A B I L E E N A R E
I T E M S N E W S W E A T L A T R I N E
O N T H E G O A L A R M R E A C T I O N
S H E A D A C H E S T L A N D E N I A L
```

a. Definitions:

(1) The redirection of an emotion from the original object to a more acceptable object: _____

(2) Attributing your own feelings to someone else: _____

(3) Nonspecific response of the body to any demand made on it: _____

14

(4) Reaction in which a startled animal stops all activity and turns toward the stimulus that startled it: _____

(5) A way of dealing with unwanted data by ignoring it: _____

(6) First stage of an acute stress response:

_____

(7) Return to an earlier mode of behavior:

_____

(8) Exhaustion of physical or emotional strength from chronic stress:

_____

(9) Unconscious translation of an emotional conflict into a physical symptom:

_____

b. Among the words or phrases hidden in the grid are six things that can TRIGGER STRESS in many individuals. List those six potential stress triggers.

(1)

(2)

(3)

(4)

(5)

(6)

c. List five situations, not included in the puzzle, that you personally find stressful.

(1)

(2)

(3)

(4)

(5)

d. Among the words or phrases hidden in the puzzle are six potential REACTIONS of patients or others TO ILLNESS OR INJURY. List the reactions you found in the puzzle.

(1)

(2)

(3)

(4)

(5)

(6)

e. Also among the words in the puzzle are three REACTIONS sometimes seen IN BYSTANDERS AT A MASS CASUALTY INCIDENT. List those reactions.

(1)

(2)

(3)

f. People dealing with loss usually proceed through five STAGES OF GRIEF, which are all named in the puzzle. List them.

(1)

(2)

(3)

(4)

(5)

g. The grid also contains six SYMPTOMS OF IMPENDING BURNOUT. List them.

   (1)

   (2)

   (3)

   (4)

   (5)

   (6)

h. List two more symptoms of impending burnout that were not mentioned in the puzzle.

   (1)

   (2)

2. When faced with a perceived threat, the body reacts with a "fight-or-flight" response. From your own experience, list four signs or symptoms of the fight-or-flight response.

   a.

   b.

   c.

   d.

3. In the following paragraphs are described behaviors of different individuals under stress. For each description, fill in the defense mechanism that the individual is apparently using.

   a. Your partner has been irritable and ill-tempered ever since he arrived for work today. You are doing your best to keep a low profile and not annoy him further, but nonetheless he snaps at you, "You sure are in a lousy mood today." Your partner is showing the mechanism of defense known as _____ _____.

   b. You are called by a very distraught woman to tend to her husband, who has been having chest pain. When you reach the patient's house, he says, "I can't understand why my wife called for an ambulance; I'm just having a little indigestion, that's all." His face is gray, and he is sweating profusely. He is using the psychologic defense mechanism known as _____.

   c. An 18-year-old woman is extricated from a wrecked automobile in which her boyfriend remains trapped. She says she has lost all sensation in her hands and feet. She does not appear terribly upset about that fact, and you cannot find any signs of injury on her body. She is using the psychologic defense mechanism called _____.

   d. At the scene of an accident, you are trying to extricate an entrapped front-seat passenger who is seriously injured. The driver, who has not suffered any apparent injury, is giving you a hard time. "Be careful, will you! #&!@! Don't drop her! Watch what you're doing!!" He is very aggressive toward you, but you realize that his behavior is simply a _____ of the anger he feels toward himself for having caused the injury to his passenger.

4. You are among the first ambulance personnel to reach the scene of a train derailment involving at least 60 casualties. There is a lot of panic and confusion at the scene. Among the bystanders you encounter are the following:

   A. A man in his late 20s who runs over to you and volunteers to help. He says he was a medic in the army. He talks very fast, makes wisecracks, runs over to another ambulance crew, then back to you.

   B. Another former medic who is standing off to the side looking very pale. He is sweating profusely and says he feels sick to his stomach.

   C. A young woman who is running among the casualties screaming, "Oh my God, oh my God! Dead! Dead! Dead! Everyone's dead! Oh my God!"

   D. A young woman who is sitting near the wrecked train, staring straight ahead.

   E. A young man who complains that he is paralyzed in both arms.

a. Which of the bystanders described could you recruit to help you out with various tasks at the scene?

b. Describe how you would deal with each of the other bystanders.

_____

_____

_____

_____

_____

_____

_____

_____

_____

_____

_____

_____

_____

_____

_____

5. You are called to the scene of a bad road accident in which a semitrailer plowed head-on into a passenger car. The driver of the car is pinned inside his vehicle, very seriously injured. You manage to gain access to the victim and start tending to him while you await help in what will be a lengthy extrication procedure. The patient is still conscious, and he asks you, "Am I going to die?" There is, in fact, a high probability that he *will* die. Describe how you would reply to this patient's question.

_____

_____

_____

_____

_____

_____

_____

_____

6. You are called to a suburban neighborhood where a 5-year-old boy ran out into the street and was struck by a car. The child's parents are at the scene and are being restrained by police. The child has sustained severe head injuries, and he goes into cardiac arrest only moments after you arrive. You start CPR and do all you can, but nothing seems to help. Meanwhile, your medical director arrives at the scene and, after assessing the situation, instructs you to stop CPR; she pronounces the child dead. Describe what measures you would take at that point to help the child's parents cope with their loss.

_____

_____

_____

_____

_____

_____

_____

_____

_____

7. As the previous two questions suggest, being a paramedic is a stressful job. For some, the stresses are too much, and burnout occurs. The time to start thinking about burnout—and about how to prevent it—is now, during your training; for now is the time to develop strategies that will keep burnout from happening to you. Describe some of the steps *you* plan to take to keep from burning out as a paramedic.

_____

_____

_____

_____

_____

_____

_____

_____

_____

_____

_____

_____

_____

_____

5
Medical Terminology

1. Refer to the root words you learned in this chapter to decipher the meaning of the following medical terms:

   a. Adenoma: _____

   b. Thoracotomy: _____

   c. Hypoglycemia: _____

   d. Oliguria: _____

   e. Anesthesia: _____

   f. Dyspnea: _____

   g. Bradycardia: _____

   h. Hemiparesis: _____

   i. Dermatitis: _____

   j. Gastrectomy: _____

   k. Leukopenia: _____

   l. Intercostal: _____

   m. Polycythemia: _____

   n. Endocardial: _____

   o. Perinephric: _____

   p. Hemorrhage: _____

   q. Retropharyngeal: _____

   r. Transtracheal: _____

   s. Hepatomegaly: _____

   t. Neuropathy: _____

2. Use a medical dictionary to look up the following words, and write the dictionary definition beside each word:

   a. Anasarca:

   b. Cryptorchidism:

   c. Diplopia:

   d. Hansen's disease:

   e. Kehr's sign:

3. Hidden in the puzzle below are 23 medical terms constructed from root words learned in this chapter. First try to find the hidden terms. Then use the terms you have found to fill in the definitions that follow the puzzle.

```
S P E R I C A R D I T I S I D E D
P E P P Y P O R C H I E C T O M Y
C H O L E C Y S T I T I S O R E S
E L L I S Y A R T H R O S I S M E
P A Y E U S M A L L R E D D O G S
H A U L B T I N H E P A T O M A T
A R R M D O N G R U R A L N E P H
L A I Y E S T I N K R D I G D N E
A L A A R C O O L O S E S P I E S
L U L L M O R G M C T N M E A A I
G O N G A P E R D Y S I M I L E A
I R D I L Y S A N T O T T T A K E
A Q U A D R I P L E G I A I D E D
R H I N O R R H E A R S A S S I S
P A S T A C H Y C A R D I A L E R
```

Definitions:

a. Cutting into a vein: _____

b. Inflammation of the gallbladder: _____

c. Excessive urination: _____

d. Visualization of blood vessels: _____

e. Pain in the joints: _____

f. Inflammation of the membrane that surrounds the heart: _____

g. White blood cell: _____

h. Tumor of the liver: _____

i. Looking at (inside) the bladder: _____

j. Runny nose: _____

k. Paralysis of all four extremities: _____

l. Absence of breathing: _____

m. Inflammation of the ear: _____

n. Rapid heart rate: _____

o. Surgical removal of a testicle: _____

p. Headache: _____

q. Disorder of sensation: _____

r. Urine (products) in the blood: _____

s. Beneath the skin: _____

t. Pain in muscles: _____

u. In the middle posterior area: _____

v. Inflammation of a gland: _____

w. Disease of joints: _____

4. Use the Glossary of Common Medical Abbreviations at the back of your textbook to help you solve this crossword puzzle.

ACROSS

1. Chronic obstructive pulmonary disease
4. Self-contained underwater breathing apparatus
9. Venereal disease
10. Left eye
12. Intramuscular
13. Past medical history
15. Cancer
16. Acquired immunodeficiency syndrome
18. Distal interphalangeal joint
21. Delirium tremens
22. Immediately
24. As needed
25. Normal sinus rhythm
27. Last menstrual period
29. Aspirin
30. Liter
31. Carbon monoxide
33. Esophageal obturator airway
35. See 6 down
37. Right upper quadrant
39. Situation normal, all fouled up
41. Complete blood count
42. Gonorrhea
43. Ringer's lactate
45. Transient ischemic attack
47. Ventricular tachycardia
48. Mobile intensive care unit
50. Normal saline
51. Four times a day
52. By mouth
53. Millimeters of mercury

DOWN

1. Cerebrovascular accident
2. Overdose
3. Dead on arrival
5. Central nervous system
6. Twice a day
7. Acute myocardial infarction
8. See 12 across
11. Sudden infant death syndrome
14. Hematocrit
15. Central venous pressure
17. Deep tendon reflex
19. Paroxysmal supraventricular tachycardia
20. Within normal limits
23. As much as desired
25. Nothing by mouth
26. See 10 across
28. Milliequivalent
29. As soon as possible
32. Operating room
34. Arteriosclerotic cardiovascular disease
35. Blue Cross
36. Discontinue
38. Urinary tract infection
40. Upper respiratory infection
44. Left costal margin
46. Water
48. Morphine (alternative term)
49. Ultramodern
50. Nasogastric

5. Concealed in the grid below are 17 terms relating to location, position, and motion that we learned in this chapter. Find the hidden words, and then use them to fill in the blanks in the sentences that follow.

```
S P A B D U C T I O N L Y
P R I N F E R I O R I F A
R O B O T U M P I R E L R
O N S U P E R I O R M E E
X E X T R A R I D E E X C
I C E R E C T I L L D I U
M L A T E R A L O T I O M
A D D U C T I O N R A N B
L S U P I N E O P O L I E
A D I S T A L K R I P E N
S E X T E N S I O N C E T
```

a. A person lying faceup on his back is lying
_____.

b. The wrist is _____ to the elbow.

c. When your leg is straight, it is in
_____.

d. A person standing upright is standing
_____.

e. Moving your arm *away* from your body is called _____.

f. The nose is _____
to the left ear.

g. The nose is _____ to the toes.

h. The hips are _____
to the lips.

i. The umbilicus is in the _____
of the body, on the _____
surface.

j. A person who is lying down is _____
_____. If he is lying face-down, he is said to be _____
_____.

k. Movement of an extremity *toward* the midline of the body is called _____.

l. The act of bending an extremity at a joint is called _____.

m. The heel is _____ to the toe.

n. The knee is _____ to the ankle.

o. The shoulder is _____ to the spine.

6. Use the diagram below to answer the following questions.

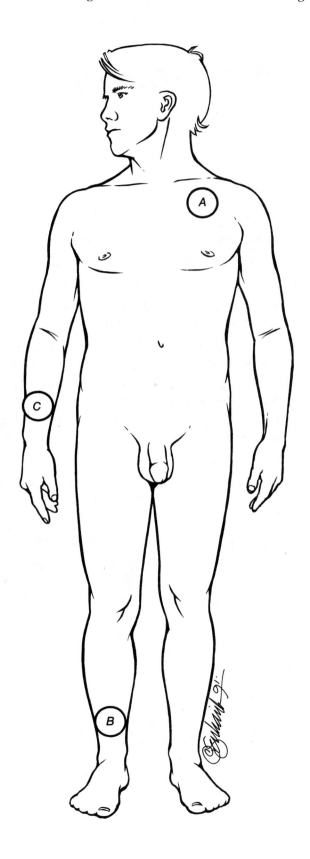

a. Describe the position of the wound at point A.

b. Describe the position of the wound at point B.

c. Describe the position of the wound at point C.

d. Mark an "X" on the diagram corresponding to a point about 2 fingerbreadths superior and 2 fingerbreadths lateral to the umbilicus on the left.

e. Mark a "Y" on the diagram corresponding to a point on the anteriomedial surface of the proximal right thigh.

f. Mark a "Z" on the diagram corresponding to a point on the lateral aspect of the left leg 2 fingerbreadths inferior to the knee.

6
The Primary Survey: Overview

1. In responding to emergencies outside the hospital, the paramedic must always proceed according to a standard set of priorities. Why is that list of priorities necessary in emergency care in general and in *prehospital* emergency care in particular?

   _____

   _____

   _____

   _____

   _____

   _____

   _____

   _____

   _____

2. You are called to the scene of a road accident in which a semitrailer jackknifed off the road into a ravine. The bystander who reported the accident from a highway telephone was too agitated to give much information, but he did mention that a passenger was lying on the ground beside the truck and "not moving at all." When you reach the scene, you will perform all of the following actions. Arrange the actions in the sequence in which you will carry them out.

a. Check the passenger for a pulse; if he has no pulse, start external chest compressions.

b. Stabilize any fractures among the casualties.

c. Determine whether you need backup support.

d. Examine the scene closely to determine the possible mechanisms of injury.

e. Determine whether there are any hazards to the rescuers.

f. Determine whether the passenger is breathing; if not, start artifical ventilation.

g. Do a head-to-toe physical examination of each casualty.

h. Package the casualties for transport.

i. Determine whether you will need special equipment to gain access to the driver of the truck.

j. Make sure the passenger has an open airway.

k. Control any bleeding you detect in the passenger.

l. Take a detailed history from the driver.

(1) ____   (5) ____   (9) ____

(2) ____   (6) ____   (10) ____

(3) ____   (7) ____   (11) ____

(4) ____   (8) ____   (12) ____

3. With regard to potential hazards at the scene, list at least three questions you need to answer for yourself at the accident described in question 2 before you approach the disabled vehicle and start treating the casualties.

   a.

   b.

   c.

4. It is useful to consider the dying process as a series of steps or way stations along a pathway from life to death. List the way stations along the pathway from life to death, and put an asterisk beside those steps where it is possible to take measures to reverse the dying process.

   a.

   b.

   c.

   d.

   e.

   f.

5. A gas leak in the downtown area led to a large explosion. You are called to the scene of the explosion, in which several people were injured by flying glass and debris. There is a great deal of noise and confusion at the scene. A middle-aged woman is lying unconscious on the sidewalk. She is covered with blood. Arrange the following steps of her management in the correct sequence.

   a. Determine if she has a pulse; if not, start external chest compressions.

   b. Find the source of bleeding, and control the bleeding.

   c. Open her airway.

   d. Cover any wounds with sterile dressings.

   e. Determine whether she is breathing; if not, start artificial ventilation.

      (1) ——

      (2) ——

      (3) ——

      (4) ——

      (5) ——

6. At the end of this question there is a coded message containing one of the most important points that we learned in this chapter. To decode the message, first fill in the words defined below; then use the letters from those words to fill in the corresponding letters in the coded message.

a. Cessation of breathing ___ ___ ___ ___ I ___ ___ ___ ___ ___ ___   ___ R R ___ ___ ___
                          52 36 46 4   13 73 58 17 9 45   19   72 31 34

b. First priority in the primary survey ___ ___ ___ ___ ___ ___
                                        62 56 5 43 33 10

c. Occurs when the heart stops ___ ___ ___ ___ ___ ___ ___ L ___ ___ A ___ ___
                               75 42 6 70 35 23 44   55 48   1 59

d. Biologic death occurs when there is irreversible damage to the ___ ___ ___ ___ ___
                                                                  74 49 8 39 57

e. Agreement by the patient to accept treatment ___ ___ N ___ ___ ___ ___
                                                27 51   61 15 25 38

f. Lying faceup ___ ___ ___ ___ ___ ___
                65 12 32 28 20   3

g. When cells are deprived of oxygen they ___ ___ ___ ___ ___ ___ T ___
                                          11 68 50 18 29 71   54

h. Abbreviation for milliequivalent ___ ___ ___
                                    7 64 67

i. Root word meaning "air" ___ ___ ___ ___ ___ ___
                           47 22 60 30 53 24

j. Part of the hemoglobin molecule containing iron ___ ___ ___ ___
                                                   2 69 63 66

k. A growth on the skin ___ E ___ ___ ___
                        37   14 21 40

l. What to say if you're offered $1,000,000 ___ E ___
                                            16   26

Secret Message: ___ ___ ___   ___ ___ ___ ___ ___ ___ ___   ___ ___ ___ ___ ___ ___   ___ ___   ___ ___
                 1 2 3   4 5 6 7 8 9 10   11 12 13 14 15 16   17 18   19 20

___ ___ ___ ___ ___ ___ ___ ___ ___ ___ ___   ___ ___ ___ ___ ___ ___   ___ ___   ___ ___ ___ ___ ___ ___
21 22 23 24 25 26 27 28 29 30 31   32 33 34 35 36 37 38   39 40   41 42 43 44 45 46

___ ___ ___ ___ ___ ___ ___ ___ ___   ___ ___   ___ ___ ___   ___ ___ ___ ___
47 48 49 50 51 52 53 54 55   56 57   58 59 60   61 62 63 64

___ ___ ___ ___ ___ ___ ___ ___: ___ ___ ___.
65 66 67 68 69 70 71 72   73 74 75

7
The Airway

1. The bank robber Willie Sutton was once asked why he chose to rob banks, and he is alleged to have replied, "Because that's where the money is." That rather straightforward explanation has sometimes been called "Sutton's Law": "Go where the money is." In the care of the critically ill and injured, the money is more often than not in the AIRWAY, which is why we give it so much attention. And since we shall be hearing a lot about the structures that make up the airway, it is important to know their names. Label the diagram below with the names of the structures indicated.

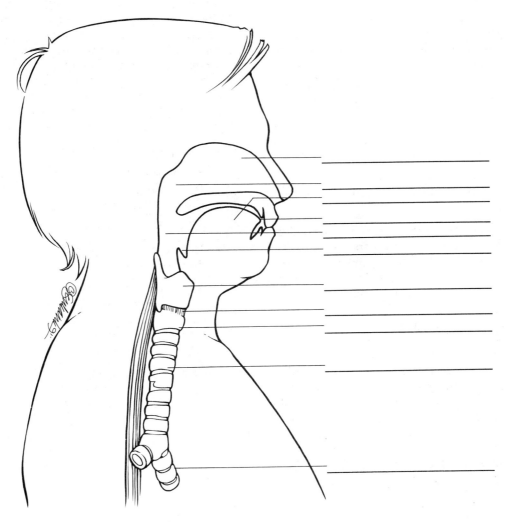

2. Obstruction of the upper airway is an immediate threat to life. The upper airway may become obstructed in several ways. List four causes of upper airway obstruction, and put an asterisk beside the most common cause.

a.

b.

c.

d.

3. For each of the patients described below, indicate which of the following is the best method for opening the airway.

A. Head tilt–chin lift

B. Triple airway maneuver

C. Jaw thrust only

_____ A construction worker found unconscious on the ground after falling 30 feet from a scaffolding.

_____ A 35-year-old man found unconscious from a drug overdose; he is breathing spontaneously.

_____ A 45-year-old man in cardiac arrest from a probable heart attack. You have arrived at his side without any ancillary equipment.

_____ Another 45-year-old man in cardiac arrest from a probable heart attack. You have a pocket mask with you.

_____ A 15-year-old boy who dove into a shallow pool and struck his head on the bottom. Bystanders removed him from the pool before you arrived. He is unconscious but breathing spontaneously (and noisily) when you arrive.

4. It's been a slow shift, so you decide to grab a quick dinner at Joe's Steak 'n Lobster Place. You park your rig outside and find a table near the door, in case you have to leave in a hurry on a call. You've just had your medium-rare sirloin placed in front of you when you notice a woman at the next table looking distinctly unwell. You ask her if there is anything the matter. "I don't know," she says in a very squeaky voice. "I have this lump in my throat, and I feel like I'm going to die," whereupon she collapses to the floor.

a. This woman is most likely suffering from

A. Food poisoning   D. Anaphylaxis
B. Choking   E. Hysteria
C. Strep throat

(Circle the best answer.)

b. The treatment you need to give most urgently, therefore, is to

A. Pump out her stomach
B. Give her 6 to 10 manual thrusts
C. Have her gargle with salt water
D. Give epinephrine 1 : 1,000, 0.5 ml SQ
E. Give diazepam (Valium), 10 mg IM

(Circle the best answer.)

5. You finish dealing with the woman described in question 4—having transferred her to the hospital—and return to Joe's Steak 'n Lobster Place in hopes that they haven't already fed your sirloin to the dog. Happily, Joe has kept your steak waiting for you, and he whips it into the microwave to rewarm it. At last the steak is back in front of you, along with a generous order of french fries. You lift your knife and fork to dig in when out of the corner of your eye you see a strange pantomime occurring two tables away. A middle-aged man in a business suit suddenly pushes himself away from the table, clutches his neck, and lurches to his feet. He staggers a few paces, then pitches to the floor—all in complete silence.

a. The man is showing signs of

A. Food poisoning   D. Anaphylaxis
B. Choking   E. Hysteria
C. Strep throat

(Circle the best answer.)

b. The treatment you need to give most urgently, therefore, is to

A. Pump out his stomach
B. Give him manual thrusts
C. Have him gargle with salt water
D. Give epinephrine 1 : 1,000, 0.5 ml SQ
E. Give diazepam (Valium) 10 mg IM

(Circle the best answer.)

6. You are having a barbecue in the backyard one Sunday. The beer has been flowing freely, and everyone is in a jolly mood. You tell a funny story, and everyone present starts laughing uproariously, including one of your friends who had just taken a big bite out of his hot dog. Suddenly he starts coughing violently. His face gets very red.

   a. At that point you should

      A. Tilt his head back and attempt to ventilate

      B. Perform a quick finger sweep to remove accessible obstructing material

      C. Give manual thrusts

      D. Reach into his throat with the barbecue tongs and try to snare the hot dog

      E. Encourage him to keep coughing

      (Circle the best answer.)

   b. That course of action does not seem to help. Your friend becomes completely silent, and his face turns a dusky gray as he struggles to breathe. You should now

      A. Tilt his head back and attempt to ventilate

      B. Perform a quick finger sweep to remove accessible obstructing material

      C. Give manual thrusts

      D. Reach into his throat with the barbecue tongs and try to snare the hot dog

      E. Encourage him to keep coughing

      (Circle the best answer.)

   c. That doesn't work either. Your friend collapses unconscious to the ground. List the next four steps you would take.

(1)

(2)

(3)

(4)

   d. Meanwhile an ambulance has arrived (someone had the wit to phone 911!), and a couple of paramedics come stampeding through your flower garden carrying what looks like all the equipment from their rig. Now that you have equipment available, what steps should you take?

      (1)

      (2)

      (3)

7. In mastering the use of any given piece of equipment, it is essential to learn not only *how* to use the equipment but also *when* to use it (and when *not* to use it). Artificial airways can be enormously helpful when applied in the appropriate circumstances; they can be downright dangerous when used in inappropriate circumstances. Fill in the table below to summarize the indications and contraindications for the oropharyngeal airway and the nasopharyngeal airway.

	Oropharyngeal Airway	Nasopharyngeal Airway
Use for:		
Do not use for:		

8. Indicate which of the following statements about suctioning are true and which are false.

   a. Any patient who is to be suctioned should first be preoxygenated for at least 3 minutes.

   TRUE   FALSE

   b. Keep the suction turned off as you insert the catheter into the patient's mouth.

   TRUE   FALSE

   c. Suction for only 2 minutes at a time.

   TRUE   FALSE

   d. Use a tonsil-tip catheter only under direct vision.

   TRUE   FALSE

   e. Once a patient is intubated, suction through the endotracheal tube every 5 to 10 minutes to keep the tube free of secretions.

   TRUE   FALSE

9. The principal *hazard* associated with endotracheal suctioning is _____. That hazard can be minimized by: _____

   _____.

10. Endotracheal intubation has several advantages over other methods of airway control. List four advantages of endotracheal intubation.

    a.

    b.

    c.

    d.

11. Despite all its advantages, endotracheal intubation is not for all patients. Like every other medical procedure, it has specific indications. List three indications for endotracheal intubation.

    a.

    b.

    c.

12. Endotracheal intubation is not without potential complications. The most serious acute complications can, however, be avoided by meticulous attention to correct technique. List two potential complications of endotracheal intubation and indicate

- How each can be avoided
- How each can be detected and corrected if it does occur

a. Complication: _____

    (1) This complication can be avoided by

    (2) If it does occur, this complication can be detected by

    (3) Once detected, this complication can be corrected by

b. Complication: _____

    (1) This complication can be avoided by

    (2) If it does occur, this complication can be detected by

    (3) Once detected, this complication can be corrected by

13. Hidden in the grid below are 26 words relating to this chapter—the names of 18 pieces of equipment used in orotracheal intubation and the names of 8 anatomic structures you will see as you intubate. See if you can find them all; then answer the questions following the grid.

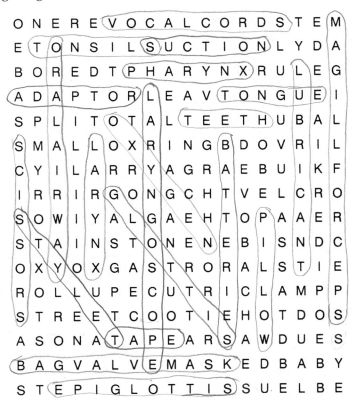

O N E R E V O C A L C O R D S T E M
E T O N S I L S U C T I O N L Y D A
B O R E D T P H A R Y N X R U L E G
A D A P T O R L E A V T O N G U E I
S P L I T O T A L T E E T H U B A L
S M A L L O X R I N G B D O V R I L
C Y I L A R R Y A G R A E B U I K F
I R R I R G O N G C H T V E L C R O
S O W I Y A L G A E H T O P A A E R
S T A I N S T O N E N E B I S N D C
O X Y O X G A S T R O R A L S T I E
R O L L U P E C U T R I C L A M P P
S T R E E T C O O T I E H O T D O S
A S O N A T A P E A R S A W D U E S
B A G V A L V E M A S K E D B A B Y
S T E P I G L O T T I S S U E L B E

a. What additional equipment or supplies, besides those listed in the grid, will you need if you decide to do a blind nasotracheal intubation?

b. Which of the items of equipment listed in the grid will you *not* need for blind nasotracheal intubation?

14. For endotracheal intubation to proceed smoothly, it is essential to position the patient correctly in order to bring his trachea into alignment with his mouth and pharynx. To do so, you need to _____ the patient's neck and _____ his head.

15. An intubation attempt should take no longer than _____ seconds. The easiest way to keep track of the time is to:

16. You are struggling to intubate a 30-year-old body builder who collapsed while working out at the local health club. You found him in cardiac arrest. Despite the fact that you have positioned him just as the textbook instructs, you can't seem to bring his vocal cords into view; they remain hidden just above your laryngoscope blade.

a. To bring the cords into view, you ask your partner to:

b. That maneuver also accomplishes another useful thing, namely:

c. With your partner's help, you get a lovely view of the vocal cords. But just as you reach for the endotracheal tube, the light on your laryngoscope flickers and dies. What will you do *now*?!

d. You manage at last to insert the endotracheal tube. Now you need to make sure that the tube is really in the trachea. List two ways of verifying that the endotracheal tube is in the right place.

(1)

(2)

17. In some EMS systems, paramedics are authorized to use paralyzing drugs to facilitate endotracheal intubation. While such drugs undoubtedly make life easier for the paramedic, they may make life quite precarious for the *patient*! What is the principal hazard of administering a neuromuscular blocking agent to a patient who needs to be intubated?

18. One should be especially cautious about using neuromuscular blocking agents in patients who, because of their anatomy or for other reasons, may be difficult to intubate. List four anatomic features that should alert you to the possibility of a difficult intubation.

a.

c.

b.

d.

19. At the end of this question, there is a secret message containing one of the most important lessons of this chapter. First fill in the words defined below; then use the letters from those words to decode the secret message.

a. Windpipe __ __ __ C __ __ __
            74 77 80   41 55 6

b. Main branch of (a) defined above __ __ __ __ C __ __ __
                                     29 18 61 3   50 35 82

c. Branch of (b) defined above __ R __ __ __ __ __ __ __
                                71   73 14 20 75 25 16 59 54

d. Voice box __ __ R __ __ __ __
             60 44   72 48 62

e. Trapdoor that protects the airway __ __ __ G __ __ __ __ I __
                                      9 43 46   39 2 27 68   52

f. Space between the lungs __ __ __ __ __ S __ I __ __ __
                           78 13 70 32 30   40   36 28 10

g. Opening between the vocal cords __ __ __ __ __ __ S
                                   64 24 4 49 17 38

h. Touching a person without his consent __ __ __ __ __ R __
                                          53 67 5 8 79   63

i. Wrongful conduct that gives rise to a lawsuit __ __ R __
                                                 37 33   45

j. Absence of breathing __ __ __ __ __
                        23 11 26 76 51

k. What the prefix *inter-* means B __ __ __ __ __ __
                                   65 7 57 22 69 34

l. Not now __ __ __ __
           12 21 58 56

m. Not a good shape for the human head __ __ __ __ __ __
                                       1 47 81 31 42 15

n. Article __ __
           19 66

Secret Message: __ __   __ __ __   __ __ __ __ __ __ __   __ __ __ __ __ __ __ __ __ __ __ __
                1 2   3 4 5   6 7 8 9 10 11 12   13 14 15 16 17 18 19 20 21 22 23 24

__ __ __ __ __ __ __ __ __ __   __ __ __ __ __   __ __ __   __ __ __ __ __ __ __   __ __ __
25 26 27 28 29 30 31 32 33 34   35 36 37 38 39   40 41 42   43 44 45 46 47 48 49   50 51 52

__ __ __ __   __ __ __ __   __ __ __ __ __ __ __ __ __ __   __ __   __ __ __ __ __   __ __ __ __ __.
53 54 55 56   57 58 59 60   61 62 63 64 65 66 67 68 69 70   71 72   73 74 75 76 77   78 79 80 81 82

20. Nasotracheal intubation is an excellent technique for establishing control over the airway under selected circumstances. In other circumstances, it is preferable to insert the endotracheal tube through the mouth; and in yet other circumstances, it may be necessary to establish an airway surgically, by cricothyrotomy. For each of the patients described below, indicate

    N   Blind nasotracheal intubation is the preferred technique
    O   Orotracheal intubation is the preferred technique
    C   Cricothyrotomy is the preferred technique

    _____ A 60-year-old man in cardiac arrest.

    _____ A 22-year-old woman with complete airway obstruction from laryngeal edema.

    _____ A 26-year-old accident victim with clear fluid draining from his nose and left ear.

    _____ An 18-year-old man in coma from a drug overdose.

    _____ A 42-year-old woman extricated from a wrecked car; she is unconscious and has a depressed skull fracture at the back of her head.

    _____ A 58-year-old man in pulmonary edema; he has been taking Coumadin (an anticoagulant drug) ever since his heart attack last year.

    _____ A 6-year-old boy who choked on a piece of meat.

    _____ A 50-year-old man who was given succinylcholine (a paralyzing drug) prior to an intubation attempt; the attempt failed, and afterward it became impossible to maintain his airway by manual methods (head tilt, etc.).

21. You are attempting a blind nasotracheal intubation on a 60-kg 24-year-old who took an overdose of sleeping pills. You have succeeded in advancing the tip of the endotracheal tube just beyond the oropharynx.

    a. As you continue to advance the tube, how can you tell whether the tip is moving toward the glottis (as opposed to the esophagus)?

    b. As you are advancing the tube, you become aware that the bleeps from the cardiac monitor are getting farther apart. What has happened, and what should you do about it?

    c. As you try again to advance the tube, you notice gastric contents creeping up the back of the patient's throat, a process called _____. What is the danger associated with that process?

       What should you do about it?

    d. The tip of the endotracheal tube is finally just where you want it—poised above the vocal cords awaiting the final push into the trachea. At what point in the respiratory cycle will you give the tube that final push?

22. In some EMS systems, the esophageal obturator airway (EOA) is used as an aid to ventilating a patient. Like any other device, the EOA should be used in the appropriate circumstances. List three *contraindications* to use of the EOA.

    a.

    b.

    c.

23. Indicate which of the following statements about the EOA are true and which are false.

    a. The main indication for the EOA is pulmonary edema.

       TRUE   FALSE

    b. The patient should be preoxygenated before an attempt is made to insert the EOA.

       TRUE   FALSE

    c. The patient should be placed in the "sniffing" position for EOA insertion.

       TRUE   FALSE

    d. It often requires considerable force to insert the EOA into the esophagus.

       TRUE   FALSE

    e. The EOA eliminates the need to tilt the patient's head back for artificial ventilation.

       TRUE   FALSE

    f. In an unconscious patient, an endotracheal tube should be inserted before the EOA is removed.

       TRUE   FALSE

    g. When intubating a patient who has an EOA in place, it is unnecessary to see the vocal cords to ensure proper placement of the endotracheal tube.

       TRUE   FALSE

24. The EOA is not without potential hazards. For each of the complications listed below, describe the error in technique that was probably responsible for the complication.

    a. Perforation of the esophagus:

    b. Rapid gastric distention and regurgitation:

    c. Inadequate ventilation of the lungs:

8
Breathing

1. Concealed in the grid below—written across, down, and diagonally—are 35 words relating to what we have studied in this chapter. See how many you can find. You will need most of them to answer questions 2 and 3!

```
S A G L O T T I S U N A R E S C A B S
C H A T A C K I D I A P H R A G M R Y
D A Y E L R A P I T R A Y P I S T O L
B U R P V S Y R L Y O A P H A R Y N X
T I E B E E T N I E R R E Y T R I C K
I P S I O R O R X N U M R P E I G H T
D I P H L N V A I N A R C O L L O U H
A B I S U R D E A D S P A C E R V S Y
L R R S S N A I N O O T R A C H E A P
V O A M I S T R O T A R B R T J R B O
O N T A P N E A T X I L I B A S T E X
L C I O X Y G E N T I L A I S I E B E
U H O L O C O U G H A D A A I G X A M
M I N U T E V O L U M E E T S H U L I
E O H Y P O V E N T I L A T I O N G A
A L L P L U M P N E U M O T H O R A X
B E F A I N T E R C O S T A L S N O W
```

36

2. Imagine you are an oxygen molecule floating past someone's face, minding your own business, just as that person is starting to take a deep breath. As his _____ and _____ contract, the volume of his chest _____ (increases or decreases?), so the pressure inside the chest (intrathoracic pressure) _____ (increases or decreases?). As a consequence, air is sucked in through the _____, and you are swept along with it.

After having a shower and completing a security check in the nasal hairs, you enter the _____. You then proceed down the _____, through the _____, and into the _____. (Had you gone down the esophagus instead, you would eventually have been expelled from the stomach as part of a _____.) Moving a little farther, you find yourself at a crossroads, called the _____, where you can either take a left turn into the left _____ or a right turn into the right _____. You choose the straighter, shorter path, to the _____. The airway in which you are travelling branches many times into smaller and smaller _____, until finally you reach a tiny sac at the end of the road, an _____. There you find the first opportunity to cross a membrane into a capillary and board a red blood cell for the journey to peripheral tissues. (Up to this point in your journey, you have been travelling only in _____, that is, the part of the airway where gas exchange does not take place.)

Some of your friends who started the journey with you did not make it as far as you did. One of them accidently tickled the throat on his way down the airway and got expelled with gale force by a _____, which is the airway's most powerful mechanism for eliminating foreign material. Another of your colleagues found himself recruited into a hiccup, also known as _____.

Yet another friend of yours made the journey all the way down the airway only to find the air spaces at the end of the line collapsed, a situation called _____. It had come about when a little bleb on the surface of the lung ruptured, allowing air to enter the space between the visceral and parietal _____, and thereby creating a small _____. The net effect was that blood reaching the collapsed alveoli could not pick up any _____ like yourself, but rather had to return to the left heart as if it had never passed through the lungs at all, a situation called _____. If a very large proportion of alveoli are nonfunctional (e.g., collapsed, filled with fluids), then a large part of the blood circulating through the lungs will be similarly affected, and the person's arterial PO_2 will fall below normal (i.e., below about 60 mm Hg), a condition known as _____.

Sometimes scattered alveoli collapse simply because a person doesn't take deep enough breaths to keep all his alveoli inflated. The body therefore has a mechanism to help periodically pop open collapsed alveoli, and that is to _____. Do so now, before you proceed to the next question.

3. The exchange of gases among the tissues, lungs, and atmosphere is called _____. The movement of air in and out of the lungs (more specifically, the flushing of _____ out of the lungs by breathing) is called _____, and its effectiveness is determined by the volume of air inhaled or exhaled each minute, that is, the _____ (= respiratory rate × _____). If that volume of air inhaled each minute is *less* than normal, the arterial PCO_2 _____ (falls or rises?), and the blood gases show _____ (excess CO_2 in the blood). We call that situation _____, that is, breathing that is insufficient to remove excess CO_2 from the body. The most extreme example occurs when a person is not breathing at all (respiratory arrest, or _____).

On the other hand, when someone breathes very deeply or very rapidly (or both), his PCO_2 will _____ (rise or fall?); that is, he will develop _____. We refer to that situation—when excessive breathing lowers the PCO_2 below about 35 _____ (mm Hg)—as _____.

4. All ambulances conforming to United States Department of Transportation specifications have the stretcher on the *left* side of the patient compartment, rather than on the right side. That design was chosen to take into account a particular feature of human anatomy.

   Explain what feature of respiratory anatomy makes it preferable to site the stretcher on the left side of the ambulance.

   _____

   _____

   _____

   _____

   _____

   _____

5. A person is breathing quietly 12 times a minute with a tidal volume of 500 ml.

   a. Calculate his *minute volume*.

   b. List two things that could cause his minute volume to *decrease*.

   (1)

   (2)

   c. If the person's minute volume does decrease, what changes will you see in his arterial blood gases?

6. Ordinarily, we measure the blood gases in a sample of *arterial* blood. Suppose that when you were drawing the blood sample to send to the blood gas laboratory, you accidently took the blood from a vein rather than from an artery. In that case, the PO_2 reading would probably be considerably _____ (lower or higher?) than expected, while the PCO_2 reading would be somewhat _____ (lower or higher?) than expected. That is because venous blood has not yet passed through the pulmonary capillaries, where _____ is taken up from the alveoli and _____ is given off into the alveoli.

7. You are doing a shift in the emergency room, and the laboratory phones down with a blood gas report. You notice that the PCO_2 reported is quite high (hypercarbia)—about 55 torr.

   a. List four conditions that could have produced an elevated level of carbon dioxide in the patient's blood.

   (1)

   (2)

   (3)

   (4)

   b. What can be done to normalize the patient's PCO_2?

8. The laboratory phones down another blood gas report. "You'd better check on this guy," the lab technician says. "His PO_2 is only 48." As you sprint off to alert the doctor about the blood gas results, you review in your mind the conditions that can cause hypoxemia.

   a. List six conditions that can cause hypoxemia.

   (1)

   (2)

   (3)

   (4)

   (5)

   (6)

   b. What is the treatment for hypoxemia?

9. Breathing is normally controlled by a respiratory center in the brainstem. In a healthy person, the primary stimulus to breathe is a _____ (rise or fall?) in the level of _____ (oxygen or carbon dioxide?) in the blood.

   In some patients with chronic obstructive pulmonary disease, that mechanism is no longer fully operative, and *their* principal stimulus to breathe is a _____ (rise or fall?) in the level of _____ (oxygen or carbon dioxide?) in the blood.

10. Oxygen is a drug, and like any other drug, it should be given when there are indications for its use. List six indications for administering oxygen to a patient.

    a.

    b.

    c.

    d.

    e.

    f.

11. Sometimes the patient himself will "tell" you, through his symptoms and signs, that either his oxygenation, his ventilation, or both are insufficient—that he is suffering from acute respiratory insufficiency. List four signs of acute respiratory insufficiency.

    a.

    b.

    c.

    d.

12. You are involved in a search-and-rescue mission to find a middle-aged hiker lost in the woods. At last you find him, sitting down propped against a tree. He tells you that he experienced severe chest pain and could not go on. Since there is a strong possibility that he is suffering an acute myocardial infarction (heart attack), you and your partner will have to carry him back to the ambulance, about a 40-minute walk. You hook the patient up to oxygen via nasal cannula at a flow rate of 5 liters per minute. You notice that the pressure gauge on your E cylinder is reading 800 psi. How long is the oxygen in the E cylinder going to last? Is that going to be long enough to get the patient back to the ambulance? (Show your calculations.)

13. Oxygen is stored in cylinders at pressures up to 2,000 psi, which means that oxygen cylinders have to be treated with respect! List six safety precautions that should be observed when using or storing oxygen cylinders.

    a.

    b.

    c.

    d.

    e.

    f.

14. For each of the patients described below, indicate the most appropriate device for giving that patient oxygen. You may choose among

    A. Nasal catheter
    B. Two-pronged nasal cannula
    C. Simple face mask
    D. Venturi mask
    E. Partial rebreathing mask
    F. Nonrebreathing mask
    G. Pocket mask with added oxygen
    H. Bag-valve-mask with oxygen reservoir
    I. Demand valve/mask

    (Note: You may use any of the above items once, more than once, or not at all.)

    _____ A 60-year-old man in severe respiratory distress from pulmonary edema.

    _____ A 52-year-old man complaining of crushing chest pain.

    _____ An accident victim in cardiac arrest; you are doing one-rescuer CPR, because your partner is busy with another casualty.

    _____ An 81-year-old woman who suddenly stopped speaking this morning and cannot move her left arm or left leg.

    _____ A 22-year-old who has overdosed with heroin; he is unconscious and breathing shallowly 6 times per minute.

    _____ A 32-year-old accident victim who was thrown forward against the steering wheel; he is coughing up blood, and his lips look rather blue.

    _____ A middle-aged man who collapsed in the street; he is in cardiac arrest by the time you arrive.

    _____ A child rescued unconscious from a house fire.

15. As we learned in Chapter 6, respiratory arrest occurs quite a way down the pathway from life to death. List six things that can cause a person to stop breathing, and put an asterisk (*) beside the most common cause.

    a.

    b.

    c.

    d.

    e.

    f.

16. How can you tell if someone has suffered a respiratory arrest?

17. A person who has suffered respiratory arrest will need _____ (controlled or assisted?) ventilation.

    a. What is the difference between controlled and assisted ventilation?

    b. What is the objective of *any* form of artificial ventilation?

18. You are sitting at the movies on your night off when you notice someone a few rows ahead of you suddenly slump over. You leap like a gazelle over several rows of seats to reach the person's side, and you discover that he has stopped breathing. So you drag him into an aisle and start mouth-to-mouth ventilation. How can you tell if you are actually getting air into his lungs?

    a.

    b.

    c.

19. As you continue mouth-to-mouth ventilation on the patient described in question 18, you reflect that you would like to avoid causing gastric distention, for you would prefer not to deal with the mess that might follow.

    a. What can you do to minimize gastric distention during artificial ventilation?

       (1)

       (2)

    b. Despite your best efforts, however, you notice the man's belly starting to get larger. What should you do?

    c. After about another 3 or 4 minutes, his belly is *much* larger, and you are finding it very hard to ventilate him. What should you do now?

20. After your experience in the movie theater, you promise yourself that you will never go *anywhere* without a pocket mask in your pocket, not only to make things more pleasant for yourself, but also because the pocket mask has several advantages over other methods of giving artificial ventilation. List four advantages of a pocket mask.

    a.

    b.

    c.

    d.

21. Your partner loves to use the demand valve; he says it's much easier to push a button than to squeeze a bag, and he doesn't see what virtue there is in doing things the hard way. You are trying to persuade him that while the demand valve has its place, it is not ideally suited for many situations that require controlled ventilation. Give three reasons why.

    a.

    b.

    c.

22. In fact, in the majority of situations that require artificial ventilation in the field, an automatic transport ventilator (ATV) is preferred over a demand valve. List two advantages of the ATV over the demand valve.

    a.

    b.

23. The purpose of artificial ventilation in respiratory arrest is twofold: (1) to remove carbon dioxide from the lungs, and (2) to furnish oxygen to the lungs. Most patients in respiratory arrest in fact need all the oxygen they can get, so it is useful to know how much oxygen each method of artificial ventilation can deliver. Fill in the following table with that information.

Method of Artificial Ventilation	O_2 Concentration Delivered
Mouth-to-mouth	
Pocket mask	
Pocket mask with O_2 at 12 L/min	
Bag-valve-mask (BVM)	
BVM with O_2 at 12 L/min	
BVM with O_2 at 12 L/min plus O_2 reservoir	
Demand valve	

24. List three situations in which information from pulse oximetry could be helpful to you in the field.

    a.

    b.

    c.

25. A 53-year-old man calls for an ambulance because of shortness of breath. You find him in severe respiratory distress, with foam bubbling out of his mouth. Your examination reveals signs of congestive heart failure (a condition in which fluid backs up into the lungs and interferes with gas exchange). The patient's pulse oximeter reading when you first arrive shows an oxygen saturation (SaO_2) of 86 percent.

    a. That reading is

        A. Normal for the patient's age
        B. Abnormally high
        C. Abnormally low
        D. Probably an artifact

        (Circle the best answer.)

    b. What measure should you take immediately?

    You treat the patient according to your protocol for congestive heart failure (we'll learn more about all that in Chap. 23), and his condition improves markedly. Now the SaO_2 reading is 96 percent. You move the patient to a stretcher and bring him out to the ambulance for transport. When you have him loaded in the ambulance, you notice that the SaO_2 is now reading 85 percent. The patient, however, still looks comfortable and is not in any respiratory distress. So you conclude that the reading on the pulse oximeter must be an error.

    c. List four potential sources of error in a pulse oximetry reading:

        (1)

        (2)

        (3)

        (4)

26. You are attempting a blind nasotracheal intubation on an unconscious patient who took an overdose of sleeping pills. When you think you have the endotracheal tube in place, you check out the end-tidal carbon dioxide monitor that you've snapped onto the endotracheal tube. Its color is purple, indicating that the air being exhaled through the tube contains less than 0.5% carbon dioxide.

    a. What can you conclude from that reading?

    b. What action should you take?

9
Circulation

1. Hidden in the grid below are 23 words related to concepts we have studied in this chapter. First find the words, then use them to fill in the blanks in the statements that follow the grid.

```
S  T  I  X  I  P  H  O  I  D  E  A  L  A  T
TH A  C  I  D  L  E  Y  E  I  N  S  A  N  E
E  V  E  R  Y  E  L  O  P  E  D  E  M  A  R
M  B  A  H  Y  P  E  R  T  O  N  I  C  E  Y
O  R  A  I  N  S  C  O  G  H  T  O  Y  R  T
G  O  A  S  Y  S  T  O  L  E  N  O  A  O  H
L  S  H  O  E  T  R  A  Y  M  O  R  N  B  R
O  M  H  T  I  C  O  L  L  O  I  D  O  I  O
B  O  A  O  C  A  L  M  E  L  P  I  S  C  C
I  S  I  N  C  R  Y  B  A  Y  O  A  I  L  Y
N  I  L  I  I  K  T  I  P  S  S  I  S  O  T
G  S  I  C  K  O  E  S  L  I  T  E  D  G  E
S  C  A  T  I  O  N  C  E  S  A  L  I  N  E
```

0.9%

a. Intravenous solution containing large molecules like protein: __Colloid__.

b. Intravenous solution that does *not* contain large molecules like protein: __Crystalloid__. One example of such a solution is normal __Saline__.

c. A compound whose pH is *less* than 7.0 is called a(n) __Acid__, while a compound whose pH is *greater* than 7.0 is called a(n) __Base__.

d. A(n) __Electrolyte__ is a substance that dissociates into charged components in water. A positively charged molecule, like Na$^+$, is a(n) __Cation__, while a negatively charged molecule, like Cl$^-$, is called a(n) __Anion__.

e. When two solutions of different solute concentration are placed on either side of a semipermeable membrane, the *more* concentrated solution is said to be __Hypertonic__ with respect to the less concentrated solution. Conversely, the *less* concentrated solution is considered __Hypotonic__ with respect to the more concentrated solution. If the two solutions have the *same* concentration, they are said to be __Isotonic__. Thus, for example, 4% saline is __Hypertonic__ with respect to the plasma; Ringer's solution is __Isotonic__ with respect to the plasma; and ½ normal saline (0.45% NaCl) is __Hypotonic__ with respect to the plasma. If you place red blood cells in a solution like ½ normal saline, the cells will rupture; that is, __Hemolysis__ will occur.

f. When two solutions of different solute concentration are placed on either side of a semipermeable membrane, water will move *from* the solution of _____ (higher or lower?) solute concentration *to* the solution of _____ (higher or lower?) solute concentration. The process by which water migrates in that fashion is called _____.

g. The most important component of the red blood cell, or _____, is an iron-containing protein called _____, which binds oxygen in the lungs and releases oxygen in the tissues. When that protein is not saturated with oxygen, it imparts a bluish color to the blood, which is reflected in a bluish color of the skin called _____.

h. When there is failure of tissue perfusion for any reason, the resulting state is called _____. One way that state can come about is if there is cardiac standstill or _____. However that state of inadequate tissue perfusion occurs, one of the immediate results is that the body cells, unable to obtain enough oxygen, switch to _____ metabolism.

i. A now somewhat controversial treatment for shock is the military anti-shock trousers, or _____, also known as the _____.

j. When performing cardiac compressions, one must be careful not to compress over the lower, cartilaginous portion of the sternum, called the _____, lest one lacerate the patient's liver.

k. The cardinal sign of *over*hydration is _____.

2. Three components are required for a functioning circulatory system. If any one of those components is impaired, shock may result. List the three necessary components, and indicate beside each one what type of shock will occur if that component is damaged.

Component	Type of Shock Resulting from Damage
_____	_____
_____	_____
_____	_____

3. For each of the following statements about CPR, indicate whether the statement is true or false.

a. To determine whether the patient has a pulse, palpate gently over the radial artery for 10 seconds.

TRUE   FALSE

b. For chest compressions to be effective, the patient must be supine on a hard surface.

TRUE   FALSE

c. The correct compression point on an adult is over the lower third of the sternum.

TRUE   FALSE

d. You should allow more time for the relaxation phase than for the compression phase, to give the heart time to refill between compressions.

TRUE   FALSE

e. After every 4 to 5 cycles of 15 compressions and 2 ventilations, you should take a 1-minute break to rest your arms and check for a spontaneous pulse.

TRUE   FALSE

4. Whether or not CPR is effective depends a great deal on how it is performed. List five measures you can take to perform CPR with maximal effectiveness.

a.

b.

c.

d.

e.

5. For each of the patients in cardiac arrest described below, indicate whether

   A. CPR *should* be started.

   B. CPR should *not* be started.

   _____ A 12-year-old boy fished out of a swimming pool unconscious about 10 minutes before you arrived.

   _____ A man who looks to be about 70 years old who collapsed downtown 15 minutes before you arrived.

   _____ A vagrant found in cardiac arrest in an alley on a snowy morning; no one knows how long he has been there.

   _____ A *very* pregnant woman critically injured in an automobile accident; she has an open skull fracture, and pieces of her brain are splattered inside the car.

   _____ A 25-year-old man known to have AIDS who suffered cardiac arrest when he accidently came in contact with a high-tension electric cable.

   _____ A 40-year-old woman with advanced breast cancer who has told her family that she doesn't want "any heroic measures."

6. You are called, along with two other ambulances, to the scene of a two-car collision on the interstate highway. You find the driver of one of the cars slumped over the steering wheel. He is covered with blood and in cardiac arrest. In performing CPR on this patient, you will have to make certain modifications in the usual technique. List three ways in which CPR for this patient will differ from that applied to, say, a person who collapsed from a heart attack.

   a.

   b.

   c.

7. Hypovolemia and dehydration occur when fluids are lost from the body.

   a. List five ways in which a person can lose fluids.

   (1)

   (2)

   (3)

   (4)

   (5)

   b. If a person does not replace the fluids he loses, he will soon become dehydrated. Which of the following is NOT a sign of dehydration?

   A. Weak, rapid pulse
   B. Skin that "tents" when pinched
   C. Sunken eyes
   D. Edema of the feet and ankles
   E. Fainting on standing up

   c. What is the most important treatment for a person who is dehydrated?

8. In choosing an intravenous fluid for any given patient, it is important to know what effects that fluid will have on the patient's overall fluid balance. Some fluids tend to remain within the vascular space, while others move quickly out of the vascular space and into the interstitial or intracellular compartment. For each of the following situations, indicate whether the intravenous fluid preferred initially would be:

   A. 5% dextrose in water (D5/W)

   B. Lactated Ringer's solution

   C. Hetastarch (Hespan)

   _____ A 30-year-old man injured in an automobile accident. He is confused and disoriented. His skin is cold and clammy. His pulse is 128, respirations 24 and shallow, and blood pressure (BP) is palpable at 80 mm Hg.

_____ A 28-year-old construction worker who collapsed at the work site on a very hot day. His skin is cool and sweaty, pulse is 100, and BP is 100/60.

_____ A 22-year-old woman rescued from a structural fire with burns over 45 percent of her body. Current vital signs are pulse 88, respirations 20 and labored, and BP 110/80.

_____ A 48-year-old man with crushing chest pain. Pulse 100 and irregular, respirations 18, and BP 180/100.

_____ A 30-year-old man complaining of very severe abdominal pain. His abdomen is exquisitely tender, and he winces every time the ambulance goes over a bump. His pulse is 110 and regular, respirations 24 and shallow, and BP 100/70.

_____ A 16-year-old boy who has had 3 days of severe diarrhea. His skin "tents" when you pinch it. His pulse is 120, respirations 22, and BP 100/60.

9. For each of the patients described below, indicate whether his or her arterial blood gases are most likely to show:

   A. Respiratory acidosis

   B. Respiratory alkalosis

   C. Metabolic acidosis

   D. Metabolic alkalosis

_____ A very anxious 18-year-old boy complaining of stabbing pains in his chest. He is breathing deeply 30 times per minute.

_____ A 50-year-old woman in cardiac arrest.

_____ A diabetic complaining of extreme thirst and of having to urinate all the time. His breath smells fruity.

_____ A young woman who has been vomiting all night. (Hint: Gastric juice is very high in acid.)

_____ A young man with a heroin overdose. You find him comatose, breathing shallowly 6 times per minute.

_____ A cardiac arrest victim given too much sodium bicarbonate during resuscitation.

a. What treatment would you give the patient(s) found in respiratory acidosis?

b. What treatment would you give the patient(s) found in respiratory alkalosis?

10. You are transporting a patient from the local community hospital to a regional trauma center. The patient's vital signs are stable when you start the transport. He has a unit of blood running. Shortly after you set out, the patient begins complaining of severe back pain. Soon thereafter he breaks out in a cold sweat, his lips take on a bluish tinge, and his neck veins seem to bulge out. You check his pulse, and it is 60. A few minutes later, when you check it again, it is 110.

   a. The patient is showing signs of

      A. An allergic reaction to the transfusion
      B. A hemolytic reaction to the transfusion
      C. An air embolism
      D. A pyrogenic reaction to the transfusion
      E. Thrombophlebitis

   b. List the steps you will take to deal with the situation.

11. The type of shock one will see most frequently in the prehospital sphere is hemorrhagic shock. It is very important to detect hemorrhagic shock early and to start treatment early. To do so, one must have a high index of suspicion in assessing patients at risk of hemorrhagic shock, which means one must be aware of the situations in which hemorrhagic shock is likely to come about. List four causes of hemorrhagic shock.

    a.

    b.

    c.

    d.

12. A middle-aged man was struck by a car as he was crossing the street. You find him lying by the side of the road, complaining of severe pain in his abdomen, where the car hit him. You would like to make an assessment of his state of perfusion. How will you assess the following?

    a. His *peripheral* perfusion:

    b. The perfusion to his *vital organs*:

13. It is easier to remember the signs and symptoms of shock if one understands the mechanisms by which those signs and symptoms occur. List four signs or symptoms of shock, and beside each, explain what change in the body causes that sign or symptom.

Sign or Symptom	Mechanism That Causes the Sign or Symptom

14. You are called to a downtown bar in which firearms were deployed to settle a difference of opinion. You find a man lying on the floor of the bar, unconscious, his trouser leg soaked in blood. List *in the sequence in which you would perform them* the steps you would take in treating this patient.

15. Being skilled in a procedure means not only knowing *how* to perform the procedure, but also knowing *when* to perform it. Accordingly, fill in the boxes below.

Patients Who Need IVs for Fluid Replacement	Patients Who Need IVs to Keep a Vein Open

Patients Who May Benefit from the MAST (PASG)	Patients for Whom the MAST (PASG) Is Contraindicated

16. All of the patients described below are experiencing one or another problem related to their intravenous therapy. Identify the problem in each case, and explain what you will do to deal with it.

a. The patient is a 59-year-old man with severe chest pain on whom you have started a "keep-open" IV. It is a long way to the hospital, and about 10 minutes into the transport, he starts complaining of breathing difficulty. You notice that his respirations have become more rapid, and when you listen to his chest, you can hear bubbly noises. Meanwhile, you suddenly notice that the liter bag of IV fluid is empty.

(1) What is the patient's problem?

(2) What are you going to do about it?

b. You have started an IV on a frail old lady. After a few minutes, you notice that the IV is infusing more and more slowly. You open the clamp wide, but that doesn't help. You lower the IV bag below the stretcher; there is no blood return into the tubing. Then you check the IV site. There seems to be a lump in the skin, and the skin feels quite cool.

(1) What is the patient's problem?

(2) What are you going to do about it?

(3) What other things might cause an IV to slow down or stop?

c. You are starting an IV near the wrist of a petite young woman. When the IV catheter enters the vein, bright red blood comes spurting back in your face.

(1) What is the patient's problem?

(2) What are you going to do about it?

d. You are transporting a patient between hospitals. The patient has an IV already running (it was started earlier in the day by the paramedics who brought the patient to the first hospital). The patient complains of pain at the IV site, and you notice that it is red, hot, and swollen.

(1) What is the patient's problem?

(2) What are you going to do about it?

(3) How could this problem have been prevented?

17. You have started an IV on a bakery worker suffering from heat exhaustion. Your physician instructs you to run the IV at 200 ml per hour. Your administration set delivers 10 drops per milliliter. At what rate (how many drops per minute) do you have to run the infusion in order to give 200 ml per hour? (Show your calculations.)

18. You have started a "keep-open" IV with a microdrip infusion set (which delivers 60 drops/ml). Your instructions are to run the IV at 30 ml per hour. At what rate (how many drops per minute) should you set the flow? (Show your calculations.)

19. And now for another secret message of great importance to those who will be caring for the critically ill and injured in the field. Solve the puzzle in the usual fashion.

a. The flow of blood through tissues __ __ R __ __ __ __ __ __

48 71   38 10 35 8 54 58

b. Breast bone __ __ __ __ __ __ M

52 15 61 29 64 46

c. White blood cell __ __ __ __ __ __ __ __ __

33 67 28 56 20 50 42 12 17

d. Clot formation in an inflamed vein __ __ __ __ __ __ __ __ __ __ __ __ I __ __ __

9 16 40 21 70 60 2 23 53 14 41 36   69 63 26

e. 60 percent of body weight __ __ __ __ __

6 68 51 30 66

f. Gaseous waste product of metabolism __ __ __ __ __ __ __ __ __ X I __ __

55 32 24 18 43 72   1 13 4   22 25

g. Air in one breath __ I __ __ __ __ volume

73 59 7 19

h. One cause of of hypoxemia __ H __ __ __

47 44 3 65

i. 200 psi is the __ __ __ __ residual

45 57 31 37

j. Lower extremities __ __ __ __

34 49 62 27

k. 2,000 pounds __ __ __

5 39 11

Secret Message: __ __ __ __ __ __ __ __ __ __ __ __ __ __ __ __ __ __ __ __ __ __

1 2   3 4 5   6 7 8 9   10 11 12 13 14   15 16 17   18 19 20 21 22

__ __ __ __ __ __ __ __ __ __ __ __ __ __ __ __ __ __ __ __ __ __ __ __ __ __ __ __ __

23 24 25 26 27 28 29 30   31 32 33 34 35   36 37 38 39 40 41   42 43 44   45 46 47 48 49 50 51

__ __ __ __ __ __ __ __ __ __ __ __ __ __ __ __ __ __ __ __ __ __.

52 53 54 55 56   57 58 59   60 61 62 63 64   65 66 67 68 69 70 71 72 73

10
Overview of Pharmacology

1. Once again, let's start with a little treasure hunt. Hidden in the grid below are medications in a variety of forms as well as some other terms relating to medications—23 terms from this chapter in all. Find the hidden words, and use them to fill in the statements that follow the grid.

```
C A P S U L E M U L S I O N
S A G E F A R M V I L L O S
U Y S E X S I R I P I L I U
P A R E N T E R A L L I N S
P I L U V E R Y L I K N T P
O U L A P T R A D E N A M E
S U L L E N T I C K Y M E N
I N A V I L L A C T E E N S
T S O L U T I O N N O N T I
O P P O S L A X T O A T O O
R I T A B L E T I I L M R N
Y R O O T R O T E R O D E S
B I T I N C T U R E E N A D
S T E A M S H A M P U L E R
```

a. Preparation of a drug for external use, usually to relieve some discomfort:
   a _____ or a
   _____.

b. Aqueous suspension of an insoluble drug:
   _____.

c. Preparation of a volatile substance dissolved in alcohol: _____.

d. Dilute alcoholic extract of a drug:
   _____.

e. Drug suspended in sugar and water:
   _____.

f. Oil distributed in small globules in water:
   _____.

g. Drug shaped into a ball or oval, often coated to disguise an unpleasant taste:
   _____.

h. Cylindrical gelatin container enclosing a dose of medication: _____.

i. Resembles h, but not made of gelatin and does not separate: _____.

j. Powdered drug that has been molded or compressed into a small disc:
   _____.

k. Drug mixed in a firm base that melts at body temperature: _____.

l. Medication impregnated onto adhesive that is applied to the surface of the skin: _____.

m. Semisolid preparation for external application, usually containing a medicinal substance: _____.

n. Like e above, but with alcohol! _____.

o. Concentrated preparation of a drug made by putting the drug into solution and evaporating off the excess solvent to a prescribed standard: _____.

p. Liquid containing one or more chemical substances *entirely dissolved*, usually in water: _____. That liquid may be supplied as a single dose in a sealed glass container, called a(n) _____ or in a multidose _____ with a rubber stopper.

q. Preparation of finely divided drug whose ingredients separate out on standing: _____.

r. Any route of administration other than through the digestive tract: _____.

s. Lasix is the _____ of the drug whose _____ is furosemide.

2. In an ideal pharmaceutical world, any given drug would have exactly the same effect every time it was administered. We do not, however, live in an ideal world, and the action of a drug may be influenced by a variety of factors. List five factors that can affect the actions of a drug, and explain in what way each factor can do so.

a.

b.

c.

d.

e.

3. The speed with which a drug reaches its target organ is influenced primarily by the drug's route of administration into the body. List the routes of drug administration in the order of their speed of absorption, starting with the route by which drugs are absorbed the *fastest*.

Fastest route: _____

_____

_____

_____

_____

_____

_____

_____

_____

Slowest route: _____

4. Not every route of administration can be used for every drug. There are only five drugs, for example, that may be administered via the endotracheal route. List them.

a.

b.

c.

d.

e.

5. What prevents a drug, once it has been taken into the body, from exerting its effect forever?

a.

b.

REVIEW OF DECIMALS

Before we move on to dosage calculations, we need to be sure that our skills in manipulating decimal fractions are in good shape! If you are already a whiz at decimals, skip this section and proceed straight to question 7. If, however, you think you could use some review and practice with decimals (or you want to see if you really *are* a whiz), continue on with this section.

The metric system, as we learned in the textbook, is based on multiples or derivatives of 10—that is, the decimal system. Thus one must be fully at ease with the workings of the decimal system to be comfortable in a metric world.

Decimals consist of a WHOLE NUMBER (the number before the decimal point), a DECIMAL POINT, and a DECIMAL FRACTION (the number after the decimal point).

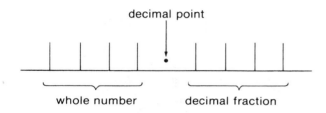

The position of the number in relation to the decimal point gives the number its *place name*; one place to the right of the decimal point is called *tenths,* two points to the right is called *hundredths,* and so on.

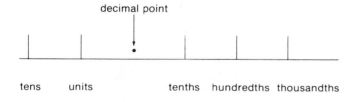

For example:

$$.6 = \text{six-tenths} = \frac{6}{10}$$

$$.07 = \text{seven-hundredths} = \frac{7}{100}$$

$$.008 = \text{eight-thousandths} = \frac{8}{1,000}$$

To eliminate the confusion that might arise from overlooking the decimal point and reading the decimal fraction as a whole number, a zero is placed to the *left* of the decimal when there is no whole number (e.g., the decimal fraction fourteen-hundredths is written 0.14). Adding zeroes to the *right* of the decimal fraction does not change its value either.

$$0.5 = 0.50 = 0.500, \text{ that is,}$$

$$\frac{5}{10} = \frac{50}{100} = \frac{500}{1,000}$$

TO ADD AND SUBTRACT DECIMALS, line up the decimal points and add zeroes to the right of the decimal fraction.

EXAMPLE: Addition

$1.5 + 21.65$

Solution

```
  1.50
+21.65
 23.15
```

EXAMPLE: Subtraction

$23.15 - 1.5$

Solution

```
 23.15
- 1.50
 21.65
```

MULTIPLICATION OF DECIMALS is carried out in exactly the same fashion as multiplication of whole numbers, except for the placement of the decimal point in the product. To determine this, count the number of decimal places in the numbers to be multiplied and count from the right of the product to locate the decimal point.

EXAMPLE: Multiplication

125×0.5

Solution

```
   125
×  0.5
  62.5   (product)
```

When MULTIPLYING BY 10, just move the decimal point *one* place to the right.

EXAMPLE: Multiplication by 10

12.5×10

Solution

$$
\begin{array}{r}
12.5 \\
\times\ \ \ 10 \\
\hline
125.0
\end{array}
$$

1.25×10

Solution

$$
\begin{array}{r}
1.25 \\
\times\ \ \ 10 \\
\hline
12.50
\end{array}
$$

When MULTIPLYING BY 100, move the decimal *two* places to the right.

EXAMPLE: Multiplication by 100

12.5×100

Solution

$$
\begin{array}{r}
12.5 \\
\times\ \ \ 100 \\
\hline
1,250.0
\end{array}
$$

Thus when multiplying a decimal by a multiple of 10, just move the decimal point to the *right* by the number of zeroes found in the multiple of 10. For example, 1,000 has three zeroes; if we multiply 1.25 by 1,000, we move the decimal point three places to the right, obtaining a product of 1,250.

DIVIDING BY DECIMALS is the same as dividing by whole numbers, except one must keep account of the decimal point. Recall the terminology of division: In the problem 24 ÷ 6 = 4, 24 is the *dividend*, 6 is the *divisor*, and 4 is the answer or *quotient*. With decimals (except if the dividend is also a decimal), keep the decimal point in the quotient above the decimal point in the dividend:

$$4\overline{\smash{\big)}\,2.4} \quad \overset{.6}{}$$

The divisor must always be a whole number. Thus, in the problem

$$0.4\overline{\smash{\big)}\,2.4}$$

make 0.4 a whole number by moving the decimal point one point to the right. However, we cannot move the decimal point in the divisor without moving the decimal point in the dividend the same num-

ber of places, so 2.4 becomes 24.0, and the problem thus becomes

$$4\overline{\smash{\big)}\,24.0} \quad \overset{6.0}{}$$

Remember to keep the decimal point in the quotient lined up with the new location of the decimal point in the dividend.

To DIVIDE A DECIMAL BY MULTIPLES OF 10, the rule is the opposite of that for multiplication by 10s; that is, move the decimal point to the *left* by the number of zeroes in the divisor.

EXAMPLE: Division by 10

$5.0 ÷ 10$

Solution

$$10\overline{\smash{\big)}\,5.0} \quad \overset{0.5}{}$$

EXAMPLE: Division by 100

$5.0 ÷ 100$

Solution

$$100\overline{\smash{\big)}\,5.0} \quad \overset{0.05}{}$$

Having reviewed the basic principles, let's practice with a few exercises.

6. Solve the following problems:

   a. $4.237 + 1.989 =$

   b. $11.4 - 9.62 =$

   c. $0.2 \times 3.413 =$

   d. $3.5 ÷ 0.5 =$

   e. $0.05 + 31.2 + 2 + 0.0006 =$

   f. $0.05 - 0.025 =$

   g. $\dfrac{2400\ ml}{70\ kg \times 2.2\ lb/kg} =$

   h. $\dfrac{12.45 + 0.08 - 3.125}{0.5 \times 2.2} =$

   i. $4.892 \times 100 =$

   j. $113.56 ÷ 1,000 =$

   k. $0.061 \times 1,000 =$

   l. $3.6 ÷ 100 =$

7. Now that we're comfortable with decimals, we can apply the decimal operations we've learned to the metric system. For example, it should now be fairly simple to convert the following volumes expressed in liters to milliliters:

   a. 1.5 liters = _____ milliliters

   b. 5 liters = _____ milliliters

   c. 0.6 liters = _____ milliliters

   d. 9.4 liters = _____ milliliters

   e. 0.02 liters = _____ milliliters

   f. 0.5 liters = _____ milliliters

   Similarly, it should be no problem to convert milliliters to liters:

   g. 300 milliliters = _____ liters

   h. 1,500 milliliters = _____ liters

   i. 10,000 milliliters = _____ liters

   j. 50 milliliters = _____ liters

   k. 2,000 milliliters = _____ liters

   l. 500 milliliters = _____ liters

8. Exactly the same calculations are required to convert between grams and milligrams:

   a. 1,500 milligrams = _____ grams

   b. 325 milligrams = _____ grams

   c. 3,500 milligrams = _____ grams

   d. 75 milligrams = _____ grams

   e. 10,000 milligrams = _____ grams

   f. 100 milligrams = _____ grams

   g. 5 grams = _____ milligrams

   h. 12 grams = _____ milligrams

   i. 0.5 grams = _____ milligrams

   j. 0.025 grams = _____ milligrams

   k. 0.001 gram = _____ milligrams

   l. 3.25 grams = _____ milligrams

9. Now let's start using these breathtaking arithmetic skills for some practical problems.

   You are called to attend to a 25-year-old woman who overdosed on diazepam (Valium). You find the empty pill bottle beside her. According to the label, the bottle had contained 50 tablets of 5 mg each.

   a. Assuming that the patient took all the tablets in the bottle, how many milligrams of the drug did she ingest? _____

   b. That is equivalent to how many *grams*? _____

   c. You radio your base for instructions. The base physician tells you to start an IV with normal saline. The objective will be to get 2 liters of fluid in over the next 2 hours. How many liters will the patient need to receive per *minute* in order to receive 2 liters over 2 hours? _____

   d. That is equivalent to _____ ml per minute.

   e. Because the woman is comatose and one cannot be 100 percent sure that the diazepam is the sole cause of her coma, the physician also instructs you to give 50 ml of 50% dextrose (D50). Fifty milliliters of 50% dextrose contains _____ grams of dextrose.

10. You are called to the home of a middle-aged man who is suffering severe chest pain. When you get him hooked up to the cardiac monitor, you notice that he is having frequent premature beats. The base physician tells you to administer 80 mg of lidocaine by IV push. You have a prefilled syringe containing lidocaine in a concentration of 20 mg per milliliter.

    a. What volume of lidocaine should you inject? _____ ml

    b. Your physician says you'd better hang up a lidocaine drip as well. He wants you to run it at a rate of 2 mg per minute. You have a vial of lidocaine for infusion that contains 1 gm of lidocaine. You started your intravenous infusion with a 500-ml bag of D5/W and a micro-drip infusion set (60 gtt/ml). If you add the contents of the vial of lidocaine (1 gm) to the bag of IV fluid (500 ml), what concentration of lidocaine will you have in the bag? _____ mg/ml

    c. How fast will you have to run the IV to give the patient 2 mg of lidocaine per minute as ordered? _____ ml/min, which is equivalent to _____ gtt/min

d. "Now," says the doctor at the other end of the radio, "we'd better do something about the patient's pain. Let's give him morphine, 0.1 mg per kilogram, by very slow IV push." The patient tells you that he weighs 175 pounds. What is his weight in kilograms?
_____ kg

e. If the dosage of morphine is 0.1 mg per kilogram, you need to give _____ mg of morphine.

f. Your Tubex cartridge contains morphine in a concentration of 10 mg per milliliter. How many milliliters of morphine do you need to administer to give the dosage you calculated above? _____ ml

g. You give the morphine as ordered, and almost immediately thereafter, the patient's pulse slows to 52 per minute. You report that turn of events to the base physician, and he says, "You'd better get a dose of atropine in fast. Give him the usual—0.01 mg per kilogram." You ferret around in the drug box and pull out a multidose vial of atropine. The label says that it contains atropine in a concentration of 1 mg per milliliter. What volume of atropine should you draw up into your syringe to give the patient the dosage ordered?
_____ ml

11. On the very next call, you have to treat a patient who is in cardiogenic shock. The physician instructs you to start a metaraminol (Aramine) drip. He tells you to add 100 mg of metaraminol to a 250-ml bag of D5/W and run it through a microdrip infusion set at 0.2 mg per minute.

a. The metaraminol in your drug box is in the form of 10-ml vials with a concentration of 10 mg per milliliter. How many milliliters of that solution do you need to add to the IV bag?
_____ ml

b. After you have added that volume of metaraminol, what will be the resultant concentration of the drug in the IV bag?
_____ mg/ml

c. What *volume* of fluid do you have to give the patient each minute to give the dosage ordered (0.2 mg/min)? _____
ml/min

d. Since your microdrip infusion set delivers 60 drops (gtt) per milliliter, that means you have to give _____ gtt per minute to administer 0.2 mg per minute.

12. When you finish your shift, you have a splitting headache from making all those calculations, so you call the base physician for advice on what to do for your headache. He says, "Take two aspirin and call me in the morning." Since you never take *any* medication without examining it closely first, you inspect the label on the aspirin bottle. You find that each aspirin tablet contains 325 mg of aspirin. If you take two tablets, therefore, you will be taking _____ mg of aspirin, which is the same as _____ gm of aspirin.

13. A bulletin is circulated to all paramedics in your EMS agency that a new drug, Panacea, is soon going to be added to the medications you are authorized to administer. You figure you'd better learn the important facts about Panacea now, before you are called on to use it, so you grab a notebook and head for the hospital library. List seven items of information you must find out about the drug before you administer it to a patient.

a.

b.

c.

d.

e.

f.

g.

14. A mistake in administering a drug can be fatal. One cannot, therefore, be too careful when it comes to administration of medications. List eight safety precautions you can take to minimize the possibility of making a mistake or otherwise causing harm with a medication.

a.

b.

c.

d.

e.

f.

g.

h.

15. For each of the following statements regarding drawing up and administering drugs, indicate whether the statement is true or false.

a. If the contents of a vial or ampule are cloudy or discolored, you may still administer the solution so long as it has not passed its expiration date.

TRUE   FALSE

b. To withdraw medication from an ampule, first inject an equivalent amount of air into the ampule.

TRUE   FALSE

c. Disinfect the rubber stopper of a vial with an alcohol swab before inserting a needle into the vial.

TRUE   FALSE

d. Intramuscular injections should be avoided in patients suspected to be suffering a heart attack.

TRUE   FALSE

e. To give an intramuscular injection, insert the needle into the muscle at an angle of 45 degrees.

TRUE   FALSE

f. As soon as you have completed giving an injection, swiftly recap the needle on the syringe.

TRUE   FALSE

g. Medications given down an endotracheal tube should be diluted in about 100 ml of sterile water.

TRUE   FALSE

16. And now for our secret message, a very important fact to remember about administering drugs in an emergency.

    a. Condition for which a drug is recommended   __ __ D __ __ __ __ __ __ __
                                          53 45   7 62 14 30 43 34 3

    b. Action of increased intensity after several doses of
       a drug   __ __ M __ __ __ __ __ __ __
               18 29   16 20 51 47 57 8 40

    c. Drug that increases body activity   __ __ __ __ __ L __ __ __
                                59 5 37 15 26   49 55 12

    d. Drug that decreases body activity   __ __ P __ __ __ __ __ __ __
                                1 9   13 33 36 46 21 38 56

    e. Oxygen-carrying pigment in the blood   __ __ M __ __ L __ __ __ __
                                 60 54   23 6   48 27 10 58

    f. Standing orders   __ __ __ __ __ __ __ L
                  50 24 4 42 61 41 2

    g. Trauma   I __ __ __ __ Y
               11 39 19 22

    h. What to wear on cold feet   __ __ __ __ __
                        26 44 28 63 17

    i. Sandwich fish   __ __ __ __
               52 35 32 31

Secret Message: __ __   __ __ __   __ __ __ __   __ __ __ __ __ __ __ __ __ __ __ __ __   __ __
                  1 2   3 4 5   6 7 8 9   10 11 12 13 14 15 16 17 18 19 20 21 22   23 24

__ __ __ - __ __ __ __ __ __ __ __ __   __ __ __ __ __ __ __ __ __ __   __ __   __
25 26 27   28 29 30 31 32 33 34 35 36   37 38 39 40 41 42 43 44 45 46   47 48   49

__ __ __ __ __ __ __   __ __   __ __ __ __ __.
50 51 52 53 54 55 56   57 58   59 60 61 62 63

Stop and Review I

Remember what a tort is? Or the difference between proximal and distal? Can you still identify the structures of the airway? Calculate how much oxygen is left in a cylinder? If the answer to any of those questions was negative, this section is for you. We have covered an enormous amount of material in the past 10 chapters. It's time to pause and consolidate some of what we've learned.

1. We will start with a secret message. Decode it in the usual fashion.

   a. Outer covering of the lungs __ __ __ __ __ __ A __   __ L __ U __ __
                                    7 51 26 15 54 3   36   49   45   23 20

   b. Structure in the larynx __ __ __ __ L __ __ __ __
                               44 31 9 55   48 2 24 53

   c. Profuse sweating __ __ __ P __ __ __ __ __ __ S
                        18 11 35   57 47 39 30 52 43

   d. Windpipe __ __ __ __ __ __ A
                56 50 22 21 29 6

   e. 110 pounds = __ __ __ __ __ kg
                    1 8 14 28 34

   f. PO means "by __ __ U __ __ "
                    12 13   37 5

   g. Wrongful conduct that gives rise to a suit __ O __ __
                                                  10   17 27

   h. Collapse of alveoli __ __ __ __ __ C __ __ S __ S
                           16 4 38 33 25   42 41   19

   i. Idea __ O __ I O __
            40   46   32

Secret Message:

__ __ __   __ __ __   __ __ __ __ __ __   __ __   __ __ __ __ __ __ __
1 2 3   4 5 6   7 8 9 10 11 12   13 14   15 16 17 18 19 20 21

__ __ __ __ __ __   __ __ __   __ __ __ __   __ __ __ __ __ __ __ __ __ __ __
22 23 24 25 26 27   28 29 30   31 32 33 34   35 36 37 38 39 40 41 42 43 44 45

__ __   __ __ __   __ __   __ __ __ __ __.
46 47   48 49 50   51 52   53 54 55 56 57

59

2. For each of the cases described below, indicate whether

   A. You may treat the patient without obtaining his expressed consent.

   B. You may *not* treat the patient without obtaining his expressed consent.

_____ A 9-year-old child struck by a car. He is bleeding profusely. His parents cannot be located.

_____ A 42-year-old man injured in an automobile accident in which his car was totally demolished. He has bruises on his forehead. He seems confused. He says, "I'm all right. Let me alone. Just call me a taxi."

_____ A 58-year-old man with chest pain. His wife phoned for an ambulance. The man says, "It's nothing, just indigestion." He refuses to be examined or treated.

_____ A 30-year-old woman pulled from the surf in cardiac arrest.

_____ A 25-year-old man injured in a barroom altercation. He is bleeding profusely from his nose and mouth. He smells strongly of alcohol. He is very belligerent and shouts at you, "Leave me alone, you creeps. If you come any closer, I'll knock your teeth in."

_____ An 80-year-old woman who fainted at home. Her son found her on the floor and called for an ambulance. She is conscious when you arrive. She says to you, "You are all very sweet, but one can't live forever, you know, and I don't much fancy hospitals."

If you elected *not* to treat any of the patients described above, explain what steps you *would* take.

_____

_____

_____

_____

_____

_____

_____

_____

_____

_____

_____

3. The way a person reacts to illness or injury will be largely determined by the mechanisms that person has developed over the years for dealing with stressful situations. List five common reactions to illness and injury.

   a.

   b.

   c.

   d.

   e.

4. Use your knowledge of medical root words to figure out the meaning of the following terms:

   a. Cephalalgia: _____

   b. Thoracentesis: _____

   c. Myasthenia: _____

   d. Hysterectomy: _____

   e. Hypoglycemia: _____

   f. Anesthesia: _____

   g. Cardiogenic: _____

   h. Rhinitis: _____

   i. Tachypnea: _____

   j. Hemiparesis: _____

   k. Oliguria: _____

   l. Thrombocytopenia: _____

5. You are called to the scene of a multivehicle accident on the interstate highway. As you approach the accident scene, you begin making your initial survey of the situation, which is the first step in the primary survey. List four questions you need to answer in making your survey of the accident scene.

   a.

   b.

   c.

   d.

6. Airway adjuncts can be very helpful in ensuring a patent air passage, but one needs to use the right adjunct in the right situation. Fill in the table below to remind yourself what to use (and not to use) when.

Adjunct	Indicated for:	Do not use in:
Oropharyngeal airway		
Esophageal obturator airway		
Endotracheal intubation		

7. Hidden in the grid below are 24 words relating to the respiratory system—20 of them are structures of the respiratory system or the chest; the remainder have to do with respiratory function or dysfunction. Find the hidden words, for you will need some of them to answer the questions that follow the grid.

```
C L E V E R I B S P A S M I S
A R P H R A G R R N E S T A T
R N I T W I P O L O U V R E E
G A G C A R I N A S N O A I R
O L L O P A C E E D C C M N
C V O U E I S H R A P A H O U
O E T T N O D I P T I L E U M
U O T I T G F O O H L C A T S
G L I P A I S L E Y A O S H O
H U S S L E S E O L A R Y N X
A S I G H E M A T U D D Y O P
V A L L E C U L A V I S H N O
E V E N T H O R A X I S T E X
N E T T L E D I A P H R A G M
```

a. Absence of breathing: _____.

b. Most effective way to expel a foreign body from the airway: _____.

c. Periodic deep inhalation to re-open collapsed alveoli: _____.

d. Protective reflex elicited by stimulating the back of the throat (but often absent in coma): _____.

e. Paired structures responsible for voice production: _____. The space between them is called the _____.

f. The breast bone is called the _____. _____. The prominence on the breast bone that lies opposite the second intercostal space is called the _____.

g. The structure behind the base of the tongue that shields the entrance to the larynx during swallowing is called the _____. The groove between that structure and the base of the tongue, where the tip of a curved laryngoscope blade comes to rest, is called the _____.

8. A passenger riding in a car is breathing quietly 12 times per minute, taking in 500 ml of air with each breath.

    a. What is his minute volume?
      _____ ml per minute

    b. The car is struck by a semitrailer. The passenger suffers injury to his cervical spine, which paralyzes him from the neck down (his intercostal muscles are also affected). His respiratory rate increases to 20 per minute, but his tidal volume falls to 200 ml. What is his minute volume now? _____ ml per minute

    c. What effect do you expect that change in minute volume to have on the patient's arterial PCO_2? _____ _____

    d. That, in turn, will cause the patient's pH to _____ (rise or fall?).

    e. The resulting derangement in his acid-base balance is called a _____ (respiratory or metabolic?) _____ (acidosis or alkalosis?).

    f. What treatment is required?
      _____

9. It's a cardiac arrest in a fourth floor walk-up apartment. You grab the jump kit and the handiest D cylinder from the ambulance, while your partner takes the drug box and defibrillator, and you sprint up the four flights of stairs to the patient's apartment. While your partner starts CPR, you "crack" the oxygen cylinder, hook up the oxygen to a bag-valve-mask, and open the flow control to 10 liters per minute. As you do so, you notice the reading on the presure gauge is 900 psi. How much time do you have before you need to switch to a fresh cylinder? _____ minutes (The cylinder constant for a D cylinder is 0.16. Show your computations.)

10. The method of choice for opening the airway of a trauma victim is

    A. Head tilt–chin lift

    B. Head tilt–neck lift

    C. Head tilt only

    D. Chin lift only

    E. Triple airway maneuver

    (Circle the best answer.)

11. The MAST is most appropriately used for

    A. Patients with head injury

    B. Patients with pelvic fracture

    C. Patients with chest injury

    D. All of the above

    E. None of the above

    (Circle the best answer.)

12. A 35-year-old man was the driver of a car that rammed head-on into an oncoming truck. When you reach the scene of the accident, you find the patient unconscious. There is a lot of blood in the passenger compartment of the car. Arrange the following steps in his management in the order in which you would perform them.

    A. Start an IV.

    B. Check for a pulse (if absent, start chest compressions).

    C. Apply the MAST.

    D. Check for hazards at the scene.

    E. Check for breathing (if absent, start artificial ventilation).

    F. Control external bleeding.

    G. Open the airway.

    (1) ____
    (2) ____
    (3) ____
    (4) ____
    (5) ____
    (6) ____
    (7) ____

13. Indicate whether each of the following statements is true or false.

    a. One of the earliest signs of hypovolemic shock is a fall in the blood pressure.

       TRUE   FALSE

    b. Patients in hypovolemic shock tend to suffer metabolic acidosis.

       TRUE   FALSE

    c. The intravenous fluid of choice to provide volume to a patient in hypovolemic shock is 5% dextrose in water (D5/W).

       TRUE   FALSE

    d. A patient may go into shock without losing any blood or fluid from his body.

       TRUE   FALSE

    e. In osmosis, water moves from a solution of lower solute concentration to a solution of higher solute concentration.

       TRUE   FALSE

    f. If the patient's abdomen starts to get distended during CPR, you should immediately apply pressure over the epigastrium to expel the air from the stomach.

       TRUE   FALSE

14. You are ordered to give a lidocaine drip at a rate of 2 mg per minute. You have on hand
- A vial containing 50 ml of 4% lidocaine
- A 500-ml bag of D5/W
- A microdrip administration set that delivers 60 gtt per milliliter

    a. How many *grams* of lidocaine are in the vial? _____ gm
(Show your calculations.)

    b. When you add the contents of the vial to the IV bag, what will be the concentration of lidocaine in the IV bag? _____ gm/ml

    c. How many milliliters per minute (ml/min) will the patient have to receive to get the dosage ordered (2 mg/min)? _____ ml/min

    d. How many *drops* per minute (gtt/min) is that equivalent to? _____ gtt/min

15. One final secret message, which by now should not be a secret!

 a. Bubble in the circulation ___ ___ ___ ___ ___ B ___ ___ ___ ___ ___
                48 11 25 33 19 13 44 21 36 12

 b. Having an osmotic pressure less than that of plasma ___ Y ___ ___ ___ O ___ ___ ___
                            5 42 52 40 22 8 23

 c. Hives ___ ___ ___ I ___ ___ ___ I ___
       18 43 35 9 46 32 38

 d. Opposing effects of a drug on another drug ___ ___ ___ ___ ___ ___ N ___ ___ M
                    28 49 15 30 51 2 27 34

 e. Where to check for a pulse ___ ___ ___ ___ ___ I ___
             29 17 31 45 37 50

 f. Nontherapeutic drug action: side ___ ___ ___ E ___ ___
               6 1 14 41 4

 g. May be incompetent to give consent ___ E ___ ___ ___ ___ E ___
               16 10 24 39 47 26

 h. Rant ___ ___ ___ E
      3 20 7

Secret Message: ___ ___ ___ ___ ___ ___ ___ ___ ___ ___ ___ ___ ___ ___ ___ ___ ___ ___ ___ ___
        1 2 3 4 5 6 7 8 9 10 11 12 13 14 15 16 17 18 19 20

___ ___ ___ ___ ___ ___ ___ ___ ___ ___ ___ ___ ___ ___ ___, ___ ___ ___ ___ ___
21 22 23 24 25 26 27 28 29 30 31 32 33 34 35 36 37 38 39 40

___ ___ ___, ___ ___ ___ ___, ___ ___ ___ ___ ___!
41 42 43 44 45 46 47 48 49 50 51 52

11
Obtaining the Medical History

1. You are called to the accident scene pictured below.

a. List four potential sources of information about what happened to the patient or about his medical background.

(1)

(3)

(2)

(4)

b. List four pieces of information you can derive simply from observing the scene.

(1)

(2)

(3)

(4)

c. List four reasons why it is necessary to take a history from the driver of the car.

(1)

(2)

(3)

(4)

d. Before you do so, however, you need to take some preliminary steps. List them.

_____

_____

_____

_____

_____

_____

_____

_____

_____

_____

_____

_____

_____

_____

_____

_____

_____

_____

_____

_____

_____

_____

_____

_____

2. For each of the following questions from a patient interview, indicate whether it is

    A. A well-phrased question

    B. A poorly phrased question

____ What seems to be the problem?

____ When did all this start?

____ Did the pain start when you were exerting yourself?

____ What is the pain like?

____ Is the pain sharp or dull?

____ Do you get short of breath when the pain comes on?

____ Has the pain gotten worse since it started?

____ How has the pain changed since it started?

____ What were you doing when the pain started?

____ Have you ever had pain like this before?

____ What medications do you take regularly?

____ Are you allergic to any medications?

____ What else is bothering you, besides the pain?

3. A patient's chief complaint is "pain in my gut."

    a. List six questions you would ask in eliciting the *history of the present illness.*

       (1)

       (2)

       (3)

       (4)

       (5)

       (6)

    b. List four questions you would ask about his *other medical history.*

       (1)

       (2)

       (3)

       (4)

4. Hidden in the grid below are 17 symptoms and 17 signs. Find the symptoms and signs and list them under the appropriate headings beneath the grid.

```
D T H I R S T O J A U N D I C E Y O
D I L A T E D P U P I L S B U R Y F
I N S U L I P H A R Y N B R U I S E
A D O T D I D Y S P N E A T A R O V
N I R V E R T P E T N U N C P S T E
A G E C A N N O T A R E N Y A S H R
U E T S C A D T S A L I A A L E E T
S S H C W H E E Z I N G D N L I A R
E T R R S E E N D O S E S O O D R E
A I O A L A K S O N O W I S R I T E
F O A M E D H I T M E P A I N S B T
A N T P A A G O R P A C E S O W U H
T C O S R C O N B L A C K E Y E R E
I E T R A H H A B U T I O V S L N B
G T O R C E T A B W R I N K E L I L
U R C T H A T A C H Y P N E A I R A
E Y E H E P M A T H U N G E R N N H
R E A D I Z Z Y S P E L L A U G H S
```

Symptoms

_____
_____
_____
_____
_____
_____
_____
_____
_____
_____
_____
_____
_____
_____

Signs

_____
_____
_____
_____
_____
_____
_____
_____
_____
_____
_____
_____
_____
_____

5. In the medical history below, circle and label

- The chief complaint
- The history of the present illness
- The other medical history

The patient is a 50-year-old man who called for an ambulance because of a severe headache. The headache started without warning about four hours earlier and got progressively worse. It was in the back part of the head, near the neck, and it radiated upward and around to the front. Nothing seemed to make it better or worse. The patient describes the headache as throbbing and very severe. He has never had a headache like this before. Along with the headache, he felt sick to his stomach, but he didn't vomit. He also felt as though he would pass out. He is under a doctor's care for diabetes, and he takes Diabinase daily for his diabetes. He also takes "a water pill" every morning. He denies any allergies.

12
Physical Assessment

1. By the time you have finished describing the patient's general appearance, even in only a sentence or two, the physician at the other end of the radio should already have a good general picture of the patient and of the urgency of the patient's situation. What parameters are included in the description of a patient's "general appearance"?

   a.

   b.

   c.

   d.

   e.

2. You are called to the scene of a road accident in which a car plowed into a utility pole. The driver of the car is sitting on the grass beside his wrecked vehicle looking dazed and confused. What parameters would you use to assess his level of consciousness, and how would you report your findings?

   _____

   _____

   _____

   _____

   _____

   _____

3. Before performing a detailed head-to-toe survey or even taking the vital signs, it is customary to make a quick check for obvious injuries. Why not simply wait until those injuries are detected during the head-to-toe survey?

   _____

   _____

   _____

   _____

   _____

   _____

   _____

   _____

4. In evaluating the patient's general appearance, we make a note, among other things, of the color, warmth, and degree of moisture of the patient's skin. For each of the skin conditions listed below, indicate whether it is most likely to be associated with

   A. Shock

   B. Heat stroke

   C. Cold exposure

   D. Fever

   _____ Hot, red, dry

   _____ Hot, red, wet

   _____ Cold, white, dry

   _____ Cold, pale, clammy

5. Measure the vital signs of a classmate or family member.

   a. Describe your findings:

     Temperature:

     Pulse:

     Respirations:

     Blood pressure:

   b. If the room had been very noisy, what alternative method could you have used for measuring the systolic blood pressure?

   c. Why is it customary to keep one's hand on the pulse when one measures the respiratory rate?

6. Match the following abnormal respiratory noises with the description that best fits each:

   A. Snoring

   B. Gurgling

   C. Stridor

   D. Crackles

   E. Wheezes

_____ Fine, crackling sounds produced by airways popping open

_____ High-pitched, whistling sounds produced by air moving through narrowed small airways (bronchioles)

_____ Rasping sound that signals partial upper airway obstruction by the tongue

_____ Sound made by fluid in the pharynx or larynx

_____ Harsh inspiratory squeak produced by severe narrowing of the upper airway, as in laryngeal edema

7. For each of the following sets of vital signs taken in adults, indicate whether the vital signs are within the range of normal. If they are not, indicate in what way they are abnormal and what underlying condition they may suggest to you from your experience as an EMT or from what we have learned so far in this text.

   a. Pulse = 120, thready, and regular
      Respirations = 20, shallow, slightly labored
      Blood pressure = 90 systolic (by palpation)

     (1) These vital signs are _____ (normal or abnormal?).

     (2) If they are abnormal, what is abnormal about them?

     (3) If they are abnormal, what do they suggest to you about what might be wrong with the patient?

   b. Pulse = 72, full, and regular
      Respirations = 4 and snoring
      Blood pressure = 110/70

     (1) These vital signs are _____ (normal or abnormal?).

     (2) If they are abnormal, what is abnormal about them?

     (3) If they are abnormal, what do they suggest to you about what might be wrong with the patient?

     (4) Suppose you had the additional information that the patient's pupils were extremely constricted. Would that help you interpret the vital signs? How?

c. Pulse = 60, full, slightly irregular
Respirations = 30 and deep; no unusual odors
on the breath
Blood pressure = 200/140

    (1) These vital signs are _____
(normal or abnormal?).

    (2) If they are abnormal, what is abnormal
about them?

    (3) If they are abnormal, what do they suggest
to you about what might be wrong with the
patient?

    (4) Suppose you had the additional informa-
tion that the patient's pupils were unequal—one was midposition, the other
widely dilated. Would that help you interpret the vital signs? How?

d. Pulse = 56, full, and regular
Respirations = 12 and unlabored
Blood pressure = 120/65

    (1) These vital signs are _____
(normal or abnormal?).

    (2) If they are abnormal, what is abnormal
about them?

    (3) If they are abnormal, what do they suggest
to you about what might be wrong with the
patient?

8. Match each of the signs listed below with the
phrase that best describes its possible diagnostic
significance. (Note: More than one sign may have
the same diagnostic significance.)

A. Ecchymoses around the eyes
B. Fruity odor to the breath
C. Stridor
D. Pitting edema of both feet
E. Paralysis of upward gaze
F. Muffled heart sounds
G. Battle's sign
H. Patient lies very still; cries out when stretcher
is jarred
I. Pinpoint pupils
J. Cyanosis of the lips
K. Capillary refill takes 5 seconds
L. Restlessness
M. Absent pulse
N. Retraction of the suprasternal muscles
O. Jugular veins distended to 10 cm with the pa-
tient sitting
P. Crackling sensation in the skin over the chest
Q. Distended, bruised abdomen in trauma victim
R. Pain on compression of the iliac crests
S. Priapism
T. No movement or sensation in the right arm or
leg
U. S₃ gallop
V. Clear fluid draining from the ear

____ Narcotics overdose

____ Cardiac arrest

____ Heart failure

____ Skull fracture

____ Stroke

____ Hypoxemia

____ Respiratory distress

____ Shock

____ Diabetic ketoacidosis

____ Spinal cord injury

____ Increased right ventricular pressure

____ Laryngeal edema

____ Pelvic fracture

____ Fluid/blood in the pericardium

____ Intra-abdominal bleeding

____ Peritonitis

____ Fracture of the orbit (eye socket in the skull)

____ Pneumothorax

9. In examining a person who has been injured ("trauma patient"), we look for different signs than we would if examining an ill person ("medical patient"). Fill in the table below to indicate what you would look for in particular when examining the different body regions of a trauma patient and a medical patient.

Body Region	Trauma Patient	Medical Patient
Head		
Neck		
Chest		
Abdomen		
Back		
Extremities		

10. And now for our secret message. Once you have decoded it, please *don't* keep it a secret!

   a. Crackling sounds from airways popping open (old terminology) __ __ __ __ __
                                                          53 24 5 59 35

   b. Paralysis on one side of the body __ __ __ __ __ __ __ __ __ A
                                                 21 10 44 27 40 56 17 64 13

   c. Swelling __ __ __ M __
                2 61 22   55

   d. Weakness on one side of the body __ __ M __ P __ __ __ __ __ __
                                        38 28   32   46 48 52 7 62 14

   e. Colorless, odorless gas vital to life __ __ Y __ __ __
                                 18 42   33 6 63

   f. Cardiac standstill A __ __ __ __ __ __ __
                        12 39 31 20 47 58 23

   g. Passage of water across a semipermeable membrane __ __ M __ __ __ __
                        15 29   41 3 45 8

   h. Position of patient's head for endotracheal intubation __ __ __ __ __ I __ G
                        11 34 49 19 37   16

   i. Ecchymosis over the mastoid __ A __ __ __ __ 'S sign
                      57   4 51 26 43

   j. mm Hg __ __ __ __
          30 36 1 25

   k. Number of lives a cat has __ I __ __
                 54   9 60

   l. What to say when a patient offers you a "joint" __ O
                       50

Secret Message: __ __ __ __ __ __ __ __ __ __ __ __   __ __   __ __ __   __ __   __ __ __
                  1 2 3 4 5 6 7 8 9 10 11 12   13 14   15 16 17   18 19   20 21 22

__ __ __ __ __ __ __ __   __ __ __ __ __   __ __   __ __ __ __ __ __ __ __ __
23 24 25 26 27 28 29 30   31 32 33 34 35   36 37   38 39 40 41 42 43 44 45 46

__ __   __ __ __ __ __ __ __ __   __ __ __ __ __ __ __ __.
47 48   49 50 51 52 53 54 55 56   57 58 59 60 61 62 63 64

13
Medical Reporting and Record Keeping

It does precious little good to take a careful history and conduct a thorough physical examination if you cannot communicate your findings to others. To do so, you need to know how to organize those findings in such a way that other medical professionals will really hear what you have to say.

1. To begin with, you need to know which information belongs in the patient's history and which should be reported as part of the physical examination. Label each of the following statements to indicate whether it is

A. The chief complaint

B. Part of the history of the present illness

C. Part of the patient's other medical history

D. Part of the description of the patient's general appearance

E. Part of the vital signs

F. Part of the head-to-toe survey

G. Part of the treatment

H. Part of the patient's condition during transport

_____ a. There was no pedal edema (edema of the feet).

_____ b. The patient is allergic to penicillin.

_____ c. The pain came on while he was watching television.

_____ d. The blood pressure was 190/110.

_____ e. He was given oxygen by nasal cannula at 4 liters per minute.

_____ f. The patient is a 51-year-old man with chest pain.

_____ g. The chest was clear.

_____ h. His skin was cold, pale, and sweaty.

_____ i. The patient was transported in a semisitting position.

_____ j. Nothing seemed to make the pain better or worse.

_____ k. The pulse was 52 and full, with an occasional premature beat.

_____ l. The neck veins were not distended.

_____ m. There was no cyanosis of the lips.

_____ n. The patient takes Maalox and cimetidine regularly.

_____ o. He also felt nauseated.

_____ p. His abdomen was soft and nontender.

_____ q. His respirations were 20 per minute and unlabored.

_____ r. He was sitting in a chair and appeared to be frightened.

_____ s. He is under the care of Dr. Tums for an ulcer.

_____ t. He was alert and fully oriented.

_____ u. He denies any shortness of breath.

_____ v. An IV was started with D5/W to a KVO rate.

_____ w. The pain radiates down his left arm.

_____ x. The blood pressure came down to 170/90 during transport.

_____ y. He describes the pain as squeezing.

_____ z. Heart sounds were clear.

Now, rearrange the statements above into the order in which they should be presented.

(1) _____   (10) _____   (19) _____
(2) _____   (11) _____   (20) _____
(3) _____   (12) _____   (21) _____
(4) _____   (13) _____   (22) _____
(5) _____   (14) _____   (23) _____
(6) _____   (15) _____   (24) _____
(7) _____   (16) _____   (25) _____
(8) _____   (17) _____   (26) _____
(9) _____   (18) _____

2. Now let's try the same exercise with the victim of trauma. First label each of the following statements to indicate whether it is

A. The chief complaint

B. Part of the history of the present illness

C. Part of the patient's other medical history

D. Part of the description of the patient's general appearance

E. Part of the vital signs

F. Part of the head-to-toe survey

G. Part of the treatment

H. Part of the patient's condition during transport

_____ a. The right leg was severely angulated at the mid-femur.

_____ b. The pulse was 92, somewhat weak, and regular.

_____ c. Bystanders say that the car that hit him was travelling very fast.

_____ d. He has a Medic Alert tag that says he is a diabetic.

_____ e. There is a bruise on the left forehead.

_____ f. His skin is cool, pale, and moist.

_____ g. He was secured to a backboard.

_____ h. The patient is a middle-aged man who was struck by a car while crossing the street.

_____ i. Respirations were 30, deep, and noisy; BP was 160/100.

_____ j. The patient was unconscious and did not withdraw from painful stimuli.

_____ k. An oropharyngeal airway was inserted, and oxygen was given by nasal cannula at 4 liters per minute.

_____ l. He apparently staggered into the street without looking, as if he were drunk.

_____ m. The chest wall was stable, and breath sounds were equal bilaterally.

_____ n. We put the right leg in a traction splint.

_____ o. The pupils were equal, midposition, and reactive to light.

_____ p. There was no change in his condition during transport.

_____ q. There was no blood or fluid draining from his nose or ears.

_____ r. His abdomen was soft.

_____ s. The dorsalis pedis pulses were equal.

Now, arrange the statements above in the correct order for presentation.

(1) _____   (8) _____   (15) _____
(2) _____   (9) _____   (16) _____
(3) _____   (10) _____   (17) _____
(4) _____   (11) _____   (18) _____
(5) _____   (12) _____   (19) _____
(6) _____   (13) _____
(7) _____   (14) _____

3. In the following case history, circle or label

• The chief complaint

• The history of the present illness

• The other medical history

• The general appearance

• The vital signs

• The head-to-toe survey

• The treatment given

• Pertinent negatives

The patient is a 49-year-old man who called for an ambulance because of chest pain. The pain was "squeezing" in character, radiated to the left shoulder and jaw, and had been present for 2 hours. The pain was accompanied by increasing difficulty in breathing, relieved somewhat by sitting upright. The patient denied nausea, vomiting, sweating, or palpitations. He is known to be a heart patient and takes nitroglycerin at home; he took two nitroglycerin today, without relief. He denies any history of hypertension or diabetes. He has been treated for peptic ulcer in the past.

On physical examination, the patient was sitting bolt upright; he appeared alert and apprehensive and was in moderate respiratory distress, breathing shallowly 30 times per minute. Pulse was 130, weak and regular and BP 200/90. His neck veins were distended to the angle of the jaw at 45 degrees. Wet crackles were heard at both lung bases, and auscultation of the heart revealed a gallop rhythm. The abdomen was not distended. There was 1+ presacral and ankle edema.

The patient was given oxygen by nasal cannula at 6 liters/minute and transported to Montefiore Hospital in a semisitting position. His vital signs remained stable throughout transport.

4. An ambulance run report, or trip sheet, must also contain other information—besides that contained in a traditional medical history. List at least one other item of information that needs to be recorded on a trip sheet, and explain why that information is important.

   a. Information that should be recorded:

   b. Why that information is important:

5. Give two reasons why you should make certain that your trip sheet is as accurate and complete as possible.

   a.

   b.

14
Mechanisms of Trauma

1. A 2,000-pound automobile is travelling at 20 mph when it strikes a pedestrian.

   a. What happens to the kinetic energy of the vehicle at the moment of impact?

   b. If the vehicle had weighed 6,000 pounds instead of 2,000 pounds, what difference would that have made in terms of its kinetic energy?

   c. If the vehicle had been travelling 60 mph rather than 20 mph, what difference would that have made in terms of its kinetic energy?

2. A car travelling at 50 mph goes out of control and slams into a concrete wall. That sequence of events in fact produces three separate collisions, each involving a transfer of kinetic energy. What objects are involved in each collision, and what happens to the kinetic energy in each case?

   a. Collision 1:

   b. Collision 2:

   c. Collision 3:

3. For each of the injuries listed below, indicate whether it is most likely to be associated with

   A. A head-on collision

   B. A lateral collision

   C. A rear-end collision

   D. A pedestrian struck by an oncoming car

   (Note: Some injuries may be associated with more than one type of accident.)

   _____ "Whiplash" injury

   _____ Lateral rib fractures

   _____ Fracture of the tibia/fibula

   _____ Fracture of the patella

   _____ Fracture of the humerus

   _____ Cervical spine injury

4. Careful inspection of a wrecked vehicle can enable the rescuer to detect injuries among the victims that might not otherwise be obvious. For each of the vehicular findings mentioned below, list the injuries that are likely to be associated.

Vehicular Clue	Injuries To Be Alert For
Bashed-in dashboard	_____
	_____
	_____
	_____
	_____
Broken steering wheel	_____
	_____
	_____
	_____
	_____

Spider-web crack in
windshield

_____
_____
_____
_____

Door on driver's
side smashed in

_____
_____
_____
_____

Front-seat
occupants
wearing three-
point seat belts

_____
_____
_____
_____

5. You are summoned to the scene of a smoky apartment-house fire. When you arrive, one of the firefighters directs you to a casualty who has been carried to a spot just beyond the fire lines. The firefighter tells you that the man jumped from a window.

a. What further information do you need to obtain about this patient to evaluate the potential seriousness of the injuries he might have sustained making that jump?

(1)

(2)

(3)

(4)

b. Assuming that he landed on his feet, what injuries might you expect him to have suffered?

6. On your very next call, you are summoned to a housing project where a 2-year-old child managed to crawl over the edge of a second-story balcony and fall into the playground below. What sort of injuries would be most likely in this child, and why?

_____
_____
_____
_____
_____

7. You are called to a somewhat disreputable downtown area for a "man shot." You finally locate the patient lying in the center of a small group of men, some of them apparently intoxicated and all of them talking at once.

a. What is the *first* action you will take on reaching the scene?

b. What information do you need to obtain regarding the shooting incident?

c. What will you look for in particular in conducting the physical examination?

8. A fire at a warehouse of a large construction company ignites their stock of dynamite and produces an explosion that shatters windows for blocks around. As you respond to the scene, you review in your mind the different kinds of injuries you might soon have to deal with. List the four categories of injuries that can be produced by an explosion, and give at least one example of each.

Category of Injury   Example(s)

_____   _____

_____   _____

_____   _____

_____   _____

9. Among the patients you treat at the scene of the explosion is a young man who had been taking a walk about half a block from the construction company when the explosion occurred. The man states that the blast "knocked me clear off my feet." He complains of a "tight feeling in my chest" and blurry vision. On physical examination, he appears somewhat confused; he cannot tell you the date or what day of the week it is. His vital signs are pulse = 100, full and regular; respirations = 30 and somewhat shallow; BP = 120/80. His skin is warm and dry. Aside from a little dried blood in the left ear canal, there are no other physical findings. What injuries do you think this patient has suffered? What is the evidence for thinking so?

Injury   Evidence

_____   _____

_____   _____

_____   _____

_____   _____

10. Many important secrets regarding a patient's injuries may be encoded within the vehicle in which he was travelling or the scene in which he is found—just as the secret message at the end of this question is encoded in the words defined below. Fill in the words and decode the message.

a. Oscillation around the vertical axis ___ ___ ___
                                                         76 37 93

b. Point at which an object penetrates the body ___ ___ ___ R ___ ___ ___ ___   ___ O ___ ___ ___
            86 33 79   64 45 41 3   8   51 69 26

c. Mandible ___ ___ ___
             73 23 1

d. Likely to be fractured by dashboard impact ___ ___ ___ ___ ___ ___ A
                  43 21 27 15 81 16

e. May also be fractured by dashboard impact ___ ___ M ___ ___
               53 59   74 31

f. May be dislocated after dashboard impact ___ ___ ___
             6 71 82

g. May be lacerated by steering wheel ___ ___ I ___
             63 13   78

h. Blood in the pleural space ___ ___ ___ ___ ___ ___ ___ ___ X
          90 96 22 32 5 47 84 75 44

i. May be fractured in lateral collision ___ ___ M ___ ___ ___ ___
          28 77   70 55 42 35

j. Another injury from a lateral collision ___ ___ ___ ___ L   ___ ___ ___ ___ ___
          52 65 48 14   40 2 25 19 46

k. Two organs apt to suffer deceleration injury in a fall ___ ___ L ___ ___ ___ and L ___ ___ ___ ___
          95 67 7 36 4   18 61 56 83

l. Below; toward the feet ___ ___ ___ ___ ___ ___ ___ R
          94 72 30 54 92 9 39

m. Opening between the vocal cords ___ L ___ ___ ___ ___ ___
          24   88 34 89 80 49

n. Vital information from the dispatcher A ___ ___ ___ ___ ___ ___
           87 17 60 29 12 66

o. Banned insecticide ___ ___ ___
          11 20 38

p. Something a paramedic should not be I ___ ___ ___ ___ ___ ___ ___ ___ E
          10 57 91 58 62 50 68 85

Secret Message: ___ ___ ___ ___   ___ ___ ___   ___ ___ ___ ___ ___ ___ ___ ___ ___ ___   ___ ___
         1 2 3 4   5 6 7   8 9 10 11 12 13 14 15 16 17   18 19

___ ___ ___ ___ ___ ___ ___,   ___ ___ ___   ___ ___ ___ ___ ___   ___ ___ ___ ___   ___ ___ ___ ___ ___ ___ ___ ___   ___ ___ ___
20 21 22 23 24 25 26   27 28 29   30 31 32 33 34   35 36 37 38   39 40 41 42 43 44 45 46   47 48 49

___ ___ ___ ___ ___ ___ ___ ___   ___ ___ ___ ___ ___ ___ ___ ___   ___ ___ ___ ___ ___   ___ ___ ___ ___ ___ ___
50 51 52 53 54 55 56 57   58 59 60 61 62 63 64 65   66 67 68 69 70   71 72 73 74 75 76

___ ___ ___ ___ ___   ___ ___ ___ ___ ___ ___   ___ ___ ___ ___ ___ ___ ___ ___ ___.
77 78 79 80 81   82 83 84 85 86 87   88 89 90 91 92 93 94 95 96

15
Wounds and Burns

1. Human skin is a quite remarkable all-weather coat whose design features enable it to serve a variety of critical functions for us.

   a. Label the components of the skin in the diagram below.

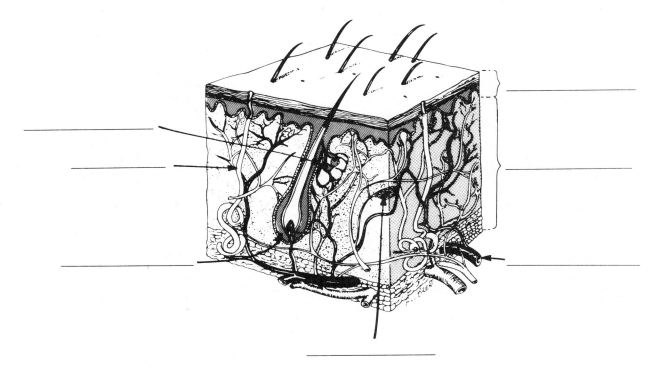

   b. We can appreciate the possible consequences of injury to the skin if we understand what functions healthy, intact skin performs for us. List four functions performed by the skin in a healthy person.

   (1)   (3)

   (2)   (4)

2. Examine the injuries shown.

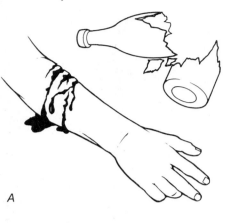

A

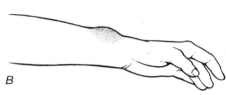

B

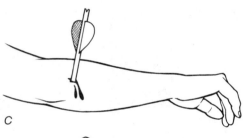

C

D

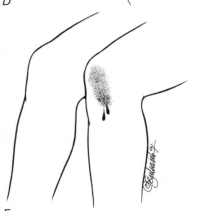

E

a. Injury A is called a(n) _____.
   The appropriate treatment is:

b. Injury B is called a(n) _____.
   The appropriate treatment is:

c. Injury C is called a(n) _____.
   The appropriate treatment is:

d. Injury D is called a(n) _____.
   The appropriate treatment is:

e. Injury E is called a(n) _____.
   The appropriate treatment is:

3. Hidden in the grid below are 27 words or phrases that should sound familiar after having read Chapter 15. Locate the hidden words and phrases, and then use them to answer the questions that follow the grid.

```
P S E X I T W O U N D E D S C A M
B L I S T E R S T W H I L E A M A
R C A N O E O F F M A T B U R N K
A R C C G O T D E R M I S S D E I
S U H B E E T A S C A L D A I S D
S T A N D R D Y N A S C O M A I N
Y U R L R E A N S Y N O T A C A E
C U R I E L L T A P N E A U A N Y
O L I O D O L I I S U N B U R N D
U R N O N O T W R O A T H U R E A
G I G H E A R H E I N L U T E U M
H O A R S E N E S S U C H M S P A
P A N E S T H E S I A M D A T A G
L A T I N E N Z Y M E L A N I N E
A S H Y P E R E S T H E S I A R T
N E A R A W A S P A R A L Y S I S
```

a. An abrasion is sometimes called a(n) _____
_____.

b. A jagged cut is a(n) _____.

c. The skin derives its color from granules of pigment called _____.

d. These three words are associated with *first-*degree burns:
_____
_____
_____

e. These three words are associated with *second-*degree burns:
_____
_____
_____

f. These two words are associated with *third-*degree burns:
_____
_____

g. Suspect that a victim of flame burns has suffered respiratory injury if any of the following signs are present:
_____
_____
_____
_____
_____
_____

h. Injury from a high-voltage electric source or from lightning may produce any of the following:
_____
_____
_____
_____
_____
_____
_____
_____

4. You are summoned to Bugsy's Butcher Shop to tend to the proprietor, Bugsy Butterfingers, who dropped a meat cleaver on his left leg. There is a large gash in the left calf, and it is bleeding profusely.

    a. List five methods you might use to try to control the bleeding, and put an asterisk next to the method likely to be the most effective.

    (1)

    (2)

    (3)

    (4)

    (5)

    b. Suppose Bugsy's wound had been on the forearm rather than on the leg. Which artery could you have compressed in that case to help control the bleeding?

5. One of Bugsy's employees, Frank Fillet, becomes so distracted watching you care for his boss that he accidently chops off two of his fingers while preparing an order of steaks.

    a. How will you treat Frank's injury?

    b. What will you do with the two fingers lying on the chopping board?

6. Yet another worker in the butcher shop, Hercules Hamburger, had been watching, slack-jawed and transfixed, as this drama was unfolding. So intent was he on the spectacle that he did not realize his right hand had entered the meat grinder—not until, that is, the hand became engaged in the grinding blades. Hearing his screams, a customer rushes over to where Hercules is standing and manages to shut off the meat grinder, but not before Hercules' hand and forearm have been badly mangled. You already have your hands full with Bugsy and Frank, so you instruct the good Samaritan who shut off the meat grinder, "Have him lie down, and try to control the bleeding—I'll be with him in just a minute." Obligingly, the customer grabs a piece of rope that he finds behind the counter, winds it around Hercules' upper arm, and slips a ball-point pen into the knot to serve as a Spanish windlass. He twists the rope as tight as he possibly can, secures the pen, and uses the butcher's apron to wrap the entire hand and arm.

    Although the customer was trying to be helpful, in fact he made several very serious mistakes. List them.

    _____

    _____

    _____

    _____

    _____

    _____

7. You are called to the scene of a smoky apartment-house fire to treat a man who jumped from his bedroom window about 15 feet above the ground. What you observe at first glance is the following: He is now lying unconscious on the ground. His trousers are smoldering. His beard is partly burned off, and his lips are swollen. His left leg is splayed out a peculiar angle. List in the correct sequence the steps you would take in managing this patient.

    _____

    _____

    _____

    _____

    _____

    _____

    _____

    _____

    _____

    _____

8. If you chose to intubate the trachea of the patient described in the previous question, give two reasons why.

    a.

    b.

    (If you chose *not* to intubate the trachea, you'd better have some good reasons why not!)

9. On examining the patient, you find burns covering the following areas:

    The whole right leg (front and back)
    The anterior left leg
    The anterior trunk
    The whole right arm

    a. Use the Rule of Nines to calculate what percentage of the patient's body surface area is burned: _____ percent. (Show your calculations.)

    b. If the patient weighs 154 pounds, at what rate should you run his IV? Use the Parkland formula to calculate the rate (and don't forget to convert his weight to kilograms first!). (Show your calculations.)
    IV rate = _____ ml/hr

c. If you have a standard infusion set that delivers 10 gtt per milliliter, at how many drops per minute do you have to run the IV to deliver the volume you calculated?
IV rate = _____ gtt/min

d. What intravenous fluid will you use?

10. While you are securing the IV on the patient described in the previous questions, firefighters lead his wife over to you (they just rescued her from another room). A quick check does not reveal any injuries, but you give her oxygen by nasal cannula anyway, because of her exposure to smoke. Meanwhile, you take advantage of the opportunity to get some information about her husband. List five questions you would ask this woman regarding her husband and what happened to him.

    a.

    b.

    c.

    d.

    e.

11. Meanwhile, the firefighters bring you yet another victim of the fire, a college student who climbed down a fire escape in back of the building. He suffered burns to the right side of his body and complains of severe pain in the right arm. On examination you find the following:

- The *right arm* is mottled red and exquisitely sensitive to the lightest touch (even the breeze blowing past it causes pain).
- The *right flank* is fiery red and also very painful.
- The *right lower leg* has a leathery appearance. In places you can see thrombosed veins beneath the surface. When you touch the skin with a sterile needle, the patient does not feel the pinprick.

a. The burn on the right arm is probably
   _____ degree.
   The appropriate treatment for that burn is:

b. The burn on the flank is probably
   _____ degree.
   The appropriate treatment for that burn is:

c. The burn on the right leg is probably
   _____ degree.
   The appropriate treatment for that burn is:

12. In the course of a busy week, you are called on to treat eight burn victims in a variety of circumstances. In each case, you have to determine whether the victim has suffered a critical burn, for if so, he or she must be evacuated directly to the Regional Burn Center, which is 24 miles away; noncritical burns, on the other hand, can be managed by the community hospital right in town. Here is a description of the patients you saw. Beside each description, indicate whether

  A. The patient has a critical burn and should be brought to a burn center.

  B. The patient does not have a critical burn and can be managed in the community hospital.

_____ A 2-year-old child who overturned a pot of soup from the stovetop onto himself; both legs and the anterior trunk are burned.

_____ A 57-year-old diabetic woman with a scald burn of her left lower leg.

_____ A 28-year-old housewife with a scald burn of her entire right arm.

_____ A lineman who suffered an electric shock. There is a small bull's-eye entrance wound on the left hand; you cannot find the exit wound. The lineman did not fall. His left leg feels rock hard.

_____ A 22-year-old short-order cook with second-degree burns over both anterior thighs, sustained when he spilled a pot of soup.

_____ A 34-year-old woman rescued from a burning building, where she had been trapped in her smoke-filled bedroom. She has second-degree burns of the right forearm. She is coughing up sooty sputum.

_____ A 25-year-old man who tripped and fell onto the hibachi on the back porch as he was preparing to barbecue some steaks. His hand went straight into the bed of red-hot charcoal, and his shirt caught fire. He has third-degree burns of the left hand and forearm, and second-degree burns of the anterior chest.

_____ A plumber who spilled a bottle of industrial-strength liquid drain cleaner down the front of his trousers.

13. You are called to treat the victim of a tenement fire, a middle-aged man who apparently fell asleep in an armchair while holding a lit cigarette. You arrive at the scene just as he is being carried unconscious from the building, his clothes still smoldering.

   a. Listed below, in random order, are the steps you will have to take in managing this patient. Arrange the steps in the correct sequence.

   A. Administer oxygen.

   B. Start an IV.

   C. Open the airway manually.

   D. Put out the fire.

   E. Remove the victim's clothing.

   F. Pass a nasogastric tube into his stomach.

   G. Determine the extent and depth of the burn.

   H. Intubate the trachea.

   I. Cover the burns with sterile dressings.

   J. Obtain first set of vital signs.

   (1) ____   (6) ____
   (2) ____   (7) ____
   (3) ____   (8) ____
   (4) ____   (9) ____
   (5) ____   (10) ____

   b. In examining the patient, you find that he has mixed second- and third-degree burns of his entire left leg and posterior right leg, extending into his groin. There are also second-degree burns over most of the left forearm.
      What percent of his body is burned?
      _____ percent. (Show your calculations.)

   c. Does he have a critical burn? Explain the reason for your answer.

   d. In doing the secondary survey, you are unable to detect either a dorsalis pedis or an anterior tibial pulse in the left foot.
      What do you think is the most likely reason?

   e. What are you going to do about it?

14. Indicate which of the following statements about chemical burns are true and which are false.

   a. If you know the identity of the chemical that caused the burn, it is preferable to start treatment with a chemical antidote (e.g., to apply a weak acid to an alkali burn and vice versa).

   TRUE   FALSE

   b. When a person has been burned by a chemical agent, the skin should be flushed for a minimum of 30 minutes with copious amounts of water.

   TRUE   FALSE

   c. It is important to use only sterile water to flush a chemical burn, lest you contaminate the burn wound.

   TRUE   FALSE

   d. In burns caused by hot tar, it is crucial to remove the tar from contact with the skin as quickly as possible to prevent systemic tar poisoning.

   TRUE   FALSE

   e. If chemicals have splashed into someone's eyes, the eyes should be irrigated with a steady stream of water for at least 30 minutes.

   TRUE   FALSE

15. You are called to a construction site 20 miles out of town for a "man electrocuted." According to the person who telephoned your dispatcher, one of the construction workers apparently bulldozed through a buried electric cable. He dismounted his bulldozer and picked up the cable to toss it aside, not realizing that it was live, and his hand "froze" to the cable.

 a. En route to the call, you review in your mind the types of injuries that may occur in connection with electrocution. You remember that there may be three different types of burns.

   (1)

   (2)

   (3)

 b. You also recall that high-voltage electricity may cause a variety of nonburn injuries. List six possible injuries or abnormal conditions that you need to be alert for in this patient.

   (1)

   (2)

   (3)

   (4)

   (5)

   (6)

 c. When you reach the construction site, you see a knot of agitated people over at one end of the site. One of them is holding a long two-by-four, with which he apparently jarred the victim loose from the cable. The victim is lying very still and appears to be unconscious. The free end of the cable is now arcing along the ground like an angry snake. List the steps you will take in dealing with this situation in the sequence in which you will perform them.

16. The electric shock victim described in question 15 quickly regains consciousness. You find on questioning that he has no significant medical history. On examination, vital signs are normal. There is an entrance wound on his right hand and an exit wound on his right foot. He complains of excruciating pain in his left leg. The base physician gives you orders by radio to administer 24 mg of morphine intravenously.

 a. What is the usual therapeutic dosage of morphine sulfate? _____ mg per kilogram

 b. Assuming that this patient weighs 70 kg, what would be the approximate dosage for him? _____ mg
 In view of that, do you think the doctor's order was correct? _____

 c. Once you get the matter of the dosage straightened out, you are ready to give the morphine. List three potential side effects that you should be prepared to deal with.

   (1)

   (2)

   (3)

17. Since you will have a relatively long transport time in bringing the electric shock victim to hospital, the doctor also orders you to give 1 mEq per kilogram of sodium bicarbonate and 0.5 gm per kilogram of mannitol intravenously.

  a. The sodium bicarbonate in your drug box comes in the form of 50-ml syringes containing 1 mEq per milliliter of sodium bicarbonate. How many milliliters will you have to inject? (Recall that the patient weighs 70 kg. Show your calculations.) _____ ml

  b. List three other indications for sodium bicarbonate, besides electric shock.

  (1)

  (2)

  (3)

  c. List two *contraindications* to giving sodium bicarbonate.

  (1)

  (2)

  d. List three potential side effects of sodium bicarbonate.

  (1)

  (2)

  (3)

  e. With regard to the mannitol that the physician ordered, what dosage of mannitol will this 70-kg patient require? _____ gm

  f. In your drug box, you have a 15% solution of mannitol in a 500-ml bottle. How many milliliters of mannitol will you have to infuse to give the dosage you just calculated? (Show your calculations.) _____ ml

  g. List three contraindications to giving mannitol.

  (1)

  (2)

  (3)

  h. Suppose this patient had a history of congestive heart failure. Which of the drugs that the physician ordered would then be contraindicated in this case?

18. You are out for a day's fishing with some friends on a cloudy Saturday. You are all sitting on the shore of a lake, leaning up against some nice tall trees, trading horror stories from work while waiting for the fish to bite. Suddenly there is a loud clap of thunder, and rain starts pouring down. List three things you can do to minimize your chances of being struck by lightning.

    a.

    b.

    c.

19. A couple of miles down the road, your partner was spending his afternoon off at a Little League baseball game in the ball field beside the junior high school, and that loud clap of thunder you heard in fact came from a lightning bolt that hit the playing field. A few moments later, you hear your partner calling over his two-way radio for help (you never go anywhere without your two-way radio, which makes you an excellent candidate for early burnout), so you and your buddies pile into your car and tear over to the Little League field. There, the first thing you notice is at least half a dozen people lying motionless on the playing field in the pouring rain.

    a. What should you do *first*?

    b. Which victim(s) should be treated first?

16
Injuries to the Head, Neck, and Spine

1. Hidden in the grid below are 37 words you encountered in this chapter. Find the hidden words and use them to answer the questions that follow the grid.

```
P A C E D F R O N T A L K C L I P A C T
S A T E U T O N I C E R E B U L B O O T
C O H B R A I N S T E M P U M A N A R E
A C O L A E L I Z M A T P U B L I S N O
L C R A M A B A Y D A E L O A D H A E M
P I A M A T E R G E O N C E R V I C A L
U P C A T E L A O P E T D O G A I R E V
B I I C E L L C M S A O L I G O L A M E
A T C E R V E H A L P R O R B I T L E R
L A I R M A I N Y E S I I N G L O B E T
M L I E U P N O S E T U N E H A E M O E
A E R B R U N I C O S M T A T T L E R B
X O D R E P I D U R A L L U L A K E E R
I S I U M I L L I M E E T E R F L E A A
L A S M L L O I N S C E R E B E L L U M
L I C E S L F O R A M E N M A G N U M B
A S C L E R A I D I M E N I N G E S I A
D E T E R S T E P I S T A X I S T A N D
```

a. The brain and spinal cord are bathed in a liquid called _____ .

b. Three membranes, collectively called the _____ , enclose and protect the brain. Those membranes are named

   (1) _____
   (2) _____
   (3) _____

   The outermost of those layers folds over to form a partition known as the _____ . When bleeding (usually from a torn artery) occurs between that outermost membrane and the skull, the resulting collection of blood is called a(n) _____ hematoma.

c. Outside of those membranes is the hard, bony covering of the brain, the _____ . That, in turn, is covered by the _____ , whose toughest, tendinous layer is known as the _____ .

d. The brain itself has several functional divisions. The part of the brain responsible for higher functions is the _____ , each hemisphere of which consists of four lobes, the _____ lobe, _____ lobe, _____ lobe, and _____ lobe. The part of the brain responsible for coordination of skilled movements is the _____ . Vital functions, such as the state of consciousness, are regulated in the _____ , one part of which, the _____ houses the centers that control breathing and cardiac action.

e. A fixed, immovable joint where bones of the skull come together is called a _____ .

f. The facial bones include the cheekbone, called the _____ , the upper jaw, or _____ , and the lower jaw, or _____ .

g. Trauma to the face often results in a nosebleed, or _____ .

h. The eyeball, or _____ , fits into a depression in the skull called the _____ . The structure that gives the eye its color is the _____ , which regulates the opening in the center of the eye, called the _____ . Anterior to those two components of the eye is the _____ , a crystal-clear extension of the otherwise white _____ covering the eyeball. Behind the pigmented structure of the eye is the _____ , which focuses light on the retina.

i. The spinal column consists of 33 bones piled one on top of the other. Each bone is called a(n) _____ , and between every two such bones there is a cushion, called a _____ , that acts as a shock absorber. It is customary to divide the spinal column into four regions: The first 7 spinal bones, in the neck, constitute the _____ spine; the next 12, which articulate with the ribs, make up the _____ spine; beneath them are 5 bones of the _____ spine; then come 5 fused bones of the _____ spine that articulate with the pelvis. And finally come the 4 fused bones of the coccyx, or tailbone.

   Which sections of the spinal column are more likely to be injured in accidents involving strong acceleration-deceleration forces?

   Why those particular sections?

2. When a person sustains a blow to the head, often it is not the injury to the head itself that has the most lethal potential but rather the rise in intracranial pressure that occurs in the wake of head injury.

   a. Explain in a few words the way(s) in which a rise in intracranial pressure may occur. What is it that causes the pressure inside the skull to rise?

   b. Why is an elevated intracranial pressure a Bad Thing? What harm can it do?

3. In a head-injured patient, as in any other patient, first priority goes to the *airway*. There are a number of things that may jeopardize the airway in a person who is found unconscious after suffering major trauma involving the head. List three things that may jeopardize the airway in such circumstances.

   a.

   b.

   c.

4. Score each of the patients described below according to the AVPU scale and the Glasgow Coma Scale:

   a. The patient is found unconscious. He opens his eyes in response to a loud voice. He does not follow commands, but he pulls his hand away when pinched and makes a few garbled noises that you cannot understand.

      AVPU score _____
      Glasgow coma score _____

   b. The patient is found apparently unconscious, but he opens his eyes at the sound of your voice. He can follow simple commands, but he is a bit confused and cannot tell you what month it is or what day of the week it is.

      AVPU score _____
      Glasgow coma score _____

   c. The patient is found unconscious. He does not open his eyes when pinched or try to pull away from the painful stimulus, but instead his arms flex spasmodically across his chest while his legs go into hyperextension. He makes no sound.

      AVPU score _____
      Glasgow coma score _____

   d. The patient is found conscious. He gives you a coherent account of what happened to him, and he can follow simple commands.

      AVPU score _____
      Glasgow coma score _____

5. Taking the history of a head-injured patient may provide important clues to the nature of the injury he suffered and its potential seriousness. List five questions that need to be answered in taking the history of a head-injured patient:

   a.

   b.

   c.

   d.

   e.

6. Presented below are the vital signs and skin condition of three patients who suffered head injury in motor vehicle accidents. In each case, indicate whether the clinical findings are most consistent with

   A. Neurogenic shock

   B. Hypovolemic shock

   C. Rising intracranial pressure

   ____ Skin cool and sweaty. Pulse 110, regular, and somewhat weak; respirations 24, shallow, and regular; blood pressure 80 systolic.

   ____ Skin hot and dry. Pulse 50, full, and regular; respirations 10, with occasional long pauses; blood pressure 210/110.

   ____ Skin warm and dry. Pulse 72, full, and regular; respirations 20, regular; blood pressure 80 systolic.

7. The head-to-toe survey may also provide evidence of significant head injury. List three signs that would suggest the presence of skull fracture.

   a.

   b.

   c.

8. You are called to attend a patient injured in an altercation that took place in a downtown drinking establishment. In the course of the dispute, someone broke a whiskey bottle over the patient's head. You find the patient conscious, bleeding profusely from his scalp, and in a distinctly unfriendly frame of mind, which he manifests by hurling tables and chairs in all directions while screaming uncomplimentary names at his assailants. List the steps you would take in treating this patient.

9. Each of the patients described below sustained a blow to the head.

   a. In each case, indicate whether the clinical findings are most consistent with

      A. A concussion
      B. A cerebral contusion
      C. An epidural hematoma
      D. A subdural hematoma

   ____ The patient was the driver of a vehicle that was struck from the left side by another car. The door on the driver's side is dented in. The patient is conscious, but witnesses say that he was "out cold" for a few minutes immediately after the accident. He complains of headache and pains in his left hip and left leg. His skull is tender to palpation in the area just superior to the left ear. While he is under your care, his level of consciousness deteriorates until he is unconscious altogether, and his respirations become very slow.

   ____ The patient was another participant in the barroom brawl mentioned in the previous question. This patient was "knocked out cold" for a few minutes. Now he seems alert, but he cannot remember what happened. He complains of a little dizziness. His vital signs are normal.

   ____ The patient was a front-seat passenger in a car that careened into a utility pole. He is confused and sleepy when you find him. His speech is slurred, and there is weakness of the right leg. He becomes more and more lethargic while under your care and vomits twice. The left pupil seems to be getting larger than the right.

   ____ The patient was an unrestrained front-seat passenger in a car involved in a head-on collision with another car. He apparently struck his head on the windshield, for the windshield in front of the patient is cracked. The patient is found unconscious. His left pupil is larger than the right. His pulse is 56, and his BP is 190/90. Respirations are irregular.

   b. In fact, in the field it will not be important to make a precise diagnosis of the type of head injury sustained. What *will* be enormously important, however, is to recognize the signs of increasing intracranial pressure, for those are *danger signals* that demand immediate evacuation of the patient. Three of the patients described above were showing such signs. List five signs of increasing intracranial pressure.

      (1)

      (2)

      (3)

      (4)

      (5)

   c. List, in the correct sequence, the steps you would take in managing a patient who has sustained head injury.

10. Injuries to the face may be quite frightening to look at, but facial injuries do not by themselves ordinarily pose an immediate threat to life. However, facial injuries may be associated with *other* conditions or injuries that *can* threaten life or limb. List three potentially serious or life-threatening conditions that may be associated with maxillofacial trauma.

    a.

    b.

    c.

11. In examining a victim of trauma, what findings would lead you to suspect maxillofacial fracture? List five signs of maxillofacial fracture.

    a.

    b.

    c.

    d.

    e.

12. In the course of one shift, you have to treat three different patients whose chief complaint is a nosebleed. For each of the patients described below, indicate whether the most appropriate treatment would be

    A. To pinch the nostrils shut

    B. To insert anterior and posterior nasal packs

    C. To cover the nostrils lightly with a sterile gauze pad

    _____ A 68-year-old man who says that his nose just started bleeding without any warning. He tells you that he is under treatment for high blood pressure, but you find his blood pressure to be normal and his pulse rapid.

    _____ A 42-year-old man involved in a motor vehicle accident. You don't see any evidence of injury to his nose, but rather watery blood is oozing from it.

    _____ A 16-year-old boy who says that his nose started bleeding after he sneezed. He is holding a bloody handkerchief against his nose.

13. While enjoying a weekend off at a ski resort, you happen to see a young lady trip over the steps at the lodge and fall. As you rush to her assistance, you see blood coming from her mouth, and closer inspection reveals that she has knocked one of her lower teeth entirely out. What steps should you take?

    _____

    _____

    _____

    _____

    _____

    _____

    _____

    _____

    _____

    _____

    _____

    _____

    _____

14. You of course volunteer to accompany the young lady to the nearest hospital, some 2 hours away by road. Just as you are pulling away from the ski resort in a friend's car, the resort manager comes running after you, waving for you to stop. "I have someone else here who needs to go to the hospital," he says. Behind him, two ski instructors are leading a young man who seems to be groping along. The patient had been involved in a fistfight and now has two black eyes. Describe what you would examine in checking this patient's eyes, and indicate what is the most important part of the examination.

15. During deer-hunting season, two young backpackers were strolling through the woods when hunters, mistaking the pair for deer, discharged their crossbows at them. One arrow entered the eye of the first backpacker, while another arrow went straight through the cheek of the second backpacker.

    a. Describe the steps you would take in treating the backpacker with the arrow in his eye.

    b. Describe the steps you would take in treating the backpacker who has an arrow impaled in his cheek.

16. In the old cowboy movies, one of the standard ways of preventing the bad guys from making their getaway was to tie a rope securely between two trees on either side of the road, at a height about 8 or 9 feet off the ground. When the bad guys came galloping down the road, the rope would catch them across the chest or neck and throw them from their horses.

    Imagine, then, that you are the Dodge City paramedic, called to attend a bad guy who has just been thrown from his horse after riding precipitously into a rope stretched across the road. You find the bad guy lying on the road moaning. His voice is quite hoarse as he replies to your questions about what happened, and he seems very short of breath. On examination, you find a prominent bruise over the anterior neck. The patient's face and neck appear bloated, and the skin there has a crinkly feel to it.

    a. What serious injury or injuries do you have to consider in this patient, given the mechanisms of injury and the findings on examination?

    b. List the steps you would take in treating this patient.

17. A 12-year-old boy lost control of his bicycle as he was riding down a long, steep hill into town. At the base of the hill, his front wheel struck the curb, and he was catapulted from the bicycle straight through the show window of the local wedding dress shop. When you arrive, you find him bleeding from multiple lacerations. The most profuse bleeding seems to be coming from a large laceration on the left side of his neck.

    a. What are the principal dangers associated with that laceration of the neck?

    b. List the steps you would take in treating the boy's neck wound.

18. In a patient who has sustained potential injury to his spinal cord, it doesn't pay to wait until there are symptoms and signs of spinal cord damage—for by then it may be too late to prevent permanent disability. The only sure way to prevent such disability is to *anticipate* spinal injury under the appropriate circumstances and to handle the patient in a way that will protect his spinal cord from damage. List eight circumstances in which you should assume that the spine has been injured.

a.

b.

c.

d.

e.

f.

g.

h.

19. A middle-aged man was the driver of a car that ran head-on into a truck parked on the opposite side of the road. You find the driver of the car unconscious in his wrecked vehicle.

a. Describe how you would open and maintain the patient's airway.

b. Continuing with the primary survey, you note that the patient's respirations are very shallow; he seems to be breathing mostly with his abdominal muscles.
   What further steps are needed at this point?

c. Proceeding with your assessment, you find that the patient's skin is warm and dry. His pulse is 72 and regular, respirations are 24 and shallow, and blood pressure is 70 systolic.
   What is the most likely explanation of those findings?

d. What further steps do you now need to take in managing this patient?

20. A 15-year-old boy was shot in the abdomen during a gang dispute. You find him lying supine on the sidewalk. He is conscious, alert, and crying out, "I can't move my legs! I can't move my legs!" You find an entrance wound just to the left of the umbilicus. You cannot find an exit wound. On examination, sensation is absent from the toes up to the bottom of the ribs. The patient cannot move either leg, but he has normal strength in both hands.

a. At approximately what level of the spinal cord has this boy probably been injured?

b. Suppose that your examination also revealed a blood pressure of 80 systolic. What could you conclude from that finding?

21. We conclude this lesson with another secret message. Decode it in the usual fashion.

a. Tendinous layer of the scalp   __ __ __ __ __
                                            70   14   21   91   76

b. Pigmented structure of the eye   __ __ __ __
                                           86   12   59   23

c. Membrane that lines the eyelids   __ __ __ __ __ __ __ __ __ __ __
                                        66   5   28   51   88   19   81   1   63   33   47

d. Opening in the occipital bone   __ __ R __ __ __ __   __ __ __ __ __ M
                                    43   40   44   9   46   26   4   68   20   90   36

e. Eyeball   __ __ __ B __
            73   35   87   78

f. Pins-and-needles sensation   __ __ __ __ __ __ __ __ __ __ __
                            10   37   53   60   6   29   2   54   84   24   65

g. Middle meningeal membrane   __ R __ __ __ __ __ __ __ __
                            34   57   85   30   15   79   27   55

h. The skin   __ __ __ __ __ __ M __ __ __
           39   69   62   3   25   52   31   41   7

i. Ringing in the ears   __ __ __ __ __ __ U __
                  16   49   83   50   71   13   64

j. Coughing up blood   __ __ M __ __ __ Y __ __ __
                45   22   11   56   38   93   8   74

k. Cushion between two vertebrae   __ __ __ C
                                 48   18   92

l. Not hard   __ __ __ __
           17   42   80   77

m. Rib with which T10 articulates   __ __ __ __ __
                              75   32   61   58   67

n. Epistaxis is bleeding from the   __ __ __ E
                            72   82   89

Secret Message: __ __ __   __ __ __ __   __ __ __ __ __ __ __ __ __   __ __ __ __ __ __
                   1   2   3   4   5   6   7   8   9   10   11   12   13   14   15   16   17   18   19   20   21   22

__ __ __ __   __ __   __ __ __   __ __ __ __ __ __ __ __ __ __   __ __   __
23   24   25   26   27   28   29   30   31   32   33   34   35   36   37   38   39   40   41   42   43   44

__ __ __ __ - __ __ __ __ __ __ __   __ __ __ __ __ __ __   __ __   __   __ __ __ __ __ __ __ __
45   46   47   48   49   50   51   52   53   54   55   56   57   58   59   60   61   62   63   64   65   66   67   68   69   70   71   72   73

__ __ __ __ __   __ __   __ __ __ __ __ __ __ __ __ __ __ __ __.
74   75   76   77   78   79   80   81   82   83   84   85   86   87   88   89   90   91   92   93

17
Chest Injuries

1. Hidden in the grid below are the structures of the chest along with some chest injuries—22 words in all. Find the hidden words, then use them to answer the questions that follow the grid.

```
U S C A P U L A M E N T I T
C I S A L A D B A R I B S R
L S P L E E N T R O I L E A
U P N E U M O T H O R A X C
N I C U R L I V E R N T S H
G N F L A I L L N E S C A E
S E V E N A C A V A T S H A
E A H S T O M A C H A T T I
T H E M O T H O R A X E L S
C L A V I C L E F D U R A L
H A R M E D I A S T I N U M
B A T H E S O P H A G U S T
B I R D I A P H R A G M M Y
```

a. The thoracic cavity lies within a bony, protective cylinder. The _____ encircle the whole thorax, articulating with the thoracic _____ posteriorly and the _____ anteriorly. Also forming part of the bony protection on each side of the chest is the strong shoulder blade, or _____, posteriorly and the collar bone, or _____, anteriorly. The inferior boundary of the thoracic cavity is formed by the _____.

b. The _____ nearly fill the thoracic cavity. Each of them is covered with a smooth, slippery membrane called the visceral _____; a similar membrane, the parietal _____, lines the inner wall of the thoracic cavity. Ordinarily there is no space between those two membranes. Injury to the chest, however, may

101

permit air to enter between the two membranes, creating a _____;
blood can also accumulate in the space between the two membranes, a situation called
_____.

c. Some of the most important organs of the body are located in a region in the center of the thoracic cavity called the _____.
The structures located there include the
_____,
_____,
_____,
_____,
_____,
and _____.

d. When two or more ribs are broken in two or more places, a condition called _____
_____ chest may develop.
Tamponade occurs when the _____
_____ becomes filled with blood, preventing the heart from contracting normally.

e. Because of the way the diaphragm is shaped, several abdominal organs actually lie partially or almost wholly within the chest, for example the _____,
the _____,
and the _____. Those organs are thus liable to be injured whenever there is serious thoracic trauma.

2. A 26-year-old woman was an unrestrained front-seat passenger in a car that was involved in a head-on collision. You find her lying unconscious on the front seat, her face covered with blood. The dashboard on her side is dented in, and the windshield in front of her is smashed.

a. List four things that might jeopardize the *airway* in this patient.

(1)

(2)

(3)

(4)

b. Specify precisely what you would check in assessing her *breathing* in the primary survey.

c. What steps would you take at this point to ensure adequate breathing?

d. Specify precisely what you would check in assessing her *circulation* in the primary survey.

3. A 22-year-old man was shot at close range by a "friend" wielding a shotgun. You find the patient slumped in a chair in considerable respiratory distress. There is a ragged 2-inch hole in his left anterior chest, and the left chest does not seem to move with respirations.

a. This patient is suffering from

A. A simple pneumothorax
B. A tension pneumothorax
C. An open pneumothorax
D. A spontaneous pneumothorax
E. Traumatic asphyxia

(Circle the best answer.)

b. What steps would you take to manage this situation?

4. For each of the patients described below, indicate whether the most likely diagnosis is

A. Tension pneumothorax
B. Massive hemothorax
C. Flail chest
D. Cardiac tamponade
E. Traumatic asphyxia

and list the steps of prehospital management.

_____ A 20-year-old driver of a car that rammed a utility pole at high speed. He is in severe distress. His pulse is rapid and feeble, and every so often you can hardly palpate a pulse at all. His neck veins are distended. There is a steering wheel imprint on his chest. The rib cage is stable. Breath sounds are equal bilaterally. It is too noisy to hear heart sounds. You are 30 minutes from the nearest hospital.

Steps of management:

_____ A 23-year-old driver of a car that rammed a utility pole at high speed. His face, neck, and chest are cyanotic and look very bloated. His eyes are bloodshot and bulging. He is vomiting blood. Breathing is labored. His pulse is rapid and very weak. The chest looks caved-in. You are 5 minutes from a trauma center.

Steps of management:

_____ A 70-year-old driver of a car that rammed a utility pole at high speed. He is conscious but in severe respiratory distress. The pulse is 92, strong, and slightly irregular. Neck veins are flat. There are bruises on the anterior chest and point tenderness along the left sternal border and over the left fifth, sixth, seventh, and eighth ribs in the anterior axillary line. The chest seems to move asymmetrically on respiration. Breath sounds seem equal. It is too noisy to hear heart sounds. You are 10 minutes from the hospital.

Steps of management:

_____ A 42-year-old front-seat passenger in a car that was struck from the right side by an ambulance that ran a red light. The patient is in severe respiratory distress. Her pulse is rapid and very weak. Her skin is cold and sweaty. The neck veins are distended. Breath sounds are decreased on the right side of the chest, which is hyperresonant to palpation. It's too noisy to hear heart sounds. You are 15 minutes from the nearest hospital.

Steps of management:

_____ A 22-year-old man who was stabbed in the left chest. The patient is in severe distress. His pulse is rapid and very weak. His skin is cold and sweaty. His neck veins are flat. Breath sounds are decreased in the left chest, which is dull to percussion. It's too noisy to hear heart sounds. You are 15 minutes from the nearest hospital.

Steps of management:

5. Many if not most serious chest injuries cannot be specifically identified in the field. An understanding of the mechanisms of injury, however, should enable you to anticipate the injuries that *might* be present in any given case and thereby to assess the potential urgency of the situation. For each of the mechanisms of injury or associated injuries listed below, indicate the serious chest injury or injuries that are likely to be present.

If you find:	The patient may have suffered:
Steering wheel imprint on anterior chest	
Caved-in door on driver's side	
Fall from a height	
Bullet entrance wound in fifth left intercostal space	
Fracture of ribs 5–7 in a young man	
Fracture of first and second ribs	

6. A 71-year-old woman was crossing the street when she was struck by a car and thrown to the ground. She is complaining of severe pain in her right chest (she points to the exact spot, over the fifth right rib in the anterior axillary line). She says the pain is much worse when she coughs or takes a deep breath. On examination, she is conscious and alert and leaning toward her right side. Her skin is warm and moist. There is no cyanosis. Her pulse is 88 and regular; respirations are 24 and shallow. Blood pressure is 160/90. The neck veins are flat. There is no tracheal deviation. There is extreme tenderness over the right fifth rib in the anterior axillary line. Breath sounds are diminished over the right chest, which sounds somewhat hollow to percussion. The rest of the exam seems to be within normal limits.

a. This woman is probably suffering from

b. What is the principal danger associated with the type of injury or injuries she has suffered?

c. What treatment is necessary in the field?

d. As you are transporting the woman to the hospital, a 20-minute drive from the accident scene, she suddenly becomes very restless and agitated and complains that she can't breathe. Her skin becomes cold and sweaty, and her pulse gets very weak. Her neck veins seem to bulge out.

   (1) What do you think has happened?

   (2) What measures will you take?

7. You are called to the scene of a two-car collision. A convertible going south on the interstate apparently jumped the median divider and plowed head-on into a station wagon travelling in the northbound lane. The driver of the convertible is lying unconscious on the road. Your primary survey reveals gurgling respirations; broken teeth; flat neck veins; asymmetric chest movement; cold, sweaty skin; weak, rapid pulse; poor capillary refill; and brisk bleeding from wounds on the scalp and neck. You are 10 minutes from a trauma center. List in order the steps you would take in this case.

8. Today's secret communication is the most important message you should take with you regarding injuries to the chest.

   a. Sac surrounding the heart __ __ __ __ __ __ __ __ __ M
   45 26 68 39 48 55 15 32 61 80

   b. Accumulation of blood in "a" above __ __ __ __ __ __ __ __ __
   7 57 19 44 37 63 23 83 11

   c. Injury with paradoxical chest motion __ __ __ __ L __ H __ __ __
   29 75 14 65   72   9 4 17

   d. Shallow breathing leads to __ __ __ __ R __ __ __ B __ __
   54 76 25 22   27 59 46   1 73

   e. Symptom of tension pneumothorax D __ __ __ __ __ __
   16 66 58 5 52 34

   f. Sign of tension pneumothorax __ H __ __ __ __
   12   42 67 21

   g. Region of the spine articularing with ribs __ H __ __ __ __ __ C
   41   18 81 43 10 77

   h. Inflammation of the ear O __ __ __ __ __
   2 69 64 28 38

   i. Ecchymosis behind the ear B __ __ __ __ __' __ __ __ __
   50 60 53 74 62 13   40 71 35 8

   j. Inflammation of the eyelid membrane C __ __ __ U __ __ __ __ V __ __ __ __
   6 36 79   78 31 70 49   3 51 30 24

   k. To stray, veer off D __ V __ __ __ __
   82   33 20 56 47

Secret Message: __ __ __ __ __ __ __ __ __ __ __ __ __ __ __ __ __ __ __ __ __ __
1 2 3 4 5 6 7 8 9 10 11 12 13 14 15 16 17 18 19 20 21 22

__ __ __ __ __ __ __ __ __ __ __ __ __ __ __ __ __ __ __ __ __ __ __ __ __ __ __ __ __ __
23 24 25 26 27 28 29 30 31 32 33 34 35 36 37 38 39 40 41 42 43 44 45 46 47 48 49 50 51 52

__ __ __ __ __ __ __ __ __ __ __ __ __ __ __ __ __ __ __ __ __ __ __ __
53 54 55 56 57 58 59 60 61 62 63 64 65 66 67 68 69 70 71 72 73 74 75 76

__ __ __ __ __ __ __.
77 78 79 80 81 82 83

18
Injuries to the Abdomen and Genitourinary Tract

1. The structures that make up the digestive and genitourinary systems are, like the 22 structures named in the grid below, largely hidden from view. Find the hidden words and then use them to answer the questions that follow the grid.

```
P R O P R O S T A T E D E
E A T S O A P P E N D I X
S T O M A C H A L K A K E
O G V E I N E N D E R I C
P H A R Y N X C O R E D O
H U R L I V E R U D E N L
A N Y O L D B E E M L E O
G O S H J B I A S C O Y N
U R E T E R L S P A T O G
S T R A J A E A V E N U E
H E E D U D U O D E N U M
Y E A R N A M E N D I P S
A R M O U T H I R D E L F
D R E A M S U R E T H R A
```

a. These three structures of the digestive system lie outside the abdomen: the _____
_____,
the _____,
and the _____.

b. Digestion of protein begins in the _____
_____. From there the partially digested food proceeds into the first portion of the small intestine, the _____, where powerful enzymes from the _____

carry out further digestion of protein and starch. Meanwhile, bile produced in the _____ and stored in concentrated form in the _____ participates in the breakdown of fat. The emulsified food moves on through the second and third portions of the small bowel, called the _____ and _____, respectively, and then enters the first portion of the large bowel, the _____. At the junction of the small and large bowels there is a wormlike

106

structure, the _____, whose principal function in adults seems to be to make work for surgeons. Proceeding through the ascending, transverse, and descending _____, waste products of digestion reach the _____ and are expelled through the _____ _____.

c. The organ responsible for producing urine is located in the retroperitoneum and is called the _____. Urine flows from that organ to the bladder through a tube called the _____; and from the bladder, urine exits the body through a passage called the _____.

d. In the female, the womb, or _____, sits just behind the bladder within the pelvis. On each side of it there is an _____, the organ that produces female hormones and eggs.

e. Among the structures listed in the grid, which ones are found in the intrathoracic abdomen?

   (1) _____
   (2) _____
   (3) _____

f. Among the structures listed in the grid, which ones are found in the retroperitoneum?

   (1) _____
   (2) _____
   (3) _____

g. List two other structures found in the retroperitoneum.

   (1) _____
   (2) _____

h. List two structures found in the left upper quadrant.

   (1) _____
   (2) _____

2. Label the following drawings.

   a. Write in the names of the *hollow organs* pictured in the drawing.

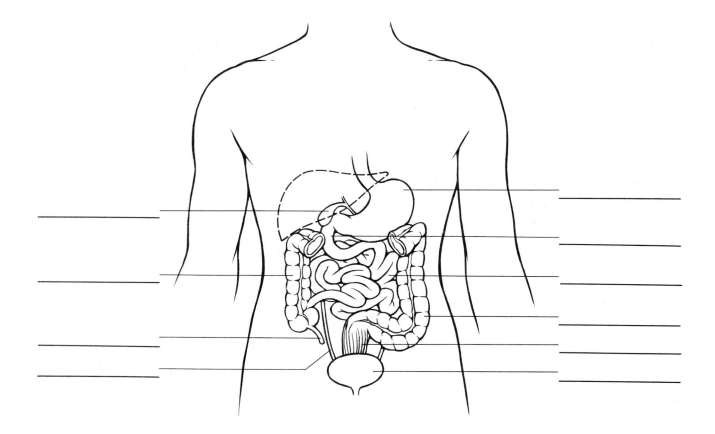

b. Write in the names of the *solid organs* pictured in the drawing.

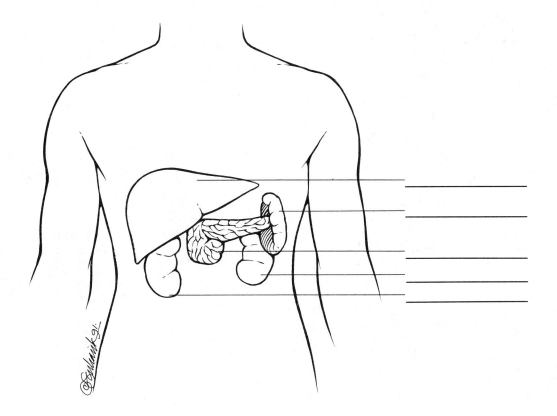

3. For each of the patients described below, given the mechanisms of injury and the clinical findings described, indicate whether he or she is *most* likely to have suffered

   A. Diaphragmatic tear
   B. Ruptured spleen
   C. Liver laceration
   D. Torn intestine
   E. Injury to the kidney
   F. Torn or ruptured bladder

List the steps of treatment for each case. (Note: A patient may have sustained more than one of the injuries listed.)

_____ A 15-year-old girl who was kicked in the left side by a horse. She is conscious and alert. Her pulse is rapid. She has a bruise over the left tenth rib in the anterior axillary line and has severe tenderness at that point.
  Steps of management:

_____ A 50-year-old man who was a passenger in a car that slammed into a wall. He was wearing a lap seat belt. He complains of shortness of breath and abdominal pain. He winces when he coughs. His vital signs are pulse 92 and regular, respirations 36 and shallow, and blood pressure 120/80.
  Steps of management:

_____ An 18-year-old man shot in the right upper quadrant by his girlfriend wielding a .38 special at a distance of about 10 feet. The patient is conscious. He has cold, sweaty skin and a weak, rapid pulse. There is an entrance wound in the right upper quadrant, about 2 finger-breadths below the costal margin in the mid-clavicular line. The exit wound is near the left buttock.
  Steps of management:

_____ A 60-year-old man struck by a car as he was crossing the street. He complains of severe pain over the eleventh and twelfth ribs posteriorly. The pain is made worse by taking a deep breath. There is marked tenderness to palpation over the eleventh and twelfth ribs posteriorly, and there seems to be a mass in the left flank.
  Steps of management:

_____ A 42-year-old construction worker extricated from underneath a pile of concrete blocks that caved in on top of him. He is unconscious. His skin is cold and clammy. His pulse is very weak. There are no bruises on the chest, which moves symmetrically with respiration. The abomen is not rigid, but there seems to be a fullness in the center of the lower quadrant. The pelvis is unstable.
  Steps of management:

4. You are called to the scene of a road accident in which an apparently intoxicated 25-year-old driver plowed his car into a bridge abutment at high speed. The front end of his vehicle is accordioned against the bridge. As you approach the disabled vehicle, your keen powers of observation enable you to perceive that the patient is conscious (he is screaming obscenities at a police officer). Describe the steps in evaluating this patient for possible abdominal injuries. What things in particular will you be looking for?

_____

_____

_____

_____

_____

_____

_____

_____

_____

_____

_____

_____

_____

_____

_____

_____

_____

_____

_____

_____

_____

_____

_____

5. A 20-year-old man was the unrestrained driver of a car that was struck from the side by another vehicle, causing the empty bucket seat beside him to be jammed into his right side. On your arrival at the accident scene, you find the victim conscious, but anxious and restless. His skin is cold and sweaty. His vital signs are pulse 140 and thready, respirations 40 and shallow, and blood pressure 72/40. There is a bruise over the right lower ribs. A large portion of the small bowel is eviscerated through an avulsion in the right side of the abdomen. The right elbow appears to be fractured. List the steps you would take in managing this case.

_____

_____

_____

6. During the usual Saturday night festivities at the local Knife & Gun Club, a 16-year-old male is stabbed with a hunting knife in the left lower quadrant of the abdomen. When you arrive, you find him lying on the ground moaning. The knife is still embedded up to its hilt in the victim's abdomen. His skin is warm and moist. Vital signs are pulse 100, respirations 32, and blood pressure 100/80. List the steps you would take in managing this case.

_____

_____

_____

_____

_____

_____

_____

_____

_____

_____

19
Fractures, Dislocations, and Sprains

1. Hidden in the grid below are 26 parts of the human skeleton. See how many you can find. Then use the words you've found to answer the questions that follow the grid.

```
A P P E N D I C U L A R C H A
I S C H I U M T A S K U L L C
D I S H C H E F I B U L A I R
U M O U N T T P U B I S V E O
S P L M E A A N T O I L I U M
T H E E C S C A P U L A C M I
E A C R A T A E A L O L L A O
R L R U E R R O T N A V E L N
N A A S N I P T E A X I A L E
U N N E A L A A L I B I T E R
M X O A T L L O L L A U R O I
B U N M E T A T A R S A L L B
A S P I N E T A R R A D I U S
D O L T R O C H A N T E R S M
```

a. The part of the skeleton made up of the upper and lower extremities is called the _____ skeleton. The rest of the skeleton, the part made up of the _____,
_____,
_____,
and _____, is called the _____ skeleton.

b. The highest point of the shoulder is called the _____.

c. The pelvis is made up of three bones, the _____,

_____,
and _____. The three come together laterally to form the depression, called the _____ in which the head of the thigh bone fits.

d. "Translate" the following into technical terminology:
(1) Shoulder blade: _____
(2) Collar bone: _____
(3) Funny bone: _____
(4) The funny part of the funny bone: _____
(5) The bone that articulates with the funny

112

bone and whose name sounds funny: _____

(6) Knee cap: _____
(7) Shin bone: _____
(8) Finger bone: _____
(9) "Hip bone": greater _____
_____

e. The bone that runs along the thumb side of the forearm is called the _____
_____. It articulates at the

wrist with the carpal bones, which in turn articulate with the _____ bones of the hand.

f. The _____, the smaller bone of the lower leg, forms the lateral _____ in its distal articulation with the _____ bones. Those in turn articulate with the _____ bones of the foot.

2. Fill in the labels on the skeleton pictured below.

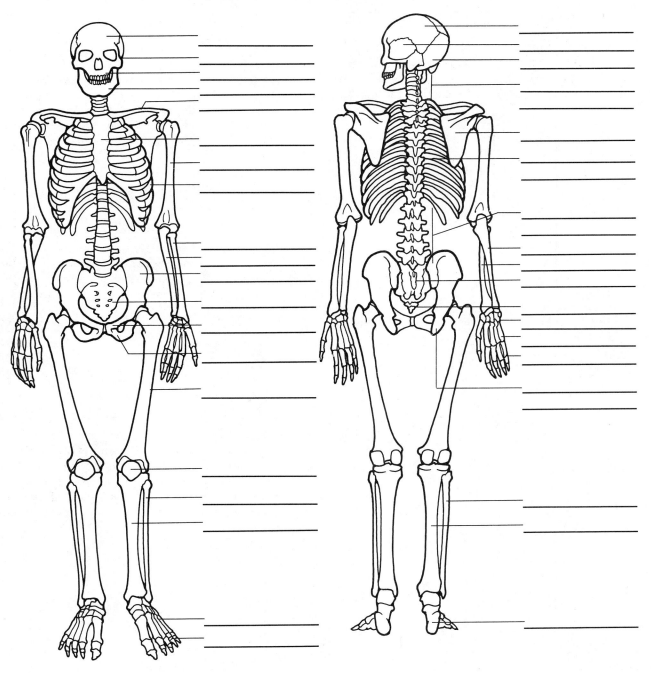

3. Question: What did the acetabulum say to the femur?

   Answer: "What's a nice bone like you doing in a joint like this?"

   List the names of the nice bones that make up the following joints:

Joint	Bones That Make Up the Joint
Shoulder	_____
Elbow	_____
Wrist	_____
Hip	_____
Knee	_____
Ankle	_____

4. A variety of different mechanisms can lead to musculoskeletal injury. List five such mechanisms in the table below, and give an example of an injury that can be produced by each of the mechanisms you listed.

Mechanism of Injury	Example

5. There are injuries that frequently come in pairs because they share a common mechanism of injury—so when you find one of such a pair, you should be alert for the presence of the other. For each of the following cases, indicate what *other* injury or injuries you would look for in particular, given the injury already detected.

   a. A young man jumped from a second-story window to escape a fire. He complains of severe pain in the left heel, which is quite black-and-blue. What other injury or injuries might you expect to find in this patient?

   b. A 50-year-old woman was the front-seat passenger in a car that was hit head-on by an oncoming vehicle. Her right knee is bruised and swollen. What other injury or injuries might you expect to find in this patient?

   c. A 60-year-old man fell sideways onto his outstretched hand. There is ecchymosis and tenderness at the base of his thumb. What other injury or injuries might you expect to find in this patient?

   d. A construction worker has been extricated from under a pile of concrete blocks that fell on top of him, pinning him prone, when part of a building collapsed. He has bruising over the left shoulder blade, and he cannot move the shoulder on that side. What other injury or injuries might you expect to find in this patient?

6. To detect a fracture, you have to know what a fractured extremity looks like and feels like. Fill in the following signs and symptoms of fractures:

Unnatural shape   __ __ F __ __ __ __ __ __

Reduced length   __ __ __ R __ __ __ __ __ __

Cardinal symptom   __ A __ __

Black-and-blue mark   __ __ C __ __ __ __ __ __ __

Grating   __ __ __ __ __ T __ __

Disability   __ __ __ __   __ __   U __ __

Protecting from movement   __ __ __ R __ __ __ __

Hurts to touch it   __ __ __ __ __ __ E __ __

Patient may report this   __ __ __ __ __   __   S __ __ __

Strange moves   __ __ __ __ __ __ __ __   __ __ __ I __ __

Edema   __ __ __ __ __ __ __ G

Seen in open fracture   __ __ __ __ __ __ __   __ __ __ __   __ N __ __

7. For each of the following patients, list the most likely diagnosis, answer any questions asked about the patient, and describe how you would manage the case.

a. A 14-year-old boy fell from his skateboard onto his extended right elbow. The elbow is massively swollen and ecchymotic. The right hand is cool and pale, and the patient cannot feel pinprick over the dorsum of the hand in the web space between the thumb and index finger.

(1) What is the most likely diagnosis?

(2) Is there any particular danger in this case? _____ If so, what is the danger?

(3) How would you manage this case?

b. The mother of the boy just described fell over her son's skateboard as she was rushing to his assistance, and her outstretched left hand took the brunt of the impact as she hit the ground. As she walks toward the ambulance, she is gripping the dorsum of her left wrist with her right hand and holding the left wrist against her abdomen. When you inspect the left wrist from the side, it has a peculiar curve, rather like that of a dinner fork.

(1) What is the most likely diagnosis?

(2) Is there any particular danger in this case? _____ If so, what is the danger?

(3) How would you manage this case?

c. A front-seat passenger in a car that hit a tree is found with his right hip flexed, adducted, and internally rotated. The right leg looks shorter than the left leg. There are no other obvious injuries, and vital signs are normal.

(1) What is the most likely diagnosis?

(2) Is there any particular danger in this case? _____ If so, what is the danger?

(3) How would you manage this case?

d. The driver of the vehicle in the same accident is unconscious behind the wheel. His skin is cold and sweaty. When you are extricating him from the vehicle, you notice that his hips are unstable.

(1) What is the most likely diagnosis?

(2) Is there any particular danger in this case? _____ If so, what is the danger?

(3) How would you manage this case?

e. As your 250-pound partner leaps gracefully from the ambulance to attend to the victims of the road accident, his ankle everts and buckles underneath him. "Ow," he says, "that is rather painful." He manages to complete his work at the scene by hopping around on one foot, but by the time he gets back to the station, his ankle is quite swollen and hurts a lot. Aside from the swelling, there is no obvious deformity and no ecchymosis.

(1) What is the most likely diagnosis?

(2) Is there any particular danger in this case? _____ If so, what is the danger?

(3) How would you manage this case?

f. You are watching the championship football game pitting your local high school team against last year's regional champions. Your quarterback, who is about 5 feet 6 inches and weighs perhaps 135 pounds, is looking to pass when he gets sacked and buried under a horde of 200-pound defensive linemen from the other team. When they unstack the linemen, your quarterback is very slow in getting up. Of course, you race over to offer your assistance. After peeling off the boy's shirt, shoulder pads, and other gear, you notice that his chest is not symmetric: There seems to be a hollow area just to the left of the sternum, at the base of the neck, and that spot is very tender. The boy, meanwhile, is quite pale, and he gasps, "I'm choking."

(1) What is the most likely diagnosis?

(2) Is there any particular danger in this case? _____ If so, what is the danger?

(3) How would you manage this case?

h. Another 25-year-old man was shot in the thigh at close range. The left thigh is swollen compared to the right, and the left leg as a whole looks shorter than the right leg. The left dorsalis pedis pulse seems weaker than that on the right side.

(1) What is the most likely diagnosis?

(2) Is there any particular danger in this case? _____ If so, what is the danger?

(3) How would you manage this case?

g. A 25-year-old man was struck by a car while crossing the street. The bumper caught him in the middle of his shin. His lower leg is severely angulated and bleeding from an open wound. He complains of severe pain in his leg and of "pins-and-needles" in his foot.

(1) What is the most likely diagnosis?

(2) Is there any particular danger in this case? _____ If so, what is the danger?

(3) How would you manage this case?

(4) If your management of the case included a splint, why did you use a splint? List three reasons for splinting an injured extremity.

(a)

(b)

(c)

i. You are spending a weekend on the ski slopes. Sailing down a particularly challenging hill, you see a skier stopped in the middle of the slope admiring the view. Seconds later, about five other skiers come careering down the slope and, one after another, pile into the stationary skier. When the pile is unravelled, the skier at the bottom is found to have a severely deformed right knee, which seems to be swelling before your eyes.

(1) What is the most likely diagnosis?

(2) Is there any particular danger in this case? _____ If so, what is the danger?

(3) How would you manage this case?

j. A 12-year-old boy was run over by a trolley car. You find the boy lying on the tracks. He is conscious and complaining of severe pain "all over." His left arm is about 3 feet away.

(1) What is the most likely diagnosis?

(2) Is there any particular danger in this case? _____ If so, what is the danger?

(3) How would you manage this case?

8. Fractures of the forearm or lower leg may be complicated by a compartment syndrome when there is significant bleeding and swelling within one of the tight muscular compartments of the injured limb. A compartment syndrome, by cutting off the blood supply, can jeopardize the whole limb, so it is important to recognize the symptoms and signs that suggest that a compartment syndrome may be developing. List six symptoms and signs of compartment syndrome.

a.

b.

c.

d.

e.

f.

9. Looking for the signs of compartment syndrome is, in fact, only part of the assessment of an injured extremity. Review the case of the man injured on the ski slope (question 7.i), and list the steps you would take in examining him.

   _____

   _____

   _____

   _____

   _____

   _____

   _____

   _____

10. Indicate whether each of the following statements about splinting is true or false.

    a. Severely angulated fractures should be straightened before they are splinted.

       TRUE　　　　　　　　FALSE

    b. An air splint is a good choice for a humeral shaft fracture.

       TRUE　　　　　　　　FALSE

    c. Fractures involving joints should be straightened before splinting to prevent distal ischemia.

       TRUE　　　　　　　　FALSE

    d. A traction splint is contraindicated in an open femoral fracture, because traction may drag broken bone ends back into the wound.

       TRUE　　　　　　　　FALSE

    e. Fingers or toes should be left out of the splint so that distal circulation can be monitored.

       TRUE　　　　　　　　FALSE

    f. For a victim of multitrauma in unstable condition, one should splint the whole axial skeleton as a unit, on a long backboard, rather than take time to splint individual fractures.

       TRUE　　　　　　　　FALSE

    g. Air splints may lose pressure with increasing altitude or temperature.

       TRUE　　　　　　　　FALSE

11. You are called to the scene of a hit-and-run accident. A 14-year-old boy is lying unconscious in the street, surrounded by a crowd of highly agitated people. No one actually saw how the accident happened. At first glance, you can see that the boy's right thigh is angulated, and the trouser leg on the side is soaked in blood.

    a. Arrange the steps in his management, listed below, in the correct sequence.

    _____ Start an IV.

    _____ Take the vital signs.

    _____ Cut away the trouser leg.

    _____ Determine whether he is breathing (he is).

    _____ Secure patient to backboard.

    _____ Apply the MAST while holding the right leg in traction.

    _____ Put manual pressure on the bleeding site.

    _____ Open the airway (chin lift).

    _____ Start transport.

    _____ Move the patient to a backboard.

    _____ Check for a carotid pulse (pulse is present).

    _____ Check for a dorsalis pedis pulse on the right.

    _____ Do AVPU check.

    _____ Check for open or tension pneumothorax.

    _____ Put a pressure dressing over open wound of leg.

    b. Have any steps been omitted? _____
       If so, what steps?

12. And now for this lesson's BIG SECRET! Decode the secret sentence in the usual fashion to find out the most important message of Chapter 19.

   a. Joint formed by the femur and tibia __ __ __ __
      9 35 67 48

   b. Cavity housing the femoral head __ __ __ N __ __ __
      65 28 22   60 54 40

   c. Funny bone __ __ __ __
      5 53 17 74

   d. Articulation __ __ __ N __
      18 70 62   13

   e. Where the pelvic bones meet anteriorly __ __ __ P __ __ __ __ __   P __ __ __ __
      68 64 37   46 29 77 21 8   2 75 41 23

   f. Shoulder blade __ __ __ __ __ __ A
      32 76 34 30 19 15

   g. Process below the femoral neck __ __ __ __ __ __ N __ __ __
      50 20 7 4 72 42   63 56 26

   h. Hand bone __ __ __ __ C __ __ __ A __
      38 73 69 14   49 61 57   6

   i. Where the metatarsals are __ __ __ __
      55 31 66 71

   j. Tube from kidney to the bladder U __ __ __ __ __
      58 44 51 12 47

   k. Do this to the distal end of a
      traction splint __ __ __ V __ __ __
      27 11 39   25 45 33

   l. Stingy person __ __ __ __ __
      1 59 3 10 24

   m. Charged particle __ __ N
      36 52

   n. Facial twitch __ __ C
      43 16

Secret Message: __ __ __ __ __ __ __ __ __ __ __ __ __ __ __   __ __ __ __ __ __ __ __   __ __ __ __ __ __
                 1 2 3 4 5 6 7 8 9 10 11 12 13 14 15   16 17 18 19 20 21 22 23   24 25 26 27 28 29

__ __ __ __   __ __   __ __ __ __ __ __ __ __ __   __ __ __ __ __ __   __ __   __ __ __ __.
30 31 32 33   34 35   36 37 38 39 40 41 42 43 44   45 46 47 48 49 50   51 52   53 54 55 56

__ __ __ __ __ __ __ __   __ __ __ __   __ __   __ __ __   __ __ __ __.
57 58 59 60 61 62 63 64   65 66 67 68   69 70   71 72 73   74 75 76 77

20
Multiple Injuries: Summary of Advanced Trauma Life Support

1. Only 1 out of 10 victims of trauma is critically injured. But for that 1 patient out of 10, every minute that elapses between the time of his injury and the time he reaches the operating room reduces his chances of survival. For that reason, all those who deal with the case in its pre–operating room phase need to act as efficiently as possible. List three ways that you, as a paramedic, can save seconds or minutes of the "Golden Hour" without compromising the care of the patient.

   a.

   b.

   c.

2. One sure way to *waste* time at the scene of an accident (or at any call) is to make a dozen trips back and forth to the ambulance to fetch equipment and supplies that you left behind. A well-organized paramedic will take with him or her everything needed for the primary survey and initial stages of management. Assume you have been called to the scene of a road accident. Among the equipment listed below, mark an "X" beside that which you would grab to take along on your *first* dash from the ambulance to the patient. If any equipment you need has been left off the list, add it at the end and explain why you need it.

____	MAST	____	Contact lens remover
____	Long-leg air splint	____	Stethoscope
____	Drug box	____	Flashlight
____	Portable suction unit	____	Triangular bandages
____	Oxygen cylinder	____	Chemical cold packs
____	OB kit	____	Cervical collar
____	Pocket mask	____	Traction splint
____	Oropharyngeal airways	____	Nonrebreathing mask
____	Intravenous fluid bags	____	Long backboard/straps
____	Dressing materials	____	Oral thermometer
____	Large-bore IV cannulas	____	Fire extinguisher
____	Head immobilizer	____	Bed pan
____	Self-adhering roller bandage	____	Heavy-duty scissors
____	Selection of board splints	____	Emesis basin
____	Wheeled cot stretcher	____	Hand-held radio
____	ECG monitor	____	Band-Aids

Other equipment that might be needed:

_____

_____

_____

_____

_____

_____

_____

_____

_____

____ MAST	____ Contact lens
____ Long-leg air splint	remover
____ Drug box	____ Stethoscope

3. Whether a patient is suffering from injury or from a medical problem, the objective of the primary survey is the same: To detect life-threatening conditions. For the victim of trauma, however, the particular details one is looking for in the primary survey are different from those one seeks in the medical patient. Fill in the following table to indicate what you would look for at each step of the *primary* survey of an injured patient found unconscious.

Survey Step	What I Would Look for at This Step
AIRWAY	
BREATHING	
CIRCULATION	
DISABILITY	

4. For each of the following patients, indicate whether the patient is

    C In critical condition (the "load-and-go" category)

    N Not in critical condition

and list the steps of management you would take in the field and in transport.

_____ A 62-year-old driver of a car hit from the side. The door on the driver's side is smashed in. The patient is conscious, in respiratory distress. The left chest is bruised, tender, and does not move symmetrically on respiration. The skin is warm. Pulse is 92 and slightly irregular, respirations 30 and shallow, and blood pressure 136/82.

a. What steps would you take at the scene?

b. What steps would you take during transport?

_____ A 24-year-old driver of a car involved in a head-on collision. He was not wearing a seat belt. The windshield on the driver's side has a spider-web crack. The patient is confused, and his breath smells of alcohol. The skin is warm. Breathing seems labored. The left pupil is larger than the right. Pulse is 56 and regular, respirations 24 and deep, and blood pressure 190/110.

a. What steps would you take at the scene?

b. What steps would you take during transport?

_____ One rainy day, a car bomb was detonated in front of a foreign consulate, and a number of bystanders were injured by flying debris, including jagged pieces of metal torn from the car's body. The first casualty you come upon is bleeding from multiple sites, including a deep gash on the right side of the neck and a laceration that has partially severed the right leg at the groin. The leg laceration is gushing blood; it is too proximal to be benefitted by a tourniquet. It's hard to evaluate skin condition in the rain. Pulse is around 100 and somewhat weak; respirations are 30 per minute.

a. What steps would you take at the scene?

b. What steps would you take during transport?

_____ A second casualty from the car bombing, a young man, was sideswiped by a piece of flying debris, which made a clean 14-inch incision straight across his abdomen. He is conscious and in moderate distress. Pulse is 104 and regular, respirations 28 and slightly labored, and blood pressure 104/70. What looks to be a major proportion of the patient's intestines are outside the abdomen.

a. What steps would you take at the scene?

b. What steps would you take during transport?

_____ A third casualty from the car bombing is another young man in considerable respiratory distress. There is a 2-inch wide hole in his right chest through which you can hear air being sucked in on inhalation. His skin is warm. His pulse is 108 and regular; respirations are 30 per minute and gasping; blood pressure is 112/64.

a. What steps would you take at the scene?

b. What steps would you take during transport?

_____ A 56-year-old woman was struck by a car as she was crossing the street. You find her lying in the street, near the curb, her left leg severely angulated and bleeding. She is conscious. There is no tenderness to palpation over the chest or spine (you don't want to take off her shirt there in the middle of the street to inspect the chest). Her skin is warm. Pulse is 108 and regular, respirations 28, and blood pressure 132/90. There is an open fracture of the left tibia. The dorsalis pedis pulses are equal, and sensation to pinprick is intact in both feet.

a. What steps would you take at the scene?

b. What steps would you take during transport?

_____ A 59-year-old man who was the driver of a car that plowed into a bridge abutment in the wee hours of the morning. The patient is conscious, but very restless. He is sweating profusely. His chest is stable (it's too dark to see whether there are bruises). He can move all his extremities. The pulse is 82, respirations are 28, and blood pressure is 100/70.

a. What steps would you take at the scene?

b. What steps would you take during transport?

_____ A back-seat passenger in the same car, a 52-year-old woman, was wearing a lap seat belt. She is shrieking, "My legs, my legs!" Her skin is warm. She has no tenderness over the chest, and the chest wall is stable. Pulse is 82 and regular, respirations 30 and slightly shallow, and blood pressure 106/76. The patient cannot move her legs, and there is no sensation to pinprick from the toes up to around the iliac wings.

a. What steps would you take at the scene?

b. What steps would you take during transport?

_____ A construction worker fell from a third-story scaffolding to the pavement below. When you arrive, he is unconscious and not breathing. You cannot detect a carotid pulse.

a. What steps would you take at the scene?

b. What steps would you take during transport?

_____ A passenger in a car that was struck from the right side by a truck running a red light. The right-hand front door of the car is rammed in, deforming the passenger compartment of the car. The patient, a middle-aged woman, is conscious and in considerable distress. Her skin is cold and moist. Her neck veins are distended. Her chest moves only minimally on respiration, and you have difficulty hearing breath sounds on the right. You can't really assess the percussion note because of all the noise at the scene. The woman's pulse is 120 and weak, and her respirations are 36 and shallow.

a. What steps would you take at the scene?

b. What steps would you take during transport?

_____ A 32-year-old man jumped from a second-story window of a burning building and landed on his feet in the flower garden beneath. He is conscious and complaining of severe pain in his heels. His skin is warm. There are second- and third-degree burns over both legs posteriorly. There is tenderness over L2. Both heels are exquisitely tender to palpation.

a. What steps would you take at the scene?

b. What steps would you take during transport?

5. Generally there isn't time at the scene of a serious accident to take a detailed history from each injured person. But we still need to acquire information that may bear on the subsequent management of the patient. List the information you should try to obtain in taking a history from the victim of trauma.

6. In the secondary survey of a multitrauma victim, you will need to look for very specific clues to specific injuries. Fill in the table below to indicate what in particular you will be looking for as you examine each part of the body.

Body Region	What I Will Be Looking for in Particular
HEAD	
NECK	
CHEST	
ABDOMEN	
EXTREMITIES	

7. We conclude with a secret message, in the fervent hope that by now the message is no longer a secret to any paramedic:

a. Inner layer of the skin   __ __ __ M __ __
                                43 76 15   5 25

b. Outermost layer of the meninges   __ __ __ __   M __ __ __ __
                                      53 78 57 27   36 86 65 2

c. Athlete's brain   __ __ __ __ __ __ __ __ __ M
               26 91 56 51 32 16 84 8 60

d. Cheek bone   __ __ __ __ M __
           41 10 71 74   19

e. Movement *away* from the midline of the body   A __ __ __ __ __ __ __ __
                                    37 77 14 54 61 69 94 89

f. Wasting away of a tissue   __ __ __ __ P __ __
                 67 20 73 82   47 58

g. End of a long bone   __ __ __ P __ __ __ __ __
             22 72 63   87 85 81 44 34

h. Where two bones meet   __ __ __ __ __
              13 30 50 83 46

i. Knee cap   __ __ __ __ __ __ A
        18 55 92 42 9 39

j. Connects bone to bone   __ __ __ A __ __ __ __
             62 11 90   93 48 29 4

k. Flexor surface of the forearm   __ __ __ A __
                 68 59 52   79

l. Occurrence   __ __ __ __ __ __ __ __
       40 97 75 3 17 88 28 24

m. It comes after cause   __ __ __ __ __ __
         80 64 49 33 6 31

n. The pulse is one   __ __ __ __ L   __ __ __ __
         95 38 35 7   66 21 98 70

o. TV news network   __ __ __
        1 45 12

p. Not out   __ __
      96 23

Secret Message: __ __ __ __ __ __ __ __ __ __   __ __ __ __ __ __ __   __ __ __ __ __ __ __ __
               1 2 3 4 5 6 7 8 9 10   11 12 13 14 15 16 17   18 19 20 21 22 23 24 25

__ __ __ __ __ __   __ __   __ __ __ __ __ __ __ __ __ __   __ __   __ __ __   __ __ __ __ __;
26 27 28 29 30 31   32 33   34 35 36 37 38 39 40 41 42 43   44 45   46 47 48   49 50 51 52 53

__ __ __ __ __   __ __ __   __ __ __ __ __ __ __ __ __ __   __ __ __ __ __ __ __ __ __ __
54 55 56 57 58   59 60 61   62 63 64 65 66 67 68 69 70 71   72 73 74 75 76 77 78 79 80 81

__ __ __ __,   __ __ __ __   __ __ __   __ __ __ __ __ __!
82 83 84 85   86 87 88 89   90 91 92   93 94 95 96 97 98

21
The Multicasualty Incident

1. You've been assigned to do a shift at the 911 switchboard, since the regular dispatcher is home with the flu. You have scarcely gotten the headset clamped over your ears when the first call comes through. "Oh, it's terrible, it's terrible!" someone is shouting into the telephone. "So many bodies. It's terrible."

   "Now, Ma'am," you say, "just try to calm down and tell me all about it so that we can send help."

   "It's just terrible. The train. It went right off the tracks and down the embankment."

   List the information you need to try to obtain from the caller, the actions you would take, and at what point you would take those actions.

   _____

   _____

   _____

   _____

   _____

   _____

   _____

   _____

   _____

   _____

   _____

   _____

   _____

   _____

   _____

   _____

   _____

   _____

   _____

   _____

2. As it turns out, the train derailment occurred when a commuter train struck a tanker truck at a level crossing where the signal and gate were apparently out of order. The tanker truck, which was carrying chlorine gas, overturned at the crossing, and gasoline is leaking from it. The train slid down an embankment on its side. The relative positions of the vehicles involved are shown in the figure on the next page.

   Your partner is the first paramedic to reach the scene. Mark an "X" on the drawing to indicate where he should station his ambulance. Also, circle what you think would be the best place to establish (a) a triage area and (b) a staging area.

   What other services, besides EMS, will be needed at the scene?

   _____

   _____

   _____

   _____

   _____

   _____

   _____

   _____

   _____

   _____

   _____

   _____

   _____

   _____

   _____

   _____

   _____

   _____

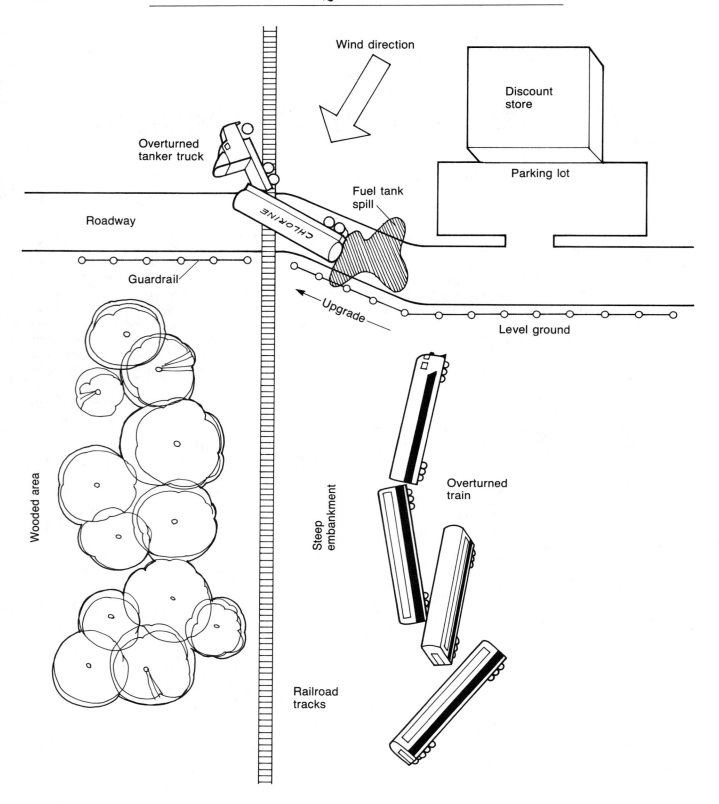

3. Hearing the first vehicles report out for the scene on her portable scanner at home, the dispatcher drags herself from her sickbed and appears at 911 headquarters to take over her regular job. ("I thought you guys could use some help," she coughs.) You are immediately sent to the disaster scene to join your regular crew there. When you arrive, your crew chief waves vaguely in the direction of a truck parked nearby and instructs you to set up a triage area. "All the equipment is in the truck," he says.

a. List the equipment that should be at *every* stretcher position.

b. What other equipment should be centrally located in the triage area so that it is readily accessible for any patient who needs it?

4. You have scarcely organized the triage area when the first casualties start arriving there, as they are hauled out of the wreckage by firefighters and other rescue personnel. Before you realize what is happening, someone thrusts a stack of triage tags into your hand and says, "Sort these victims out, will you?" You shout for other paramedics to come and help as you start moving from casualty to casualty, affixing triage tags to their clothing. Six rescuers come over to help; everyone else is tied up with casualties still inside the train.

a. For each of the casualties described below, indicate which triage tag you would assign:

R RED TAG: First priority patient—treat immediately.
Y YELLOW TAG: Second priority patient.
G GREEN TAG: Lowest priority patient—treat after higher priority patients are taken care of.
B BLACK TAG: Hopelessly injured or dead: Do not treat.

_____ Patient is conscious. His skin is warm. Abdominal viscera are hanging out of his belly.

_____ Patient is unconscious and breathing. The left pupil is larger than the right.

_____ Patient is unconscious. His face is bashed in. He is making gurgling noises as he breathes, and blood is bubbling from his mouth.

_____ Patient is conscious. One eye is hanging out of its socket.

_____ Patient is unconscious. His head has been crushed, and a large proportion of his cerebral matter seems to have spilled out onto the ground.

_____ Patient is conscious and gasping. His neck veins are distended.

_____ Patient is conscious. He has a severely angulated fracture of the lower leg.

_____ Patient is unconscious. He is not breathing and has no pulse.

_____ Patient is conscious. He has a 2-inch hole in his anterior right chest through which you can hear air being sucked on inhalation.

_____ Patient is conscious but confused and agitated. His skin is cold and sweaty.

_____ Patient is unconscious and not breathing, but a carotid pulse is still present.

_____ Patient is conscious. He complains that he cannot move his legs.

_____ Patient is decapitated.

_____ Patient is conscious. He is bleeding profusely from a gash in the neck.

_____ Patient is sitting with his eyes wide open looking blankly out into space. He is breathing and has a strong pulse but does not respond when you talk to him or pinch him.

_____ Patient is conscious. He has multiple small cuts over his face and arms.

_____ Patient is unconscious. You cannot immediately detect the cause.

_____ Patient is conscious. He says he has no feeling in his hands and feet.

b. What is the minimum number of ambulances that will be required to deal with the patients you have triaged so far? (Assume that each ambulance has a crew of two or three.) _____

5. As care of the accident victims proceeds, it is important to fill in pertinent details on each casualty's triage tag. List the information that should be recorded, if it can be obtained, on the triage tag.

_____

_____

_____

_____

_____

_____

_____

_____

_____

_____

_____

_____

6. Described below are several people who were removed from the train wreck apparently uninjured.

   a. Mark an "X" beside those who you think could be mobilized to help out at the scene.

_____ Young man in a business suit who is dashing from one casualty to another, "just to check how everyone is doing." He tells you he is a fully trained EMT with his local volunteer fire department. "I'm an expert on the Dow-Jones and broken bones," he says. "Whoops, gotta run, I think they need me over there."

_____ Young woman in a white uniform, looking pale and dazed. "I'm a nurse," she tells you, "but I don't know if I can handle this. I feel like I'm going to throw up."

_____ Another man in a business suit, running from one person to another, saying, "We're all going to die here. There's a truck with chlorine gas up there. We're all going to die here."

_____ Middle-aged man carrying a briefcase, looking dazed and stunned. "It's just like 'Nam," he says, "when I was a medic. Just like 'Nam. All the noise. All the blood."

_____ The casualty described earlier who is just sitting, staring blankly into space, and who does not respond when you talk to him or touch him.

_____ Teenage boy who comes over to you and asks, "You guys need any help? We took an EMT course in high school, and I passed the state exam."

   b. Having selected responsible people from among those just described, list three tasks you can assign to them.

   (1)

   (2)

   (3)

7. You find that there are not enough ambulances currently at the scene to transport all the casualties. Some casualties will have to wait for the arrival of other ambulances or for vehicles returning to make a second or even a third trip. All of the patients you triaged are ready to be evacuated. At the moment, you have seven ambulances at the scene.

   a. For each of the patients you have already triaged, described below in the condition in which you first saw them, assign a priority (1–4) for evacuation (e.g., "1" for first priority, "2" for second priority).

   b. Taking into account the fact that you can evacuate a casualty who will not need ongoing medical attention en route in the same vehicle with a casualty who is severely injured, put an asterisk beside those lower priority casualties who should be sent out with the first wave of departing ambulances.

_____ Patient is conscious. His skin is warm. Abdominal viscera are hanging out of his belly.

_____ Patient is unconscious and breathing. The left pupil is larger than the right.

_____ Patient is unconscious. His face is bashed in. He is making gurgling noises as he breathes, and blood is bubbling from his mouth.

_____ Patient is conscious. One eye is hanging out of its socket.

_____ Patient is unconscious. His head has been crushed, and a large proportion of his cerebral matter seems to have spilled out onto the ground.

_____ Patient is conscious and gasping. His neck veins are distended.

_____ Patient is conscious. He has a severely angulated fracture of the lower leg.

_____ Patient is unconscious. He is not breathing and has no pulse.

_____ Patient is conscious. He has a 2-inch hole in his anterior right chest through which you can hear air being sucked on inhalation.

_____ Patient is conscious but confused and agitated. His skin is cold and sweaty.

_____ Patient is unconscious and not breathing, but a carotid pulse is still present.

_____ Patient is conscious. He complains that he cannot move his legs.

_____ Patient is decapitated.

_____ Patient is conscious. He is bleeding profusely from a gash in the neck.

_____ Patient is sitting with his eyes wide open looking blankly out into space. He is breathing and has a strong pulse but does not respond when you talk to him or pinch him.

_____ Patient is conscious. He has multiple small cuts over his face and arms.

_____ Patient is unconscious. You cannot immediately detect the cause.

_____ Patient is conscious. He says he has no feeling in his hands and feet.

8. We close with a secret message about incidents involving many victims.

a. Sorting of victims by severity of injury _ _ _ _ _ _
   39 26 22 12 53 34

b. Place for ambulances at a disaster _ _ _ _ _ _ _   _ _ _ _
   6 60 20 35 17 2 43   56 49 65 3

c. Smaller bone of the lower leg _ I _ _ _ _
   47 64 19 13 9

d. Form of cardiac arrest _ _ _ _ _ _ L _
   38 59 27 41 32 29   52

e. Heart muscle _ _ _ _ _ _ _ I _ _
   63 15 48 8 5 54 46 11 4

f. Ringing in the ears _ I _ _ I _ _ _
   57 24 61 25 62 10

g. Phalanx of the lower extremity _ _ _
   14 45 37

h. What you'll take at the end of the course _ _ _ _
   42 55 16 50

i. Balance precariously _ _ _ _ _ R
   18 31 28 21 40

j. Emergency Rx for this is Preparation H _ _ M _ _ _ _ _ _ _ _ _
   51 58 44 36 66 33 23 1 30 7

Secret Message: _ _   _   _ _ _ _   _ _ _ _ _ _ _ _   _ _ _ _ _ _ _ _ _,
                 1 2   3   4 5 6 7   8 9 10 11 12 13 14 15   16 17 18 19 20 21 22 23 24

_ _ _   _ _   _ _ _   _ _ _   _ _ _ _ _ _ _ _   _ _ _ _
25 26 27 28 29 30 31 32 33 34 35 36 37 38 39 40 41 42 43 44 45 46

_ _ _   _ _ _   _ _ _ _ _ _ _ _   _ _ _ _ _ _.
47 48 49 50 51 52 53 54 55 56 57 58 59 60 61 62 63 64 65 66

Stop and Review II

It's time again, now that we have completed the unit on trauma, to pause and consolidate the material we have covered up to now.

1. We shall start with a secret message. Decode it in the usual fashion.

   a. Outermost layer of skin __ __ __ __ E __ __ __ __

6 52 14 34   30 48 21 16

   b. Black-and-blue mark __ __ __ __ __ M __ __ __ __

25 40 15 50 58   2 33 26 59

   c. Vein of the neck __ __ G __ __ __ __

28 44   24 5 56 46

   d. Partially torn off tissue is __ __ __ L __ __ __

12 62 29   22 51 1

   e. Completely severed tissue is __ __ P __ __ __ __ E __

39 55   60 20 10 4   8

   f. Most superficial burn __ __ __ __ __ degree

45 54 9 36 49

   g. Drug to promote urine flow in electric burn __ A __ __ __ __ __ L

11   27 3 31 19 43

   h. mm Hg __ __ __ __

41 17 38 57

   i. 110 pounds equals F __ __ __ __ kg

35 18 7 42

   j. Carries oxygenated blood A __ __ __ __ __

61 37 63 53 64

   k. Combining word meaning "bone" __ __ __ __ O

47 23 13 32

Secret Message: __ __ __ ' __ __ __ __ __ __ __ __ __ __ __ __

1 2 3 4   5 6 7   8 9 10 11 12 13 14 15   16 17 18 19   20 21 22 23 24 25

__ __ __ __ __ __ __ __ __ __ __ __ __ __ __ __ __ __ __ __ __ __ __

26 27 28 29 30 31 32 33   34 35 36 37 38 39 40 41   42 43 44   45 46 47 48   49 50 51

__ __ __ __ __ __ __ __ __ __ __ __ __ .

52 53 54 55 56 57 58   59 60 61 62 63 64

132

2. Every state in the United States defines certain cases as "coroner's cases," that is, cases of death that you are obliged to report to law enforcement authorities. While regulations vary somewhat from state to state, there are certain categories of cases that are nearly universally regarded as coroner's cases. List three such categories.

    a.

    b.

    c.

3. It is critically important to recognize a person who is choking so that appropriate measures can be taken quickly enough to prevent that person's dying from hypoxemia.

    a. List three signs of choking.

        (1)

        (2)

        (3)

    b. List the steps in treating a conscious, choking victim (assume that you have with you any equipment you might need).

4. A 34-year-old man has been injured in a road accident in which his head apparently struck the windshield with some force. When you first reach the scene, the patient is unconscious. He is breathing 8 times per minute, inhaling 500 ml of air with each breath.

    a. What is his minute volume? _____ per minute

    b. Is that volume greater or less than normal?
    _____

    c. Therefore, we can conclude that the patient's arterial PCO_2 will tend to _____ (increase or decrease?), so his pH will _____ (increase or decrease?). The net effect will be an acid-base disorder called a _____ (respiratory or metabolic?) _____ (acidosis or alkalosis?). The way you can help correct that abnormality is to _____
    _____
    _____
    _____.

    d. One reason to try to correct hypoventilation in a head-injured patient is that hypoventilation may, through its effects on acid-base balance just mentioned, worsen cerebral edema and thereby accelerate the increase in intracranial pressure. How would you know if this patient is developing an increase in intracranial pressure? List five signs of increasing intracranial pressure.

        (1)

        (2)

        (3)

        (4)

        (5)

    e. Here are the findings of your initial neurologic assessment of the patient:

        • He opens his eyes only when pinched, not when spoken to.
        • He pulls his whole arm and shoulder away when you pinch his hand.
        • He makes garbled sounds that you cannot understand.

        (1) What is his AVPU rating? _____
        (2) What is his score on the Glasgow Coma Scale? _____

5. The driver of the same vehicle mentioned in the previous question is found conscious but very restless. He keeps asking you, "Can't you give me some water? I'm so thirsty—please give me something to drink." His skin is cold and sweaty. You do not see any external signs of serious injury.

   a. Do you think this patient has been seriously injured? _____ Explain the reasons for your answer.

   b. You decide to start an IV with lactated Ringer's, which is a _____ (colloid or crystalloid?) solution. Your protocol calls for administering 200 ml per hour in these circumstances. You have an administration set that delivers 10 drops per milliliter. At how many drops per minute will you have to set the infusion rate in order to deliver 200 ml per hour? ____ gtt/min (Show your calculations.)

   c. A few minutes after you adjust the IV rate, you notice that the IV has slowed down to the point that it is hardly flowing at all. List the steps you would take to try to identify and solve the problem with the IV.

6. Listed below are some of the routes by which a medication can be administered. Arrange the list in order, according to the speed of absorption into the body, starting with the route by which medications are absorbed the *fastest*.

   a. Subcutaneous injection

   b. Endotracheal spray

   c. Topical application

   d. Intravenous injection

   e. Sublingual tablet

   f. Oral (swallowed)

   g. Intracardiac injection

   h. Rectal (suppository)

   i. Intramuscular injection

   (1) ____   Fastest route
   (2) ____
   (3) ____
   (4) ____
   (5) ____
   (6) ____
   (7) ____
   (8) ____
   (9) ____   Slowest route

7. Patient assessment consists largely of detective work—searching for and interpreting clues to form a picture of the patient's problem. At the scene of an accident or, for that matter, in the patient's home, there may be several sources of information about the patient. List four potential sources of information about the patient and what has happened to him.

   a.

   b.

   c.

   d.

8. One of the most lethal objects in a motor vehicle is the steering wheel. Whenever you find structural damage to a steering wheel—or, indeed, whenever there is significant deformity to the front end of a car involved in an accident—you must be alert for the presence of the "ring of injuries" that impact with the steering wheel may have produced in the driver of the car. List six injuries that may be associated with steering wheel trauma.

   a.

   b.

   c.

   d.

   e.

   f.

9. You are summoned to a house fire where the firefighters have just rescued a young man from a particularly smoky part of the building. He is unconscious, and you notice that his clothes are smoldering.

   a. Whenever a person has been unconscious in a smoky environment, you have to worry about the possibility of respiratory injury. List five signs that should lead you to suspect the presence of respiratory injury in a burned patient.

      (1)

      (2)

      (3)

      (4)

      (5)

   b. What is the *first* step you should take in dealing with this patient?

   c. In due course, you remove his clothing and examine him from head to toe, to evaluate the depth and extent of the burn. You find the following:

      • Third-degree burns of the posterior surfaces of both legs, extending well into the buttocks and groin
      • Second-degree burns of the entire left arm and a hand-sized patch of the left flank

      (1) What percentage of the patient's body has been burned? ____%
      (2) Does the patient have a critical burn? ____ If yes, according to what criteria?

   d. Use the Parkland formula to calculate the rate at which you should run the patient's IV. Assume that he weighs 70 kg and that your infusion set delivers 10 gtt per milliliter. (Show your calculations.)
   The IV should be run at ____ gtt/min.

   e. After a few minutes of oxygen therapy, the patient regains consciousness and begins complaining of excruciating pain, especially in his groin and left arm. Medical command instructs you to administer morphine.

      (1) What is the correct dosage of morphine for this patient?

(2) By what route should it be given?

(3) List three possible adverse side effects that you should be ready to deal with.

(a)

(b)

(c)

10. A passenger car has been involved in a head-on collision with a pickup truck. When you arrive at the scene, you find the driver of the passenger car propped up against a tree, where he had been placed by bystanders who pulled him from the wreckage. The patient has numerous cuts on his face and arms and is in severe respiratory distress. He seems confused. His skin is cold, gray, and sweaty, and his pulse is rapid and very weak. He can barely talk, but he manages to gasp, "Can't breathe. . . ." You notice that the veins of his neck are bulging out. List in order the steps you would take in assessing and treating this patient.

_____

_____

_____

_____

_____

_____

_____

_____

11. A 22-year-old man was shot in the right chest with a handgun at a range of 10 feet. There is an entrance wound in the right midclavicular line about 2 fingerbreadths below the right nipple. A slightly larger exit wound is visible 3 inches (7.5 cm) to the right of the vertebral column just below the lowest rib. What organs are most likely to have been in the path of the bullet?

_____

_____

_____

_____

_____

_____

_____

_____

_____

_____

12. A middle-aged woman was struck by a car and sustained an open fracture of the left femoral shaft.

a. How can you determine if the circulation to the left leg is compromised?

b. How can you determine whether there is damage to the nerve supply to the leg?

13. As you were heading toward the call described in the previous question, which came in simply as a "pedestrian struck by a car," you were busy in the back of the ambulance collecting the equipment to take with you as soon as you reached the scene. Since you had no way of knowing how badly the pedestrian was hurt, you figured you had better prepare for the worst—a "load-and-go" situation. What equipment would you assemble to take to the patient on your first trip from the ambulance?

_____

_____

_____

_____

_____

_____

_____

_____

14. In the next chapter, we shall be considering respiratory emergencies, so now is a good time to review the anatomy of the respiratory tract. Label the drawing below with the names of the structures indicated.

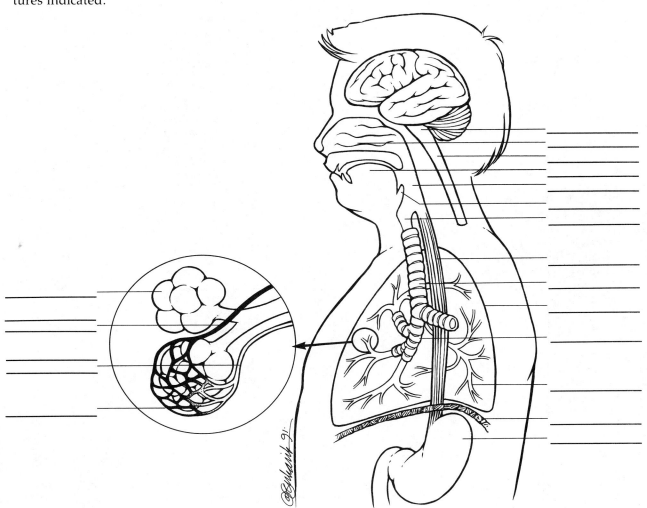

15. Here's a little exercise for a long winter's night.

ACROSS

1. Largest vein: vena _____
5. Meningeal layer
11. pH less than 7
12. Blood minus RBCs
18. Poisonous gas
19. Charged particle
20. Abbr. for "regarding"
21. Osteopathic physician
23. Product of anaerobic metabolism
24. Bladder outlet
28. Bicarbonate is one
30. Beverage for off-duty hours
31. Goes with he or she
32. Title for 21 across
33. What *endo* means
34. Campus in Storrs, CT
35. _____ now, pay later
36. Crystalloid solution
37. Time until your next holiday
38. Biggest of the arteries
41. Nurse
42. What not to provoke
43. 0.001 gm
44. Strong as an _____
45. Nosebleed
47. Chemical symbol of chromium
49. British blood
51. Goes with gevalt
52. Laryngectomee's opening
55. Space agency
58. What a flail chest is
63. Reside
65. Roman 40
66. mm Hg
67. Occurs in spinal shock
72. Low cholesterol spread
73. The way out
74. Bitter drug taken orally
75. One of the vital signs
76. His sign means skull fx
79. Nostrils
81. Poisonous
82. When you should withhold oxygen from a dyspneic patient
83. Amateur radio
84. Transgress
85. Abbr. for "bile container"
87. What to call an angry patient with a .38 special
88. Absence of vocalization
93. What you think with
96. By mouth
97. Bulge in an artery
98. Subterfuge
99. Between the ribs
102. Blood that doesn't get oxygenated while in the lungs

103. Disinfect the skin
104. Opposite of medial
105. *This typeface*
107. Emergency department
109. Abbr. for "that is"
110. Boston's airport
113. Folks to recall on April 15
115. To _____ or not to be
116. Overdose, in short
118. Diaphoresis
120. Has no pulse, flat EEG
122. Attaches to a syringe
123. Roof of the mouth
124. Map marking
125. Wish for
126. Emergency room, for short

DOWN

1. Tracheal bifurcation
2. Elastic bandage
3. Roman numeral 6
4. Movement *toward* the midline
6. Not chronic
7. Word for heart
8. 79% of the air we breathe
9. Goes with "aah"
10. Religious inscription
12. Membrane covering the lungs
13. Voice box
14. Current that induces tetany
15. Goes with hemo- and homeo-
16. Referring to the cheeks
17. Collapse of alveoli
22. _____ thee I sing
25. Watery swelling
26. Absence of O_2
28. Eructation
29. Abbr. for "foreign body"
31. See 33 across
39. Poetic form of *over*
40. Absence of a pulse
46. Sick
48. Will never replace an EMT
50. Opposite of a "mini"
53. In the center
54. Fat tissue
56. No paramedic is one of these
57. Unable to speak
58. Connects kidney to bladder
59. Occurs when you need a bigger dose for the same effect
60. Plural of *is*

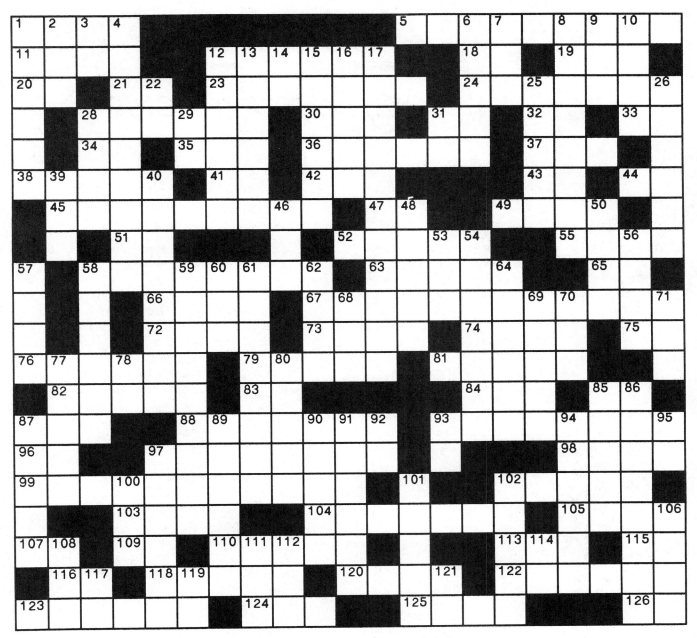

61. Branch of the trachea
62. Always
64. Syrup containing alcohol
68. Laceration inflictor
69. Dress style
70. What every patient needs
71. Nothing by mouth
77. Negatively charged particle
78. Good sedative
80. Miscarry
85. Sign of respiratory distress
86. Characteristic of ribs
87. Vertebral column
89. Often get in the way at mass casualty incidents
90. Type of antelope
91. No man is one of these
92. Morning hours

93. Means the same as *ml*
94. Contusion
95. Best paramedic in town
97. No pulse = cardiac _____
100. Nickname for adrenaline
101. Pertaining to kidneys
102. Splint for clavicular fx
106. Lecherous smile
108. The worst diagnosis
111. What to row with
112. Abbr. for "drops"
114. See 20 across
117. 100 ml
119. Nominative of us
121. Paramedics have a "can-_____" attitude

22
Respiratory Emergencies

1. You are called to an office building for a "possible heart attack." On arriving, you are somewhat surprised to find that the patient is a secretary who looks about 22 years old—not at all like your usual heart attack patient. The woman looks pale and anxious, however, and complains of stabbing pains in her chest that came on "out of the blue." She also complains of a "funny tingly feeling in my lips." On examination, her pulse is 110 and regular, respirations are 30 and unlabored, and blood pressure is 140/84 without significant variation during the respiratory cycle. There are no abnormal physical findings except that the patient's hands look a bit odd, almost like claws.

   a. What is the most probable diagnosis in this case?

   b. What steps will you take in managing this case?

   c. This woman's arterial PCO_2 is probably _____ (higher or lower?) than normal. Explain why.

2. An accident victim who has sustained injury to the cervical spinal cord may develop weakness or paralysis of his respiratory muscles. If so, such a patient may not have the strength to inhale as deeply as he otherwise would. Thus his minute volume will _____ (increase or decrease?), leading to a(n) _____ _____ in his arterial PCO_2.

   The correct management in the field of such a patient's respiratory problem is to

   _____
   _____
   _____
   _____
   _____

3. a. Shunt is best defined as
      A. An elevated arterial PCO_2
      B. An elevated arterial PO_2
      C. The proportion of the circulation that passes through the tissues without giving up its oxygen
      D. The proportion of the circulation that passes through the lungs without taking up oxygen
      E. Hypoxemia plus hypercarbia

      (Circle the best answer.)

   b. When there is significant shunt, it points to a problem in
      A. The respiratory center of the brain
      B. The spinal cord or the respiratory muscles
      C. The upper airway
      D. The lower airway
      E. The alveoli

      (Circle the best answer.)

c. List six conditions that can cause shunt, and explain how each of those conditions leads to shunt.

Condition	How It Leads to Shunt

d. The prehospital management of shunt from any cause is to give OXYGEN. What are the *contraindications* to oxygen therapy?

4. You are called late one night to the Koff family residence for a "man who can't breathe." The patient's wife answers the door, quite distraught, and hurries you into the bedroom blurting, "This is the worst it's ever been. I kept telling him to leave those cigarettes alone—the doctor's been saying the same thing—but do you think he listens? Might as well be talking to a brick wall."

In the bedroom, you find a heavy-set man about 60 years old sitting up at the edge of the bed in obvious respiratory distress. In fact, his "obvious" respiratory distress will be obvious only if you know the *signs* of respiratory distress.

a. List four signs of respiratory distress.   b. What steps will you take at this point?

(1)

(2)

(3)

(4)

c. In due course, you learn that the patient called for an ambulance because he wakened from sleep unable to breathe. List six questions you need to ask in taking his history.

(1)   (4)

(2)   (5)

(3)   (6)

d. As you proceed systematically through the physical assessment of this patient, you will be looking for some specific abnormalities at each step. In the following table, indicate what in particular you will be looking for as you examine each part of the body indicated.

Part of the Body	What I Will Be Looking for in Particular
General appearance	
Vital signs	
Head	
Neck	
Chest	
Abdomen	
Extremities	

e. In the course of the secondary survey, you learn that the patient has been a three-pack-per-day cigarette smoker for about 45 years. He "keeps a cough," but lately it has been worse than usual, and he's been bringing up a lot more sputum. His feet have also begun swelling, to the point that he can hardly get his shoes on anymore. (Most of this you learn from the patient's wife; the patient is too short of breath to provide more than two or three words at a time.)

On physical examination, you find a number of abnormalities, including those listed in the following table. Beside each of the abnormal findings listed, indicate the possible significance of the finding, that is, what it tells you about the patient's underlying physiology.

Abnormal Finding	Possible Significance of the Finding
Confusion	
Irregular pulse	
Crackles and wheezes	
Right upper quadrant fullness and tenderness	
Ankle edema	

f. This patient is most likely suffering from
   A. Pulmonary embolism
   B. Decompensated chronic obstructive pulmonary disease (COPD)
   C. Pneumonia
   D. Pickwickian syndrome
   E. Acute asthmatic attack

(Circle the best answer.)

g. What steps will you take in managing this patient?

h. Should oxygen be withheld from this patient or given in very low doses only? _____ If so, why? If not, why not?

i. Since you are some distance from the hospital, the physician at medical command orders you to give aminophylline.

   (1) What are the therapeutic effects of aminophylline?

   (2) What is the dosage?

   (3) What side effects do you have to be alert for?

   (4) Are there any contraindications to giving aminophylline to *this particular patient*? _____ If there are, what are they, and what should you do about it?

   (5) Is there a safer, more effective drug for this patient? _____ If so, what is the drug, and how is it administered?

5. You are summoned to the scene of a "fender bender" accident during evening rush hour on the freeway, to attend to the driver of a car that rear-ended another vehicle. Fortunately, both vehicles were travelling at the typical rush hour crawl. There is scarcely any damage to either car, "but," says the police officer at the scene, "that driver doesn't seem to be, uh, all there."

The person to whom the police officer is referring is still sitting behind the wheel of his car. At a glance, you estimate that he weighs about 350 pounds. On questioning, he does not seem to remember how the accident happened. "I must have dozed off," he says, and promptly does just that, although he wakens promptly to the sound of your raised voice.

a. This patient is most likely suffering from

   A. Pulmonary embolism

   B. Decompensated COPD

   C. Pneumonia

   D. Pickwickian syndrome

   E. Acute asthmatic attack

   (Circle the best answer.)

b. What do you think accounts for his drowsiness?

c. What steps will you take in managing this patient?

6. The call is for a 68-year-old woman complaining of severe shortness of breath. She tells you that she "caught a chill" the day before, and since then she has felt feverish and sick. She has been coughing a little bit, but it hurts to cough, so she tries not to. On physical examination, she looks very ill. Her skin is flushed and hot. Her pulse is 112 and slightly irregular, respirations are 28 and labored, and blood pressure is 160/90. The neck veins are flat. There are crackling sounds in the left side of the chest.

a. This patient is most likely suffering from

   A. Pulmonary embolism

   B. Decompensated COPD

   C. Pneumonia

   D. Pickwickian syndrome

   E. Acute asthmatic attack

   (Circle the best answer.)

b. What steps will you take in managing this patient?

7. You are summoned to the campus of the local community college to see a 20-year-old student, who is sitting with one of his friends in an office in the administration building, laboring to breathe. He is too short of breath to reply to your questions except in one or two words. When you ask him if he has taken any medications, he points to his jacket pocket, from which you remove three inhalers (Intal, Vanceril, and Bronkometer) along with two pill bottles (Bricanyl and Tedral).

On physical examination, he appears to be in considerable distress. He is sitting bolt upright, leaning forward. His skin is cold and wet. Vital signs are pulse 144 and regular; respirations 36 and shallow, with a prolonged expiratory phase; and blood pressure 130/86 on inhalation, 150/90 on exhalation. There is retraction of the neck muscles on inhalation. The neck veins are not distended. The chest looks enlarged and is hyperresonant to percussion. You do not hear wheezing or much of anything else on auscultation of the chest. The epigastrium seems to be sucked in on inhalation. There is no pedal edema.

a. This patient is most likely suffering from

A. Pulmonary embolism

B. Decompensated COPD

C. Pneumonia

D. Pickwickian syndrome

E. Acute asthmatic attack

(Circle the best answer.)

b. List five symptoms or signs present in this case that suggest this patient is severely ill.

(1)

(2)

(3)

(4)

(5)

c. What steps will you take in managing this patient?

d. Medical command orders you to administer TERBUTALINE.

(1) For what purpose is terbutaline given in asthma?

(2) What is the correct dosage of terbutaline in these circumstances?

(3) By what route is it given?

(4) What are the *contraindications* to giving terbutaline?

(5) What *side effects* may occur from giving terbutaline?

e. You are also instructed to help the patient take a dose from his BRONKOMETER inhaler. Are there any contraindications to giving the Bronkometer solution in this situation? _____
If yes, what are the contraindications and what should you do about it?

8. Not every patient who presents with dyspnea and wheezing has bronchial asthma. List four other conditions that can produce wheezing.

   a.

   b.

   c.

   d.

9. A 56-year-old man calls for an ambulance because of severe dyspnea. His wife, who greets you at the door, tells you, "My husband, he's a heart patient. Please get him to the hospital quickly. I think he's having another heart attack."

   You find the patient in the living room, sitting in an armchair in obvious distress. "Hit me like a ton of bricks," he gasps. "Not like the heart attack"—gasp—"Can't get air"—gasp —"Hurts to breathe."

   On physical examination, his skin is cool and moist. Vitals are pulse 120 and regular, respirations 32 and shallow, and blood pressure 174/96. The neck veins look a bit distended, but otherwise there are no abnormal findings.

   a. This patient is most likely suffering from

      A. Pulmonary embolism
      B. Decompensated COPD
      C. Pneumonia
      D. Pickwickian syndrome
      E. Acute asthmatic attack

      (Circle the best answer.)

   b. What steps will you take in managing this patient?

10. You are called to the scene of a three-alarm fire in a phonograph record warehouse. The first casualty carried to your ambulance is a middle-aged firefighter who was overcome by smoke. He seems very groggy.

    a. What is the *first* thing you should do?

    b. List four questions that you would like answered about this patient and his exposure.

       (1)

       (2)

       (3)

       (4)

    c. In examining the firefighter, what would you be looking for in particular? That is, what signs would alert you to the possibility of respiratory injury? List five of them.

       (1)

       (2)

       (3)

       (4)

       (5)

d. Among those signs, which one should alert you to the possibility that complete upper airway obstruction is imminent?

If that sign is present, what action will you take?

e. While you are examining the patient, he starts "coming around," and by the time you finish your assessment, he insists he feels fine and wants to return to fighting the fire. What should you do at this point? What steps should you take?

11. You are attending a barbecue at a friend's house when you hear a commotion out by the swimming pool. You rush outside to find a neighbor's teenage son under the water, not moving. Several other boys are clutching the side of the pool, panting for breath.

a. What steps should you take?

b. It turns out that the boy is in respiratory arrest, so you start mouth-to-mouth ventilation. Meanwhile, an ambulance that someone summoned has arrived. Now that you have equipment available, what else will you do?

c. You radio for further orders, and the doctor at medical command instructs you to administer SODIUM BICARBONATE.

(1) What are the *indications* for giving sodium bicarbonate?

(2) What are the *contraindications*?

(3) What is the *dosage*?

(4) Are there any *side effects* you need to watch out for?

12. You decide to take a week's vacation doing some climbing in the Canadian Rockies. Of course, you are carrying a medical kit, because it's hard for you to accept the idea that you are *really* on vacation. On your first day out, one of your buddies starts complaining of a headache—"probably because I didn't sleep real well last night," he says. You're a little concerned that he might be suffering from the altitude, but he shrugs it off and insists that you all keep going.

a. How could you check at that point whether your friend is suffering from a serious case of acute mountain sickness?

b. As things turn out, you decide to continue climbing. About an hour later, you feel a tug on the rope and look back to see your friend really dragging. He seems out of breath. Now you're really concerned. List five symptoms or signs that would suggest your friend is suffering from high-altitude pulmonary edema.

(1)

(2)

(3)

(4)

(5)

c. Assuming that you do find signs of high-altitude pulmonary edema, what steps should you take to treat your friend?

13. When your next vacation comes up, you decide you won't make the same mistake twice: no more mountains, where emergencies will spoil your relaxation. So instead you sign up for a cruise to the West Indies—a week of sun and sand and steel bands. On the ship with you are a group of scuba enthusiasts, who don't miss any opportunity to explore the local coral reefs each time you anchor.

One fine afternoon, as you are sunning yourself on deck with a rum swizzle in hand, you hear a commotion off to the starboard side of the ship. You leap from your chair and peer over the rail to see some of the diving crowd in a state of agitation in the rubber raft from which they've been diving. One of their number is lying motionless in the raft, and another two are just emerging from the water and climbing into the raft to join them. The captain, meanwhile, having spotted the situation, has already lowered a winch to bring up the raft and everyone in it.

As soon as the divers are back aboard the ship, you race to the side of the diver who is uncon-

scious. His friends tell you that he was the least experienced of their group. He had surfaced first, and a minute or so after being pulled onto the raft, he complained of chest pain and his voice had sounded funny. Then he just blacked out.

a. What do you think has happened to this diver?

b. What steps should you take to manage this situation?

c. About an hour later, while you are monitoring the condition of the diver pending more definitive treatment, you hear one of his friends who was in the water with him saying to another member of the group, "Gee, my back is sure killing me. I must have pulled a muscle when I did my back flip off the raft. The hell of it is that I can't pee either." You prick up your ears when you hear that, for that story makes you suspect that the speaker has suffered _____.

d. What steps will you take to manage *his* problem?

14. The secret message from this chapter had better not be a secret! Decode it in the usual fashion.

   a. Hypoxemia plus hypercarbia __ __ __ __ __ __ A
                                  52 64 37 20 36 25 58

   b. Blood leaves the lungs through the pulmonary __ __ __ __
                                                    8 14 44 1

   c. Sensation that the room is spinning __ __ __ __ __ G __
                                           3 62 31 18 40   54

   d. 33 __ __ __ is equivalent to 1 ATA
          30 48 16

   e. Crackles in the lungs __ __ __ __ S
                             10 38 22 28

   f. Sound of upper airway obstruction __ __ __ __ __ __ __
                                         59 43 15 50 23 32 5

   g. A COPD __ __ __ __ __ __ __ M __
             9 33 49 19 26 63 4   34

   h. Top of the head __ __ __ __ __ X
                       13 47 61 39 2

   i. 80% of the air we breathe __ __ __ __ __ __ __ __
                                 35 17 60 55 24 27 12 6

   j. Cantankerous __ __ __ __ R __
                    21 46 45 7   56

   k. Wimp's cousin __ __ __ __
                     11 41 51 57

   l. First half of a wit __ I __
                           42   53

Secret Message: __ __ __ __ __   __ __ __ __ __   __ __ __ __ __   __ __ __ __ __ __ __ __
                 1 2 3 4 5   6 7 8 9 10   11 12 13 14 15   16 17 18 19 20 21 22 23

__ __ __ __ __ __   __ __ __ __   __ __ __   __ __ __ __ __ __ __   __ __
24 25 26 27 28 29   30 31 32 33   34 35 36   37 38 39 40 41 42 43   44 45

__ __ __ __ __ __ __ __ __ __ __   __ __ __ __ __ __ __ __!
46 47 48 49 50 51 52 53 54 55 56   57 58 59 60 61 62 63 64

23
Cardiovascular Emergencies

1. The average red blood cell logs hundreds of miles every day commuting around the cardiovascular system. Pictured below are the systemic and pulmonary circulations as seen by a red blood cell. Start at the arrow below, and see whether *you* can find your way from the vena cava to the aorta, and name the structures you pass en route.

Aorta ←

Structures traversed en route:

_____ valve

_____

_____ valve

_____

Pulmonary _____

_____

_____

Pulmonary _____

_____ valve

_____ valve

_____

↑
START HERE

Inferior vena cava

2. Identify the structures in the drawing below and on the next page.

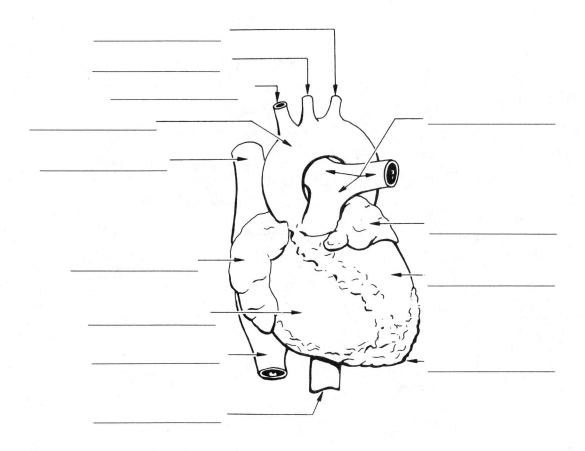

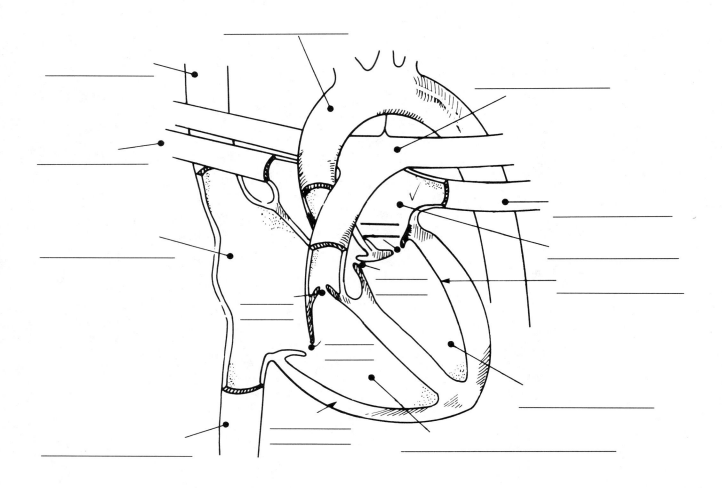

3. For each of the following symptoms or signs, indicate whether it is most likely to be associated with

   A. Left heart failure

   B. Right heart failure

   ____ Dyspnea

   ____ Jugular venous distention

   ____ Swelling of the feet

   ____ Crackles on auscultation

   ____ Hepatomegaly

   ____ Sacral edema

   ____ Pink, frothy sputum

4. The arteries that supply the heart are called the _____. They arise from the _____ and branch into (a) the _____ artery, which supplies the left ventricle, and (b) the _____ _____, which supplies the right atrium and right ventricle. The main *vein* of the heart crosses the heart in a groove that separates the atria and ventricles, called the _____, to empty finally into the _____, which in turn empties into the right atrium.

5. Identify the major blood vessels of the body from the descriptions.

   a. Empties into left atrium   — — — M — — — — —   — — — — —

   b. Artery of the wrist   — A — — — — —

   c. Neck veins   J — — — — — — — —

   d. First aortic arch artery   — — — O — — — — — — —

   e. Drains lower body   — — — — — — — R   — — — — —   — — — —

   f. Drains upper body   — — — — — — — — V — — —   — — — — —

   g. Artery supplying the scalp   — E — — — — — — —

   h. Artery for measuring blood pressure   — — — — — I — —

   i. Another wrist artery   — — N — —

   j. Major vein of the arm   — — S — — — —

   k. Artery supplying the arm   — — — — — A — —

   l. Major vein of the leg   — — — — — N — — —

   m. Where to check for a pulse   — — — — — D   — — — — — —

   n. Sometimes used for an IV   — — — — A — — — —   — — — — —

   o. Largest artery in the body   — — R — —

   p. Artery behind the knee   — — — — T — — — —

   q. Artery behind a malleolus   — — — — E — — — —   — — — — — — —

   r. Takes blood to the lungs   — — — — — — — R —   — — — — — —

   s. Artery of the foot   — — — — — I —   — — — — —

   t. Artery of the groin   — E — — — — —

   u. Third aortic arch artery   S — — — — — — — — —

6. a. Suppose a person at rest has a heart rate of 72 per minute and a stroke volume of 75 ml per beat. What is his cardiac output? _____ ml/min

   b. Now he runs to catch a bus. His heart speeds up to 100 per minute, and his stroke volume increases to 90 ml per beat. What is his cardiac output now? ____ ml/min

7. a. List at least one thing that might increase cardiac *preload*.

   b. What effect does an increased preload have on cardiac output, and why does it have that effect?

   c. List at least one thing that might increase cardiac *afterload*.

   d. What effect does increasing the afterload have on cardiac output?

   e. What is the immediate effect on cardiac afterload of each of the following?
      (1) Norepinephrine _____
      (2) Isoproterenol _____
      (3) Nitroglycerin _____
      (4) Phenylephrine _____
      (5) Hypertension _____

8. For each of the following, indicate whether it is associated with

   A. The sympathetic nervous system

   B. The parasympathetic nervous system

   _____ Vagus nerve

   _____ Acetylcholine

   _____ Tachycardia

   _____ Propranolol

   _____ Sweating

   _____ Valsalva maneuver

   _____ Vegetative functions

   _____ Atropine

   _____ Fight/flight response

   _____ Carotid massage

   _____ Alpha receptor

   _____ Paralyzed in spinal cord injury

   _____ Bradycardia

   _____ Norepinephrine

   _____ Labetalol

   _____ Dilated pupils

   _____ Increased salivation

9. Below you will find a list of medications and a drug box. Store the medications in the correct compartments of the box.

   propranolol   atropine   low-dose dopamine
   epinephrine   isoproterenol   high-dose dopamine
   norepinephrine   labetalol   neostigmine
   metaraminol   phenylephrine   chlorpromazine
   isoetharine   albuterol   terbutaline

| | PARASYMPATHETIC AGENTS | SYMPATHETIC AGENTS | |
		ALPHA AGENTS	BETA AGENTS
Agonist*			
Blocker			

*An agonist is a stimulating drug (as opposed to an *antagonist*, or blocking drug).

10. Electrolytes play an important role in myocardial function. The depolarization of the myocardial cell, for example, occurs when the extracellular cation _____ suddenly begins to flow into the cell, changing its net charge.

    Drugs such as verapamil and nifedipine work by blocking the uptake of another electrolyte, namely _____.

    We learned in Chapter 9 (remember?) that an excess of one particular electrolyte, _____, may produce a tall, pointy T wave on the ECG.

11. Follow the dots on the diagram below to outline the normal pathway of electric conduction through the heart, and list the structures that the electric impulse passes through on the way.

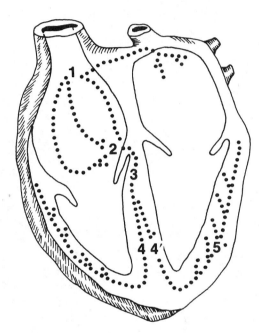

Structures:

1.

2.

3.

4.

5.

Among those structures, list three that can function as a pacemaker, and state the intrinsic firing rate of each.

Structure	Intrinsic Firing Rate
_____	_____
_____	_____
_____	_____

12. Identify each of the components of the following labelled ECG.

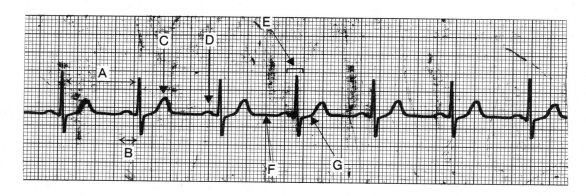

a.   e.

b.   f.

c.   g.

d.

13. You are called to attend a 54-year-old man complaining of chest pain.

a. List six questions you would ask in taking the history.

   (1)

   (2)

   (3)

   (4)

   (5)

   (6)

b. In the course of taking the history, you learn that the patient has had several other symptoms as well. For each of the symptoms listed below, state the possible significance (i.e., what it suggests about the underlying pathophysiology).

Symptom	Suggests
Dyspnea	
Palpitations	
Dizziness	
Sweating	

c. In conducting the physical examination, you find several abnormal physical signs, listed below. For each sign listed, indicate its possible significance.

Physical sign	Possible significance
Patient seems confused.	
Skin is cold and pale.	
Pulse is very irregular.	
Crackles/wheezes in the chest.	

d. Here is the patient's ECG rhythm strip. Answer the questions that follow the strip.

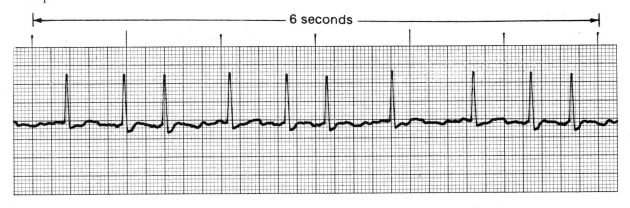

RHYTHM: _____ regular _____ irregular
RATE: _____ per minute
P WAVES: _____ present _____ absent
    If present, is there a P before every QRS? _____ yes _____ no
        Is there a QRS after every P? _____ yes _____ no
P–R INTERVAL: _____ seconds
QRS complexes: _____ normal _____ abnormal
Name of rhythm: _____
Treatment: _____

14. You are called to an apartment building for a "possible heart attack." A middle-aged man who lives alone in one of the apartments apparently collapsed after climbing the stairs to his flat. You find him in cardiac arrest in the entranceway to his apartment, with a bag of spilled groceries around him. You are able to restore a sinus rhythm with a defibrillating shock, but the patient remains unconscious. While you ready the patient for transport, your partner makes a quick sweep through the bathroom to check out the medicine cabinet. He returns with several bottles of medications, labelled as follows:

Lanoxin   Aldalat
Isordil   Diuril
Aldomet

What can you conclude about the patient's past medical history from this collection of drugs? Be specific: Which drugs suggest which conclusions?

15. List seven risk factors for coronary artery disease, and put an asterisk (*) beside those risk factors that can be modified or eliminated by changes in behavior.

a.

b.

c.

d.

e.

f.

g.

16. A 51-year-old man called for an ambulance because of chest pain. He says that the pain came on very suddenly, "like a thunder bolt," about half an hour ago, as he was bending down to tie his shoelaces, and it has been there ever since—the worst pain he's ever had in his life. He describes the pain as "like a knife ripping through me." He denies any significant past medical history. On physical examination, he is obviously in very severe distress. His pulse is 92 and regular; his respirations are 24 and shallow; and his blood pressure is 120/62 (right arm) and 144/88 (left arm). There are no abnormal findings on head-to-toe survey.

a. This patient is most likely suffering from

    A. Angina pectoris
    B. Acute myocardial infarction
    C. Dissecting aortic aneurysm
    D. Acute pulmonary embolism
    E. Hyperventilation syndrome

(Circle the best answer.)

b. What steps will you take in managing this patient?

c. About 5 minutes after your arrival at the scene, the patient starts to become very restless. His face grows pale, and his skin becomes cold and sweaty. You take another set of vitals, and now the pulse is 110 and thready; the blood pressure (left arm) is 90/80. The neck veins are distended. What do you think has happened?

d. What action will you take?

17. A 42-year-old man calls for an ambulance because of chest pain. He states that the pain is "squeezing" in character and came on during a squash game. He stopped playing and sat down for a while, and the pain went away after about 5 minutes; but the whole experience "really shook him up" because he's never had anything like that happen before. He does not appear to be in severe distress at the moment. His vital signs are pulse 82, respirations 24, and blood pressure 152/88 in both arms.

a. This patient is most likely suffering from

   A. Angina pectoris

   B. Acute myocardial infarction

   C. Dissecting aortic aneurysm

   D. Acute pulmonary embolism

   E. Hyperventilation syndrome

   (Circle the best answer.)

b. What steps will you take in managing this patient?

c. Here is the patient's ECG rhythm strip. Answer the questions that follow the strip.

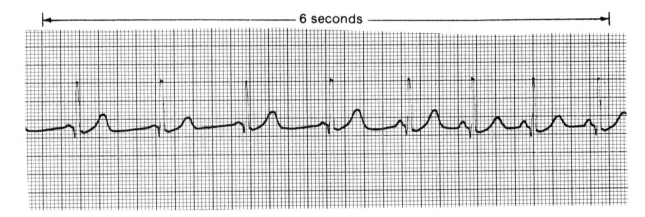

RHYTHM: ____ regular ____ irregular
RATE: ____ per minute
P WAVES: ____ present ____ absent
     If present, is there a P before every QRS? ____ yes ____ no
       Is there a QRS after every P? ____ yes ____ no
P–R INTERVAL: ____ seconds
QRS complexes: ____ normal ____ abnormal
Name of rhythm: _____
Treatment: _____

18. A 35-year-old woman calls for an ambulance because of chest pain. She says the pain came on suddenly half an hour earlier. It is located in the left chest and made worse by coughing or taking a deep breath. The patient has no significant past medical history and takes no medications regularly except the "Pill" (oral contraceptive). On physical examination, she is in moderate distress. Her pulse is 110 and regular, respirations are 40 and shallow, and blood pressure is 110/60 in both arms. There are no abnormal findings on head-to-toe survey.

a. This patient is most likely suffering from

   A. Angina pectoris

   B. Acute myocardial infarction

   C. Dissecting aortic aneurysm

   D. Acute pulmonary embolism

   E. Hyperventilation syndrome

(Circle the best answer.)

b. What steps will you take in managing this patient?

19. A 48-year-old man calls for an ambulance because of chest pain. He says that the pain came on gradually over the past couple of hours. "At first I thought it was something I ate." He describes the pain as "heavy, like an elephant is sitting on my chest." He also feels rather sick to his stomach. On physical examination, the patient looks very apprehensive. His skin is cold and sweaty. His vital signs are pulse of 72 and regular, respirations 20, and blood pressure 180/110 (right arm) and 178/110 (left arm). There are no abnormal findings on head-to-toe survey.

a. This patient is most likely suffering from

   A. Angina pectoris

   B. Acute myocardial infarction

   C. Dissecting aortic aneurysm

   D. Acute pulmonary embolism

   E. Hyperventilation syndrome

(Circle the best answer.)

b. What steps will you take in managing this patient?

c. The doctor orders MORPHINE for pain.

   (1) What are the *contraindications* to giving morphine?

   (2) What is the *dosage*, and how is it given?

   (3) What adverse *side effects* should you be prepared to deal with?

d. The doctor didn't pay much attention to the patient's story. Here is the patient's ECG rhythm strip after he received the morphine. Answer the questions that follow the strip.

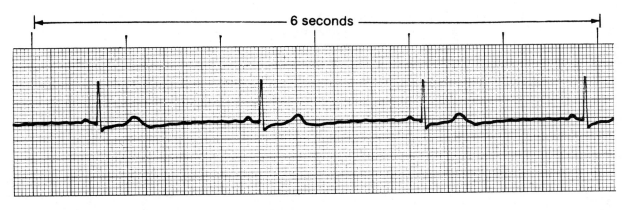

RHYTHM: _____ regular _____ irregular
RATE: _____ per minute
P WAVES: _____ present _____ absent
     If present, is there a P before every QRS? _____ yes _____ no
               Is there a QRS after every P? _____ yes _____ no
P–R INTERVAL: _____ seconds
QRS complexes: _____ normal _____ abnormal
Name of rhythm: _____
Treatment: _____

e. You report the ECG findings to medical command and are instructed to give ATROPINE.

(1) What are the *contraindications* to giving atropine?

(3) What adverse *side effects* should you be prepared to deal with?

(2) What is the *dosage*, and how is it given?

20. A 35-year-old woman calls for an ambulance because of chest pain. She says the pain came on suddenly half an hour earlier. She describes the pain as "like a knife" in the middle of her chest. She says she also feels dizzy and has a funny, tingling sensation in her lips. On physical examination, she seems very apprehensive. Her pulse is 100 and regular, respirations are 32, and her blood pressure is 140/82 in both arms. There are no abnormal findings on head-to-toe survey except that the patient's fingers seem oddly contorted, with her thumbs curled in toward the palms.

a. This patient is most likely suffering from

   A. Angina pectoris

   B. Acute myocardial infarction

   C. Dissecting aortic aneurysm

   D. Acute pulmonary embolism

   E. Hyperventilation syndrome

(Circle the best answer.)

b. What steps will you take in managing this patient?

c. Here is the patient's ECG rhythm strip. Answer the questions that follow the strip.

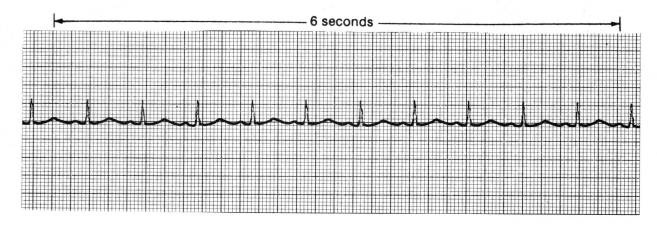

6 seconds

RHYTHM: _____ regular _____ irregular
RATE: _____ per minute
P WAVES: _____ present _____ absent
     If present, is there a P before every QRS? _____ yes _____ no
       Is there a QRS after every P?   _____ yes _____ no
P–R INTERVAL: _____ seconds
QRS complexes: _____ normal _____ abnormal
Name of rhythm: _____
Treatment: _____

21. You are called to see a patient whose chief complaint is shortness of breath. In gasps, he tells you that for nearly a week now he has been waking up in the middle of the night short of breath. When that happens, he has to get up and walk around to obtain relief. The same thing happened tonight, but this time he couldn't get his breath back. When you ask about his medical history, he just gestures toward some medicine bottles on the bedside table. You inspect them and find Diazide, Catapres, and Tums. You also notice a pack of cigarettes on the bedside table. On physical examination, the patient is clearly in severe respiratory distress. The pulse is 72 and slightly irregular; respirations are 48 and labored; blood pressure is 210/100 in both arms. The neck veins are flat. The chest is full of wheezes. The abdomen is soft. There is no peripheral edema.

    a. This patient is most likely suffering from

        A. Right heart failure

        B. Left heart failure

        C. Cardiogenic shock

        D. Acute decompensation of chronic bronchitis

        E. An acute asthmatic attack

        (Circle the best answer.)

    b. What steps will you take in managing this patient?

    c. The doctor at medical control instructs you to administer NITROGLYCERIN.

        (1) For what purpose has the doctor ordered nitroglycerin? That is, what *therapeutic effects* is he trying to obtain?

        (2) What are the *contraindications* to giving nitroglycerin?

        (3) What is the correct *dosage*, and how is it given?

        (4) What are the possible adverse *side effects*?

    d. The doctor also instructs you to administer FUROSEMIDE.

        (1) For what purpose has the doctor ordered furosemide; that is, what *therapeutic effect* is he trying to obtain?

        (2) What are the *contraindications* to giving furosemide?

        (3) What is the correct *dosage*, and how is it given?

        (4) What are the possible adverse *side effects*?

e. Here is the patient's ECG rhythm strip **before treatment.** Answer the questions that follow the strip.

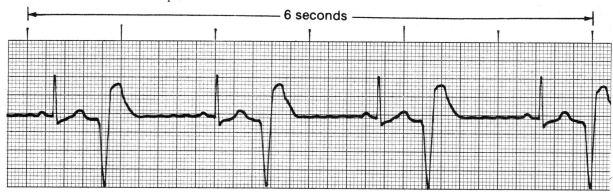

6 seconds

RHYTHM: _____ regular _____ irregular
RATE: _____ per minute
P WAVES: _____ present _____ absent
      If present, is there a P before every QRS? _____ yes _____ no
      Is there a QRS after every P?   _____ yes _____ no
P–R INTERVAL: _____ seconds
QRS complexes: _____ normal _____ abnormal
Name of rhythm: _____
Treatment: _____

22. You are called to see a 62-year-old man complaining of severe chest pain. He says that the pain came on an hour earlier and that it feels "like a thousand-pound weight on my chest." The patient is very restless and seems confused at moments, so it is hard to get much history. On physical examination, he is obviously in marked distress. His skin is pale and cold. His pulse is 124 and thready; respirations are 32 and shallow; blood pressure is 90/62.

a. This patient is most likely suffering from

  A. Right heart failure

  B. Left heart failure

  C. Cardiogenic shock

  D. Acute decompensation of chronic bronchitis

  E. An acute asthmatic attack

(Circle the best answer.)

b. What steps will you take in managing this patient?

c. The doctor instructs you to start a DOPA-MINE infusion for this patient.

    (1) What are the *contraindications* to giving dopamine?

    (2) What is the correct *dosage*, and how is it given?

    (3) What are the possible adverse *side effects*?

d. The doctor also orders NITROUS OXIDE for analgesia.

    (1) Why didn't he order morphine in this case?

    (2) What are the *contraindications* to giving nitrous oxide?

    (3) What is the correct *dosage*, and how is it given?

    (4) What are the possible adverse *side effects*?

23. You are called to see a patient whose chief complaint is dyspnea. He tells you, in gasps, that for several nights he's been waking up around 3:00 A.M. unable to breathe, and he has to get up and go over to the window to catch his breath. Tonight, even that didn't help. "Must be the damn cigarettes," he wheezes. He tells you that he "keeps a cough," but lately he's been bringing up much more sputum than usual. On physical examination, he is in obvious respiratory distress, coughing periodically. His lips look rather blue. His pulse is 102 and irregularly irregular; his respirations are 60 and labored; and his blood pressure is 170/94 in both arms. His neck veins are distended to the angle of the jaw. His chest is a veritable symphony of crackles and wheezes. There is a tender fullness in the right upper quadrant of the abdomen. Both feet are swollen well above the ankles.

a. This patient is most likely suffering from

    A. Right heart failure
    B. Left heart failure
    C. Cardiogenic shock
    D. Acute decompensation of chronic bronchitis
    E. An acute asthmatic attack

    (Circle the best answer.)

b. What steps will you take in managing this patient?

c. When you report in to medical command on this patient, the doctor instructs you to give AMINOPHYLLINE by infusion.

    (1) What are the *contraindications* to giving aminophylline?

    (2) What is the correct *dosage*, and how is it given?

    (3) What are the possible adverse *side effects*?

24. You are called to the sixty-second floor of a downtown office building for a "seizure case." The patient turns out to be a middle-aged black executive who apparently had a seizure during a meeting at work. He is now lying on the floor, groggy, complaining of a severe headache. His speech seems a bit garbled as he denies ever having had a seizure before. On physical examination, he appears to be in moderate distress. His pulse is 62 and regular; respirations are 20; and blood pressure is 240/158 in the right arm, 236/156 in the left arm. There is widespread twitching of his muscles, but otherwise there are no abnormal findings on the head-to-toe survey.

   a. What do you think is wrong with this patient?

   b. What steps will you take in managing this case?

   (4) If you are using (as you should!) a microdrip infusion set that gives 60 gtt/per milliliter, at what rate (in gtt/min) do you have to run the infusion to deliver the correct dosage of labetalol? ＿＿ gtt/per minute.

   (5) What are the possible adverse *side effects* of labetalol?

   c. When you go to bring the patient to the ambulance for transport, you are chagrined to discover that none of the elevators are working due to some sort of short circuit in the building. You radio medical command to notify the doctor of your predicament (somehow you don't feel up to carrying the patient and all your gear down 62 flights of stairs); the doctor decides that since there may be a significant delay in evacuating the patient, you had better start treatment right where you are. She therefore instructs you to start a LABETALOL drip.

   (1) What are the *contraindications* to giving labetalol?

   d. Had the patient been more alert (and therefore less at risk of aspirating anything given orally), the doctor probably would have ordered NIFEDIPINE, since it is much easier than labetalol to administer under field conditions.

   (1) What is the *dosage* of nifedipine for this situation?

   (2) How is it administered?

   (3) What are the *contraindications*?

   (2) What is the correct *dosage*, and how is it given?

   (4) What *side effects* may occur after nifedipine administration?

   (3) You add 2 ampules (200 mg in 40 ml) of labetalol to a 60-ml bag of D5/W, which yields a concentration of ＿＿ mg per milliliter.

25. You are called to a suburban home for a middle-aged man with chest pain. Only moments after you enter the bedroom where he is sitting and set down your gear, the patient's eyes suddenly roll back and he collapses in his chair, unconscious.

    a. What steps will you take at that point?

    b. Your partner meanwhile has whipped out the defibrillator/monitor and applied the quick-look paddles to the patient's chest. Here is the patient's rhythm strip. Answer the questions that follow the strip.

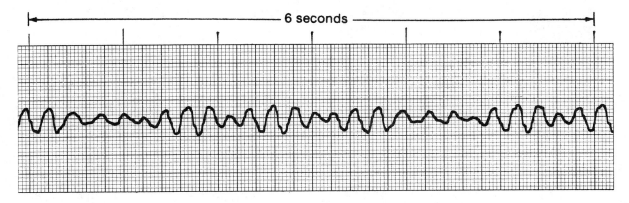

```
RHYTHM: _____ regular _____ irregular
RATE: _____ per minute
P WAVES: _____ present _____ absent
        If present, is there a P before every QRS? _____ yes _____ no
                   Is there a QRS after every P?    _____ yes _____ no
P–R INTERVAL: _____ seconds
QRS complexes: _____ normal _____ abnormal
Name of rhythm: _____
Treatment: _____
```

c. Your treatment is successful, and the patient comes around. You notify medical command of the situation and are instructed to give LIDOCAINE by bolus and infusion.

   (1) What are the *contraindications* to giving lidocaine?

   (2) What is the correct *dosage,* and how is it given?

   (3) What are the possible adverse *side effects?*

d. You give the lidocaine as instructed, but 5 minutes after you get the infusion going, the patient again loses consciousness and the ECG again shows the same rhythm as before. Once again, you manage to bring the patient around. This time, the doctor instructs you to give BRETYLIUM, as a bolus and infusion.

   (1) What are the *contraindications* to giving bretylium?

   (2) What is the correct *dosage,* and how is it given?

   (3) What are the possible adverse *side effects?*

26. You are called for a "man down" in the local shopping mall. The "man down" turns out to be a woman who looks to be in her sixties. Bystanders state that she collapsed about 15 minutes before you got there.

    a. What steps will you take at this point?

    b. You find she has no pulse. What will you do next?

    c. When you apply monitoring electrodes, you get the following rhythm strip. Answer the questions that follow the strip.

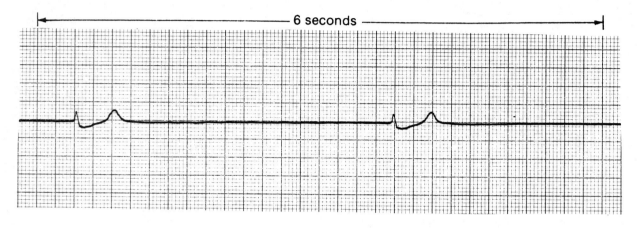

    RHYTHM: _____ regular _____ irregular
    RATE: _____ per minute
    P WAVES: _____ present _____ absent
       If present, is there a P before every QRS? _____ yes _____ no
                Is there a QRS after every P? _____ yes _____ no
    P–R INTERVAL: _____ seconds
    QRS complexes: _____ normal _____ abnormal
    Name of rhythm: _____
    Treatment: _____

    d. According to your protocols for this situation, you administer EPINEPHRINE to the patient.

       (1) What is the correct _dosage_ of epinephrine for this situation, and how is it given?

       (2) What if you haven't been able to start an IV?

27. a. You are standing around the local emergency room one fine day, staring vaguely at the monitor in one of the patient cubicles (as you avail yourself of free coffee and donuts), when you notice the following rhythm on the monitor. Answer the questions that follow the strip.

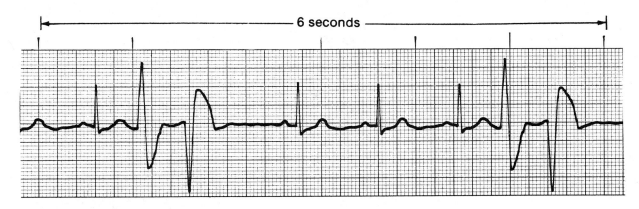

RHYTHM: _____ regular _____ irregular
RATE: _____ per minute
P WAVES: _____ present _____ absent
    If present, is there a P before every QRS? _____ yes _____ no
                Is there a QRS after every P?   _____ yes _____ no
P–R INTERVAL: _____ seconds
QRS complexes: _____ normal _____ abnormal
Name of rhythm: _____
Treatment: _____

b. The doctors and nurses are all occupied with a resuscitation in the "crash room," so you enter the cubicle to get a better look at the patient and the monitor. As you approach the patient, the rhythm on the monitor suddenly changes to that seen on the strip below, and the patient loses consciousness. Answer the questions that follow the strip.

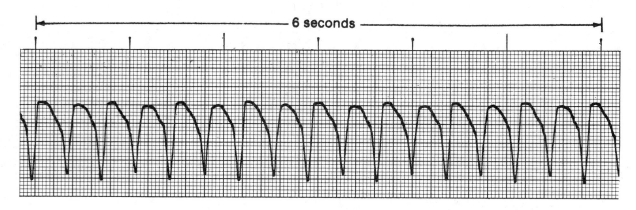

RHYTHM: _____ regular _____ irregular
RATE: _____ per minute
P WAVES: _____ present _____ absent
       If present, is there a P before every QRS? _____ yes _____ no
              Is there a QRS after every P?   _____ yes _____ no
P–R INTERVAL: _____ seconds
QRS complexes: _____ normal _____ abnormal
Name of rhythm: _____
Treatment: _____

c. Assuming that the resuscitation equipment had not been tied up in another room and you could use whatever equipment you needed, what treatment would you have given this patient? (Be specific.)

28. A 26-year-old woman presents with a "dizzy spell."

  a. On finding a rapid pulse, you immediately hook up the monitor, and here is what you see. Answer the questions that follow the strip.

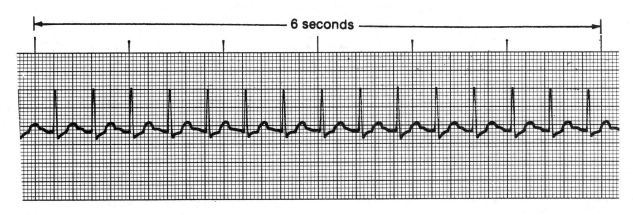

───── **6 seconds** ─────

RHYTHM: _____ regular _____ irregular
RATE: _____ per minute
P WAVES: _____ present _____ absent
    If present, is there a P before every QRS? _____ yes _____ no
         Is there a QRS after every P? _____ yes _____ no
P–R INTERVAL: _____ seconds
QRS complexes: _____ normal _____ abnormal
Name of rhythm: _____
Treatment: _____

  b. You try to convert the rhythm with carotid sinus massage, but without success. You radio for instructions, and the physician tells you to give PROPRANOLOL.

   (1) What are the *contraindications* to giving propranolol?

   (2) What is the correct *dosage*, and how is it given?

   (3) What are the possible adverse *side effects*?

  c. Nowadays, the first-line drug for this dysrhythmia is ADENOSINE.

   (1) What are the *contraindications* to giving adenosine?

   (2) What is the correct dosage, and how is it given?

   (3) What are the possible adverse *side effects*?

  d. Sometimes VERAPAMIL is used instead of propranolol in the treatment of this dysrhythmia.

   (1) What are the *contraindications* to giving verapamil?

   (2) What is the correct *dosage*, and how is it given?

   (3) What are the possible adverse *side effects*?

29. You are called to see a 46-year-old man with chest pain. He says that the pain started about 4 hours earlier and "feels like a vise around my chest." It was not relieved by nitroglycerin. The patient is a known diabetic and takes insulin. On physical examination, he is pale and apprehensive. Vital signs are pulse of 62 and slightly irregular, respirations 24, and blood pressure 200/110 in both arms. There are no abnormal findings on the head-to-toe survey.

a. Here is the patient's ECG rhythm strip. Answer the questions that follow the strip.

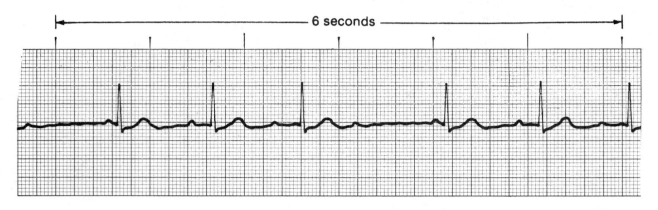

RHYTHM: _____ regular _____ irregular
RATE: _____ per minute
P WAVES: _____ present _____ absent
　　　　If present, is there a P before every QRS? _____ yes _____ no
　　　　　　　Is there a QRS after every P?　_____ yes _____ no
P–R INTERVAL: _____ seconds
QRS complexes: _____ normal _____ abnormal
Name of rhythm: _____
Treatment: _____

b. Is this patient a good candidate for thrombo-lytic therapy? _____ Explain why or why not.

30. You are called to see a man who has fainted at work. His colleagues have propped him up on a sofa. He seems very confused, and when you ask him what's wrong, he just says, "Dizzy. . . ." Taking his wrist, you notice a quite irregular pulse, so you immediately hook up the monitor. Here is what you see. Answer the questions that follow the strip.

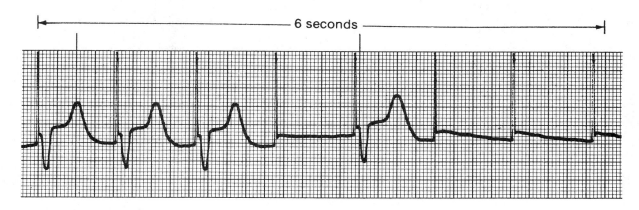

RHYTHM: _____ regular _____ irregular
RATE: _____ per minute
P WAVES: _____ present _____ absent
        If present, is there a P before every QRS? _____ yes _____ no
            Is there a QRS after every P? _____ yes _____ no
P–R INTERVAL: _____ seconds
QRS complexes: _____ normal _____ abnormal
Name of rhythm: _____
Treatment: _____

31. A 42-year-old woman calls for an ambulance because of chest pain. You find her
     in moderate distress, but fully alert. Her skin is warm and moist. Her pulse is
     72, full, and regular; respirations are 18 and unlabored; blood pressure is 150/84
     in both arms. When you hook up the monitor, you see the following. Answer
     the questions that follow the strip.

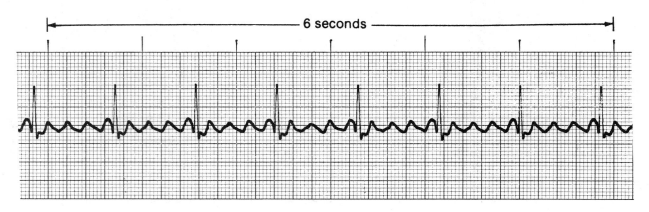

RHYTHM: _____ regular _____ irregular
RATE: _____ per minute
P WAVES: _____ present _____ absent
       If present, is there a P before every QRS? _____ yes _____ no
             Is there a QRS after every P?   _____ yes _____ no
P–R INTERVAL: _____ seconds
QRS complexes: _____ normal _____ abnormal
Name of rhythm: _____
Treatment: _____

32. A 32-year-old Peace Corps volunteer has been invalided home after suffering a severe case of malaria in East Africa. You are dispatched to the airport to pick him up and transport him to the hospital. You enter the aircraft and help him to the ambulance. He looks pale and complains of fatigue. When you ask him about medications, he said he is taking quinidine for his malaria, since it was resistant to all the more usual medications. You hook him up to the monitor, just to give him "VIP treatment," and this is what you see. Answer the questions that follow the strip.

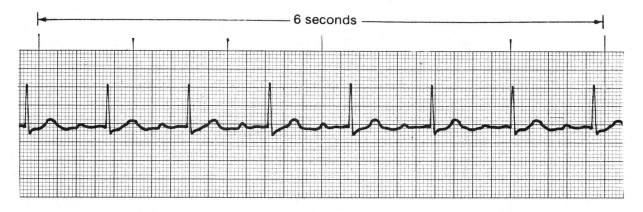

RHYTHM: _____ regular _____ irregular
RATE: _____ per minute
P WAVES: _____ present _____ absent
           If present, is there a P before every QRS? _____ yes _____ no
                 Is there a QRS after every P?   _____ yes _____ no
P–R INTERVAL: _____ seconds
QRS complexes: _____ normal _____ abnormal
Name of rhythm: _____
Treatment: _____

33. A 26-year-old man was involved in a motorcycle accident on a lonely country
    road, half an hour out of town. You find him lying beside the wreckage of his
    Harley-Davidson, complaining that he can't move his legs. On physical exami-
    nation, there is no evidence of external bleeding beneath all his leather clothing.
    The skin is warm and moist. Pulse is about 72 and regular, respirations are 28,
    and blood pressure is 80/50. The patient has no sensation to pinprick below the
    umbilicus, and he cannot move either leg.

    a. Here is the patient's ECG rhythm strip. Answer the questions that follow the
       strip.

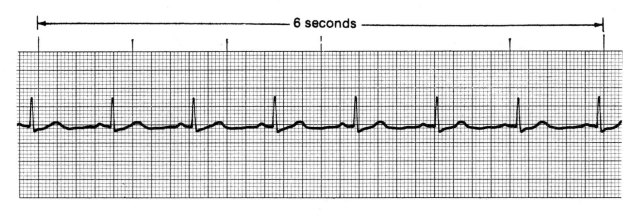

```
RHYTHM: _____ regular _____ irregular
RATE: _____ per minute
P WAVES: _____ present _____ absent
         If present, is there a P before every QRS? _____ yes _____ no
                        Is there a QRS after every P?   _____ yes _____ no
P–R INTERVAL: _____ seconds
QRS complexes: _____ normal _____ abnormal
Name of rhythm: _____
Treatment: _____
```

    b. You report your findings to the physician, and   (2) What is the correct *dosage*, and how is it
       he instructs you to start a NOREPINEPHRINE   given?
       drip.

       (1) What are the *contraindications* to giving
           norepinephrine?   (3) What are the possible adverse *side effects*?

34. A 43-year-old man calls for an ambulance because of crushing chest pain radiating down his left arm. Here is the patient's ECG rhythm strip. Answer the questions that follow the strip.

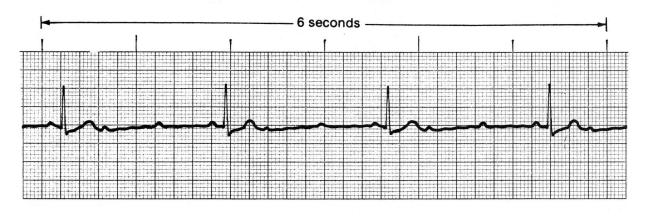

RHYTHM: _____ regular _____ irregular
RATE: _____ per minute
P WAVES: _____ present _____ absent
　　　　If present, is there a P before every QRS? _____ yes _____ no
　　　　　　　　Is there a QRS after every P? _____ yes _____ no
P–R INTERVAL: _____ seconds
QRS complexes: _____ normal _____ abnormal
Name of rhythm: _____
Treatment: _____

35. A 56-year-old man calls for an ambulance because of "indigestion." He says he began to feel very sick to his stomach around mid-morning. He vomited once, and he feels as if he has a lot of gas. You notice that he has the hiccups. He also looks awfully scared for someone who just has indigestion. Here is the patient's ECG rhythm strip. Answer the questions that follow the strip.

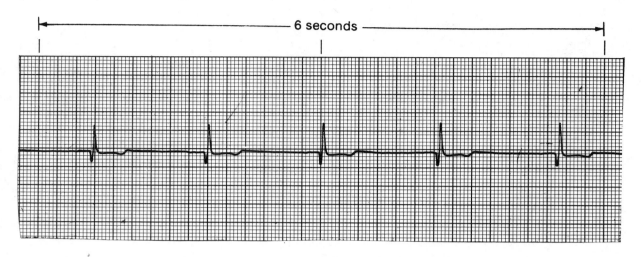

RHYTHM: _____ regular _____ irregular
RATE: _____ per minute
P WAVES: _____ present _____ absent
       If present, is there a P before every QRS? _____ yes _____ no
              Is there a QRS after every P? _____ yes _____ no
P–R INTERVAL: _____ seconds
QRS complexes: _____ normal _____ abnormal
Name of rhythm: _____
Treatment: _____

36. The family of a 76-year-old woman calls for an ambulance after the woman fainted while preparing Sunday dinner. She is lying on the sofa when you arrive, conscious but somewhat confused. Here is the patient's ECG rhythm strip. Answer the questions that follow the strip.

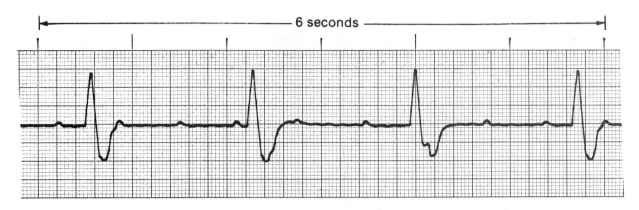

RHYTHM: _____ regular _____ irregular
RATE: _____ per minute
P WAVES: _____ present _____ absent
        If present, is there a P before every QRS? _____ yes _____ no
        Is there a QRS after every P? _____ yes _____ no
P–R INTERVAL: _____ seconds
QRS complexes: _____ normal _____ abnormal
Name of rhythm: _____
Treatment: _____

37. You are called to the home of a 68-year-old man who experienced the onset of "crushing" chest pain shortly after breakfast, about half an hour ago. When you arrive, he is sitting on the living room sofa. His face looks very pale, almost gray. His skin is cold and sweaty. He appears frightened. In the course of your management of this patient, you obtain the following 12-lead ECG:

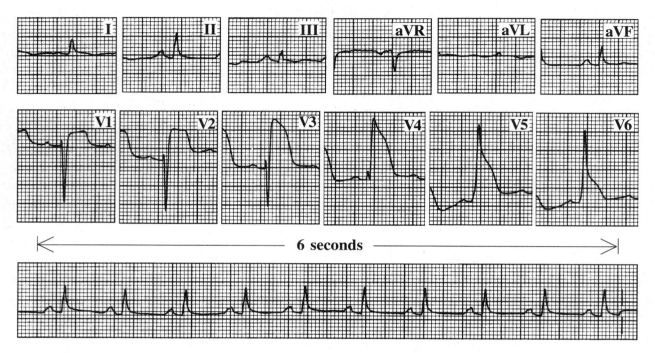

a. Analyze the ECG and rhythm strip, and answer the following questions:

RHYTHM: _____ regular _____ irregular
RATE: _____ per minute
P WAVES: _____ present _____ absent
       If present, is there a P before every QRS? _____ yes _____ no
               Is there a QRS after every P? _____ yes _____ no
P–R INTERVAL: _____ seconds
QRS complexes: _____ normal _____ abnormal
Name of rhythm: _____

Q WAVES deeper than 2 mm: _____ not present
                           _____ present in leads _____
S–T SEGMENTS: _____ normal
              _____ elevated in leads _____
              _____ depressed in leads _____
T WAVES INVERTED _____ only in lead aVR (normally inverted)
                    _____ in leads _____

Portion(s) of the heart affected: _____ inferior wall _____ lateral wall
                              _____ anterior wall _____ other

Pathophysiologic process: _____ ischemia _____ injury _____ infarction

b. What steps will you take in managing this patient?

c. Because of your prompt notification to the receiving hospital, the emergency room staff was fully prepared for his arrival and was able to administer thrombolytic therapy within only a few minutes of admitting the patient. You stop by to check on the patient the next morning, and this is his ECG then:

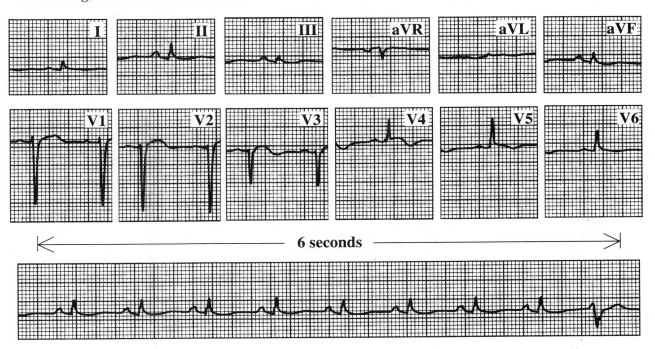

How is this ECG different from the one you took on the same patient 24 hours earlier? Do you think that thrombolytic therapy helped?

38. A 74-year-old man calls for an ambulance because he's been "feeling poorly." It's nothing he can really pin down. He's just been feeling very weak and washed out for the last few days, so he thought maybe he ought to go to the hospital and have a doctor take a look at him. There are no striking findings on physical examination, but because of his age and the vague nature of his complaints, you decide to take a 12-lead ECG. This is what it looks like:

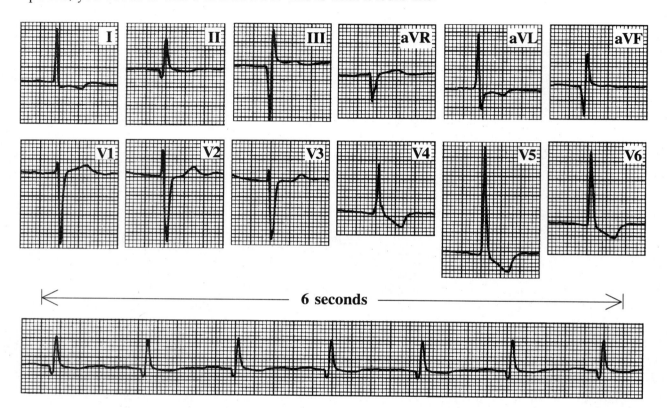

6 seconds

a. Fill in the information required:

```
RHYTHM: _____ regular _____ irregular
RATE: _____ per minute
P WAVES: _____ present _____ absent
      If present, is there a P before every QRS? _____ yes _____ no
            Is there a QRS after every P?   _____ yes _____ no
P–R INTERVAL: _____ seconds
QRS complexes: _____ normal _____ abnormal
Name of rhythm: _____

Q WAVES deeper than 2 mm: _____ not present
                          _____ present in leads _____
S–T SEGMENTS: _____ normal
              _____ elevated in leads _____
              _____ depressed in leads _____
T WAVES INVERTED _____ only in lead aVR (normally inverted)
                 _____ in leads _____

Portion(s) of the heart affected: _____ inferior wall _____ lateral wall
                                  _____ anterior wall _____ other

Pathophysiologic process: _____ ischemia _____ injury _____ infarction
```

b. What steps will you take in managing this patient?

39. A 64-year-old man had the onset of "heavy" chest pain about 18 hours ago. He kept putting off calling for an ambulance, in hopes that the pain would go away by itself, but finally he just felt too sick to hold out any longer. When you arrive, he is in bed, looking pale and ill. In the course of your management of this patient, you obtain the following 12-lead ECG. Examine the ECG and fill in the information that follows it.

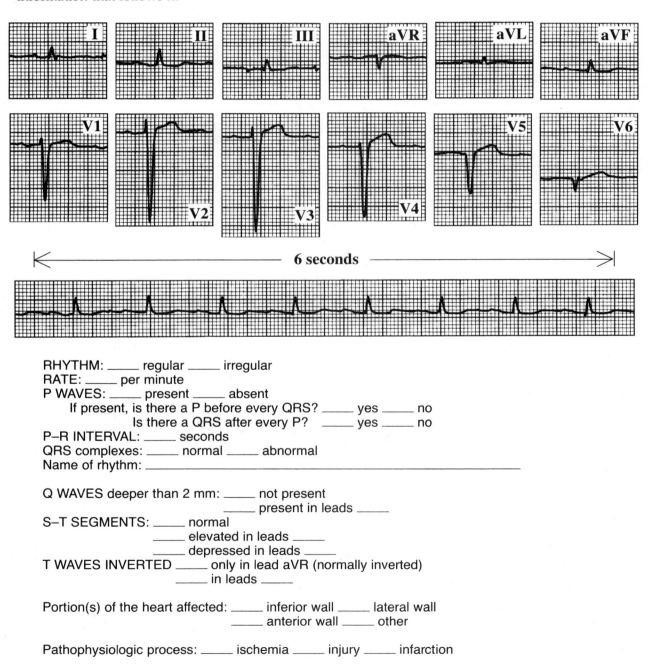

6 seconds

RHYTHM: _____ regular _____ irregular
RATE: _____ per minute
P WAVES: _____ present _____ absent
    If present, is there a P before every QRS? _____ yes _____ no
            Is there a QRS after every P? _____ yes _____ no
P–R INTERVAL: _____ seconds
QRS complexes: _____ normal _____ abnormal
Name of rhythm: _____

Q WAVES deeper than 2 mm: _____ not present
                              _____ present in leads _____
S–T SEGMENTS: _____ normal
                _____ elevated in leads _____
                _____ depressed in leads _____
T WAVES INVERTED _____ only in lead aVR (normally inverted)
                      _____ in leads _____

Portion(s) of the heart affected: _____ inferior wall _____ lateral wall
                               _____ anterior wall _____ other

Pathophysiologic process: _____ ischemia _____ injury _____ infarction

40. And finally, our thought for the day. Decode the message in the usual fashion.

   a. Outpouching of a blood vessel   __ __ __ __ __ __ __ M
                                                 35 46   5   19 53 23   8

   b. Resistance against which the ventricle contracts   __ __ __ __ __ L __ __ __
                                                       2   43 57 14 27   50 30 47

   c. Delta waves are seen in   __ __ __ __ __ -Parkinson-White syndrome
                                     9 40 31 51 16

   d. To defibrillate, turn the "synch" switch   __ __ __
                                         24 34 52

   e. To cardiovert, turn the "synch" switch   __ __
                                       15   6

   f. Profuse sweating   __ __ __ __ __ __ __ S __ S
                    28 13 17   1 10 42 36 49   32

   g. Tissue anoxia   __ S __ __ __ __ __ __
                4   18 56 45 22 48 26

   h. Drug taken for angina (abbr.)   __ __ __
                            33 20 55

   i. Vasoconstrictor drug in cigarettes   __ __ __ __ __ __ N __
                            41 54 37 11   3 29   21

   j. Room at the top   A __ __ __ __
                      44   7 39 25

   k. Score in football   __ __
                  38 12

Secret Message: __ __ __ __ __ __ __ __   __ __ __   __ __ __   __ __   __ __ __ __ __
                   1   2   3   4   5   6   7   8   9 10 11   12 13 14   15 16   17 18 19 20 21

__ __ __ __ __ __ __ __ __ __   __ __ __ __ __ __ __ __ __ __   __ __ __ __ __
22 23 24 25 26 27 28 29 30 31   32 33 34 35 36 37 38 39 40 41   42 43 44 45 46

__ __ __   __ __   __ __ __ __ __ __ .
47 48 49   50 51   52 53 54 55 56 57

24
Unconscious States

1. Hidden in the grid below are 30 words relating to this chapter. Find the hidden words and then use them to answer the questions that follow the grid.

```
P S Y C H O G E N I C E G U Y D I E
O A T H E I L A D Y S A R T H R I A
R P E A A N U D N I K S T U P O R T
O O I L T S G R A N D M A L T W O H
V L A C S U M M E R W A S N A S T Y
E Y E O T L S L I M N O T T R Y U P
R P A H R I H E A D I N J U R Y E O
D H I O O N E S P O T A G U E O U T
O A E L K A M E N I N G I T I S K H
S G P E E C H A S S L E S C Y C L E
E I S H Y P O G L Y C E M I A D E R
G A G L A S S M E N D S P N E U M M
O X E S A S S Y A C T O R T A R R I
D A M N E S I A P O L Y U R I A T A
A R S N E C L A M P S I A M E C E E
I S H E A D A C H E K U S S M A U L
A P O L Y D I P S I A M E S E C A S
```

a. When a person appears to be asleep but can be roused by speaking to him, he is said to be _____. When he cannot be roused by vocal stimuli but can still be wakened by a painful stimulus, his condition is then called _____. But when neither speaking nor applying painful stimuli will waken the person, then he is in _____.

b. List 11 possible causes of an unconscious state.

(1)

(2)

(3)

(4)

(5)

(6)

(7)

(8)

(9)

(10)

(11)

c. Many, if not most, of the things you listed that can cause an unconscious state can also cause seizures. Another cause of seizures that occurs only during pregnancy is a condition called _____.

d. One thing that needs to be differentiated from a seizure is a simple faint, or _____.

e. A seizure may be preceded by warning sensations, called a(n) _____. In a generalized motor seizure, also called a _____ seizure, the patient then falls to the ground rigid and shortly thereafter begins convulsive movements. After the seizure, when the patient wakes up, he will often complain of _____. If the patient does *not* wake up, but goes on to have another one or more seizures, the condition is called _____.

f. Symptoms of a stroke may include _____, _____, and _____. Stroke may be the result of thrombosis, embolism, or hemorrhage. A subarachnoid hemorrhage is one that occurs beneath the arachnoid membrane covering the brain. Recall that the other two protective layers surrounding the brain are the pia mater and the _____ mater.

g. If the patient with a stroke (or any other patient, for that matter) does not have an intact _____ reflex, the patient's airway is in immediate jeopardy.

h. Diabetic ketoacidosis occurs when a diabetic has taken relatively too little _____ for his or her needs. The symptoms of diabetic ketoacidosis include _____, _____, and _____. A patient in ketoacidosis will also often show a characteristic respiratory pattern called _____ breathing.

2. You are called to a somewhat rundown apartment building where the police have forcibly entered an apartment after neighbors reported that the occupant of the apartment hadn't been seen in a few days and was not answering his telephone. Inside, you find a man who looks to be about 30 lying unconscious on a sofa in the living room. Some neighbors are milling around, giving information to the police officers.

a. Without knowing anything more about this patient, you already know that he is in danger simply by virtue of being unconscious. List three dangers that threaten him because of his unconscious state.

(1)

(2)

(3)

b. List six questions you would ask the neighbors about the patient.

(1)

(2)

(3)

(4)

(5)

(6)

c. Besides the neighbors, what other sources of information might be present? What places in the apartment would you check? What would you be looking for?

d. When you examine the patient, you detect the following findings. For each finding listed, indicate its possible diagnostic significance.

Finding	Possible Diagnostic Significance
Cold, dry skin	
Pulse = 110, thready BP = 90/60	
Respirations = 12 and shallow	
Pupils dilated and do not react to light	
Breath smells of alcohol	
Left arm is cold and blue	

e. In assessing this patient's level of consciousness, you find the following:
- He does not open his eyes.
- His arms flex when you pinch his leg.
- He does not make any sound in response to your calling his name or pinching him.

(1) In view of those findings, he is best described as:

A. Drowsy
B. Lethargic
C. Comatose
D. Stuporous
E. Obtunded

(Circle the best answer.)

(2) His Glasgow coma score is _____ .

f. List in order the steps in managing this patient.

g. Among the medications usually given to a patient in coma of unknown cause is 50% DEXTROSE (D50).

(1) What are the *contraindications* to giving D50?

(2) What is the usual *dosage,* and how is it administered?

(3) What are the potential *adverse side effects* of D50?

(4) When D50 is given to a patient in coma of unknown cause, another drug is usually given first. What is that other drug?

a. Why is it given?

b. What is the *dosage,* and how is it administered?

3. Over the course of a week of ambulance runs, five patients are found in coma. You don't have any information about any of them except for the medications found at the scene or on the patient's person. Nonetheless, based on those medications, you can make an educated guess at least as to each patient's underlying illnesses. For each of the comatose patients whose medications are listed below, indicate the most probable underlying illness(es).

a. Patient #1 is carrying Luminal and Dilantin in her purse.
Probable underlying illness(es):

b. Patient #2 has Diuril, Aldomet, and Inderal in the bathroom medicine cabinet.
Probable underlying illness(es):

c. Patient #3 has Micronase on his bedside table.
Probable underlying illness(es):

d. Patient #4 has a small bottle of Cordarone in his jacket pocket.
Probable underlying illness(es):

e. A vial of Iletin is found in Patient #5's refrigerator.
Probable underlying illness(es):

4. A 22-year-old woman is found unconscious in her apartment. Her roommate, who is nearly hysterical, tells you between sobs, "I went away for the weekend, and when I got back tonight, I found her like this. She won't die, will she?" A neighbor arrives and helps calm the roommate while you and your partner carry out the primary survey. That accomplished, you proceed to the secondary survey. You find that the patient wakens to a painful stimulus but rapidly returns to sleep. Her skin is warm and flushed and "tents" when you pinch it. Her vital signs are pulse 110 and regular, respirations 30 and deep, blood pressure 90/60. The eyes look sunken. Pupils are 5 mm, equal, and reactive. The breath smells like Juicy Fruit gum. The neck is not rigid. The chest is clear. The abdomen is soft. There are multiple needle marks and skin changes over the anterior thighs. Completing your examination, you ask the patient's roommate, "Ma'am, is your friend by chance a diabetic?"

"Oh, didn't I mention that?" sniffles the roommate.

List the steps in treating this patient (including the steps of the primary survey that you already carried out).

5. You are called to a local shopping mall for a "man down." When you arrive at the scene, you are directed to a shoe store where a man, who looks to be about 60, is lying on the floor, conscious but very groggy.

   a. In trying to remember the particular conditions that can cause fainting, you first recall that most episodes of fainting occur because not enough blood is reaching the brain. In general terms, there are only two underlying mechanisms that can be responsible:

   (1)

   (2)

b. Now it all starts to come back to you, and you can easily recall at least six possible causes of a syncopal episode.

   (1)

   (2)

   (3)

   (4)

   (5)

   (6)

c. List four questions you would ask of the patient and bystanders in trying to narrow down the diagnostic possibilities.

   (1)

   (2)

   (3)

   (4)

d. List the steps in managing this patient.

6. You are called to an office building where a young salesman apparently had a seizure while waiting for a meeting with his boss.

a. List six possible causes of seizures.

(1)

(2)

(3)

(4)

(5)

(6)

b. The secretary in whose office the patient had been waiting when the seizure occurred tells you that he had been "acting sort of strange" before the seizure. He'd complained of a headache and was very restless and irritable, which was entirely out of character for him ("Usually he's such a sweetheart!"). Then he just fell to the ground and "started jerking all over."

On examining the patient, you find him still unconscious, although he does respond to being pinched by pulling his arm away and mumbling some incomprehensible words. He is no longer seizing. His skin is cold, pale, and clammy. His vital signs are pulse 120 and weak, respirations 16 and unlabored, and blood pressure 130/44. His pupils are about 6 mm, equal, and reactive to light. There are no unusual odors on the breath. The neck is not rigid. The only finding on head-to-toe survey is hyperactivity of the deep tendon reflexes.

List the steps in treating this patient.

c. As you finish carrying out the steps you just listed, you are very gratified to see that the patient rapidly becomes fully alert. "Gee, I sure am sorry to have caused you people all this trouble," he says. "I knew I shouldn't have skipped breakfast." What do you think caused his seizure?

d. What advice will you give this patient?

7. The very next call is for yet another patient having seizures. This time it is one of the city's homeless whom the police found lying in an alley. He is having a generalized motor seizure when you arrive. It lasts about 3 minutes, then subsides. You quickly open the airway by jaw lift, start oxygen, and prepare to start an IV, but before you can do so, the patient has another generalized motor seizure that lasts about 3 minutes.

a. Urgent treatment measures will take priority over the secondary survey. But when you do get around to examining this patient, what will you look for in particular?

b. List the steps in the prehospital management of this patient.

c. What medication is given in the field for repeated seizures?

(1) What are the *contraindications*?

(2) What is the correct *dosage* in the present situation, and how is it administered?

(3) What possible adverse *side effects* might occur?

8. For each of the items listed below, indicate whether it is most likely to be associated with

A. Thrombotic stroke
B. Embolic stroke
C. Hemorrhagic stroke

Note: An item may be associated with more than one form of stroke.

_____ Atrial fibrillation

_____ Atherosclerosis

_____ Excruciating headache

_____ Birth control pills

_____ Often presents with a seizure

_____ Usually preceded by transient ischemic attacks (TIAs)

_____ Patient was on the toilet when it happened

_____ Usually occurs during the night or early morning hours

_____ One pupil fixed and dilated

_____ Sickle cell disease

_____ Patient is often a hypertensive

_____ Stiff neck

_____ Neurologic deficit evolves gradually over hours to days

_____ Typical findings: blood pressure = 230/130, pulse = 48, respirations = 30 and deep

9. You are called to the home of a 68-year-old woman for a "possible stroke." Arriving at the scene, you are greeted at the door by the woman's daughter. "I phoned and phoned all morning," she said, "and when no one answered, I figured I'd better come and check. I found Mother lying in the bathroom." You proceed to the bathroom, where you find the patient lying on the floor. She is conscious but does not seem to be able to answer your questions—she just makes garbled noises. Her skin is warm and dry. Her vitals are pulse 70 and slightly irregular, respirations 20 and unlabored, and blood pressure 190/120. On head-to-toe survey, there is no evidence of head injury, but the face looks a bit lopsided, and tears are streaming down. The pupils are 4 mm, equal, and reactive. The gag reflex is absent. The right arm and right leg are flaccid. There is no evidence of injury.

a. Do you think the patient is right-handed or left-handed?_____ How did you reach that conclusion?

b. List the steps in treating this patient.

10. And, above all, remember today's message (after you've decoded it in the usual fashion).

   a. Period following a seizure   P __ __ __ __ __ __ __ __
                                                     75 3 25 63 55 48 81 30

   b. Type of stroke due to blocked blood supply   __ __ __ __ __ __ I __
                                               16 83 65 77 11 49   37

   c. Usual source of that blockage   __ __ R __ __ __ __ __
                                19 26   33 28 5 9 45

   d. Less common source of blockage in stroke   __ __ __ __ __ __ __
                                        44 67 21 59 41 2 20

   e. Underlying disease in most strokes   __ __ __ __ __ __ S __ __ __ __ __ __ I __
                              56 76 53 17 22 66   80 36 50 79 43 10   27

   f. Parasympathetic blocker   __ __ __ __ __ I __ __
                        73 4 70 40 13   46 54

   g. Good K$^+$ source if taking diuretics   __ __ __ __ __ __
                               61 8 74 14 57 12

   h. Yellow skin discoloration   __ __ __ __ __ I __ __
                        1 35 82 64 42   7 23

   i. Type of reassurance to give a stroke patient   __ __ __ __ __ __
                                    39 47 58 6 32 15

   j. First item of info to ask a patient   __ __ __ __
                           18 68 72 62

   k. Doctor's charge   __ __ __
                 69 78 84

   l. Phalanx of the foot   __ __ __
                 60 71 29

   m. What paramedics never do   __ __ __ __
                 31 38 51 34

   n. Indefinite article   __ __
               24 52

Secret Message: __ __ __ __   __ __ __ __ __ __ __   __   __ __ __ __ __ __ __ __   __ __ __ __ __ __
                 1 2 3 4   5 6 7 8 9 10 11   12   13 14 15 16 17 18 19 20   21 22 23 24 25 26

__ __ __ __ __ __   __ __   __ __ __ __ __ __ __   __ __ __ __   __ __ __   __ __ __ __
27 28 29 30 31 32   33 34   35 36 37 38 39 40 41   42 43 44 45   46 47 48   49 50 51 52

__ __   __ __ __ __ __ __   __ __   __ __   __ __ __ __   __ __ __ __   __ __ __ __ __ __ __
53 54   55 56 57 58 59 60   61 62   63 64   65 66 67 68   69 70 71 72   73 74 75 76 77 78 79

__ __ __ __ __.
80 81 82 83 84

25
Acute Abdomen

1. Pictured below is an abdomen. It may not *look* like an abdomen, but hidden inside it are 20 abdominal structures. Find them and sort them according to the categories listed after the grid.

```
T A P E R I T O N E U M O
G P R A N K S T E E R A V
R A G S T O I L I V E R A
A N L A D L E D U S T E R
V C A L M E S E N T E R Y
E R S O B L A D D E R B Y
N E T P I L E U M A Y J O
A A O C L I A O R T A E M
C S M O E E N D O R A J A
A B A L D S E E D O N U T
V Y C O U S I N V E R N E
A S H N C T C U T E R U S
T R E C T U M M Y T U M S
```

GASTROINTESTINAL SYSTEM

_____

_____

_____

_____

_____

_____

_____

_____

URINARY SYSTEM

_____

_____

_____

VASCULAR SYSTEM

_____

_____

_____

REPRODUCTIVE SYSTEM

_____

_____

OTHER

_____

_____

2. A 42-year-old man complains of crampy abdominal pain that builds up to a peak, then subsides, then builds up again. When you ask where the pain is, he points to the general area of the umbilicus, but when you palpate his abdomen, the part that is tender is in the left lower quadrant. He tells you that he has been vomiting nearly since the pain started, about 6 hours ago.

   a. What *type* of abdominal pain is this?

   b. What *mechanism* is most likely to produce this type of pain?

   c. Give an example of a condition that can produce this type of pain.

3. A 15-year-old girl complains of sharp pain in the right lower quadrant. The pain is made worse by coughing or moving around. The spot she points to is the spot that is most tender to palpation. She lies very still, with her right leg flexed at the hip and knee.

   a. What *type* of abdominal pain is this?

   b. What *mechanism* is most likely to produce this type of pain?

   c. Give an example of a condition that can produce this type of pain.

4. When abdominal pain is felt at some point distant from the pathologic process that is causing the pain, it is called "referred pain." Give two examples of referred pain. For each example, name the underlying condition and state the place to which the pain is commonly referred.

   a. Condition: _____
      Pain commonly referred to: _____
   b. Condition: _____
      Pain commonly referred to: _____

5. A 49-year-old woman calls for an ambulance because of abdominal pain.

   a. List six questions you would ask in trying to learn more about this patient's chief complaint.

      (1)

      (2)

      (3)

      (4)

      (5)

      (6)

   b. In taking the history, you of course keep in mind that not all abdominal pain comes from the abdomen. List four conditions occurring *outside* the abdomen that can produce abdominal pain.

      (1)

      (2)

      (3)

      (4)

6. In the course of a busy week (Is there any other kind?), you have several calls for patients with abdominal pain. Each time you have to evaluate a different story and a different set of physical findings. Among the findings in the patients you cared for were those listed below. For each finding, explain its clinical significance.

Finding	What the Finding Tells Me
Coffee-ground vomitus	
Severe bradycardia	
Melena	
Tenting of the skin	
Patient very still	
Pulsatile abdominal mass	
Rigid abdomen	

7. It is not necessary in the field to make a specific diagnosis of a patient's abdominal pain, but it *is* necessary to be able to recognize when a potentially life-threatening situation exists. Any patient with abdominal pain showing symptoms or signs of shock must be considered to be in danger. To recognize that danger, you must be able to spot the symptoms and signs of shock. Recall them now, and list six symptoms and signs of shock.

a.

b.

c.

d.

e.

f.

8. A 54-year-old man calls for an ambulance because of severe pain in his lower back of 2 hours' duration. "I thought maybe I strained it when I was changing a tire yesterday," he says, "but this pain isn't like anything I've ever had." He also notes, "I keep feeling that I have to move my bowels." On physical examination, he looks pale and apprehensive, but is fully alert. His pulse is 124 and regular, respirations are 20 and unlabored, and blood pressure is 100/70. The chest is clear. On inspecting the abdomen, you notice that the skin looks mottled. The patient is quite obese, so it's difficult to palpate for masses, but you note there is no rigidity. You have trouble feeling the femoral pulses, and both legs are cool and pale. This patient's findings are most consistent with

A. Peptic ulcer disease

B. Diverticulitis

C. Mesenteric ischemia

D. Leaking abdominal aortic aneurysm

E. Ureteral colic

F. None of the above

(Circle the best answer.)

9. A 42-year-old man calls for an ambulance because of "burning" epigastric pain of several hours' duration. He says that yesterday he noticed his bowel movement was "black as pitch," and about an hour ago he vomited some "stuff that looked like coffee grounds." He also feels quite dizzy. He takes no medications except Mylanta "for my heartburn." On physical examination, he looks pale and anxious, and he sits leaning forward. His skin is cold and sweaty. His pulse is 140 and regular; his respirations are 20 and slightly labored; his blood pressure is 90/60. His abdomen is diffusely tender, especially over the epigastrium. There is guarding but no real rigidity. Peripheral pulses are intact. This patient's findings are most consistent with

A. Peptic ulcer disease

B. Diverticulitis

C. Mesenteric ischemia

D. Leaking abdominal aortic aneurysm

E. Ureteral colic

F. None of the above

(Circle the best answer.)

10. A 70-year-old woman calls for an ambulance because of abdominal pain of 4 hours' duration. "I just knew I shouldn't have eaten all that rich food," she says. "It never agrees with me. Oh, I hate to cause everyone so much bother." And she starts to cry. On questioning, she says she had some diarrhea, but it didn't relieve the pain. Her past medical history is notable for two previous acute myocardial infarctions. On physical examination, the woman appears to be in considerable distress. Pulse is 108 and slightly irregular; respirations are 20 and shallow; blood pressure is 160/100 in both arms. The chest is clear. The abdomen is quite distended, but it is soft, and there is very little if any tenderness to palpation. Pedal pulses are difficult to palpate. This patient's findings are most consistent with

A. Peptic ulcer disease

B. Diverticulitis

C. Mesenteric ischemia

D. Leaking abdominal aortic aneurysm

E. Ureteral colic

F. None of the above

(Circle the best answer.)

11. On the first hot day of the summer, a 35-year-old construction worker calls for an ambulance because of "excruciating" abdominal pain. His wife admits you to the house, where you find the patient in the bedroom, writhing about on the bed, tears rolling down his face. "I can't take it, I can't take it," he says. "Please give me something for the pain." The wife says that he came home from work complaining of back pain and then pain in his groin, and it just got worse and worse. He has been vomiting for the past hour or so. On physical examination, he is clearly in severe distress. His pulse is 124 and regular, respirations are 30, and blood pressure is 160/80. There is some guarding in the abdomen and tenderness on the left side, but no rigidity. This patient's findings are most consistent with

A. Peptic ulcer disease

B. Diverticulitis

C. Mesenteric ischemia

D. Leaking abdominal aortic aneurysm

E. Ureteral colic

F. None of the above

(Circle the best answer.)

12. A 46-year-old man calls for an ambulance because of severe abdominal pain of 2 hours' duration. "It's not really pain," he tells you. "It's more like indigestion, but it's got to be the worst indigestion I've ever had. I feel like . . . like I'm going to die." The pain is located in the epigastrium and does not radiate. The patient says he also feels very nauseated and has vomited twice since the pain started. On physical examination, he looks pale and apprehensive. His skin is cold and sweaty. His pulse is 42 and regular; his respirations are 24 and somewhat shallow; his blood pressure is 170/106 in both arms. There is some abdominal guarding, but no real tenderness. This patient's findings are most consistent with

A. Peptic ulcer disease

B. Diverticulitis

C. Mesenteric ischemia

D. Leaking abdominal aortic aneurysm

E. Ureteral colic

F. None of the above

(Circle the best answer.)

13. A 52-year-old woman called for an ambulance because of severe abdominal pain. She says the pain started a couple of days ago as a kind of steady ache (she points to the left lower quadrant), and it just kept getting worse and worse. Now her whole abdomen hurts. It's been 2 days since she had a bowel movement. On physical examination, the patient is in obvious distress. She lies very still on the stretcher and cries out with pain when your partner accidently bumps the stretcher. Her pulse is 128 and regular; respirations are 28 and shallow; blood pressure is 150/80. The abdomen is slightly distended, and it does not move with respiration. On palpation, it feels like a slab of concrete. The pedal pulses are equal. This patient's findings are most consistent with

    A. Peptic ulcer disease
    B. Diverticulitis
    C. Mesenteric ischemia
    D. Leaking abdominal aortic aneurysm
    E. Ureteral colic
    F. None of the above

    (Circle the best answer.)

14. Which of the patients described in questions 8 through 13 would you consider to be in a potentially life-threatening situation?
    Patient(s) ————————————————
    List the steps you would take in treating the patients you consider to be in serious condition from an acute abdomen.

    ————————————————————
    ————————————————————
    ————————————————————
    ————————————————————
    ————————————————————
    ————————————————————
    ————————————————————
    ————————————————————
    ————————————————————
    ————————————————————
    ————————————————————
    ————————————————————
    ————————————————————
    ————————————————————
    ————————————————————
    ————————————————————

15. Many patients with chronic renal failure are kept alive by periodic hemodialysis. While dialysis does remove toxic wastes from the blood and help restore fluid and electrolyte balance, it does not by any means solve all the patient's problems. Patients maintained on long-term dialysis for chronic renal failure are much more vulnerable than patients with normal kidneys to a whole gamut of serious medical problems. List eight medical problems to which patients with chronic renal failure are particularly susceptible.

    a.

    b.

    c.

    d.

    e.

    f.

    g.

    h.

16. The following ambulance calls involve dialysis patients. For each situation described, indicate what you think is the problem and what you would do about it.

  a. A patient is due for dialysis today but says he feels "too weak and dizzy even to get out of bed." His ECG shows a rate of 40 per minute, flattened P waves, wide QRS complexes, and tall, pointy T waves. You are 30 minutes from the hospital.

   (1) What do you think is the problem?

   (2) What steps will you take to manage the problem?

  b. The patient calls for an ambulance because of dyspnea that wakened him from sleep. You find him sitting bolt upright, struggling for breath and coughing up foamy, pink sputum. The lungs are full of crackles. The ECG shows sinus tachycardia (120/min). Blood pressure is 190/120.

   (1) What do you think is the problem?

   (2) What steps will you take to manage the problem?

  c. The patient just got home from a dialysis session at the local kidney center. He complains of a severe headache and nausea. He has vomited twice since getting home. On physical examination, he seems a little confused. His pulse is 56 and regular, respirations are 16, and blood pressure is 180/102.

   (1) What do you think is the problem?

   (2) What steps will you take to manage the problem?

17. Finally, a thought to comfort you if you feel overwhelmed by the list of things that can cause an
acute abdomen. Decode it in the usual way.

  a. Pulsating mass in the abdomen   __ __ __ __ __ Y __ __
                                           68 54 34 41 77   22 48

  b. Large bowel   __ __ L __ __
                  25 9   52 4

  c. Left upper quadrant organ   __ __ __ __ R __ __ __
                           23 59 72 30   6 37 74

  d. Retroperitoneal organ   __ __ __ __ __ Y
                      53 12 46 2 63

  e. Hollow upper quadrant organ   __ __ __ M __ __ __
                        81 60 71   39 29 20

  f. First segment of the small bowel   __ __ __ __ __ __ __ M
                           7 80 35 11 21 15 67

  g. Fluid stored in the gallbladder   __ __ L __
                   45 26   3

  h. Gastrointestinal organs in the mouth   __ __ __ __ __
                          51 76 43 19 62

  i. Inflammation of "e" above   __ __ __ __ R __ __ __ __
                   14 44 64 61   73 10 28 33

  j. Renal calculus   __ __ __ __ __
              17 57 1 50 5

  k. Positively charged particle   __ __ __ __ __ __
                 40 31 69 78 47 38

  l. Feeling   __ M __ __ __ __ __
           18   79 66 70 55 8

  m. Pressure measurement used in diving   __ __ __
                        36 75 56

  n. Not a friend   __ __ __
            27 16 49

  o. French water   __ __ __
            24 13 32

  p. __ __ __ or miss
    58 65 42

Secret Message: __ __ __   __ __ __ __   __ __ __   __ __ __ __ __ __ __ __   __ __ __
                    1 2 3   4 5 6 7   8 9 10   11 12 13 14 15 16 17 18   19 20 21

__ __ __ __ __ __ __ __   __ __ __ __ __   __ __   __ __   __ __ __ __ __   __ __ __ __ __ __ __
22 23 24 25 26 27 28 29   30 31 32 33 34   35 36   37 38   39 40 41 42 43   44 45 46 47 48 49 50

__ __   __ __ __ __   __ __ __ __   __ __ __   __ __ __ __ __ __ __ __ __
51 52   53 54 55 56   57 58 59 60   61 62 63   64 65 66 67 68 69 70 71 72

__ __   __ __ __ __ __ __ __ .
73 74   75 76 77 78 79 80 81

26
Anaphylaxis

1. Hidden in the grid below are 19 signs and symptoms of an anaphylactic reaction. Find the signs and symptoms, then sort them out according to the organ system they affect, and describe the mechanism that produces each.

```
T A S K D E W H E E Z E S T
U I N H A I L O F T O D A Y
R A G D O G A A V E L I N G
T A C H Y C A R D I A N G E
I S B I T E K S R I B R I P
C P L U N C H E S H E E N S
A R O M A O H N E D E M A H
R U A N A U S E A L W A V E
I R T M U G A S S Y P A P A
A I I L P H O S A T R E A D
L T N D Y S R H Y T H M I A
T U G O F L U S H I N G E C
A S T R I D O R M O U S E H
A L R E A D Y S P N E A N E
```

SIGNS AND SYMPTOMS	MECHANISM
CARDIOVASCULAR	
angina	decreased coronary blood flow

RESPIRATORY

_____   _____
_____   _____
_____   _____ _____
_____   _____
_____   _____
_____   _____

GASTROINTESTINAL

_____   _____
_____   _____
_____   _____
_____   _____

CUTANEOUS

_____   _____
_____   _____
_____   _____
_____   _____

NERVOUS SYSTEM

_____   _____

2. When an antigen combines with a specific antibody on the surface of a mast cell, the mast cell looses its chemical bombs ("degranulates," to use the technical term), releasing a variety of powerful mediators, such as histamine and serotonin. List six effects produced by those mediators.

a.

b.

c.

d.

e.

f.

3. a. Which of the following patients is most likely to be suffering from an anaphylactic reaction? (For those who are *not*, indicate what you think they *are* suffering from.)

 A. A 25-year-old man is dining at a fast-food joint. Suddenly he grows very pale, lurches back from the table clutching his throat, with his eyes popping. He staggers to his feet, then collapses to the floor—all in complete silence. His problem is most likely _____.

 B. You are summoned for a 60-year-old man having a "bad reaction" to a medicine. Earlier in the day, the patient was prescribed erythromycin for a respiratory infection. Now he complains of severe abdominal distress and nausea. On physical examination, his skin is slightly pale and cool. His pulse is 72 and regular; his respirations are 22 and unlabored; his blood pressure is 160/94. His problem is most likely _____

 _____.

 C. A 22-year-old man is found sitting on the sidewalk in marked distress. He tells you hoarsely that he just got "a shot" at the VD clinic down the street, and right after he was given the shot and sent home, he started to feel "real strange." He says

he got hot and itchy all over, and now he feels like he's going to die. On physical examination, his face looks quite flushed and puffy. His pulse is 140 and thready; his respirations are 32 and shallow; and his blood pressure is 110/60. His problem is most likely _____.

b. Describe how you would manage the patient among the three described above who *is* having an anaphylactic reaction.

c. After you report in to medical command, the physician instructs you, in addition, to give DIPHENHYDRAMINE.

 (1) What are the *contraindications* to giving diphenhydramine?

 (2) What are the correct *dosage* and *route of administration* in this case?

 (3) What *side effects* of diphenhydramine should you anticipate?

d. The physician also instructs you to start an AMINOPHYLLINE infusion.

   (1) In this situation, what are the therapeutic effects of aminophylline?

   (2) What are the *contraindications* to giving aminophylline?

   (3) In what *dosage* should aminophylline be given?

   (4) What are the potential *side effects* of giving aminophylline to this patient?

4. You are called to the suburban home of a 52-year-old man with "shortness of breath." You learn that while gardening, the patient was stung by a bee; several minutes later he noticed a tight feeling in his chest. Now, 15 minutes after the sting, he looks flushed and very apprehensive. His vital signs are pulse 124 and slightly irregular, respirations 36 and shallow, and blood pressure 90/60.

   a. List the steps in managing this patient.

b. One of the drugs that you will be giving is EPINEPHRINE. List the possible adverse effects of epinephrine if given in excessive dosage.

c. When you report in to medical command, the doctor instructs you, in addition, to give 200 mg of HYDROCORTISONE IV.

   (1) What are the *contraindications* to giving hydrocortisone?

   (2) What *side effects* should you anticipate?

5. Besides bees, what other agents are commonly responsible for anaphylactic reactions? List at least four.

6. Our thought for today comes to us in a somewhat squeaky voice. Decode it in the usual fashion.

a. Protective protein ___ ___ ___ ___ B ___ ___ ___
　　　　　　　　　　 59　40　8　16　　51　32　56

b. Substance that evokes "a" above ___ ___ ___ ___ G ___ ___
　　　　　　　　　　　　　　　　　 24　7　50　30　　27　34

c. Form of definition "b" that produces hypersensitivity ___ ___ L ___ ___ ___ ___ ___
　　　　　　　　　　　　　　　　　　　　　　　　　　 3　44　　61　19　35　6　28

d. Overwhelming allergic reaction ___ ___ ___ ___ ___ Y ___ ___ ___ ___ ___
　　　　　　　　　　　　　　　　　1　31　42　23　47　　43　33　57　10　21

e. Chemical mediator of "d" ___ ___ ___ ___ ___ ___ ___ N ___
　　　　　　　　　　　　　　 55　20　13　41　52　49　26　　36

f. Possible cause of "d" ___ ___ ___ ___
　　　　　　　　　　　　 9　22　53　2

g. Pruritus ___ ___ C ___
　　　　　　 48　4　　12

h. What capillaries do in "d" ___ ___ ___ ___
　　　　　　　　　　　　　　 38　37　5　54

i. Wife of a person who suffers "d" ___ ___ ___ ___ W
　　　　　　　　　　　　　　　　　 46　58　17　45

j. Wrongful conduct that gives rise to a suit ___ ___ ___ ___
　　　　　　　　　　　　　　　　　　　　　 60　18　15　11

k. What the prefix *ad-* means ___ ___
　　　　　　　　　　　　　　　 29　39

l. Abbreviation for "drop" G ___ ___
　　　　　　　　　　　　　　 25　14

Secret Message: ___ 　 ___ ___ ___ ___ ___ ___ ___ 　 ___ ___ ___ ___ 　 ___ ___ ___ ___ ___ ___ ___ 　 ___ ___ 　 ___
　　　　　　　　　1　　2　3　4　5　6　7　8　　9　10　11　12　　13　14　15　16　17　18　19　　20　21　　22

___ ___ ___ ___ ___ ___ ___ 　 ___ ___ 　 ___ ___ ___ ___ ___ ___. 　 ___ ___ ___ ___ , 　 ___ ___ ___ ___ ___
23　24　25　26　27　28　29　　30　31　　32　33　34　35　36　37　　38　39　40　41　　42　43　44　45　46

___ ___ ___ 　 ___ ___ 　 ___ ___ ___ ___ ___ ___ ___ ___ ___ ___.
47　48　49　　50　51　　52　53　54　55　56　57　58　59　60　61

27
Poisons, Drugs, and Alcohol

1. Hidden in the grid below are 25 commonly abused drugs. Find the drugs and then match them with their street names listed beneath the grid.

```
M E T S W I N I C O T I N E D
O E L L I B R I U M P I R E S
M A T E N I C E B O U G H T O
E L P H E N O B A R B I T A L
T C O C A I N E A P C O S S I
H Y D R O M O R P H O N E M P
A E R E O F P A C I F I C E E
D I R T X P A H P N F O O T Y
O H C O D E I N E E E R N H O
N E A L I M D U E T E M A A T
E L F S U N D R M E A L L D E
S P U D H O P E I S A M A R T
T A M A R I J U A N A D I I A
A M Y T A L S T A T E M I N K
C H L O R A L H Y D R A T E E
```

STIMULANT DRUGS

Ice: _____
Stardust: _____
Bambita: _____
Footballs: _____
Ecstasy: _____
Eve: _____
Java: _____
Fag: _____

NARCOTIC DRUGS

Horse: _____
Miss Emma: _____
Fours: _____
Dillies: _____
Dollies: _____
Auntie: _____

205

BARBITURATES AND OTHER SEDATIVES

Red devils: _____

Yellow jackets: _____

Bluebirds: _____

Roche-tens: _____

Mickey: _____

Rose: _____

Grass: _____

Hash: _____

HALLUCINOGENS

Elephant: _____

Acid: _____

Button: _____

2. You are called to the home of a frantic young couple who discovered their 3-year-old happily consuming the contents of a bottle from the cleaning cupboard. List five questions you would ask in taking the history of the incident.

a.

b.

c.

d.

e.

3. A middle-aged man is found unconscious in his garage. He has left a suicide note on the car windshield, but the hood of the car is cold, so you are reasonably sure the engine has not been run recently. List five things to which you would give particular attention in the physical examination of this patient.

a.

b.

c.

d.

e.

4. For each of the patients described below, indicate whether
   V   You *should* induce vomiting
   N   You should *not* induce vomiting

_____ A 3-year-old child who ingested an unknown plant about 10 minutes ago. He is awake and alert.

_____ A 24-year-old man who downed an unknown quantity of Liquid Plumr in a suicide attempt 15 minutes ago.

_____ A 2-year-old who took a few swigs of pretty red furniture polish before being apprehended 20 minutes ago.

_____ A 38-year-old man experiencing "heavy" pain in his chest after popping a few amphetamine pills to "be up for a business meeting."

_____ A 20-year-old woman who swallowed 50 Valium pills about 10 minutes earlier in a suicide attempt—then panicked and called for an ambulance.

_____ A 22-year-old woman found in her apartment with empty, unmarked pill bottles on her bedside table. She is very drowsy and her speech is slurred.

_____ A 2-year-old child who apparently ingested the entire contents of a bottle of his mother's diet pills. He had a grand mal seizure just before your arrival.

_____ A 15-year-old girl who ingested about 50 phenobarbital pills 10 minutes before your arrival. She tells you, "I didn't really want to die. I just panicked when I found out I was pregnant."

_____ A 3-year-old child apprehended in the act of polishing off a bottle containing 250 Yumyum Ninja Multivitamins.

5. A 15-year-old boy swallowed about 35 of his father's antihypertensive pills in a suicide gesture after a family argument. You arrive at the scene, some 30 minutes' distance from the nearest hospital, about 15 minutes after the ingestion. In a telephone consultation with Poison Control, you are advised to induce vomiting and then follow up with activated charcoal. The boy is fully alert, and vital signs are all normal.

   a. What drug is used to induce vomiting?

      (1) What is the correct *dosage* for a patient of this age?

      (2) What are the *contraindications* to giving this drug?

      (3) What are the possible *side effects*?

   b. What is the purpose of giving ACTIVATED CHARCOAL? That is, what is the therapeutic effect?

      (1) List three poisonings in which activated charcoal is *not* effective:

         (a)

         (b)

         (c)

      (2) What is the *dosage* of activated charcoal for this patient?

   c. List in order the steps in treating this patient.

6. A 35-year-old man ingested "about a tablespoon" of Drano crystals 10 to 15 minutes before your arrival. He is fully alert and complaining of severe pain in his throat and chest. His lips and mouth are very red, and there are still crystals sticking to the mucous membranes in his mouth.

   a. List the steps in treating this patient.

   b. Should you induce vomiting?

   c. Should you give activated charcoal?

7. You are summoned to a location by the railway tracks where the local down-and-outs hang out. A police officer at the scene gestures toward two of the group congregated there. "They looked in pretty bad shape," he says, "so I thought I'd better call you folks to come have a look."

   "Been drinking real bad stuff," one of the group chimes in. "Told 'em to stay away from that rotgut—you can go blind from drinkin' stuff like that."

   a. The first patient is in severe respiratory distress. He says he hasn't had a drink since the previous day, when he drank "some stuff they left lying around the gas station—I don't know what it was—tasted pretty good." He says he threw up a few times about 6 hours after that. On physical examination, the patient is alert. There is no alcohol odor on his breath. His vital signs are pulse 120 and regular, respirations 36 and noisy, and blood pressure 180/105. The pupils are midposition, equal, and reactive to light. The gag reflex is present. The chest is full of crackles.

      (1) What do you think is this patient's problem?

      (2) List the steps you would take in managing this patient.

b. The second patient appears intoxicated. His speech is slurred, and he can scarcely walk. "Why ish it shnowing in Sheptember?" he mumbles. His breath smells of alcohol. His pulse is 108 and regular, his respirations are 30 and deep, and his blood pressure is 140/86. There is no evidence of head injury. The pupils are about 6 mm and equal and react sluggishly to light. The gag reflex is present. The chest is clear. The abdomen is very tender and nearly rigid to palpation.

(1) What do you think is this patient's problem?

(2) List the steps you would take in managing this patient.

8. You are called to the home of a 46-year-old woman who swallowed an unknown quantity of silver polish in a suicide attempt. A bevvy of agitated family members are hovering around her, all talking at once. As far as you can determine, the ingestion took place sometime during the past hour. While your partner telephones Poison Control for a rundown on the exact composition of that brand of silver polish, you examine the patient. You find her very confused and sleepy. There is a funny smell on her breath that you can't quite place—a little like marzipan. The skin is flushed. The pulse is 132 and thready, respirations are 32 and labored, and blood pressure is 90/64.

a. What do you think is this patient's problem?

b. What *drug* is indicated to treat this problem, in order to "buy time" until you reach the emergency room?

c. How is it given?

d. What *side effects* should you anticipate?

e. List the steps you would take in managing this patient.

9. You are called to a suburban home by a frantic mother whose 2-year-old has ingested kerosene he found in the garage. She is not sure how much the child took; but pointing to the soft drink bottle in which the kerosene was stored, she says, "I think it was full before." The bottle is now half empty, but you notice there is kerosene spilled on the garage floor and on the child's clothing. On examination, he smells strongly of kerosene but is alert and in no apparent distress. What steps will you take in managing this patient?

10. While it is advisable to consult Poison Control for definitive identification of any ingested substance, it is nonetheless worthwhile to have a general knowledge of the categories of poisons and some of the more commonly encountered examples of each category. Fill in the box below with examples of each type of poison mentioned.

Type of Poison	Examples
Strong acid	
Strong alkali	
Volatile hydrocarbon	
Toxic plant	

11. You are staying with a bunch of friends at their cabin in the mountains for a nice ski weekend. Your host takes considerable pride in the cabin, which he built himself. "Snug as a bug in a rug," he says, "not a draft in the place." You have to admit that he did a good insulation job and that the place is nice and cozy from the Franklin stove in the corner.

    When you get up the next morning, your friend's wife, who knows of course that you're a paramedic, says, "Will you have a look at the baby? She's sick with something. She's been throwing up all morning." You don't know much about babies, and you don't feel so hot yourself, but you take a look at the baby. You find her pale and dehydrated, with a bounding pulse but no fever. As you are examining her, she has a grand mal seizure. "It must be the flu," says the baby's mother, "because I'm coming down with something too. I feel real sick to my stomach." Meanwhile, your friend, just getting up, says, "Boy, do I have a headache; it's like Niagara roaring through my skull."

    a. What do you think is the baby's problem?

    b. What steps should you take in this situation?

12. One fine Sunday afternoon, you are called to a suburban home for a "possible heart attack." On arrival, you find a middle-aged man, clad in shorts and a T-shirt, sprawled out on the sofa in the living room. "I don't know what happened," he says. "I was just sitting outside on the lawn, and I started to feel real dizzy and sick to my stomach. And real weak. And there's this tight feeling in my chest. . . ."

    "It's that stuff Mr. Dimbledirt was spraying," his wife chimes in. "I'm sure of it. Why he has to spray his precious roses precisely when *we're* sitting in the garden is beyond me."

    While you begin your assessment of the patient, your partner goes next door to talk with Mr. Dimbledirt. You find the patient in considerable distress. His skin is pale and diaphoretic. His vital signs are pulse 42 and regular, respirations 28 and labored, blood pressure 140/80. The pupils are very constricted. The patient is salivating profusely, and his breath smells like garlic. The neck veins are flat. The chest is full of wheezes. As you are completing the examination, your partner returns carrying a bottle labelled "Parathion."

    a. What do you think is this patient's problem?

    b. What *drug* is used to treat this problem?

    c. What are the *contraindications* to giving that drug?

    d. What is the correct *dosage* in this situation?

e. How will you know when you have given enough of the drug?

f. List all the steps in treating this patient.

13. You are called to a local junior high school where a 12-year-old boy had a grand mal seizure. The school nurse, who is kneeling on the floor of the boys' restroom beside the child, tells you that the child has no known seizure history. The boy is unconscious but can be roused by painful stimulus. You cannot find any abnormalities on physical examination save for signs that he indeed just had a seizure (slight bleeding of the tongue, incontinence). A search of his pockets, however, reveals a few small bottles of typewriter correction fluid. What steps will you take in managing this patient?

14. Leading the local Boy Scout troop on a trek through the woods one Saturday, you are constrained to deal with a few misadventures. Describe how you would manage each.

a. One boy is stung by a bee and is howling in pain.

b. Another boy discovers a tick firmly attached to his leg.

c. A third boy, availing himself of an outhouse found en route, lets out a squeak of pain: "Ah-ah-oww! Something bit me in the . . . ah-ah-ow!" he howls. You tell him to pipe down and behave like a Boy Scout, but you start to become concerned when he complains of severe cramps. You reach a roadside telephone and call for an ambulance. By the time the ambulance arrives, the boy is very restless. He vomits several times, and his abdomen feels like a rock.

(1) What do you think bit him?

(2) What drug may help relieve his pain?

(3) What are the *contraindications* to giving that drug?

(4) What is the *dosage*?

(5) List all the steps in treating this boy.

15. The next weekend, when you are on duty, you are called to the very same woods for a snakebite victim. You find a young hiker sitting on the ground with his trouser leg rolled up, clutching his leg.

a. What symptoms and signs would suggest to you that the bite is truly envenomed?

b. You conclude from your assessment of the patient that he *has* suffered an envenomed snakebite. List the steps of treatment.

16. You are attending an EMS conference in a southern coastal resort, and you decide to take an afternoon off and enjoy the beach. You are no sooner ensconced in your deck chair, gin and tonic in hand, with a friend tending to the barbecue, than you hear a commotion and see a swimmer being pulled from the water. You rush over of course, and you find the swimmer writhing on the ground crying, "My legs, oh, it hurts, my legs. . . ." You notice there are some little structures stuck to his legs. What steps can you take to help this patient?

17. Having managed that emergency with your usual finesse, you mix yourself a fresh gin and tonic and settle back into your deck chair, only to hear yet more shouts at the shoreline. Cantering back there, you find a young boy screaming in pain. Beside him is the starfish that he just dropped in a hurry, after it punctured his hand. What steps can you take to help this patient?

18. The sun is already getting low in the sky by the time you sink back into your deck chair and close your eyes. You are quickly roused from your reverie by the voice of someone standing over you. "Hey, mister, you a doctor or somethin'?"
"No," you reply, "I'm a paramedic."

"Do you s'pose you could take a look at this?" The questioner presents a set of abraded knuckles for your inspection.
"It doesn't look very serious to me," you say, hoping he will go away. "How did it happen?"
He looks embarrassed. "Oh, I guess you could call it a difference of opinion. First he hit me here in the neck, and then I landed this left to his mouth."
How would you manage this patient?

19. You're folding up your deck chair when you happen to see a jogger running erratically down the beach toward you. His shorts are torn, and there is blood trickling down one leg. "What happened to you?" you ask.
"Some big Doberman tackled me as I was running. I figured the best thing to do was keep running to where I left my car."
You note the tooth marks and a laceration on the runner's left leg. How would you manage this patient?

Returning to your hotel, you encounter one of your friends who is attending the same conference. "Been goofing off at the beach, I see," he says, taking in your sunburn.
"It wasn't like that at all," you tell him. "All I did was take care of medical emergencies."
"Sure, sure," he says.

20. You are called to an apartment building in a somewhat unsavory area of town for an "unconscious man." Arriving there, you find several young people, all of whom seem to be under the influence of one drug or another, hovering over one of their friends, who is indeed unconscious.

  a. List five questions to ask in taking the history of the unconscious patient.

     (1)

     (2)

     (3)

     (4)

     (5)

  b. List five things to which you would pay particular attention in conducting the physical examination.

     (1)

     (2)

     (3)

     (4)

     (5)

  c. The patient's friends are not very informative, and the physical examination does not yield unequivocal evidence to suggest a particular cause of the coma, although the pulse is a bit slow (60/min) and so are the respirations (10/min). The patient is deeply unconscious and has no gag reflex. List the steps you would take in managing this patient.

21. Goldilocks and the three bears had a party at which drugs and booze were used very freely. By the end of the party, Goldilocks and her furry friends had all overdosed on one drug or another. Checking out the premises, you find syringes, a crack pipe, a bottle containing some phencyclidine (PCP) pills, and another with one or two pentobarbital (Nembutal). Try to figure out who overdosed on what, and in each case, list the steps you would take in managing the patient. (Note: Assume that the dosages for bears are the same as for people.)

  a. GOLDILOCKS is deeply comatose. She doesn't respond even to being pinched. Her pulse is 112 and weak, respirations are 14 and shallow, and blood pressure is 70 systolic. Her skin feels quite cold. Her pupils are widened and scarcely react at all when you shine a light in them. Her breath smells of alcohol.

     (1) Goldilocks has probably taken an overdose of _____.
     (2) List the steps you would take in managing this problem.

  b. PAPA BEAR looks positively "wired." He is dancing around the premises with a broom, and when you ask him to please sit down, he says he can't sit down—he has to keep moving. He is sweating visibly. His pulse is 120 and bounding, respirations are 20 and unlabored, and the blood pressure is 200/100. His paws are rather shaky.

     (1) Papa Bear has probably taken an overdose of _____.
     (2) List the steps you would take in managing this problem.

c. MAMA BEAR is sitting drowsily on the sofa. She keeps nodding off to sleep, and it's getting more and more difficult to wake her. Her vitals are pulse 52, respirations 8 and deep, and blood pressure 90/60. Her pupils are very constricted.

(1) Mama Bear has probably overdosed on

_____.

(2) List the steps you would take in managing this problem.

d. BABY BEAR is standing in the middle of the room staring blankly in front of him. He is bleeding profusely from his left foot, where he evidently sliced off one of his toes with a carving knife. He does not seem to be in any pain. He does not, in fact, seem to be in this world at all. He is just standing there, holding the carving knife. But when you start to approach, he says, "If any more of you CIA agents come near me, I'll cut you to pieces."

(1) Baby Bear has probably overdosed on

_____.

(2) List the steps you would take in managing this problem.

e. In treating one of these patients, you had to give NALOXONE (Narcan), so of course you were completely familiar with the properties of that drug.

(1) What are the *indications* for giving naloxone?

(2) What are the *contraindications*?

(3) What are the possible *side effects*?

22. You are called one morning to a well-appointed apartment building for a middle-aged businessman complaining of severe abdominal pain. He describes the pain as sharp, steady, and radiating from the epigastrium straight through into his back. He has been vomiting since last night. You have a feeling that alcohol may be a part of this problem, and you ask the patient how much alcohol he normally consumes. "Oh, an occasional highball at lunch," he says, "nothing out of the ordinary."

a. List five clues that, if present, would tend to reinforce your suspicion that the patient has a drinking problem.

(1)

(2)

(3)

(4)

(5)

b. If the patient *is* an alcoholic, he will be much more vulnerable than a nondrinker to a whole host of medical problems. List seven conditions to which alcoholics are more prone than the general population.

(1)

(2)

(3)

(4)

(5)

(6)

(7)

c. As you are taking the patient's vital signs, his eyes suddenly deviate to the left, his whole body becomes rigid, and then he falls to the floor in a grand mal seizure. His wife, who has been uncommunicative up to this point, now tells you, "He drinks much more than he said. But he hasn't had a drink in almost 2 days now."

(1) List the steps in managing this patient.

(2) Suppose that before he wakes up fully, the patient has another seizure. What will you do then?

23. A middle-aged man is found unconscious in an alley downtown. His clothing is dishevelled, and he smells strongly of alcohol.

   a. List eight possible causes of his unconscious state *besides* alcohol.

   (1)

   (2)

   (3)

   (4)

   (5)

   (6)

   (7)

   (8)

b. List the steps in managing this patient.

c. Among the medications routinely given in a situation such as this are 50% dextrose and thiamine.

   (1) Why is THIAMINE given, and in what dosage is it given?

   (2) What are the possible adverse *side effects* of 50% DEXTROSE?

24. You are called to police lockup for a "man gone crazy." The desk officer tells you that the prisoner had been picked up 3 days earlier for vagrancy and had seemed all right until this morning, when he started throwing things around his cell. He has been completely out of control ever since. You follow a police officer into the cell block and shortly find yourself in the center of a tremendous din. During a struggle that preceded your arrival, the patient had been handcuffed to the bars of his cell, but he is still wild-eyed and thrashing around. You introduce yourself as a paramedic and inquire politely what seems to be the trouble.

   "The rats," he says. "Don't you see the rats crawling on the ceiling?" He is sweating profusely.

   a. This patient is showing signs of _____ _____.

   b. List the steps you will take in managing this patient.

25. And finally our thought for the day. Decode it in the usual fashion.

a. Wood alcohol ___ ___ ___ ___ ___ ___ ___ ___
67 8 69 38 74 9 22 53

b. Pupillary constriction ___ ___ ___ ___ ___ ___
47 26 55 78 7 16

c. Mandible ___ ___ ___
59 44 25

d. Abnormally low body temperature ___ ___ ___ ___ ___ ___ ___ ___ M ___ ___
28 49 4 32 45 70 51 61   39 5

e. Kerosene is one ___ Y ___ ___ ___ ___ ___ ___ ___ ___
2   63 21 66 73 48 42 50 12 37

f. Inhaling through a cloth soaked in volatile liquid ___ ___ ___ ___ ___ ___ G
46 75 64 11 52 58

g. Substance used to "cut" heroin ___ ___ ___ C
27 29 54

h. Itching ___ ___ ___ ___ ___ ___ ___ ___
19 72 60 56 57 6 13 76

i. Street name for peyote ___ ___ ___ ___ ___ N
41 18 1 10 68

j. Found in egg yolks, meat, cream, etc. C ___ ___ ___ ___ ___ ___ ___ ___ L
33 20 30 71 24 17 43 65 36

k. Given to every patient in coma G ___ ___ ___ ___ ___ ___
35 23 31 34 40 77

l. Requirement ___ ___ ___ ___
14 3 62 15

Secret Message: ___ ___ ___   ___ ___ ___ ___ ___ ___ ___   ___ ___ ___ ___ ___   ___ ___ ___ ___ ___ ___ ___ ___ ___
1 2 3   4 5 6 7 8 9 10   11 12 13 14 15   16 17 18 19 20 21 22 23 24

___ ___ ___ ___   ___ ___ ___ ___ ___ ___ ___   ___ ___   ___ ___ ___   ___ ___ ___ ___ ___ ___   ___ ___ ___
25 26 27 28   29 30 31 32 33 34 35   36 37   38 39 40   41 42 43 44 45 46   47 48 49

___ ___   ___ ___ ___   ___ ___   ___ ___ ___ ___ ___ ___ ___   ___ ___ ___ ___   ___ ___ ___ ___ ___   ___ ___ ___ ___ ___ ___ .
50 51   52 53 54   55 56   57 58 59 60 61 62 63   64 65 66 67   68 69 70 71 72   73 74 75 76 77 78

28
Communicable Diseases

1. This time around, we shall *start* with a secret message, because the message is vitally important. If you read the chapter in the textbook, the message will not be any big secret.

   a. Object that transmits a disease agent   __ __ __ __ __ __
                                                      82 73 39 20 26 60

   b. Type of microbe that causes hepatitis   __ __ __ __ __
                                                    87 64 33 74 56

   c. Skin test to detect TB   __ __ __ __ __ __ U __
                        50 13 4 88 85 91   93 43 21

   d. Sign of hepatitis   __ __ __ __ __ U __
                29 24 41 63 15   70

   e. Painful complication of mumps   __ __ __ __ __ __ I __
                            32 75 47 76 40 1   80

   f. Symptom of gonorrhea   __ __ __ U __ __ __
                  57 72 65   35 53 17

   g. Sign of measles   __ __ __ __
               89 9 38 2

   h. Sign of TB   __ I __ __ __ __   __ __ __ __ __ __
          78 52 28 66   6 68 86 77 42 59

   i. Another sign of TB   __ __ U __ __
               27 67 31 71

   j. Symptom of hepatitis   __ __ __ I __ __ __
              10 46 7 45 55 84

   k. Another symptom of hepatitis   __ __ U __ __ __
                   49 19 8 5 81

   l. Bluish skin in hypoxemia   C __ __ __ __ __ __ __
                    90 69 30 54 62 58 22

   m. Protective reflex   __ __ __
             18 92 12

   n. What arteries do in neurogenic shock   __ I __ __ __ __
                          79 94 14 34 3

   o. Good source of K^+ B __ __ __ __ __
                61 37 25 44 51

   p. Nickname for U.S. transportation agency   __ __ __
                        16 48 83

   q. Caffeine-containing drink   __ __ __
             23 11 36

Secret Message: __ __ __   __ __ __ __   __ __ __ __ __ __ __ __ __   __ __ __ __ __ __ __
               1 2 3   4 5 6 7   8 9 10 11 12 13 14 15 16   17 18 19 20 21 22 23

__ __ __ __ __ __ __ __   __ __   __ __ __ __ __ __ __ __ __ __ __ __   __
24 25 26 27 28 29 30 31   32 33   34 35 36 37 38 39 40 41 42 43 44 45   46

__ __ __ __ __ __ __ __ __ __   __ __ __ __ __ __ __   __ __   __ __   __ __ __ __   __ __ __ __
47 48 49 50 51 52 53 54 55 56   57 58 59 60 61 62 63   64 65   66 67   68 69 70 71   72 73 74 75

__ __ __ __ __   __ __ __ __ __   __ __ __ __ __   __ __ __ __ .
76 77 78 79 80   81 82 83 84 85   86 87 88 89 90   91 92 93 94

2. Match the following words with the definition that best fits each.

   A. Reservoir
   B. Carrier
   C. Fomite
   D. Incubation period

   E. Communicable period
   F. Nosocomial
   G. Contamination
   H. Infection

   _____ Time during which a person is capable of transmitting his disease to someone else.

   _____ Local or systemic disease process caused by a microorganism.

   _____ Inanimate object that can transmit disease microorganisms from one person to another.

   _____ Place where microorganisms live and multiply.

   _____ Time between exposure to a microorganism and the development of symptoms.

   _____ Relating to a hospital or other health care setting.

   _____ Presence of harmful microorganisms on or in a person, animal, or object.

   _____ One who harbors an infectious agent and can transmit it to others, although not himself ill.

3. For each of the illnesses in the box below, list its usual mode(s) of transmission and the measures a paramedic can take to minimize the risk of contracting the illness from a patient.

Disease	Mode(s) of Transmission	Protective Measures
AIDS		
Hepatitis type A		
Hepatitis type B		
Meningitis		
Mumps		
Syphilis		
Tuberculosis		

4. You are called to transport a 22-year-old college student from the college infirmary to the hospital. The nurse tells you that the student has a high fever. He complains of a severe headache and stiff neck, and he seems rather confused. He vomits twice en route to the hospital.

   a. This patient is likely to be suffering from

   _____ .

   b. The paramedic can minimize the risk of catching this patient's illness by:

5. A 54-year-old man calls for an ambulance after he coughed up some blood. He says that over the past several weeks he's been waking up in the middle of the night with his pajamas and bedclothes soaked through with sweat. He's lost about 25 pounds in the last 2 or 3 months, and today he started noticing some blood in his sputum.

   a. This patient is likely to be suffering from

   _____ .

   b. The paramedic can minimize the risk of catching this patient's illness by:

6. A 28-year-old man calls for an ambulance because he "feels lousy." He says that for a week or so, he hasn't had any energy at all. He doesn't feel like eating; he doesn't feel like doing anything; he just feels "done in." Even cigarettes "taste like cow dung." This morning, he noticed that his urine was very dark, and he got panicky. On examination, you observe that his eyes have a yellow tinge and that there are needle tracks on his arms.

   a. This patient is likely to be suffering from

   _____ .

   b. The paramedic can minimize the risk of catching this patient's illness by:

7. You are called to transport an 8-year-old boy who fell and sustained a laceration to his forehead. "I told him to stay in bed," his mother says, "but no, he has to go horsing around with his brother." According to the mother, both children have been sick for a week with a fever and sore throat. On examining the 8-year-old, you find a 2-inch laceration on the left side of the forehead, and you control the bleeding with pressure. He does seem a little warm, and the angles of his jaw are indistinct, as if there is something swollen there.

   a. This patient is likely to be suffering from

   _____ .

   b. The paramedic can minimize the risk of catching this patient's illness by:

8. It's back to the college infirmary for another patient with a fever—this time a 19-year-old woman. She complains of headache and says the light bothers her a lot. Her eyes are reddened, and she is coughing. She has a blotchy, red rash over her face and neck, and when you are examining her throat you notice some little white spots on the mucous membranes in her mouth.

   a. This patient is likely to be suffering from

   _____ .

   b. The paramedic can minimize the risk of catching this patient's illness by:

9. Indicate whether each of the following statements about AIDS is true or false.

    a. AIDS is a highly contagious communicable disease.

    TRUE   FALSE

    b. Approximately 1.0 to 1.5 million Americans are infected with the AIDS virus.

    TRUE   FALSE

    c. Patients with AIDS are abnormally susceptible to many infectious diseases.

    TRUE   FALSE

    d. AIDS can be acquired through casual contact, such as shaking hands with an HIV-positive patient.

    TRUE   FALSE

    e. Approximately one-quarter of AIDS patients in the United States are intravenous drug users.

    TRUE   FALSE

    f. An HIV-positive patient can transmit the AIDS virus even if he does not have clinical signs of AIDS.

    TRUE   FALSE

    g. Many health workers have acquired AIDS through contact with the blood or body fluids of AIDS patients.

    TRUE   FALSE

    h. The majority of AIDS cases that have occurred in health workers as a result of occupational exposure have been among EMS personnel.

    TRUE   FALSE

10. List the ways in which AIDS can be transmitted.

11. You are called late one night to the scene of a two-car collision on the interstate. One of the vehicles involved in the accident skidded into a ditch and flipped upside down. The driver is unconscious inside. There is blood and broken glass everywhere. At the least, you are going to have to deal with this patient's bleeding, stabilize his spine, extricate him, and start an IV.

    a. List at least four precautions you will take to protect yourself from possible infection during the care and extrication of this patient.

    (1)

    (2)

    (3)

    (4)

    b. List the routine measures you will employ for cleaning the ambulance and its equipment after this call.

    c. While you are putting fresh linens on the stretcher, your partner emerges from the "crash room" where the patient has been taken. "You oughta see that guy's eyes," he says, "they're yellow as a canary. I didn't notice it in the vehicle, but with these fluorescent lights, you can't miss it."

    Given that information, what further measures should you take

    (1) To protect yourself from infection?

    (2) To disinfect the vehicle and its equipment?

12. Carry out the following research project before you begin employment as a paramedic.

   a. Check off the illnesses you had as a child or up to this point:
      ____ Measles
      ____ Mumps
      ____ Chickenpox
      ____ German measles (rubella)
      ____ Polio
      ____ Hepatitis B

   b. Check off the immunizations you have had up to this point, and fill in the dates (obtain the records from your family doctor or the clinic where you received your immunizations):

      ____ Measles Date immunized: _____
      ____ Mumps   Date immunized: _____
      ____ Rubella Date immunized: _____
      ____ DPT (diphtheria/pertussis/tetanus)
          #1   Date immunized: _____
          #2   Date immunized: _____
          #3   Date immunized: _____
      ____ Most recent tetanus booster
               Date immunized: _____

      ____ Oral polio #1
               Date immunized: _____
      ____ Oral polio #2
               Date immunized: _____
      ____ Oral polio #3
               Date immunized: _____
      ____ Hepatitis B
               Date immunized: _____

   c. Based on the data you have compiled above, what immunizations do you need to get before you start work?

13. Examine Figures 9-33, 9-34, 9-35, and 15-3 in your textbook. What is wrong with those pictures?

29
Emergencies in the Elderly

1. Patients over 65 years old account for one-third of all ambulance calls today. As the population continues to age, that percentage can be expected to increase even further. It is therefore important for paramedics to understand the special problems and challenges posed by caring for the elderly. List five characteristics of the elderly that make it particularly challenging to diagnose their problems correctly and to provide them with appropriate care.

   a.

   b.

   c.

   d.

   e.

2. There are many misconceptions about the elderly and the process of aging that are widespread among the public (and also, regrettably, among health professionals), resulting in inaccurate stereotypes of the elderly. Indicate which of the following statements about the elderly are true and which are false.

   a. The rate of aging is the same in a 35-year-old as in an 80-year-old.

      TRUE   FALSE

   b. Mental deterioration and some degree of dementia are an inevitable part of the aging process.

      TRUE   FALSE

   c. Elderly people are more likely than younger individuals to seek emergency care for minor, nonserious complaints.

      TRUE   FALSE

   d. The pain mechanism is often depressed among the elderly.

      TRUE   FALSE

   e. Major hearing loss is universal among the elderly.

      TRUE   FALSE

3. The process of aging in our society is nearly always accompanied by social and psychologic stresses that may have an enormous impact on health. List two potentially stressful changes that tend to occur in a person's life as he or she approaches "golden age."

   a.

   b.

4. The normal aging process produces changes in nearly every organ system of the body. It is important to know what constitutes a *normal* age-related change, so that such a change will not be mistaken for a sign of disease (and, conversely, so that signs of disease will not be written off as "just part of getting old"). For each of the organ systems named below, list two changes that occur in its structure or function as a normal consequence of aging.

Organ System	Normal Age-Related Changes
CARDIOVASCULAR	
RESPIRATORY	
RENAL	
DIGESTIVE	
MUSCULOSKELETAL	
NERVOUS	
HOMEOSTATIC	

5. For each of the "symptoms and signs" listed below, indicate whether it is

   N   A *normal* part of the aging process that sooner or later occurs in every person
   D   An indication of a *disease* process

   _____ Decreased skin turgor   _____ Loss of teeth

   _____ Dyspnea   _____ Mental confusion

   _____ Joint pains   _____ Decrease in height

   _____ Depressed gag reflex   _____ Deafness

   _____ Cessation of menstrual periods in women   _____ Urinary incontinence

6. In younger patients, the chief complaint often has considerable value in localizing the patient's underlying problem. A middle-aged man suffering a myocardial infarction, for example, will usually complain of pain or discomfort in his chest, while a young person with pneumonia usually will have a cough and a fever. Among the elderly, on the other hand, the response to serious illness tends to be less specific. List four responses to illness common among seriously ill elderly patients.

   a.

   b.

   c.

   d.

7. Obtaining an accurate history from an elderly patient requires considerable skill, for there are a number of obstacles to history-taking among the elderly that do not exist when talking with younger patients. List four obstacles to obtaining a medical history from an old person, and indicate what steps you can take to overcome each of them.

   a. Obstacle:

      What I can do to try to overcome the obstacle:

   b. Obstacle:

      What I can do to try to overcome the obstacle:

   c. Obstacle:

      What I can do to try to overcome the obstacle:

   d. Obstacle:

      What I can do to try to overcome the obstacle:

8. One way to try to ensure that you don't miss anything important in the patient's history is to ask some general screening questions, irrespective of the patient's chief complaint. Suppose an 80-year-old woman has called for an ambulance because she feels "tired and weak." List ten general screening questions you would ask to assess the status of her major organ systems.

   a.

   b.

   c.

   d.

   e.

   f.

   g.

   h.

   i.

   j.

9. You are called to the apartment of a 78-year-old woman who fell down.

    a. List five questions you would ask in taking the history of the present illness.

      (1)

      (2)

      (3)

      (4)

      (5)

    b. List the information you should obtain about the patient's past (other) medical history.

    c. List six things you would look for in particular in performing the physical examination.

      (1)

      (2)

      (3)

      (4)

      (5)

      (6)

    d. In conducting the physical examination, you will of course be keeping an eye out for those injuries to which old people are particularly vulnerable. List three injuries to which elderly patients are more susceptible.

      (1)

      (2)

      (3)

    e. On examining the patient, you find the following: She is alert and mostly oriented, although a bit confused about the date. Her vital signs are pulse 62 and regular, respirations 28 and unlabored, and blood pressure 122/88. There is no evidence of head injury. There is no tenderness over the neck or ribs. There are some crackles audible at both lung bases. The abdomen is soft. The left leg is flexed abducted and appears shorter than the right; the patient cries out when you so much as touch it. All the peripheral pulses are difficult to find, but the temperature of the left leg seems about the same as that of the right. List in detail the steps in managing this patient.

10. In a middle-aged patient, the clinical presentation of such conditions as acute myocardial infarction or congestive heart failure is usually straightforward. In an elderly person with the same problem, the clinical presentation may be much less clear-cut. List at least two symptoms or signs that are commonly part of the clinical presentation of acute myocardial infarction and of congestive heart failure in the elderly.

Condition	Possible Signs and Symptoms in the Elderly
ACUTE MYOCARDIAL INFARCTION	
CONGESTIVE HEART FAILURE	

11. One of the most common presenting symptoms among the elderly is an acute confusional state (delirium). List five conditions likely to present as delirium in the elderly.

    a.

    b.

    c.

    d.

    e.

12. You are called to a shopping center where an elderly man tripped on a potted plant and fell, sustaining a minor laceration to his arm. As you are applying a dressing to the laceration, you notice that he seems very listless and depressed. How would you go about evaluating this patient's risk for suicide? What questions would you ask him?

    _____
    _____
    _____
    _____
    _____
    _____
    _____
    _____
    _____
    _____
    _____
    _____
    _____
    _____
    _____
    _____
    _____
    _____

13. The best drug for an elderly patient is very often *no* drug, for the likelihood of suffering adverse drug reactions increases sharply with advancing age. EMS providers need to be careful not to add to the problem by giving elderly patients medications that cause toxic effects. List four drugs used in prehospital emergency care that are especially likely to produce adverse reactions in the elderly.

a.   c.

b.   d.

14. Our thought for today is something every EMS provider needs to bear in mind whenever caring for the elderly. Decode the message in the usual way.

a. What aging is *not* __ __ __ __ __ __ __
   36 89 83 67 30 28 6

b. Major cause of trauma in the elderly   F __ __ __ __ __ __
   11 21 51 71 46 33

c. May be absent in infection in the elderly   __ __ __ __ R
   70 87 66 14

d. *Always* a sign of serious illness when seen acutely in the elderly   __ __ __   F __ __ __ __ __
   49 41 2   59 92 13 75 55

e. Increase in the size of an organ or tissue   __ __ P __ __ __ __ __ __ __ __
   47 22   38 80 72 7 34 10 29 27

f. Elderly patient at high risk for suicide   __ I __ __ __ __ __
   43   5 94 25 64 20

g. Even if dehydrated, an old person may not be   __ __ __ __ __ __ __
   16 44 69 37 53 76 9

h. If the patient can't hear, this won't help   __ __ __ __ __ I __ __
   40 78 35 95 12   62 88

i. False stereotype of the elderly   K __ __ __ __ __
   90 65 77 63 86

j. Poor proprioception causes problems in   __ __ __ __ __ C __
   58 1 52 82 74   45

k. Pertaining to the inferoposterior orifice   __ __ __ __
   54 15 26 60

l. Ideal body weight   __ __ __ __
   8 79 50 17

m. Risk factor for acute myocardial infarction   __ __ __ __   __ __ X
   57 19 24 91   73 3

n. What caring for the elderly isn't   __ __ __ __
   81 26 31 93

o. Highway division   __ __ __ __
   4 61 85 48

p. Fluorescent light   __ __ __ __
   42 18 84 68

q. Driver's organization   __ __ __
   56 32 39

Secret Message: __ __   __ __ __ __ __ __ __   __ __ __ __ __ __ __   __ __ __ __ __ __
                 1 2   3 4 5 6 7 8 9   10 11 12 13 14 15 16   17 18 19 20 21 22

__ __ __ __ __ __   __ __ __   __   __ __ __ __   __ __ __ __ __ __   __ __ __ __   __ __
23 24 25 26 27 28   29 30 31   32   33 34 35 36   37 38 39 40 41 42   43 44 45 46   47 48

__ __ __ __ __   __ __   __ __ __ __ __ __ __ __ __   __ __ __ __   __ __   __ __ __ ' __
49 50 51 52 53   54 55   56 57 58 59 60 61 62 63 64   65 66 67 68   69 70   71 72 73

__ __ __   __ __ __   __ __ __ __ __ __   __ __   __ __ __ __ __   __ __ __ .
74 75 76   77 78 79   80 81 82 83 84 85   86 87   88 89 90 91 92   93 94 95

30
Pediatric Emergencies

1. Match the following statements with the age group(s) most applicable to each.

   A. Infant

   B. Toddler

   C. Preschooler

   D. Grade-school child

   E. Adolescent

   _____ May be interested to learn about the equipment in your vehicle.

   _____ Can be distracted by jangling keys and cooing noises.

   _____ Wants to be treated as an adult.

   _____ Particularly fearful of cuts and mutilating injuries.

   _____ Should be examined on mother's lap.

   _____ Can provide at least some of the history.

   _____ Most likely to bite, kick, and spit.

   _____ Their physical examination should be done in toe-to-head order.

   _____ For this age group, a pimple may be seen as a catastrophe.

   _____ Most likely to be the victim of abuse.

   _____ Fontanelles not yet closed.

2. You are called to the scene of an accident in which a 6-year-old child was struck by a car as he darted into the street in front of his home. The child is lying on the street, surrounded by a small knot of people including his very distraught parents.

   a. Given the mechanisms of injury, list at least three injuries you need to look for in particular in this child.

      (1)

      (2)

      (3)

   b. As you are kneeling beside the injured child, carefully going through the steps of the primary survey, the child's father (who looks like a pro wrestler) charges over and starts shouting at you: "What the h--- do you think you're doing with my kid? Stop messing around and get him to a *hospital*. Can't you see he's hurt bad? He's going to die here while you dingbats muck about." [The father's actual comments are less polite but cannot be quoted verbatim in a genteel textbook.]

   (1) What are your feelings at this moment?

   (2) How will you deal with this situation?

c. On checking the child's vital signs, you find the following: pulse = 120 and regular; respirations = 24 and unlabored; blood pressure = 90/60. Which of the following conclusions can be drawn from those vital signs?

    (1) The child is going into shock.

    (2) The child has increasing intracranial pressure.

    (3) The vital signs are normal for a child of that age.

    (4) There is probably significant intrathoracic injury.

    (5) There is probably significant intra-abdominal bleeding.

3. Indicate which of the statements below are true and which are false.

    a. A child who is seriously ill or injured will always be agitated and showing clear signs of distress.

    TRUE   FALSE

    b. A sunken anterior fontanelle in an infant suggests meningitis or head injury.

    TRUE   FALSE

    c. Neonates are nose breathers, so nasal congestion may compromise their breathing.

    TRUE   FALSE

    d. Infants and small children rely mainly on their abdominal muscles to breathe.

    TRUE   FALSE

    e. Grunting is a sign of respiratory distress in infants.

    TRUE   FALSE

4. You are called around 1:00 A.M. for a child who "can't breathe." A haggard father greets you at the door and tells you that his 2-year-old Tammy has had "a little cold" for a couple of days but otherwise seemed fine. ("It didn't slow her down a bit.") Tonight, however, she began coughing, and the cough kept getting worse. Indeed, even as you are walking toward the child's room, you can hear a loud barking noise. On reaching Tammy's room, you see a very agitated 2-year-old struggling in her mother's lap. Her nostrils are flaring with each inhalation, and there are retractions of her neck muscles. Her lips are bluish. She flails and has a

fit of dry coughing as you start to come near. Eventually, you manage to measure a pulse of 160 per minute and a respiratory rate of 52 per minute. When you try to auscultate the child's chest, however, she grabs your stethoscope and yanks it out of your ears.

    a. The vital signs are _____ (normal or abnormal?) for a child of this age.

    b. The most likely diagnosis is _____ _____.

    c. What steps will you take in managing this child?

5. You are called for a 4-month-old infant in respiratory distress. His mother says that he's been "off his feed" for a couple of days and has been sneezing a lot. On examination, you notice that the baby seems to be breathing like a rabbit. The pulse is 180, respirations are 60, and blood pressure is 90/60. There is diffuse wheezing throughout the chest.

    a. The vital signs are _____ (normal or abnormal?) for a child of this age.

    b. The most likely diagnosis is _____ _____.

    c. What steps will you take in managing this child?

6. You are called for a 2½-year-old having difficulty breathing. The mother says that she left little Bobby playing quietly in his room, and when she returned half an hour later, she found him in severe respiratory distress. She thinks he's had a slight cold lately, but nothing serious. "You know, it's just one runny nose after another all winter with them. Each one gives it to the others, and I've got five little ones—so I can't always keep track of who has a runny nose."

   You find Bobby in severe respiratory distress. He makes high-pitched squeaks when he tries to inhale, and his eyes look like they are popping out of his head. His lips are blue. You place the back of your hand on his forehead and note that the skin does not feel abnormally warm.

   a. The most likely diagnosis is _____ _____.

   b. What steps will you take in managing this child?

   c. As you are in the midst of treating this baby's problem, he stops breathing altogether. How many breaths per minute should you give in ventilating this baby?

   d. Where will you check for a pulse?

   e. You find that the pulse is absent. What is the correct compression point for external chest compressions?

   f. How many chest compressions should you give per minute? _____

   g. The monitor shows ventricular fibrillation. Assuming that the child weighs 12 kg, what is the defibrillation dosage?
      _____ joules

h. In the course of resuscitating this baby, you have to give several drugs. For each, list the correct dosage for this baby.

   (1) Epinephrine: _____

   (2) Lidocaine: _____

   (3) Atropine: _____

i. Which of those drugs may be given by endotracheal tube if you can't get an IV line established?

j. Which of those drugs may be given by intraosseous infusion if you can't get an IV line established?

7. You are called to see a 4-year-old who is "very sick." His mother says that he was fine until a few hours ago when he began complaining of a sore throat. Since then, he would not eat or drink anything, and he is very feverish. You find the child sitting very still, bolt upright in bed, with his chin thrust forward. He does not reply to your questions, but only nods or shakes his head slightly. Saliva is dribbling out of the corners of his mouth. His skin feels very hot. His pulse is 140, respirations are 40 and quiet, blood pressure is 90/60. The chest is clear.

   a. The vital signs are _____ (normal or abnormal?) for a child of this age.

   b. The most likely diagnosis is _____ _____.

   c. What steps will you take in managing this child?

   d. What is the special danger threatening this child?

8. You are called to see a 2½-year-old child who is "very sick." "I don't know what happened," says the child's mother. "He seemed well enough all morning, but late this afternoon I noticed he was looking peculiar. Got a fever too." On examination, the child indeed looks ill. His skin is hot and sweaty. His pulse is 136 and regular, respirations are 24 and very deep, and blood pressure is 90/60. You do not find any other abnormal findings on physical examination. While you are examining the child, he vomits, and there appear to be some white particles in the vomitus.

a. The most likely diagnosis is_____
_____.

b. What steps will you take in managing this child?

(3)

(4)

(5)

b. List the steps you would take in managing this case.

9. You are called to a field about 6 miles outside of town where a 6-year-old child in the first-grade nature study class is having difficulty breathing. The teacher says that she noticed him lagging behind the others several times during the morning, and finally she found him sitting by himself under a tree, struggling to breathe. You find the child still sitting under the tree, but apparently dozing. It is difficult to waken him, and when he does open his eyes, he just stares at you blankly. When you ask him whether he has taken any medicine today, he just shakes his head and seems to doze again.

On examination, the child's pulse is 160 and somewhat weak, respirations are 52 and shallow, and blood pressure is 90/60 on exhalation and 50 systolic during inhalation. The lips look bluish. There is retraction of the neck muscles. The chest does not seem to move with respiration, and it sounds like an empty barrel when you tap on it. You can hardly hear any breath sounds at all. On the child's wrist is a Medic Alert bracelet inscribed, "Asthmatic."

a. List at least five signs that suggest this child is having a very serious asthmatic attack.

(1)

(2)

10. The very same evening, you are called to see a child who is "short of breath." The child is a known asthmatic.

a. List five questions you would ask the child and his parents in taking the history.

(1)

(2)

(3)

(4)

(5)

b. The medications we give in the treatment of asthma are aimed at reversing the underlying pathophysiologic processes. For each such process listed below, give an example of a medication used to counteract it.

Pathophysiologic Process	Medication Used to Counteract It
Bronchospasm	_____
Dehydration/mucous plugging	_____
Edema of bronchial walls	_____
Hypoxemia	_____
Acidosis	_____

c. Your protocol calls for giving ALBUTEROL for an acute asthmatic attack.

   (1) What are the relevant *contraindications* to albuterol?

   (2) What are the possible adverse *side effects* of albuterol?

   (3) What is the correct *dosage,* and how is the drug administered?

11. You are called to a downtown apartment for a "very sick baby." A frightened looking young mother greets you at the door and hurries you into the bedroom, where a baby is lying very still in its crib. You observe at once that the baby's color is grayish and that it is not breathing. When you touch the baby to open the airway, you can feel that the skin is cold. Describe what you will do from that point on.

12. You are called for a 2-year-old child who is "having a fit." En route to the call, you review in your thoughts the possible causes of seizures in children.

    a. List five causes of seizures in children.

       (1)

       (2)

       (3)

       (4)

       (5)

b. List five questions you should ask in taking the child's history.

   (1)

   (2)

   (3)

   (4)

   (5)

c. List five things you would look for in particular in examining the child.

   (1)

   (2)

   (3)

   (4)

   (5)

d. You learn that the child never had a seizure before. On examining him, you find that he is no longer seizing but is still somewhat drowsy. His skin is very hot, so you take an axillary temperature and get a reading of 39°C (102.2°F). The pupils are equal and reactive. The neck is supple. The chest is clear. Describe how you would manage this case.

13. You are summoned to a local high school where a 14-year-old girl is having a seizure. The school nurse tells you that the child has never had a seizure in school before. This seizure came on while the girl was in the auditorium watching a movie. The seizure lasted about 5 minutes. One of the teachers then carried the girl to the nurse's office. The nurse was in the midst of trying to contact the girl's mother when the child had another grand mal seziure. Now, as you are speaking with the nurse, you witness a third grand mal seizure that lasts about 6 minutes.

a. List the steps in treating this patient.

b. What drug is used in the emergency treatment of repeated seizures?

c. What are the *contraindications* to giving that drug?

d. What are the possible adverse *side effects*?

e. What is the dosage for children, and how is it administered?

14. You are called to attend a 10-month-old baby who sustained burns to the foot when he "stepped on a cigarette." Something about the story sounds fishy to you, and you find yourself on the alert for evidence that the child has been abused.

a. What's "fishy" about the story?

b. List 10 possible clues—in the history, the physical examination, or the behavior of the child or his parents—that might substantiate your suspicion that this is an abused child.

(1)

(2)

(3)

(4)

(5)

(6)

(7)

(8)

(9)

(10)

c. By the time you finish examining the child, you are privately convinced that the baby was deliberately burned and that, furthermore, it has been burned and beaten in the past. How should you manage this case?

d. Suppose the child's parent refuses to allow the child to be transported to the hospital? What should you do then?

15. Indicate which of the following statements about trauma in children are true and which are false.

    a. An infant falling from a height is most likely to sustain injury to the head.

    TRUE   FALSE

    b. The method of choice for opening the airway of a small child who has been struck by a car is head tilt–chin lift.

    TRUE   FALSE

    c. To insert an oropharyngeal airway in a small child, introduce the airway tip-upward, then rotate it 180 degrees and slide it into place.

    TRUE   FALSE

    d. Because of the increased resistance to air flow of a child's tiny airways, the only means of giving effective artificial ventilation to a child is with the demand valve.

    TRUE   FALSE

    e. A 10-kg toddler need lose only about 200 ml (less than 8 oz) of blood to be in severe shock.

    TRUE   FALSE

    f. Hypotension is an early response to blood loss in infants and small children.

    TRUE   FALSE

16. List six signs suggestive of hypovolemic shock in infants and small children.

    a.

    b.

    c.

    d.

    e.

    f.

17. Upon completing the extended primary survey of any seriously injured person, of any age, the paramedic must make a decision whether to transport at once or to proceed to the secondary survey. List 10 indications for immediate transport ("load-and-go") of injured infants and children.

    a.

    b.

    c.

    d.

    e.

    f.

    g.

    h.

    i.

    j.

18. In examining the injured infant or child, you need to know exactly what you're looking for, so that each second spent on the head-to-toe survey will be well invested. In the following box, indicate what in particular you would be looking for as you examine each part of the body mentioned.

Body Area	What I Would Be Looking for in Particular
HEAD	
NECK	
CHEST	
ABDOMEN	
EXTREMITIES	

19. You are called to treat an 18-month-old baby who fell off a second-floor balcony to the ground 5 meters (about 15 feet) below. On examination, you find the baby conscious but drowsy. Vital signs are pulse 80 and regular, respirations 16, and blood pressure 100/70. There is a bruise on the left forehead. The pupils are equal and reactive to light. The point of maximal impulse is in the midclavicular line. Breath sounds are equal bilaterally. The abdomen does not appear distended. The baby is moving all extremities. List the steps in the prehospital management of this case.

20. You are called to the scene of a motor vehicle accident on the interstate highway in which a car jumped the median divider and plowed head-on into an oncoming vehicle. Among the injured are two children, both back-seat passengers in the vehicle that was hit. Both children have been removed from the wrecked car by well-meaning bystanders.

a. The first child is about 4 years old and is lying listlessly on the ground. His skin feels cool. His pulse is 160 and difficult to palpate, his respirations are 48, and his blood pressure is 90/60 on both inhalation and exhalation. You find no signs of head injury. The pupils are equal and reactive. The neck veins are not distended. The PMI is in the midclavicular line. There are no bruises on the chest. Breath sounds are impossible to hear in all the noise. There is a seat belt mark across the anterior abdomen, which looks somewhat distended. Capillary refill takes 3 seconds. The right arm appears broken. List the steps in the prehospital management of this case.

b. The second child looks to be about 2 years old and is gasping for breath. The upper airway seems clear, but not much air is moving in and out of the chest. The lips are bluish. The trachea seems to be slanting to the left. It is impossible to auscultate breath sounds in all the noise at the scene. The PMI is in the anterior axillary line. The abdomen looks slightly distended but not bruised. List the steps in the prehospital management of this case.

21. You are called to the scene of a smoky house fire just as one of the firefighters is emerging from the building carrying a baby. "He was in the thick of it," the firefighter tells you. "Out cold when I found him." The baby still seems very drowsy.

    a. Should this infant be intubated? _____ Why or why not?

    b. List five indications for the immediate intubation of an infant or small child who has been in a fire.

       (1)

       (2)

       (3)

       (4)

       (5)

22. You are all settled in to watch a football game on your day off when a neighbor comes running in, carrying her protesting 2-year-old. "Johnny did it AGAIN!" she wails.

    "Did what?" you ask, not really wanting to know the answer.

    "He put peanuts in BOTH ears."

    "Now, Johnny," you address the little tyke, "why did you do a naughty thing like that?" (And why on my day off? you add silently to yourself.)

    "He can't hear you," says Johnny's mother. "He's got peanuts in his ears."

    How will you manage this case?

    _____
    _____
    _____
    _____
    _____
    _____
    _____
    _____
    _____

23. Indicate which of the following statements about advanced life support measures in children are true and which are false.

    a. The first step in assembling the equipment for pediatric intubation is to check the cuff on the endotracheal tube you have selected.

       TRUE   FALSE

    b. A straight blade is preferred for pediatric intubation.

       TRUE   FALSE

    c. In intubating infants, the laryngoscope blade is slipped beneath the epiglottis, to lift it up, rather than into the vallecula.

       TRUE   FALSE

    d. The narrowest point in an infant's airway is the opening between the vocal cords.

       TRUE   FALSE

    e. Universal precautions are unnecessary in starting IVs on infants and children.

       TRUE   FALSE

    f. A burned infant should be given about 50 ml/kg/hr of IV fluids.

       TRUE   FALSE

24. Pictured below is your pediatric drug box, which is in a bit of a mess, everything jumbled together. Straightening it out one day, you find 18 medications, one important ancillary "drug," and a few things that shouldn't be in the box. First find the medications, and make yourself a list of the correct pediatric dosage of each. Then find and remove whatever shouldn't be in the drug box.

```
A P L O L L I P O P S Y C H E S T
D R A M I N O P H Y L L I N E P T
O I L A L B U T E R O L L U P I R
P O P E R A Z I N C R U S T I D T
A R C H O L I D O C A I N E N E E
M O O N E U N U C H T C I D E R E
I S M A N N I T O L E R S D P I A
N O O N C C H E R E R O N Y H I T
E R R T O H A Y N A B I C A R B R
I M P A L A L A D I U M A L I U O
S O H Y D R O C O R T I S O N E P
T R I C Y C L E S N A P P L E S I
O P N A L O X O N E L M T R E E N
W H E N H A R R Y H I T I Z Z I E
P I S T U L E S E E N A G N O L T
O N E S A U D I A Z E P A M E L A
P E D I S O E T H A R I N E L A R
```

Drug	*Correct Dosage*
_____	_____
_____	_____
_____	_____
_____	_____
_____	_____
_____	_____
_____	_____
_____	_____
_____	_____
_____	_____
_____	_____
_____	_____
_____	_____
_____	_____
_____	_____
_____	_____
_____	_____
_____	_____

Ancillary "drug": _____

Things to remove: _____
_____

25. Finally, our thought for the day. Decode it in the usual fashion.

a. Increased blood flow to a tissue __ __ P __ __ E __ __ __
                                                12 34   21 56   7 46 26

b. Soft spot on an infant's head __ __ __ __ __ __ __ __ E
                                 42 50 62 41 19 48 36 9 28

c. Having a fever __ __ __ __ __ __ E
               51 3 53 22 30 10

d. Major parasympathetic nerve __ __ __ __ __
                           20 1 47 57 18

e. Type of burn seen often in abused infants __ __ __ L __
                                 49 58 17   15

f. Where to start the examination of a toddler __ __ __ __
                             59 43 39 45

g. One cause of wheezing __ __ __ __ __ __
                  8 24 55 16 25 37

h. Gland of the mouth __ __ __ __ __ __ __ __
               6 29 38 60 2 33 44 23

i. Forehead __ __ __ __
         35 4 52 32

j. What an ambulance may be to a child (or grown-up) __ __ A __ __
                                     54 11 31 5

k. Pad for scrubbing B __ __ __ __ __
              40 13 27 14 61

Secret Message: __
          1   2 3 4 5   6 7 8 9 10   11 12 13 14 15   16 17 18   19   20 21 22 23

__ __ __ __ __   __ __ __ __ __ __.   __ __   __ __ __ __ __   __ __ __
24 25 26 27 28   29 30 31 32 33 34   35 36   37 38 39 40 41   42 43 44

__ __ __ __ __   __ __   __ __ __ __ __ __ __ __ __ __ __.
45 46 47 48 49   50 51   52 53 54 55 56 57 58 59 60 61 62

Stop and Review III

Confess! You've forgotten what the galea aponeurotica is. Clearly it's time to pause and review.

1. We'll start with a search for bones. Hidden in the grid below are 29 bones or parts of bones of the human body. Find the lost bones, and then fill in the blanks that follow the grid.

```
S C R A N I U M P I R Z O T S A
P H A L A N X C O C C Y X I T M
A N D I A P H Y S I S G O B R A
T S I I S C H I A C R O M I O N
S A U N G L E N O I D M A A C D
I C S I L A F T A R S A L S H I
S R A L L V I T A I L U L N A B
T U C P B I B P U B I S E E N L
E M A R U C U M U L U S O L T E
R M R O P L L M A X I L L A E R
N U P E R E A O F F E M U R R Y
U R A A C A L C A N E U S M A T
M A L H U M E R U S T Y T O G S
```

a. List the bones you found:

_____ _____ _____ _____
_____ _____ _____ _____
_____ _____ _____ _____
_____ _____ _____ _____
_____ _____ _____ _____
_____ _____ _____ _____

b. Bony protuberance on the ankle joint: _____

c. Socket in the shoulder bone for the humeral head: _____

d. Cup-shaped socket for the femoral head: _____

e. Shaft of a long bone: _____

f. Process below the femoral neck: _____

g. Highest point of the shoulder: _____

2. Imagine you are an oxygen molecule just about to be inhaled into someone's left nostril. Your instructions are to make your way to a pulmonary capillary, where you are to hitch a ride on a red blood cell and travel to the right big toe. But now, at the threshold of the nostril, the journey seems very complicated. See if you can find your way to the pulmonary capillary on the following map of the airway, and list in order the structures of the airway you will traverse en route.

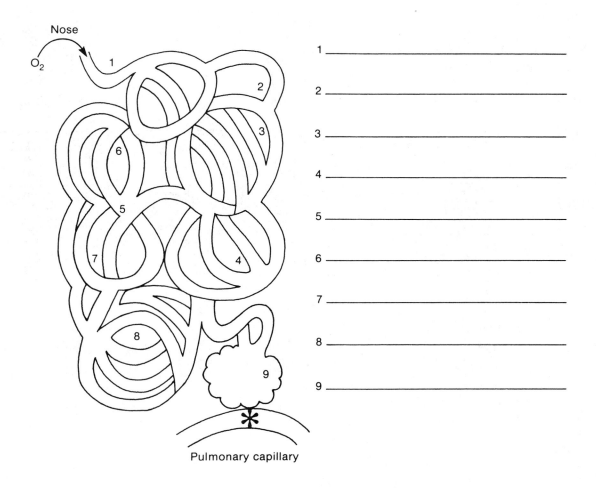

1. _____

2. _____

3. _____

4. _____

5. _____

6. _____

7. _____

8. _____

9. _____

3. Shortly after a sudden thunder squall, you are summoned to a local golf course where one of the golfers was apparently struck by lightning while teeing off from the seventh hole. Grabbing a jump kit, you proceed on foot across the green with the golf course manager, while your partner takes the vehicle around to an access road. The rain is pelting down, and there is still a lot of lightning and thunder. You find the stricken golfer lying unconscious on the green.

a. List the steps you will take while waiting for your partner to arrive with the ambulance.

b. You find that the golfer is in cardiac arrest. Your partner pulls up with the ambulance. What steps will you take now?

c. Here is the golfer's ECG rhythm strip. Answer the questions beneath the strip.

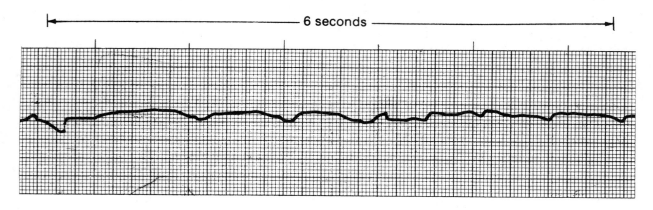

RHYTHM: _____ regular _____ irregular
RATE: _____ per minute
P WAVES: _____ present _____ absent
    If present, is there a P before every QRS? _____ yes _____ no
        Is there a QRS after every P? _____ yes _____ no
P–R INTERVAL: _____ seconds
QRS complexes: _____ normal _____ abnormal
Name of rhythm: _____
Treatment: _____

d. After only a few minutes of CPR, the patient's pulse is restored. List any further treatment that might be indicated.

4. List at least six circumstances in which you should suspect spinal cord injury has occurred.

   a.   d.

   b.   e.

   c.   f.

5. A 50-year-old man was the driver of a car that plowed into a concrete wall. You find the driver in considerable distress, laboring to breathe. The front of his chest bears a steering wheel imprint and seems to cave in during inhalation and bulge out during exhalation.

   a. Where do you go from here? That is, list the steps you would take from this point on (including assessment and treatment).

   b. Here is the patient's ECG rhythm strip. Answer the questions beneath the strip.

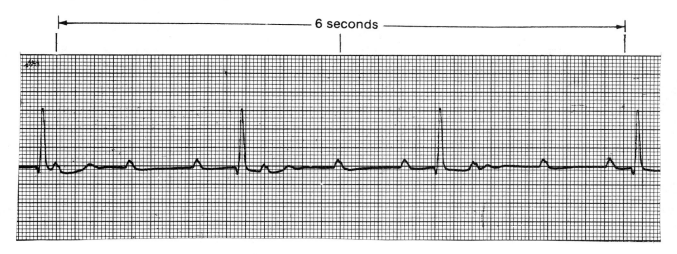

RHYTHM: _____ regular _____ irregular
RATE: _____ per minute
P WAVES: _____ present _____ absent
    If present, is there a P before every QRS? _____ yes _____ no
                 Is there a QRS after every P? _____ yes _____ no
P–R INTERVAL: _____ seconds
QRS complexes: _____ normal _____ abnormal
Name of rhythm: _____
Treatment: _____

6. The organs of the abdomen are sometimes classified according to whether they are hollow or solid, for the type of injury to which an organ is susceptible depends to a large extent on its structure.

   a. List the hollow and solid organs of the abdominal cavity.

   Hollow Organs   *Solid Organs*

   _____   _____
   _____   _____
   _____   _____
   _____   _____
   _____   _____

   b. Which of those organs is most likely to be injured in association with

      (1) Fracture of the left ninth and tenth ribs anteriorly: _____

      (2) Fracture of the eleventh and twelfth ribs posteriorly: _____

      (3) Fracture of the pelvis: _____

      (4) Stab wound to the right upper quadrant: _____

      (5) Primary blast injury: _____

7. One of the more dangerous acute complications of a fracture is the development of a compartment syndrome, which—if not treated quickly—will lead to lifelong disability. It is therefore essential to be able to detect the symptoms and signs of a developing compartment syndrome. List six symptoms and signs of compartment syndrome, and indicate which of them are early signs and which are late signs.

   a.

   b.

   c.

   d.

   e.

   f.

8. You are called to the scene of a highway accident in which a car swerved off the road, rolled over twice, and finally came to a stop upside down in a ditch. The driver was apparently thrown from the vehicle, and he is lying—unconscious and bleeding—about a meter (3 feet) from the vehicle. You notice smoke coming from the vehicle. Arrange the steps of management below in the correct sequence.

   a. Start transport.

   b. Control obvious external hemorrhage.

   c. Start an IV with lactated Ringer's solution.

   d. Check the pupils.

   e. Look, listen, and feel for breathing.

   f. Immobilize the patient on a backboard.

   g. Assess pulses and capillary refill.

   h. Administer oxygen.

   i. Cut the patient's clothing along the seams.

   j. Move the patient to safety.

   k. Check the chest for open wounds, unequal breath sounds.

   l. Open the airway, with cervical spine stabilization.

   m. Assess the level of consciousness (AVPU scale).

   n. Conduct the secondary survey.

   o. Suction the mouth, and insert an oropharyngeal airway.

   p. Notify the receiving hospital of the patient's condition and your estimated time of arrival.

      (1) ____
      (2) ____
      (3) ____
      (4) ____
      (5) ____
      (6) ____
      (7) ____
      (8) ____
      (9) ____
      (10) ____
      (11) ____
      (12) ____
      (13) ____
      (14) ____
      (15) ____
      (16) ____

9. In an incident involving many casualties, it is necessary to assign priorities for evacuation when the number of casualties exceeds the number of ambulances immediately available. Suppose that you are triage officer at a train wreck involving scores of injured. Ambulances are starting to assemble in the staging area, getting ready to transport the casualties that you indicate. For each of the casualties whose injuries are listed, assign an evacuation priority from 1 (highest priority) to 5 (lowest priority).

_____ Conscious but can't move his legs

_____ Has a sprained left ankle

_____ Massive maxillofacial trauma

_____ Flail chest

_____ Fractured radius/ulna

_____ Deteriorating level of consciousness; injury unknown

_____ Second- and third-degree burns over 27 percent of the body surface area

_____ Eye hanging out of its socket

_____ Very restless, with cold, clammy skin and weak, rapid pulse

_____ Open fracture of the tibia

_____ Removed from burning passenger car with facial burns and stridor

_____ Weak rapid pulse; distended neck veins; equal breath sounds; muffled heart sounds

10. You are called to a third-floor walk-up apartment to attend to "Uncle Bernie," who—according to the niece who called for the ambulance—is "doing poorly." You learn that Uncle Bernie is 69 years old and has "lung troubles." Over the past several days, he's been coughing more than usual and bringing up a lot of "evil-looking" sputum. He has stopped going out (usually he at least takes a stroll to the corner grocery every morning to buy his cigarettes), and he's also been sleeping badly.

You find Uncle Bernie sitting upright in a chair, laboring to breathe. You estimate he weighs about 100 kg (220 lb), and probably 10 kg of that is edema fluid in his legs. He seems very confused, and he becomes suspicious and agitated when you approach ("Don't want no CIA agents here," he says). He tears off the blood pressure cuff as fast as you can put it on, but you do manage to count a pulse of about 80 and a respiratory rate of 40 per minute. The patient's lips are bluish. His neck veins are distended. He won't let you put a stethoscope on his chest, but you can hear his wheezes and crackles even without the stethoscope.

a. List the steps in managing this patient.

b. Here is the patient's ECG rhythm strip. Answer the questions beneath the strip.

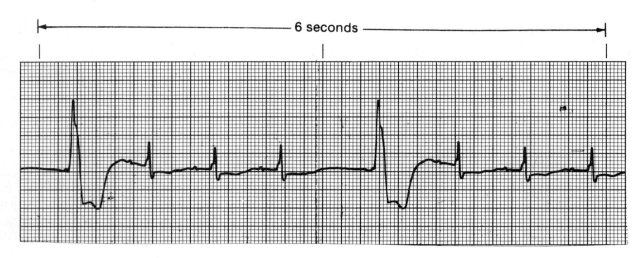

6 seconds

RHYTHM: _____ regular _____ irregular
RATE: _____ per minute
P WAVES: _____ present _____ absent
　　　If present, is there a P before every QRS? _____ yes _____ no
　　　　　　Is there a QRS after every P? 　_____ yes _____ no
P–R INTERVAL: _____ seconds
QRS complexes: _____ normal _____ abnormal
Name of rhythm: _____
Treatment: _____

11. You are called to a downtown office building where a 52-year-old businessman is having severe chest pain. En route, you review some facts about chest pain and coronary artery disease.

a. List six risk factors for coronary artery disease.

(1)

(2)

(3)

(4)

(5)

(6)

b. On reaching the scene, you find a middle-aged man in considerable distress. He says the pain is "heavy—like someone is sitting on my chest." It came on an hour earlier and was not relieved by nitroglycerin (he tried three tablets). The patient's face is a grayish color, and he looks scared. His skin is cold and wet. List in order the steps in assessing and managing this patient.

c. Here is the patient's ECG rhythm strip. Answer the questions beneath the strip.

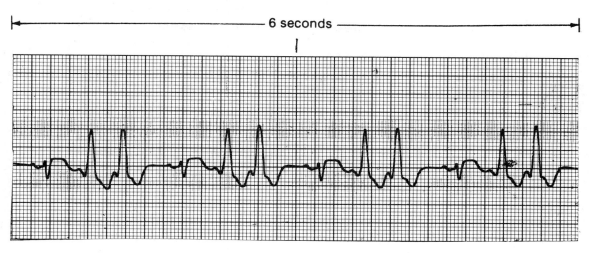

6 seconds

RHYTHM: _____ regular _____ irregular
RATE: _____ per minute
P WAVES: _____ present _____ absent
      If present, is there a P before every QRS? _____ yes _____ no
               Is there a QRS after every P? _____ yes _____ no
P–R INTERVAL: _____ seconds
QRS complexes: _____ normal _____ abnormal
Name of rhythm: _____
Treatment: _____

12. You are called to a department store where a woman who appears to be about 60 years old has been found unconscious in the ladies' restroom.

   a. List eight possible causes of coma.

     (1)

     (2)

     (3)

     (4)

     (5)

     (6)

     (7)

     (8)

   b. On examining the woman, you do not find an immediately obvious reason for her unconscious state. List the steps you would take in managing this patient.

c. Here is the patient's ECG rhythm strip. Answer the questions beneath the strip.

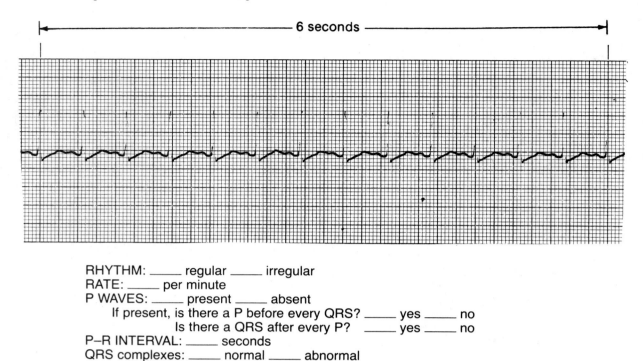

|← —————————————— 6 seconds —————————————— →|

RHYTHM: _____ regular _____ irregular
RATE: _____ per minute
P WAVES: _____ present _____ absent
      If present, is there a P before every QRS? _____ yes _____ no
               Is there a QRS after every P?　_____ yes _____ no
P–R INTERVAL: _____ seconds
QRS complexes: _____ normal _____ abnormal
Name of rhythm: _____
Treatment: _____

13. A 68-year-old woman calls for an ambulance because of severe abdominal pain. She says the pain came on earlier in the day, after she'd had "a big, rich lunch that I knew I shouldn't be eating." The pain has gotten more and more severe since then. She has had some diarrhea, but it did not relieve the pain. On physical examination, the woman is clearly in severe distress. Her vital signs are pulse 102 and regular, respirations 32, and blood pressure 170/100. The chest is clear. The abdomen is distended, but it is soft to palpation and does not seem unusually tender. List the steps in treating this patient.

14. You are dining out on your night off at Fish Fare, a deluxe local restaurant. As you are just about to dig into your red snapper, you notice a woman at a nearby table looking distressed. "Aunt Gertrude, what's the matter?" asks another woman at the table.

"I don't know," squeaks the distressed woman. "I feel so peculiar. Like there's a lump in my throat. And my chest feels so tight."

Without waiting to hear another word, you bolt over to the telphone, dial 911, and ask for an ambulance posthaste. Then you go over to the woman in distress and introduce yourself as a paramedic. You notice that the woman's face is very flushed, and her eyes look puffy. Her pulse is weak and rapid.

"Oh dear, I think I'm going to be sick," she says.

Just then the ambulance pulls up.

List the steps in treating this patient.

15. You are standing by at a three-alarm fire when a woman is brought down a ladder by firefighters and carried to your ambulance. "The whole apartment was full of smoke," one of the firefighters tells you, "everything smoldering—carpets, mattresses, furniture." The woman is conscious but confused. She complains of a severe headache. Her vital signs are pulse 120 and thready, respirations 40 and labored, and blood pressure 160/90. You find no evidence of burns or other injury.

a. What is your major concern in this patient, given the history and her symptoms and signs?

b. List the steps you would take in managing this patient.

16. List eight medical problems to which alcoholics are particularly susceptible.

a.

b.

c.

d.

e.

f.

g.

h.

17. With all the hysteria over AIDS, it is crucial that health professionals be as knowledgeable as possible on the subject.

a. List three ways that AIDS can be transmitted from one person to another.

(1)

(2)

(3)

b. List three things you can do to minimize the risk of acquiring HIV from a patient.

(1)

(2)

(3)

18. You are called to attend a 78-year-old man who is "feeling poorly." He states that since the morning he's been feeling very weak and dizzy, and about an hour ago he began to get quite short of breath as well. On physical examination, he seems a little confused. His pulse is about 70 and somewhat irregular, his respirations are 40 and slightly labored, and his blood pressure is 160/80. There are crackles throughout both lungs.

a. List the steps you would take in managing this patient.

b. Here is the patient's ECG rhythm strip. Answer the questions beneath the strip.

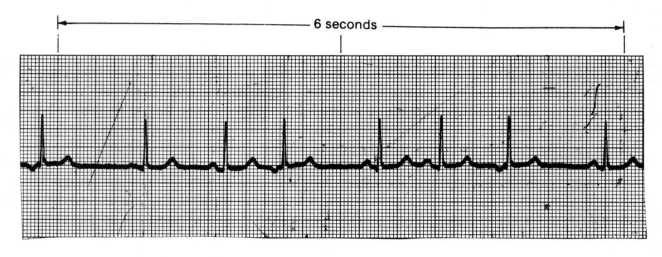

RHYGHM: _____ regular _____ irregular
RATE: _____ per minute
P WAVES: _____ present _____ absent
     If present, is there a P before every QRS? _____ yes _____ no
                Is there a QRS after every P? _____ yes _____ no
P–R INTERVAL: _____ seconds
QRS complexes: _____ normal _____ abnormal
Name of rhythm: _____
Treatment: _____

19. Asthma is common in children, so it's important to be able to distinguish a mild asthmatic attack from one that is potentially life-threatening. List at least five signs that an asthmatic attack is very severe and warrants urgent transport to the hospital.

a.

b.

c.

d.

e.

20. A parting thought. Decode it in the usual way.

a. Drug used to treat seizures ___ ___ ___ ___ ___ ___ M
   70 59 49 22 64 36 2

b. Drug for every comatose patient ___ ___ ___ ___ ___ ___ ___ ___
   12 29 38 68 31 11 43 55

c. Fainting ___ ___ ___ C ___ ___ ___
   26 61 6   37 1 69

d. Weakness of one side of the body ___ ___ ___ ___ ___ ___ ___ ___ ___ S
   51 5 33 28 62 53 24 56 8 41

e. Slurring of speech ___ ___ ___ ___ ___ ___ ___ ___ ___ A
   27 35 52 57 63 50 10 16 4

f. Womb ___ ___ ___ ___ U ___
   44 7 66 54   58

g. Carries blood depleted of oxygen ___ ___ ___ ___
   65 48 21 67

h. Pediatric endotracheal tube does not have one of these ___ ___ ___ ___
   45 23 30 15

i. Vomiting blood ___ ___ ___ ___ ___ ___ ___ ___ ___ S
   34 39 40 42 3 14 18 25 19 13

j. Complete ___ ___ ___ ___ ___
   9 46 17 60 20

k. Overdose, for short ___ ___
   32 47

Secret Message: ___ ___ ___ ___ ___ ___ ___ ___   ___ ___ ___   ___ ___ ___   ___ ___ ___ ___   ___ ___ ___ ___ ___ ___ ___ ___
               1 2 3 4 5 6 7 8   9 10 11   12 13 14   15 16 17 18   19 20 21 22 23 24 25 26

___ ___ ___   ___ ___ ___ ___   ___ ___ ___ ___ ___ ___ ___ ___ ___.   ___ ___ ___ ___
27 28 29   30 31 32 33   34 35 36 37 38 39 40 41 42   43 44 45 46

___ ___ ___ ___ ___ ___   ___ ___ ___   ___ ___ ___ ___ ___ ___   ___ ___ ___ ___ ___ ___ ___ ___ ___.
47 48 49 50 51 52   53 54 55   56 57 58 59 60 61   62 63 64 65 66 67 68 69 70

21. You are called one fine Monday morning to the home of a 68-year-old man complaining of "pressure" in his chest. He says the feeling came on right after breakfast and he hasn't been able to shake it. When you ask him to describe the feeling in more detail, he makes a fist and says, "It's a kind of squeezing." His face is pale, and he is sweating noticeably. His past medical history is unremarkable except for his being a heavy smoker with a chronic cough. His skin is cold and clammy.

   a. Here is the patient's 12-lead ECG with a rhythm strip on lead II. Fill in the information requested after the ECG:

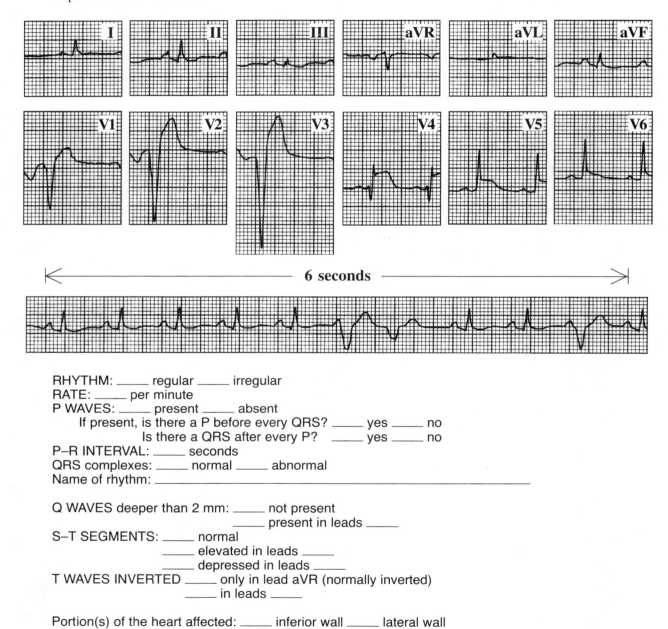

RHYTHM: _____ regular _____ irregular
RATE: _____ per minute
P WAVES: _____ present _____ absent
        If present, is there a P before every QRS? _____ yes _____ no
                Is there a QRS after every P? _____ yes _____ no
P–R INTERVAL: _____ seconds
QRS complexes: _____ normal _____ abnormal
Name of rhythm: _____

Q WAVES deeper than 2 mm: _____ not present
                              _____ present in leads _____
S–T SEGMENTS: _____ normal
                    _____ elevated in leads _____
                    _____ depressed in leads _____
T WAVES INVERTED _____ only in lead aVR (normally inverted)
                       _____ in leads _____

Portion(s) of the heart affected: _____ inferior wall _____ lateral wall
                                    _____ anterior wall _____ other

Pathophysiologic process: _____ ischemia _____ injury _____ infarction

b. What steps will you take in managing this patient?

22. Not long after you have safely delivered the previous gentleman to the emergency room, you are called to a downtown office building for a man who "feels bad." The patient is 52 years old and looks ill. He says, "It must be something I ate—I overdid it a bit at my daughter's wedding last night. Now I feel really sick to my stomach and gassy." Here is his 12-lead ECG:

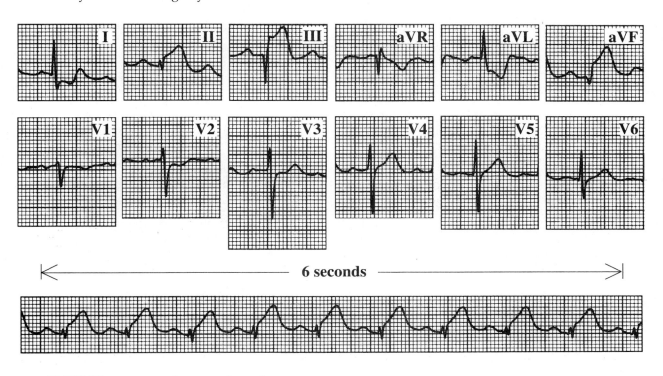

RHYTHM: _____ regular _____ irregular
RATE: _____ per minute
P WAVES: _____ present _____ absent
　　　If present, is there a P before every QRS? _____ yes _____ no
　　　　　　　Is there a QRS after every P?　_____ yes _____ no
P–R INTERVAL: _____ seconds
QRS complexes: _____ normal _____ abnormal
Name of rhythm: _____

Q WAVES deeper than 2 mm: _____ not present
　　　　　　　　　　　　　_____ present in leads _____
S–T SEGMENTS: _____ normal
　　　　　　　_____ elevated in leads _____
　　　　　　　_____ depressed in leads _____
T WAVES INVERTED _____ only in lead aVR (normally inverted)
　　　　　　　　　_____ in leads _____

Portion(s) of the heart affected: _____ inferior wall _____ lateral wall
　　　　　　　　　　　　　　_____ anterior wall _____ other

Pathophysiologic process: _____ ischemia _____ injury _____ infarction

31
Heat Exposure

1. The core temperature of the human body at any given moment represents a balance between the heat produced by the body and that shed by the body.

   a. List the potential sources of body heat and the mechanisms by which body heat can be dissipated.

   Sources of Body Heat

   (1) _____

   (2) _____

   (3) _____

   Ways of Shedding Heat

   (1) _____

   (2) _____

   (3) _____

   (4) _____

   b. The body's mechanisms for dissipating excess heat have certain limitations. All of the mechanisms, first of all, depend on _____ _____ to shunt blood from the core to the body surface. Three of the body's cooling mechanisms, furthermore, require a temperature gradient between the body and the outside in order to be effective. None of those three mechanisms— _____ _____, _____, or _____ —can work if the outside is not at least a few degrees cooler than the body core. Finally, one of the body's cooling mechanisms is dependent on the ambient humidity. When the humidity is high, that mechanism—namely _____ —is ineffective in lowering the core temperature.

   c. A hatless hiker standing still on a mountaintop on a windless day loses heat from his head by _____. A breeze picks up. Now the hiker loses heat by _____ _____ as well.

   d. A white-water enthusiast who capsizes his canoe in a swift-running stream loses body heat by _____.

   e. A soldier on maneuvers in the desert, in ambient temperatures of over 37.7°C (100°F) can shed heat only by _____.

2. The body's normal response to entering a hot environment can place considerable stress on a person who has a limited cardiovascular reserve. Explain why.

3. Anyone can succumb to a heat wave, but some people are more vulnerable than others. List five factors that increase a person's risk of suffering significant heat illness in response to heat stress.

   a.

   b.

   c.

   d.

   e.

4. You are called to the local high school playing field on a hot, sticky August afternoon to deal with a "casualty" of preseason training, a 16-year-old fullback who "became crazy" during practice. You see him over near the goalposts, where several of his teammates are trying to restrain him. "None of my boys ever messed around with drugs before," the coach tells you, "and I sure never would have pegged Chuck as a junkie. But I don't know how else to explain his behavior. He's been touchy all afternoon, and he just started acting crazy."

   You find the fullback agitated and combative. He seems completely disoriented. His skin is warm and sweaty. His vital signs are pulse 120 and bounding, respirations 30 and shallow, blood pressure 150/90, and oral temperature 41.7°C (107°F). The pupils are widely dilated and react only sluggishly to light.

   a. This boy is most likely suffering from _____
      _____.

   b. List the steps in managing this case.

5. The following day, it is even hotter, but mercifully the humidity has dropped considerably. You are called to the very same playing field for another casualty of preseason training, this time a 14-year-old running back. You find him lying in midfield writhing in pain. "I swear I didn't clip him," one of the other players is insisting. "I didn't even get near him. He just fell down by himself."

   "Sure, sure," says the coach, who is trying to massage the cramps out of the boy's legs. When you ask the boy what his problem is, he just moans and says, "My legs, my legs."

   On examination, his skin is cool and sweaty. His pulse is 100 and regular, respirations are 30 and shallow, blood pressure is 110/70, and oral temperature is 37°C (98.6°). There are no signs of injury to the extremities.

   a. This boy is most likely suffering from
      _____.

   b. List the steps in managing this case.

6. "As long as you folks are already here," says the coach, "maybe you could take a look at our quarterback. I think he's coming down with something, and I have to decide whether to send him home."

You find the quarterback sitting on the bench looking quite miserable. He says that his girlfriend has mononucleosis and he thinks he may be coming down with it too because he feels very tired and achy. On examination, he is sweating profusely, and his skin feels clammy. His pulse is 110 and somewhat weak, his respirations are 28 and shallow, his blood pressure is 100/60, and his oral temperature is 39.4°C (103°F).

a. This boy is most likely suffering from _____
   _____.

b. List the steps in managing this case.

   What advice should you give the football coach?

7. On the very same day, you are called to a local supermarket for a "sick baby." You arrive to find a nearly hysterical woman who looks scarcely out of her teens holding a comatose baby. "I just left her in the car for a minute while I ran in to buy a couple of things," she says, although you note three full shopping bags in her cart. The baby, a 6-month-old, is unconscious (AVPU score = U). Pulse is 180, respirations are 60, blood pressure is 100/80, and rectal temperature is 43.3°C (110°F).

a. This baby is most likely suffering from _____
   _____.

b. List the steps in managing this case.

8. Paramedics, like other public safety personnel, do not have the luxury of postponing heavy exertion until weather conditions are favorable; they must do their job whatever the weather, which means they may be exposed to a significant risk of heat illness during periods of high temperature.

a. List five measures you can take to reduce your risk of becoming ill from the heat.

   (1)

   (2)

   (3)

   (4)

   (5)

b. If you do start to experience early symptoms of heat illness, you must stop your activities immediately. But to do so, you need to be able to recognize the warning symptoms of heat illness when they occur. List four warning symptoms of heat illness.

   (1)

   (2)

   (3)

   (4)

32
Cold Exposure

1. No one would ever suffer cold injury if they simply heeded the advice of their mother. Mothers always know, even without taking a paramedic course, how to keep warm on cold days. Listed below are several statements we have all doubtless heard at least once from Mother. Each statement reflects an intuitive knowledge of the ways in which the body generates and loses heat. For each statement, identify the mechanism of heat generation or heat loss to which Mother was referring and explain why Mother was right.

   a. "Don't go out without a hat and scarf; it's freezing out there."
   Mother was right because:

   b. "Stop rolling around in the snow. You'll get a death of a chill."
   Mother was right because:

   c. "Get out of those wet clothes this minute."
   Mother was right because:

   d. "Those skates are much too tight. Your toes will fall off."
   Mother was right because:

   e. "Make sure you wear your windbreaker. It's blowing a gale out there."
   Mother was right because:

   f. "Eat. Eat. You have to have something to keep going in this weather."
   Mother was right because:

2. Without Mother's advice, the body has only a limited repertoire of defenses against the cold. List three ways the body can defend itself against a drop in core temperature.

   a.

   b.

   c.

3. Although anyone can suffer cold injury, certain factors *predispose* a person to suffer ill effects from the cold.

   a. List four factors that predispose a person to suffer frostbite when exposed to freezing conditions.

   (1)

   (2)

   (3)

   (4)

   b. List four factors that predispose a person to suffer hypothermia.

   (1)

   (2)

   (3)

   (4)

4. Indicate which of the following statements about frostbite are true and which are false.

   a. A partially frostbitten extremity is best warmed in front of a campfire or heater.

   TRUE   FALSE

   b. In deep frostbite, the extremity feels cold and rock hard.

   TRUE   FALSE

   c. If rescue circumstances require it, a patient with deep frostbite may walk on a frostbitten leg without causing major additional damage to the limb.

   TRUE   FALSE

   d. Antibiotic ointment should be applied gently over frostbitten areas to prevent infection.

   TRUE   FALSE

   e. A frostbitten extremity will be excruciatingly painful until it is rewarmed.

   TRUE   FALSE

   f. Frost nip most often affects the tips of the ears, nose, fingers, and toes.

   TRUE   FALSE

5. Hypothermia affects every system in the body. In the following table, list some of the effects of a drop in core temperature on each body system mentioned.

Body System	Effects of Hypothermia
Central nervous system	
Cardiovascular system	
Respiratory system	
Muscular system	
Metabolic system	

6. You are enjoying a week off at a mountain ski resort. On your first morning there, the manager of the resort asks for volunteers to join a search-and-rescue party that is going out to look for three skiers who failed to return to the lodge the previous night. You of course volunteer, and you set off with a team on skis to comb the slopes. You are all carrying two-way radios so that you can summon a snowmobile to help transport the lost skiers if you find them. Eventually you locate two of the skiers, about 15 miles from the ski lodge, dug into a makeshift shelter in the snow (and unaware that only about 50 meters away, beyond a stand of trees, is an empty cabin). Both skiers are alert.

a. The first skier tells you that he lost all sensation in his left leg sometime during the night. On examination the leg is white, cold, and very hard. Describe how you would manage this patient.

b. The second skier says, "I think I've got the same problem in my left foot." On examination, the foot has a waxy, white appearance. The skin feels very stiff, but there is "give" underneath when you press down hard on the skin. How would you manage *this* patient?

c. Not long after those two skiers have been evacuated on stretchers by snowmobile, you find the third skier. He is sitting up against a tree, unconscious. Apparently he did not realize that he had come within a hundred meters of the main road. His skin is very cold. You cannot detect any pulse. His pupils are dilated and unreactive. But he does seem to be breathing, although only about once or twice a minute. You radio for a paramedic-staffed ambulance to meet you at the road.

(1) Describe the management of the patient until the ambulance comes and en route to hospital.

(2) This patient is at considerable risk of ventricular fibrillation. List five things that could trigger ventricular fibrillation in these circumstances.

(a)

(b)

(c)

(d)

(e)

7. You and your crew are at the local lake on a chilly November afternoon, covering an annual speedboat race that invariably produces a few minor casualties (mostly from indigestion among the picnicking spectators). Making a hairpin turn at high speed, one of the speedboats capsizes. After what seems a very long time, you see the boat's driver bob to the surface (he is wearing a life jacket) and start trying to swim for shore. Describe the actions you should take in this situation.

8. During the first spell of bitter cold weather of the season, you are called to the downtown bus terminal for a "man down." When you reach the scene, a police officer waves you over. "Sorry to bother you folks with this," he says. "Just a vagrant who's been sleeping in the place for a few days, and probably all he needs is a night in the lockup to sober up." You find the patient, being restrained by another police officer, over in a corner. His speech is slurred, and he staggers when he tries to walk. His breath smells of wine. His skin is pale and cold.

   a. List at least three diagnoses you must consider in this case.

   (1)

   (2)

   (3)

b. In view of the diagnostic possibilities, describe how you would manage this case.

9. The stories that many of us learned as children contain many cautionary tales about cold exposure.

   a. When the three little kittens lost their mittens, they became most vulnerable to this cold injury: _____

   b. Sitting on an ice-cold tuffet on a winter day, Little Miss Muffet was losing heat from her body by _____.

   c. Who is at greater risk of suffering hypothermia—Jack Sprat or his wife? _____
   _____

   d. Before venturing outside to try out his new ice skates, little Jack Horner retreated to a corner and ate his Christmas pie. Was that a good idea? Why or why not?

   e. Swinging about in the treetop is baby in his cradle. When the wind blows, the cradle will rock. When the wind blows, furthermore, baby will lose heat from his body by the process called _____.

10. Now our thought for the day. Decode it in the usual fashion.

a. Part of the body surrounding the core ___ ___ ___ ___ L
    25 45 71 61

b. Continued fall in temperature after removal
   from cold ___ ___ ___ ___ ___ D ___ ___ ___
   51 43 8 37 19   67 65 54

c. What makes a cold day colder ___ ___ ___ ___
   17 28 3 1

d. Local cold injury without tissue damage ___ ___ ___ ___ ___   ___ ___ P
   66 47 2 57 13   52 39

e. Sign of second-degree cold injury and of second-degree burn ___ L ___ ___ ___ ___ ___
   27   42 56 40 72 36

f. Don't give this to a hypothermic patient ___ ___ ___ ___ ___
   59 4 14 73 9

g. Often occurs in hypothermia H ___ ___ ___ ___ L ___ C ___ ___ ___ ___
   53 11 24 76   41   46 10 49 21

h. Highly insulated person ___ ___ ___ ___ ___
   69 6 30 44 64

i. Type of rewarming to avoid in severe hypothermia ___ ___ ___ ___ ___ ___ ___ L
   48 34 5 31 15 75 18

j. What to wear on your hands on cold days ___ ___ ___ ___ ___ ___ ___
   20 62 7 35 68 32 50

k. How the skin feels in second-degree frostbite ___ ___ ___ ___
   22 60 70 38

l. Partner of teeter ___ ___ ___ ___ ___ ___
   63 55 12 26 16 23

m. Game that no one wins ___ ___ ___
   29 74 33

n. Key person in the Me Generation ___
   58

Secret Message: ___ ___   ___ ___ ___   ___ ___ ___ ___ ___ ___ ___   ___ ___   ___ ___ ___ ___ ___ ___   ___
1 2   3 4 5   6 7 8 9 10 11 12   13 14   15 16 17 18 19 20   21

___ ___ ___ ___ ___ ___ ___ ___ ___ ___ ___   ___ ___ ___ ___ ___ ___ ___ ___ ___   ___ ___   ___ ___ ___ ___ ___   ___ ___
22 23 24 25 26 27 28 29 30 31 32   33 34 35 36 37 38 39 40 41   42 43   44 45 46 47 48   49 50

___ ___ ___   ___ ___ ___ ___ ___ ___ ___ ___ ___ ___ ___   ___ ___   ___ ___ ___ ___ ___ ___ ___ ___ ___ ___
51 52 53   54 55 56 57 58 59 60 61 62 63 64   65 66   67 68 69 70 71 72 73 74 75 76

33
Radiation Exposure

1. a. The three forms of ionizing radiation of concern to EMS providers are

   (1)

   (2)

   (3)

   b. Of those forms of radiation, _____ _____ can be stopped by something as thin as a piece of paper. _____ can be stopped by heavy clothing. But _____ cannot be stopped except by lead shielding, a concrete wall, or a similar heavy barrier.

   c. In view of the fact that the first two forms of radiation mentioned are so easily blocked, why do we need to worry about them at all?

   d. What measures should be taken at the scene of a "dirty" radiation accident to protect oneself from those two forms of radiation?

2. When responding to a "dirty" radiation accident, rescuers must try to limit the patient's and their own exposure to the radiation source as strictly as possible. The three most effective ways to limit one's dosage from a radioactive source are

   a.

   b.

   c.

3. You are called to the infirmary of a local factory to see an employee who was injured in an unspecified "industrial accident." The plant manager who escorts you in explains, "There was a nasty accident. The red warning light in the "hot room" wasn't functioning, and one of our workers went in there when we had a powerful emitter unshielded. I don't know how many rads he got— we've got our engineers measuring the emissions now—but it was certainly a few hundred."

   You find the patient lying quietly in the infirmary looking very pale. He complains of feeling weak and very sick to his stomach. There are no abnormal findings on physical examination.

   a. What safety precautions are necessary in handling this patient?

   b. Is there any evidence at the moment that the patient may have sustained serious radiation injury? _____ If so, what is the evidence?

c. The plant's radiation safety officer arrives, having completed some measurements at the site of the exposure. He tells you that the patient spent 15 minutes exposed to radioactive emissions of 2,000R per hour. What was the patient's total radiation exposure? _____R

d. The patient had been working only 1 foot away from the radiation source. Had he been working 5 feet away, his exposure would have been considerably less. How much less?

4. You are called to the scene of a transport accident in which a truck carrying radioactive waste overturned and caught fire. When you arrive, fire fighters have just extinguished the fire, but there is still a lot of smoke. The driver of the truck is pinned inside the crushed cabin. Indicate which of the following statements about handling this call are true and which are false.

a. The ambulance should be parked upwind from the wrecked truck.

TRUE   FALSE

b. Once the fire is extinguished, the danger of radioactive contamination has passed.

TRUE   FALSE

c. The driver should be carefully examined from head to toe, then extricated from the truck cabin on short and long backboards.

TRUE   FALSE

d. If extrication will require more than a minute or two, rescuers should work in shifts.

TRUE   FALSE

e. A dosimeter film badge should be clipped onto your protective clothing before you enter an area potentially contaminated with radioactive dust.

TRUE   FALSE

f. Once the patient is removed from the wreckage, first priority goes to decontaminating him.

TRUE   FALSE

5. In the case described in the previous question, Civil Defense workers arrive and determine that the radioactive emission rate 1 foot from the overturned truck is 1,000R per hour.

a. If the driver was trapped for 15 minutes, approximately what radiation exposure did he receive? _____R

b. By moving him 20 feet away from the wrecked vehicle, you can reduce his (and your) exposure rate to _____R per hour.

c. List the steps you would take before moving the patient out of the contaminated work zone.

6. Our thought for the day is easily forgotten at a radiation accident.

   a. Radiation absorbed dose __ __ __
                              39 9 14

   b. Electron of the atom   B __ __ __ particle
                                50 57 31

   c. Helium nucleus __ __ __ __ __ particle
                     62 10 21 2 35

   d. Sign of serious radiation exposure __ __ __ __ __ __ __ G
                                         49 16 59 7 18 24 45

   e. Charged particle __ __ __
                       60 48 11

   f. One safeguard against radiation exposure __ I __ __
                                               1   4 42

   g. Another safeguard against radiation exposure __ I __ __ __ __ __ __
                                                    43   15 27 58 66 54 20

   h. Where to park with respect to a radiation accident U __ __ __ __ __
                                                           38 30 64 61 6

   i. Site of a famous radiation accident __ __ __ __ __ __ B __ __
                                          46 19 3 51 26 55   32 29

   j. Disfigure __ __ __ __ __ __
                52 47 17 22 8 53

   k. Adolescent __ __ __ __
                 63 37 44 56

   l. Digit of the foot __ __ __
                        34 65 40

   m. What to say to a photographer __ H __ __ __ __
                                     41   12 5 33 25

   n. Katherine's nickname __ __ __ __
                           36 28 23 13

Secret Message: __ __ __   __ __ __ __ __ __   __ __ __ __ __   __ __   __ __ __
                 1 2 3   4 5 6 7 8 9 10 11 12 13 14 15 16 17   18 19 20

__ __ __ __ __ __ __   __ __ __ __ __ __   __ __ __ __   __ __ __ __ __ __ __ __ __ __
21 22 23 24 25 26 27   28 29 30 31 32 33   34 35 36 37   38 39 40 41 42 43 44 45 46 47

__ __ __ __   __ __ __ __ __ __ __ __ __ __ __ __ __ __ __.
48 49 50 51   52 53 54 55 56 57 58 59 60 61 62 63 64 65 66

34
Hazardous Materials

1. The next time you're driving on the interstate highway, or even along the main street of your city or town, start noticing the USDOT placards on the trucks passing by. Make a note of the code numbers, and look them up later in the USDOT handbook. You may be surprised to find how many potentially hazardous materials are passing through your region every day. Listed in the grid below are 20 hazardous materials that might move through your town by truck or rail during an average day. How many can you find? Are you prepared to deal with a major accident involving any one of them?

```
P O N G A S A H O L L Y O N
I A N T I M O N Y O U Y O I
C S A C O U M A R I N B E T
R B U H U F F O T E R R O R
I U F L U O R I N E V O L I
C T R O F F E E T I R M A C
A Y E R O U N D O F A I D A
C R A I N D R A I N U N I C
I I R N E S T I B I N E R I
D C R E I L C U C U M E N D
E A T S O D I U M A T T E R
A C I G A R E T T E C A O I
N I T R O G E N G A S I N G
A D R H Y M E T H A N E D E
```

2. While it's axiomatic in EMS that you never know what you may find at a call until you reach the scene, nonetheless there are certain types of calls that should start red lights flashing in the back of your brain: ALERT! Possible hazmat call! Listed below are some calls to 911 during a busy month. Mark an "H" beside those calls that are apt to involve hazardous materials, and indicate what sort of hazardous materials might be involved in each case you marked.

_____ Two-car collision downtown _____
_____

_____ Apartment-house fire _____
_____

_____ Three municipal workers collapsed in a sewer
_____
_____

_____ Two police officers injured in a riot _____
_____

_____ Fire in a garden supply store warehouse _____
_____

_____ Semitrailer overturned on the interstate _____
_____

_____ Two "men down" on the maintenance staff of the municipal swimming pool _____
_____

_____ Freight train struck car on level crossing _____
_____

_____ Fire in a furniture factory _____
_____

3. You are called to the scene of a railway accident in which the last 5 cars of a 12-car freight train derailed and toppled onto a highway below, crushing motor vehicles beneath them. Before approaching the derailed freight cars and the injured motorists underneath them, you want to make sure those train cars were not carrying a hazardous cargo. List three potential sources of information regarding the nature of the train's cargo.

a.

b.

c.

4. You manage to determine that one of the derailed cars was carrying liquid chlorine, and as a matter of fact, you can already smell chlorine in the air. List the steps you would take at this point (assume that you are in the first public safety vehicle to reach the scene).

5. Indicate which of the following statements regarding hazmat incidents are true and which are false.

a. If there are no unusual odors at the scene of a transport accident, it is safe to assume that hazardous materials are not involved.

TRUE   FALSE

b. EMS personnel at a hazmat incident may become contaminated with toxic materials by touching a patient who is contaminated.

TRUE   FALSE

c. In decontaminating a hazmat victim, one should use a brush to scrub the skin briskly with strong soap and lots of water.

TRUE   FALSE

d. When decontamination is carried out at the scene, it is unneccessary to notify the receiving hospital that you are bringing in a hazmat case.

TRUE   FALSE

e. It is preferable that an ambulance team that was not involved in treating and decontaminating the patient be summoned to transport the patient to the hospital.

TRUE   FALSE

35
Obstetrics and Emergency Childbirth

1. Concealed in the grid below are 25 words we learned in this chapter. Find the words, and use them to fill in the blanks in the statements that follow the grid.

```
G R A A F I A N F O L L I C L E C
A I L H E A P R O V U L A T E C H
M A U M B I L I C A L C O R D R I
E R M O P E A L L R V T E G R O N
N I T N R F C L O Y A U R R O W E
A P E R I N E U M P G I L A V N S
R A R E M O N T O R I L O V E I E
C E M L I S T R U I N A V I A N X
H O M A P L A I N S A W N D O G S
E A T B A B Y I C R I E D T V U P
R I B O R B O N E S U T E R U S T
Y O U R A Y P R E P A R T U M B Y
A B O R T I O N C E I C H E E S E
```

This is a story about how babies are made. Babies do not come in packages delivered by the stork. Babies are the result of _____! In fact, our story begins at _____, the time when a girl first starts having menstrual periods. Each menstrual cycle thereafter is a preparation for pregnancy.

On around the fourteenth day of the cycle, women _____, that is, a _____ _____ located in the left or right _____ ruptures, with the release of an egg, or _____. If a sperm should happen along just about the time when the egg is released, fertilization may take place, usually in the _____,

where the fertilized egg remains for about 3 days before entering the _____ and implanting into the endometrium. Between the third and eighth week of development, the fertilized egg is called a(n) _____. Thereafter, it is called a(n) _____ until delivery. After delivery, it is officially a(n) _____.

Specialized structures develop during pregnancy to support the developing baby. The baby is enclosed in a fluid-filled _____ _____. It is nourished by a large, vascular organ of pregnancy called the _____, which attaches to the baby via the _____.

At about 40 weeks after conception, the baby

reaches maturity, or _____, and is ready to make its debut in the world. (When a baby is expelled early, before the twentieth to twenty-eighth week of gestation, the woman is said to have had a miscarriage, or _____.) At that point, the woman goes into _____, the process by which the baby is expelled from the womb, and the pregnant, or _____, womb begins contracting. As it does so, the _____ progressively effaces and dilates until the womb becomes continuous with the birth canal, or _____. The period of uterine contractions will be of shorter duration in a _____, a woman who has already had a delivery in the past, than in a nullipara. Delivery is imminent when the presenting part becomes visible, that is, when _____ occurs. At that point, it is important to control the rate at which the baby emerges, for otherwise there may be injury to the external genitalia (_____) or to the skin between the anus and the opening of the birth canal, an area called the _____. All events occurring before delivery are called antepartum, or _____, while those occurring after delivery are called postpartum.

2. By the second or third week of pregnancy, the placenta starts to develop inside the maternal uterus. The placenta is a specialized organ of pregnancy whose overall task is to nurture the developing fetus. List four specific functions that the placenta carries out for the fetus.

   a.

   b.

   c.

   d.

3. A 22-year-old woman calls for an ambulance because of vaginal bleeding. She states that she is "about 3 months pregnant" and that the bleeding started yesterday, when she thinks she passed some tissue. She has used about 10 sanitary nap-

kins since then. On examination, her skin feels cool and wet. Her pulse is 120 and weak, and her blood pressure is 90/60.

a. This woman is likely to be experiencing

   A. A threatened abortion
   B. An inevitable abortion
   C. An incomplete abortion
   D. A missed abortion
   E. A septic abortion

(Circle the best answer.)

b. List the steps in the prehospital management of this patient.

4. A 32-year-old woman calls for an ambulance because she is "feeling poorly." She states that she is "about 6 months along" in a pregnancy. She has not had any prenatal care. She had some vaginal bleeding "early on," but it lasted only a few days and then stopped. Now for several days, the patient has felt vaguely unwell. She has had a brownish vaginal discharge, and "things are very quiet in there." On physical examination, the patient does not appear in any distress. Her pulse is 74 and regular, respirations are 18 and unlabored, and blood pressure is 120/80. On abdominal examination, you can feel the uterine fundus just above the pelvic brim; it feels quite hard. You are not able to hear fetal heart tones, but the room is noisy, so you are not sure what to make of that finding.

a. This woman is likely to be experiencing

   A. A threatened abortion
   B. An inevitable abortion
   C. An incomplete abortion
   D. A missed abortion
   E. A septic abortion

(Circle the best answer.)

b. List the steps in the prehospital management of this patient.

5. A 20-year-old primigravida calls for an ambulance because of vaginal bleeding. She states that she is in her fourth month of pregnancy and has been fine up to now, but this morning she noticed some bleeding. She denies abdominal pain or cramping. On physical examination, there are no abnormal findings.

a. This woman is likely to be experiencing

A. A threatened abortion

B. An inevitable abortion

C. An incomplete abortion

D. A missed abortion

E. A septic abortion

(Circle the best answer.)

b. List the steps in the prehospital management of this patient.

6. You are called to a suburban home for a "sick girl." The patient is a 16-year-old girl with a high fever. She insists on giving you her history privately, without her parents in the room. When her parents have exited, the girl tells you that she had gone that morning to "some hole in the wall" to have an abortion. A few hours after she got home, she started to feel sick, and she has been having a bad-smelling, bloody vaginal discharge ever since. On examination, she looks very ill. Her pulse is 120 and weak, respirations are 28 and shallow, blood pressure is 80/60, and oral temperature is 40°C (104°F).

a. This woman is likely to be experiencing

A. A threatened abortion

B. An inevitable abortion

C. An incomplete abortion

D. A missed abortion

E. A septic abortion

(Circle the best answer.)

b. List the steps in the prehospital management of this patient.

7. You are called to the home of a weeping 26-year-old woman in the fifteenth week of pregnancy. "It's happening again," she sobs, "I just know it's happening again." She tells you that she has had three miscarriages in the past and that this morning she started having severe abdominal cramps and bleeding, "just like all the other times." She has used six sanitary napkins since the bleeding started about 3 hours ago. On physical examination, she is very distraught. Her pulse is 110 and regular, respirations are 24 and unlabored, blood pressure is 110/70, and she is afebrile. On palpating the abdomen, you can feel the uterine contractions.

a. This woman is likely to be experiencing

   A. A threatened abortion

   B. An inevitable abortion

   C. An incomplete abortion

   D. A missed abortion

   E. A septic abortion

   (Circle the best answer.)

b. List the steps in the prehospital management of this patient.

8. You are called to the home of a 36-year-old grand multip whose chief complaint is bleeding. She is in her eleventh pregnancy and "due any day now." She states that the bleeding, of bright red blood, started a few hours ago, without any warning. She has not had any cramps or other symptoms, and "the baby is still kicking like a football player." On physical examination, the woman looks a little pale and apprehensive. Her pulse is 124 and regular, respirations are 28 and unlabored, and blood pressure is 100/68; she is afebrile. On gentle palpation, you find the abdomen soft. The fundus is at the level of the xiphoid, and fetal heart tones are audible. The fetal heart rate is 140 per minute.

a. List three possible causes of this woman's bleeding.

   (1)

   (2)

   (3)

b. Of those three causes, which do you think is the most likely cause in her case?

c. List the steps you will take in managing this patient.

9. You are called to see a 28-year-old woman in her thirty-fifth week of pregnancy after she had a "fainting spell." The patient's husband greets you at the door and tells you, "We were just sitting there talking—Agnes was lying in bed and I was sitting in the chair—and suddenly I look over and I see that she's out cold. Not sleeping, just out." The patient has meanwhile regained consciousness. She says she feels rather dizzy and has a slight headache, but otherwise feels all right. She denies vaginal bleeding. On physical examination, her pulse is 104 and regular, her respirations are 24 and unlabored, and her blood pressure is 90/60. When you have her roll onto her side, and then recheck her vitals a couple of minutes later, her pulse becomes 88 per minute and her blood pressure is 120/72. Her fundus is nearly at the level of the xiphoid, and fetal heart tones are present at a rate of 160 per minute.

   a. This woman is most probably suffering from

      A. Inevitable abortion

      B. Preeclampsia

      C. Eclampsia

      D. Abruptio placenta

      E. Supine hypotensive syndrome

      (Circle the best answer.)

   b. List the steps in the prehospital care of this patient.

10. You are called to a downtown department store, where an obviously pregnant woman has fallen and twisted her ankle. You find her surrounded by a knot of agitated people, none of them more agitated than the store manager. As you are checking the woman's pedal pulses, you notice that *both* ankles are swollen, not just the one she injured. You decide you had better get a set of vital signs, since you vaguely remember learning that vital signs should be measured in *every* patient, especially every *pregnant* patient. In this woman, you find the pulse is 110 and regular, respirations are 20 and unlabored, and blood pressure is 150/90. As you are taking the radial pulse, you notice that the patient's hands seem puffy. It is too noisy in the store to even bother trying to listen for fetal heart tones, but the woman tells you that the baby is "kicking away."

    a. This woman is most probably suffering from

       A. Inevitable abortion

       B. Preeclampsia

       C. Eclampsia

       D. Abruptio placenta

       E. Supine hypotensive syndrome

       (Circle the best answer.)

    b. List the steps in the prehospital care of this patient.

c. En route to the hospital, you find yourself locked in a traffic jam on the freeway. Meanwhile, your patient starts complaining of cramping abdominal pains. "I've never had a baby before," she says, "but I think these are labor pains." While you look helplessly at the line of cars stretching endlessly to the front and the rear of the ambulance, the woman's eyes suddenly roll back, and she has a grand mal seizure. What steps will you take *now*?

11. A 26-year-old woman in her thirtieth week of pregnancy was the driver of a car that skidded off the road and plowed head-on into a tree. The woman was wearing a shoulder/lap seat belt. Sitting in the passenger seat of the same car was a woman in her twenty-eighth week of pregnancy (they were returning together from a natural childbirth class), also wearing a seat belt. En route to the call, you try to review in your mind the injuries you will need to look for in particular, for you remember that pregnancy makes a woman more vulnerable to trauma.

   a. List five anatomic or physiologic changes of pregnancy that affect a woman's susceptibility or response to trauma.

   (1)

   (2)

   (3)

   (4)

   (5)

b. On reaching the scene of the accident, you find the driver of the car conscious, still sitting behind the wheel of the car. She complains of thirst. On physical examination, her skin is cool and moist. Her pulse is 120 and regular, respirations are 24 and shallow, and blood pressure is 110/68. There is a steering wheel bruise on the upper abdomen. The abdomen is not particularly tender, and it is not rigid. The conditions are too noisy to try to hear fetal heart tones. List the steps in managing this patient.

c. The front-seat passenger is also fully conscious. She complains of a "whiplash," but otherwise thinks she feels all right. "At least the baby's all right," she says. "I can feel him moving around." On physical examination, her skin is warm and moist. Her pulse is 100 and regular, respirations are 20 and unlabored, and her blood pressure is 124/70. You do not find any evidence of injury. Can you conclude that there has been no injury to the fetus? ____ Explain the reason for your answer.

12. Labor proceeds through three well-defined stages, whose duration depends to some extent on whether the woman has ever delivered a baby before.

	FIRST STAGE OF LABOR	SECOND STAGE OF LABOR	THIRD STAGE OF LABOR
Begins with			
Ends with			
Duration in a nullipara			
Duration in a multipara			

13. For each of the cases described below, indicate whether

    T   There is time to **transport** the woman to the hospital for delivery
    D   You will have to assist in emergency **delivery** in the field

    For each case that you decide requires prehospital delivery, indicate what, if any, complications you need to anticipate.

_____   A 20-year-old woman in her first pregnancy. She says her bag of waters broke about 6 hours ago. Now her contractions are about 2 minutes apart, and she feels a need to move her bowels. You are 20 minutes from the hospital. What, if any, complications may occur?

_____   A 25-year-old nullipara (gravida 1, para 0) who has been in labor for 9 hours. Her contractions are 4 to 5 minutes apart. You are 20 minutes from the hospital. What, if any, complications may occur?

_____   A 32-year-old multip (gravida 10, para 8) who has been in labor about 5 hours. Her contractions are 3 minutes apart. She says she thinks the baby's coming. You are 10 minutes from the hospital. What, if any, complications may occur?

_____   A 30-year-old gravida 4, para 3 who has been in labor for 6 hours. She had two of her three children by cesarean section. Her contractions are 2 minutes apart, and she is crowning. You are 5 minutes from the hospital. What, if any, complications may occur?

_____ A 28-year-old gravida 1, para 0 whose contractions started 24 hours ago. They do not come at regular intervals, and they have not gotten much more intense since they started. You are 25 minutes from the hospital.
What, if any, complications may occur?

_____ A 24-year-old gravida 3, para 2 who announces, as you enter her flat, "Hurry, the twins are coming any minute!" She says she has been in labor "quite a while," and you time her contractions as coming less than 2 minutes apart. You are 20 minutes from the hospital.
What, if any, complications may occur?

14. For each of the following statements about assisting at a childbirth outside of the hospital, indicate whether the statement is true or false.

a. If you are transporting a woman in labor, and she begins crowning when you are only a minute or two from the hospital, you should instruct her to cross her legs until you reach the emergency room.

TRUE   FALSE

b. If the fetal heart rate is less than 120 per minute, the fetus is in danger.

TRUE   FALSE

c. A woman should be discouraged from sitting up or squatting for delivery of her baby since those positions are unphysiologic and increase the demand on the mother's energy.

TRUE   FALSE

d. If the baby is coming fast, it is more important to control the delivery than to drape the mother with sterile towels.

TRUE   FALSE

e. If the cut ends of the umbilical cord are oozing blood, you should unclamp them and reapply the clamps more tightly.

TRUE   FALSE

f. If the placenta has not delivered within 20 minutes of the baby's delivery, you should exert gentle traction on the umbilical cord while you vigorously massage the uterus.

TRUE   FALSE

g. With the exception of buttocks breech, all other abnormal presentations must be delivered in the hospital.

TRUE   FALSE

15. You are assisting in the delivery of a baby in the lingerie section of a downtown department store.

a. The baby's head delivers spontaneously, and you notice that it is covered with a membrane. What should you do?

b. You deal with that problem successfully. The next thing you notice is that the umbilical cord is wound tightly around the baby's neck. What should you do about *that*?

c. List the steps in carrying out the remainder of the delivery (second and third stage).

d. At 1 minute after birth, the baby's body is pink, but its extremities are dusky. Its pulse is 120. It is moving vigorously and shrieking like a banshee. What is the Apgar score? _____

16. During another one of those weekends off at the ski lodge, when you are cheerfully snowed in, one of the other guests arrives in the lounge and asks, "Does anyone here know anything about delivering a baby? My wife seems to be in labor." You shrivel up into a corner of your chair, hoping someone else will come forward, but there don't seem to be any obstetricians among the skiers. So, with a sigh, you stand up and follow the distraught husband to his room. There you find a woman in active labor, already crowning. Inspecting the presenting part, you note that it looks awfully smooth, and it has a sort of crack running down the middle.

   a. You realize you are dealing with _____
   _____.

   b. Describe how you will manage this case.

17. The day after you get back to work, your very first call is another "possible OB." The patient is a 24-year-old in her first pregnancy whose labor started about 10 hours earlier. "This wasn't supposed to happen for another month and a half," she tells you. The contractions are now about 2 minutes apart. When you inspect her to see whether she is crowning, you see a short length of umbilical cord protruding from her vagina. Describe how you will manage this case.

18. You have just finished delivering the placenta after an uneventful "OB" call at the home of a 28-year-old multip. The family is all crowded around, admiring the new baby boy that has joined their number, when the mother suddenly complains of a sharp pain in her chest and says, "It's getting hard to breathe." You quickly get a set of vital signs and find that her pulse is 140 per minute, her respirations are 40 per minute and shallow, and her blood pressure is 90/60.

   a. What do you think may have happened?

   b. Describe how you will manage this case.

19. You are called to the home of a 30-year-old gravida 6, para 5 who has gone into labor. "It's twins," she announces as soon as you come in the door. "I'm carrying twins, and they're coming at any moment, I can feel it." And indeed, when you examine the woman, you find that she is crowning.

   a. Describe the special measures necessary in this case.

   b. After delivery of the placenta, the mother continues bleeding quite briskly per vagina.
   Did this woman have any risk factors for postpartum hemorrhage? ___ If so, what risk factor(s)?

c. List three other risk factors for postpartum hemorrhage.

   (1)

   (2)

   (3)

d. Describe how you will manage this situation.

20. And finally to our thought for the day. Decode it in the usual fashion.

  a. Woman who has had more than one pregnancy M __ __ __ __ __ __ __ __ __ A
                                                     17 9 36 65 15 42 52 1 54 29

  b. Toxemia with seizures __ __ __ __ __ __ __ __ A
                        24 48 7 61 33 41 51 27

  c. Female sex hormone __ S __ __ __ __ __ __
                    11   57 71 39 72 34 20

  d. Ovum __ __ __
         56 21 67

  e. Pregnancy __ __ __ __ __ __ __ O __
            44 10 35 62 6 22 50   66

  f. Fertilized ovum from third to eighth week of life __ __ __ __ __ O
                                      37 69 8 18 76

  g. Organ anterior to the uterus B __ __ __ __ __ __
                    53 46 12 16 70 28

  h. Presenting part in a breech __ __ __ __ __
                 40 2 74 64 49

  i. Can precipitate a miscarriage __ __ __ __ __ __
                55 59 13 3 23 25

  j. Unlucky number __ __ __ __ T __ __ __
          30 26 4 38   73 43 14

  k. Human gestation period __ __ __ __ months
            5 19 45 68

  l. Response to "It's a boy!" __ __ __ __ __
           75 58 63 60 31

  m. Not out __ __
        32 47

Secret Message: __ __ __ __ __ __ __ __ __ __ __ __ __ __ __ __ __ __ __ __ __ __ __ __
                 1 2 3 4 5 6 7   8 9 10 11 12 13 14 15   16 17 18 19 20 21   22 23 24

__ __ __ __ __ __ __ __ __ __ __ __ __ __ __ __ __ __ __ __ __ __ __ __ __
25 26 27 28 29   30 31 32 33 34 35 36 37 38   39 40   41 42 43 44 45 46 47 48 49

__ __ __ __ __ __ __ - __ __ __ __ __ __ __ __ __ __ __ __ __ __ __ __ __ __ __ __.
50 51   52   53 54 55 56   57 58 59 60 61 62 63 64 65 66 67   68 69 70 71 72 73 74 75 76

36
Neonatal Care and Transport

1. Hidden in the grid below are 17 terms related to emergency childbirth and care of the newborn. You will need to use those terms to fill in the blanks in the statements that follow the grid. See how many you can find.

```
U M B I L I C A L A R T E R Y E
T A P R E M A T U R E E N A T E
E N D R A P E R I N E U M C O L
R N U M B I L I C A L V E I N G
U S M O O N W A R P E E L D O E
S H E E L V E S C N E V A O R T
D U C T U S A R T E R I O S U S
O R O P H A R R Y A N G R I S H
V E N A C A V A Y I Z T T S T O
E S I F O R A M E N O V A L E C
S H U N T A N D P E C K P O C K
N O M E A N E O N A T E S T E W
```

Oxygenated blood from the _____ _____ enters the fetus in the _____. It flows through the liver into the inferior _____. Leaving that vessel, a large proportion of the oxygenated blood flows directly across the _____ _____ through a hole called the _____, thereby bypassing the lungs. When blood goes from the right side of the heart to the left side of the heart without picking up oxygen in the lungs, we call it a _____. Another direct connection, the _____

_____, links the fetal pulmonary artery to the _____. Both those connections close very soon after birth. After circulating through the fetus, blood enters a(n)

_____ to return to the placenta.

The newborn, or _____, is very vulnerable to hypothermia. It is important to try to prevent hypothermia from occurring in the newborn, because hypothermia may lead to _____, which in turn may lead to _____. A baby born before the thirty-eighth week of pregnancy or weighing less than 2.5 kg is considered to be _____ _____ and is at higher risk of hypothermia.

When fetal stool, called _____, is expelled into the amniotic fluid, it may find its way into the fetal airway before birth and then be aspirated deep into the airway when the baby takes its first breath. The result may be a complete failure to breathe at all, called _____.

The womb: _____

The organ where eggs reside:

_____

The region between the vagina and the anus:

_____

2. You are called to attend a 38-year-old multip in active labor at home. She has not had any prenatal care. She tells you that "this baby is a month late according to my calendar and is sure a long time in coming." Her contractions started about 10 hours ago and are now 2 minutes apart. Her "bag of waters" broke 10 minutes before your arrival, and you notice greenish stains on the bedclothes. The woman says she feels as if she has to move her bowels.

a. Are there any indications that this may be a complicated delivery or that you may have problems with the baby after delivery? _____. If so, list the risk factors in this delivery.

b. List four other risk factors, not present in this case, that indicate a high likelihood of complications during delivery or immediately thereafter.

(1)

(2)

(3)

(4)

c. You immediately set up for delivery—and none too soon! You scarcely have your gloves on before the baby is crowning, and a moment later, the head is delivered. It is covered with a thick, greenish substance. List the steps you would take at this point.

d. What further steps should you take when the baby is fully delivered?

3. You are called to a movie theater where a 23-year-old gravida 4, para 3 went into active labor while watching *Return of the Spider Monster.* You find the patient in a cold, drafty ladies' room, sitting on the floor, panting. "I'm only in my seventh month," she says. "This can't be happening." As she makes that statement, the baby's head delivers spontaneously, so you scramble to the floor to control the rest of the delivery. Within seconds, you find yourself holding a very red, wrinkled, little baby.

   a. List the steps you would take at this point, in the sequence in which you would perform them.

   b. At what point would you clamp and cut the baby's umbilical cord? (Explain the reasoning behind your answer.)

   c. What factors are likely to promote hypothermia in this baby?

   d. It is important to prevent the baby from losing heat because hypothermia may have some very serious adverse consequences. List two possible adverse consequences of hypothermia in a premature newborn.

      (1)

      (2)

   e. What steps can you take to try to prevent the baby from becoming hypothermic?

   f. What other special measures should be taken in caring for this baby, beside ensuring that it stays warm?

4. You are called to a downtown apartment for a "sick woman." You arrive to find a teenage girl sitting on the toilet, having given birth only seconds before. The placenta has not yet delivered. You quickly fish the newborn out of the toilet.

   a. List the steps you would take at this point.

   b. What would be the indications for starting artificial ventilation on this baby?

   c. As it turns out, the baby has one of those indications, so you start artificial ventilation with a bag-valve-mask and 100% oxygen. After a minute, you reassess the baby and find that its heart rate is 84 per minute. What should you do now?

   d. After another minute or so, you reassess again. The baby's heart rate is now 56 per minute. What should you do?

   e. Under what circumstances should you administer epinephrine to this baby?

   f. If ordered to give epinephrine, what dosage will you give? (The baby weighs 3 kg.) _____ How will you give it?

5. For each of the following statements regarding care of the newborn, indicate whether the statement is true or false.

   a. Deep pharyngeal suctioning may stimulate the vagus nerve in a newborn and cause severe bradycardia.

   TRUE   FALSE

   b. Even slight meconium staining of the amniotic fluid indicates a need to intubate the newborn immediately after delivery.

   TRUE   FALSE

   c. If the fetal heart rate is less than 120 per minute at any point during labor, you should roll the mother onto her side and give her supplemental oxygen to breathe.

   TRUE   FALSE

   d. Clamping and cutting of the umbilical cord should ordinarily be carried out after the cord stops pulsating.

   TRUE   FALSE

   e. Hypothermia in the newborn may lead to the reestablishment of right-to-left shunting and consequent hypoxemia.

   TRUE   FALSE

   f. Most newborns who require resuscitation will need full CPR.

   TRUE   FALSE

37
Gynecologic Emergencies

1. You are summoned to a downtown apartment for a "sick woman." On arrival, you find a 24-year-old woman complaining of severe abdominal pain.

   a. List 10 questions you would ask in taking this woman's history.

      (1)   (6)

      (2)   (7)

      (3)   (8)

      (4)   (9)

      (5)   (10)

   b. List three things you would look for in particular in performing the physical examination.

      (1)

      (2)

      (3)

2. You are called to see a 20-year-old woman with abdominal pain. She states that she "finally got her period" the day before, about a month or so late, and that this morning she started having quite severe, crampy abdominal pain in the middle of her abdomen. She has already used almost a whole box (one dozen) of sanitary napkins. On examination, she appears to be in moderate distress. Her pulse is 92 and regular while sitting, 104 while standing; respirations are 20 and unlabored; and blood pressure is 110/70. There is moderate tenderness to palpation in the lower quadrant medially.

a. This woman is most likely to be experiencing

   A. A threatened abortion

   B. An inevitable abortion

   C. A septic abortion

   D. An ectopic pregnancy

   E. Pelvic inflammatory disease

   (Circle the best answer.)

b. List the steps you would take in managing this patient.

3. A 25-year-old woman calls for an ambulance because of abdominal pain. She says the pain started yesterday and has just gotten worse and worse. It is a "heavy," aching pain in the lower abdomen. This afternoon, she started having chills as well, and she threw up once. Her LMP was 5 days ago and was normal. She uses an intrauterine device (IUCD) for contraception. On physical examination, the patient looks ill. Her skin feels hot and dry. Her pulse is 110 and regular while sitting, 116 standing; respirations are 24 and unlabored; and the blood pressure is 122/74. The abdomen is *very* tender to palpation in all quadrants.

a. This woman is most likely to be experiencing

   A. A threatened abortion

   B. An inevitable abortion

   C. A septic abortion

   D. An ectopic pregnancy

   E. Pelvic inflammatory disease

   (Circle the best answer.)

b. List the steps you would take in managing this patient.

4. A 24-year-old woman calls for an ambulance because "I think I have appendicitis." She says she's been having some crampy pain in the right lower quadrant for a couple of days, but today it got much worse. She can't remember exactly when her last menstrual period was, "but I think I'm getting my period now, because I had some spotting this morning." She is certain, in any case, that she couldn't possibly be pregnant. On physical examination, she appears anxious and in moderate distress. Her skin is cool and moist. Her pulse is 100 and regular sitting, 124 standing; her respirations are 24 and regular; her blood pressure is 110/70. Her abdomen is very tender to palpation.

   a. This woman is most likely to be experiencing

      A. A threatened abortion

      B. An inevitable abortion

      C. A septic abortion

      D. An ectopic pregnancy

      E. Pelvic inflammatory disease

      (Circle the best answer.)

   b. List the steps you would take in managing this patient.

5. Ectopic pregnancy is more likely in some women than in others. List two factors that predispose a woman to ectopic pregnancy.

   a.

   b.

6. Three findings in the history make up the classic diagnostic triad for ectopic pregnancy, and a woman who has those three findings must be considered to be suffering from ectopic pregnancy until proved otherwise. What three findings make up the classic triad for ectopic pregnancy?

   a.

   b.

   c.

7. For each of the following statements regarding the management of a rape victim, indicate whether the statement is true or false.

   a. The paramedic should take a detailed history of the rape incident to enable the victim to ventilate her feelings about what happened.

      TRUE   FALSE

   b. All superficial wounds and abrasions suffered by a rape victim should be carefully cleaned and covered with sterile dressings before transport, to prevent infection.

      TRUE   FALSE

   c. The patient should be discouraged from cleaning up before being examined in the emergency room.

      TRUE   FALSE

   d. The rape victim's external genitalia should be routinely inspected for injury.

      TRUE   FALSE

   e. If the victim of rape does not wish to be examined at the hospital, she should be transported to the home of a friend or relative.

      TRUE   FALSE

   f. The diagnosis on your trip sheet for a victim of sexual assault should read "Alleged rape" rather than "Rape."

      TRUE   FALSE

38
Disturbances of Behavior

1. Hidden in the grid below are 21 things other than psychiatric illness that can cause disturbances of behavior. How many can your find?

```
A B E E P C P R U N E B A T
H M R A I D R Y R A P R O E
H Y P O G L Y C E M I A D E
L X P H M S E H M E L I I N
O E R E E I T F I L E N G S
A D A A R T D R A I P T I Y
F E E D A T A E O N S U T P
E M A I L L E M P K Y M A H
V A I N C S E N I L E O L I
E I N J O D Y I S N O R I L
R G L U H O L Y P I E R S I
T H Y R O T O X I C O S I S
S T A Y L O C O C A I N E T
```

2. For each of the symptoms and signs listed below, indicate whether it is

O More typical of *organic* brain syndrome
P More typical of *psychiatric* illness
B Apt to be seen in *both* organic and psychiatric illness

____ Obsessional thinking

____ Flat affect

____ Delirium

____ Distractibility

____ Compulsions

____ Visual hallucinations

____ Confabulation

____ Anxiety

____ Coma

____ Circumstantial thinking

3. Indicate whether each of the following statements about the approach to a disturbed patient is true or false.

   a. The most important thing a paramedic can do to help a disturbed patient is to remain calm and steady.

   TRUE   FALSE

   b. There should be a maximum sense of urgency in evacuating a disturbed patient to the hospital, since there is nothing that can be done to help the patient in the field.

   TRUE   FALSE

   c. It is essential to correct a patient's misinterpretations of reality.

   TRUE   FALSE

   d. The disturbed patient should be reassured that everything will turn out all right.

   TRUE   FALSE

   e. The paramedic should remain with the disturbed patient at all times until the emergency room staff takes over the patient's care.

   TRUE   FALSE

   f. Police intervention is usually required to transport a disturbed patient against his or her will.

   TRUE   FALSE

4. The following is the transcript of an interview between an inexperienced paramedic and a disturbed patient. The interview illustrates several errors in approach. Read the interview through. Then list the points in the interview that you think could have been handled or phrased in a better way.

   PARAMEDIC (entering an apartment in which there is a lot of noise and confusion): OK, which one of you is the patient?

   Someone points to a young woman crouching in a corner, crying.

   PARAMEDIC (approaching the woman and standing in front of her): Now, dearie, what's the trouble?

   Patient continues crying.

   PARAMEDIC: Now come on, get hold of yourself. Big girls don't cry.

   PATIENT (sobbing): Everything's just so hopeless.

   PARAMEDIC: Things are never hopeless. You're probably just making a mountain out of a mole-

   hill, and by tomorrow you'll wonder what you were making such a big fuss about.

   Patient sits crying to herself.

   PARAMEDIC: Well, if you don't want to tell me what's wrong, maybe one of your friends here can tell me. Is there anyone here who can tell me what's going on?

   Immediately the noise and confusion resume, as everyone starts talking at once. The patient huddles farther into the corner.

   List the things you think were done incorrectly in this interview (include errors of omission and errors of commission).

   _____

   _____

   _____

   _____

   _____

   _____

   _____

   _____

   _____

   _____

   _____

   _____

5. For each of the symptoms and signs listed, indicate whether it is indicative of a disturbance of

   A. Consciousness
   B. Motor activity
   C. Speech
   D. Thinking
   E. Affect or mood
   F. Memory
   G. Orientation
   H. Perception

   _____ The patient cannot name three objects that you listed out loud 5 minutes earlier.

   _____ The patient is pacing up and down.

   _____ The patient smiles pleasantly as he tells you that his daughter was run over by a truck.

   _____ The patient keeps shifting his attention from you to the television or to the window.

   _____ The patient seems to be having a conversation with an invisible friend.

   _____ The patient thinks it's 1931.

_____ The patient also thinks that he is Albert Einstein.

_____ He tells you, "All the world is my kingdumbell and I'm the pellmellery scullop."

_____ The patient is terrified of spiders.

_____ He puts two fingers to his forehead in a salute every time he finishes speaking.

_____ He complains of palpitations, nausea, tightness in his chest, and numbness around his lips.

_____ He thinks that the sound of the wind is someone calling his name.

6. You are called to a downtown apartment building for a "sick man." Reaching the corridor outside the man's apartment, you are intercepted by a neighbor who had called for the ambulance. "I feel a little silly troubling you folks," she says, "but Mr. Crosby next door—he's just not himself lately—doesn't even poke his head out of that apartment, doesn't want to see no one—he just says, "Go away," when I knock. So I got to worrying. I mean I don't even think he's got himself anything to eat in there."

You knock at Mr. Crosby's door. There isn't any response. You knock several more times.

"Who's there?" someone finally says.

"We're paramedics, from the city ambulance service."

"Well, what do you want with me?"

"We just want to talk with you a bit," you say. "There are folks worried about you."

It takes some persuading, but finally Mr. Crosby opens the door and admits you to his apartment. The place is in complete disarray, and it appears as if no one has washed a dish or tidied up in months. Here and there you note an empty liquor bottle lying around on the floor.

"So what do you want?" Mr. Crosby asks listlessly.

a. Where would you go from here? List some of the questions you would ask Mr. Crosby at this point.

b. In the course of your interview with Mr. Crosby, which seems to go very slowly, you learn that he is a 62-year-old widower. He has one son ("I never hear from him"). He used to be a watchmaker, "but I haven't been worth anything since I got this arthritis 10 years ago." In response to your query about why he has stopped going out of the apartment, he says, "What's there to go out for? Anyway, I don't have the energy to go rambling around the city."

"Don't you have to shop for food?" you ask.

"What for? I don't feel much like eating these days anyway."

This patient is showing clear symptoms of depression. List the symptoms of depression present in this case.

c. List four other symptoms or signs of depression.

(1)

(2)

(3)

(4)

d. List the risk factors for suicide present in this patient's history.

e. List four other risk factors for suicide.

(1)

(2)

(3)

(4)

f. List three questions you would ask to try to evaluate the patient's risk of suicide.

(1)

(2)

(3)

b. What symptoms and signs led you to that conclusion?

c. Are there any other diagnoses you need to take into consideration? ____ If so, what diagnoses?

d. How will you manage this patient?

7. You are called to a downtown office building for a "possible heart attack." Reaching the building, you are escorted into an office by a harried looking businessman. "It's my secretary," he says. "She's having some kind of cardiac attack." In the midst of a buzzing group of people, you see a woman who looks to be about 24 years old sitting wide-eyed and pale. People are fanning her with file folders and trying to get her to drink some water. You make your way through the crowd and ask the woman what her problem is.

"Can't breathe," she gasps. "Chest all tight (gasp). Feel like I'm going to pass out (gasp). Everything is unreal (gasp), like I'm dying (gasp)."

"Quick! Quick!" squeaks one of the bystanders. "Get her to the hospital!"

Ignoring the chorus demanding that you leave immediately for the hospital, you begin taking the woman's vital signs. Her pulse is 112 and regular, her respirations are 30 and deep, and her blood pressure is 160/88. You notice that her skin is cold and sweaty and her hands are shaking.

a. What do you think is this patient's problem?

8. You are called to a downtown bar to see a man who has apparently become disruptive there. A police officer meets you at the entrance to the bar. "Listen," he says, "the barkeep called *us* to deal with an unruly customer, but personally I think the guy's a psycho case—so I thought maybe you folks ought to take a look at him."

You enter the bar and find a well-dressed but dishevelled man pacing rapidly up and down. "One week from today," he is announcing, "one week from today, I'll be one of the richest men in America. I'm putting together a business empire now that will rule Wall Street." He is talking a mile a minute, cracking jokes, and gesturing extravagantly. He catches sight of you and your partner and says, "Well, hello fellas. Bartender, give these fine young people a drink, on me. They do a great public service. This country was built on public service, yes indeed it was. So give them a public service drink."

"You haven't paid for the drinks you already ordered," says the bartender.

"Listen, fathead, I said give these nice people a drink."

"Uh, sir," you break in, "we're not allowed to drink while on duty. And we thought maybe you'd like to take a little ride with us to the hospital."

"Hospital? What do I need to go to the hospital for? Never felt better in my life. By next week, I'll be able to *buy* the hospital, buy this bar too, buy the whole damned town."

One of the police officers says, "Maybe you *ought* to go with them, sir, just to get a checkup."

"Any of you puts a hand on me," replies the man, "I'll sue the whole lot of you. Assault. Battery. False imprisonment. I'll sue you for the whole lot, and let me tell you, you don't want to tangle with *my* team of lawyers. Best legal talent in the country. You wouldn't stand a chance."

a. What do you think is this man's problem?

b. What symptoms and signs led you to that conclusion?

c. How will you manage this patient?

9. You are called to a downtown street corner where several police officers are standing around apparently trying to talk to a somewhat wild-eyed man who could be anywhere from 55 to 75 years old. He is dressed in about six layers of tattered clothes and wearing a naval officer's cap. He clearly hasn't had a bath, shave, or haircut in weeks. "He was just walking down the middle of Main Street," says one of the police officers, "as if he didn't even notice the traffic—and all those horns blowing, people screeching on their brakes."

You introduce yourself to the man and ask whether you can be of help. He mumbles something that sounds like, "Dogs and cats."

"Sorry," you say, "I didn't quite catch what you said."

"Salt and pepper," he says. "Black and blue, I didn't, dontcha know, I didn't."

The police officer gives you a meaningful look.

How will you manage this case?

_____
_____
_____
_____
_____
_____
_____
_____
_____
_____
_____
_____
_____
_____
_____
_____
_____
_____
_____
_____
_____
_____
_____
_____

10. A middle-aged woman calls for an ambulance because "my son is acting real strange." When you arrive at the designated address, the woman greets you at the door. She tells you that her 20-year-old son won't come out of his room. He's been in there for 2 days now. Sometimes she hears him talking to someone, but there isn't anyone else there. "I'm sure it's all that karate stuff," she says. "It just went to his head, made him crazy, all that black belt business."

    You go up to the son's room and knock on the door.

    "You're not going to get me," says a voice from the other side of the door. "You won't take me alive."

    "Sir, we're paramedics. We've just come to talk with you."

    "You can't fool me. I know you're from the FBI. Well, you'll have to shoot me to take me."

    You try the door and find it's unlocked. Inside, a young man clothed in karate garb is sitting in an armchair, gripping the armrests.

    You introduce yourselves again. The patient looks away.

    "You won't take me alive," he says again in a monotone. He looks suddenly toward the wall. "I know, I know," he says to the wall.

    "Who are you talking to?" you ask.

    He looks startled. "The voices said you would come. They killed John Lennon, and the FBI is after me. The voices said not to let you take me alive."

    a. This patient is showing signs of

    A. A panic attack

    B. Psychosis

    C. Depression

    D. Mania

    E. Disorganization

    (Circle the best answer.)

    b. Are there any indications that he might become violent? _____ If so, what are the indications?

    c. How will you manage this case?

11. Certain situations have a higher potential for violence than others. List five situations or classes of patients that should activate the paramedic's "nose for danger."

    a.

    b.

    c.

    d.

    e.

12. Our thought for the day can be decoded in the usual fashion.

   a. Seeing or hearing things that
      aren't there   __ __ __ __ __ __ __ __ __ __ __ __
                      62 106 87 7   31 68 11 51 22 93 56 14 103

   b. A fixed, false idea   __ __ __ U __ __ __ __
                          39 80 112   76 34 53 92

   c. Repetitive expression of a single idea   __ __ __ __ E __ __ __ __ __ __ I __ __
                                       98 83 81 71   17 97 107 73 90   65 35

   d. Intense, irrational fear   __ __ __ __ __ __
                     58 2 94 78 24 84

   e. Having two opposite feelings at once   __ __ B __ __ __ __ __ __ __ __
                           6 49   88 5 99 111 46 85 61 108

   f. Describing repetitive, purposeless behavior   __ __ E __ __ __ __ __ __ __ __ __
                            47 95   19 91 30 1 113 21 50 33

   g. Disorientation and impaired understanding   __ __ N __ __ __ __ __ __
                          105 77   54 75 89 67 63 26

   h. Type of memory loss   __ __ __ __ E   __ __ A __ __
                  109 38 66 110   45 104   52 4

   i. Speech disorder with compulsive repetition of
      sounds heard   __ __ __ O __ __ __ I __
              16 36 29   64 43 32   69

   j. Feeling of uneasiness   __ __ X __ __ __ __ __
                9 42   101 40 72 60

   k. Inability to sit still   R __ __ __ __ __ __ __ __ __ __
              102 48 10 37 25 59 28 13 18 57 79

   l. Affect that shows little or no feeling is called   __ __ __ __
                          15 70 41 100

   m. Flight of ideas is a disorder of   __ __ __ __ G __ __
                    74 96 12 8   55 27

   n. Syphilis is one   __ __ __
               44 23 86

   o. Jealousy   __ N __ __
          3   82 20

Secret Message: __ __ __   __ __ __ __ __ __ __ __ __ __   __ __   __ __ __ __ __
                      1 2 3   4 5 6 7 8 9 10 11 12 13   14 15   16 17 18 19 20

__ __ __ __ __ __ __   __ __ __ __ __ __   __ __ __ __ __ __ __   __ __
21 22 23 24 25 26 27   28 29 30 31 32 33   34 35 36 37 38 39 40   41 42

__ __ __ __ __ __ __ __ __ __   __ __   __ __ __   __ __ __ __ __ __ __ __ __ __ __ __ __
43 44 45 46 47 48 49 50 51 52   53 54   55 56 57   58 59 60 61 62 63 64 65 66 67 68 69 70

__ __ __ __ __ __ .   __ __ __ __ __ __ __   __ __ __   __ __ __ __ __ __   __ __   __ __ __
71 72 73 74 75 76   77 78 79 80 81 82 83   84 85 86   87 88 89 90 91 92   93 94   95 96 97

__ __ __ __ __ __ __   __ __ __ __ __ __ __ __ __ .
98 99 100 101 102 103 104   105 106 107 108 109 110 111 112 113

39
Communications and Dispatching

1. You have just been appointed Communications Director for your regional EMS operation, and you have been asked to draw up plans for an EMS communications system. To do so, you have to figure out who needs to communicate with whom in such a system and what is the best technical means (pager, radio, land-line, or cellular phone) to achieve each link in the communications chain. Fill in the blanks below with the answers you have come up with.

a. _____ needs to be able to talk with _____. The best technical means of establishing that link is _____.

b. _____ needs to be able to talk with _____. The best technical means of establishing that link is a _____.

c. _____ needs to be able to talk with _____. The best technical means of establishing that link is _____.

d. _____ needs to be able to talk with _____. The best technical means of establishing that link is _____.

e. _____ needs to be able to talk with _____. The best technical means of establishing that link is _____.

f. _____ needs to be able to talk with _____. The best technical means of establishing that link is _____.

2. For each of the following statements, indicate whether the statement is most applicable to

V   VHF radio
U   UHF radio
C   Cellular telephone

____ Best means for calling the base from sky-scraper row downtown

____ Best means for calling the base from a rural, wooded area

____ Best means for sending a 12-lead ECG to medical command

____ Best means for calling a patient's family doctor

____ FCC-preferred for routine voice communications

____ FCC-approved for one-lead ECG transmission

____ Can be monitored by someone with a scanner

3. You are planning a radio system for your ambulance service, which consists of six vehicles serving an area of 150 square miles. List the components you will need, and state the function of each component.

Component	Function

4. Below is a transcript of a transmission between a paramedic unit in the field and a local hospital. The transmission does *not* follow the guidelines for good radio communications. Read through the transmission, and then list all the errors in it that you could find.

AMBULANCE: Medic 12 to County Hospital.
HOSPITAL: Who's calling County Hospital?
AMBULANCE: This is Medic 12.
HOSPITAL: Go ahead, Medic 12.
AMBULANCE: Be advised that we are en route to your location with Maggie Jones, a lady well endowed with adipose tissue who's complaining of SOB.
HOSPITAL: Could you please 10-9 that chief complaint?
AMBULANCE: What's the matter, are you deaf or something? S.O.B. S as in silly, O as in old, B as in bag. Stand by for the ECG. [Pause.]
AMBULANCE: Medic 12 to County Hospital. Did you get the strip?
HOSPITAL: Yes.
AMBULANCE: Say again.
HOSPITAL: Yes, we received the strip. The doctor wants to know how old the patient is.
AMBULANCE: She's 58.
HOSPITAL: And does she have any medical history?
AMBULANCE: Yeah, she's a cardiac patient and takes digitalis, Tenormin, Slow-K, Diuril, and a whole bunch of other stuff here.
HOSPITAL: Did you get any vitals?
AMBULANCE: That's affirmative. The BP is 180/120, the pulse is 44, and the respirations are, let's see, here it is, the respirations are 30.
HOSPITAL: Doctor's orders are to give 1 mg of atropine IV.
AMBULANCE: That's a 10-4. Will do.
HOSPITAL: What's your ETA?
AMBULANCE: About 10 minutes.
HOSPITAL: We'll see you then.
AMBULANCE: Roger. Pop a few doughnuts into the microwave for us, will you?

What's wrong with that transmission?

_____
_____
_____
_____
_____
_____
_____
_____
_____
_____
_____
_____
_____
_____
_____

5. Spell out each of the following words in the international phonetic alphabet:

    a. THE: _____

    b. QUICK: _____

    _____

    c. BROWN: _____

    _____

    d. FOX: _____

    e. JUMPED: _____

    _____

    f. OVER: _____

    g. LAZY: _____

    h. DOG: _____

6. The following statements come from a patient's case history. Arrange them in the correct order for transmission by radio to medical command.

    a. Pulse is 50 and regular, respirations are 36 and deep, and BP is 180/126.

    b. The patient has a history of high blood pressure.

    c. The deep tendon reflexes are hyperactive.

    d. Her daughter says the patient complained of a severe headache before she collapsed.

    e. The patient was still conscious when we arrived, but she rapidly lost consciousness.

    f. The patient is a 60-year-old woman who collapsed in the bathroom while sitting on the toilet.

    g. We are administering oxygen at 4 liters per minute by nasal cannula.

    h. The patient's medications include nitroglycerin and Aldomet.

    i. Her left pupil is larger than the right and does not react to light.

    j. She was apparently well until this morning.

    k. Her neck is somewhat stiff.

    l. She was hospitalized 6 years ago for an AMI.

    (1) _____   (5) _____   (9) _____

    (2) _____   (6) _____   (10) _____

    (3) _____   (7) _____   (11) _____

    (4) _____   (8) _____   (12) _____

7. To the paramedic knee-deep in mud trying to extricate the victim of a road traffic accident, the dispatcher's job looks pretty easy. In fact, the job is not easy at all. List four tasks the dispatcher has to perform to ensure that the EMS system operates as it should.

    a.

    b.

    c.

    d.

8. You are covering for the dispatcher during his lunch break. ("Don't worry about a thing," you tell him as he heads out the door. "This job's a piece of cake.") The dispatcher has no sooner departed than the telephone rings. You answer on the first ring, and a caller blurts out, "There's been a terrible accident. Oh my God, it's terrible, it's terrible," and he starts sobbing. List the questions you will ask this caller, and indicate at what point you will dispatch an ambulance.

    _____

    _____

    _____

    _____

    _____

    _____

    _____

    _____

    _____

    _____

    _____

    _____

    _____

    _____

9. Our thought for the day is something to keep in mind every time you pick up the radio mike.

   a. Radio system on two frequencies $\underline{}\ \underline{}\ \underline{}\ \underline{}\ \underline{}$ X

30 9 16 52 36

   b. Channel with a lot of interference $\underline{}\ \underline{}\ \underline{}\ \underline{}\ \underline{}$

45 23 58 10 49

   c. Transmission of physiologic data by radio $\underline{}\ \underline{}\ \underline{}\ \underline{}\ \underline{}$ L $\underline{}\ \underline{}\ \underline{}\ \underline{}\ \underline{}\ \underline{}$

50 20 44 14 39   6 37 56 25 28 7

   d. Miniature transmitter for rebroadcasting signals $\underline{}\ \underline{}$ P $\underline{}\ \underline{}\ \underline{}\ \underline{}$ R

13 27   51 48 55 17

   e. One cps $\underline{}\ \underline{}\ \underline{}\ \underline{}$ Z

26 34 40 11

   f. Portion of the radio frequency spectrum $\underline{}\ \underline{}\ \underline{}$ D

38 41 21

   g. Sound of a telephone $\underline{}\ \underline{}\ \underline{}\ \underline{}$

33 53 24 60

   h. Best way to find out a patient's chief complaint $\underline{}\ \underline{}\ \underline{}$

29 54 19

   i. Letter *N* in international phonetic alphabet $\underline{}\ \underline{}$ V $\underline{}\ \underline{}\ \underline{}\ \underline{}\ \underline{}$

59 8   2 35 1 46 5

   j. Errors $\underline{}\ \underline{}\ \underline{}\ \underline{}\ \underline{}$

22 32 4 3 15

   k. Principal $\underline{}\ \underline{}\ \underline{}\ \underline{}$

47 12 31 42

   l. Which patient needs TLC $\underline{}\ \underline{}\ \underline{}$

18 57 43

Secret Message: $\underline{}\ \underline{}\ \underline{}\ \underline{}\ \underline{}\ \underline{}\quad \underline{}\ \underline{}\ \underline{}\quad \underline{}\ \underline{}\ \underline{}\ \underline{}\ \underline{}\quad \underline{}\ \underline{}\ \underline{}\ \underline{}\ \underline{}\ \underline{}\ \underline{}\ \underline{}$

1 2 3 4 5 6   7 8 9   10 11 12 13 14   15 16 17 18 19 20 21 22

$\underline{}\ \underline{}\quad \underline{}\ \underline{}\ \underline{}\quad \underline{}\ \underline{}\ \underline{}\ \underline{}\ \underline{},\quad \underline{}\ \underline{}\ \underline{}\ \underline{}\ \underline{}\ \underline{}\ \underline{}\ \underline{}:\quad \underline{}\ \underline{}\ \underline{}\ \underline{}\ \underline{}\ \underline{}$

23 24   25 26 27   28 29 30 31 32   33 34 35 36 37 38 39 40   41 42 43 44 45 46

$\underline{}\ \underline{}\ \underline{}\quad \underline{}\ \underline{}\quad \underline{}\ \underline{}\ \underline{}\ \underline{}\ \underline{}\ \underline{}\ \underline{}\ \underline{}\ \underline{}.$

47 48 49   50 51   52 53 54 55 56 57 58 59 60

40
Rescue and Extrication

1. It's been a while since you straightened out the big tin box that houses all your rescue stuff. The box is pictured below. Eighteen items of rescue gear are jumbled up inside. Locate all your rescue equipment in the box. Make a list of what you've got, and indicate the possible use of each item in a rescue/extrication situation.

```
T U M M Y I T C H O C K S
I S H A M M E R C Y O M E
N O S T I S H O V E L L A
S H A C K S A W S L O B S
N R G O R Y N B R E R O H
I N O N E E D A M E S L A
P I G P E N W R X S N T R
O P G L E N I D E E E C D
O F L A R E N A R A T U H
F R E I N D C A V I C T A
O U S T E S H L E P V T T
S N A P O R T O P O W E R
O G L O V E S T E D O R R
```

Item	Use in a Rescue Situation	Item	Use in a Rescue Situation
_____	_____	_____	_____
_____	_____	_____	_____
_____	_____	_____	_____
_____	_____	_____	_____
_____	_____	_____	_____
_____	_____	_____	_____
_____	_____	_____	_____
_____	_____	_____	_____
_____	_____	_____	_____

2. In the accident scene pictured below are at least six hazards. Find the hazards, and describe what action you would take to deal with each.

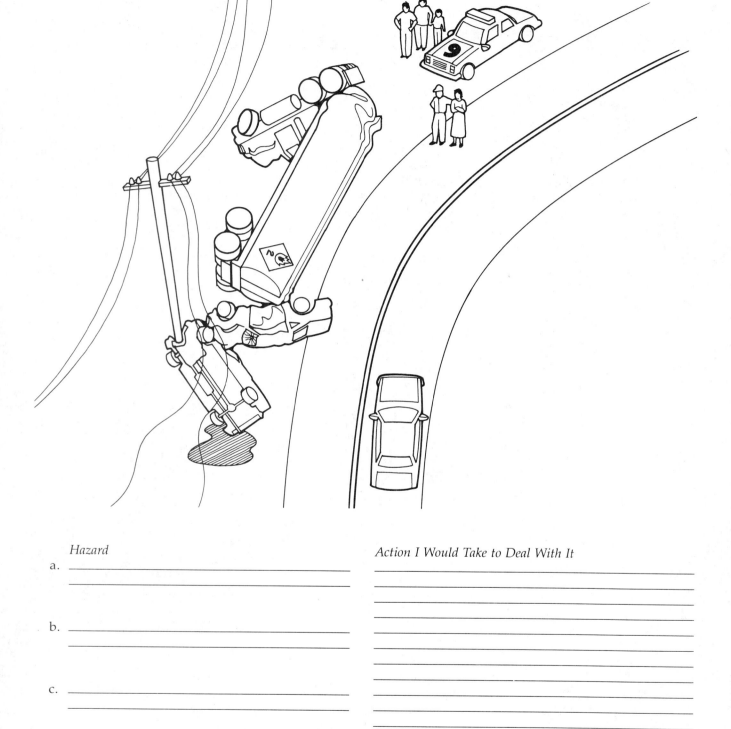

Hazard   *Action I Would Take to Deal With It*

a. _____

b. _____

c. _____

d. _____

e. _____
_____

_____

f. _____
_____

_____
_____
__ __
_____
_____
_____
_____
_____
_____

3. For each of the following statements about rescue and extrication, indicate whether the statement is true or false. If the statement is false, explain *why* it is false.

a. The primary function of a paramedic in an extrication is to direct the disentanglement of the patient from the wreckage.

TRUE   FALSE because _____
_____
_____

b. The most efficient access to a patient in a badly damaged vehicle is usually through a window on the passenger side of the vehicle.

TRUE   FALSE because _____
_____
_____

c. Care of the accident victim should start even before the victim is removed from the vehicle.

TRUE   FALSE because _____
_____
_____

d. The paramedic should use a "hot stick" and wear insulated gloves to remove downed wires that are in contact with a disabled vehicle.

TRUE   FALSE because _____
_____
_____

e. The best way to prevent the battery in a wrecked vehicle from shorting out and causing an explosion is to disconnect the battery wires.

TRUE   FALSE because _____
_____
_____

f. A disabled vehicle that is upright on four wheels still needs to be stabilized before anyone enters to reach the injured inside.

TRUE   FALSE because _____
_____
_____
_____

4. You and your crew (two other paramedics) are called to the scene of a highway accident just outside of town. Arriving at the scene, you see a late-model sedan accordioned against a utility pole. The windshield is shattered. The driver is unconscious, bleeding, and tightly pinned between the steering wheel and the seat. There are no passengers.

a. List in order the steps you would take. Include details of how you would reach the patient.

b. List the actions you would take after the patient has been transferred to the care of emergency room personnel.

Stop and Review IV

We have covered a lot of material in 40 chapters—much more than can be reviewed in a single exercise. So in this last review section, we shall simply take a sampling of some of the topics of the previous 40 chapters. If you draw a blank on any of the questions, go back and review the material in more detail.

1. List four symptoms or signs of choking.

   a.

   b.

   c.

   d.

2. List three indications for endotracheal intubation in the prehospital setting.

   a.

   b.

   c.

3. You are treating a middle-aged man who has been injured in a road accident and is pinned inside the wreckage. You are administering oxygen by non-rebreathing mask at a flow rate of 10 liters per minute. The pressure gauge on your portable E cylinder reads 800 psi. The cylinder constant for an E cylinder is 0.26 liters/psi. How much more time do you have before you have to get a fresh E cylinder? (Show your calculations.)

4. List eight indications for administering oxygen.

   a.

   b.

   c.

   d.

   e.

   f.

   g.

   h.

   List contraindications to administering oxygen.

5. Jumbled up in the grid below are 40 structures of the human body. Find the structures and then sort them out according to the organ system to which they belong.

```
S L I V E R I F Y S H O P S
P E A S P U B I S C H I U M
L I A C E T A B U L U M P T
A F A R A B R U T E R U S T
N L A M G R R L O R B I T E
T A T L A S P A N C R E A S
I R R O L T R A I A O O R K
B Y I I L O E L L N N L A I
I N U M B M P R O U C H O D
A X M O L A B I A S H O R N
F A T R A C H E A T U I T E
T E A M D H O P Y N S L A Y
A I M E D L O L L E T E N T
R E S U E D U O D E N U M A
S O V A R Y E N O L U M B A
A V E I N O V A G U S R I E
L E T C U R E T E R M B A T
```

CARDIOVASCULAR SYSTEM

_____

_____

_____

NERVOUS SYSTEM

_____

_____

_____

_____

_____

MUSCULOSKELETAL SYSTEM

_____

_____

_____

_____

_____

_____

_____

_____

_____

_____

URINARY SYSTEM

_____

RESPIRATORY SYSTEM

_____

_____

_____

GASTROINTESTINAL SYSTEM

_____

_____

_____

_____

_____

FEMALE REPRODUCTIVE SYSTEM

_____

_____

_____

6. List six symptoms and signs of hypovolemic shock.

a.

b.

c.

d.

e.

f.

7. List five drugs that may be given via an endotracheal tube when an IV cannot be rapidly established.

a.

b.

c.

d.

e.

8. A 52-year-old man calls for an ambulance because of chest pain.

   a. List six questions you would ask in taking the *history of the present illness.*

   (1)   (4)

   (2)   (5)

   (3)   (6)

   b. Here is the patient's ECG rhythm strip. Answer the questions that follow the ECG.

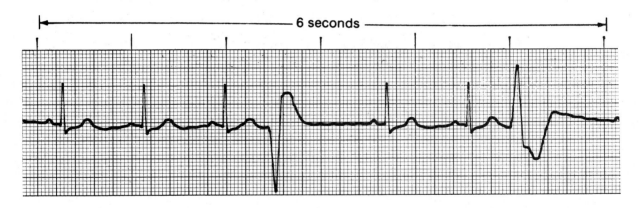

   RHYTHM: _____ regular _____ irregular
   RATE: _____ per minute
   P WAVES: _____ present _____ absent
         If present, is there a P before every QRS? _____ yes _____ no
                       Is there a QRS after every P?   _____ yes _____ no
   P–R INTERVAL: _____ seconds
   QRS complexes: _____ normal _____ abnormal
   Name of rhythm: _____
   Treatment: _____

9. When called to a road accident, the paramedic needs to examine not only the patient but also the _vehicle_, for the type of damage that the vehicle sustained may provide clues to the patient's injuries. For each type of vehicular damage listed below, list the type(s) of injuries most likely to be associated.

Vehicular Damage	_Look for These Injuries_
Deformed steering column	_____
	_____
	_____
	_____
	_____
Driver's door staved in	_____
Front windshield cracked	_____
Dashboard on passenger side deformed	_____
	_____
	_____

10. List five methods for the control of external hemorrhage, and indicate which method is the most effective.

   a.

   b.

   c.

   d.

   e.

11. You are called late one night for a "man down" in a somewhat disreputable section of the city. Arriving at the scene, you find a shabbily dressed man of middle age slumped unconscious in an alley. He is not carrying any wallet or identification. The police say they've no idea how long he has been there. On examination, the man is unresponsive to painful stimulus. His skin is cool and dry. Vital signs are pulse 53 and regular, respirations 32 and deep, and blood pressure 200/120. The lighting isn't good enough to allow an assessment for Battle's sign or coon's eyes, but you can determine that there is no blood or fluid coming from the ears or nose. The left pupil is dilated and does not react to light. The breath smells of alcohol. The chest is clear. The abdomen is soft. The legs appear somewhat stiff, and it's hard to flex them.

   a. List five causes of unconsciousness, and put an asterisk beside the one you think is the most likely cause in this case.

   (1)

   (2)

   (3)

   (4)

   (5)

   b. List the steps you would take in treating this patient.

12. Match the musculoskeletal injury in column A with the complication or other injury in column B most likely to be associated with it.

Column A
Pelvic fracture

Calcaneal fracture

Humeral shaft fracture

Posterior dislocation of the clavicle

Elbow fracture

Posterior dislocation of the hip

Open fracture

Patellar fracture

Column B
Fracture of L1/L2 of the spine

Volkmann's ischemic contracture

Posterior dislocation of the hip

Foot drop

Wrist drop

Pneumothorax

Infection

Ruptured bladder

13. List eight "load-and-go" situations.

a.

b.

c.

d.

e.

f.

g.

h.

14. List four signs of respiratory distress.

a.

b.

c.

d.

15. You are called to a college dormitory to treat a young man who "can't breathe." The patient's roommate tells you that the patient is an asthmatic and has been "wheezy" all day. The patient himself can scarcely give you any history because he's too short of breath to talk. When you ask him what medications he has already taken today, he gestures to his Ventolin and Intal inhalers and a bottle of Tedral tablets on his bureau. On physical examination, he looks pale and apprehensive. He is sitting upright, leaning forward, struggling to breathe. His pulse is 140 and somewhat weak, his respirations are 40 and very shallow, and his blood pressure is 120/70 on exhalation and 100/65 on inhalation. His chest is hyperresonant, and breath sounds are very hard to hear.

a. List the steps you would take in treating this patient.

b. Here is the patient's ECG rhythm strip. Answer the questions that follow the ECG.

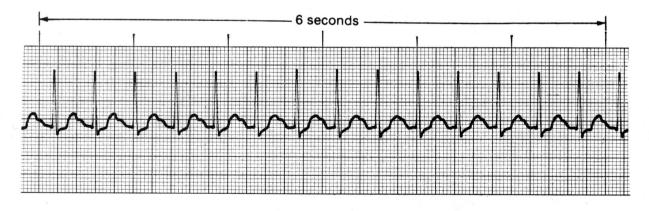

RHYTHM: _____ regular _____ irregular
RATE: _____ per minute
P WAVES: _____ present _____ absent
      If present, is there a P before every QRS? _____ yes _____ no
            Is there a QRS after every P? _____ yes _____ no
P–R INTERVAL: _____ seconds
QRS complexes: _____ normal _____ abnormal
Name of rhythm: _____
Treatment: _____

16. A 62-year-old woman calls for an ambulance because of shortness of breath. She says she was wakened from sleep by a suffocating sensation and she had to get up and pace around in order to catch her breath at all. She takes medicines for "blood pressure," but she can't remember where she put them. On physical examination, you find an agitated woman in considerable distress. She seems confused. Her skin is cool and wet. Her pulse is around 110 and erratic, her respirations are 40 and noisy, and her blood pressure is 190/116. Her neck veins are not distended. Her chest is full of wheezes and crackles. Her abdomen is soft. She has 2+ ankle edema.

a. List the steps you would take in treating this patient.

b. Here is the patient's ECG rhythm strip. Answer the questions that follow the ECG.

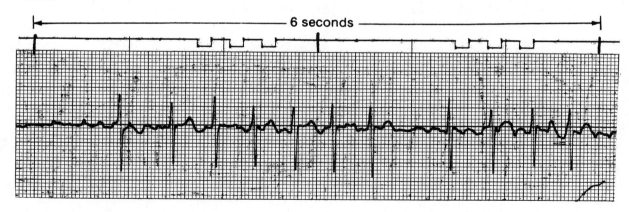

RHYTHM: _____ regular _____ irregular
RATE: _____ per minute
P WAVES: _____ present _____ absent
    If present, is there a P before every QRS? _____ yes _____ no
              Is there a QRS after every P?   _____ yes _____ no
P–R INTERVAL: _____ seconds
QRS complexes: _____ normal _____ abnormal
Name of rhythm: _____
Treatment: _____

17. You are called one fine autumn morning for a "possible stroke." You arrive at the designated address, a small wooden house about 10 minutes from the hospital, and are greeted at the door by a middle-aged woman. "I just came by to check on Mother this morning," the woman says, "and I found her very confused. She also seems to have wet the bed, and she's never had a problem like that before. As a matter of fact, she's never been sick before. The only medicine she's ever taken are Carter's Little Liver Pills, and don't ask me how she decided she needed those."

In the living room, you find a frail-appearing 78-year-old woman sitting in her nightdress. She is awake but confused; she knows who she is, but not where she is or what day, month, or year it is. Her speech is slurred, and she responds only slowly to questions. Her skin feels cold and dry. Her pulse is around 40 and weak, respirations are 16, and her blood pressure is 106/70 and very faint to auscultation. The right side of the patient's face seems to be drooping. Her breath has a fruity smell. Her chest is clear. Her abdomen is soft. Her right arm and leg are weaker than the left.

a. List the steps you would take in treating this patient.

b. Here is the patient's ECG rhythm strip. Answer the questions that follow the ECG.

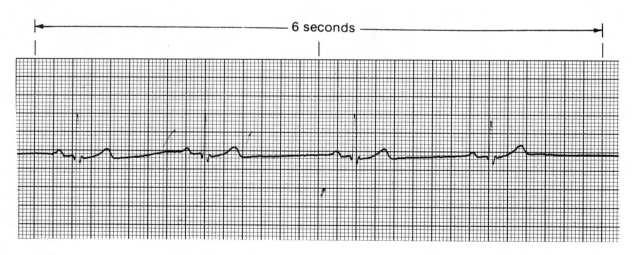

RHYTHM: _____ regular _____ irregular
RATE: _____ per minute
P WAVES: _____ present _____ absent
    If present, is there a P before every QRS? _____ yes _____ no
        Is there a QRS after every P? _____ yes _____ no
P–R INTERVAL: _____ seconds
QRS complexes: _____ normal _____ abnormal
Name of rhythm: _____
Treatment: _____

c. The treatment of this woman's dysrhythmia required the use of a certain drug, namely

_____.

(1) List the *indications* for giving that drug.

(2) List the *contraindications* to giving that drug.

(3) List the *side effects* of that drug.

(4) What *dosage* did you give?

18. For each of the following statements, indicate whether the statement is true or false.

a. A hypoglycemic person may appear to be drunk.

TRUE   FALSE

b. A patient who has fainted should be helped into a sitting position.

TRUE   FALSE

c. If a patient with a stroke is unable to speak, he or she is also unable to understand what others are saying.

TRUE   FALSE

d. The induction of vomiting is contraindicated in a patient who has swallowed a volatile hydrocarbon like lighter fluid.

TRUE   FALSE

e. The best way to avoid contracting or spreading a communicable disease is to wash your hands after every call.

TRUE   FALSE

f. Elderly patients are usually hypochondriacs.

TRUE   FALSE

19. List eight medical problems to which alcoholics are particularly susceptible.

a.

b.

c.

d.

e.

f.

g.

h.

20. List eight clues that would lead you to suspect that an injured child was the victim of physical abuse.

a.

b.

c.

d.

e.

f.

g.

h.

21. List four risk factors for postpartum hemorrhage.

a.

b.

c.

d.

22. A 25-year-old woman calls for an ambulance because of abdominal pain. She says that the pain started the previous day as cramping in the right lower quadrant. It just kept getting worse and worse, and now her whole abdomen hurts and she even has pain in her right shoulder. When you ask her about her last menstrual period, she says, "I finally got my period this morning, 2 weeks late. I was really starting to worry." On physical examination, the woman seems restless and apprehensive. Her skin is cool and damp. Her pulse is 100 and regular, respirations are 28, and blood pressure is 106/60. The chest is clear. The abdomen feels hard and is diffusely tender.

a. List the steps you would take in treating this patient.

b. Here is the patient's ECG rhythm strip. Answer the questions that follow the ECG.

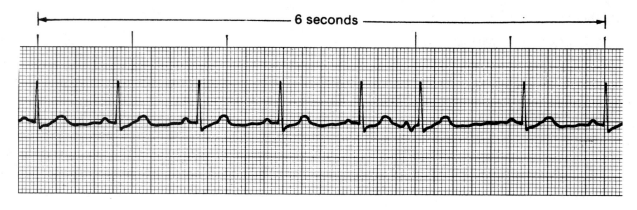

RHYTHM: _____ regular _____ irregular
RATE: _____ per minute
P WAVES: _____ present _____ absent
      If present, is there a P before every QRS? _____ yes _____ no
                Is there a QRS after every P? _____ yes _____ no
P–R INTERVAL: _____ seconds
QRS complexes: _____ normal _____ abnormal
Name of rhythm: _____
Treatment: _____

23. A 53-year-old woman calls for an ambulance because of "heaviness in my chest." Here is her ECG rhythm strip. Answer the questions that follow the strip.

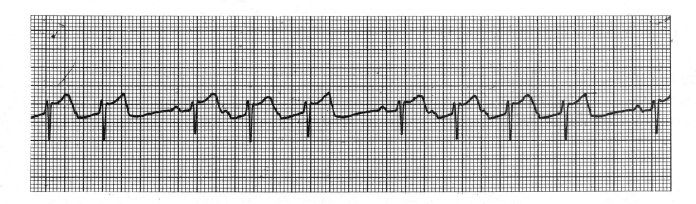

RHYTHM: _____ regular _____ irregular
RATE: _____ per minute
P WAVES: _____ present _____ absent
        If present, is there a P before every QRS? _____ yes _____ no
               Is there a QRS after every P? _____ yes _____ no
P–R INTERVAL: _____ seconds
QRS complexes: _____ normal _____ abnormal
Name of rhythm: _____
Treatment: _____

24. A 75-year-old man called for an ambulance because of "heavy" chest pain that started half an hour ago when he was trying to change a tire on his car. The patient has a history of angina, and he took a nitroglycerin tablet when the pain started, but it didn't help. You find him sitting on the back steps of his house, looking pale and apprehensive. His skin is cool and damp. The pulse seems rather rapid. Blood pressure is 180/100. Respirations are 32 per minute.

a. Here is the patient's 12-lead ECG. Fill in the information required.

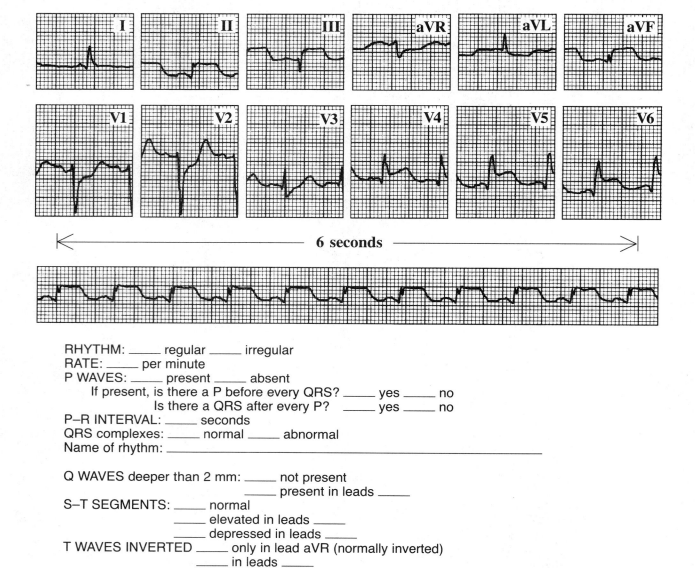

RHYTHM: _____ regular _____ irregular
RATE: _____ per minute
P WAVES: _____ present _____ absent
        If present, is there a P before every QRS? _____ yes _____ no
        Is there a QRS after every P?   _____ yes _____ no
P–R INTERVAL: _____ seconds
QRS complexes: _____ normal _____ abnormal
Name of rhythm: _____

Q WAVES deeper than 2 mm: _____ not present
                          _____ present in leads _____
S–T SEGMENTS: _____ normal
              _____ elevated in leads _____
              _____ depressed in leads _____
T WAVES INVERTED _____ only in lead aVR (normally inverted)
                 _____ in leads _____

Portion(s) of the heart affected: _____ inferior wall _____ lateral wall
                                  _____ anterior wall _____ other

Pathophysiologic process: _____ ischemia _____ injury _____ infarction

b. Is this patient a candidate for thrombolytic therapy? _____ Why or why not?

25. A 65-year-old waitress at the local diner calls for an ambulance because of sharp
    pains in her chest, "probably from eating the rot we serve here," she tells you.
    The pain started about an hour after lunch and has continued for 2 or 3 hours.
    The waitress seems in moderate distress. Her vital signs are unremarkable, and
    there are no pathologic findings on physical exmaination. Here is her ECG. Fill
    in the information required.

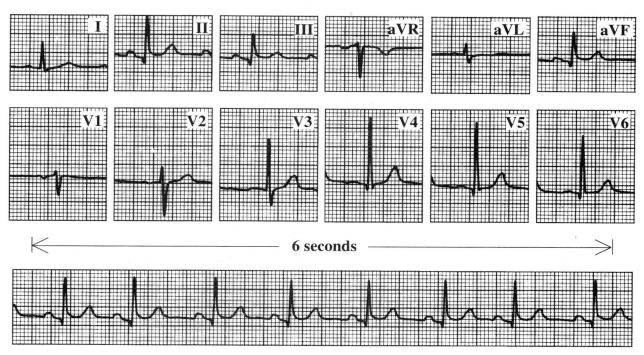

RHYTHM: _____ regular _____ irregular
RATE: _____ per minute
P WAVES: _____ present _____ absent
       If present, is there a P before every QRS? _____ yes _____ no
                      Is there a QRS after every P?   _____ yes _____ no
P–R INTERVAL: _____ seconds
QRS complexes: _____ normal _____ abnormal
Name of rhythm: _____

Q WAVES deeper than 2 mm: _____ not present
                          _____ present in leads _____
S–T SEGMENTS: _____ normal
              _____ elevated in leads _____
              _____ depressed in leads _____
T WAVES INVERTED _____ only in lead aVR (normally inverted)
                 _____ in leads _____

Portion(s) of the heart affected: _____ inferior wall _____ lateral wall
                                  _____ anterior wall _____ other

Pathophysiologic process: _____ ischemia _____ injury _____ infarction

26. You are called to a nursing home to see an elderly woman who is "feeling poorly." She states that she just feels "washed out." She does not complain of any pain. Her pulse is not abnormal. Her blood pressure is 160/98, and her respirations are 24 per minute.

 a. Here is her 12-lead ECG. Fill in the information required.

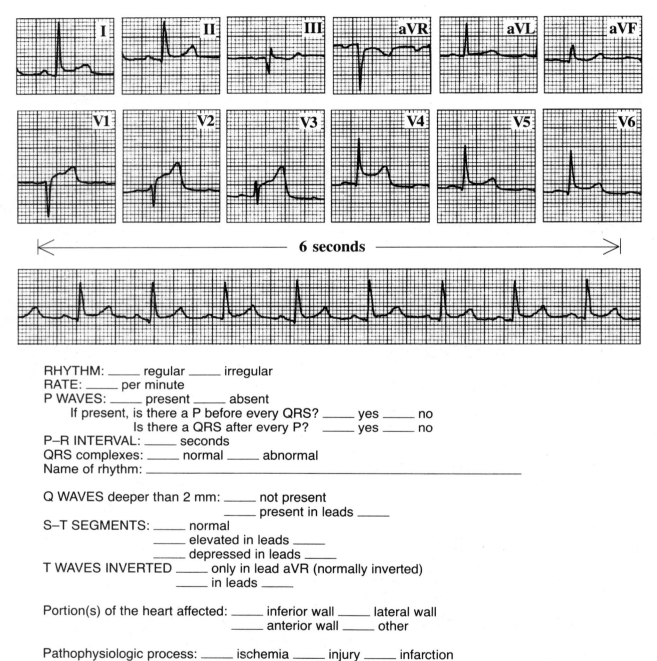

RHYTHM: _____ regular _____ irregular
RATE: _____ per minute
P WAVES: _____ present _____ absent
      If present, is there a P before every QRS? _____ yes _____ no
             Is there a QRS after every P? _____ yes _____ no
P–R INTERVAL: _____ seconds
QRS complexes: _____ normal _____ abnormal
Name of rhythm: _____

Q WAVES deeper than 2 mm: _____ not present
                          _____ present in leads _____
S–T SEGMENTS: _____ normal
              _____ elevated in leads _____
              _____ depressed in leads _____
T WAVES INVERTED _____ only in lead aVR (normally inverted)
              _____ in leads _____

Portion(s) of the heart affected: _____ inferior wall _____ lateral wall
                                  _____ anterior wall _____ other

Pathophysiologic process: _____ ischemia _____ injury _____ infarction

 b. List the steps in managing this patient.

27. You are called to a physician's office to transport a 75-year-old man to the hospital. The physician says that his patient had come in that morning "to get something for his gas pains." The physician took an ECG and noticed that it had changed significantly since the patient's previous ECG a year ago. Here is the ECG. Fill in the information required.

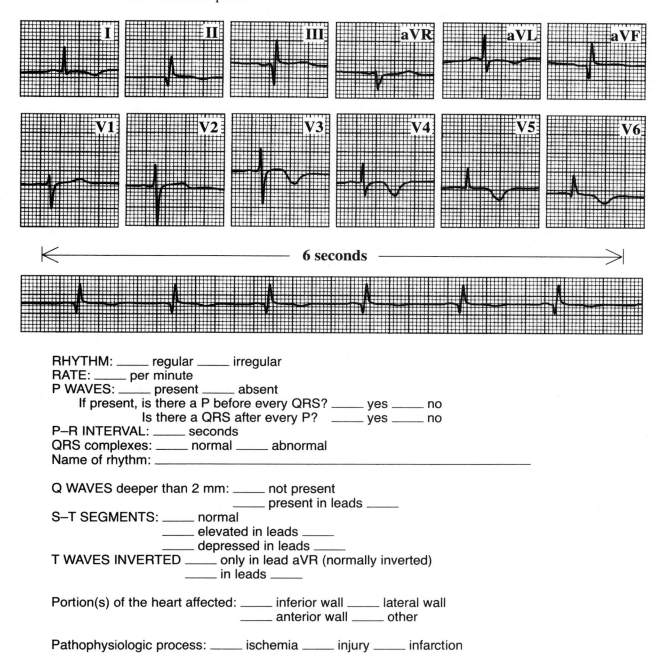

6 seconds

RHYTHM: _____ regular _____ irregular
RATE: _____ per minute
P WAVES: _____ present _____ absent
        If present, is there a P before every QRS? _____ yes _____ no
                Is there a QRS after every P? _____ yes _____ no
P–R INTERVAL: _____ seconds
QRS complexes: _____ normal _____ abnormal
Name of rhythm: _____

Q WAVES deeper than 2 mm: _____ not present
                                _____ present in leads _____
S–T SEGMENTS: _____ normal
               _____ elevated in leads _____
               _____ depressed in leads _____
T WAVES INVERTED _____ only in lead aVR (normally inverted)
                       _____ in leads _____

Portion(s) of the heart affected: _____ inferior wall _____ lateral wall
                                       _____ anterior wall _____ other

Pathophysiologic process: _____ ischemia _____ injury _____ infarction

28. And finally, our thought for the year. Decode it in the usual way.

a. Abnormally rapid breathing __ __ C __ __ __ __ __ __
    92 14   54 32 56 69 46 50

b. Increased blood flow to a tissue __ __ __ __ __ __ __ __ A
    2 27 17 28 83 41 4 37

c. Retroperitoneal organ __ __ D __ __ __
    51 59   24 65 93

d. Branch of the trachea __ __ __ __ C __ __ __
    64 12 21 61   40 79 74

e. Transmitting physiologic data by radio __ __ L __ __ __ __ __ __ __
    1 71   52 9 55 85 87 77

f. Weakness __ A __ __ __ __ __
    10   72 18 63 88 6

g. Vascular abdominal tissue __ __ __ __ __ __ __ __ Y
    49 73 66 35 26 53 60 90

h. Ear inflammation __ __ __ __ __ __
    89 7 82 44 23 20

i. Affect __ __ __ __ __ O __
    3 36 78 48 8   22

j. Sound made by little feet __ __ __ __ E __ __ __ __ __ E __
    86 68 16 75 80   42 25 70 58 19

k. What *tachy-* means __ __ __ __
    81 43 30 39

l. Water moving across a semipermeable membrane __ __ __ __ __ __ __
    11 84 29 5 76 91 33

m. Immediate __ __ __ __ A __ __
    45 15 38 67 47 13

n. Abbreviation for "right away" __ __ __ __
    31 62 57 34

Secret Message: __ __ __   __ __ __ __   __ __ __ __ __ __ __ __ __   __ __ __ __ __ __   __ __
    1 2 3   4 5 6 7   8 9 10 11 12 13 14 15 16   17 18 19 20 21 22   23 24

__ __ __   __ __ __   __ __ __ __ __ __   __ __   __ __ __   __ __ __ __ __ __ __.   __ __ __ __
25 26 27   28 29 30   31 32 33 34 35 36   37 38   39 40 41   42 43 44 45 46 47 48   49 50 51 52

__ __ __   __ __ __ __ __ __ __ __,   __ __ __ __   __ __ __ __ __ __ __ __ __
53 54 55   56 57 58 59 60 61 62 63   64 65 66 67   68 69 70 71 72 73 74 75 76

__ __ __ __   __ __ __ __ __   __ __ __ __ __ __ __ __.
77 78 79 80   81 82 83 84 85   86 87 88 89 90 91 92 93

ANSWERS

1
Roles and Responsibilities of the Paramedic

1. There is bound to be some variation among the lists that different people compile to describe the attributes of the "ideal paramedic." Your list should, though, include most of the following:

   a. **Caring,** compassionate

   b. **Calm** under pressure

   c. **Courteous**

   d. **Friendly**

   e. **Knows his** (or her) **stuff**

   f. **Knows his** (or her) **limitations**

   g. Shows **leadership ability;** takes charge

   h. **Efficient** and **well-organized**

   i. **Professional**

   j. Pays **attention to details**

   k. Takes **pride** in doing a good job

   l. **Dependable**

   m. **Neat,** clean, scrubbed, polished

   The important point about this question is that in answering it—and in making a list of what *you* consider the most important attributes of a good paramedic—you are defining the goals toward which you yourself should work. The paramedic you want on the scene to treat someone you care about is the kind of paramedic you should strive to be.

2. Again, there are many possible answers to this question because paramedics have many responsibilities. Among those that were mentioned in the textbook are

   a. Responsibility for the **care of the vehicle** and its gear

   b. Responsibility to make a **prompt, efficient response** to an emergency

   c. Responsibility for rapidly gaining **control of a scene,** managing bystanders, and removing patients from possible hazards

   d. Responsibility for **protecting the patient's interests**

   e. Responsibility for **stabilizing the patient** prior to transport and ensuring continuing care en route to the hospital

   f. Responsibility for supplying a **thorough and accurate report** of the patient's history, physical findings, and treatment to the doctor or nurse who takes over the patient's care

3. Also among the responsibilities of a paramedic is the responsibility for mastering a whole gamut of new skills that you were not permitted to deploy as an EMT-A. Among those new skills are

   a. Endotracheal **intubation**

   b. **Suctioning** through an endotracheal tube

   c. **Intravenous cannulation**

   d. Cardiac **rhythm interpretation**

   e. Cardioversion and **defibrillation**

   f. Administration of **medications** by various routes

   g. In some systems, cricothyrotomy, translaryngeal jet ventilation, and needle decompression of a pneumothorax

   If you mentioned any five of the above, mark your answer correct.

4. Medical control is the **supervision by a physician** that provides the legal framework within which a paramedic is permitted to work. Medical control is important not solely for legal reasons but also **to ensure the highest possible standard of care** for the patient.

5. Medical control, in fact, takes several forms.

   a. Examples of *prospective* medical control:

      (1) Establishment of **training standards** for paramedics
      (2) Establishment of **protocols** and standing orders
      (3) Deciding on **operational guidelines** for the system

   b. Examples of *immediate* medical control:

      (1) **Interpretation of telemetered electrocardiogram** by base station physician
      (2) **Voice orders** by base station physician to administer a certain dosage of a certain drug

   c. Examples of *retrospective* medical control:

      (1) Weekly **debriefing** sessions among paramedics, emergency room nurses, and emergency room doctors to discuss difficult cases
      (2) Statistical **analysis** of all ambulance calls of the preceding month **to evaluate response times**

6. Retrospective medical control can be a form of continuing medical education. Among some of the other ways to keep your skills fresh and your knowledge up to date are

   a. Reading professional **journals**

   b. Participating in **workshops** or conferences

   c. **Teaching** others

   d. Arranging for periodic **manikin practice**

   e. **Reviewing your textbook!**

   Perhaps you had some other ideas as well. What is important is not *how* you keep your skills sharp and your knowledge current, but only that you do so. Find the strategy that works best for you—but keep in mind your state's CME requirements as well.

7. Were you able to find all 25 words?

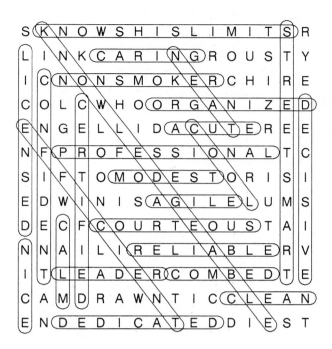

a. A paramedic who has passed the written and practical examinations of the National Registry of Emergency Medical Technicians is said to be **certified.**

b. When a paramedic obtains official permission from a state agency to practice as a paramedic in that state, the paramedic is **licensed.**

c. Being a **professional** means conforming to the standards of conduct and performance in a given area.

2
EMS Systems

1. The links in the EMS chain are

   a. RECOGNITION of the emergency and FIRST AID by bystanders (which means **public education**)

   b. INITIATION of the EMS RESPONSE (i.e., **activating the system**)

   c. TREATMENT AT THE SCENE by members of the EMS system

   d. TRANSPORTATION WITH ADVANCED LIFE SUPPORT in a suitable vehicle

   e. TREATMENT IN THE HOSPITAL

   f. COMMUNICATIONS

   g. EDUCATION and TRAINING

   h. PLANNING and ORGANIZATION

   i. EVALUATION and RESEARCH

2. If John Q. Citizen is to make optimal use of the EMS system in his community, he must know

   a. **How to recognize an emergency** when it happens

   b. **How to call for help** (what phone number to call, what information to give to the EMS dispatcher)

   c. **What to do until help arrives** (e.g., how to perform CPR, how to stop bleeding)

3. In a modern EMS system, some treatment is initiated at the scene, even if it may not be possible to stabilize the patient completely before transport.

   a. Treatment is started at the scene **to improve the patient's chances of survival or to lessen the risk of further injury.** For example, delaying the initiation of CPR or defibrillation until the patient in cardiac arrest reaches the hospital will almost certainly eliminate the patient's chances for survival. Similarly, moving a patient who has sustained fractures without first stabilizing the fractured extremities in some fashion is very likely to result in further injury.

   b. A patient who has suffered **major trauma,** especially if he has **internal bleeding** or is in **shock,** cannot be completely stabilized before transport. He will have to be moved without unnecessary delay to the nearest appropriate medical facility, with stabilizing measures performed en route to the hospital. (We will deal with this matter in considerably more detail in Chapter 20 when we discuss advanced trauma life support.)

4. Transportation of the sick or injured patient to the hospital is now part of the process of prehospital emergency *care.* Therefore today's ambulance transport requires the following:

   a. **Ambulances that meet minimal design specifications** (hearses just won't do anymore!).

   b. **Medical equipment aboard the ambulances—** sometimes quite sophisticated medical equipment, such as a defibrillator.

   c. If advanced life support is required, the ambulance must be staffed with **personnel at least at the level of paramedic,** and the paramedics must be in radio contact with a physician.

You should have listed at least two of the above three features of transport for a correct answer.

5. Let's see what kind of judgments you made about where to bring your patients:

__C__   A 20-year-old woman, rescued at 10 A.M. from a house fire, with third-degree burns over 35 percent of her body.

A third-degree burn of this magnitude is a critical burn, and a patient with a critical burn needs to be in a burn unit. Doodleberry General houses the regional burn center, so that is the place to take this woman.

__C,D__   A 42-year-old man involved in a vehicular accident around midnight; he is found unconscious, in shock, with massive trauma to the chest.

This one is a judgment call. The patient is critically injured, and there's no doubt that he belongs in a regional trauma center. The question is whether he is going to stay alive long enough to get there. (At a distance of 30 miles, it's probably at least a 30-minute drive. And at that distance, you won't save much time calling for the helicopter; by the time it gets into the air, you could already be halfway to the University Hospital by road.) So if you choose to go first to Doodleberry General—about 15 minutes away—to see if they can stabilize the patient there, you couldn't be faulted. This is a prime case for consulting by radio with your medical director and letting him or her make the final decision.

__C__   A 14-year-old boy who sustained a probable fracture to the forearm while skateboarding to school.

There's no reason why Ambling Community Hospital can't handle a simple fracture that occurs during the day, especially when they have an orthopedic surgeon on the staff.

__D__   A construction worker who fell 30 feet from a scaffolding and complains that he can't move his legs.

A patient suspected of having sustained a spinal cord injury—which means *any* patient who has fallen from a considerable height, not just one who is already showing signs of spinal cord transection like this man—belongs in a major trauma center (or a specialized spinal cord injury unit, if there is one within a reasonable distance). The extra 15 minutes or so it may take to get to the trauma center will not make a difference in the case as described.

__B__   A 51-year-old man who experienced crushing chest pains after supper.

Babcockle County Hospital ought to be able to handle a possible acute myocardial infarction (heart attack), since they have a coronary care unit. There is no reason to take the patient any farther from his home.

__A__   A 12-year-old girl who suffered an acute asthmatic attack during school.

During daylight hours, the community hospital is staffed well enough to handle a routine case, like an asthmatic attack. Probably the emergency room nurses at Ambling Community Hospital know the patient from previous visits, which will be helpful all around.

__B__   A cardiac arrest victim, with CPR in progress, who had collapsed during a morning meeting in his office.

When you're doing CPR in transit, you don't want to have to travel very far, so Babcockle County is a good destination—probably not more than about 6 minutes away. Why not go to the Community Hospital? The reason is that if you do succeed in resuscitating this patient, he will need to be in a coronary care unit, and the Community Hospital hasn't got one. So it's preferable to take him to the hospital where he can be admitted.

__A__   A 20-year-old man with abdominal pain suspected to be acute appendicitis.

There's no reason why the Community Hospital can't handle this one. Granted, if the call came in at night, the surgeon, laboratory technician, x-ray technician, and possibly the operating room team would have to be called in from home, but an hour's delay shouldn't make much difference. In a case of this sort, the patient's preference should also be taken into consideration (he may, for instance, have a family doctor who practices at Babcockle County and thus prefer to be taken there).

Did you come up with the same choices as those listed above? Were you influenced by the coffee and doughnuts awaiting you in the nurses' lounge at Ambling Community Hospital?!

6. As we shall learn in more detail in Chapter 39, an EMS communications system has to provide for at least the following linkages:

   - **Citizen to dispatch center**
   - **Dispatch center to ambulances**
   - **Dispatch center to hospitals**
   - **Dispatch center to medical control**
   - **Dispatch center to other services**
   - **Ambulance to hospitals**
   - **Paramedic to medical control**

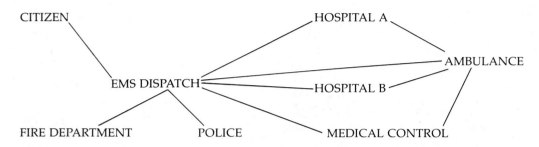

7. There are an almost endless number of issues that must be addressed in establishing an EMS system. Here are five examples:

   a. Where will the ambulances be stationed?

   b. How many levels of service will the system include? EMT-As only? EMT-As plus first responders? EMT-As, first responders, and paramedics?

   c. Who will be responsible for medical command?

   d. How will ambulances restock after a call? (Will they be allowed to restock from emergency room supplies at each hospital?)

   e. Who will make the transport decision, that is, the decision *where* to bring the patient (a thorny issue!)?

   How many other issues did you come up with?

8. Again, there are as many possible research projects as there are problems in EMS delivery. Here's one simple project:

   Review all the trip sheets of cardiac arrest calls for the past year to determine the average response time. Are you getting to all the arrests within 5 minutes? If not, are there ways you could move faster? Should you introduce another tier into your system, such as first responders, who could get to any given location more quickly?

3
Medicolegal and Ethical Issues

1. How many of the 25 words did you find?

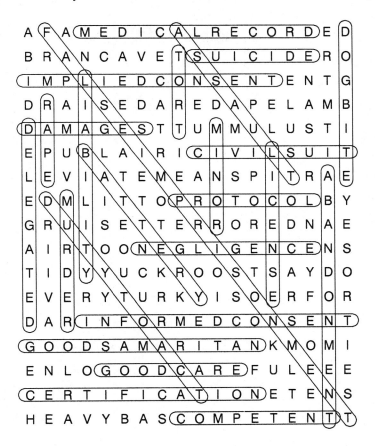

a. The intentional and unjustified detention of a person against his will: **false imprisonment**

b. An action instituted by a private individual against another private individual: **civil suit**

c. Official written procedure for diagnosis, triage, treatment, or transport: **protocol**

d. Compensation for injury: **damages**

e. Assumption on behalf of a person unable to give permission for treatment that he would have done so: **implied consent**

f. Act providing limited immunity from liability to persons who stop and help at the scene of an emergency: **Good Samaritan**

g. Permission to practice a profession granted by a state agency: **license**

h. The process by which a professional organization grants recognition to someone who has met its qualifications: **certification**

i. The actions of a paramedic in the field are considered the **delegated** practice of a physician.

j. A patient's voluntary agreement to be treated, after being told about the risks and benefits of the proposed treatment: **informed consent**. In order to give that agreement, a person must be conscious and mentally **competent**.

k. A finding in civil cases that the balance of evidence shows the defendant was responsible for the plaintiff's injuries: **liability**

l. To create in another person a fear of immediate bodily harm: **assault**

m. Wrongful act that gives rise to a civil action: **tort**

n. Abrupt termination of contact with the patient without giving him sufficient opportunity to find another equally qualified health professional to take over his care: **abandonment**

o. Legal obligation of public ambulance services to respond to a call for help in their jurisdiction: **duty to act**

p. Any act of touching another person without that person's permission: **battery**

q. An act of omission or commission that results in injury to a patient: **negligence**

r. Two examples of reportable cases: **dog bite** and **rape**

s. Two examples of coroner's cases: **suicide** and **murder**

t. Permission from the parent or legal guardian is required to treat a **minor.**

u. The paramedic's best defense against being sued: **good care**

v. The paramedic's best defense if he does have to go to court as a witness or defendant: **medical record**

2. Depending on which state act you used to answer this question, the answers may vary. Using the Florida Good Samaritan Act, the answers are as follows:

a. **Any person,** including a doctor, who stops to give help is protected under the Florida Good Samaritan Act.

b. The preconditions for immunity from liability under the Florida act are that the person giving help (1) **does not charge money** for his services and (2) **acts as an ordinary reasonable prudent person would have acted in the same circumstances.**

c. Excluded from protection, by implication, are those who charge for their services and those who act negligently.

3. To prove negligence, a plaintiff must demonstrate

a. That an **injury** occurred

b. That the paramedic had a **duty to act**

c. That there was a **breach of that duty**

d. That the **failure to act appropriately was the proximate cause of the plaintiff's injury**

4. The requirements for consent are as follows:

   a. From a conscious, mentally competent adult, consent must be **informed**—that is, the proposed procedures must be fully explained to the patient, including the risks of treatment and the risks of not being treated, in a way the patient can understand.

   b. To treat a child, consent must be obtained from the **natural parent or legal guardian.** Only if there is an immediate threat to the child's life may treatment be undertaken without parental consent.

5. The six emergency calls present difficult dilemmas. In several of the cases described, there is no single "right" answer. In such cases, or whenever you have any doubts, it is essential to confer with your medical director for help in making a decision.

   a. A 12-year-old boy has fallen at school and sprained his ankle. The school authorities have so far been unable to reach the boy's parents.
   The boy's injury is not life-threatening, nor is it likely to be appreciably aggravated by waiting another hour or so. Tell the school authorities to keep trying to reach the boy's parents and call you back when they have gotten permission to have the boy treated.

   (b.) A middle-aged woman is found in cardiac arrest.
   This is a classic case of **implied consent.**

   c. A young man called for an ambulance after his 19-year-old girlfriend swallowed a large number of sleeping pills. She is awake and refuses treatment. She says, "Go away and let me die."
   This is a tough one. Some people would argue that any person who attempts suicide is, by definition, not mentally competent and therefore not able to give informed consent (or informed refusal). But you can't depend on that argument to protect you from a charge of technical assault and battery if you touch the patient or false imprisonment if you take her to the hospital against her will. Ask the boyfriend if the patient is under psychiatric care; if so, perhaps her psychiatrist can be enlisted to help. In states where suicide is a felony, you may call in the police for help. In any event, contact Medical Command for advice.

   d. A 20-year-old man has taken PCP (a psychedelic drug that often induces violent behavior) and has tried to gouge out his eyes. He is bleeding profusely from the face and screaming, "Don't come near me."
   Even though this patient is clearly *not* mentally competent, his life is not in immediate jeopardy (but *yours* may be if you try to get too close to him!). The best thing to do in this situation is call for police backup. In all probability, this patient will have to be forcibly restrained, and the police are the only ones permitted to authorize that action.

   (e.) A 14-year-old boy was knocked from his bicycle and run over by a truck. He is unconscious and bleeding. Both legs appear fractured. Bystanders do not know the boy or his parents.
   Another classic example of **implied consent.**

   f. A 43-year-old man has crushing chest pain. His wife called for the ambulance. The man says he doesn't need an ambulance; he just has indigestion. His face is gray, and he is sweating profusely.
   This patient is probably having a heart attack and very definitely needs to be in the hospital—but the only legal way to get him there is through patient, sympathetic persuasion. You will need to spend time talking with him, trying to understand his fears, and explaining to him the possible consequence of ignoring his symptoms. If despite your best efforts at persuasion he still refuses treatment and transport, you may not transport him against his will. But be sure to "leave the door open," so that he feels free to call you back later if he should change his mind.

6. The criteria for determining whether a patient is mentally competent include

   a. **Orientation** to person, place, and time

   b. **Absence of signs of mental impairment** from alcohol, drugs, head injury, and so on

   c. Evidence that the **patient understands the nature of his condition**

   d. Evidence that the **patient can describe a reasonable plan for follow-up care.**

7. A paramedic's trip sheet should contain

   a. **Date** and **times**

   b. **History** elicited from patient and bystanders

   c. **Observations of the scene**

   d. Findings on **physical examination**

   e. All **treatments** given

   f. Any **changes in the patient's status**

8. Reportable cases differ from state to state, but often include most of the following:

   a. **Child abuse**

   b. **Elder abuse**

   c. **Injury sustained during commission of a felony**

   d. **Drug-related** injuries

   e. **Childbirth** occurring outside a medical facility

   f. **Rape**

   g. **Animal bites**

   h. Certain **communicable diseases**

9. What is classified as a coroner's case also varies from state to state, but the list usually includes

   a. **Homicide**

   b. **Suicide**

   c. Any other **violent or unexpected death**

   d. **Death of a prison inmate**

10. Clearly each person will have his or her own private code of right and wrong. The paramedic's guiding principle, however it is worded, should be based on **overriding concern for the welfare of the patient.**

11. Did you manage to decode the secret message?

    a. **abandonment**

    b. **duty to act**

    c. **protocol**

    d. **witness**

    e. **gag**

    f. **W.H.O.**

    g. **Rh**

    h. **few**

    Secret Message: DO WHAT'S BEST FOR THE PATIENT AND YOU WON'T GO WRONG.

4
Stress Management

1. How well did you do with the puzzle? Did you find all 30 words? Here they are:

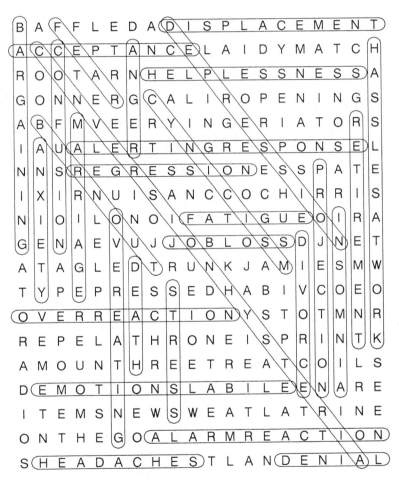

a. Definitions:

(1) The redirection of an emotion from the original object to a more acceptable object: **displacement** (e.g., someone who gets angry at you when he is really angry at himself)

(2) Attributing your own feelings to someone else: **projection**

(3) Nonspecific response of the body to any demand made on it: **stress**

(4) Reaction in which a startled animal stops all activity and turns toward the stimulus that startled it: **alerting response**

(5) A way of dealing with unwanted data by ignoring it: **denial**

(6) First stage of an acute stress response: **alarm reaction**

(7) Return to an earlier mode of behavior: **regression**

(8) Exhaustion of physical or emotional strength from chronic stress: **burnout**

(9) Unconscious translation of an emotional conflict into a physical symptom: **conversion hysteria**

b. Potential STRESS TRIGGERS named in the puzzle were:

(1) **Death**
(2) **Divorce**
(3) **Marriage**
(4) **Retirement**
(5) **Job loss**
(6) **Hassles at work**

c. Only you can know what situations you personally find stressful. A representative list might include things such as

(1) Taking exams
(2) Having to deal with angry or aggressive people
(3) Having to meet a deadline
(4) Walking into a room full of strangers
(5) Looking down from a height

The important thing is to be honest with yourself and make as accurate a list as possible of the things that put *you* under stress—for only by being in touch with your feelings will you be able to deal with them.

d. The potential REACTIONS of patients or others TO ILLNESS OR INJURY listed in the puzzle were

(1) **Fear**
(2) **Anxiety**
(3) **Helplessness**
(4) **Depression**
(5) **Anger**
(6) **Confusion**

You might also have mentioned the defense mechanisms of **denial, regression, projection,** and **displacement.**

e. Three REACTIONS sometimes seen IN BYSTANDERS AT A MASS CASUALTY INCIDENT are

(1) **Overreaction**
(2) **Conversion hysteria**
(3) **Depression**

If you mentioned **anxiety,** that is also correct.

f. The five STAGES OF GRIEF that people dealing with loss usually proceed through are

(1) **Denial**
(2) **Anger**
(3) **Bargaining**
(4) **Depression**
(5) **Acceptance**

g. Six SYMPTOMS OF IMPENDING BURNOUT listed in the puzzle are

   (1) **Fatigue**
   (2) **Cynicism**
   (3) **Emotions labile**
   (4) **Insomnia**
   (5) **Headaches**
   (6) **Overeating**

h. Among the symptoms of impending burnout that are not mentioned in the puzzle, you could have mentioned any of the following:

   (1) **Abuse of drugs or alcohol**
   (2) **Loss of interest in hobbies**
   (3) **Declining physical health**
   (4) Feeling of **tightness in the muscles**
   (5) Feelings of **helplessness and hopelessness**

2. When faced with a perceived threat, the body reacts with a "fight-or-flight" response. Different symptoms predominate in different people, but among the most common are

   a. **Cold sweat**

   b. **Pounding heart**

   c. **Dry mouth**

   d. Feeling **"energized"**

3. Were you able to spot the mechanisms of defense being deployed by those around you?

   a. When your irritable partner snaps at you, "You sure are in a lousy mood today," he is showing the mechanism of defense known as **projection,** for he is projecting his own feelings onto you.

   b. The middle-aged man with chest pain who insists, "I'm just having a little indigestion, that's all," is using the psychologic defense mechanism known as **denial,** for he is trying to deny the frightening significance of his symptoms.

   c. The 18-year-old woman who says she has lost all sensation in her hands and feet is showing symptoms of **conversion hysteria.** She has converted her distress over the accident into a symptom: loss of sensation in the hands and feet.

   d. The driver is very aggressive toward you, but you realize that his behavior is simply a **displacement** of the anger he feels toward himself for having caused the injury to his passenger.

4. a. At the scene of the train derailment, the bystander most likely to be able to perform a useful role will be **bystander B,** the young man who is standing off to the side looking a little green around the gills. He is suffering a normal reaction to such a stressful event, and he will most likely "snap out of it" if you give him something constructive to do. It may also be possible to mobilize **bystander D** from her dazed condition; if not, she will have to be removed from the immediate area of the wreckage and supervised along with other disabled bystanders.

   b. As to those bystanders who will *not* be useful to you:

   Bystander A: This young man is showing signs of *overreaction,* and he will only get in the way. He needs to be removed from the triage area and placed under the supervision of a calmer person.

   Bystander C: This woman is showing signs of *blind panic.* She must also be removed from the triage area—as quickly as possible, lest her panic infect others—and placed under supervision.

   Bystander E: This man is suffering from *conversion hysteria.* He will not be able to help. Remove him from danger, and evacuate him with the "walking wounded."

5. There is no single "correct" answer to the dilemma posed in this question: How do you reply to a patient when he asks, "Am I going to die?" There are, though, some general guidelines:

- **Do not try to minimize the seriousness of the patient's situation.** Most patients who are near death *know* at least that they are in serious condition. If you are merrily chirping, "There, there, everything is going to be fine," the patient will simply assume that (a) you don't understand the situation or (b) it is forbidden for him to speak to you honestly about his fears. Those are *not* the messages you want to convey!
- **Do not, on the other hand, take away all hope.** As long as a person is alive, there is hope for him.

In the situation described, therefore, you might say something like this: "Sir, your situation is very serious, but we have an excellent rescue team here, with the best medical backup, and we're going to do everything we can to save your life." Also let the patient know that you are willing to listen to what he has to say, to transmit any messages he has for other people, and so forth.

6. The case of the child killed in a traffic accident is one of the most difficult a paramedic may have to deal with, for it is hard enough coping with your own feelings in those circumstances without having to cope with the feelings of others at the scene. Nonetheless, your job isn't done when the child has died, for at that very moment, the parents become the "patient." Among the things you can do for them are the following:

- **Give the parents some time alone with the body of the child.** Provide them with privacy, for example by putting the child's body inside the ambulance, shielded from the stares of curious onlookers, and letting the parents sit there beside their child for a few minutes.
- **Do not use euphemisms for the word** *dead*.
- **Arrange for social support.** Ask the parents if there is someone they would like called—a friend, a relative, a clergyman; or recruit a neighbor to come and be with them.
- **Accept the feelings of the parents,** even if *you* might react differently. If they are angry and aggressive, remind yourself that they are not really angry at you, and do *not* respond to their anger in kind.

7. Strategies for preventing burnout will vary from one person to another, for different people have different temperaments. But most effective strategies will include at least some of the following:

- **Take care of your own health:**
  Get enough REST.
  Eat a balanced DIET.
  Get regular EXERCISE.
  Treat your body with respect (avoid cigarettes, drugs).
- **Give yourself some "me" time every day.**
- **Learn how to relax.** Forget the job when you finish your shift.
- **Do not make unreasonable demands on yourself or others.**
- **Stay in touch with your feelings.**
- **Debrief after tough calls.**

5
Medical Terminology

Learning the language of medicine is like learning any other "foreign" language: It takes practice. This lesson was a start, and in the rest of the textbook and study guide, there will be a lot more practice with new vocabulary. So don't worry if you are not yet fluent in Medispeak. The words you need to know will appear over and over again; and by the time you have finished reading the textbook and doing all the exercises, you will be surprised to see just how much vocabulary you have mastered.

1. Were you able to decipher all the medical terms? The secret is to take the word apart into its component roots:

   a. Adenoma: **tumor of a gland** (adeno- + -oma)

   b. Thoracotomy: **incision into the chest** (thoraco- + -otomy)

   c. Hypoglycemia: **deficient blood sugar level** (hypo- + glyco- + -emia)

   d. Oliguria: **very small urine output** (oligo- + -uria)

   e. Anesthesia: **absence of sensation** (an- + -esthesia)

   f. Dyspnea: **difficulty in breathing** (dys- + -pnea)

   g. Bradycardia: **slow heart rate** (brady- + -cardio)

   h. Hemiparesis: **weakness of one half (side) of the body** (hemi- + -paresis)

   i. Dermatitis: **inflammation of the skin** (dermato- + -itis)

   j. Gastrectomy: **surgical removal of the stomach** (gastro- + -ectomy)

   k. Leukopenia: **deficiency of white blood cells** (leuko- + -penia)

   l. Intercostal: **between ribs** (inter- + costo-)

   m. Polycythemia: **many (excessive) cells in the blood** (poly- + -cyto + -emia)

   n. Endocardial: **within the heart**—actually, inner layer of the cardiac muscle (endo- + cardio-)

   o. Perinephric: **around the kidney** (peri- + nephro-)

   p. Hemorrhage: **profuse bleeding**—blood bursting forth (hemo- + -rrhagia)

   q. Retropharyngeal: **back of the throat** (retro- + pharyngo-)

   r. Transtracheal: **across the trachea** (trans- + tracheo-)

   s. Hepatomegaly: **enlargement of the liver** (hepato- + -megaly)

   t. Neuropathy: **disease of nerves** (neuro- + -pathy)

2. A good medical dictionary can provide a lot of useful information—about the pronunciation of a word, its roots, and its different meanings.

   a. Anasarca: **Generalized massive edema affecting all parts of the body.**

   b. Cryptorchidism: **Developmental defect characterized by failure of the testes to descend into the scrotum.**

   c. Diplopia: **Double vision.**

   d. Hansen's disease: **Leprosy.** (In some dictionaries, this entry will appear under *disease*.)

   e. Kehr's sign: **Pain in the left shoulder following rupture of the spleen.** (In some dictionaries, this entry will appear under *sign*.)

329

3. Were you able to find all 23 words in the grid?

Definitions:

a. Cutting into a vein: **phlebotomy**

b. Inflammation of the gallbladder: **cholecystitis**

c. Excessive urination: **polyuria**

d. Visualization of blood vessels: **angiography**

e. Pain in the joints: **arthralgia**

f. Inflammation of the membrane that surrounds the heart: **pericarditis**

g. White blood cell: **leukocyte**

h. Tumor of the liver: **hepatoma**

i. Looking at (inside) the bladder: **cystoscopy**

j. Runny nose: **rhinorrhea**

k. Paralysis of all four extremities: **quadriplegia**

l. Absence of breathing: **apnea**

m. Inflammation of the ear: **otitis**

n. Rapid heart rate: **tachycardia**

o. Surgical removal of a testicle: **orchiectomy**

p. Headache: **cephalalgia**

q. Disorder of sensation: **dysesthesia**

r. Urine (products) in the blood: **uremia**

s. Beneath the skin: **subdermal**

t. Pain in muscles: **myalgia**

u. In the middle posterior area: **dorsomedial**

v. Inflammation of a gland: **adenitis**

w. Disease of joints: **arthrosis**

4. A crossword puzzle is an excellent place for abbreviations. A medical record is a less suitable place for abbreviations. Use abbreviations sparingly in your reports, and make sure that those abbreviations you do use are absolutely unambiguous.

	C	O	P	D		S	C	U	B	A			I	
	V	D		O	S		N		I	M		P	M	H
C	A			A	I	D	S		D	I	P			C
V		W		D	T						S	T	A	T
P	R	N		N	S	R		O			V		D	
	L	M	P			A	S	A		T		L	
C	O		E	O	A		S				B	I	D
	R	U	Q		S	N	A	F	U		C	B	C
	T		G	C		P		R	L				
	T	I	A		V	T		M	I	C	U		N	S
		Q	I	D		P	O		M	M	H	G	

5. Were you able to spot all 17 words?

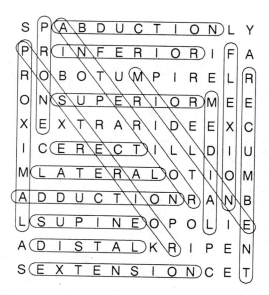

a. A person lying faceup on his back is lying **supine.**

b. The wrist is **distal** to the elbow.

c. When your leg is straight, it is in **extension.**

d. A person standing upright is standing **erect.**

e. Moving your arm *away* from your body is called **abduction.**

f. The nose is **medial** to the left ear.

g. The nose is **superior** to the toes.

h. The hips are **inferior** to the lips.

i. The umbilicus is in the **midline** of the body, on the **anterior** surface.

j. A person who is lying down is **recumbent.** If he is lying facedown, he is said to be **prone.**

k. Movement of an extremity *toward* the midline of the body is called **adduction.**

l. The act of bending an extremity at a joint is called **flexion.**

m. The heel is **posterior** to the toe.

n. The knee is **proximal** to the ankle.

o. The shoulder is **lateral** to the spine.

6. Look over the diagram again. How well did you describe the location of the various wounds?

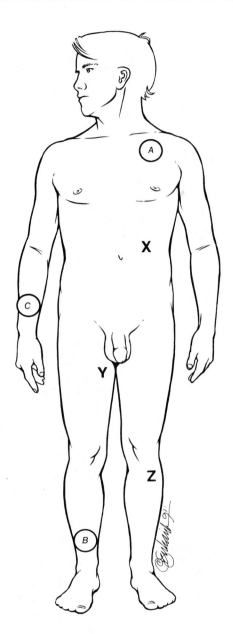

(To check how well you described the location, read your description aloud to a classmate and see if he or she can point to the location accurately on your body! A doctor receiving your report by radio will be in the same situation as your classmate—trying to picture from your words just where the injury is. That is why it is important to be able to describe location with precision.)

a. Wound A is on the **left anterior chest,** slightly **lateral to the sternum** (breast bone) and **inferior to the clavicle** (collar bone). (In fact, it is in what is called the midclavicular line.)

b. Wound B is on the **anterior** surface of the **distal right leg.**

c. Wound C is on the **posterior** (or dorsal) surface of the **right forearm,** about 3 inches **proximal to the base of the right thumb.**

d–f. Check the diagram to see whether you inflicted wounds X, Y, and Z in the correct places!

6
The Primary Survey: Overview

1. Priorities of management are, in fact, essential in every type of patient care, but nowhere are they more essential than in emergency care of the ill and injured outside the hospital. The reason is that in the uncontrolled and often chaotic environment of the prehospital scene, **it is easy to forget what to do first** if you don't have a set of priorities that you know by heart. Furthermore, when dealing with the *critically* ill and injured, it is **essential to detect and correct life-threatening conditions as quickly as possible;** a fixed set of priorities enables the rescuer to address the more important problems first and the less important problems later.

2. Now let's see whether *you* got your priorities straight!

   First you need to take care of certain essential preliminaries, before you even approach the accident victims:

   (1) __e__ Determine whether there are any **hazards** to the rescuers.

   (2) __c__ Determine whether you need **backup** support.

   (3) __i__ Determine whether you will need **special equipment** to gain access to the driver of the truck.

   Then you can address yourself to the first victim, the passenger lying unconscious beside the truck. In dealing with *any* unconscious patient, the order of priorities is **A-B-C:**

   (4) __j__ Make sure the passenger has an open **airway.**

   (5) __f__ Determine whether the passenger is **breathing;** if not, start artificial ventilation.

   (6) __a__ Check the passenger for a **pulse;** if he has no pulse, start external chest compressions.

   (7) __k__ Control any **bleeding** you detect in the passenger.

   Only now can you move on to the various components of the **secondary survey** (this is assuming that the driver of the vehicle is conscious and does not require attention to *his* ABCs):

   (8) __d__ Examine the scene closely to determine the possible **mechanisms of injury.**

   (9) __l__ Take a detailed **history** from the driver.

   (10) __g__ Do a **head-to-toe physical examination** of each casualty.

   Once the secondary survey is complete, you may start readying the casualties for transport.

   (11) __b__ **Stabilize** any **fractures** among the casualties.

   (12) __h__ **Package** the casualties for transport.

   As we shall learn later on, sometimes it will not be possible to complete, or even to start, the secondary survey in the field; the patient's condition may be too unstable. But the primary survey is always initiated in the field, in the sequence given.

3. In considering potential hazards at this particular accident scene, the questions you need to ask include

   a. Is the vehicle carrying **hazardous materials?** (We shall learn in Chapter 34 how to recognize a vehicle that is transporting hazardous materials.)

   b. Is the vehicle in an **unstable position,** liable to tip over or to slide farther down the ravine?

c. Is there a fire or a **danger of fire** (spilled gasoline)?

d. Are there **downed electrical wires** on or near the disabled vehicle?

e. Is there a **traffic hazard?**

(Give yourself full points if you listed any three of the above answers.)

4. The steps in the pathway from life to death are

a. Loss of meaningful communication

*b. Loss of consciousness

*c. Airway obstruction

*d. Respiratory arrest

*e. Cardiac arrest

f. Irreversible brain damage (biologic death)

*Points at which the process can sometimes be reversed by timely intervention.

5. This question, involving the arrangement of steps of management in the correct sequence, will occur over and over again, in modified forms, throughout the book. You may have hesitated over the question this time; but by the time you complete this book, you will be able to reel off the correct sequence of patient management in your sleep and—more important—you should be able to carry out the correct sequence of patient management automatically at the scene of any emergency.

(1) __c__ Open her **airway.**

(2) __e__ Determine whether she is **breathing;** if not, start artificial ventilation.

(3) __a__ Determine if she has a **pulse;** if not, start external chest compressions.

(4) __b__ Find the source of **bleeding,** and control the bleeding.

(5) __d__ Cover any wounds with sterile dressings.

6. There will also be many vocabulary exercises in this book, for learning the terminology of emergency medicine is essential to communicating with other health care personnel. How well did you do with this exercise?

a. **respiratory arrest**

b. **airway**

c. **clinical death**

d. **brain**

e. **consent**

f. **supine**

g. **suffocate**

h. **mEq**

i. **pneumo**

j. **heme**

k. **nevus**

l. **yes**

Secret Message: THE PRIMARY SURVEY OF AN UNCONSCIOUS PATIENT IS ALWAYS PERFORMED IN THE SAME SEQUENCE: ABC.

7
The Airway

The first letter of the rescue alphabet is A, for Airway. We consider the airway first because the airway *comes* first—not only in the alphabet, but also in the care of every patient.

1. The structures of the airway are shown below.

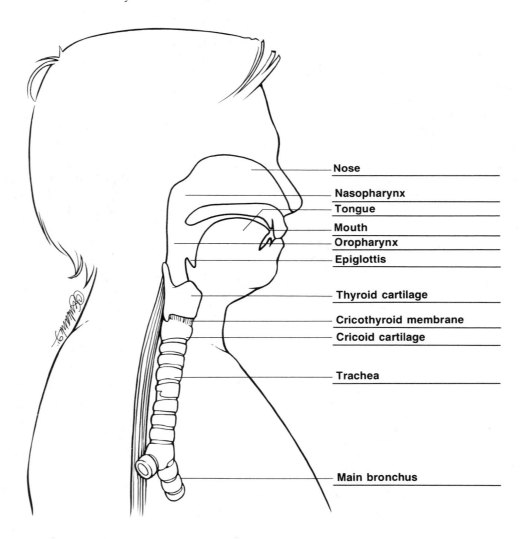

Nose

Nasopharynx

Tongue

Mouth

Oropharynx

Epiglottis

Thyroid cartilage

Cricothyroid membrane

Cricoid cartilage

Trachea

Main bronchus

2. The upper airway may become obstructed by

   *a. The **tongue**

   b. A **foreign body**

   c. **Swelling** (edema)

   d. **Trauma** to the face or neck

3. The method you choose for opening a patient's airway will depend a good deal on the condition in which you find the patient.

   __C__ A construction worker found unconscious on the ground after falling 30 feet from a scaffolding.
   Given the mechanisms of his injury (a fall from a height), this patient must be assumed to have suffered a cervical spine injury until proved otherwise. Therefore you should open his airway by the only maneuver mentioned that does not require motion of the neck, the **jaw thrust.**

   __A__ A 35-year-old man found unconscious from a drug overdose; he is breathing spontaneously. For this patient, who requires only a maneuver to bring the base of the tongue away from the back of the throat, and for whom there is no contraindication to movement of the neck, **head tilt–chin lift** should be ideal.

   __A__ A 45-year-old man in cardiac arrest from a probable heart attack. You have arrived at his side without any ancillary equipment.
   Having run to the patient without any equipment, you are going to have to start CPR with mouth-to-mouth ventilation, for which **head tilt–chin lift** is standard procedure. Next time perhaps you'll remember at least to keep a pocket mask in your pocket (see Chap. 8).

   __B__ Another 45-year-old man in cardiac arrest from a probable heart attack. You have a pocket mask with you.
   As we shall see in the next chapter, to ventilate through a pocket mask, you need to perform a **triple airway maneuver** from the vertex. (Where is the vertex? If you don't remember, check the Glossary for this chapter!)

   __C__ A 15-year-old boy who dove into a shallow pool and struck his head on the bottom. Bystanders removed him from the pool before you arrived. He is unconscious but breathing spontaneously (and noisily) when you arrive. This is the classic scenario for a cervical spine injury, so make sure you don't move the boy's neck; open his airway with the **jaw thrust** only.

4. a. The woman who collapses after complaining of feeling a "lump" in her throat is most likely suffering from **anaphylaxis** (answer **D**); the "lump" in her throat and the squeaky quality of her voice were doubtless signs of laryngeal swelling. Food poisoning (answer **A**) is unlikely to cause symptoms so quickly, and the symptoms most commonly produced are vomiting and diarrhea, not laryngeal edema and collapse. Had the woman been choking (answer **B**), she would either be coughing violently (partial obstruction) or aphonic (complete obstruction) while struggling to breathe. It is extremely unlikely that anyone would collapse from a strep throat (answer **C**). And you would be taking a *big* chance if you decided to write the woman's collapse off as hysterical (answer **E**).

   b. The treatment of choice for anaphylaxis is **epinephrine** 1 : 1000, 0.5 ml SQ (answer **D**). None of the other treatments mentioned is anywhere near appropriate! (If you had trouble understanding the dosage mentioned, don't worry; we shall be learning about such things in great detail when we come to the discussion of pharmacology in Chap. 10.)

5. a. The patient described in this question is showing classic signs of **choking** (answer **B**): He gives the universal distress sign for choking (clutches his neck), staggers, and falls—all without making a sound. The reason he isn't making a sound is because no air is moving past his vocal cords, which means that his upper airway is completely obstructed—and *that* means that HE IS GOING TO DIE IF YOU DON'T ACT AT ONCE!

   b. The most urgent priority is to try to expel the foreign body from his airway, which means giving him **manual thrusts.** There's no reason to pump his stomach (answer **A**), for his problem is what *didn't* make it into his stomach, not what did! Clearly he is not in any shape to gargle with salt water (answer **C**), nor would it help him if he could. At the moment, he doesn't need epinephrine (answer **D**), although he may need it very soon, if his airway obstruction is not relieved and he suffers cardiac arrest as a consequence. And he certainly doesn't need a sedative such as diazepam (answer **E**); he's already sedated quite enough by his hypoxemia. (What's hypoxemia? Check the Glossary if you don't remember.)

Both this question and the one preceding it illustrate why it's not a good idea to try to grab a quick dinner while you're on duty. Caroline's Law of Dining on Duty states: If you are going to get called to a cardiac arrest during your shift, the call is going to come at the precise moment that the pizza you ordered comes out of the oven.

6. Even when you're off duty, dining can be hazardous, especially when people have had a few drinks and are making merry, as this question illustrates.

   a. When your friend starts to choke on his hot dog, as evidenced by his paroxysm of violent coughing, the *first* thing you should do is **encourage him to keep coughing** (answer E). A cough generates air flows of gale-force velocity—far more powerful than anything you could generate artificially by, for example, manual thrusts (answer C). Sticking your finger in the mouth of a panicky, choking person (answer B) is a good way to lose a finger; and reaching blindly into the throat with *any* instrument, let alone barbecue tongs (answer D), is as likely to produce a rather messy tonsillectomy as it is to snare a wayward hot dog. There's no point in trying to ventilate your friend artificially (answer A); he's still got some air exchange by his own efforts, and blowing into his mouth may just force the hot dog farther down his airway.

   b. When coughing fails to expel the foreign object and your friend becomes completely obstructed (as evidenced by his aphonia), *that* is

the time to **give manual thrusts** (answer C). He's still conscious, so the finger sweep (answer B) and head tilt (answer A) are still inappropriate. The barbecue tongs (answer D) are *always* inappropriate. And there's no point now in encouraging him to keep coughing (answer E); if he *could* cough, he would.

   c. When the manual thrusts don't work and your friend becomes unconscious, your next steps should be as follows:

      (1) Open his mouth (tongue-jaw lift), and perform a quick **finger sweep** to remove any accessible obstructing material.
      (2) Then try to **open the airway** by head tilt–chin lift.
      (3) **Attempt to ventilate** mouth-to-mouth.
      (4) If you cannot force air past the obstruction, give **manual thrusts** until the foreign body is expelled from the victim's airway.

   d. When the paramedics arrive with all their gear, you finally have the means to take definitive action. At that point you should take the following steps:

      (1) Try to visualize the obstructing material by **direct laryngoscopy**, snare it with a Magill forceps or strong suction under direct vision, and remove it.
      (2) **Open the patient's airway** by head tilt–chin lift. See whether he is breathing.
      (3) If he is not breathing, give **artificial ventilation** with **supplemental oxygen**.

7. Knowing *when* to deploy a piece of equipment is just as important as knowing *how* to deploy it.

	Oropharyngeal Airway	Nasopharyngeal Airway
Use for:	Deeply unconscious patient who has no gag reflex, especially if being ventilated by bag-valve-mask Bite-block for intubated patient	Semiconscious patient
Do not use for:	Patient with intact gag reflex	Patient with: Trauma to the nose Suspected basilar skull fracture (blood or clear fluid draining from nose)

8. One of the most important things to remember about suctioning is that SUCTIONING REMOVES AIR AS WELL AS LIQUIDS.

   a. Any patient who is to be suctioned should first be preoxygenated for at least 3 minutes. **TRUE.** The patient will be virtually without an oxygen supply during the suctioning process, so he needs as much oxygen on board as possible to tide him over the period of suctioning.

   b. Keep the suction turned off as you insert the catheter into the patient's mouth. **TRUE.** Suction as you *withdraw* the catheter, not as you insert it.

   c. Suction for only 2 minutes at a time. **FALSE!** Do not suction for more than 15 *seconds* at a time. Two minutes is far too long to be without oxygen (try holding your breath for 2 minutes and see how *you* like it!).

   d. Use a tonsil-tip catheter only under direct vision. **TRUE.** Never jam *any* firm object blindly into someone's throat.

   e. Once a patient is intubated, suction through the endotracheal tube every 5 to 10 minutes to keep the tube free of secretions. **FALSE!** Remember Caroline's first rule about suctioning through an endotracheal tube? The rule is very simple: DON'T. There are exceptions to the rule—when secretions are so copious that you are unable to ventilate the patient (that happens sometimes in pulmonary edema). But if you can manage not to suction an intubated patient in the field, that is all to the good, for the likelihood under field conditions of introducing bacteria into the patient's lungs is very high.

9. The *principal* hazard associated with endotracheal suctioning is **hypoxemia,** as a consequence of removing the oxygen from the airway. That hazard can be minimized by **preoxygenating the patient** for at least 3 minutes before *every* suctioning attempt.

10. Endotracheal (ET) intubation provides the most definitive control over a patient's airway. The advantages of endotracheal intubation over other methods are many; if you mentioned any four of the following, give yourself full points:

   a. The cuffed ET tube **protects the airway from aspiration.**

   b. ET intubation permits **intermittent positive pressure ventilation with 100% oxygen.**

   c. The ET tube provides **access for suctioning** tracheobronchial secretions.

   d. Ventilation through an ET tube **does not cause gastric distention.**

   e. An ET tube **guarantees a patent airway.**

   f. An ET tube enables **delivery of aerosolized drugs** directly into the lung for rapid absorption into the bloodstream.

11. The *indications* for endotracheal intubation include

   a. **Cardiac arrest**

   b. **Deep coma** with absent cough and gag reflex

   c. **Imminent danger of upper airway obstruction**

12. Possible acute *complications* of endotracheal intubation include

   a. Accidental **intubation of the esophagus**

      (1) This complication can be *avoided* by
         (a) **Positioning the patient correctly** for intubation
         (b) **Seeing the tube pass through the vocal cords**
         (c) **Checking for breath sounds** over both lungs after intubation
      (2) If it does occur, intubation of the esophagus can be *detected* by
         (a) **Gurgling noises over the epigastrium** during ventilation
         (b) **Absence of breath sounds** over the lungs during ventilation
         (c) Failure of the patient to "pink up" on ventilation
      (3) Once detected, accidental intubation of the esophagus can be *corrected* by **immediately withdrawing the endotracheal tube and ventilating the patient with a bag-valve-mask.** No further attempt to intubate the patient should be made until the patient has been reoxygenated for at least 3 minutes.

   b. Accidental **intubation of a bronchus** (usually the right main bronchus)

      (1) This complication can be *avoided* by **cutting the endotracheal tube to an appropriate length before inserting it.**

(2) If it does occur, bronchial intubation can be *detected* by **absence of breath sounds over one lung** (usually the left).

(3) Once detected, bronchial intubation can be *corrected* by **slowly drawing the tube back until breath sounds become audible in both lungs.**

13. Were you able to find all 26 words?

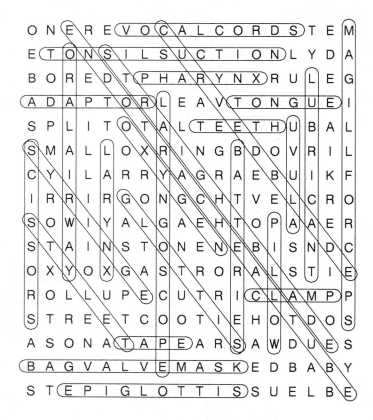

In this exercise, you had to *hunt* for all the intubation equipment. In the field, you should never have to hunt for your equipment! It should be all assembled and checked before you start any given procedure.

a. The additional supplies you will need for blind nasotracheal intubation are

   (1) **Cardiac monitor**
   (2) **Phenylephrine** topical spray
   (3) **Topical anesthetic spray**
   (4) **Atropine,** 0.01 mg per kilogram drawn up in a syringe

b. The items of equipment listed in the grid that are *not* necessary for blind nasotracheal intubation are

   (1) **Stylet**
   (2) **Oral airway**

If you also listed the laryngoscope, curved and straight blades, and Magill forceps, you are clearly very confident that you will succeed in getting the tube in blindly. Overconfident. Nothing is a sure thing, and in dealing with life-threatening emergencies, you always need a contingency plan. So even when you intend to do a *blind* nasotracheal intubation, have all the equipment available for a standard intubation—just in case you can't get the tube in blindly.

14. To get the mouth, pharynx, and trachea in alignment, you need to place the patient in the "sniffing position," by **flexing his neck** and **extending his head.**

15. An intubation attempt should take no longer than **20** seconds. The easiest way to keep track of the time is to **hold your own breath** as you intubate.

16. Probably this body builder has a short, very muscular neck, which is a classic situation for a difficult intubation.

    a. When the cords won't come into view, ask your partner to **apply downward pressure on the cricoid cartilage.**

    b. That maneuver also accomplishes another useful thing, namely it **squeezes the esophagus shut** against the vertebral column, thereby preventing regurgitation during the intubation attempt.

    c. When your laryngoscope gives up the ghost in the middle of an intubation, remove the laryngoscope from the patient's mouth; then **insert your left index and middle fingers into the patient's mouth and lift up on the tongue and epiglottis. Guide the endotracheal tube** along your index finger, or between your index and middle finger, **into the trachea.**

    d. When you've finally got the tube in, you need to verify its position. To do so, ventilate through the tube and

       (1) **Look to see if the chest rises** with each ventilation.
       (2) **Listen for breath sounds** on both sides of the chest with each ventilation.

17. The principal hazard of using a neuromuscular blocker is that it **converts a breathing patient with some sort of airway into a nonbreathing patient without any airway**—so if you are unable to intubate within 20 seconds and you have trouble maintaining an airway manually, the patient will need a surgical airway urgently.

18. Anatomic features that forewarn of a difficult intubation include

    a. **Short, thick neck** ("bull" neck)

    b. **Receding chin**

    c. **Overbite**

    d. **Large or swollen tongue**

19. The secret message at the end of this question should *not* be any secret to those who read the chapter carefully. Were you able to decode it?

    a. **trachea**

    b. **bronchus**

    c. **bronchiole**

    d. **larynx**

    e. **epiglottis**

    f. **mediastinum**

    g. **glottis**

    h. **battery**

    i. **tort**

    j. **apnea**

    k. **between**

    l. **then**

    m. **dented**

    n. **an**

    Secret Message: DO NOT ATTEMPT ENDOTRACHEAL INTUBATION UNTIL THE PATIENT HAS BEEN WELL OXYGENATED BY OTHER MEANS.

20. There are various techniques for obtaining definitive control of the airway. Knowing which technique to use when is essential.

    __O__ A 60-year-old man in cardiac arrest.
    This is one of the classic indications for **orotracheal intubation.** Blind nasotracheal intubation is not feasible, since the patient is not breathing, and cricothyrotomy is unnecessary when there is no obstruction above the larynx.

    __C__ A 22-year-old woman with complete airway obstruction from laryngeal edema.
    Here you don't have much choice, for you won't be able to get *any* tube into the trachea from above. The only hope is to create an airway *below* the point of obstruction by **cricothyrotomy.**

    __O__ A 26-year-old accident victim with clear fluid draining from his nose and left ear.
    One must assume, on account of the fluid draining from this patient's ear, that he has suffered a basilar skull fracture. It is therefore possible that the delicate bone separating the nasopharynx from the brain has also been shattered. Under those circumstances, it is

simply too risky to jam any kind of tube into the patient's nose, lest one intubate the brain rather than the trachea. The patient should be intubated, but by the **orotracheal** route.

N An 18-year-old man in coma from a drug overdose.

This is a classic indication for **nasotracheal intubation**—a patient in coma who still has spontaneous respirations.

N A 42-year-old woman extricated from a wrecked car; she is unconscious and has a depressed skull fracture at the back of her head.

If the lady has a depressed skull fracture, it means that very powerful forces were applied to the back of her head. And if very powerful forces were applied to the back of her head, we have to assume, until proved otherwise, that she suffered *cervical spine injury* as well. So we don't want to move her neck any more than absolutely necessary. In skilled hands, blind **nasotracheal intubation** is less likely than orotracheal intubation to require motion of the neck.

O A 58-year-old man in pulmonary edema; he has been taking Coumadin (an anticoagulant drug) ever since his heart attack last year.

Ordinarily, pulmonary edema in a conscious patient would be an indication for *naso*tracheal intubation. The hooker here is that the patient is taking anticoagulant medications, so he is at risk of suffering excessive hemorrhage if the delicate tissues of the nasal cavity are traumatized. For that reason, we need to stick to **orotracheal intubation** in this case—although whatever route we choose, we are in for a struggle: Patients in pulmonary edema tend to be *very* panicky.

O A 6-year-old boy who choked on a piece of meat.

We are going to have to perform direct laryngoscopy anyway, in order to try to visualize and remove the piece of meat; so as long as the boy needs airway control (e.g., if he is unconscious), we might as well slip in an **orotracheal** tube while we have the laryngoscope in place and the vocal cords in view. Cricothyrotomy might be reasonable *in an adult*, but it's best to avoid cricothyrotomy in children, since the potential for complications is considerable.

C A 50-year-old man who was given succinylcholine (a paralyzing drug) prior to an intubation attempt; the attempt failed, and afterward it became impossible to maintain his airway by manual methods (head tilt, etc.)

Since your intubation attempt has failed and you can't maintain an airway manually, you don't have any options! It's either a **cricothyrotomy** or a long ride to the cemetery. That's why it is important to think twice about using neuromuscular blockers in the prehospital setting.

21. Nasotracheal intubation doesn't always go smoothly, and one needs to be prepared to spend a little time getting it right.

   a. You can tell that the tip is moving toward the glottis by

      (1) Putting your ear over the tube and **hearing and feeling the movement of air through the tube.**

      (2) **Seeing misting inside the tube** (from condensation of the patient's breath).

   b. When the bleeps from the monitor start getting farther and farther apart, it means that the **patient's heart is slowing down** (i.e., she is developing **bradycardia**). You must immediately

      (1) **Stop advancing the tube.**

      (2) Attach the tube to an **oxygen** source.

      (3) Give **atropine,** 0.6 mg IV, to speed up the patient's heart. (We shall learn a lot more about atropine and its actions in Chap. 23; don't panic if you don't understand at this point why it is being administered.)

   c. The passive backflow of gastric contents from the stomach up the esophagus and into the throat is called **regurgitation,** and it is NOT a Good Thing. Regurgitation is dangerous because the gastric contents—which may include stomach acids along with the triple cheeseburger the patient had for lunch—are prone, once they have reached the laryngopharynx, to get sucked down the trachea and into the lungs (a process called **aspiration**). The lungs don't like gastric acid and triple cheeseburgers; they respond by developing a chemical pneumonia, sometimes serious enough to be fatal.

      If you *see* gastric contents creeping up the back of the patient's throat as you are intubating, immediately ask your partner to apply **cricoid pressure,** which will squeeze the esophagus shut between the cricoid cartilage and the cervical vertebrae and thereby prevent any more material from ascending into the pharynx.

d. The tip of the endotracheal tube should be advanced through the vocal cords **at the beginning of inhalation,** when the cords are open most widely.

22. The esophageal obturator airway (EOA) is *contraindicated* in

    a. **Children under 16** years old (or any very small patient)

    b. Patients known to have **esophageal or liver disease**

    c. Patients known to have **swallowed corrosive substances**

23. If you are going to use the EOA in your ambulance service, you need to be fully aware of its indications and drawbacks.

    a. The main indication for the EOA is pulmonary edema.
       FALSE. The main indication for the EOA—indeed, the *only* indication—is CARDIAC ARREST.

    b. The patient should be preoxygenated before an attempt is made to insert the EOA.
       Absolutely **TRUE!** Start CPR with some other means of ventilation (mouth-to-mouth, pocket mask, bag-valve-mask) and give supplemental oxygen while you get set up to insert the EOA.

    c. The patient should be placed in the "sniffing" position for EOA insertion.
       FALSE. The sniffing position is designed to bring the mouth, pharynx, and *trachea* into alignment, so that an endotracheal tube will slip easily into the trachea. You don't want the *EOA* to slip easily into the trachea! So the head is, in fact, flexed a bit forward for EOA insertion.

    d. It often requires considerable force to insert the EOA into the esophagus.
       FALSE!! What requires force is jamming the

EOA through the wall of the esophagus into the mediastinum. NEVER USE FORCE TO INSERT THE EOA. If you meet resistance, withdraw the obturator slightly and try again.

    e. The EOA eliminates the need to tilt the patient's head back for artificial ventilation.
       FALSE. The EOA is basically just a mask, like any other mask, and ventilating through a mask requires that the airway be kept open by correct positioning of the patient's head.

    f. In an unconscious patient, an endotracheal tube should be inserted before the EOA is removed.
       TRUE. Removal of the EOA is almost invariably accompanied by a mess, as the contents of the stomach rapidly follow the obturator in its exit from the esophagus. If the patient is still unconscious and his airway is not protected by a cuffed endotracheal tube when that mess arrives in the laryngopharynx, a considerable part of the mess is going to end up in the trachea.

    g. When intubating a patient who has an EOA in place, it is unnecessary to see the vocal cords to ensure proper placement of the endotracheal tube.
       FALSE. The esophagus is quite distensible, and if you are not watching what you are doing, there is nothing to prevent the endotracheal tube from entering the esophagus to keep the EOA company. You MUST see the tip of the endotracheal tube pass through the vocal cords.

24. Incorrect use of the EOA may lead to serious complications:

    a. Perforation of the esophagus may come about from **trying to force the EOA against resistance.**

    b. Rapid gastric distention and regurgitation will occur if the **obturator is accidently inserted into the trachea rather than the esophagus—** for all the air blown into the mask will then inflate the stomach rather than the lungs.

    c. Inadequate ventilation of the lungs will occur if the **rescuer fails to maintain proper backward tilt of the patient's head.**

8
Breathing

Breathing is something we don't think about much—until there's a problem. Nothing is more frightening than being unable to breathe, perhaps because our bodies instinctively "know" what lies beyond a few minutes of apnea.

1. Were you able to find all that new vocabulary?

2. Now let's imagine ourselves to be oxygen molecules taking that stroll down someone's airway. As his **diaphragm** and **intercostals** contract, the volume of his chest **increases,** so the pressure inside the chest (intrathoracic pressure) **decreases.** As a consequence, air is sucked in through the **nares,** and you are swept along with it.

   After having a shower and completing a secu-

rity check in the nasal hairs, you enter the **pharynx.** You then proceed down the **larynx,** through the **glottis,** and into the **trachea.** (Had you gone down the esophagus instead, you would eventually have been expelled from the stomach as part of a **burp.**) Moving a little farther, you find yourself at a crossroads, called the **carina,** where you can either take a left turn into the left **bron-**

chus or a right turn into the right **bronchus.** You choose the straighter, shorter path, to the **right.** The airway in which you are travelling branches many times into smaller and smaller **bronchioles,** until finally you reach a tiny sac at the end of the road, an **alveolus.** There you find the first opportunity to cross a membrane into a capillary and board a red blood cell for the journey to peripheral tissues. (Up to this point in your journey, you have been travelling only in **dead space,** that is, the part of the airway where gas exchange does not take place.)

Some of your friends who started the journey with you did not make it as far as you did. One of them accidently tickled the throat on his way down the airway and got expelled with gale force by a **cough,** which is the airway's most powerful mechanism for eliminating foreign material. Another of your colleagues found himself recruited into a hiccup, also known as **singultus.**

Yet another friend of yours made the journey all the way down the airway only to find the air spaces at the end of the line collapsed, a situation called **atelectasis.** It had come about when a little bleb on the surface of the lung ruptured, allowing air to enter the space between the visceral and parietal **pleura,** and thereby creating a small **pneumothorax.** The net effect was that blood reaching the collapsed alveoli could not pick up any **oxygen** like yourself, but rather had to return to the left heart as if it had never passed through the lungs at all, a situation called **shunt.** If a very large proportion of alveoli are nonfunctional (e.g., collapsed, filled with fluids), then a large part of the blood circulating through the lungs will be similarly affected, and the person's arterial PO_2 will fall below normal (i.e., below about 60 mm Hg), a condition known as **hypoxemia.**

Sometimes scattered alveoli collapse simply because a person doesn't take deep enough breaths to keep all his alveoli inflated. The body therefore has a mechanism to help periodically pop open collapsed alveoli, and that is to **sigh.**

3. The exchange of gases among the tissues, lungs, and atmosphere is called **respiration.** The movement of air in and out of the lungs (more specifically, the flushing of **carbon dioxide** out of the lungs by breathing) is called **ventilation,** and its effectiveness is determined by the volume of air inhaled or exhaled each minute, that is, the **minute volume** (= respiratory rate × **tidal volume**). If that volume of air inhaled each minute is *less* than normal, the arterial PCO_2 **rises,** and the blood gases show **hypercarbia** (excess CO_2 in the blood). We call that situation **hypoventilation,** that is, breathing that is insufficient to remove excess CO_2 from the body. The most extreme example occurs when a person is not breathing at all (respiratory arrest, or **apnea**).

   On the other hand, when someone breathes very deeply or very rapidly (or both), his PCO_2 will **fall;** that is, he will develop **hypocarbia.** We refer to that situation—when excessive breathing lowers the PCO_2 below about 35 **torr** (mm Hg)—as **hyperventilation.**

4. The stretcher is placed on the left side of the ambulance because of the anatomy of the tracheobronchial tree. The right bronchus comes off the trachea at much less of an angle than the left, so it is much more likely to provide an easy path for aspirated foreign materials if the right side of the body is dependent. For that reason, unconscious patients should be transported in the lateral recumbent position, **right side up.** If you place a patient in that position and you put the stretcher on the *right* side of the ambulance, the patient will be facing the *wall* of the ambulance! That makes it difficult for you to carry out such maneuvers as suctioning his mouth, observing the size of his pupils, and so on. The patient should be facing *you*, not the wall.

5. How good is your arithmetic?

   a. Minute volume = tidal volume × respiratory rate
       = 500 ml/breath × 12 breaths/minute
       = **6,000 ml** (6 liters)

   b. The minute volume will *decrease* if
      (1) The **tidal volume is decreased** (shallow breaths, as in spinal cord injury), or
      (2) The **respiratory rate slows** (as in heroin overdose)

   c. If the minute volume does decrease, the arterial blood gases will show a **rise in PCO_2,** because carbon dioxide will not be removed efficiently, so it will accumulate in the blood. (Unless one stops breathing altogether, or very nearly so, decreases in minute volume do not affect the *oxygenation* of the blood as dramatically.)

6. If you drew your blood gas sample from a vein instead of an artery, the **PO₂** reading you got back from the laboratory would be considerably **lower** than expected, while the **PCO₂** reading would be somewhat **higher** than expected. That is because venous blood has not yet passed through the pulmonary capillaries, where **oxygen** is taken up from the alveoli and **carbon dioxide** is given off into the alveoli.

7. Hypercarbia occurs when a person is not moving enough air in and out of his lungs to remove the carbon dioxide being produced by metabolism.

   a. Hypercarbia can be caused by

      (1) Diabetic **ketoacidosis** (increased CO₂ production)
      (2) Narcotic **overdose** (decreased respiratory rate)
      (3) **Spine injury** (decreased tidal volume)
      (4) **Rib fracture** (decreased tidal volume—because it *hurts* to take breaths of normal volume)

   b. The way to help normalize the PCO₂ of a hypercarbic patient is to **increase his minute volume,** that is, to assist his ventilations so that his tidal volume is larger (and perhaps give an extra breath here and there, to increase his respiratory rate as well).

8. a. Conditions that can cause hypoxemia include

      (1) **Pulmonary edema**
      (2) **Pneumonia**
      (3) **Near drowning**
      (4) **Chest trauma**
      (5) **Airway obstruction**
      (6) **Pneumothorax**
      (7) **Inhalation of smoke or toxic fumes**
      (8) **Respiratory arrest**

      Any six of the above will do for a correct answer.

   b. The treatment for hypoxemia is to **give oxygen!** That may sound obvious, but it is truly remarkable how many hypoxemic patients arrive at the emergency room by ambulance *without* oxygen being administered. DON'T BE STINGY WITH OXYGEN!!

9. In a healthy person, the primary stimulus to breathe is a **rise** in the level of **carbon dioxide** in the blood.

   In some patients with chronic obstructive pulmonary disease, that mechanism is no longer fully operative and *their* principal stimulus to breathe may be a **fall** in the level of **oxygen** in the blood.

10. Indications for oxygen therapy include

    a. **Pulmonary edema**

    b. **Pneumonia**

    c. **Near drowning**

    d. **Chest trauma**

    e. **Airway obstruction**

    f. **Pneumothorax**

    g. **Inhalation of smoke or toxic fumes**

    h. **Respiratory arrest**

    Any six of the above will do for a correct answer.

11. Signs of respiratory insufficiency include

    a. **Tachypnea** (rapid breathing)

    b. **Hyperpnea** (abnormally deep breathing)

    c. **Use of accessory muscles** to breathe

    d. **Nasal flaring**

    e. **Cyanosis** (bluish tinge to the lips and nail beds)

    If you mentioned **dyspnea**—a *feeling* of shortness of breath—that's all right, but technically speaking, dyspnea is a symptom, not a sign. We shall learn the difference in Chapters 11 and 12.

12. **The oxygen is going to run out!**

$$\frac{\text{Duration}}{\text{of flow}} = \frac{(\text{gauge pressure} - 200 \text{ psi}) \times C}{\text{flow rate}}$$

$$= \frac{(800 \text{ psi} - 200 \text{ psi}) \times 0.26}{5 \text{ liters/minute}}$$

$$= \textbf{31 minutes}$$

Only if you let the cylinder run down all the way to zero will you manage to squeeze 40 minutes' worth of oxygen out of it, but you will have to make sure you keep up your pace as you trudge through the woods carrying the stretcher. If you are starting to drag, you'd better decrease the flow rate to the nasal cannula to about 4 liters per minute. And *next time*, make sure you take a FULL oxygen cylinder with you!

13. Safety precautions around oxygen cylinders include the following:

    a. **No smoking!**

    b. **No grease.**

c. Keep **out of extreme heat.**

d. Use the **right valve.**

e. **All valves closed when not in use.**

f. Cylinders **firmly secured.**

g. Keep your **face and body to the side** of the cylinder.

14. Choosing the appropriate means of delivering oxygen to a patient is as important as getting the right dosage of a drug. A patient who needs a high concentration of oxygen may get very little benefit from a device that can deliver only a low concentration. In this question, you had to figure out not only which patients needed more oxygen than others but also which patients needed assisted or controlled ventilation, as opposed to those patients who could breathe all right on their own.

  I   A 60-year-old man in severe respiratory distress from pulmonary edema.
Pulmonary edema is the primary indication for the **demand valve,** for not only does the demand valve deliver the very high concentration of oxygen (100%) required, but it delivers that oxygen under positive pressure, which may help drive fluid out of the alveoli.

  B   A 52-year-old man complaining of crushing chest pain.
A middle-aged man with chest pain is having a heart attack until proved otherwise. Since there is no reason to suspect a significant degree of shunt, the moderate oxygen concentrations delivered by a **two-pronged nasal cannula** should be sufficient. A *simple face mask* (C) will give about the same concentrations, so that answer is also correct; but most patients find the nasal cannula less confining.

  G,A   An accident victim in cardiac arrest; you are doing one-rescuer CPR, because your partner is busy with another casualty.
The optimal device for giving artificial ventilation during CPR is a **pocket mask,** although you may tire rather quickly if you have to keep going back and forth between the patient's chest and his vertex. Alternatively, you could give mouth-to-mouth ventilation and supplement the oxygen in your exhaled air by inserting a **nasal catheter** in your own nose.

  B   An 81-year-old woman who suddenly stopped speaking this morning and cannot move her left arm or left leg.
We are talking about a probable stroke. Again,

as in the patient with the heart attack, there is no evidence of significant shunt, so moderate concentrations of oxygen will do. Thus the **nasal cannula** should be sufficient.

  H,I   A 22-year-old who has overdosed with heroin; he is unconscious and breathing shallowly 6 times per minute.
This patient is hypoventilating and therefore needs some form of *assisted ventilation* to help clear CO_2 from his lungs—the oxygen concentration is a secondary consideration. Either the **bag-valve-mask** or the **demand valve/mask** can be used to augment the patient's tidal volume.

  F   A 32-year-old accident victim who was thrown forward against the steering wheel; he is coughing up blood, and his lips look rather blue.
This patient does have a significant shunt: He has blood in his airway, and he is showing signs of hypoxemia (his blue lips). So he needs oxygen in high concentration, and the **nonrebreathing mask** is the best way to give it. Granted, the demand valve (I) provides 100% oxygen, but this patient does not *need* oxygen under pressure—indeed it might be dangerous to his damaged lung.

  G,H   A middle-aged man who collapsed in the street; he is in cardiac arrest by the time you arrive.
A patient in cardiac arrest needs controlled ventilation with as much oxygen as possible. The **bag-valve-mask** can furnish a higher oxygen concentration, but it takes a lot of skill to ventilate properly with it. The **pocket mask** may provide only about 50% oxygen, but it enables the rescuer to give very good ventilation volumes. So take your pick.

  F   A child rescued unconscious from a house fire.
We have to assume that this child's alveoli are full of all the wrong gases (carbon monoxide, other toxic fumes, and smoke) and that as a consequence he has a big shunt; so he needs oxygen in high concentrations, which only the **nonrebreathing mask** will provide.

15. The causes of respiratory arrest include

  *a. Airway **obstruction by the tongue** in an unconscious person

  b. **Choking**

  c. **Laryngeal edema**

  d. **Respiratory center depression** (drugs, head injury)

e. **Stroke**

f. **Electric shock**

g. **Primary cardiac arrest**

16. To diagnose respiratory arrest, first **open the airway;** then **look, listen, and feel** for breathing:

    a. LOOK at the chest to see whether it rises and falls.

    b. LISTEN over the nose and mouth for the sound of air flow.

    c. FEEL with your cheek over the nose and mouth for the movement of air.

17. A person who has suffered respiratory arrest will need **controlled ventilation.**

    a. In *controlled* ventilation, the rescuer has to breathe for the patient. In *assisted* ventilation, by contrast, the patient *is* breathing spontaneously, and the rescuer simply **boosts the tidal volume.**

    b. With *any* form of artificial ventilation, the primary objective is to **normalize the PCO$_2$ by moving air in and out of the lungs.** Controlled ventilation also aims to supply oxygen to the alveoli.

18. You can gauge the effectiveness of mouth-to-mouth ventilation by

    a. Seeing the patient's **chest rise and fall** with each breath you give

    b. **Feeling the compliance of the patient's lungs** in your own lungs

    c. **Hearing and feeling air escape** through the patient's mouth during his passive exhalation

19. a. To minimize gastric distention during artificial ventilation, you need to

    (1) **Keep the patient's airway fully open,** and

    (2) **Avoid excessive ventilation volumes.** Blow in only that volume of air needed to make the chest rise.

    b. When the patient's belly starts to distend despite your best efforts, **reposition his head to try to improve the airway** and **pay more attention to the ventilation volumes.** Do not, at that point, take any action to try to relieve the gastric distention.

    c. When, however, the patient's gastric distention begins to interfere seriously with your ability to get any air into his lungs, you will

have to **attempt to decompress the stomach.** It will not be a pleasant job. Roll the patient quickly to his side, facing away from you, and press firmly over his epigastrium. He will probably regurgitate, perhaps massively, so be prepared to sweep his mouth free of vomitus before you roll him back supine.

If you answered either of those "What should you do?" questions with the phrase, "Call an ambulance!", give yourself an extra point. Unless you want to spend the night doing CPR all by yourself in the movie theater, you should send someone for help at the very outset.

20. The advantages of the pocket mask over other devices for giving artificial ventilation include

    a. Its immediate **availability** (assuming you remember to carry it in your pocket).

    b. Its **adaptability;** it can be deployed with or without supplemental oxygen.

    c. Its potential to be **used as a simple face mask** if the patient resumes breathing.

    d. Its **effectiveness;** it is much easier to maintain a good seal with a pocket mask (and therefore deliver good volumes) than with a bag-valve-mask.

21. The demand valve has its drawbacks and should not be used indiscriminately. Among its limitations:

    a. The high pressures generated by the demand valve lead quickly to **gastric distention** in the nonintubated patient.

    b. The high pressures also make it **unsuitable for use in children.**

    c. The **very dry gases** can damage the respiratory tract tissues if the demand valve is used for more than a few minutes to ventilate through an endotracheal tube.

22. The automatic transport ventilator is very nearly the ideal ventilator for prehospital use. Among its advantages over a demand valve are the following:

    a. The ATV can be set to **deliver a specific tidal volume at a specific rate.** With the demand valve, you can only guess what volume you are delivering to the patient.

    b. The ATV delivers oxygen at a **lower flow rate over a longer period** than the demand valve (flow rates of 15–30 liters/min over 1–2 seconds, rather than 50–150 liters/min over less than a second. What that means, practically speaking, is that the ATV is **less likely than the demand valve to cause gastric distention.**

c. In the intubated patient, the ATV acts as a volume-cycled ventilator to provide artificial ventilation to the patient automatically. That in turn **frees the rescuer for other tasks**, since he does not have to sit pushing a button on the demand valve.

23. Different modes of delivering controlled ventilation have different properties in terms of the maximum concentration of oxygen they can deliver.

Method of Artificial Ventilation	O₂ Concentration Delivered
Mouth-to-mouth	16–18%
Pocket mask	16–18%
Pocket mask with O₂ at 12 L/min	40–50%
Bag-valve-mask (BVM)	21%
BVM with O₂ at 12 L/min	40%
BVM with O₂ at 12 L/min plus O₂ reservoir	90%
Demand valve	100%

24. This was, in fact, a rather unfair question, for at this point in the course the student is not yet familiar enough with specific emergencies to be able to know when the pulse oximeter would be most useful. In general, any time you have a patient whose state of oxygenation may be in jeopardy, the pulse oximeter can help you keep tabs on things:

a. A patient with **trauma to the chest,** in whom pneumothorax or hemothorax (or both) may interfere with oxygenation

b. A patient in **pulmonary edema,** who has a large shunt because of fluid in his alveoli

c. A patient **undergoing endotracheal intubation**

d. A patient **undergoing suctioning**

e. A patient having a **severe asthma attack** or deterioration of **chronic lung disease**

f. A **near-drowning victim**

Give yourself full points if you listed any three of the above or any three similar situations. By the time you finish reading this book, you will have a much clearer idea of the types of calls in which a pulse oximeter could be useful to you.

25. The patient in congestive heart failure has fluid in his alveoli, and for that reason a portion of his cardiac output is not picking up any oxygen as it passes through the lungs (a situation we call *shunt*). It is not surprising, therefore, that his oxygen saturation is reduced.

a. The SaO_2 reading of 86 percent is **abnormally low** (answer 3). A normal reading would be between 97 and 99 percent on room air. There's no reason to suspect an artifact (erroneous reading), for the reading is quite consistent with the patient's clinical presentation.

b. The measure you need to take immediately when you see a reading like that (or, even without a pulse oximeter, when you see a patient in respiratory distress) is to **administer oxygen.** (What would be the best device for administering oxygen in this patient?)

c. Possible sources of an erroneous reading in this patient include the following:

(1) **Bright ambient light** may be interfering with the reading. Cover the sensor with a towel or aluminum foil if you suspect that's the problem.
(2) Check whether the **patient is moving.** The oximeter may confuse patient motion for a pulse.
(3) The sensor may be picking up **venous pulsations.** Move it to a different finger or to the ear lobe and recheck.
(4) If it's cold in the ambulance and the patient's peripheral blood vessels constrict as a consequence, the resulting **poor perfusion** of the extremities may lead to false oximetery readings.

26. Probably the primary indication for using an end-tidal carbon dioxide monitor is to check the placement of an endotracheal tube in a *spontaneously breathing, normally perfused patient.*

a. In the case described, one can conclude that **the endotracheal tube is in the esophagus.** If the tube were in the trachea, as it's supposed to be, the carbon dioxide concentration of the exhaled gas ought to be at least 2 percent, translating into a tan or yellow color on the sensor.

b. The action you should take right away is to deflate the cuff and **remove the endotracheal tube.** Let the patient breathe 100% oxygen for at least 3 minutes before you make another attempt to intubate.

9
Circulation

1. Like the words in the grid below, the signs of shock may remain hidden to those who don't look for them carefully.

a. Intravenous solution containing large molecules like protein: **colloid.**

b. Intravenous solution that does *not* contain large molecules like protein: **crystalloid.** One example of such a solution is normal **saline.**

c. A compound whose pH is *less* than 7.0 is called an **acid,** while a compound whose pH is *greater* than 7.0 is called a **base.**

d. An **electrolyte** is a substance that dissociates into charged components in water. A positively charged molecule, like Na^+, is a **cation,** while a negatively charged molecule, like Cl^-, is called an **anion.**

e. When two solutions of different solute concentration are placed on either side of a semipermeable membrane, the *more* concentrated solution is said to be **hypertonic** with respect to the less concentrated solution. Conversely, the *less* concentrated solution is considered **hypotonic** with respect to the more concentrated solution. If the two solutions have the *same* concentration, they are said to be **isotonic.** Thus, for example, 4% saline is **hypertonic** with respect to the plasma; Ringer's solution is **isotonic** with respect to the plasma; and ½ normal saline (0.45% NaCl) is **hypotonic** with respect to the plasma. If you place red blood cells in a solution like ½ normal saline, the cells will rupture; that is, **hemolysis** will occur.

f. When two solutions of different solute concentration are placed on either side of a semipermeable membrane, water will move *from* the solution of **lower** solute concentration *to* the solution of **higher** solute concentration. The process by which water migrates in that fashion is called **osmosis.**

g. The most important component of the red blood cell, or **erythrocyte,** is an iron-containing protein called **hemoglobin,** which binds oxygen in the lungs and releases oxygen in the tissues. When that protein is not saturated with oxygen, it imparts a bluish color to the blood, which is reflected in a bluish color of the skin called **cyanosis.**

h. When there is failure of tissue perfusion for any reason, the resulting state is called **shock.** One way that state can come about is if there is cardiac standstill or **asystole.** However that state of inadequate tissue perfusion occurs, one of the immediate results is that the body cells, unable to obtain enough oxygen, switch to **anaerobic** metabolism.

i. A now somewhat controversial treatment for shock is the military anti-shock trousers, or **MAST,** also known as the **PASG.**

j. When performing cardiac compressions, one must be careful not to compress over the lower, cartilaginous portion of the sternum, called the **xiphoid,** lest one lacerate the patient's liver.

k. The cardinal sign of *over*hydration is **edema.**

2. Three components are required for a functioning circulatory system:

Component	Type of Shock Resulting from Damage
PUMP (heart)	**Cardiogenic shock**
VOLUME (blood)	**Hypovolemic shock**
TUBING (arteries)	**Neurogenic shock**

3. There is no doubt that CPR saves lives when performed correctly. There is equally no doubt that CPR will be ineffective and even possibly injurious if performed incorrectly.

a. To determine whether the patient has a pulse, palpate gently over the radial artery for 10 seconds.
FALSE. Palpate lightly for 5 to 10 seconds, yes, but *not* the radial pulse; check for a *carotid* pulse in the neck.

b. For chest compressions to be effective, the patient must be supine on a hard surface.
TRUE. If the patient is not recumbent, blood will not reach vital organs like the brain; if he is on a soft surface, compressions will depress the surface (e.g., a mattress) and not the patient's chest.

c. The correct compression point on an adult is over the lower third of the sternum.
TRUE.

d. You should allow more time for the relaxation phase than for the compression phase, to give the heart time to refill between compressions.
FALSE. Allow equal time for the compression phase and the relaxation phase, or give slightly more time to the *compression* phase.

e. After every 4 to 5 cycles of 15 compressions and 2 ventilations, you should take a 1-minute break to rest your arms and check for a spontaneous pulse.
FALSE! Take your coffee break *after* CPR, not during it! For during that minute that you're resting, the patient's brain and other organs are not getting any oxygen whatsoever, not even the very marginal supply that you were furnishing with CPR. So during your 1-minute rest, brain cells are dying in droves. DO NOT INTERRUPT CPR FOR MORE THAN ABOUT 7 SECONDS AT A TIME.

4. Here are some of the things you can do to make CPR as effective as possible:

   a. Keep the **airway fully open.**

   b. **Avoid excessive inflation pressures** during artificial ventilation.

   c. Maintain **correct hand position** on the chest.

   d. Keep your **compressions smooth and regular.**

   e. Keep your **fingers off the chest** during compressions.

   f. Keep your **shoulders directly over the sternum.**

   g. **Do not interrupt CPR** for more than 7 seconds at a time.

   If you mentioned any four of the above, give yourself full points.

5. Deciding when it is appropriate to start CPR is usually a straightforward process, but sometimes it can be a very difficult decision indeed, involving a person's most basic attitudes and values. There is not always a "right" answer.

   _A_ A 12-year-old boy fished out of a swimming pool unconscious about 10 minutes before you arrived.

   Probably no one will argue about this one. To begin with, we tend, whether rightly or wrongly, to "give it our best try" when a child is the patient. Secondly, we don't really know how long the child has been in cardiac arrest. And, even if he has been in arrest for the whole 10 minutes, if the water in the pool was colder than body temperature, the immersion may have given him a slightly larger margin of safety by cooling the brain (and thereby reducing its metabolic need for oxygen). So by all means, start CPR!

   _A_ A man who looks to be about 70 years old who collapsed downtown 15 minutes before you arrived.

   Unless you've got something against senior citizens, this patient falls under the "benefit-of-the-doubt rule." We know that he *collapsed* 15 minutes ago, but we have no idea when he actually went into cardiac arrest. It may have been only moments before you arrived, and there may be every chance of saving him.

   _A_ A vagrant found in cardiac arrest in an alley on a snowy morning; no one knows how long he has been there.

   Here's another patient who comes under the "benefit-of-the-doubt" rule. First of all, we don't know when his heart stopped beating. Secondly, as we shall learn when we study cold exposure, even if the cardiac arrest occurred an hour ago, there may be every chance of saving the patient—for his chilled condition may have protected him from hypoxic injury. Were you influenced by the fact that he is a "vagrant"? In fact, you don't even really know *that!* He may be a leading citizen who had an insulin reaction and lost consciousness in the snow. And even if he *is* a "vagrant," he is one of the people you have chosen to serve by becoming a paramedic.

   _A_ A *very* pregnant woman critically injured in an automobile accident; she has an open skull fracture, and pieces of her brain are splattered inside the car.

   If you came to the conclusion that there was little or no chance of reviving this woman, you were probably correct. But what you have to take into account is that when a woman is in the advanced stages of pregnancy, you are dealing with *two* patients, not one—and CPR may save the life of the patient *inside;* that is, it may sustain the fetus until an emergency cesarean section can be performed in the hospital.

   _A_ A 25-year-old man known to have AIDS who suffered cardiac arrest when he accidently came in contact with a high-tension electric cable.

   This is another case presented to help you examine your attitudes. If you did not want to start CPR on this patient, why not? "Because he will die anyway"? Perhaps he will, but that could be 5 or 10 years down the line, and his family and friends might want to have him around for those 5 or 10 years. Because you are afraid of catching AIDS from him? That, as we shall learn in Chapter 28, is not a legitimate reason for denying CPR or any other treatment to a patient.

   _B_ A 40-year-old woman with advanced breast cancer who has told her family that she doesn't want "any heroic measures."

   Here we have a different situation altogether— a patient in the last stages of a terminal disease who has *expressed a clear wish not to receive heroic treatment.* Such wishes should be respected.

Do you agree with the answers given above? If not, why not? Discuss your reactions with your classmates.

6. CPR for the victim of trauma must take into account the patient's possible injuries and his special needs.

    a. In **opening the airway,** one must avoid any maneuver that may aggravate a cervical spine injury; therefore one should use **jaw thrust, jaw lift,** or **chin lift** *without head tilt* to open the airway.

    b. Assessment of the **circulation** in a trauma patient must include **checking for and controlling severe external bleeding.**

    c. CPR by itself will not save the life of a severely injured patient. Therefore one must **start CPR and get moving.**

7. a. Abnormal losses of fluids can take place through

        (1) **Vomiting** or **diarrhea** (gastrointestinal losses)
        (2) **Fever** or **hyperventilation** (insensible losses)
        (3) **Sweating**
        (4) **Peritonitis** or **pancreatitis** ("third space" losses)
        (5) **Burns** (plasma losses)

    b. If a person does not replace his fluid losses, he will become dehydrated. The signs of dehydration do NOT include **edema** (answer **D**), which is the cardinal sign of *over*hydration.

    c. The most important *treatment* for a dehydrated person is to give him **fluids.** In some instances, it will be possible to give him fluids by mouth, but severe dehydration will almost always require intravenous fluids.

8. In choosing an intravenous fluid, one needs to consider both the properties of the fluid and the condition of the patient:

C   A 30-year-old man injured in an automobile accident. He is confused and disoriented. His skin is cold and clammy. His pulse is 128, respirations 24 and shallow, and blood pressure (BP) is palpable at 80 mm Hg.
If ever there was a case for giving colloid, this patient in hemorrhagic shock is it. If, however, you answered **B** (lactated Ringer's solution), there are many trauma experts who would support your decision.

B   A 28-year-old construction worker who collapsed at the work site on a very hot day. His skin is cool and sweaty, pulse is 100, and BP is 100/60.
This man is severely dehydrated and probably suffering from heat exhaustion. He has lost water and salt from his body by sweating, so water and salt are what we need to give him back.

B   A 22-year-old woman rescued from a structural fire with burns over 45 percent of her body. Current vital signs are pulse 88, respirations 20 and labored, and BP 110/80.
Here is a woman *at risk* of shock, but apparently not in shock yet. She needs fluids to replace the plasma that she is losing across her skin. Hetastarch is a rather expensive way to give her those fluids, when lactated Ringer's will do the trick, at least for the time being.

C   A 48-year-old man with crushing chest pain. Pulse is 100 and irregular, respirations 18, and BP 180/100.
This patient with symptoms of acute myocardial infarction needs a **keep-open IV** with a minimum of fluid and salt; D5/W fits the bill.

B   A 30-year-old man complaining of very severe abdominal pain. His abdomen is exquisitely tender, and he winces every time the ambulance goes over a bump. His pulse is 110 and regular, respirations 24 and shallow, and BP 100/70.
This young man is showing signs of peritonitis—an inflammation of the lining of the abdomen—and can be expected to be losing fluid into the abdominal cavity, a so-called third space loss. That fluid is lost to the circulation just as surely as if it had leaked outside the body. The patient is at risk for shock and so needs an intravenous fluid that will remain longer than D5/W in the intravascular space. Lactated Ringer's is the fluid of choice (there's no need here for colloid, at least not in the prehospital stage).

B   A 16-year-old boy who has had 3 days of severe diarrhea. His skin "tents" when you pinch it. His pulse is 120, respirations 22, and BP 100/60.
Once again, we have a patient who has lost water and electrolytes and is approaching shock. We need to give him back at least some of what he has lost; lactated Ringer's will give him water along with sodium, potassium, calcium, and chloride, which is a good start.

9. Understanding changes in the body's acid-base balance is really not all that difficult if you think about the production and disposal of carbon dioxide (CO_2).

__B__ A very anxious 18-year-old boy complaining of stabbing pains in his chest. He is breathing deeply 30 times per minute.

The boy is apparently *hyperventilating,* that is, ventilating in excess of his need to excrete CO_2. One would therefore expect the level of CO_2 in his blood to fall, which would in turn lower the overall carbonic acid in the blood, leading to *alkalosis.* It is a **respiratory alkalosis** because the source of the problem is in the patient's breathing.

__C__ A 50-year-old woman in cardiac arrest.

This woman has two problems, from the viewpoint of acid-base balance. First of all, she can't get rid of the CO_2 that her tissues are producing (she isn't breathing), so CO_2, and therefore carbonic acid, build up in the blood. Secondly, since her cells aren't getting oxygen, she has had to switch to *anaerobic metabolism,* which means a higher output of acid. The net effect is *acidosis*—a **metabolic acidosis** because the excess acids are the result of metabolic processes.

__C__ A diabetic complaining of extreme thirst and of having to urinate all the time. His breath smells fruity.

Here's another patient producing too much acid—in his case, the ketoacids of diabetes out of control—so once again this is **metabolic acidosis.**

__D__ A young woman who has been vomiting all night. (Hint: Gastric juice is very high in acid.) If you paid attention to the hint, this patient should not have posed too difficult a problem. She is *losing* acid, through vomiting, so the balance is going to swing to the alkaline side. It is a **metabolic alkalosis** by exclusion: It has nothing to do with any problem in the respiratory system.

__A__ A young man with a heroin overdose. You find him comatose, breathing shallowly 6 times per minute.

With a markedly reduced minute volume such as this patient has (how do we know that?), the body cannot eliminate CO_2 normally—so CO_2 accumulates in the blood. The result of CO_2 accumulation, as always, is *acidosis*—in this instance, **respiratory acidosis,** because the source of the problem lies in the failure to breathe adequately.

__D__ A cardiac arrest victim given too much sodium bicarbonate during resuscitation.

The effect of bicarbonate is to neutralize acids (which is why some people take bicarbonate of soda for "acid stomach"), that is, to tilt the balance toward *alkalosis.* In this case it is a **metabolic alkalosis** because it has nothing to do with the respiratory system.

a. For the patient found in *respiratory acidosis* (the heroin overdose), the treatment is to **assist ventilations** in order to improve the minute volume and blow off the excess CO_2.

b. The patient in *respiratory alkalosis* (the fellow who is hyperventilating) needs to be **calmed and reassured** so that he will slow down his breathing (see Chap. 22).

10. a. The patient who develops back pain, diaphoresis, cyanosis, and so forth during a blood transfusion is showing signs of a **hemolytic reaction to the blood transfusion** (answer **B**).

b. To deal with this situation, you need to

(1) **STOP THE TRANSFUSION!** Disconnect the blood bag and save it for testing.
(2) Keep the **IV line open** with D5/W (if signs of shock develop, switch to normal saline or Ringer's).
(3) **Draw a blood sample** (red-top tube) from a site other than the IV line.
(4) **Notify the physician** and request orders.

11. Causes of hemorrhagic shock include

    a. **External bleeding**

    b. Blunt **chest trauma**

    c. Blunt **abdominal trauma**

    d. **Fractures** of the pelvis or femur

    e. **Ruptured ectopic pregnancy**

    f. **Bleeding ulcer**

12. In assessing the state of perfusion:

    a. One can judge *peripheral* perfusion by checking **capillary refill.**

    b. The best indicator in the field of *perfusion of vital organs* is the patient's **state of consciousness.**

13. Knowing the mechanisms that produce symptoms and signs makes it much easier to remember those symptoms and signs.

Sign or Symptom	Mechanism That Causes the Sign or Symptom
Restlessness	Possibly hypoxemia
Cold, clammy, pale skin	Peripheral vasoconstriction, the body's attempt to shunt blood away from the "nonvital" periphery to more vital internal organs (like the brain)
Weak, rapid pulse	The pulse is weak because (a) the volume is reduced and (b) the arteries are narrowed. It is rapid because the body has to cycle the remaining red blood cells faster to furnish the same amount of oxygen (each red blood cell must make more trips).
Rapid breathing	When not enough oxygen is reaching the brain, the brainstem sends signals to the respiratory muscles to increase the minute volume. One way to do that is to increase the respiratory *rate.* (What is another way?)
Confusion	When the brain isn't being perfused adequately, it can't think straight.

14. You are called to a bar to attend a bleeding, unconscious man. The place is full of noise and confusion—unruly customers, police, curiosity seekers. THIS IS THE TIME TO REMEMBER YOUR PRIORITIES: A-B-C.

    First, before you even enter that bar, make certain that the police have the situation under control. (If you did not include that step in your answer, you do not get ANY points for your answer and, furthermore, you are a very poor risk for life insurance!) LOOK FIRST TO YOUR OWN SAFETY, remember?

    a. Open the patient's **airway.**

    b. Check whether he is **breathing.** If not, start artificial ventilation.

    c. Check whether he has a **pulse.** If he does not have a pulse, start external chest compressions.

    d. Cut away the patient's trouser leg, and **find the source of his bleeding.** When you've found it, **control the bleeding with direct pressure on the wound,** preferably applied over a sterile dressing. Check quickly for other lower extremity injuries.

    e. Apply the **MAST,** and inflate it to about 30 to 40 mm Hg.

    f. **Transfer the patient** to the vehicle (he should be on a backboard by now, since you had the MAST on a backboard).

    g. **Get under way** to the hospital, and **start an intravenous infusion** en route. Complete your survey as time permits.

15. Were you able to sort out who needs what?

Patients Who Need IVs for Fluid Replacement	Patients Who Need IVs to Keep a Vein Open
Hypovolemic shock Risk of hypovolemic shock: • External bleeding • Ulcer • Vaginal bleeding • Abdominal trauma • Pelvic/femur fracture • Widespread burns • Heat exhaustion Neurogenic shock MAST indications	Risk of cardiac arrest Seizures Coma Congestive heart failure

Patients Who May Benefit from the MAST (PASG)	Patients for Whom the MAST (PASG) Is Contraindicated
Diffuse lower extremity bleeding Pelvic fracture Neurogenic shock Hypovolemic shock with signs of poor perfusion	Chest injury Head injury Pulmonary edema Any injury above the level of the MAST

16. Intravenous lines are supposed to help save lives, but they may cause problems (most of which can be prevented!).

   a. (1) *You* are the patient's problem! You weren't keeping an eye on the IV. The 59-year-old man who is suddenly short of breath has most probably developed **circulatory overload** because his "keep-open" IV became a "runaway IV" and poured an extra liter of fluid into his vascular space in a very short period of time.
   (2) What you need to do is **slow the IV to keep-open, sit the patient up with his legs dangling,** and **radio your physician for further instructions.** (Why not discontinue the IV altogether?)

   b. (1) The frail old lady probably has very frail veins, and your IV has apparently ruptured the wall of one of those veins and **infiltrated.**
   (2) What you have to do is **discontinue the IV, and start a new one at another site,** if she really needs it. If not, wait until you reach the emergency room, where a new IV can be inserted under more controlled conditions.
   (3) Other things that might cause an IV to slow down include **tightening of the clamp,** a **kink in the tubing,** the tip of the catheter resting up against the wall of the vein, **flexion at a joint** causing the vein to kink, and the **IV bottle hung too low.**

   c. (1) When bright red blood comes spurting back in your face, it's a pretty good indication that you have **accidently cannulated an artery.**
   (2) What you need to do is **immediately withdraw the catheter** and **hold firm pressure over the puncture site** for at least 5 minutes.

   d. (1) A painful, red, swollen venipuncture site is a sign of **thrombophlebitis.**
   (2) The treatment is to **discontinue the IV,** and put a warm compress over the puncture site.
   (3) The likelihood of thrombophlebitis can be minimized by
      (a) Adequate **disinfection of the skin** before venipuncture
      (b) **Wearing sterile gloves** to start an IV
      (c) Covering the puncture site with a **sterile dressing**
      (d) **Securing the catheter** firmly so it can't wobble around inside the vein.

17. To give the baker 200 ml per hour with a macrodrop set:

$$\text{gtt/min} = \frac{\text{volume to be infused} \times \text{gtt/ml of administration set}}{\text{total time of infusion in minutes}}$$

$$= \frac{200 \text{ ml} \times 10 \text{ gtt/ml}}{60 \text{ minutes}}$$

$$= \textbf{approximately 33 gtt/min}$$

18. For the patient who needs only a keep-open line:

$$\text{gtt/min} = \frac{30 \text{ ml} \times 60 \text{ gtt/ml}}{60 \text{ minutes}}$$

$$= \textbf{30 gtt/min}$$

19. Did you decode the secret message? Now engrave it in your memory!

   a. **perfusion**

   b. **sternum**

   c. **leukocyte**

   d. **thrombophlebitis**

   e. **water**

   f. **carbon dioxide**

   g. **tidal**

   h. **shunt**

   i. **safe**

   j. **legs**

   k. **ton**

   Secret Message: DO NOT WAIT UNTIL THE BLOOD PRESSURE FALLS BEFORE YOU SUSPECT SHOCK AND BEGIN TREATMENT!

10
Overview of Pharmacology

Throughout the remainder of the textbook, we will be making reference to various drugs, dosages, and routes of administration. This chapter is intended to provide a general framework for understanding the properties of the specific medications we shall study as we go along.

1. First, of course, we have to learn some new terminology. The words seem obscure only until you've seen them once or twice—then they become familiar.

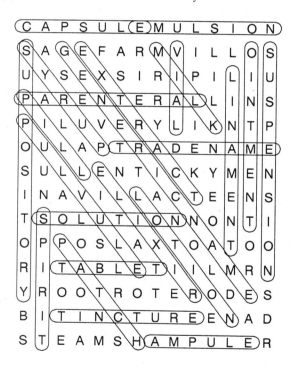

a. Preparation of a drug for external use, usually to relieve some discomfort: a **lotion** or a **linament.**

b. Aqueous suspension of an insoluble drug: **milk.**

c. Preparation of a volatile substance dissolved in alcohol: **spirit.**

d. Dilute alcoholic extract of a drug: **tincture.**

e. Drug suspended in sugar and water: **syrup.**

f. Oil distributed in small globules in water: **emulsion.**

g. Drug shaped into a ball or oval, often coated to disguise an unpleasant taste: **pill.**

h. Cylindrical gelatin container enclosing a dose of medication: **capsule.**

i. Resembles "h", but not made of gelatin and does not separate: **pulvule.**

j. Powdered drug that has been molded or compressed into a small disc: **tablet.**

k. Drug mixed in a firm base that melts at body temperature: **suppository.**

l. Medication impregnated onto adhesive that is applied to the surface of the skin: **patch.**

m. Semisolid preparation for external application, usually containing a medicinal substance: **ointment.**

n. Like "e" above, but with alcohol! **elixir.**

o. Concentrated preparation of a drug made by putting the drug into solution and evaporating off the excess solvent to a prescribed standard: **extract.**

p. Liquid containing one or more chemical substances *entirely dissolved,* usually in water: **solution.** That liquid may be supplied as a single dose in a sealed glass container, called an **ampule,** or in a multidose **vial** with a rubber stopper.

q. Preparation of finely divided drug whose ingredients separate out on standing: **suspension.**

r. Any route of administration other than through the digestive tract: **parenteral.**

s. Lasix is the **trade name** of the drug whose **generic name** is furosemide.

2. Among the factors that may influence the effects of a drug are the following:

   a. The **age of the patient:** Elderly patients, for example, may react differently to drugs than do younger patients.

   b. The patient's **weight,** which will determine the ultimate concentration of a given dose within the body tissues.

   c. The patient's **physical condition** and health problems: Impaired renal function, for example, may hinder excretion of a drug and allow it to accumulate to toxic levels in the body.

   d. **Individual variation:** What is a therapeutic dose for one patient may be too little or too much for another.

   e. **Route of administration:** A drug given by mouth, for example, will take longer to have an effect than one give intravenously.

   f. **Dosage:** A drug may have one effect at a low dose and a different effect at a higher dose. (As we shall learn in Chap. 23, that is precisely the case with dopamine.)

3. Rates of absorption vary according to the route of administration, as follows:

Fastest route:	Intracardiac
	Intravenous
	Endotracheal
	Inhalation
	Sublingual injection
	Sublingual tablet
	Intramuscular injection
	Subcutaneous injection
	Rectal
	Oral
Slowest route:	Topical

4. If you remember "NAVEL," you will remember the drugs that may be administered through an endotracheal tube:

   a. **Naloxone** (Narcan)

   b. **Atropine**

   c. **Valium** (diazepam)

   d. **Epinephrine**

   e. **Lidocaine** (Xylocaine)

5. Two mechanisms prevent a drug that has been taken into the body from exerting its effect forever:

   a. **Excretion** of the unchanged drug, mostly through the lungs and the kidneys

   b. **Inactivation** of the drug by metabolic processes (biotransformation), mostly in the liver

6. Confess! You used your pocket calculator to do the arithmetic with decimals. There's nothing wrong with that (I used mine to prepare this answer section)—so long as you understand the principles involved; for one day you may not be able to find your pocket calculator when you need it to compute a dosage, so you'd better know how to get along without it!

   a. $4.237 + 1.989 = $ **6.226**

   b. $11.4 - 9.62 = $ **1.78**

   c. $0.2 \times 3.413 = $ **0.6826**

   d. $3.5 \div 0.5 = $ **7**

   e. $0.05 + 31.2 + 2 + 0.0006 = $ **33.2506**

   f. $0.05 - 0.025 = $ **0.025**

   g. $\dfrac{2400 \text{ ml}}{70 \text{ kg} \times 2.2 \text{ lb/kg}} = $ **15.5844 ml/lb**

   h. $\dfrac{12.45 + 0.08 - 3.125}{0.5 \times 2.2} = $ **8.55**

   i. $4.892 \times 100 = $ **489.2**

   j. $113.56 \div 1,000 = $ **0.11356**

   k. $0.061 \times 1,000 = $ **61**

   l. $3.6 \div 100 = $ **0.036**

7. To get back and forth between liters and milliliters, we need to be good at dividing and multiplying by 1,000:

   a. 1.5 liters = **1,500** milliliters

   b. 5 liters = **5,000** milliliters

   c. 0.6 liter = **600** milliliters

   d. 9.4 liters = **9,400** milliliters

   e. 0.02 liter = **20** milliliters

   f. 0.5 liter = **500** milliliters

   g. 300 milliliters = **0.3** liter

   h. 1,500 milliliters = **1.5** liters

   i. 10,000 milliliters = **10** liters

   j. 50 milliliters = **0.05** liter

   k. 2,000 milliliters = **2** liters

   l. 500 milliliters = **0.5** liter

8. Multiplying and dividing by 1,000 will also get us back and forth between grams and milligrams:

   a. 1,500 milligrams = **1.5** grams

   b. 325 milligrams = **0.325** gram

   c. 3,500 milligrams = **3.5** grams

   d. 75 milligrams = **0.075** gram

   e. 10,000 milligrams = **10** grams

   f. 100 milligrams = **0.1** gram

   g. 5 grams = **5,000** milligrams

   h. 12 grams = **12,000** milligrams

   i. 0.5 gram = **500** milligrams

   j. 0.025 gram = **25** milligrams

   k. 0.001 gram = **1** milligram

   l. 3.25 grams = **3,250** milligrams

9. The young woman who overdosed on diazepam (Valium) provides you with an opportunity to try out your skills in computaton.

   a. If she took 50 tablets of 5 mg each, her total dosage was 50 tablets $\times$ 5 mg/tablet = **250 mg**.

   b. That is equivalent to **0.25 gm**.

   c. If you want to give 2 liters of fluid over 2 hours:

   $$\frac{2 \text{ L}}{2 \text{ hr}} = \frac{2 \text{ L}}{120 \text{ min}}$$

   $$= \textbf{0.017 L/min} \text{ (approximately)}$$

   d. 0.017 liter per minute is equivalent to **17 ml per minute**.

   e. By definition, 50% dextrose contains *50 gm of dextrose per 100 ml* of solution. But we are giving 50 ml, not 100 ml. So we can solve the problem as follows:

   $$\frac{50 \text{ gm}}{100 \text{ ml}} = \frac{x \text{ gm}}{50 \text{ ml}}$$

   $$100x = 50 \times 50$$

   $$100x = 2,500$$

   $$x = \textbf{25 gm}$$

10. Suppose you left your pocket calculator behind at the home of that young woman who took the overdose. Will you be able to figure out the dos-

ages for this man who may be suffering a heart attack?

a. If your prefilled syringe contains lidocaine in a concentration of 20 mg per milliliter and you need to give 80 mg:

$$\frac{\text{Volume to be}}{\text{administered}} = \frac{\text{desired dose (mg)}}{\begin{array}{c}\text{concentration}\\\text{on hand (mg/ml)}\end{array}}$$

$$= \frac{80 \text{ mg}}{20 \text{ mg/ml}}$$

$$= \textbf{4 ml}$$

b. It is not unusual to follow up a "lidocaine push" by a lidocaine infusion. In this case, you have added 1 gm of lidocaine to 500 ml:

$$\frac{1 \text{ gm}}{500 \text{ ml}} = \frac{1,000 \text{ mg}}{500 \text{ ml}} = \textbf{2 mg/ml}$$

c. The doctor wants you to give 2 mg per minute.

$$\frac{\text{mg/min}}{\text{mg/ml}} = \frac{2 \text{ mg/min}}{2 \text{ mg/ml}} = \textbf{1 ml/min}$$

If the infusion set gives you 60 drops per milliliter:

$$\text{gtt/ml} \times \text{ml/min} = \text{gtt/min}$$

$$60 \text{ gtt/ml} \times 1 \text{ ml/min} = \textbf{60 gtt/min}$$

d. If the patient weighs 175 pounds, his weight in kilograms is

$$\frac{175 \text{ lb}}{2.2 \text{ lb/kg}} = \textbf{80 kg} \text{ (79.55)}$$

e. If the dosage of morphine is 0.1 mg per kilogram, then you need to give this patient

$$0.1 \text{ mg/kg} \times 80 \text{ kg} = \textbf{8 mg} \text{ of morphine}$$

f. Your Tubex cartridge contains morphine in a concentration of 10 mg per milliliter. Therefore you need to give

$$\frac{8 \text{ mg}}{10 \text{ mg/ml}} = \textbf{0.8 ml}$$

g. As we shall learn later on, one of the possible side effects of morphine is to cause bradycardia (slowing of the heart). If you know that (and you should, if you are going to administer the drug!), you will anticipate the side effect and have the antidote, atropine, all ready in a syringe so that you *don't* have to go ferreting around in the drug box in an emergency. In any case, you are supposed to give 0.01 mg per kilogram of atropine to this pa-

tient, and your vial contains atropine in a concentration of 1 mg per milliliter.

First figure out the dosage in milligrams you need to give:

$$0.01 \text{ mg/kg} \times 80 \text{ kg} = 0.8 \text{ mg}$$

Then calculate what volume contains that dosage:

$$\frac{0.8 \text{ mg}}{1 \text{ mg/ml}} = \textbf{0.8 ml}$$

11. You don't even have time to go back to the place where you lost your calculator before you have to make yet another computation, this time to start an Aramine drip on a patient in cardiogenic shock.

a. You are supposed to add 100 mg to the IV bag, and you've got 10 mg per milliliter in each 10-ml vial.

$$\frac{100 \text{ mg}}{10 \text{ mg/ml}} = \textbf{10 ml} \text{ (1 vial)}$$

b. After you've added the 100 mg to the 250-ml bag, the resulting concentration will be

$$\frac{100 \text{ mg}}{250 \text{ ml}} = \textbf{0.4 mg/ml}$$

c. To give 0.2 mg per minute, as ordered, you need to give

$$\frac{0.2 \text{ mg/min}}{0.4 \text{ mg/ml}} = \textbf{0.5 ml/min}$$

d. With your microdrip infusion set, which delivers 60 gtt per milliliter, you will have to run the infusion at

$$0.5 \text{ ml/min} \times 60 \text{ gtt/ml} = \textbf{30 gtt/min}$$

12. It's not surprising you got a headache from all those calculations, but those are precisely the calculations you will be making every day in your work as a paramedic. So keep practicing until you can do them *without* getting a headache! Meanwhile, those two aspirin you took contained

$$325 \text{ mg/tablet} \times 2 \text{ tablets} = \textbf{650 mg} \text{ of aspirin}$$
$$= \textbf{0.65 gm} \text{ of aspirin}$$

13. The things that you need to know about Panacea before you ever administer it to a patient are

a. The **therapeutic effects** of the drug

b. The **indications** for the drug

c. The **contraindications** to the drug

d. The **dosage** in which the drug is given

e. The known **side effects**

f. The **route of administration**

g. Any other drugs or substances with which this drug is **incompatible**

14. Among the ways of trying to ensure that you do not harm anyone in the course of giving medications are the following:

a. **Make sure the physician understands the situation,** so that *he* (or *she*) won't make a mistake in choosing the right drug.

b. **Make sure you understand the physician's order.** If you have any doubts, ask him to repeat it.

c. **Repeat the order back** to the physician to confirm that you received it accurately.

d. **Verify that the patient is not allergic** to the drug ordered.

e. **Read the label** on the drug to make sure it is the drug that was ordered and to check the concentration.

f. **Inspect the ampule or vial** to make sure there are no impurities in the drug or that the expiration date has not passed.

g. **Monitor the patient** after you've administered the drug, for possible side effects. (If you know what the side effects might be, you can prepare appropriately to deal with them.)

h. **Dispose of the needle and syringe safely,** so that no one (including yourself) will get an injection that was *not* prescribed.

15. One thing that *is* true about any skill: You will not learn it solely by reading about it. Skills take *practice.* In a study guide, all we can do is see how much you *know* about the skill, not how well you can perform it.

a. If the contents of a vial or ampule are cloudy or discolored, you may still administer the solution so long as it has not passed its expiration date.
FALSE! If the contents of the vial or ampule are suspect in any way, DISCARD THE VIAL OR AMPULE!

b. To withdraw medication from an ampule, first inject an equivalent amount of air into the ampule.
FALSE. You can if you want to, but all you'll do is make bubbles. Once you've broken off the stem, the ampule is open to the air, so there is no pressure that needs to be opposed. It's when withdrawing medications from a *vial* that you need to inject air first.

c. Disinfect the rubber stopper of a vial with an alcohol swab before inserting a needle into the vial.
TRUE. The object is not to introduce germs into the vial (or into the patient).

d. Intramuscular injections should be avoided in patients suspected to be suffering a heart attack.
TRUE. Injecting anything into a person's muscle may cause the release of muscle enzymes. Ordinarily that is not a problem. But patients suspected of suffering a heart attack will undergo various laboratory tests to confirm or rule out that diagnosis, and some of those tests measure muscle enzymes (as evidence of damage to heart muscle). So giving an intramuscular injection to a patient who may be having a heart attack can create confusion in interpreting laboratory results.

e. To give an intramuscular injection, insert the needle into the muscle at an angle of 45 degrees.
FALSE. For an intramuscular injection, insert the needle at a 90-degree angle.

f. As soon as you have completed giving an injection, swiftly recap the needle on the syringe.
FALSE. Recapping a needle, especially in the chaotic conditions of an emergency, is one of the best ways to stick yourself with it. Dispose of the needle and syringe as a unit in a safe receptacle designed for that purpose.

g. Medications given down an endotracheal tube should be diluted in about 100 ml of sterile water.
FALSE, unless you want to drown the patient! By all means, dilute the medications, but use a *maximum* of 10 ml of sterile water.

16. Were you able to decode the message?

a. **indication**

b. **cumulative**

c. **stimulant**

d. **depressant**

e. **hemoglobin**

f. **protocol**

g. **injury**

h. **socks**

i. **tuna**

Secret Message: DO NOT GIVE INTRA-MUSCULAR OR SUBCUTANEOUS INJEC-TIONS TO A PATIENT IN SHOCK.

Stop and Review I

1. Pondering whether or not to start CPR? Consider the secret message from this question:

   a. **visceral pleura**

   b. **vocal cord**

   c. **diaphoresis**

   d. **trachea**

   e. **fifty**

   f. **mouth**

   g. **tort**

   h. **atelectasis**

   i. **notion**

   Secret Message: FOR THE VICTIM OF CARDIAC ARREST THE ONLY ALTERNATIVE TO CPR IS DEATH.

2. Deciding when it is permissible to treat a patient without his or her expressed consent is always a thorny problem. Observe local policies and the following guidelines:
   * Wherever possible, always *try* to obtain consent.
   * The majority of lawsuits against EMS providers have been for acts of *omission*, not acts of commission—that is, failure to treat or transport. If there is a danger to the patient's life or limb, err on the side of giving appropriate treatment.
   * Involve your superiors or base physician (or both) in your decision.

   A A 9-year-old child struck by a car. He is bleeding profusely. His parents cannot be located.
   Consent in this case is almost certainly implied, for it is hard to imagine that any parent would refuse to allow his child to be treated under such circumstances.

   A A 42-year-old man injured in an automobile accident in which his car was totally demolished. He has bruises on his forehead. He seems confused. He says, "I'm all right. Let me alone. Just call me a taxi."
   This case is less clear-cut, but it does not invite a great deal of debate. It is the kind of case where one of those acts of omission could occur. The patient has been in an accident involving enormous forces (his car was demolished). He has evidence of head injury (bruises, confusion). You would not be faulted for assuming that he might not be mentally competent at that particular moment to refuse treatment. If, on the other hand, you summoned a taxi for him, as he requested, and he died in the taxi on the way home, you would almost certainly find yourself in court.

   B A 58-year-old man with chest pain. His wife phoned for an ambulance. The man says, "It's nothing, just indigestion." He refuses to be examined or treated.
   Here is a different story. As far as we can tell, the patient is a mentally competent adult (we might disagree with his judgment, but that does not mean he is not mentally competent). Try to find out what he is afraid of (his strong denial makes it clear he is afraid of *something*). Explain, without overdramatizing it, the possible consequences of his not getting treatment. If your best efforts to persuade him to be examined and transported to hospital don't win him over, you may not treat or transport him against his will. Be sure, though, to "leave the door open," by assuring the patient that it's OK to call you back if he changes his mind.

   A A 30-year-old woman pulled from the surf in cardiac arrest.
   This is another clear-cut case of implied con-

sent. We have to assume that this woman would want her life saved.

A A 25-year-old man injured in a barroom altercation. He is bleeding profusely from his nose and mouth. He smells strongly of alcohol. He is very belligerent and shouts at you, "Leave me alone, you creeps. If you come any closer, I'll knock your teeth in."

Probably from a strictly legal point of view you *may* treat this patient, for he is apparently sufficiently intoxicated that he cannot be regarded as mentally competent to refuse treatment. Whether you *should* try to treat the patient under the circumstances described is another matter. LOOK FIRST TO YOUR OWN SAFETY! Remember? Try to calm him down by taking a nonbelligerent approach (see discussion of violence containment in Chap. 38). Involve the police if necessary. But if someone says he'll knock your teeth in, it's a good idea to take him at his word.

B An 80-year-old woman who fainted at home. Her son found her on the floor and called for an ambulance. She is conscious when you arrive. She says to you, "You are all very sweet, but one can't live forever, you know, and I don't much fancy hospitals."

There is nothing to suggest that this elderly woman is not mentally competent (the mere fact that she is 80 years old does *not* automatically mean that she is muddle-headed!). She simply doesn't want to go to the hospital, probably for very good reasons. Talk to her about her reasons; you may end up agreeing with her! Or you may discover that there is a social problem that needs to be solved first (e.g., she is worried about who will take care of her cat if she is hospitalized). But in any case, *do not assume that because the patient is elderly, she is no longer competent.* It is very tempting in such situations to direct one's attention to the son's story ("You know, mother is very elderly and can't really take care of herself. . . ."); but to allow a son or anyone else to make decisions for an elderly person is to take away whatever dignity that elderly person has left.

3. Among the common reactions to illness and injury are the following:

   a. **Realistic fears**

   b. Diffuse **anxiety,** stemming from a sense of helplessness

   c. **Depression**

   d. **Anger**

   e. **Confusion** (especially in the elderly when they become ill)

4. Did your knowledge of medical root words help you to decode the technical terms?

   a. Cephalalgia: **headache**

   b. Thoracentesis: **puncture into the thoracic cavity**

   c. Myasthenia: **weakness of muscles**

   d. Hysterectomy: **surgical removal of the uterus**

   e. Hypoglycemia: **abnormally low concentration of sugar in the blood**

   f. Anesthesia: **absence of sensation**

   g. Cardiogenic: **caused by the heart**

   h. Rhinitis: **inflammation of the nose**

   i. Tachypnea: **abnormally rapid rate of breathing**

   j. Hemiparesis: **weakness on one side of the body**

   k. Oliguria: **scanty urine output**

   l. Thrombocytopenia: **deficiency of clotting cells (platelets)**

5. The four questions you need to answer in making your survey of the scene are

   a. **Is it safe for me** to approach the victim(s)?

   b. Is there any **hazard to the patient?**

   c. Am I going to need any **help?**

   d. Do I need any **special equipment** to reach the patient?

If you do *not* ask and answer those questions at every incident scene, your career as a paramedic may be very short indeed, for you will not notice the downed high-tension line draped over the car, or the little trail of fire creeping toward the vehicle, or the bus about to plow into the disabled vehicle that is still in the middle of the road.

6. Every piece of equipment in the ambulance has its indications and sometimes contraindications. You need to be aware of both.

Adjunct	Indicated for:	Do not use in:
Oropharyngeal airway	Airway maintenance in deeply unconscious, breathing patient To improve effectiveness of bag-valve-mask ventilation	Patient who is not deeply unconscious Severe trauma in the mouth Any patient with intact gag reflex
Esophageal obturator airway	Cardiac arrest when it is not feasible to intubate the trachea	Children under 16 Patient who is not deeply unconscious Patient who has swallowed corrosives Known esophageal disease Cirrhosis of the liver
Endotracheal intubation	Cardiac arrest Deep coma Absent gag reflex Imminent danger of upper airway obstruction (e.g., respiratory burns)	Patients with intact gag reflex or likelihood of laryngospasm

7. Were you able to find all the components of the respiratory system? (Will you be able to find the landmarks for endotracheal intubation just as easily?)

a. Absence of breathing: **apnea.**

b. Most effective way to expel a foreign body from the airway: **cough.**

c. Periodic deep inhalation to reopen collapsed alveoli: **sigh.**

d. Protective reflex elicited by stimulating the back of the throat (but often absent in coma): **gag.**

e. Paired structures responsible for voice production: **vocal cords.** The space between them is called the **glottis.**

f. The breast bone is called the **sternum.** The prominence on the breast bone that lies opposite the second intercostal space is called the **angle of Louis.**

g. The structure behind the base of the tongue that shields the entrance to the larynx during swallowing is called the **epiglottis.** The groove between that structure and the base of the tongue, where the tip of a curved laryngoscope blade comes to rest, is called the **vallecula.**

8. Breathing accomplishes two quite separate and mostly unrelated jobs for the body:
   • It furnishes the body with oxygen.
   • It clears away carbon dioxide produced in metabolism and thereby plays a major role in the minute-to-minute regulation of acid-base balance.

   To receive enough oxygen, we need an intact alveolar-capillary interface, and we need to take in air that has a sufficiently high oxygen concentration; the volume of air we take in is not so important. To maintain the carbon dioxide balance of the body, however, the *volume* of air we exchange is critical, as this question should make evident.

   a. The person breathing quietly 12 times per minute with a tidal volume of 500 ml has a minute volume as follows:

   Minute volume = respiratory rate × tidal volume

   = 12 breaths/min × 500 ml/breath

   = **6,000 ml/min**
   (6 liters)

   b. After the accident, when paralysis of the respiratory muscles prevents the person from taking deep breaths (and respiratory distress and fear prompt him to increase his respiratory rate), the minute volume changes as follows:

   Minute volume = respiratory rate × tidal volume

   = 20 breaths/min × 200 ml/breath

   = **4,000 ml/min**

   The situation is much more serious than it might seem from a 33 percent reduction in minute volume. A person whose tidal volume is so small is doing little more than moving his dead space back and forth (do you remember

   what dead space is?), so there is little true alveolar ventilation and therefore little carbon dioxide removal.

   c. Since carbon dioxide will not be removed efficiently, the level of carbon dioxide in the blood will rise, so the arterial **PCO_2 will rise,** by definition a situation of **hypoventilation.**

   d. As a result, the patient's **pH will fall,** reflecting the increased acidity of his blood.

   e. The resulting derangement in his acid-base balance is called a **respiratory acidosis**—"acidosis" because the pH is lower than normal, "respiratory" because the source of the problem is in the respiratory system (the failure to breathe deeply enough).

   f. The treatment required in the acute situation is to **assist the patient's ventilations** to improve the tidal volume and flush out some of that excess carbon dioxide.

9. Next time you have to go up four flights of steps, you'll probably remember to take a full E cylinder, not a half-empty D cylinder. . . .

$$\frac{\text{Duration}}{\text{of flow}} = \frac{(\text{gauge pressure} - 200 \text{ psi}) \times C}{\text{flow rate (L/min)}}$$

$$= \frac{(900 \text{ psi} - 200 \text{ psi}) \times 0.16 \text{ L/psi}}{10 \text{ L/min}}$$

= **11 minutes**

10. The method of choice for opening the airway of a trauma victim is **chin lift only** (answer **D**). All of the other methods mentioned involve motion of the neck, which is precisely what one wishes to avoid in a seriously injured patient.

11. Among the possible indications mentioned in the question, the MAST is most appropriately used for **patients with pelvic fracture** (answer **B**). The

MAST is *contraindicated* in head injury (answer A) and chest injury (answer C).

12. Doing things in the correct sequence is as important as doing them with the correct technique. The sequences of treating critically ill and injured patients should become so automatic to you that you can perform them in your sleep—for situations that require you to deploy the skills of CPR or trauma management are almost always chaotic. If you do not have a fixed set of priorities, you will forget something crucial.

(1) __d__   **Check for hazards** at the scene.

(2) __g__   Open the **airway.**

(3) __e__   Check for **breathing;** if absent, start artificial ventilation.

(4) __b__   Check for a **pulse;** if absent, start chest compressions.

(5) __f__   Control external **bleeding.**

(6) __c__   Apply the **MAST.**

(7) __a__   Start an **IV.** (It will be easier once the MAST is inflated.)

Did you let all that blood distract you from the airway? If so, the patient may well die from asphyxia by the time you find the source of his bleeding, stop the bleeding, and get back to the airway. It takes only a moment to open an airway. REMEMBER YOUR ABCs!!

13. It wasn't really so long ago that we covered fluids and shock. How well do you remember that material?

a. One of the earliest signs of hypovolemic shock is a fall in the blood pressure.
 FALSE!!! A fall in blood pressure is a relatively *late* sign in hypovolemic shock, signalling the collapse of all the patient's compensatory mechanisms, by which time the chances of saving the patient are markedly reduced. Learn to recognize shock by its *early* signs. Better still, learn to *anticipate* shock in situations in which shock is likely to occur.

b. Patients in hypovolemic shock tend to suffer metabolic acidosis.
 TRUE. Because of poor perfusion, and therefore reduced oxygen supply, the peripheral tissues switch to *anaerobic metabolism*, which produces more acid.

c. The intravenous fluid of choice to provide volume to a patient in hypovolemic shock is 5% dextrose in water (D5/W).
 FALSE. Solutions of sugar and water pass very quickly out of the vascular space. What is required in hypovolemic shock is a fluid that will remain *within* the vascular space, at least for a while, to support the circulation. Salt solutions, such as normal saline or lactated Ringer's, are the best crystalloids for the purpose (colloids are perhaps even better).

d. A patient may go into shock without losing any blood or fluid from his body.
 TRUE. A person may bleed internally—into a body cavity like the chest or abdomen, or even into a leg—without losing a drop of blood to the outside. Similarly, in conditions such as peritonitis, a person may "lose" a very large quantity of *fluid* into the abdominal cavity. While that fluid is still inside the body, it is nonetheless lost to the vascular space as surely as if it had all leaked outside.

e. In osmosis, water moves from a solution of lower solute concentration to a solution of higher solute concentration.
 TRUE. The best way to remember the direction water moves during osmosis is to remember that the net effect is to *equalize* the concentration of fluid on either side of the membrane—so water will move from the less concentrated side to the more concentrated side.

f. If the patient's abdomen starts to get distended during CPR, you should immediately apply pressure over the epigastrium to expel the air from the stomach.
 FALSE! Pressing over the epigastrium is an excellent way to produce regurgitation, and if you're doing mouth-to-mouth ventilation, regurgitation is something you would like to avoid for your own sake, if not for the patient's sake! Should you see the abdomen starting to distend, reposition the patient's head to improve the airway, and make sure you are not giving excessive ventilation volumes. Expel the air from the patient's stomach *only as a last resort*, when gastric distention makes it impossible to give adequate ventilations.

14. This problem, which involves calculating concentrations and flow rates, is not merely a theoretical exercise; it is typical of the calculations you will

be making every day in your work as a paramedic, and a slip of the decimal point could kill someone!

a. Your vial of lidocaine contains 50 ml of 4% lidocaine, so by definition it contains

$$\frac{4 \text{ gm of lidocaine}}{100 \text{ ml}} = \mathbf{\frac{2 \text{ gm of lidocaine}}{50 \text{ ml}}}$$

b. When you add that 2 gm of lidocaine to a volume of 500 ml:

$$\frac{2 \text{ gm}}{500 \text{ ml}} = \frac{2{,}000 \text{ mg}}{500 \text{ ml}} = \mathbf{4 \text{ mg/ml}}$$

(Ignore the volume in which the lidocaine was suspended.)

c. If the patient is to receive 2 mg per minute, he must receive

$$\frac{2 \text{ mg/min}}{4 \text{ mg/ml}} = \mathbf{0.5 \text{ ml/min}}$$

d. Thus, the number of drops per minute at which you have to set the infusion is

$$0.5 \text{ ml/min} \times 60 \text{ gtt/ml} = \mathbf{30 \text{ gtt/min}}$$

15. There is at least one big difference between a patient who has been critically injured (a "trauma patient") and a patient who is critically ill (a "medical patient"): It will never be possible for the paramedic to give definitive care to a trauma patient in the field. As we shall see in Chapter 20, the object is to do a few essential things and get moving.

a. **air embolism**

b. **hypotonic**

c. **urticaria**

d. **antagonism**

e. **carotid**

f. **effect**

g. **retarded**

h. **rave**

Secret Message: FOR THE VICTIM OF TRAUMA IN CARDIAC ARREST, START CPR, LOAD, AND GO!

11
Obtaining the Medical History

1. Accident scenes like the one pictured in this question are fairly characteristic of those you will actually encounter in your work. You can learn a lot from the scene and the people there if you know what to look for and what to ask.

   a. The potential sources of information at the scene are

      (1) The **scene itself**
      (2) The **patient**
      (3) The **bystanders** at the bus stop and perhaps in the diner
      (4) Any **medical identification devices** the patient might be carrying

   b. From observing the scene, one can tell that

      (1) The driver was **driving somewhat erratically.**
      (2) Something **caused him to swerve** off the road (perhaps he saw something in the road or thought he saw something).
      (3) The **driver was conscious** when he went off the road (he was able to apply the brakes).
      (4) **Massive forces** were involved in the accident (enough to break the telephone pole).
      (5) The driver **struck his head** against the windshield.

   c. It is necessary to take a history

      (1) To find out **what happened.** *Why* did he swerve off the road? Did something cross his path? Did he suddenly feel ill?
      (2) To find out **what hurts,** i.e., to start searching for his most serious injuries.
      (3) To find out whether he has any **underlying medical problems** that might complicate his care. If, for example, he is taking anticoagulant drugs (drugs that interfere with blood clotting) after a previous heart attack, he could lose a great deal of blood from what might otherwise be a fairly minor wound.
      (4) To **gather information that might otherwise be unavailable to the hospital staff,** such as data on the mechanisms of injury.

   d. Before you start taking the history, you need to

      (1) **Clear your mind** of any preconceived ideas about the patient (e.g., "He must have been drunk.").
      (2) **Introduce yourself,** and explain your role.
      (3) **Find out the patient's name.**
      (4) Try to position yourself **at the patient's level**—lean over or crouch down near the car window.
      (5) Initiate some **physical contact,** e.g., put a hand on the patient's shoulder and instruct him not to move until you have examined him.

2. The first questions you ask the patient should be open-ended, to enable him to state his problem in his own words. Once the general outline of that problem is established, you need to ask more direct questions, but without putting words into the patient's mouth.

   A   What seems to be the problem?
   That is about as open-ended as a question can get!

   A   When did all this start?

   B   Did the pain start when you were exerting yourself?
   In this case, the question *is* putting words in the patient's mouth. It is better to ask, "What were you doing when the pain started?"

   A   What is the pain like?

__A__ Is the pain sharp or dull?
This is a good way to home in on a description of the pain without actually putting the words in the patient's mouth.

__B__ Do you get short of breath when the pain comes on?
This is the kind of yes/no question to avoid. Better to ask, "Did you have any other uncomfortable or unusual feelings along with the pain?"

__B__ Has the pain gotten worse since it started?
Same problem here. The next question is a better way of asking the same thing.

__A__ How has the pain changed since it started?

__A__ What were you doing when the pain started?

__A__ Have you ever had pain like this before?
Yes, this question does require a yes-or-no answer, but sometimes there is no way to avoid that. In this case, there is simply no other way to get at that particular information.

__A__ What medications do you take regularly?

__A__ Are you allergic to any medications?
Again, this yes/no question is acceptable, because it's the most efficient way of getting the information one is looking for.

__A__ What else is bothering you, besides the pain?

3. a. In eliciting the history of the present illness from a patient whose chief complaint is "pain in my gut," one would want to know at least the following:

   (1) Did anything in particular **provoke** the pain? What brought it on? Does anything make it worse? Does anything make it better?
   (2) What is the **quality** of the pain? What is it like?
   (3) Does the pain **radiate** anywhere? Where is it precisely?
   (4) How **severe** is the pain?
   (5) What was the **timing** of the pain; that is, when did it come on? Has it been there constantly since, or does it come and go?
   (6) Are there any **associated symptoms,** such as nausea, vomiting, diarrhea, constipation?

   b. In inquiring about the patient's *other medical history,* you need to find out

   (1) Does he have any **major underlying medical problems?** One way to find out is to ask, "Are you presently under a doctor's care for any condition?"
   (2) Does he take any **medications** regularly?
   (3) Does he have any **allergies?**
   (4) Does he have a **family doctor,** or does he go regularly to a **particular hospital?**

4. Were you able to sort out symptoms from signs? One way to do so is to consider that you can take a history (i.e., elicit all the patient's *symptoms*) over the telephone, without ever seeing the patient. On the other hand, you can observe all of the patient's *signs* even if the patient cannot communicate.

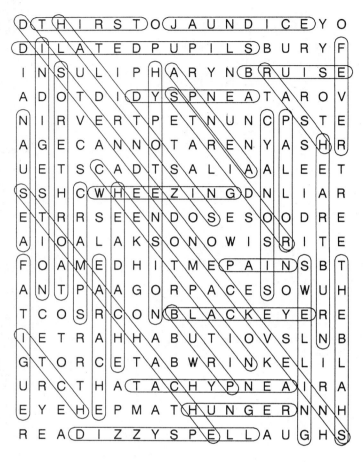

Symptoms	Signs
Sore throat	Halitosis
Nausea	Swelling
Pain	Pallor
Headache	Cyanosis
Dizzy spell	Jaundice
Dyspnea	Tachypnea
Chest pain	Bruise
Fatigue	Distended neck veins
Indigestion	Hypotension
Heartburn	Stridor
Earache	Fever
Hunger	Wheezing
Thirst	Rash
Stomachache	Black eye
Itch	Burp
Cramps	Apnea
The blahs	Dilated pupils

5. This was actually a rather unfair question. In the report printed below, we have circled the elements of the history as we expect you to have done at this stage in your training. As you learn more about diabetes, however, you will discover that the patient's diabetes may have a lot to do with his headache—so it may actually belong under the heading of "history of the present illness" rather than "other medical history." Furthermore, his "water pill," or diuretic, may have been prescribed for high blood pressure secondary to the diabetes, and that high blood pressure may also be a factor in the patient's headache. The point is that in order to know what belongs in the "history of the present illness," one must know something about different illnesses. You may therefore expect your history-taking skills to improve as your knowledge of illnesses and injuries expands.

The patient is a 50-year-old man who called for an ambulance because of a (severe headache) The ——— Chief complaint
headache started without warning about four hours earlier and got progressively worse. It was in the back part of the head, near the neck, and it radiated upward and around to the front. Nothing seemed to make it better or worse. The patient describes the headache as throbbing and very severe. He has never had a headache like this before. Along with the headache, he felt sick to his stomach, but he didn't vomit. He also felt as though he would pass out. — History of the present illness

He is under a doctor's care for diabetes, and he takes Diabinase daily for his diabetes. He also takes "a water pill" every morning. He denies any allergies. — Other history

12
Physical Assessment

Physical assessment is all about looking for *signs* of illness or injury, irrespective of what the patient may or may not have told us.

1. In assessing the patient's general appearance, we take note of

   a. The **position** in which he is found

   b. His **level of consciousness**

   c. His **behavior** and **degree of distress**

   d. Any **obvious wounds** or **deformities**

   e. The **condition of his skin** (color, temperature, moisture)

2. In assessing a patient's level of consciousness, we want to use quantifiable measurements, that is, measurements that can be replicated by others. Thus we need to observe and describe the patient's level of consciousness in terms of **specific responses to specific stimuli.** In the case of the patient described here, we would ask questions such as, "What is your full name? date of birth? address? Do you know where you are? Do you know today's date?" and record the answers. We would also record whether the speech was in any way slurred or garbled.

3. The reason for making a quick check for obvious injuries at the very outset of the secondary survey, before even taking the vital signs, is to **avoid moving an injured part of the patient's body** inadvertently before it has been properly examined and stabilized.

4. Observing the condition of the patient's skin can give us a great deal of information about his cardiovascular status, state of oxygenation, and level of stress.

   __B__ Hot, red, dry
   In classic **heat stroke,** the body cannot shed heat normally, by mechanisms such as sweating, so the skin is relatively dry; peripheral vasodilatation makes it red and hot as well.

   __D__ Hot, red, wet
   In **fever,** by contrast, the patient *can* perspire, so the skin—while hot and red from vasodilatation—is wet from perspiration, one of the body's cooling mechanisms.

   __C__ Cold, white, dry
   In **cold exposure,** the body attempts to conserve heat by shunting blood flow away from the exposed body surface. Peripheral vasoconstriction makes the skin both cold and white.

   __A__ Cold, pale, clammy
   Peripheral vasoconstriction is also at work in **shock,** in this case as the body's attempt to sustain the blood pressure in the face of volume loss. The wetness of the skin reflects one of the responses of the sympathetic nervous system to *stress:* "cold sweat."

5. The particular numbers you obtained in measuring a classmate's vital signs will, of course, differ. But in reporting your results, you should have mentioned not only the numbers but also the other salient characteristics of the vital signs. For example:

   a. Temperature: 98°F orally
   Pulse: 80, full, and regular
   Respirations: 16, regular, unlabored
   Blood pressure: 120/80

In general, when assessing the vital signs, pay attention to the following:

VITAL SIGNS

- TEMPERATURE (usually estimated only)
- PULSE
  1. Rate
  2. Force
  3. Rhythm (regular or irregular)
- RESPIRATIONS
  1. Rate
  2. Rhythm
  3. Ease
  4. Depth
  5. Abnormal noises
  6. Abnormal breath odors
- BLOOD PRESSURE

---

b. An *alternative method for measuring the blood pressure* is **by palpation of the radial pulse.** Inflate the blood pressure cuff above the estimated systolic pressure. Keep a finger on the radial pulse as you slowly deflate the cuff. The point at which you begin to feel a radial pulse is the systolic blood pressure (the needle on the pressure gauge should start to bounce at that point as well).

c. The reason for not removing one's fingers from the radial pulse when counting the respirations is to **give the patient the impression you are still counting the pulse.** As soon as a person becomes aware that his breathing is under scrutiny, it becomes very difficult to breathe naturally, and the respiratory rate may change. Thus it's preferable that the patient *not* know you are counting his breaths.

6. The funny little noises issuing from a patient's airway and lungs can be very informative.

D Fine, crackling sounds produced by airways popping open (**crackles**).

E High-pitched, whistling sounds produced by air moving through narrowed small airways (**wheezes**).

A Rasping sound that signals partial upper airway obstruction by the tongue (**snoring**).

B Sound made by fluid in the pharynx or larynx (**gurgling**).

C Harsh inspiratory squeak produced by severe narrowing of the upper airway, as in laryngeal edema (**stridor**).

7. One can often obtain an extraordinary amount of information from the patient's vital signs. Indeed, some experts in prehospital care argue that there is no need for the paramedic to gather any data about the patient *other than* the vital signs, for the latter provide enough information to decide whether the patient's condition warrants urgent treatment and transport.

a. Pulse = 120, thready, and regular
Respirations = 20, shallow, slightly labored
Blood pressure = 90 systolic (by palpation)

  (1) The vital signs are **abnormal.**

  (2) The pulse is very rapid (**tachycardia**) and weak, the respirations are at the upper limit of normal (**tachypnea**) and shallow, and the blood pressure is low (**hypotension**).

  (3) These vital signs are typical of **hypovolemic shock,** and there are few if any other conditions that will produce this picture. For confirmation, examine the skin (what would you expect the skin to show in shock?), consider the mechanisms of injury, and so on.

b. Pulse = 72, full, and regular
Respirations = 4 and snoring
Blood pressure = 110/70

  (1) These vital signs are **abnormal.**

  (2) The **respirations are extremely slow!** (The snoring indicates that the airway is also partially obstructed by the tongue, which can happen only in deep sleep or coma.)

  (3) From the vital signs only, one can conclude that **something has depressed the patient's respirations.**

  (4) Given the additional information that his pupils were extremely constricted, one could reasonably assume that the most likely cause of the patient's respiratory depression was an **overdose of a narcotic drug.**

c. Pulse = 60, full, slightly irregular
Respirations = 30 and deep; no unusual odors on the breath
Blood pressure = 200/140

(1) These vital signs are **abnormal.**
(2) The **pulse is borderline,** the respirations are abnormally rapid (**tachypnea**) and deep (**hyperpnea**), and the blood pressure is extremely high (**severe hypertension**).
(3) As we shall study in a later chapter, this constellation of vital signs is apt to be present in any condition—medical or traumatic—that produces swelling of the brain (**cerebral edema**).
(4) The finding of unequal pupils serves to substantiate the assumption that the patient has cerebral edema from some cause.

d. Pulse = 56, full, and regular
Respirations = 12 and unlabored
Blood pressure = 120/65

This set of vital signs underscores the **importance of knowing the context** in which they were obtained. They **may be normal or abnormal.** If they were taken from an Olympic athlete at rest, they are undoubtedly normal. If they were taken from a middle-aged man suffering chest pain, we would tend to be very concerned about a pulse of 56. We would say the patient had a **bradycardia** and very probably give him atropine to speed up his heart.

8. Spotting abnormal physical signs is only part of physical assessment; the other part is drawing the correct conclusions from those signs.

I   Narcotics overdose (**pinpoint pupils**)

J,M   Cardiac arrest
Of course, **absent pulse** is the cardinal sign; but after a few minutes of arrest, one would expect to see some **cyanosis of the lips** as well.

D,O,U   Heart failure
When the *right* side of the heart fails, fluid backs up behind the right heart and leaks out into the tissues, so one sees **distention of the jugular veins** and peripheral **edema.** When the *left* side of the heart fails, the lungs may fill with fluid, causing shunt and hypoxemia, so if you also wrote answers **J** (cyanosis of the lips) and **L** (restlessness), you are very sharp. The S_3 gallop may occur with failure of either side of the heart, and the really alert students of

physiology will also know that the circulation time may be considerably prolonged in heart failure, so **capillary refill** could be **prolonged** (answer **K**).

A,G,V   Skull fracture
Periorbital ecchymoses ("coon's eyes"), **Battle's sign** (ecchymoses over the mastoid bone), and the **drainage of clear fluid from the ear** are all classic signs of skull fracture.

T   Stroke
Hemiplegia is the typical pattern of paralysis in stroke (as opposed to paraplegia or quadriplegia in a spinal cord lesion).

J,L   Hypoxemia
Both **cyanosis of the lips** and **restlessness** should make you think of hypoxemia.

N,C   Respiratory distress
Retraction of the suprasternal muscles is one of several signs that a patient is struggling to breathe. It is also reasonable to call **stridor** a sign of respiratory distress; stridor is, in fact, a sign of impending respiratory catastrophe.

K,L   Shock
Prolonged capillary refill time and **restlessness** are both common signs of shock.

B   Diabetic ketoacidosis
The **fruity odor to the breath** is produced by the ketones churned out by the diabetic's disordered metabolism.

S   Spinal cord injury
Priapism may signal injury to the spinal cord.

O   Increased right ventricular pressure
The most direct indication of increased pressure in the right ventricle of the heart is **jugular venous distention.** If the increase in right ventricular pressure is chronic, one might also expect to see some **edema,** so you would not be incorrect if you also included answer **D.**

C   Laryngeal edema
Stridor should always be a tip-off to a narrowed upper airway.

R   Pelvic fracture
Genuine **pain on compression of the iliac crests** in the context of massive injury means pelvic fracture until proved otherwise.

__F__ Fluid/blood in the pericardium
It's the blood or excess fluid that **muffles the heart sounds.**

__Q__ Intra-abdominal bleeding
It's not proof positive, but when you see a **distended abdomen** in a victim of trauma, especially if there are **bruises** on the abdomen, you have to assume there is massive intra-abdominal hemorrhage and anticipate shock.

__H__ Peritonitis
When a patient **cries out each time the stretcher is jarred,** it's a good bet that his peritoneum is inflamed.

__E__ Fracture of the orbit (eye socket in the skull)
Paralysis of upward gaze is the classic sign here.

__P__ Pneumothorax
Subcutaneous emphysema can occur whenever the lung or part of the airway is disrupted and air leaks into the soft tissues. In a pneumothorax severe enough to cause an increase in intrathoracic pressure (e.g., a tension pneumothorax), one might also see **jugular venous distention,** so if you also wrote answer **O,** consider yourself very sharp. And if, in addition, you mentioned answer **L** (**restlessness**), consider yourself even sharper.

9.

Body Region	Trauma Patient	Medical Patient
Head	**Bleeding,** scalp **depression; blood** or fluid draining from the ears or nose; **eye movements; pupillary signs;** blood, vomitus, or foreign **material in mouth; blue lips**	Facial **asymmetry; icterus; pupillary signs; pallor** of the conjunctivae; **cyanosis** of the lips
Neck	**Tracheal deviation, tenderness, deformity, jugular distention**	**Jugular distention**
Chest	**Bruises, asymmetry, unequal breath sounds**	**Abnormal shape,** abnormal **breath sounds**
Abdomen	**Distention, masses, ecchymoses,** presence of **bowel sounds, rigidity**	**Distention, bowel sounds, tenderness, rigidity**
Back	**Bruises, wounds,** spinal **tenderness**	Edema
Extremities	**Deformity, bruises, movement, sensation, capillary refill**	**Edema,** equality of **pulses, strength, sensation**

10. The secret messages we present in these exercises aren't really intended to be secret. Indeed, they are generally selected from the most important messages in the chapter.

a. **rales**

b. **hemiplegia**

c. **edema**

d. **hemiparesis**

e. **oxygen**

f. **asystole**

g. **osmosis**

h. **sniffing**

i. **Battle's**

j. **torr**

k. **nine**

l. **no**

Secret Message: RESTLESSNESS IS ONE OF THE EARLIEST SIGNS OF HYPOXEMIA OR INTERNAL BLEEDING.

13
Medical Reporting and Record Keeping

1. Were you able to sort out the history from the physical assessment?

__F__ a. There was no pedal edema. (**head-to-toe survey**)

__C__ b. The patient is allergic to penicillin. (**other medical history**)

__B__ c. The pain came on while he was watching television. (**present illness**)

__E__ d. The blood pressure was 190/110. (**vital signs**)

__G__ e. He was given oxygen by nasal cannula at 4 liters per minute. (**treatment**)

__A__ f. The patient is a 51-year-old man with chest pain. (**chief complaint**)

__F__ g. The chest was clear. (**head-to-toe survey**)

__D__ h. His skin was cold, pale, and sweaty. (**general appearance**)

__H__ i. The patient was transported in a semisitting position. (**condition during transport**)

__B__ j. Nothing seemed to make the pain better or worse. (**present illness**)

__E__ k. The pulse was 52 and full, with an occasional premature beat. (**vital signs**)

__F__ l. The neck veins were not distended. (**head-to-toe survey**)

__F__ m. There was no cyanosis of the lips. (**head-to-toe survey**)

__C__ n. The patient takes Maalox and cimetidine regularly. (**other medical history**)

__B__ o. He also felt nauseated. (**present illness**)

__F__ p. His abdomen was soft and nontender. (**head-to-toe survey**)

__E__ q. His respirations were 20 per minute and unlabored. (**vital signs**)

__D__ r. He was sitting in a chair and appeared to be frightened. (**general appearance**)

__C__ s. He is under the care of Dr. Tums for an ulcer. (**other medical history**)

__D__ t. He was alert and fully oriented. (**general appearance**)

__B__ u. He denies any shortness of breath. (**present illness**)

__G__ v. An IV was started with D5/W to a KVO rate. (**treatment**)

__B__ w. The pain radiates down his left arm. (**present illness**)

__H__ x. The blood pressure came down to 170/90 during transport. (**condition during transport**)

__B__ y. He describes the pain as squeezing. (**present illness**)

__F__ z. Heart sounds were clear. (**head-to-toe survey**)

In rearranging the sentences into the correct sequence for presentation, there may be some variation in the order of sentences within a given category (e.g., the sentences that make up the "history of the present illness," which you labelled B); but all sentences from category B should precede those from category C, which should precede those from category D, and so forth.

HISTORY

Chief Complaint

(1) __F__ The patient is a 51-year-old man with chest pain.

History of the Present Illness

(2) __C__ The pain came on while he was watching television.

(3) __Y__ He describes the pain as squeezing.

(4) __W__ The pain radiates down his left arm.

(5) __J__ Nothing seemed to make the pain better or worse.

(6) __O__ He also feels nauseated.

(7) __U__ He denies any shortness of breath.

Other Medical History

(8) __S__ He is under the care of Dr. Tums for an ulcer.

(9) __N__ The patient takes Maalox and cimetidine regularly.

(10) __B__ The patient is allergic to penicillin.

PHYSICAL ASSESSMENT

General Appearance

(11) __R__ He was sitting in a chair and appeared to be frightened.

(12) __T__ He was alert and fully oriented.

(13) __H__ His skin was pale, cold, and sweaty.

Vital Signs

(14) __K__ The pulse was 52 and full, with an occasional premature beat.

(15) __Q__ His respirations were 20 per minute and unlabored.

(16) __D__ The blood pressure was 190/110.

Head-to-Toe Survey

(17) __M__ There was no cyanosis of the lips.

(18) __L__ The neck veins were not distended.

(19) __G__ The chest was clear.

(20) __Z__ Heart sounds were clear.

(21) __P__ His abdomen was soft and nontender.

(22) __A__ There was no pedal edema.

TREATMENT

(23) __E__ He was given oxygen by nasal cannula at 4 liters per minute.

(24) __V__ An IV was started with D5/W to a KVO rate.

CONDITION DURING TRANSPORT

(25) __I__ The patient was transported in a semisitting position.

(26) __X__ The blood pressure came down to 170/90 during transport.

Question: What do you think is wrong with this patient? Should anything else have been done that was not done?

2. Now that you've had some practice, this second exercise should be a little easier than the first.

__F__ a. The right leg was severely angulated at the mid-femur. (**head-to-toe survey**)

__E__ b. The pulse was 92, somewhat weak, and regular. (**vital signs**)

__B__ c. Bystanders say that the car that hit him was travelling very fast. (**present illness**)

__C,B__ d. He has a Medic Alert tag that says he is a diabetic.
Here is a good example of how knowing a little bit about an illness can change the way we look at data. On the face of things, the fact that the patient is a diabetic would seem to have nothing to do with his present problem, so answer **C** (**other medical history**) would seem appropriate. But how

did the accident happen? He staggered out into the street as if he were drunk—a description that makes one wonder, if one knows something about diabetes, whether the patient was having an insulin reaction. If you suspected so, you would classify the fact that he is a diabetic as part of the **history of the present illness,** since it may have contributed to his accident and may still be contributing to his coma.

<u>F</u>   e. There is a bruise on the left forehead. (**head-to-toe survey**)

<u>D</u>   f. His skin is cool, pale, and moist. (**general appearance**)

<u>G</u>   g. He was secured to a backboard. (**treatment**)

<u>A</u>   h. The patient is a middle-aged man who was struck by a car while crossing the street. (**chief complaint**)

<u>E</u>   i. Respirations were 30, deep, and noisy; BP was 160/110. (**vital signs**)

<u>D</u>   j. The patient was unconscious and did not withdraw from painful stimuli. (**general appearance**)

<u>G</u>   k. An oropharyngeal airway was inserted, and oxygen was given by nasal cannula at 4 liters per minute. (**treatment**)

<u>B</u>   l. He apparently staggered into the street without looking, as if he were drunk. (**present illness**)

<u>F</u>   m. The chest wall was stable, and breath sounds were equal bilaterally. (**head-to-toe survey**)

<u>G</u>   n. We put the right leg in a traction splint. (**treatment**)

<u>F</u>   o. The pupils were equal, midposition, and reactive to light. (**head-to-toe survey**)

<u>H</u>   p. There was no change in his condition during transport. (**condition during transport**)

<u>F</u>   q. There was no blood or fluid draining from his nose or ears. (**head-to-toe survey**)

<u>F</u>   r. His abdomen was soft. (**head-to-toe survey**)

<u>F</u>   s. The dorsalis pedis pulses were equal. (**head-to-toe survey**)

Rearranging the sentences into the correct sequence for presentation, we come up with the following:

HISTORY

Chief Complaint

(1) <u>H</u> The patient is a middle-aged man who was struck by a car while crossing the street.

History of the Present Illness

(2) <u>L</u> He apparently staggered into the street without looking, as if he were drunk.

(3) <u>C</u> Bystanders say that the car that hit him was travelling very fast.

(4) <u>D</u> He has a Medic Alert tag that says he is a diabetic.

Other Medical History

(Apparently none is available; the Medic Alert tag could have been listed here, as previously noted.)

PHYSICAL ASSESSMENT

General Appearance

(5) <u>J</u> The patient was unconscious and did not withdraw from painful stimuli.

(6) <u>F</u> His skin is cool, pale, and moist.

Vital Signs

(7) <u>B</u> The pulse was 92, somewhat weak, and regular.

(8) <u>I</u> Respirations were 30, deep, and noisy; BP was 160/110.

Head-to-Toe Survey

(9) <u>E</u> There is a bruise on the left forehead.

(10) <u>Q</u> There was no blood or fluid draining from his nose or ears.

(11) <u>O</u> The pupils were equal, midposition, and reactive to light.

(12) <u>M</u> The chest wall was stable, and breath sounds were equal bilaterally.

(13) __R__   His abdomen was soft.

(14) __A__   The right leg was severely angulated at the mid-femur.

(15) __S__   The dorsalis pedis pulses were equal.

TREATMENT

(16) __K__   An oropharyngeal airway was inserted, and oxygen was given by nasal cannula at 4 liters per minute.

(17) __N__   We put the right leg in a traction splint.

(18) __G__   He was secured to a backboard.

CONDITION DURING TRANSPORT

(19) __P__   There was no change in his condition during transport.

Question: What are the likely possible causes of this patient's coma?

3. The parts of the case history are labelled below.

History of the present illness {

The patient is a 49-year-old man who called for an ambulance because of chest pain. The pain was "squeezing" in character, radiated to the left shoulder and jaw, and had been present for 2 hours. The pain was accompanied by increasing difficulty in breathing, relieved somewhat by sitting upright. The patient denied nausea, vomiting, sweating, or palpitations. He is known to be a heart patient and takes nitroglycerin at home; he took two nitroglycerin today, without relief. He denies any history of hypertension or diabetes. He has

— Chief complaint

— Pertinent negatives

Other medical history { been treated for peptic ulcer in the past.

Physical examination {

On physical examination, the patient was sitting bolt upright; he appeared alert and apprehensive and was in moderate respiratory distress, breathing shallowly 30 times per minute. Pulse was 130, weak and regular, and BP 200/90. His neck veins were distended to the angle of the jaw at 45 degrees. Wet crackles were heard at both lung bases, and auscultation of the heart revealed a gallop rhythm. The abdomen was not distended. There was 1+ presacral and ankle edema.

— General appearance

— Vital signs

— Head-to-toe survey

— Pertinent negative

Treatment {
Condition during transport {

The patient was given oxygen by nasal cannula at 6 liters/minute and transported to Montefiore Hospital in a semisitting position. His vital signs remained stable throughout transport.

4. a. Besides the standard information regarding the patient's medical history and physical findings, the trip sheet should contain a **record of the times** (time the call was received, time the ambulance departed, time the ambulance reached the scene and so on).

   b. Such a record is important to **enable evaluation** of such things as **response times** or **how much time is being spent at the scene.**

5. Two reasons for making sure that your trip sheets are accurate and complete are

   a. **For the benefit of the patient,** whose subsequent care may depend on the information that you have (or have not) provided.

   b. **For your own benefit,** if the case should ever become a subject for court proceedings. The trip sheet reflects on the person who wrote it. If your trip sheet is sloppy and incomplete, a court would not be unjustified in wondering whether the care you gave the patient was also sloppy and incomplete.

14
Mechanisms of Trauma

1. In this question, we are asked to consider the forces involved when a 2,000-pound automobile travelling at 20 mph strikes a pedestrian.

   a. Some of the kinetic energy of the vehicle will remain energy of motion, assuming the vehicle keeps moving. (If the driver hits the brakes, the friction of the brakes will transform that kinetic energy into heat.) Some will be **absorbed by the vehicle** in the deformation of the bumper or hood. The remainder will be **absorbed by the pedestrian** who has been struck by the vehicle.

   b. Had the vehicle weighed 6,000 pounds instead of 2,000 pounds, that is, had its weight (mass) been tripled, its kinetic energy at any given speed would also have been **tripled,** according to the kinetic energy equation:

   $$KE = \frac{mV^2}{2}$$

   c. Had the vehicle been travelling at 60 mph instead of at 20 mph, that is, had its velocity been tripled, its kinetic energy would have been **increased nine times,** for it increases as the *square* of the velocity. That is why it is nearly impossible for a pedestrian to survive an impact with a vehicle going faster than about 40 mph, even a relatively small vehicle—the kinetic energies become overwhelming.

2. When a car travelling at 50 mph slams into a concrete wall, three distinct collisions take place:

   a. Collision 1 is **between the *automobile* and the concrete wall.** Since the automobile is both more mobile and more deformable than the concrete wall, the majority of the kinetic energy will be absorbed by the automobile, in its rebound off the wall and deformity of the front end.

   b. Collision 2 is **between the *occupant* and the automobile.** In that collision, some of the kinetic energy will be absorbed by the automobile (e.g., in denting the dashboard), but the larger proportion will be absorbed by the occupant.

   c. Collision 3 is **between the internal *organs* of the occupant and the restraining walls of his body** (e.g., the skull, the chest cage, the pelvic girdle). The majority of the kinetic energy in that collision will be absorbed by the internal organs.

3. As soon as you receive the dispatcher's instructions to respond to a head-on or rear-end collision, you should already have a picture in your mind of the type of injuries you might encounter.

   __C__ "Whiplash" injury
   That is the classic injury from a **rear-end collision,** in which the head lags behind as the body is accelerated forward.

   __B__ Lateral rib fractures
   Lateral rib fractures and lateral flail chest are most commonly seen after a **lateral collision,** in which the patient's humerus is jammed into the side of his chest. If you also mentioned a **pedestrian accident** (answer **D**), you may mark your answer correct, for being struck from the side could produce rib fracture, especially if the pedestrian is not very tall.

   __D__ Fracture of the tibia/fibula
   This is the classic initial injury when a **pedestrian is struck by an oncoming car** and the bumper catches him in the lower leg.

   __A__ Fracture of the patella
   The massive deceleration forces in a **head-on collision** hurl the unrestrained passenger for-

ward, and usually the first part of the body to come in contact with the car is the knee, which may be fractured by the force of impact.

B Fracture of the humerus
A staved-in door in a **lateral collision** may fracture the humerus on that side.

A–D Cervical spine injury
All of the accidents listed can result in cervical spine injury, each through a different combination of forces. The important point to remember is that virtually any casualty subjected to the enormous forces and kinetic energies of a motor vehicle accident is at risk of cervical spine injury. So the safest rule of thumb is TREAT EVERY ACCIDENT VICTIM AS A CERVICAL SPINE INJURY UNTIL PROVED OTHERWISE!

4. When you arrive at the accident scene, a close inspection of the scene and of the damaged vehicle(s) can provide extremely important information—information that will enable the doctors who take over the patient's care to detect and manage the patient's problems much more expeditiously. Indeed, what you observe (or fail to observe) about the accident scene could make the difference between life and death for the patient—so keep your eyes open, report what you have observed to the base physician, and record your findings on the patient's trip sheet.

Vehicular Clue	Injuries To Be Alert For
Bashed-in dashboard	Fracture of the **patella;** fracture of the **femur;** posterior **dislocation of the hip**
Broken steering wheel	Lacerations of the **mouth, chin; tracheal fracture; cervical spine** injury; **myocardial contusion, pericardial tamponade; pulmonary contusion; pneumothorax; hemothorax;** shearing of the **aorta;** shearing of the **liver, spleen, pancreas**
Spider-web crack in windshield	**Facial lacerations; skull fracture,** with or without **brain injury; cervical spine** injury
Door on driver's side smashed in	Fracture of the **clavicle, humerus;** multiple lateral **rib fractures** with or without **flail chest;** underlying **pulmonary contusion;** fracture of the **pelvis** or **hip; head injuries; cervical spine** fractures
Front-seat occupants wearing three-point seat belts	Fractures of **lower cervical and upper thoracic spine;** fractures of the **clavicle**

5. a. To evaluate the nature and potential seriousness of the jumper's injuries, you need to know

 (1) The distance (**height**) that he jumped, for that will determine the speed at which he fell and therefore the force of impact with which he hit the ground.
 (2) **How he landed:** On his feet? facedown? on his rump? That will tell you what part(s) of the body absorbed the greatest amount of kinetic energy.
 (3) **What kind of surface he landed on.** A pile of hay has a lot more give than a concrete sidewalk. The more the surface can "give," the less the falling body will have to deform.
 (4) The **physical condition of the patient** before the fall. Does he have any underlying physical problems, such as an ulcer or an enlarged spleen, that might predispose him to certain injuries?

 b. If the patient landed on his feet on a hard surface, we would be well advised to look for **calcaneal fractures, compression fractures of the L1 and L2 vertebrae,** and possibly also fractures of the **femur** and **pelvis.** Massive deceleration forces acting on internal organs may also have produced **pulmonary contusions, laceration of the spleen or liver,** or **rupture of the bladder.**

6. The 2-year-old child who fell off the second-story balcony is likely to have a different constellation of injuries. Because a child's head is much larger and heavier relative to its body than is the case with an adult, the child is more likely to **fall head-first,** so **head injuries** of all types are possible. As the head strikes the ground, the kinetic energy of the fall will also be absorbed by the neck, so it would be well to anticipate **cervical spine injury,** just as in a diving accident. If the child tried to break his fall with his outstretched hands, there may also be **fractures of the wrists and arms.**

7. How well did you do at that shooting incident? Did you come out of it alive?

 a. This question was included to see whether you remember the priorities of the primary survey, specifically the *first* priority: IS IT SAFE FOR *ME* TO APPROACH THE VICTIMS? Thus, in the case described here, the *first* thing to do on reaching the scene is to **notify the police.** Do NOT go plunging into the midst of a group of intoxicated people when there has just been a shooting. The person who did the shooting may still be present, he may still be in possession of his weapon, and there may still be enough ammunition left in it to polish off you and your crew.

b. The information you should try to obtain regarding the shooting incident includes

(1) The **type and caliber of the weapon** used.
(2) The **range** from which it was fired.
(3) The **type of bullet** used. (If possible, obtain an unfired cartridge; otherwise ask the police for a description of the ammunition.)

c. In examining the patient, look especially for

(1) The **entrance wound**
(2) **Powder residue** on the skin around the entrance wound
(3) An **exit wound** (may or may not be present)

8. Explosions produce several different types of injury, and one needs to anticipate each type; otherwise it is easy to miss the less obvious injuries.

Category of Injury	Example(s)
Primary blast injury	Ruptured eardrum; pulmonary contusion or pulmonary tears, which may produce cerebral air embolism; bowel injury
Secondary blast injury	Lacerations and impaled objects from flying debris
Tertiary blast injury	Head injury, fractures, bruises from being hurled against a hard object
Miscellaneous injuries	Inhalation of toxic fumes; burns from hot gases or from fires started by the explosion

9. The patient described in this question exemplifies how potentially life-threatening problems might be missed if one did not have a high index of suspicion for primary blast injury. The patient has very few outward signs of injury, but in fact, he has been injured seriously.

Injury	Evidence
Ruptured tympanic membrane (eardrum)	Dried blood in ear canal (not in itself serious, but an indicator that the patient did sustain at least 7-psi blast pressure)

Injury	Evidence
Pulmonary injury	Symptoms: tight feeling in the chest Signs: tachypnea and shallow breathing
Cerebral air embolism	Confusion and disorientation

Such a patient needs to receive oxygen at once. He should be placed in a left lateral recumbent position, in about 10 degrees of head-down tilt, in an attempt to trap the air bubbles in the heart chambers and keep them from proceeding on into the coronary arteries or brain. Definitive treatment will require a hyperbaric chamber, so appropriate arrangements need to be started.

10. We hope that the secret message wasn't really such a big secret.

a. **yaw**

b. **entrance wound**

c. **jaw**

d. **patella**

e. **femur**

f. **hip**

g. **chin**

h. **hemothorax**

i. **humerus**

j. **flail chest**

k. **spleen & liver**

l. **inferior**

m. **glottis**

n. **address**

o. **ddt**

p. **indecisive**

Secret Message: WHEN THE WINDSHIELD IS DAMAGED, THE FRONT SEAT OCCUPANT HAS SUFFERED CERVICAL SPINE INJURY UNTIL PROVED OTHERWISE.

15
Wounds and Burns

1. The skin is the largest organ of the human body and one of the few organs we can easily *see* from the outside of the body.

   a. The structural components of the skin are labelled below.

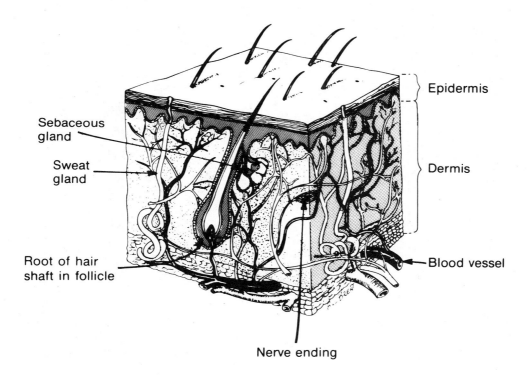

Sebaceous gland

Sweat gland

Root of hair shaft in follicle

Epidermis

Dermis

Blood vessel

Nerve ending

b. The *functions* of intact skin include the following:

   (1) It **protects** underlying tissue **from injury.**
   (2) It plays a major role in **temperature regulation.**
   (3) It **prevents excessive loss of water** from the body.
   (4) It serves as a **sense organ** for temperature, touch, and pain.

2. The skin is subject to a variety of different types of injury.

   a. Injury A is called a **laceration,** for it is a jagged tear in the skin's surface (a clean cut would be called an incision). The appropriate treatment is to **apply a pressure dressing** to stop the bleeding.

   b. Injury B is called a **contusion,** or bruise, for it is a closed wound with bleeding beneath the intact skin (which will doubtless evolve into a full-blown **hematoma**). The treatment consists of (1) application of **cold packs** to the injured area; (2) firm **compression** over the injured area; (3) **elevation** of the arm; and (4) application of a **splint** to the arm.

c. Injury C is an **impaled object,** which is a type of **puncture wound** in which the implement that made the puncture remains embedded in the wound. The treatment is to **stabilize the impaled object in place.**

d. Injury D is an **avulsion,** for a flap of skin has been torn loose from the forehead. The treatment is to **rinse the wound and the avulsed tissue** quickly with sterile saline, to flush out dirt and debris, and then **place the skin flap back in its normal position** and hold it in place with a firmly applied dressing.

e. Injury E is called an **abrasion,** or brush burn. The only treatment it needs in the field is a quick rinse and a lightly applied dressing.

3. Did you find all the injuries or signs of injury hidden in the grid? Finding clues on the patient's body requires at least as much diligence.

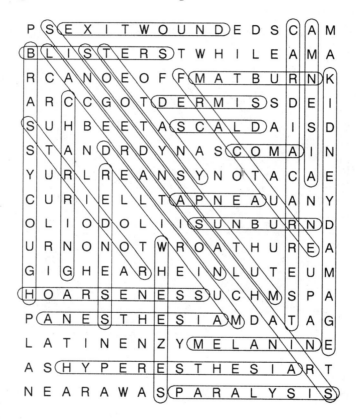

a. An abrasion is sometimes called a **mat burn.**

b. A jagged cut is a **laceration.**

c. The skin derives its color from granules of pigment called **melanin.**

d. These three words are associated with *first*-degree burns:

   sunburn
   redness
   hyperesthesia

e. These three words are associated with *second*-degree burns:

   blisters
   scald
   dermis

f. These two words are associated with *third*-degree burns:

anesthesia
charring

g. Suspect that a victim of flame burns has suffered respiratory injury if any of the following signs are present:

singed nasal hairs	**stridor**
sooty sputum	**wheezes**
brassy cough	**hoarseness**

h. Injury from a high-voltage electric source or from lightning may produce any of the following:

apnea	**paralysis**
cardiac arrest	**fracture**
kidney damage	**delirium**
exit wound	**coma**
amnesia	**tetany**

4. a. To control the bleeding from Bugsy Butterfingers' left calf, you have several methods available to you:

   *(1) **Direct manual pressure** over the bleeding site (likely to be the most effective)
   (2) **Elevation** of the bleeding extremity
   (3) **Pressure point control,** in this case by pressing over the *femoral* artery
   (4) **Splinting** the left leg
   (5) As a last resort, applying a **tourniquet**

   b. If Bugsy's wound had been on the forearm rather than on the leg, pressure over the **brachial** artery might have helped control the bleeding.

5. When Frank Fillet accidently amputates two of his fingers, you have two problems—first to treat Mr. Fillet himself, then to preserve the amputated parts in optimal condition.

   a. To treat the injury, the first priority will be to **stop the bleeding.** Probably direct pressure will be sufficient, since amputations ordinarily do not bleed profusely. Apply lots of fluffed gauze to the stumps of the fingers and bandage the whole hand in a position of function (fingers slightly flexed). The patient will doubtless require a lot of calming down; if you can remain calm, it will help a great deal.

   b. Once you have taken care of the patient, you may turn your attention to the amputated parts. **Rinse the two fingers** free of contaminants with cool, sterile saline. **Wrap** them loosely in saline-moistened sterile gauze. Then **place them in a plastic bag,** seal the bag, and place it in a **cool container** for transport. Do NOT place the amputated part in water or directly on ice!

6. Bugsy's Butcher Shop is definitely not a healthy workplace. Now poor Hercules Hamburger has also become a casualty—not only of the meat grinder that mangled his hand but also of a good Samaritan trying to help. The mistakes made in caring for Hercules include the following:

   a. **No attempt** was made **to stop the bleeding by other means,** such as direct pressure alone or in combination with pressure point control, splinting, and so on. A TOURNIQUET IS A LAST RESORT, not a first resort!

   b. **A rope should not be used as a tourniquet,** nor should any other narrow materials that can damage underlying tissues.

   c. The **tourniquet was twisted too tightly.** It is virtually never necessary to twist a tourniquet as tight as it will go; the end point is when the bleeding slows sufficiently that it can then be controlled by direct pressure.

   d. **A tourniquet should never be covered,** lest it escape attention. Our good Samaritan covered the patient's whole arm in a butcher's apron, perhaps to spare the patient the sight of his mangled extremity.

7. The patient who jumped from his bedroom window to escape a fire is in grave jeopardy. He is unconscious, so his airway is liable to be obstructed. He may have additional respiratory injury (note the burns to his face), along with head and neck injuries (note the mechanisms of injury). And he almost certainly has at least one broken bone. The steps in treating him are as follows:

   a. **Put out the fire** in his trousers!

   b. **Open his airway** with cervical spine precautions (i.e., chin lift or jaw lift only).

c. Administer **oxygen**—he's been in a smoky environment.

d. **Intubate the trachea.** This patient is unconscious, so his airway is already in jeopardy. In addition, he has almost certainly sustained airway injury—note the singed beard and swollen lips—so don't wait until laryngeal edema closes off his airway altogether. Get the endotracheal tube in while it's still relatively easy to do so.

e. Cut away the trousers, and **perform the secondary survey.** In doing so, rapidly **evaluate** the extent, depth, and severity of **the burn.**

f. **Cover the burns** with sterile dressings.

g. **Splint** the left leg and any other fractures; immobilize the patient on a **backboard.** (He fell from 15 feet, so you have to assume he injured his spine until proved otherwise.)

h. **Start an IV** (can be done en route to hospital). Note: The precise point in time at which you start the IV will be determined by the patient's overall condition and the amount of help you have at the scene. If the patient is shocky, start the IV as soon as you've secured the airway.

8. The two reasons for intubating the patient in the previous question were, as implied:

a. **The patient was unconscious,** and it must be assumed that *any* unconscious patient is incapable of protecting his airway.

b. The patient had **evidence of respiratory burns** (singed beard, burned lips) and was therefore in danger of rapidly progressive laryngeal edema.

9. To calculate the patient's fluid needs, we need first to assess the extent of his burns. Then we calculate the IV rate in the usual fashion.

a. The percentage of the patient's body that has been burned is calculated as follows:

Whole right leg	18%
Anterior left leg	9%
Anterior trunk	18%
Whole right arm	9%
TOTAL	**54%**

b. Now we have to calculate the patient's fluid needs. First, we need to convert his weight from pounds to kilograms:

$$\frac{154 \text{ lb}}{2.2 \text{ lb/kg}} = \textbf{70 kg}$$

Now, according to the Parkland formula, the patient's fluid needs over the first *8* hours will be

½ × 4 ml/kg body weight × % of body surface burned

½ × 4 ml × 70 kg × 54 = 7,560 ml

So his fluid needs *per hour* will be

$$\frac{7,560 \text{ ml}}{8 \text{ hr}} = \textbf{945 ml/hr}$$

(Practically speaking, that figure can be regarded as equivalent to 1 liter per hour, but we shall complete the calculations using the precise figures.)

Thus you will need to deliver

$$\frac{945 \text{ ml/hr}}{60 \text{ min/hr}} = 15.8 \text{ ml/min (i.e., } \textbf{16 ml/min)}$$

c. If your infusion set delivers 10 gtt per milliliter, you therefore need to set the rate of the infusion set at

10 gtt/ml × 16 ml/min = **160 gtt/min**

We included this question to give you a little practice in computing IV rates—just in case you were getting rusty. In this particular case, however, it is an academic exercise only, for in order to deliver the kind of volumes we are talking about—nearly 1 liter per hour—you will have to run the IV wide open, probably under pressure. Usually when volumes of this sort are required, it makes more sense to start a second and even a third IV line.

d. For a burned patient, give an intravenous fluid that will remain in the vascular space, such as **normal saline** or **lactated Ringer's** solution.

10. Among the questions you would like answered about the burned patient are the following:

a. **When** precisely did the burn occur? (That is, when did the fire break out?)

b. Was the patient **in a closed space** with smoke or other products of combustion?

c. Does the patient have any significant **underlying medical problems?**

d. Does the patient **take any medications** regularly? Had he taken any drugs or alcohol within the past few hours?

e. Does the patient have any **allergies?**

We already know the answers to most of the other questions we would normally ask. We can assume that the patient did not lose consciousness while still in the burning building, since he managed to jump out the window. We know what he was burned with (flame). And we know that nothing was done until the ambulance arrived. It would, however, be helpful to question the fire personnel regarding toxic products of combustion to which the patient might have been exposed.

11. The second victim of this apartment fire, the college student who got out via the fire escape, has several degrees of burn:

a. The burn on the right arm is probably **second degree.** The severe pain virtually rules out a third-degree burn, and the mottling suggests it is more serious than a first-degree burn. The appropriate treatment is to **cover the burn with cool, wet, sterile dressings.** If the application of cool dressings is not sufficient to relieve the patient's pain, it may be necessary to give him a small dose of morphine in addition.

b. The burn on the flank is probably a **first-degree** burn, although it could also be second degree (it will be impossible to tell for sure until at least another few hours). **Treat it as you would treat a second-degree burn,** since it might well be one.

c. The burn on the right leg is probably **third degree.** The leathery appearance, thrombosed veins, and absence of sensation are all characteristic. **Cover the burn with a dry sterile dressing.**

12. Determining the severity of a burn is essential for making a correct decision regarding the most appropriate hospital for a given patient.

A A 2-year-old child who overturned a pot of soup from the stovetop onto himself; both legs and the anterior trunk are burned.

This child's ticket to the burn unit is the extent of his burn—46 percent of the body surface area. Burns of any degree involving more than 25 percent of the body surface are considered critical.

A A 57-year-old diabetic woman with a scald burn of her left lower leg.
Diabetes makes any burn a potential catastrophe.

B A 28-year-old housewife with a scald burn of her entire right arm.
A scald burn is nearly always second degree, and a second-degree burn involving only 9 percent of the body surface does not ordinarily warrant hospitalization in a burn center. If, however, the hand is also involved, the burn should be considered critical.

A A lineman who suffered an electric shock. There is a small bull's-eye entrance wound on the left hand; you cannot find the exit wound. The lineman did not fall. His left leg feels rock hard.
All **electric burns** must be considered critical until proved otherwise. In this case, the rock-hard leg suggests massive damage to muscle, which may jeopardize not only the patient's leg but also his kidneys. He needs to be in a burn center.

B A 22-year-old short-order cook with second-degree burns over both anterior thighs, sustained when he spilled a pot of soup.
Again, we are dealing with probably second-degree burns affecting about 9 percent of the body surface; a community hospital ought to be able to handle a burn of that sort.

A A 34-year-old woman rescued from a burning building, where she had been trapped in her smoke-filled bedroom. She has second-degree burns of the right forearm. She is coughing up sooty sputum.
Burns complicated by respiratory injury require referral to a burn center. The circumstances of this woman's burn (trapped in a smoke-filled room) and the carbonaceous sputum both point to respiratory involvement.

A A 25-year-old man who tripped and fell onto the hibachi on the back porch as he was preparing to barbecue some steaks. His hand went straight into the bed of red-hot charcoal, and his shirt caught fire. He has third-degree

burns of the left hand and forearm, and second-degree burns of the anterior chest.
This backyard chef wins admission to the burn center by virtue of having a **burn of the hand.**

__A__   A plumber who spilled a bottle of industrial-strength liquid drain cleaner down the front of his trousers.
Just about any **deep chemical burn** merits transport to a burn center. Liquid drain cleaner, being a strong alkali, is almost sure to inflict a deep burn, for alkalis may keep burning and damaging tissues deeper and deeper in the body for hours after they first come in contact with the skin.

13. a. The order of priorities in treating a patient should become so ingrained that you can perform the appropriate steps almost automatically, no matter how horrifying the injuries or how chaotic the scene. For that reason, we shall go over priorities again and again in this book. In the case of the man carried unconscious, with his clothes smoldering, from a burning building, the correct sequence of treatment is as follows:

   (1) **D. Put out the fire!**
   (2) **C.** Open the **airway** manually.
   (3) **A.** Administer **oxygen.**
   (4) **H. Intubate** the trachea.
   (5) **F.** Pass a **nasogastric tube** into his stomach.*
   (6) **B.** Start an **IV.***
   (7) **J.** Obtain first set of **vital signs.**
   (8) **E. Remove the victim's clothing.**
   (9) **G.** Determine the **extent and depth of the burn.**
   (10) **I. Cover the burns** with sterile dressings.
   *Can be postponed until transport.

   b. The percentage of the patient's body that is burned is

Entire left leg	18%
Posterior right leg	9%
Left forearm	4%
TOTAL	**31%**

   c. The patient **has a critical burn,** for two reasons:

   (1) The burn covers **more than 25 percent of the body surface.**
   (2) The burn involves the **genitals.**

   d. If the pedal pulses are absent in a burned leg, you have to assume that **swelling from cir-**cumferential burns has cut off the circulation to the foot. If you do not act quickly in such a situation, the patient may lose his leg.

   e. What you need to do is **cool the burned leg with towels that have been soaked in cold water** and **transport the patient immediately** to the hospital.

14. The principles of treating chemical burns do not differ significantly from those of treating thermal burns. In both cases, the first priority is to *put out the fire,* but in a chemical burn, putting out the fire is a more difficult and time-consuming operation.

   a. If you know the identity of the chemical that caused the burn, it is preferable to start treatment with a chemical antidote (e.g., to apply a weak acid to an alkali burn and vice versa).
   FALSE. To begin with, hunting around for a chemical antidote simply wastes time. What is needed is to remove the offending chemical from the patient's skin as fast as possible. Many chemical antidotes, furthermore, neutralize by an exothermic reaction, that is, a reaction that produces *heat;* thus the chemical reaction with the antidote may simply add a thermal burn to the patient's chemical burn.

   b. When a person has been burned by a chemical agent, the skin should be flushed for a minimum of 30 minutes with copious amounts of water.
   TRUE. Indeed, if the agent is a strong alkali, flushing should, under optimal conditions, continue for as long as 2 hours. Consider leaving the patient at the scene, under responsible supervision, and picking him up later, after he's had time to sit under a shower for an hour or so. Check first with your medical director.

   c. It is important to use only sterile water to flush a chemical burn, lest you contaminate the burn wound.
   FALSE. You'll run out of sterile water very quickly, and you certainly won't have enough aboard your ambulance to flush a chemical burn properly. What is needed is LOTS of water, and clean water out of a tap will do just fine.

   d. In burns caused by hot tar, it is crucial to remove the tar from contact with the skin as quickly as possible to prevent systemic tar poisoning.

FALSE. The only treatment necessary in the field for a hot tar burn is to *cool* the tar down as fast as possible, to halt the burning process. The most efficient way to do so is to immerse the affected area in cold water. It is neither necessary nor desirable to try to get the tar off the skin; leave that to the emergency room staff, who have special preparations for dissolving tar. Meanwhile, the tar will serve as a sort of burn dressing and prevent contaminants from reaching the burn surface.

e. If chemicals have splashed into someone's eyes, the eyes should be irrigated with a steady stream of water for at least 30 minutes. **TRUE.** Do not use any solution other than clean water or saline to irrigate the eyes, and do not take any shortcuts.

15. Electric burns can be very deceptive, for the extent of injury may not be at all apparent from the burn that is visible on the surface of the body.

    a. The three types of *burns* that may occur from electricity are

        (1) A **contact burn,** which usually produces a bull's-eye lesion at the point of entry and sometimes also at the point of exit.
        (2) A **flash burn,** an electrothermal injury caused by the arcing of electric current.
        (3) A **flame burn,** which occurs if the electricity ignites a person's clothing or surroundings.

    b. Besides burns, electricity may cause a variety of other injuries or disorders of function, including

        (1) **Respiratory arrest**
        (2) **Cardiac arrest**
        (3) **Neurologic disorders** (seizures, coma, paralysis)
        (4) **Kidney damage**
        (5) **Fractures** and **dislocations**
        (6) **Cervical spine injuries**

    c. In dealing with this electrocuted patient lying beside a live cable, you need to take the following steps:

        (1) **Secure the scene.** Keep all bystanders well back from the live wire. Do not get within reach of the wire yourself if you are not fully trained and fully equipped to deal with power lines. Radio for help, and do not get within range of the wire until it has been inactivated. If you have

some creative idea for extricating the patient that does not require your coming within range of the cable (e.g., lassoing him and dragging him toward you), you may try such a method, but bear in mind that the patient may have a spinal injury.

        (2) As soon as it is safe to approach the patient, ensure that he has an **open airway,** taking precautions not to hyperextend his neck.
        (3) Provide **artificial ventilation or full CPR** as needed.
        (4) Administer **oxygen.**
        (5) If the patient remains unconscious, **intubate** the trachea.
        (6) Start an **IV,** and run in lactated Ringer's solution as fast as the IV will flow.
        (7) Consult the base physician for medication orders.
        (8) **Cover burns** with a sterile dressing.
        (9) **Splint fractures.**
        (10) **Immobilize the spine** on a backboard.

16. "Why should I have to learn the dosages of all these drugs," the paramedic student may well ask, "when it's the doctor who gives the order for how much of a drug to administer?" By the time you finish working out the answer to question 16, you should know the answer to the paramedic student's question as well.

    a. The usual therapeutic dosage of morphine is **0.1 mg per kilogram.**

    b. If the patient weighs 70 kg, then the correct dosage for him would be

    $0.1 \text{ mg/kg} \times 70 \text{ kg} = \textbf{7 mg}$

    Therefore, the doctor's order was **incorrect.** The doctor has ordered more than three times the usual therapeutic dose. If you are as sleepy as the doctor apparently was, you will miss his error and perhaps administer a lethal dose of morphine to the patient. *That* is why you need to know the dosage of every medication you will be administering.

    c. When you administer the morphine, you need to keep an eye out for potential side effects, including

        (1) A sudden **fall in blood pressure** (hypotension)
        (2) **Respiratory depression,** which will become noticeable as a fall in respiratory rate
        (3) **Nausea** and **vomiting**
        (4) **Bradycardia**

17. The treatment of severe electric injury may also include administration of sodium bicarbonate and mannitol, so you need to know the pharmacology of those two drugs.

a. If the patient weighs 70 kg and is supposed to receive 1 mEq per kilogram of BICARBONATE, then you will have to give

1 mEq/kg $\times$ 70 kg = 70 mEq

Since bicarbonate is supplied in a concentration of 1 mEq per milliliter,

$$\frac{70 \text{ mEq}}{1 \text{ mEq/ml}} = \textbf{70 ml}$$

which will be just about 1½ ampules.

b. Other *indications* for sodium bicarbonate include

(1) To treat **metabolic acidosis** in certain poisonings
(2) To treat **hyperkalemia**
(3) To **promote excretion of barbiturates** in some overdoses
(4) In certain cases of **prolonged CPR**

c. *Contraindications* to giving sodium bicarbonate include

(1) **Hypokalemia**
(2) **Congestive heart failure**

d. Potential *side effects* of sodium bicarbonate include

(1) **Fluid overload** because of increase in intravascular volume
(2) **Hypokalemia** and consequent cardiac dysrhythmias
(3) **Elevated arterial PCO$_2$**

e. Regarding MANNITOL, this 70-kg patient will require the following *dosage:*

0.5 gm/kg $\times$ 70 kg = **35 gm**

f. To figure out how much of a 15% solution you need to give the patient, we first need to recall that a 15% solution, by definition, contains *15 gm per 100 ml.* We know that we want to give the patient 35 gm. Therefore

$$\frac{35 \text{ gm}}{x \text{ ml}} = \frac{15 \text{ gm}}{100 \text{ ml}}$$

x = **233 ml**

g. *Contraindications* to giving mannitol include

(1) **Absence of urine output** (anuria)
(2) **Congestive heart failure**
(3) Suspected **intracranial bleeding**
(4) **Pregnancy**
(5) **Dehydration**

h. Had this patient been in heart failure, both **sodium bicarbonate** and **mannitol** would have been contraindicated. It would, however, be perfectly all right and indeed useful to give morphine.

18. Murphy's Law predicts that there will be a thunderstorm on your day off, especially if you decide to go fishing. But should you be rash enough to go fishing anyway, and should you then get caught in the thunderstorm, here are some things you can do to minimize the chances of being struck by lightning:

a. **Get away from the water.**

b. **Stay low.**

c. **Get away from objects that project from the ground,** such as the tree you're leaning against.

d. **Drop your fishing pole.**

19. When you are called to the scene of a lightning strike, especially if that scene is a golf course or stadium, you must keep in mind that you are very likely to be dealing with more than one victim.

a. The *first* thing you should do is **evaluate the whole scene** to determine how many people have been injured and who has priority for treatment. If the storm is still going on, you should at the same time **protect yourself and others** by evacuating everyone to the adjacent school building or into parked vehicles.

b. First treatment priority goes to **victims who are not breathing.**

16
Injuries to the Head, Neck, and Spine

1. Was your eye keen enough to find all 37 words? It will need to be very keen indeed to detect some of the signs of serious head injury.

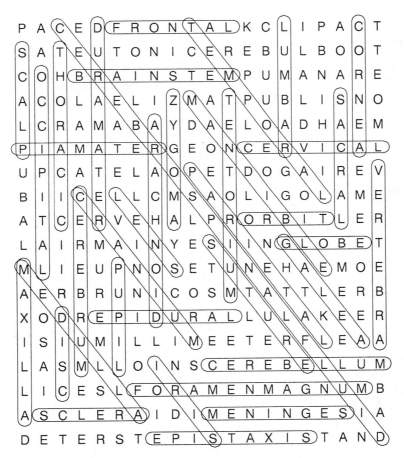

  a. The brain and spinal cord are bathed in a liquid called **cerebrospinal fluid.**

  b. Three membranes, collectively called the **meninges,** enclose and protect the brain. Those membranes are named

  (1) The **pia mater.**
  (2) The **arachnoid.**
  (3) The **dura mater.**

The outermost of those layers folds over to form a partition known as the **tentorium.** When bleeding (usually from a torn artery) occurs between that outermost membrane and the skull, the resulting collection of blood is called an **epidural** hematoma.

c. Outside of those membranes is the hard, bony covering of the brain, the **cranium.** That, in turn, is covered by the **scalp,** whose toughest, tendinous layer is known as the **galea.**

d. The brain itself has several functional divisions. The part of the brain responsible for higher functions is the **cerebrum,** each hemisphere of which consists of four lobes, the **frontal** lobe, **temporal** lobe, **parietal** lobe, and **occipital** lobe. The part of the brain responsible for coordination of skilled movements is the **cerebellum.** Vital functions, such as the state of consciousness, are regulated in the **brainstem,** one part of which, the **medulla,** houses the centers that control breathing and cardiac action.

e. A fixed, immovable joint where bones of the skull come together is called a **suture.**

f. The facial bones include the cheekbone, called the **zygoma,** the upper jaw, or **maxilla,** and the lower jaw, or **mandible.**

g. Trauma to the face often results in a nosebleed, or **epistaxis.**

h. The eyeball, or **globe,** fits into a depression in the skull called the **orbit.** The structure that gives the eye its color is the **iris,** which regulates the opening in the center of the eye, called the **pupil.** Anterior to those two components of the eye is the **cornea,** a crystal-clear extension of the otherwise white **sclera** covering the eyeball. Behind the pigmented structure of the eye is the **lens,** which focuses light on the retina.

i. The spinal column consists of 33 bones piled one on top of the other. Each bone is called a **vertebra,** and between every two such bones there is a cushion, called a **disc,** that acts as a shock absorber. It is customary to divide the spinal column into four regions: The first 7 spinal bones, in the neck, constitute the **cervical** spine; the next 12, which articulate with the ribs, make up the **thoracic** spine; beneath them are 5 bones of the **lumbar** spine; then come 5 fused bones of the **sacral** spine that articulate with the pelvis. And finally come the 4 fused bones of the coccyx, or tail bone.

   The portions of the spine most liable to be injured by powerful acceleration-deceleration forces are the **cervical** and **lumbar** segments, for they are **not anchored to any other bony structures.** The thoracic spine is held stable by the ribs, and the sacral spine is fused with the pelvis, so those portions of the spine are relatively protected from extremes of motion.

2. A blow to the head is dangerous principally because of the danger of increasing intracranial pressure.

   a. The increase in intracranial pressure may come about from either

      (1) **Swelling of the brain**
      (2) **Bleeding** within the skull

   or a combination of the two. In either case, because the skull cannot expand, any increase in volume will inevitably lead to an increase in pressure.

   b. An elevated intracranial pressure is dangerous because it **causes vital structures to be compressed.** Pressure on the medulla, for example, may lead to respiratory arrest.

3. The airway of an unconscious, head-injured patient may be jeopardized in any of three ways:

   a. By the **tongue** falling back against the posterior throat.

   b. By **blood, broken teeth,** or other products of the injury.

c. By **vomitus** (vomiting is common in head-injured patients).

4. It should be clear, after carrying out this exercise, that the Glasgow Coma Scale enables a much more precise description than the AVPU rating of the patient's level of consciousness.

  a. The patient is found unconscious. He opens his eyes in response to a loud voice. He does not follow commands, but he pulls his hand away when pinched and makes a few garbled noises that you cannot understand.
  AVPU score: somewhere between **V** and **P**
  Glasgow coma score: **10**

  b. The patient is found apparently unconscious, but he opens his eyes at the sound of your voice. He can follow simple commands, but he is a bit confused and cannot tell you what month it is or what day of the week it is.
  AVPU score: **V**
  Glasgow coma score: **13**

  c. The patient is found unconscious. He does not open his eyes when pinched or try to pull away from the painful stimulus, but instead his arms flex spasmodically across his chest while his legs go into hyperextension. He makes no sound.
  AVPU score: somewhere between **P** and **U**
  Glasgow coma score: **5**

  d. The patient is found conscious. He gives you a coherent account of what happened to him, and he can follow simple commands.
  AVPU score: **A**
  Glasgow coma score: **15**

5. In taking the history of a head-injured patient, you need to find out

  a. The **circumstances of the accident:** How did the injury occur? What were the **mechanisms of injury?**

  b. Whether the patient **lost consciousness** at any point. If so, when? For how long?

  c. Whether the patient **vomited.**

  d. What the patient's **current symptoms** are (assuming he is conscious and can tell you).

  e. Whether the patient has ingested **drugs or alcohol** within the past few hours.

  f. Whether the patient has any **significant underlying illnesses.**

6. The vital signs are called "vital" because they measure vital functions. Another reason for calling them "vital" could be because they often provide vital information.

__B__ Skin cool and sweaty. Pulse 110, regular, and somewhat weak; respirations 24, shallow, and regular; blood pressure 80 systolic.

This is the classic picture of **hypovolemic shock.** If you missed it, go back and reread Chapter 9. As a paramedic, you should be able to spot a patient in shock in the blink of an eye.

__C__ Skin hot and dry. Pulse 50, full, and regular; respirations 10, with occasional long pauses; blood pressure 210/110.
These are classic findings in head injury with **rising intracranial pressure.** The very high blood pressure, increased pulse pressure, slow pulse, and disordered respirations are all clues, as is the tendency to hyperpyrexia.

__A__ Skin warm and dry. Pulse 72, full, and regular; respirations 20, regular; blood pressure 80 systolic.
Often the tip-off to **neurogenic shock** is the fall in blood pressure without other signs of shock. The skin stays warm because the peripheral blood vessels are unable to constrict; it stays dry because sweating under stress is a response of the sympathetic nervous system, and the sympathetic nervous system is precisely what has been damaged in neurogenic shock.

7. Signs of skull fracture include

   a. **Ecchymoses behind the ears** (Battle's sign)

   b. **Ecchymoses around the eyes** ("coon's eyes")

   c. **Leakage of clear fluid (CSF) or blood from the nose or ears**

   d. Obvious **depression** in the skull

8. In treating the victim of the whiskey bottle, how well did you remember your priorities?

   a. **Eliminate the safety hazard.** So long as there are tables and chairs being launched into orbit, you and everyone else in the bar are in danger. So try to get all bystanders to leave the premises (call in police help if needed), and then, from a safe distance, see if you can calm the patient. Explain that you are paramedics and that you have come to help him. Such an explanation is often of particular importance in municipalities where paramedics wear uniforms that could be mistaken for police uniforms.

   b. When you are reasonably certain that it is safe to approach the patient, encourage him to sit down, and **examine his scalp** by palpating the scalp wound lightly with a gloved finger to make certain that the skull beneath the wound is not fractured.

   c. If there is no evidence of skull fracture, **control scalp bleeding by direct manual pressure,** and apply a pressure dressing.

   d. **Complete the secondary survey,** and manage any other injuries detected thereby.

9. a. Sometimes, but far from always, you will find patients with a classic presentation of a particular type of head injury.

   C The patient was the driver of a vehicle that was struck from the left side by another car. The door on the driver's side is dented in. The patient is conscious, but witnesses say that he was "out cold" for a few minutes immediately after the accident. He complains of headache and pains in his left hip and left leg. His skull is tender to palpation in the area just superior to the left ear. While he is under your care, his level of consciousness deteriorates until he is unconscious altogether, and his respirations become very slow.

   The tip-offs that this patient suffered an **epidural hematoma** are the site of the injury (temporal bone) and the lucid interval between two periods of unconsciousness.

   A The patient was another participant in the barroom brawl mentioned in the previous question. This patient was "knocked out cold" for a few minutes. Now he seems alert, but he cannot remember what happened. He complains of a little dizziness. His vital signs are normal.

   A **concussion** typically produces amnesia for the events immediately surrounding the injury, and the patient often complains of dizziness, headache, ringing in the ears, and similar symptoms—but there are no neurologic deficits on examination.

   D The patient was a front-seat passenger in a car that careered into a utility pole. He is confused and sleepy when you find him. His speech is slurred, and there is weakness of the right leg. He becomes more and more lethargic while under your care and vomits twice. The left pupil seems to be getting larger than the right.

   Subdural hematoma carries the worst prognosis of the various types of head injuries. This type of injury is typically produced by an accident involving powerful deceleration forces, and focal neurologic signs, such as speech disorders or hemiplegia, are not uncommon.

   B The patient was an unrestrained front-seat passenger in a car involved in a head-on collision with another car. He apparently struck his head on the windshield, for the windshield in front of the patient is cracked. The patient is found unconscious. His left pupil is larger than the right. His pulse is 56, and his blood pressure is 190/90. Respirations are irregular.

   In fact, all one could say for certain about this patient with a **cerebral contusion** is that he has signs of increased intracranial pressure. It would be impossible without a computed tomography (CT) scan or similar study to know whether the increase in intracranial pressure was indeed due solely to swelling of the brain or whether there was bleeding within the skull as well.

   b. The first, third, and fourth patients described all showed some signs of increased intracranial pressure. The typical signs of an elevated intracranial pressure include

      (1) A **deteriorating level of consciousness**
      (2) The onset of **hemiplegia**

(3) **Vomiting,** especially if sudden and not preceded by nausea

(4) **Unilateral pupillary dilatation** ("blown pupil")

(5) **Rising blood pressure** accompanied by a **slowing pulse**

(6) **Abnormal respirations** or **apnea**

c. The steps in managing a head-injured patient are as follows:

(1) Establish an **airway,** with cervical spine precautions. Keep suction close at hand in case of vomiting.

(2) If respirations are depressed, **assist breathing** with a bag-valve-mask at a rate of about 20 breaths per minute. In any case, give **100% oxygen.**

(3) **Control bleeding,** if present. Unless there are signs of hypovolemic shock, **restrict intravenous fluids.**

(4) **Prevent hyperpyrexia.** Do not cover the patient with blankets unless ambient temperature is very low.

(5) **Cover wounds** with sterile dressings.

(6) **Monitor cardiac rhythm.**

(7) **Be prepared to deal with seizures;** have *diazepam* drawn up and ready to administer on orders from the base physician to do so.

(8) **Immobilize the patient on a backboard.**

(9) **Transport** the patient **expeditiously** to the hospital.

10. Maxillofacial injuries, while not by themselves ordinarily a threat to life, are a cause of concern because they may be accompanied by other injuries or conditions that do pose a threat to life or limb, such as

a. **Airway obstruction** from blood, broken teeth, and so on

b. **Closed head injury** with increasing intracranial pressure

c. **Cervical spine injury**

11. Clues to the presence of maxillofacial fracture include

a. **Swelling** of the face

b. **Ecchymoses** over the face

c. **Crepitus** over a broken bone

d. **Malocclusion** in cases where the jaw is fractured

e. **Loss of sensation** over part of the face

f. **Paralysis of gaze** in a given direction

g. Obvious **deformity** of the face (e.g., flattening of one side)

12. Epistaxis tends to elicit a considerable amount of panic among bystanders, but it pays to stop a moment and consider the source of the "nosebleed" before you start to treat it.

B A 68-year-old man who says that his nose just started bleeding without any warning. He tells you that he is under treatment for high blood pressure, but you find his blood pressure to be normal and his pulse rapid.
This patient is most likely suffering a *posterior* nosebleed related to his chronic hypertension (if you want to double-check, shine your penlight in his mouth and see if blood is dripping down the back of his throat). He will undoubtedly need **anterior and posterior nasal packs,** and if you are any distance from the hospital, you may have to insert those packs in the field to prevent serious blood loss. (The fact that the patient's blood pressure is now "normal" is rather worrisome, especially in the light of his rapid pulse; one has to assume that he is going into shock.)

C A 42-year-old man involved in a motor vehicle accident. You don't see any evidence of injury to his nose, but rather watery blood is oozing from it.
This patient is *not* in fact suffering from a nosebleed, or not in the usual sense. What is coming out of his nose is a combination of blood and cerebrospinal fluid, so what he has doubtless suffered is a skull fracture! The treatment therefore is simply to **cover the nose lightly with a sterile dressing** to minimize the entry of contaminants into the CSF.

A A 16-year-old boy who says that his nose started bleeding after he sneezed. He is holding a bloody handkerchief against his nose.
Here we have what seems to be a simple nosebleed, which should be amenable to the time-honored method of **pinching the nostrils shut.**

13. If you are able to salvage this young woman's lost tooth, you will have made a friend for life.

a. Try to **locate the missing tooth.**

b. If you find the tooth, and if it is intact, hold it carefully by the crown while you **rinse the tooth and the empty socket** with sterile saline.

c. Line the tooth up in its correct position, and **slowly press it back into its socket.**

d. Once the tooth is in place, have the patient bite down on a gauze roll, to maintain pressure against the tooth.

14. A thorough examination of an injured eye includes assessment of

a. The **orbits** for ecchymoses, swelling, instability, and tenderness

b. The **eyelids,** for ecchymoses, swelling, and lacerations

c. The **conjunctivae,** for redness and foreign bodies

d. The **pupils,** for size, shape, equality, and reaction to light

e. **Eye movements in all directions,** for evidence of paralysis of gaze

f. Most important of all, **visual acuity**

15. It is, in fact, rather rare to encounter a patient with an impaled object, but we give considerable attention to the problem in EMT and paramedic courses because the consequences of mismanagement could be disastrous.

a. When the impaled object is in the eye, the usual principle applies: **Stabilize the impaled object in place.** For the eye, the most efficient way to do so is usually with a stack of gauze pads that has a hole in the middle. The gauze pads are passed gently over the impaled object and bandaged in place. If the impaled object is an arrow, as in the present case, it won't be possible to cover it with a paper cup as well. **Do not try to shorten the impaled object.** Just protect it from being jarred, and be sure to **patch the other eye** as well, to prevent the injured eye from moving every time the uninjured eye shifts its gaze.

b. When an object is impaled in the cheek, we have to break the usual rule about not removing an impaled object, for it will be impossible to control bleeding inside the mouth so long as the arrow is sticking through the cheek. Therefore, **gently pull the arrow out of the cheek.** Then **pack the inside of the cheek** with sterile gauze, and **apply counterpressure** with a dressing secured firmly against the outside of the cheek. Keep the patient on his side, so that he can more easily spit any blood out of his mouth (instruct him not to swallow blood, as blood in the stomach is a stimulus to vomit).

16. It is really quite remarkable how many bad guys in cowboy movies managed to get up and fight after being caught in the throat by an outstretched rope, for most mortals would be severely injured in such an accident. In the case in question:

a. The bad guy has probably suffered **severe injury to the larynx,** such as a laryngeal "fracture," as evidenced by the bruise over his throat, his hoarseness, and his subcutaneous emphysema. Furthermore, given the mechanisms of injury, one has to assume that he has suffered **cervical spine injury** as well.

b. The steps of treatment are as follows:

(1) Administer **100% oxygen,** and instruct the patient to breathe slowly (rapid inhalation may cause an unstable trachea to collapse inward). It is preferable to avoid intubating the patient in the field, but if the airway becomes compromised further, you may have no choice.

(2) **Immobilize the spine** by immobilizing the whole patient on a long backboard.

(3) **Transport the patient immediately,** preferably to a major trauma center.

17. The 12-year-old boy bleeding among the wedding dresses has one laceration that is of more concern than all the others, and that is the laceration to his neck.

a. The principal dangers associated with a laceration of the neck are **exsanguination** (because of the major blood vessels that pass through the neck) and **air embolism.**

b. The steps in treating the boy's neck wound are

(1) **Cover the wound immediately,** preferably with an airtight seal such as petrolatum gauze or plastic wrap, but even with your gloved hand if you do not have anything else immediately available.

(2) Apply a **pressure dressing** over the airtight seal.

(3) Position the boy about 15 degrees **head-down** in the **left lateral recumbent** position, to trap any air bubbles that may have entered the circulation in the right side of the heart.

18. Whenever the mechanisms of injury are such that an injury to the spine *might* have occurred, you must assume that injury to the spine *did* indeed occur and treat the patient accordingly. It is preferable to apply a backboard unnecessarily in a thousand cases than to omit the backboard in the one patient who really needed it. Therefore, suspect spinal injury and immobilize the patient in

a. Major **vehicular trauma**

b. **Diving accidents,** when the patient struck his head in diving

c. **Falls from a height**

d. Any patient with **significant injury above the clavicles**

e. Patients with **crush injury**

f. Patients injured by **lightning**

g. Patients who sustained **gunshot wounds anywhere from the head down to the lower abdomen**

h. Victims of **multiple trauma**

i. Any patients who were **found unconscious after trauma**

19. The patient described in this question fits the description of a "patient found unconscious after trauma." That is to say, this patient must be presumed to have suffered spinal cord injury.

a. Therefore, to open the airway, one must use a method that does not involve any extension of the head or neck, such as **jaw thrust,** jaw lift, or chin lift **with the head in neutral position.** At the earliest opportunity, it will be necessary to **intubate the trachea** to maintain the airway and protect against aspiration.

b. As soon as you discover that the patient's breathing is inadequate, you must **assist ventilations** with a bag-valve-mask and 100% oxygen. If the patient is unconscious, it is a good bet that he has suffered head injury, and he must not therefore be allowed to become hypercarbic. (Why?) So aim to keep his ventilatory rate around 20 per minute, with good tidal volumes.

c. The most likely (but not the sole) explanation of the patient's vital signs and skin condition—normal pulse, hypotension, and warm skin—is **neurogenic shock.**

d. The remaining steps in his treatment will include

(1) **Immobilization** on a backboard.

(2) Starting an **IV** (preferably while already en route to the hospital) with normal saline. The rate at which you run the IV may be problematic: Shock requires fluids; head injury is best treated by fluid restriction. The patient seems to have both problems. Let the base physician decide what to do about it.

20. The Cold War is over, but until the disarmament process reaches the urban streets, injuries such as that described in this question will continue to keep paramedics and other EMS personnel busy.

a. The boy has a sensory level around T8 and intact motor function at least from T1 upward. So we can assume that his injury is **no higher than T8.**

b. The boy's hypotension could mean **either neurogenic shock or hypovolemic shock.** It is very difficult, if not impossible, to distinguish between the two under these circumstances, for if the sympathetic nervous system has been disrupted by the spinal cord injury, we will not see the usual signs of shock, such as sweating and tachycardia. Furthermore, the boy's sensory deficit may mask pain from damage to intra-abdominal structures. So when we encounter shock in such circumstances, we have to TREAT IT AS HYPOVOLEMIC SHOCK UNTIL PROVED OTHERWISE.

21. The secret message of this lesson is the most important message of the whole chapter.

a. **galea**   h. **integument**

b. **iris**   i. **tinnitus**

c. **conjunctiva**   j. **hemoptysis**

d. **foramen magnum**   k. **disc**

e. **globe**   l. **soft**

f. **paresthesia**   m. **tenth**

g. **arachnoid**   n. **nose**

Secret Message: THE MOST IMPORTANT SINGLE SIGN IN THE EVALUATION OF A HEAD-INJURED PATIENT IS A CHANGING STATE OF CONSCIOUSNESS.

17
Chest Injuries

1. Like the words in the grid, injuries inside the chest may not be immediately evident.

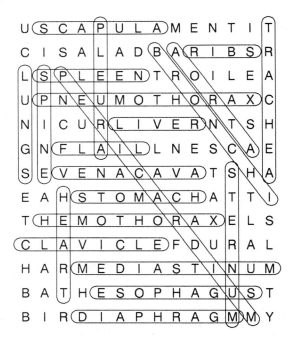

```
U S C A P U L A M E N T I T
C I S A L A D B A R I B S R
L S P L E E N T R O I L E A
U P N E U M O T H O R A X C
N I C U R L I V E R N T S H
G N F L A I L L N E S C A E
S E V E N A C A V A T S H A
E A H S T O M A C H A T T I
T H E M O T H O R A X E L S
C L A V I C L E F D U R A L
H A R M E D I A S T I N U M
B A T H E S O P H A G U S T
B I R D I A P H R A G M M Y
```

a. The thoracic cavity lies within a bony, protective cylinder. The **ribs** encircle the whole thorax, articulating with the thoracic **spine** posteriorly and the **sternum** anteriorly. Also forming part of the bony protection on each side of the chest is the strong shoulder blade, or **scapula,** posteriorly and the collar bone, or **clavicle,** anteriorly. The inferior boundary of the thoracic cavity is formed by the **diaphragm.**

b. The **lungs** nearly fill the thoracic cavity. Each of them is covered with a smooth, slippery membrane called the visceral **pleura;** a similar membrane, the parietal **pleura,** lines the inner wall of the thoracic cavity. Ordinarily there is no space between those two membranes. Injury to the chest, however, can permit air to enter between the two membranes, creating a **pneumothorax;** blood can also accumulate in the space between the two membranes, a situation called **hemothorax.**

c. Some of the most important organs of the body are located in a region in the center of the thoracic cavity called the **mediastinum.** The structures located there include the **heart, aorta, vena cava, trachea, bronchi,** and **esophagus.**

400

d. When two or more ribs are broken in two or more places, a condition called **flail** chest may develop. Tamponade occurs when the **pericardium** becomes filled with blood, preventing the heart from contracting normally.

e. Because of the way the diaphragm is shaped, several abdominal organs actually lie partially or almost wholly within the chest, for example the **spleen,** the **liver,** and the **stomach.** Those organs are thus liable to be injured whenever there is serious thoracic trauma.

2. In this case, we have a young woman who suffered unspecified deceleration injuries serious enough to render her unconscious. The damage to the car—a caved-in dashboard and smashed windshield—also hints at significant head and chest injury.

   a. The major threats to this woman's airway are

      (1) Her **tongue,** which is liable to fall back against her posterior pharynx
      (2) **Blood or broken teeth** in her mouth
      (3) **Vomitus**
      (4) Possible **injury to the airway** (e.g., ruptured larynx)

   b. In assessing the adequacy of her *breathing,* one needs to

      (1) LOOK for
         (a) **Signs of respiratory embarrassment** (nasal flaring, intercostal or supraclavicular retractions)
         (b) **Tracheal deviation**
         (c) **Obvious bruises or open wounds of the chest**
         (d) **Paradoxical movement** of any part of the chest

      (2) LISTEN for
         (a) **Sucking chest wound**
         (b) **Inequality of breath sounds**
         (c) **Dullness** or **hyperresonance** to percussion

      (3) FEEL for
         (a) **Tracheal deviation**
         (b) **Subcutaneous emphysema**
         (c) **Instability** of the rib cage

   c. What needs to be done immediately to ensure adequate breathing is

      (1) **Suction** out the mouth as needed.
      (2) Administer **100% oxygen.**

   d. To evaluate and manage the *circulation* during the primary survey, you need to

      (1) Identify and **control significant external bleeding.**
      (2) Check the **pulse** (quality, rate, regularity, presence of paradoxus).

      (3) Note the **skin condition** (color, moisture, temperature).
      (4) Check **capillary refill.**
      (5) Assess **neck veins** for distention.

3. a. The patient who suffered a shotgun wound to the chest in a "friendly" encounter has an **open pneumothorax** (answer **C**), indeed a quite significant one (a 2-inch hole would be hard not to notice!). The wound inflicted by a shotgun at close range is essentially a blast injury, so one would expect in addition a considerable amount of damage to the lung tissue beneath, probably with disruption of major blood vessels as well.

   b. The steps in managing this patient are

      (1) Make certain that the "friend" with the shotgun has left the scene or been "neutralized" by police.
      (2) **Seal the open chest wound with an occlusive dressing** as quickly as possible. Tape the dressing on three sides only, so that air can escape from it during exhalation.
      (3) Administer **100% oxygen,** preferably by nonrebreathing mask. Try to avoid giving oxygen under positive pressure.
      (4) Start **transport.**
      (5) Start an **IV** en route, with lactated Ringer's solution.

4. In working out the answers to this question, you may have noticed that the mechanisms and signs of various chest injuries may be very similar to one another. If it is hard to distinguish such injuries in the relative calm and quiet of your study, consider how difficult it is at midnight in a ditch by the side of the interstate highway in the pouring rain—which is where you will inevitably be making such determinations.

   D A 20-year-old driver of a car that rammed a utility pole at high speed. He is in severe distress. His pulse is rapid and feeble, and every so often you can hardly palpate a pulse at all. His neck veins are distended. There is a steering wheel imprint on his chest. The rib cage is stable. Breath sounds are equal bilaterally. It is too noisy to hear heart sounds. You are 30 minutes from the nearest hospital.

This patient's *distended neck veins* tell you that something is increasing pressure on the venae cavae. The two most likely possibilities are air in the pleural space or blood in the pericardium. Since the breath sounds are equal, the best bet is **cardiac tamponade,** and the apparent pulsus paradoxus supports that diagnosis. Under ideal conditions, you might also be able to appreciate that the heart sounds are muffled, but conditions in the field are seldom ideal, and even evaluating breath sounds is usually quite challenging.

Steps of management:

a. Administer **100% oxygen.**

b. **Contact medical control** for authorization to carry out **pericardiocentesis.** If you are half an hour from the hospital, the patient is unlikely to make it unless you can aspirate some of the blood from his pericardium. If you obtain permission:

   (1) Prepare the area around the xiphoid.
   (2) Attach an 18-gauge needle to a 20-ml syringe. Attach the hub of the needle to the V lead of a grounded electrocardiogram machine via an alligator clip.
   (3) With the patient in a semisitting position, insert the needle just to the left of the xiphoid; when it passes the sternum, angle it up and to the left.
   (4) When the needle pops into the pericardium, clamp it in place and withdraw as much blood as you can. Then withdraw the needle.

c. Start **transport.**

d. **Monitor** cardiac rhythm.

e. Start an **IV** with lactated Ringer's en route.

__E__ A 23-year-old driver of a car that rammed a utility pole at high speed. His face, neck, and chest are cyanotic and look very bloated. His eyes are bloodshot and bulging. He is vomiting blood. Breathing is labored. His pulse is rapid and very weak. The chest looks caved in. You are 5 minutes from a trauma center.

This is the classic picture of **traumatic asphyxia,** the so-called "bloated frog" appearance, and it bespeaks massive, often fatal chest injury.

Steps of management:

a. Establish an **airway.** Don't take time at the scene for endotracheal intubation unless absolutely necessary.

b. Administer **100% oxygen.**

c. **Immobilize** the spine.

d. Start **transport.**

e. Start at least one **IV en route.**

__C__ A 70-year-old driver of a car that rammed a utility pole at high speed. He is conscious but in severe respiratory distress. The pulse is 92, strong, and slightly irregular. Neck veins are flat. There are bruises on the anterior chest and point tenderness along the left sternal border and over the left fifth, sixth, seventh, and eighth ribs in the anterior axillary line. The chest seems to move asymmetrically on respiration. Breath sounds seem equal. It is too noisy to hear heart sounds. You are 10 minutes from the hospital.

If a patient has three ribs broken in two places, it's a good bet he's got a **flail chest.** You may not actually be able to see the paradoxical movement of the chest, especially if the patient is conscious and splinting the injured part of the chest (which he will do automatically, to reduce the pain that breathing causes him). But the nature of the injury tells you that there probably *is* a flail, and the asymmetry of chest movements supports the hypothesis.

Steps of management:

a. Administer **100% oxygen** by nonrebreathing mask.

b. **Splint the flail segment,** by having the patient hold a pillow against it or by taping the unstable segment to the adjacent stable segment.

c. Encourage the patient to take **deep breaths.** If he is unable to do so, assist ventilations *gently* with a bag-valve-mask. BE ALERT FOR PNEUMOTHORAX.

d. Start **transport.**

e. **Monitor** cardiac rhythm.

f. Start an **IV lifeline** en route, at a **keep-open rate.**

__A__ A 42-year-old front-seat passenger in a car that was struck from the right side by an ambulance that ran a red light. The patient is in severe respiratory distress. Her pulse is rapid and very weak. Her skin is cold and sweaty. The neck veins are distended. Breath sounds are decreased on the right side of the chest, which is hyperresonant to palpation. It's too noisy to hear heart sounds. You are 15 minutes from the nearest hospital.

Here again, distended neck veins point to a process that is increasing intrathoracic pressure or otherwise preventing venous return to the heart. The decrease in breath sounds on the right side tells you that the problem is in the right chest, and the hyperresonance argues for a **tension pneumothorax** there.

Steps of management:
a. Administer **100% oxygen** by nonrebreathing mask.

b. **Contact medical control** for authorization to carry out **chest decompression.** If authorization is given:

   (1) Identify the second right intercostal space in the midclavicular line.
   (2) Prep the point you have identified (with povidone-iodine).
   (3) Use a 14-gauge Intracath or whatever other 14-gauge needle is at hand to pop through into the pleural space and vent the pneumothorax. Secure the catheter or needle in place. Use a flutter valve if possible.

c. **Immobilize the spine.**

d. Start **transport.**

e. Start an **IV en route.**

__B__ A 22-year-old man who was stabbed in the left chest. The patient is in severe distress. His pulse is rapid and very weak. His skin is cold and sweaty. His neck veins are flat. Breath sounds are decreased in the left chest, which is dull to percussion. It's too noisy to hear heart sounds. You are 15 minutes from the nearest hospital.

Like the patients with cardiac tamponade and tension pneumothorax, this patient with **massive hemothorax** is showing signs of shock (cold, sweaty skin; rapid, weak pulse). But in contrast to the others, his venous pressure is low (neck veins *not* distended), which makes one suspect hypovolemia. The decreased breath sounds in the left chest indicate that something is going on there, and the dullness

to percussion suggests that fluid (blood) has taken the place of air in that side of the chest. It all adds up to massive bleeding within the chest. (Given the location of the stab wound, it is not unreasonable to consider the possibility of myocardial trauma and pericardial tamponade as well.)

Steps of management:
a. Administer **100% oxygen.**

b. Start **transport.**

c. Start at least one large-bore **IV en route.**

5. The mechanisms of injury, or easily detected injuries, may give clues to the presence of injuries that are harder to find.

If you find:	The patient may have suffered:
Steering wheel imprint on anterior chest	**Myocardial contusion, cardiac tamponade** **Aortic rupture** **Pneumothorax** or **hemothorax** **Tracheobronchial injury**
Caved-in door on driver's side	**Diaphragmatic tear**
Fall from a height	**Aortic rupture** **Pulmonary contusion**
Bullet entrance wound in fifth left intercostal space	**Cardiac tamponade** **Injury to liver, spleen, stomach, lungs** (look for exit wound)
Fracture of ribs 5–7 in a young man	**Pulmonary contusion** **Pneumothorax** and/or **hemothorax**
Fracture of first and second ribs	**Major vascular injury** **Hemothorax**

6. The elderly woman struck by a car has very well localized pain over the fifth right rib as well as diminished breath sounds and hyperresonance on that side of the chest.

a. This woman is probably suffering from **rib fracture** together with a **simple pneumothorax** on the right.

b. The principal danger associated with rib fracture is the development of **atelectasis** because of the patient's reluctance to breathe deeply. Atelectasis, in turn, predisposes the patient to develop **pneumonia.**

c. The treatment necessary in the field is as follows:

(1) Administer **100% oxygen** by nonrebreathing mask.

(2) Encourage the patient to take periodic **deep breaths;** have her splint the fractured rib against a pillow each time she does so.

(3) Given the mechanisms of injury, it would be a good idea as well to **immobilize the spine.**

d. (1) When the patient becomes suddenly shocky, while at the same time she shows signs of increased venous pressure (neck veins distended), she has probably developed a **tension pneumothorax.**

(2) If you are more than 2 to 3 minutes from the hospital when that happens, stop the vehicle and **decompress the chest** with a needle.

7. All that the primary survey has revealed to us about the man ejected from his convertible is that he has a partially obstructed airway, is bleeding, and is in shock and therefore critically injured. In fact, that is all we need to know to start appropriate treatment.

Although the following steps of treatment are listed in sequence, we shall, in practice, have to accomplish the first few steps almost simultaneously.

a. Open the **airway** by jaw thrust. As soon as the equipment to do so is available, **suction out the mouth and pharynx.**

b. With the hand that is maintaining jaw thrust, **seal off the bleeding wound of the neck.** Apply a pressure dressing as soon as possible. Then **apply a pressure dressing to the scalp wound.**

c. Administer **100% oxygen** as soon as it is available.

d. **Immobilize the spine.**

e. Start **transport.**

f. Start at least one **large-bore IV** en route. Run it wide open.

g. **Monitor** cardiac rhythm.

8. After considering the previous case, the secret message should not seem all that obscure to you.

a. **pericardium**

b. **tamponade**

c. **flail chest**

d. **hypercarbia**

e. **dyspnea**

f. **shock**

g. **thoracic**

h. **otitis**

i. **Battle's sign**

j. **conjunctivitis**

k. **deviate**

Secret Message: IT IS NOT NECESSARY TO MAKE A SPECIFIC DIAGNOSIS TO APPRECIATE THAT A PATIENT IS CRITICALLY INJURED.

18
Injuries to the Abdomen and Genitourinary Tract

1. Abdominal injuries are the most difficult to detect, but it helps considerably to know what structures are where within the abdominal cavity.

a. These three structures of the digestive system lie outside the abdomen: the **mouth,** the **pharynx,** and the **esophagus.**

b. Digestion of protein begins in the **stomach.** From there the partially digested food proceeds into the first portion of the small intestine, the **duodenum,** where powerful enzymes from the **pancreas** carry out further digestion of protein and starch. Meanwhile, bile produced in the **liver** and stored in concentrated form in the **gallbladder** participates in the breakdown of fat. The emulsified food moves on through the second and third portions of the small bowel, called the **jejunum** and **ileum,** respectively, and then enters the first portion of the large bowel, the **cecum.** At the junction of the small and large bowels there is a wormlike structure, the **appendix,** whose principal function in adults seems to be to make work for surgeons. Proceeding through the ascending, transverse, and descending **colon,** waste products of digestion reach the **rectum** and are expelled through the **anus.**

c. The organ responsible for producing urine is located in the retroperitoneum and is called the **kidney.** Urine flows from that organ to the bladder through a tube called the **ureter;** and from the bladder, urine exits the body through a passage called the **urethra.**

d. In the female, the womb, or **uterus,** sits just behind the bladder within the pelvis. On each side of it there is an **ovary,** the organ that produces female hormones and eggs.

e. Among the structures listed in the grid, the following are found in the intra-thoracic abdomen:

   (1) **Spleen**
   (2) **Stomach**
   (3) **Liver**

f. Among the structures listed in the grid, the following are found in the retro-peritoneum:

   (1) **Kidney**
   (2) **Pancreas**
   (3) **Duodenum**

g. Two other structures found in the retroperitoneum are

   (1) **Aorta**
   (2) **Inferior vena cava**

h. Two structures found in the left upper quadrant are

   (1) **Spleen**
   (2) **Stomach**

2. The organs of the abdominal cavity are correctly labelled as follows:

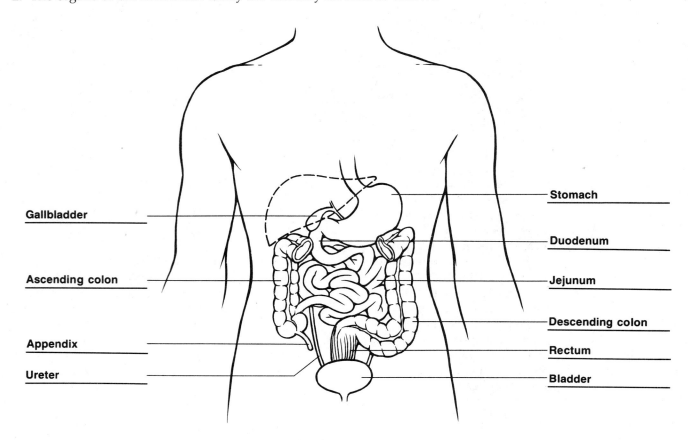

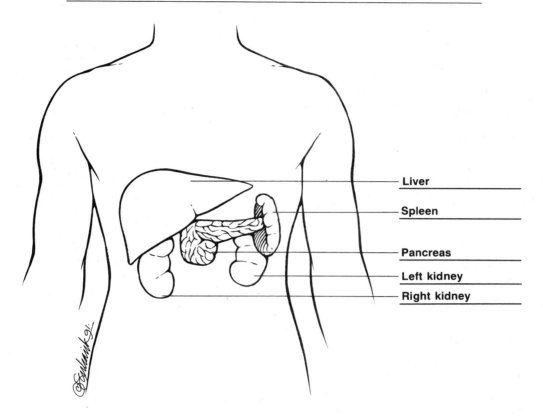

3. There is room for debate in deciding what is the correct answer to each of these questions (only the surgeon who opens the patient's belly will know the correct answer for sure). What is important is to be alert for the injuries that *might* be present in any given set of circumstances, even if there are no obvious signs of injury at the time you examine the patient.

__B__ A 15-year-old girl who was kicked in the left side by a horse. She is conscious and alert. Her pulse is rapid. She has a bruise over the left tenth rib in the anterior axillary line and has severe tenderness at that point.

The signs of fracture over the left tenth rib anteriorly should alert you to the possibility of a **ruptured spleen.**

Steps of management:

a. Administer **oxygen.**

b. **Splint** the fractured rib manually or with a pillow.

c. Encourage the patient to take **deep breaths.**

d. Start **transport.**

e. Start an **IV** en route.

__A,D__ A 50-year-old man who was a passenger in a car that slammed into a wall. He was wearing a lap seat belt. He complains of shortness of breath and abdominal pain. He winces when he coughs. His vital signs are pulse 92 and regular, respirations 36 and shallow, and blood pressure 120/80.

The classic *seat belt injuries* in accidents involving deceleration forces are **diaphragmatic tear** (from compression of the abdominal contents upward) and **tears in the intestine** (from twisting forces). If you also added **torn or ruptured bladder** (answer **F**), that is quite possible, especially if the patient's bladder was full at the time of the accident. The clinical findings point to involvement of the chest (the patient has dyspnea), perhaps from a diaphragmatic injury, and peritonitis (he winces when he coughs), which may be due to blood, urine, or digestive juices spilled within the peritoneal cavity.

Steps of management:

a. Administer **100% oxygen.**

b. **Immobilize the spine.**

c. Start **transport.**

d. Start an **IV** en route.

__C__ An 18-year-old man shot in the right upper quadrant by his girlfriend wielding a .38 special at a distance of about 10 feet. The patient is conscious. He has cold, sweaty skin and a weak, rapid pulse. There is an entrance wound in the right upper quadrant, about 2 finger-breadths below the costal margin in the mid-clavicular line. The exit wound is near the left buttock.

Steps of management:

a. Administer **100% oxygen.**

b. **Immobilize the spine** (the bullet may have ricocheted off the spinal column).

c. Start **transport.**

d. Start **two large-bore IVs** en route, and run in lactated Ringer's rapidly.

__E__ A 60-year-old man struck by a car as he was crossing the street. He complains of severe pain over the eleventh and twelfth ribs posteriorly. The pain is made worse by taking a deep breath. There is marked tenderness to palpation over the eleventh and twelfth ribs posteriorly, and there seems to be a mass in the left flank.
Fractures of the eleventh and twelfth ribs posteriorly along with a mass in the flank both point to **disruption of a kidney** with bleeding into the retroperitoneal space.

Steps of management:

a. Administer **100% oxygen.**

b. **Immobilize the spine.** (If the forces were sufficient to break two ribs in back, they were sufficient to damage the thoracic spine.)

c. Start **transport.**

d. Start an **IV** en route.

__F__ A 42-year-old construction worker extricated from underneath a pile of concrete blocks that caved in on top of him. He is unconscious. His skin is cold and clammy. His pulse is very weak. There are no bruises on the chest, which moves symmetrically with respiration. The abdomen is not rigid, but there seems to be a fullness in the center of the lower quadrant. The pelvis is unstable.
The fullness in the lower quadrant together with the pelvic fracture is highly suggestive of **a ruptured bladder.**

Steps of management: In a case of this sort, the patient's prehospital management will be dictated by the fact that he is critically injured and showing signs of shock, irrespective of the precise nature of the injuries:

a. Ensure an open **airway.**

b. Give **100% oxygen.** Assist ventilations as needed.

c. Apply and inflate the **MAST.**

d. **Immobilize the spine.**

e. Start **transport.**

f. Start **two large-bore IVs** en route, and run in lactated Ringer's rapidly.

4. The abdominal evaluation of an injured patient at the accident scene should not take more than about 30 seconds. The mechanisms of injury and his overall condition will dictate the treatment measures you have to take, so there is nothing to be gained by a painstakingly detailed abdominal assessment in the field. You should, however, note at least the following:

a. The **mechanisms of injury,** including damage to the vehicle and type of seat belt worn (if any) if the patient is the victim of a motor vehicle accident.

b. The patient's **complaints** referable to the abdomen, specifically complaints of nausea, vomiting, hematemesis, or abdominal pain.

c. **External signs of abdominal injury,** such as abrasions, contusion, seat belt marks, lacerations, or evisceration.

d. **Tenderness or rigidity** to palpation.

5. The case of evisceration described in this question is based on an actual case (see Majernik TG, et al. Intestinal evisceration resulting from a motor vehicle accident. *Ann Emerg Med* 13:633, 1984). The published case report does not record what care was given at the scene, but the care that *should* have been given at the scene is based on the fact that this patient is in shock and is as follows:

a. Administer **100% oxygen.**

b. Anticipate vomiting, and have suction at hand.

c. **Assist ventilations** with a bag-valve-mask.

d. **Cover the eviscerated bowel** with sterile aluminum foil or with sterile universal dressings that have been soaked in sterile saline. Cover the dressings, in turn, with a towel, to minimize heat loss across the wound.

e. **Immobilize the spine,** taking care not to place any straps across the eviscerated bowel. Include the right arm within the straps, to hold the fractured elbow immobile.

f. Start **transport.**

g. Start **two large-bore IVs** en route, and run in lactated Ringer's as rapidly as possible.

6. The principles of managing an impaled object in the abdomen are fundamentally the same as for an impaled object anywhere else: LEAVE THE IMPALED OBJECT IN PLACE.

a. Administer **oxygen.**

b. **Stabilize the impaled object** in place. Buttress it on all sides with universal dressings or with triangular bandages formed into "doughnut" rings. Then tape the buttress material securely, so that the knife cannot move in any direction.

c. Start **transport.**

d. Start an **IV** en route.

19
Fractures, Dislocations, and Sprains

1. Musculoskeletal injuries are usually not nearly as difficult to find as the words in this grid.

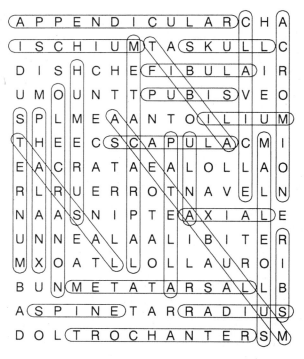

a. The part of the skeleton made up of the upper and lower extremities is called the **appendicular** skeleton. The rest of the skeleton, the part made up of the **skull, spine, sternum,** and **ribs,** is called the **axial** skeleton.
b. The highest point of the shoulder is called the **acromion.**
c. The pelvis is made up of three bones, the **ilium, ischium,** and **pubis.** The three come together laterally to form the depression, called the **acetabulum,** in which the head of the thigh bone fits.
d. Here are the "translations" into medical terminology:

   (1) Shoulder blade: **scapula**
   (2) Collar bone: **clavicle**
   (3) Funny bone: **ulna**
   (4) The funny part of the funny bone: **olecranon**
   (5) The bone that articulates with the funny bone and whose name sounds funny: **humerus**

(6) Knee cap: **patella**
(7) Shin bone: **tibia**
(8) Finger bone: **phalanx**
(9) "Hip bone": greater **trochanter**

e. The bone that runs along the thumb side of the forearm is called the **radius.**
   It articulates at the wrist with the carpal bones, which in turn articulate with
   the **metacarpal** bones of the hand.

f. The **fibula,** the smaller bone of the lower leg, forms the lateral **malleolus** in
   its distal articulation with the **tarsal** bones. Those in turn articulate with the
   metatarsal bones of the foot.

2. The bones of the skeleton are correctly labelled as follows:

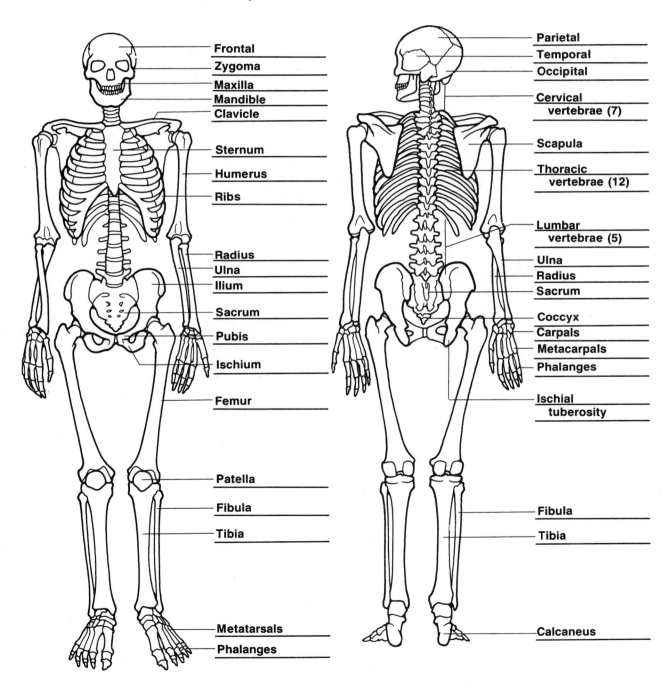

3. The bones that belong in the various joints are as follows:

Joint	Bones That Make Up the Joint
Shoulder	**Scapula, humerus**
Elbow	**Humerus, ulna**
Wrist	**Radius, ulna, carpals**
Hip	**Ilium, ischium, pubis, femur**
Knee	**Femur, tibia**
Ankle	**Tibia, fibula, tarsals**

4. When you know how an injury happened, you already know a lot about what injury you might find.

Mechanism of Injury	Example
Direct blow	Patella fractured against car dashboard
Indirect blow	Hip fractured after knee hit the dashboard
Twisting force	Ski injury, with spiral fracture of tibia
Powerful muscle contractions	Anterior shoulder dislocation from seizure
Pathologic fracture	Vertebral fracture in a patient with cancer that has spread to the spine

5. The presence of some injuries may also give clues to the possible presence of other injuries that share the same mechanism of injury.

   a. A young man jumped from a second-story window to escape a fire. He complains of severe pain in the left heel, which is quite black-and-blue.

His CALCANEAL FRACTURE mandates that you check for **fracture of the other calcaneus** as well as **fracture of the lumbar vertebrae,** especially around L1–L2.

   b. A 50-year-old woman was the front-seat passenger in a car that was hit head-on by an oncoming vehicle. Her right knee is bruised and swollen.
   This is the classic dashboard injury. The same forces that smashed up the knee may well have acted anywhere along the femur to cause a **femoral fracture** or to ram the femur backward, producing **fracture or dislocation of the hip.**

   c. A 60-year-old man fell sideways onto his outstretched hand. There is ecchymosis and tenderness at the base of his thumb.
   In this case of probable SCAPHOID FRACTURE, the forces are transmitted from the hand, along the radius and ulna, through the elbow, and up the humerus into the shoulder, so look for injuries anywhere along that axis, specifically **fracture of the distal radius/ulna, fracture/dislocation of the elbow, fracture of the shaft of the humerus, fracture/dislocation of the shoulder,** or **fracture of the clavicle.**

   d. A construction worker has been extricated from under a pile of concrete blocks that fell on top of him, pinning him prone, when part of a building collapsed. He has bruising over the left shoulder blade, and he cannot move the shoulder on that side.
   The obvious fracture is the FRACTURE OF THE SCAPULA, which is a tip-off to the powerful forces involved in the injury. Thus you need to start looking for **rib fractures, vertebral fractures,** and **damage to underlying soft tissues** (pulmonary contusion, renal injury).

6. The signs and symptoms of fracture are usually not terribly subtle:

Unnatural shape	D E F O R M I T Y
Reduced length	S H O R T E N I N G
Cardinal symptom	P A I N
Black-and-blue mark	E C C H Y M O S I S
Grating	C R E P I T U S
Disability	L O S S O F U S E
Protecting from movement	G U A R D I N G
Hurts to touch it	T E N D E R N E S S
Patient may report this	H E A R D A S N A P
Strange moves	U N N A T U R A L M O T I O N
Edema	S W E L L I N G
Seen in open fracture	V I S I B L E B O N E E N D S

7. It's all well and good to memorize the signs and symptoms of musculoskeletal injuries, but what counts is whether you can recognize the injuries when you see them and whether you then take the appropriate action.

a. We start with the boy who fell off his skateboard:

(1) The most likely diagnosis is a **fractured elbow.** If you want to be more exact, you could specify that it's a **supracondylar fracture of the humerus,** but probably it won't be possible (or necessary) in the field to know exactly what is broken and what isn't. The fact that the elbow is involved in a fracture is reason enough to feel a sense of urgency.

(2) **Yes,** there is a special danger in this case, the danger of the patient developing **Volkmann's ischemic contracture** as a result of the blood supply to his forearm being jeopardized. He's already showing signs of a compromised blood supply (his hand is cool and pale), and the broken end of the humerus is probably pinching his radial nerve as well (he has a sensory loss in the distribution of the radial nerve). Those are DANGER SIGNALS!

(3) If this boy is to retain the use of his right hand, urgent measures must be taken to restore the blood supply to the area. Those measures are best taken by an expert—an orthopedic surgeon—in the hospital; so if you are close to the hospital, **splint the elbow as you found it,** and hit the road—notifying the hospital of your ETA so that they can summon an "orthopod" (i.e., orthopedic surgeon) to be standing by in the emergency room. If you are any distance from the hospital, however, **contact medical command for orders;** you may be instructed to **apply traction along the axis of the humerus and straighten the elbow slightly,** until the patient's hand "pinks up."

b. The boy's mother tripped over his skateboard in her haste to assist him (there's a lesson in that!). She's done something to her wrist.

(1) The most likely diagnosis is a **Colles' fracture,** that is, a fracture of the distal radius and ulna. The "dinner-fork deformity" is classic for the Colles' fracture, as is the way the woman walked over to you, holding the injured wrist in her other hand and using her body as a splint.

(2) **No,** there is not ordinarily any special danger in a Colles' fracture, although you must, as always, check the circulation and neurologic function distal to the injury, just to be certain.

(3) A **padded aluminum ladder splint,** bent into a right angle at the elbow and supported in a sling is probably the most comfortable splint for this woman. But you may also use an air splint (provided it comes up over the elbow) or a padded board splint. In either of those two cases, transport the woman supine, with her splinted arm supported on a pillow, in order to **elevate the injured part.**

c. Here is another classic dashboard injury.

(1) The most likely diagnosis is **posterior dislocation of the hip.** That is what one would expect given the mechanisms of injury (deceleration forces, femur driven backward), and the patient has characteristic signs: The affected hip is flexed, adducted, and internally rotated, and the leg appears shorter than the leg on the uninjured side.

(2) **Yes,** there is a particular danger associated with posterior hip dislocation. Two dangers, in fact. The most feared complication is **avascular necrosis of the head of the femur,** which leads to total destruction of the hip joint. There is also danger of **damage to the sciatic nerve** and consequent foot drop.

(3) The most important treatment for a dislocated hip is **early reduction of the dislocation.** If you are within 20 minutes or so of the hospital, the best thing to do is **immobilize the patient on a long backboard,** generously padded with pillows, and **transport immediately.** If you are at a considerable distance from the hospital, **contact medical command.** If you are given instructions to do so, **try once to reduce the dislocation.**

d. The other victim from the same accident was the driver, found unconscious.

(1) The most likely *orthopedic* diagnosis in this case is a **fractured pelvis.** But this patient has some other very serious, even life-threatening injuries as well. Loss of consciousness in a victim of trauma means **head injury** until proved otherwise, and head injury in multitrauma means **spinal cord injury** until proved otherwise.

(2) **Yes, indeed** there is a particular danger in this case. There are several particular dangers. For starters, the patient is unconscious, so his **airway is in jeopardy.** He also seems to be in **shock,** perhaps from blood loss related to his pelvic fracture, but perhaps from blood loss elsewhere as well.

(3) In treating this patient, remember the ABCs:

A Open his **airway** (chin lift or jaw thrust); insert an oropharyngeal airway to help keep it open.

B Determine whether he is **breathing** adequately; if not, assist his breathing with a bag-valve-mask. In any event, give **oxygen.**

C Assess the **circulation** (pulse, capillary refill), and control external bleeding.

D Assess neurologic **disability** on the AVPU scale.

E **Expose** the patient for examination (which you probably won't be able to do properly until you've extricated him on a backboard from the vehicle).

Given the patient's condition, you're not going to have time to do a lot more in the field except

(a) Apply the **MAST.**

(b) Secure the patient to the **backboard.**

(c) Then **start transport.**

(d) En route, get a set of **vital signs,** if you haven't done so already.

(e) Start at least one and preferably **two large-bore IVs,** and run them wide open.

(f) Complete the **secondary survey** as best you can.

e. Apparently it's only when you get back to base that your partner mentions how much his ankle is hurting.

(1) The most likely diagnosis is a **sprained ankle,** although you can't be 100 percent sure without an x-ray.

(2) **No,** there is no particular danger associated with a sprained ankle.

(3) The treatment is to **immobilize the ankle** (e.g., air splint, pillow splint), apply a **cold pack, elevate the ankle,** and transport your partner to the emergency room to be checked over.

f. The high school quarterback who ended up under a pile of 200-pound linemen was subject to significant crushing forces.

(1) The most likely diagnosis is **posterior sternoclavicular dislocation.**

(2) **Yes,** there is a particular danger in this case, and that is **damage to critical underlying structures.** In fact, there is already evidence that such damage has occurred, for the boy says he is "choking"—an indication of possible tracheal damage.

(3) The most important aspect of this boy's treatment will be **expeditious transport to the hospital.** Administer **oxygen** en route. If he is comfortable lying down, keep him supine, with his left arm abducted and a pillow or rolled towel under his left shoulder; that position may take the pressure off the trachea or whatever structures are being compressed by the proximal end of the clavicle.

g. The pedestrian suffered a direct blow to the shin.

(1) The most likely diagnosis is an **open fracture of the tibia,** probably a transverse fracture.

(2) **Yes,** there is a particular danger associated with tibial fractures, and that is the development of a **compartment syndrome.** Indeed, the patient's paresthesias suggest that there may already be pressure on the sensory nerves supplying the foot.

(3) To treat the patient in the field, apply manual **traction** to straighten out the angulation and **splint** the limb (padded board splint, long-leg air splint). Keep the patient supine so that you can **elevate the injured leg.** Apply cold packs. **Transport** the patient **without delay,** and notify the receiving hospital to have an orthopod standing by.

h. In today's less than tranquil society, gunshot wounds are frequent sources of musculoskeletal trauma.

(1) The most likely diagnosis in this case is a **fractured femur.** The location of the wound and the shortening of the injured leg are the tip-offs.

(2) **Yes,** there is a particular danger in this case. Aside from the danger of **shock** that

attends every femoral fracture, there is apparently some **compromise to distal circulation** (the dorsalis pedis pulse is weak). There may also be a danger to *you* if the person who did the shooting is still wandering around with a loaded gun—did you bother to check on that before you ran over to attend the patient?

(3) This is another case that involves setting priorities:
   (a) Administer **oxygen.**
   (b) **Cover the open wound(s)** with sterile dressings.
   (c) Immobilize the injured leg in a **traction splint.**
   (d) Start **transport.**
   (e) Start a **large-bore IV** en route to the hospital.
   (f) Keep **rechecking the dorsalis pedis pulse.** Document all your findings.

(4) The PURPOSES OF SPLINTING in general are:
   (a) To **relieve pain**
   (b) To **prevent further injury**
   (c) To help **control bleeding**

i. The skier who ended up at the bottom of a pileup doubtless suffered a hyperextension injury of the leg.

   (1) The most likely diagnosis is **dislocation of the knee** (it may also be fractured).
   (2) **Yes,** there is a particular danger associated with that diagnosis, the danger of **damage to the popliteal artery** and consequent ischemic damage to the lower leg.
   (3) The treatment under these circumstances—where you are on the ski slopes, at some distance from a hospital—is to **try once to reduce the dislocation,** before muscle spasm makes it impossible to do so. Use a traction splint if you have one available. Otherwise apply manual traction in the long axis of the leg. Then **get the patient to the hospital as quickly as possible,** and notify the hospital in advance of your impending arrival.

j. Our last patient is the boy who was run over by the trolley car.

   (1) It doesn't take a lot of clinical acumen to diagnose a **traumatic amputation of the arm,** especially when the boy and his arm are lying several feet apart.
   (2) One could argue that the particular danger already happened. But so long as there is hope of reimplanting the severed arm, there is also a **danger of the amputated arm losing viability.**
   (3) There are two considerations here: First, and most important, is treatment of the *boy;* second is optimal handling of the severed *arm.*
      (a) Treatment of the injured boy:
         • **Cover the amputation stump** with a moist pressure dressing.
         • Complete the **secondary survey,** and treat any injuries found.
         • Start an **IV** en route to hospital.
      (b) Treatment of the amputated arm:
         • **Rinse** it free of debris with sterile saline.
         • **Wrap** it loosely in saline-moistened sterile gauze.
         • **Seal** it inside a plastic bag.
         • Place it in a **cool container,** or place chemical cold packs around the plastic bag containing the arm.

8. The compartment syndrome may be heralded by any or several of the **six Ps,** which are symptoms and signs of an ischemic limb:

   a. **Pain** is the earliest and most reliable sign.
   b. **Pallor.**
   c. **Pulselessness.**
   d. **Paresthesias.**
   e. **Paresis** or **paralysis.**
   f. **Puffiness.**

9. In examining the patient injured on the ski slope, it's a good idea to start by eliciting his **chief complaint.** While his deformed right knee may be the most obvious injury to *you,* there may be other injuries that are bothering the *patient* more. If you don't ask, you may not find out. In conducting the physical assessment, pay particular attention to

   a. The **position** in which the extremities are found (as always, compare the injured to the uninjured limb).
   b. The **circulatory status** of the injured limb. Check
      (1) **Skin condition.**
      (2) **Capillary refill.**
      (3) Distal **pulses** (anterior tibial and dorsalis pedis).

c. The **neurologic status** of the injured limb. Check

   (1) **Sensation** to pinprick over the heel and dorsum of the foot.
   (2) **Motor function:** ability to plantar flex and dorsiflex the foot.

10. Before you put on a splint, make sure you know the "rules."

   a. Severely angulated fractures should be straightened before they are splinted.
   TRUE, in order to relieve pain, prevent broken bone ends from overriding, and improve peripheral circulation.

   b. An air splint is a good choice for a humeral shaft fracture.
   FALSE. A splint is supposed to immobilize the *joint above and the joint below* the fracture. The joint *above* a humeral shaft fracture is the shoulder joint, which will not be included in the air splint.

   c. Fractures involving joints should be straightened before splinting to prevent distal ischemia.
   FALSE. Fractures involving joints should be "splinted where they lie," that is, in the position in which they are found.

   d. A traction splint is contraindicated in an open femoral fracture, because traction may drag broken bone ends back into the wound.
   FALSE. It *is* true that traction may drag broken bone ends back into the wound. It is *not* true that the traction splint is contraindicated in femoral fracture for that reason. Sometimes one has to choose the lesser of two evils, and it's a lesser evil to risk contamination of the wound than to risk ischemia to the extremity.

   e. Fingers or toes should be left out of the splint so that distal circulation can be monitored.
   TRUE. A splint that was just fine when you applied it may become too tight 10 minutes later because of swelling in the injured extremity. The only way you can tell if it has become too tight is if you can monitor the distal circulation.

   f. For a victim of multitrauma in unstable condition, one should splint the whole axial skeleton as a unit, on a long backboard, rather than take time to splint individual fractures.
   TRUE. When a person has been seriously injured, there simply isn't time to deal with the victim's fractures one by one. Securing the whole patient firmly to a backboard isn't a bad compromise though, for proper backboarding keeps a patient very nearly motionless, and that's what splinting is all about.

   g. Air splints may lose pressure with increasing altitude or temperature.
   FALSE. It's precisely the other way around. As the altitude increases or the temperature rises, air within an air splint expands, so the pressure *increases* and the air splint gets tighter—sometimes much tighter. For that reason, when you take the patient out of the snowbank into your nice warm ambulance, check and recheck his air splint to be certain it has not become too tight.

11. a. As we shall see in the next chapter, when dealing with a severely injured patient, knowing what to do is not enough. One has to know what to do *first* and what to do *next* and what to do after that. If you remember the alphabet, you'll be in good shape.

   __16__ Start an IV.

   __9__ Take the vital signs.

   __5__ Cut away the trouser leg. (Ordinarily this is step **E,** EXPOSE, but if you want to control the bleeding in the leg, which is part of step **C,** you've got to see what's bleeding.)

   __2__ Determine whether he is **breathing** (he is) (step **B**).

   __14__ Secure patient to backboard.

   __12__ Apply the MAST while holding the right leg in traction. (You will minimize movement of the patient if you have laid out the MAST on the backboard before you transferred the patient onto the backboard.)

   __6__ Put manual pressure on the bleeding site (part of step **C,** CIRCULATION).

   __1__ Open the **airway** (chin lift) (step **A**).

   __15__ Start transport.

   __10__ Move the patient to a backboard.

   __4__ Check for a carotid pulse (pulse is present) (first part of step **C,** CIRCULATION).

   __11,13__ Check for a dorsalis pedis pulse on the right. (You need to do this both before and after you have applied the splint, which in this case is the MAST.)

   __7__ Do AVPU check (step **D,** DISABILITY).

__3__   Check for open or tension pneumothorax (part of checking the adequacy of **breathing,** step **B**).

__8__   Pressure dressing over open wound of leg. (In practice, you'll do this whenever the dressing material becomes available.)

In actual practice, you will be carrying out some of the above steps very nearly simultaneously. While holding the airway open and observing the movements of the chest, for instance, you will also have a finger on the carotid pulse. But it is useful to consider the actions separately in order to review priorities.

b. **Yes,** at least one step has been omitted. **The patient was not given oxygen!**

12. Did you uncover the BIG SECRET?

    a. **knee**

    b. **glenoid**

    c. **ulna**

    d. **joint**

    e. **symphysis pubis**

    f. **scapula**

    g. **trochanter**

    h. **metacarpal**

    i. **foot**

    j. **ureter**

    k. **elevate**

    l. **miser**

    m. **ion**

    n. **tic**

    Secret Message: MUSCULOSKELETAL INJURIES RARELY POSE AN IMMEDIATE THREAT TO LIFE: PRIORITY GOES TO THE ABCs.

20
Multiple Injuries: Summary of Advanced Trauma Life Support

1. There are many ways to save time without cutting corners in the management of the critically injured, among them:

   a. **Get rolling at once** when dispatched. Don't wait until you have all the details; all you need to get on the road is the *address*—you can find out the rest en route.

   b. Know the map, and **take the shortest route to the scene.**

   c. While en route to the scene, **assemble the equipment you will need** when you get there.

   What other ideas did you come up with for saving time? It is always possible to find a more efficient way to do a job.

2. There's room for some discussion regarding what things are absolutely essential during the first few minutes with a patient who has been critically injured in a road accident. With experience, you may want to modify your list. In general, you will have to make a trade-off between all the equipment you would like to have immediately at hand and what you can comfortably carry during your first, hurried dash—often over difficult terrain—to the patient.

   _X_ MAST (consider it part and parcel of your backboard)

   ___ Long-leg air splint

   ___ Drug box

   _X_ Portable suction unit (a "must" for airway care)

   _X_ Oxygen cylinder (if you left the oxygen behind, deduct 10 points!!)

   ___ OB kit

   _X_ Pocket mask

   _X_ Oropharyngeal airways

   ___ Intravenous fluid bags

   _X_ Dressing materials

   _X_ Large-bore IV cannulas (to stick in the *chest*, not in a vein!)

   _X_ Head immobilizer

   _X_ Self-adhering roller bandage

   ___ Selection of board splints

   ___ Wheeled cot stretcher

   ___ ECG monitor

   ___ Contact lens remover

   _X_ Stethoscope

   _X_ Flashlight

   _X_ Triangular bandages

   ___ Chemical cold packs

   _X_ Cervical collar

   ___ Traction splint

   _X_ Nonrebreathing mask

   _X_ Long backboard/straps

   ___ Oral thermometer

   _X_ Fire extinguisher (if you're there before the fire department)

   ___ Bed pan

   _X_ Heavy-duty scissors

   ___ Emesis basin

   _X_ Hand-held radio

   ___ Band-Aids

   Other equipment that might be needed: Depending on the circumstances, you might require some **light rescue and extrication equipment.** And you may prefer a **bag-valve-mask** to a pocket mask. Finally, EMTs and paramedics should, in this era of AIDS, be donning plastic or rubber **gloves** when they have to come in contact with a patient's blood or secretions.

3. In conducting the extended primary survey—ABCDE—of the injured patient, it is well to keep in mind that basically there are only two things that can kill a person fast: hypoxia and exsanguination. So what you will be looking for are conditions that can rapidly bring about hypoxia or exsanguination.

Survey Step	What I Would Look for at This Step
AIRWAY	Severe **maxillofacial trauma** Mouth: **foreign materials, blood, vomitus, broken teeth** Neck: Deformity or open wound over the larynx (OPEN THE AIRWAY.)
BREATHING	Is breathing **present?** Signs of **respiratory distress** **Rate** and **depth** of respirations Is the **trachea midline?** By inspection: **bruises, open wounds, deformity, flail chest** By palpation: **instability** of rib cage By auscultation: **inequality of breath sounds** By percussion: **dullness** or **hyperresonance** (ASSIST VENTILATIONS, as needed.)
CIRCULATION	**Skin condition:** warmth, moisture, color **Pulses:** rate and quality of carotid pulse; presence or absence of femoral and radial **Neck veins** distended? **Capillary refill** time Sources of **external bleeding** (CONTROL BLEEDING.)
DISABILITY	**Pupils:** equality and reaction to light **Level of consciousness** on AVPU scale

4. By the time you have finished carrying out the primary survey, you should at least be able to determine whether the patient is in critical condition and therefore requires immediate transport ("load-and-go" situation) or whether there is time to carry out some stabilizing measures at the scene.

   C   A 62-year-old driver of a car hit from the side. The door on the driver's side is smashed in. The patient is conscious, in respiratory distress. The left chest is bruised, tender, and does not move symmetrically on respiration. The skin is warm. Pulse is 92 and slightly irregular, respirations 30 and shallow, and blood pressure 136/82.

   A **flail chest** is considered a critical injury because it can lead rapidly to hypoxia.

   a. Steps to be taken at the scene:

   (1) Establish an **airway** (cervical spine precautions).
   (2) Administer **oxygen.**
   (3) **Stabilize the flail segment** with a pillow.

   (4) **Immobilize** the patient on a long **backboard.**
   (5) **Communicate** with medical command or receiving hospital.

   b. Steps to be taken en route:

   (1) **Secondary survey.**
   (2) Large-bore **IV** with lactated Ringer's.
   (3) Recheck **vital and neurologic signs** every 5 minutes.
   (4) Be alert for development of tension pneumothorax.

   C   A 24-year-old driver of a car involved in a head-on collision. He was not wearing a seat belt. The windshield on the driver's side has a spider-web crack. The patient is confused, and his breath smells of alcohol. The skin is warm. Breathing seems labored. The left pupil is larger than the right. Pulse is 56 and regular, respirations 24 and deep, and blood pressure 190/110.

   The mechanisms of injury (note the broken

windshield) suggest head trauma, even before you have inspected the patient's head. The patient's suboptimal mental status, his unequal pupils, along with a slow pulse and high blood pressure all add up to **rising intracranial pressure.**

a. Steps to be taken at the scene:

(1) Administer **oxygen.**
(2) **Immobilize** the patient on a long **backboard.** (It may not be easy, for the patient may not be cooperative!)
(3) **Communicate** with medical command or receiving hospital.

b. Steps to be taken en route:

(1) **Secondary survey.**
(2) Start **keep-open IV** with normal saline.
(3) Be alert for seizures, vomiting.
(4) Recheck **vital and neurologic signs** every 5 minutes.

__C__ One rainy day, a car bomb was detonated in front of a foreign consulate, and a number of bystanders were injured by flying debris, including jagged pieces of metal torn from the car's body. The first casualty you come upon is bleeding from multiple sites, including a deep gash on the right side of the neck and a laceration that has partially severed the right leg at the groin. The leg laceration is gushing blood; it is too proximal to be benefitted by a tourniquet. It's hard to evaluate skin condition in the rain. Pulse is around 100 and somewhat weak; respirations are 30 per minute.

This patient earns his "load-and-go" status by virtue of **uncontrollable bleeding** from the femoral artery.

a. Steps to be taken at the scene:

(1) **Seal the open wound of the neck.**
(2) Administer **oxygen.**
(3) Try at least to **slow the bleeding** from the groin with pressure dressings and the **MAST.**
(4) **Communicate** with medical command or receiving hospital.

b. Steps to be taken en route:

(1) Two **large-bore IVs** with rapid infusion of lactated Ringer's.
(2) **Secondary survey.**
(3) Recheck **vital and neurologic signs** every 5 minutes.

__N__ A second casualty from the car bombing, a young man, was sideswiped by a piece of flying debris, which made a clean 14-inch incision straight across his abdomen. He is conscious and in moderate distress. Pulse is 104 and regular, respirations 28 and slightly labored, and blood pressure 104/70. What looks to be a major proportion of the patient's intestines are outside the abdomen.

Abdominal **evisceration** is certainly an attention-getter, but it does *not* pose an immediate threat to life.

a. Steps to be taken at the scene:

(1) Administer **oxygen.**
(2) Complete the **secondary survey.**
(3) Cover the eviscerated organs with **sterile dressings soaked in sterile saline.**

b. Steps to be taken en route:

(1) **Communicate** with medical command or receiving hospital.
(2) Start a **large-bore IV** with lactated Ringer's.
(3) Recheck **vital and neurologic signs** every 5 minutes.

__C__ A third casualty from the car bombing is another young man in considerable respiratory distress. There is a 2-inch-wide hole in his right chest through which you can hear air being sucked in on inhalation. His skin is warm. His pulse is 108 and regular; respirations are 30 per minute and gasping; blood pressure is 112/64.

An **open chest wound** is considered a critical injury because it prevents adequate ventilation of the lungs.

a. Steps to be taken at the scene:

(1) **Seal off the sucking chest wound** with an occlusive dressing taped on three sides.
(2) Administer **oxygen;** assist ventilations as needed.
(3) **Communicate** with medical command or receiving hospital.

b. Steps to be taken en route:

(1) **Secondary survey.**
(2) Start an **IV** with lactated Ringer's.
(3) Recheck **vital and neurologic signs** every 5 minutes.

__N__ A 56-year-old woman was struck by a car as she was crossing the street. You find her lying in the street, near the curb, her left leg severely angulated and bleeding. She is conscious. There is no tenderness to palpation over the chest or spine (you don't want to take off her shirt there in the middle of the street to inspect the chest). Her skin is warm. Pulse is 108 and regular, respirations 28, and blood pressure 132/90. There is an open fracture of the left tibia. The dorsalis pedis pulses are equal, and sensation to pinprick is intact in both feet.

An **open fracture of the tibia** is a serious injury with serious potential complications (such as compartment syndrome), but it does *not* pose an immediate threat to life; nor are there any signs so far of other injuries that do jeopardize the patient's life.

a. Steps to be taken in the field:

(1) **Secondary survey.**
(2) **Cover the wound** on the leg with a sterile dressing.
(3) **Straighten and splint** the fractured leg.

b. Steps to be taken en route:

(1) **Communicate** with medical command or receiving hospital.
(2) Recheck **pulse and sensation** distal to the fracture every 5 minutes.

C   A 59-year-old man who was the driver of a car that plowed into a bridge abutment in the wee hours of the morning. The patient is conscious, but very restless. He is sweating profusely. His chest is stable (it's too dark to see whether there are bruises). He can move all his extremities. The pulse is 82, respirations are 28, and blood pressure is 100/70.

Your primary survey has not given you much information regarding *where* precisely this patient has been injured, but the primary survey *has* given you unmistakable evidence that the patient is in **shock** (restlessness, profuse sweating). Don't be fooled by the slow pulse—bradycardia occurs sometimes with intra-abdominal bleeding. And DON'T WAIT FOR THE BLOOD PRESSURE TO FALL BEFORE YOU DECIDE THAT THE PATIENT IS IN SHOCK!

a. Steps to be taken at the scene:

(1) Administer **oxygen.**
(2) **Immobilize** the patient on a **long back-board.**
(3) **Communicate** with medical command or receiving hospital.

b. Steps to be taken en route:

(1) **Secondary survey.**
(2) Start two **large-bore IVs** and run in lactated Ringer's full tilt.
(3) Recheck **vital and neurologic signs** every 5 minutes.

N   A back-seat passenger in the same car, a 52-year-old woman, was wearing a lap seat belt. She is shrieking, "My legs, my legs!" Her skin is warm. She has no tenderness over the chest, and the chest wall is stable. Pulse is 82 and regular, respirations 30 and slightly shallow, and blood pressure 106/76. The patient cannot move her legs, and there is no sensation to pinprick from the toes up to around the iliac wings.

A **spinal cord injury** is a tragic injury, but ordinarily it does *not* pose an immediate threat to life unless there is a transection high in the cervical spine that paralyzes all muscles of breathing. This patient has a traumatic paraplegia, but no evidence of spinal shock or any other life-threatening condition.

a. Steps to be taken at the scene:

(1) **Secondary survey.**
(2) **Immobilize** the patient on a **long back-board.**

b. Steps to be taken en route:

(1) **Communicate** with medical command or receiving hospital.
(2) Start an **IV** with lactated Ringer's.
(3) Recheck **vital and neurologic signs** every 5 minutes.

C   A construction worker fell from a third-story scaffolding to the pavement below. When you arrive, he is unconscious and not breathing. You cannot detect a carotid pulse.

Things don't get much more critical than **cardiac arrest!**

a. Steps to be taken at the scene:

(1) Open the **airway** (cervical spine precautions).
(2) Start **CPR.**
(3) Give **oxygen** during ventilations.
(4) **Intubate** the trachea if you can do so quickly.
(5) **Immobilize** the patient on a **long back-board** with CPR ongoing.

(6) **Communicate** with medical command or receiving hospital.

b. Steps to be taken en route:

(1) Start an **IV.**
(2) Administer **medications** as required for CPR.
(3) **Defibrillate** as indicated.

__C__   A passenger in a car that was struck from the right side by a truck running a red light. The right-hand front door of the car is rammed in, deforming the passenger compartment of the car. The patient, a middle-aged woman, is conscious and in considerable distress. Her skin is cold and moist. Her neck veins are distended. Her chest moves only minimally on respiration, and you have difficulty hearing breath sounds on the right. You can't really assess the percussion note because of all the noise at the scene. The woman's pulse is 120 and weak, and her respirations are 36 and shallow.

The clues to this patient's **tension pneumothorax** are the signs of shock in the face of distended neck veins and decreased breath sounds on one side.

a. Steps to be taken in the field:

(1) Administer **oxygen.**
(2) **Decompress the chest** with a cannula in the second right intercostal space, midclavicular line.
(3) **Immobilize** the patient on a **long backboard.**
(4) **Communicate** with medical command or receiving hospital.

b. Steps to be taken en route:

(1) **Secondary survey.**
(2) Start a **large-bore IV** with lactated Ringer's.
(3) Recheck **vital and neurologic signs** every 5 minutes.

__N__   A 32-year-old man jumped from a second-story window of a burning building and landed on his feet in the flower garden beneath. He is conscious and complaining of severe pain in his heels. His skin is warm. There are second- and third-degree burns over both legs posteriorly. There is tenderness over L2. Both heels are exquisitely tender to palpation.

None of this patient's several injuries—probable **calcaneal fractures, lumbar vertebral fracture,** and **burns** of up to 18 percent of his body surface—pose an immediate threat to life.

a. Steps to be taken at the scene:

(1) **Secondary survey.**
(2) **Cover burns** with Water-Jel or a sterile sheet.
(3) **Immobilize** the patient on a **long backboard.**

b. Steps to be taken en route:

(1) **Communicate** with medical command or receiving hospital.
(2) Start an **IV** with lactated Ringer's.
(3) Recheck **vital and neurologic signs** every 5 minutes.

5. The mnemonic for taking the history of a multi-trauma victim is "Take an AMPLE history":

A   Does the patient have any **allergies?**
M   What **medications** has he taken today?
P   Is there any significant **past medical history,** especially
   • Previous operations or hospitalizations.
   • Previous problems with anesthesia.
   • Serious underlying illnesses (e.g., diabetes).
L   When did he eat his **last meal** (or drink his last drink!)?
E   What were the **events** leading up to the accident? What were the mechanisms of injury?

6. When you go over an injured patient from head to toe, it helps to know what you are looking for!

Body Region	What I Will Be Looking for in Particular
HEAD	Deformity, lacerations, CSF leak, Battle's sign, maxillofacial injury
NECK	Open wounds, subcutaneous emphysema, tracheal deviation, jugular distention, bruises over cervical spine
CHEST	Bruises, open wounds, instability, inequality of breath sounds, dullness or hyperresonance
ABDOMEN	Contusions, open wounds, evisceration, distention, rigidity, cough rebound
EXTREMITIES	Deformity, swelling, ecchymosis; pulses, movement, sensation

7. Did you succeed in decoding the secret message?

a. **dermis**

b. **dura mater**

c. **cerebellum**

d. **zygoma**

e. **abduction**

f. **atrophy**

g. **epiphysis**

h. **joint**

i. **patella**

j. **ligament**

k. **volar**

l. **incident**

m. **effect**

n. **vital sign**

o. **CNN**

p. **in**

Secret Message: CRITICALLY INJURED PATIENTS CANNOT BE STABILIZED IN THE FIELD; CARRY OUT LIFESAVING PROCEDURES ONLY, THEN GET MOVING!

21
The Multicasualty Incident

1. The information you should try to obtain from the caller is as follows:

   a. The **exact location** of the train derailment. Ask the caller to describe any LANDMARKS that might be helpful to the rescue crews in identifying the spot. As soon as you have the location, **dispatch the police, a fire company, and at least two ambulances.** Then proceed with your questions.

   b. Next, obtain the caller's **telephone number** and name, in case you are disconnected.

   c. Try to find out **how many vehicles were involved:** The train only? Did the train hit another vehicle? How many cars make up the train? **What kind of train is it?** A freight train? A commuter train? **In what condition is the derailed train?** Is it on its side? Is it on fire?

   d. Can the caller make any sort of estimate of the **number of victims?** Give her figures to choose from—10 victims? 50 victims? 100 victims?

   e. Are there any **hazards** at the scene? Since the caller cannot be expected in such circumstances to think clearly as to what constitutes a hazard, ask her specifically about FIRE, DOWNED ELECTRIC WIRES, HAZARDOUS MATERIALS, DEBRIS, and VEHICLES IN PRECARIOUS POSITIONS. Are there any strange smells that might signal toxic chemicals?

2. The locations for the first ambulance, the triage area, and the staging area are marked on the diagram below.

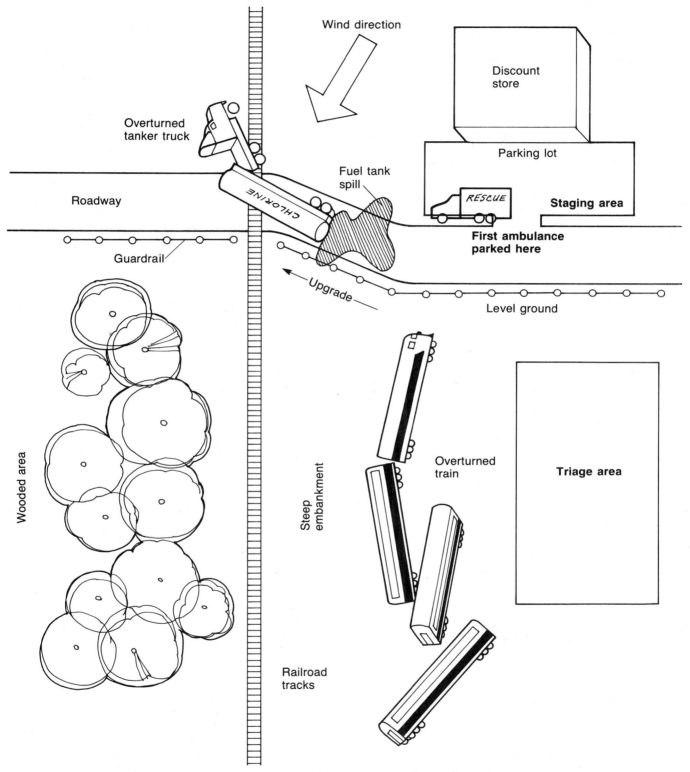

Besides EMS, the **police, fire department,** and a **hazmat team** (hazardous materials team) will be needed at the scene. It might also be useful to summon some **alternate means of transport,** such as a bus, to remove the noninjured and very lightly injured from the scene as soon as they are triaged.

3. In setting up the triage area, you need to distribute equipment in such a way that it will be easily accessible. A rescuer should not have to leave his patient to obtain something he needs to save a life. All lifesaving equipment must be within reach.

  a. At *each* stretcher position, there should be

    (1) Portable **oxygen** and **suction**
    (2) Oropharyngeal **airway**
    (3) **Bag-valve-mask**
    (4) **IV equipment** (e.g., catheters, infusion set, IV fluid, tape)
    (5) **Dressings, bandages,** and **scissors**
    (6) **Stethoscope** and **sphygmomanometer**

  b. In addition, in some central and readily visible place, you need to assemble the following:

    (1) **Prepackaged kits for emergency procedures,** including
      (a) Endotracheal intubation kit
      (b) Cricothyrotomy kit
      (c) Drug box
    (2) **MAST**
    (3) **Backboards** with all ancillary gear (straps, collars)
    (4) **Splints** of all types
    (5) **Monitor/defibrillator**

4. Triage is the most difficult task at a multicasualty incident, and it should ideally be carried out by the most highly trained and experienced medical person present.

  a. Triage decisions are rarely clear-cut, and you may wish to debate with your colleagues the triage choices listed below:

  __Y__ Patient is conscious. His skin is warm. Abdominal viscera are hanging out of his belly.
  An evisceration is a dramatic injury, but it does not pose an immediate threat to life, and there is no indication of shock.

  __R__ Patient is unconscious and breathing. The left pupil is larger than the right.
  This patient is first priority by virtue of being unconscious (and therefore unable to protect his **airway**), not because of his head injury. In fact, his signs of increased intracranial pressure earn him first priority for *evacuation.*

  __R__ Patient is unconscious. His face is bashed in. He is making gurgling noises as he breathes, and blood is bubbling from his mouth.
  Here is another **airway in jeopardy.**

  __Y__ Patient is conscious. One eye is hanging out of its socket.
  There is no threat to life here.

  __B__ Patient is unconscious. His head has been crushed, and a large proportion of his cerebral matter seems to have spilled out onto the ground.

  __R__ Patient is conscious and gasping. His neck veins are distended.
  This picture looks enough like a **tension pneumothorax** that you have to assume it *is* one.

  __G__ Patient is conscious. He has a severely angulated fracture of the lower leg.

  __B__ Patient is unconscious. He is not breathing and has no pulse.
  Difficult as it may be, you'll have to pass this patient by; you're too shorthanded to tie up one or two rescuers with a CPR effort that, in any case, has a very poor chance of success.

  __R__ Patient is conscious. He has a 2-inch hole in his anterior right chest through which you can hear air being sucked on inhalation.
  Open pneumothorax requires immediate treatment.

  __R__ Patient is conscious but confused and agitated. His skin is cold and sweaty.
  If you're short of people, this patient in **shock** can wait a bit, but only a bit, and he should be among the first to be evacuated.

  __R__ Patient is unconscious and not breathing, but a carotid pulse is still present.
  Apnea is first priority; if the patient still has a pulse, there's a good chance of pulling him through.

  __Y/G__ Patient is conscious. He complains that he cannot move his legs.
  Spinal cord injury is very serious indeed, in terms of its implications for the rest of the patient's life; but it is not an immediate threat to life and does not require any immediate stabilizing measures.

  __B__ Patient is decapitated.

  __R__ Patient is conscious. He is bleeding profusely from a gash in the neck.

  __G__ Patient is sitting with his eyes wide open looking blankly out into space. He is breathing and has a strong pulse but does not respond when you talk to him or pinch him.

This is probably a form of **hysteria.** The patient will need care, but not until those whose lives and limbs are in danger have been managed.

G   Patient is conscious. He has multiple small cuts over his face and arms.

R   Patient is unconscious. You cannot immediately detect the cause.
Simply being unconscious is sufficient—once again, it's a matter of an **airway** in jeopardy.

G   Patient is conscious. He says he has no feeling in his hands and feet.
Probably conversion hysteria.

b. If you make a rough calculation that you will need 2 rescuers for every critically injured patient (red tag), 1 rescuer for every seriously injured patient (yellow tag), and half a rescuer (!) for every patient with a minor injury, you come out needing somewhere around **20 rescuers,** which means a minimum of **7 to 10 ambulances.**

5. Triage tags are usually not very large and cannot accommodate a lot of information. But they should at least contain the most essential facts about the patient, especially if he is unconscious or for any other reason will be unable to provide information himself to the emergency room staff:

   a. **Identifying information:** name, age, address, next of kin's name and telephone number

   b. **Information about the scene:** anything that will help the emergency room staff understand the mechanisms of injury

   c. Pertinent (AMPLE) **medical history**

   d. **Physical findings:** vital and neurologic signs, any positive findings on physical examination

   e. Any **treatment** given (if a drug, the dose given, the time it was given, and the route by which it was given)

   f. **Priority** (will usually be indicated by the color of the triage tag itself)

6. a. Were you able to size up the uninjured train passengers and decide which ones could be of help?

   _____   Young man in a business suit who is dashing from one casualty to another, "just to check how everyone is doing." He tells you he is a fully trained EMT with his local volunteer fire department. "I'm an expert on the Dow-Jones and broken bones," he says. "Whoops, gotta run, I think they need me over there."
   This fellow is showing classic signs of **overreaction** and will just be a nuisance. Someone needs to move him out of the triage area and calm him down.

   X   Young woman in a white uniform, looking pale and dazed. "I'm a nurse," she tells you, "but I don't know if I can handle this. I feel like I'm going to throw up."
   This nurse is having a perfectly **normal reaction** to what must be a pretty horrific scene. She will in all probability "snap out of it" if you give her something to do.

   _____   Another man in a business suit, running from one person to another, saying, "We're all going to die here. There's a truck with chlorine gas up there. We're all going to die here."
   This man is showing signs of **blind panic,** which could infect others if he is not removed from the triage area.

   X   Middle-aged man carrying a briefcase, looking dazed and stunned. "It's just like 'Nam," he says, "when I was a medic. Just like 'Nam. All the noise. All the blood."
   Chances are good that this man, despite the indications that reactivated war memories have left him stunned, *can* be mobilized. Again, give him a job to do, and see what happens.

   _____   The casualty described earlier who is just sitting, staring blankly into space, and who does not respond when you talk to him or touch him.
   This is a form of hysterical reaction, and you will not be able to "snap him out of it."

   X   Teenage boy who comes over to you and asks, "You guys need any help? We took an EMT course in high school, and I passed the state exam."
   Welcome him with open arms—you need all the skilled help you can get!

   b. The number of tasks that can be assigned to responsible bystanders is limited only by your imagination. What needs to be done? Among the possibilities are

   (1) To **calm and comfort the emotionally disabled** people at the scene

(2) To serve as **scribe** and record the names of casualties at the scene or other important information

(3) To **assist in procedures** (e.g., cut tape for an IV, hold an IV bag aloft until an IV stand has been procured)

7. Ordinarily, patients are evacuated as soon as they are stabilized or, in the case of "load-and-go" casualties, as soon as critical interventions have been accomplished. When there are fewer transport vehicles than casualties, however, priorities have to be assigned for evacuation. In this particular case, we have only seven ambulances initially at the scene, each of which can carry one critically injured casualty and one other casualty who will not require attention and can sit up front with the driver of the ambulance. In the list below, casualties with first priority for evacuation are indicated with a "1," those with second priority with a "2," and so forth. Lower priority casualties who can be sent out with the first wave of ambulances are indicated with an asterisk (*) beside their priority rating.

__2__ Patient is conscious. His skin is warm. Abdominal viscera are hanging out of his belly.

__1__ Patient is unconscious and breathing. The left pupil is larger than the right.
With **increasing intracranial pressure,** this patient needs treatment that only a hospital can provide.

__1__ Patient is unconscious. His face is bashed in. He is making gurgling noises as he breathes, and blood is bubbling from his mouth.

__2__ Patient is conscious. One eye is hanging out of its socket.

____ Patient is unconscious. His head has been crushed, and a large proportion of his cerebral matter seems to have spilled out onto the ground.

__1__ Patient is conscious and gasping. His neck veins are distended.

__3__ Patient is conscious. He has a severely angulated fracture of the lower leg.
If there are signs of ischemia in the injured leg (the six Ps), bump him up to priority 2.

____ Patient is unconscious. He is not breathing and has no pulse.

__1__ Patient is conscious. He has a 2-inch hole in his anterior right chest through which you can hear air being sucked on inhalation.

__1__ Patient is conscious but confused and agitated. His skin is cold and sweaty.

__1__ Patient is unconscious and not breathing, but a carotid pulse is still present.

__2__ Patient is conscious. He complains that he cannot move his legs.

____ Patient is decapitated.

__1__ Patient is conscious. He is bleeding profusely from a gash in the neck.

__4__ Patient is sitting with his eyes wide open looking blankly out into space. He is breathing and has a strong pulse but does not respond when you talk to him or pinch him.
He's in no shape to sit unsupervised beside an ambulance driver!

__*4__ Patient is conscious. He has multiple small cuts over his face and arms.

__2__ Patient is unconscious. You cannot immediately detect the cause.
Ordinarily, an unconscious patient would have first priority for evacuation, but you have only seven vehicles, and there are already seven other patients in worse shape than this one; so he will have to wait until another ambulance reaches the site.

__*4__ Patient is conscious. He says he has no feeling in his hands and feet.

8. The secret message was, in fact, the cardinal rule of triage.

a. **triage**
b. **staging area**
c. **fibula**
d. **asystole**
e. **myocardium**
f. **tinnitus**
g. **toe**
h. **test**
i. **totter**
j. **hemorrhoids**

Secret Message: IN A MASS CASUALTY SITUATION, TRY TO DO THE GREATEST GOOD FOR THE GREATEST NUMBER.

Stop and Review II

1. The secret message is just a reminder about priorities.

   a. **epidermis**

   b. **ecchymosis**

   c. **jugular**

   d. **avulsed**

   e. **amputated**

   f. **first**

   g. **mannitol**

   h. **torr**

   i. **fifty**

   j. **artery**

   k. **osteo**

   Secret Message: DON'T LET DRAMATIC SOFT TISSUE INJURIES DISTRACT YOU FROM THE PRIMARY SURVEY.

2. In most jurisdictions, the following are considered coroner's cases:

   a. Obvious or suspected **homicide**

   b. Obvious or suspected **suicide**

   c. Any other **violent or unexpected death**

   d. Death of a **prison inmate**

3. Quick recognition of choking is a prerequisite to quick action.

   a. The signs of choking include

   (1) **Aphonia**
   (2) **Universal distress signal** (clutching the throat)

   (3) Dusky or **cyanotic skin**
   (4) Exaggerated or ineffectual breathing movements

   b. The steps of treating a conscious choking victim are as follows:

   (1) Determine if obstruction is complete (can he talk?). If not, **encourage him to cough.** But *if obstruction is complete:*
   (2) Apply 10 **manual thrusts.**
   (3) Keep repeating steps 2 and 3 until successful or until victim loses consciousness. *If he loses consciousness:*
   (4) Open his mouth and do a quick **finger sweep.**
   (5) Visualize the larynx (**direct laryngoscopy**), and try to remove the foreign body with a tonsil suction or Magill forceps under direct vision.

4. In this question about a head-injured patient, you had to review both some respiratory physiology along with the pathophysiology of head injury.

   a. If the patient's respiratory rate is 8 per minute and his tidal volume is 500 ml, then his minute volume is calculated as follows:

   $$\frac{\text{MINUTE}}{\text{VOLUME}} = \frac{\text{TIDAL}}{\text{VOLUME}} \times \frac{\text{RESPIRATORY}}{\text{RATE}}$$

   = 500 ml/breath × 8 breaths/min

   = **4,000 ml/min** (4 liters/min)

   b. That minute volume is smaller than normal. (Normal is around 6 liters/min.)

c. Therefore, we can conclude that the patient's arterial PCO_2 will tend to **increase,** so his pH will **decrease.** The net effect will be an acid-base disorder called a **respiratory acidosis.** The way you can help correct that abnormality is to **assist the patient's ventilations** and thereby increase his minute volume (which will blow off more carbon dioxide).

d. The signs of increasing intracranial pressure include

   (1) **Deteriorating level of consciousness**
   (2) **Hemiplegia**
   (3) **Vomiting**
   (4) **"Blown" pupil**
   (5) **Rising blood pressure with a slowing pulse**
   (6) Abnormal respirations or **apnea**

e. (1) The patient's AVPU rating is **P** (responds only to **p**ainful stimuli).
   (2) His score on the Glasgow Coma Scale is **8** points.

5. What did you make of the thirsty driver?

a. **Yes,** he is probably seriously injured. The reason for that conclusion is the **signs of shock** already evident: restlessness; cold, clammy skin; and the thirst itself.

b. You decide to start an IV with lactated Ringer's, which is a **crystalloid** solution. To calculate the IV rate, you need to recall the equation:

$$\text{gtt/min} = \frac{\text{volume to be infused} \times \text{gtt/ml}}{\text{time of infusion (in minutes)}}$$

$$= \frac{200 \text{ ml} \times 10 \text{ gtt/ml}}{60 \text{ min}}$$

$$= 33.3 \text{ gtt/min (for practical purposes, that is } \mathbf{30 \text{ gtt/min}})$$

c. The steps in troubleshooting an IV are as follows:

   (1) **Check the forearm** to make sure you didn't leave the tourniquet on!
   (2) **Straighten** the patient's arm, if bent.
   (3) **Examine the venipuncture site** for signs of infiltration (swelling, coolness).
   (4) Open the flow regulator clamp wide, and **lower the IV bag** below the level of the patient's heart; if there is no backflow, the IV has infiltrated, and you'll have to remove it and start another.
   (5) **Raise the IV bag** higher.
   (6) Close the clamp and try to **"milk" the tubing** toward the patient's arm; then reopen the clamp.

6. As important as knowing the correct dosage of a drug is knowing the route(s) by which it is administered and how fast it can be expected to take effect by any given route. The relative speed of onset of action by different routes is as follows:

   (1) __g__ Intracardiac injection (15 seconds)
   (2) __d__ Intravenous injection (30–60 seconds)
   (3) __b__ Endotracheal spray (3 minutes)
   (4) __e__ Sublingual tablet (3–5 minutes)
   (5) __i__ Intramuscular injection (10–20 minutes)
   (6) __h__ Rectal suppository (5–30 minutes, but unpredictable)
   (7) __a__ Subcutaneous injection (15–30 minutes)
   (8) __f__ Oral (30–90 minutes)
   (9) __c__ Topical application (hours to days)

7. Possible sources of information about what happened to the patient include

a. The **patient himself** (the most important source if the patient is conscious)

b. **Bystanders** or family

c. The **scene** (mechanisms of injury)

d. **Medical identification devices**

8. Injuries that can result from impact with the steering wheel include

a. Lacerations of the **mouth** and **chin**

b. **Laryngeal** and **tracheal** injury ("fracture")

c. **Cervical spine** injury

d. **Sternal fracture** with underlying **myocardial contusion** or **cardiac tamponade** or both

e. **Rib fractures** and possibly **flail chest**

f. **Pulmonary contusion** with or without **hemothorax** or **pneumothorax**

g. **Shearing of the aorta**

h. Shearing or compression of **abdominal organs**

9. In this question, a young man was rescued unconscious from a house fire.

   a. Signs suggestive of respiratory injury in a burned patient include

      (1) **Facial burns**
      (2) **Singed nasal hairs**
      (3) **Blistering** or redness **inside the mouth**
      (4) **Hoarseness, stridor,** or **brassy cough**
      (5) **Sooty sputum**
      (6) **Wheezing**

   b. The *first* step to take in managing this patient is to **PUT OUT THE FIRE** in his clothing!!!

   c. (1) To calculate the extent of his burns, you need to use a combination of the Rule of Nines and the Rule of Palms:

Posterior surface of both legs	18 percent
Whole left arm	9 percent
Hand-sized patch of left flank	1 percent
TOTAL	28 percent

   (2) The patient **does have a critical burn** on at least three counts:
      (a) He has **third-degree burns over more than 10 percent of his body.**
      (b) He has burns of **all degrees** over **more than 25 percent of his body.**
      (c) He has burns **involving the genitals.**

   d. The Parkland formula states that during the *first 8 hours* the patient should receive

   ml/8 hr = ½ × 4 ml/kg body weight × % body surface burned

   So for our patient, that means

   ml/8 hr = ½ × 4 ml × 70 kg × 28
   = 3,920 ml

   Therefore, during each hour, the patient needs to receive

   $$\text{ml/hr} = \frac{3{,}920 \text{ ml}}{8 \text{ hr}}$$

   $$= 490 \text{ ml/hr}$$

   $$\text{ml/min} = \frac{490 \text{ ml/hr}}{60 \text{ min/hr}}$$

   $$= 8 \text{ ml/min}$$

   gtt/min = 8 ml/min × 10 gtt/ml

   = 80 gtt/min

   e. (1) The dosage of morphine usually given to an adult in the field is **2 to 5 mg.**
      (2) It is usually given **intravenously,** because absorption after intramuscular administration may be erratic if the patient has any perfusion problems.
      (3) Possible *adverse side effects* include
         (a) **Hypotension**
         (b) **Bradycardia**
         (c) **Respiratory depression**
         (d) Nausea and **vomiting**

10. This is a patient who clearly has a serious chest injury. Furthermore, it is a chest injury that is increasing venous pressure. The combination of dyspnea, shock, and distended neck veins is highly suggestive of **tension pneumothorax,** so you need to proceed as follows:

    a. Administer **100% oxygen** by nonrebreathing mask.

    b. **Look** for deviation of the trachea, and **listen** for breath sounds on both sides of the chest. *If breath sounds are unequal:*

    c. **Percuss** for hyperresonance. *If one side sounds hollow:*

    d. **Decompress the chest** with a 14-gauge cannula in the second intercostal space in the midclavicular line.

    e. **Immobilize the patient** on a long backboard.

    f. **Start transport** to a trauma center.

    g. Start at least one **large-bore IV** en route.

11. What you need to remember to answer this question correctly is that ANY INJURY BELOW THE NIPPLES IS AN ABDOMINAL INJURY AS WELL AS A CHEST INJURY. The bullet apparently took a straight line through the right upper quadrant, and it could be expected to have hit the **liver, kidney,** and perhaps part of the **lung.**

12. It is essential to assess the neurovascular status of an injured limb both before and after splinting.

    a. To assess the circulation to the limb, check

       (1) **Warmth** and **color**
       (2) **Capillary refill**
       (3) **Distal pulses**—in this case the dorsalis pedis and posterior tibial

    b. To assess sensation and motor function in the lower extremity:

       (1) Test **pinprick** over the **heel** and the **dorsum of the foot.**
       (2) Test **dorsiflexion** and **plantar flexion** of the foot and toes.

13. Equipment to grab and take with you when you rush to the side of a severely injured patient should include

a. Long **backboard** with at least three straps

b. **Cervical collar** and **head immobilizer** (e.g., blanket roll)

c. Portable **oxygen** and **suction**

d. Oropharyngeal or nasopharyngeal **airways**

e. Pocket mask or **bag-valve-mask**

f. **Wound kit**

g. **MAST**

h. **Stethoscope, sphygmomanometer,** and **flashlight**

14. If you labelled the diagram correctly, you will be in good shape to start Chapter 22!

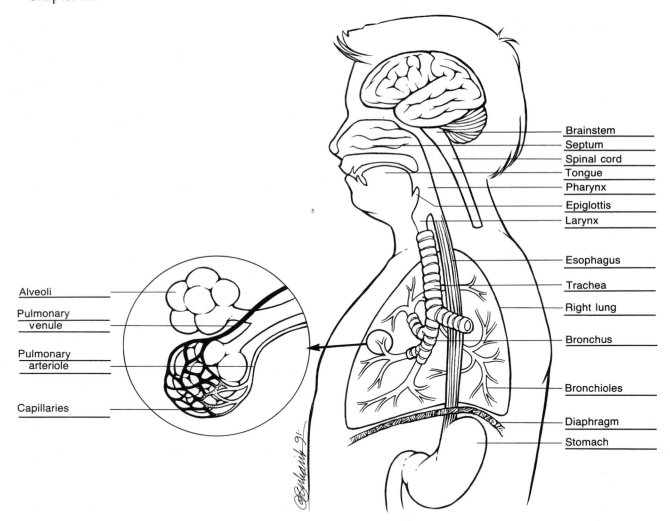

15. The crossword should have been a snap if you have been learning the vocabulary chapter by chapter.

```
C A V A . . . . . . . A R A C H N O I D
A C I D . . P L A S M A . . C O . I O N .
R E . D O . L A C T A T E . U R E T H R A
I . B U F F E R . A L E . I T . D R . I N O
N U C . B U Y . S A L I N E . E O N . O
A O R T A . R N . I R E . . M G . O X
. E P I S T A X I S . C R . H A E M . I
. R . O Y . . L . S T O M A . N A S A
D . U N S T A B L E . A B I D E . X L
U . R . T O R R . V A S O D I L A T I O N
M . E . O L E O . E X I T . P I L L . B P
B A T T L E . N A R E S . T O X I C . O
. N E V E R . C B . . S I N . G B
S I R . A P H O N I A . C E R E B R U M
P O . A N E U R Y S M . C . R U S E
I N T E R C O S T A L . R . S H U N T
N . P R E P . L A T E R A L . I T A L
E D . I E . L O G A N . N . I R S . B E
. O D . S W E A T . D E A D . N E E D L E
P A L A T E . R T E . L O N G . . E R
```

22
Respiratory Emergencies

1. a. While it is *possible* for a 22-year-old to suffer a heart attack, it is not very likely; so when you are confronted with a patient of that age complaining of chest pain, you need to think about other possibilities—such as a pulmonary embolism, a spontaneous pneumothorax, or, as this case turns out to be, **hyperventilation syndrome.** The tip-offs were the paresthesias around the mouth, the carpopedal spasm, and, incidentally, the increased respiratory rate. We mention that last because, strangely enough, often tachypnea and hyperpnea are *not* the most prominent features of hyperventilation syndrome and, as in this case, other signs or symptoms may predominate.

   b. The *steps in management* are

   (1) **Calm** and **reassure** the patient.
   (2) Help her to **take conscious control of her breathing** by telling her to breathe as you slowly count (about one number every 5 seconds).
   (3) If the acute episode passes, have the patient hyperventilate under your supervision, to duplicate her previous symptoms—so she will see how those symptoms came about. (If the acute episode *doesn't* pass, the patient needs to be evaluated in the emergency room!)

   c. This woman's arterial PCO_2 is probably **lower** than normal **because her minute ventilation is increased;** that is, she is blowing off more carbon dioxide than usual.

2. The spine-injured patient with weakness or partial paralysis of the respiratory muscles does not have the strength to inhale deeply. Thus his tidal volume will be smaller than normal, so his minute volume will also **decrease,** leading to an **increase** in his arterial PCO_2.

The correct management in the field in such a situation is to **assist the patient's ventilations** to increase the volume of each breath (tidal volume).

3. a. Shunt is best defined as **the proportion of the circulation that passes through the lungs without taking up oxygen** (answer **D**).

   b. When there is significant shunt, it points to a problem in the **alveoli** (answer **E**).

   c.

Condition	How It Leads to Shunt
Rib fracture	Pain prevents the patient from taking deep breaths; alveoli aren't inflated, so they collapse.
Pulmonary contusion	Alveoli fill with blood.
Pneumonia	Alveoli fill with pus.
Pulmonary edema	Alveoli fill with edema fluid.
Toxic inhalation	Alveoli fill with gases other than oxygen.
Pneumothorax	Atelectasis; no oxygen in collapsed alveoli.

   d. There are **no contraindications to oxygen therapy!!!**

4. The 985,500 cigarettes (give or take a few) that Mr. Koff has smoked over the past 45 years seem to be catching up with him. You can do the arithmetic yourself: 3 packs/day × 20 cigarettes/pack × 365 days/year × 45 years.

   a. Now you find him in respiratory distress. *Signs of respiratory distress* include

   (1) **Nasal flaring**

(2) **Tracheal tugging**

(3) **Retraction of intercostal muscles**

(4) Use of **accessory muscles in the neck** to assist breathing

(5) **Paradoxical respiratory movement** with sucking in of the epigastrium on inhalation (normally the belly bulges *out* on inhalation)

b. What needs to be done *immediately* on encountering a patient in this condition is to **administer oxygen,** before you ask any more questions or proceed any further with your examination. It would also be a good idea to hook the patient up to a **cardiac monitor** at this stage, for a hypoxic patient is a patient who is very likely to develop serious, possibly life-threatening cardiac dysrhythmias—and you'd like to have some warning that they are coming!

c. In *taking the history,* the following are among the things you would like to know:

(1) Regarding the dyspnea itself, the PQRST-A questions are in order:

P We already have a general idea of what **provoked** the symptoms (probably it was being in the recumbent position for several hours); but it would be useful to know what **palliates** them. Is there a position in which the patient is more comfortable? Has he taken anything to try to relieve his symptoms? If so, did it help?

Q What is the **quality** of the dyspnea? Is it the same as his usual shortness of breath or qualitatively different?

R As to **recurrence,** what we really want to know is *how long* the problem has been going on, particularly this acute episode. We also want to know how many years the patient has been smoking (although it was mentioned at the beginning of this answer section, in fact we did not obtain the information until later on).

S How **severe** is the dyspnea? Ask the patient to rate it against his usual dyspnea, in terms of ability to do specific things (e.g., walk up a flight of stairs).

T What was the **timing** of this particular attack? When specifically did it come on? What symptom came first, what came next?

A Is the patient having any **associated symptoms,** particularly cough, chest pain, fever?

(2) We shall also want to know a bit about the patient's *medical history,* particularly the **medications** he takes regularly and any **other underlying medical problems** from which he suffers.

d. In conducting the *physical assessment,* we'll be looking for some very specific signs:

Part of the Body	What I Will Be Looking for in Particular
General appearance	**Position; level of consciousness** (to indicate cerebral oxygenation); **degree of distress;** skin—**sweating, cyanosis**
Vital signs	**Tachycardia;** abnormal **respiratory rate, depth,** or **pattern; noisy breathing**
Head	**Cyanosis** of mucous membranes; **nasal flaring**
Neck	**Tracheal tugging** or **deviation;** use of **neck muscles** to breathe; distended **neck veins**
Chest	**Increased anteroposterior diameter;** abnormal or unequal **breath sounds;** inadequate **air exchange**
Abdomen	Paradoxical **respiratory movement;** painful, **palpable liver** in right upper quadrant
Extremities	Cigarette stains; **clubbing** of the fingers; pedal **edema**

e. Indeed, your careful physical assessment does turn up some meaningful findings—meaningful, that is, to one who understands how to interpret them.

Abnormal Finding	Possible Significance of the Finding
Confusion	The brain isn't getting enough oxygen.
Irregular pulse	The heart isn't getting enough oxygen; right heart failure.
Crackles and wheezes	Mucus in the bronchi and bronchospasm.
Right upper quadrant fullness and tenderness	Enlarged liver, a sign of right heart failure.
Ankle edema	Another sign of right heart failure.

f. This patient is most likely suffering from an acute **decompensation of COPD** (answer **B**).

g. The *steps of management* should include

(1) Administer **OXYGEN!!!** (You should have done that already.)
(2) Keep the patient **sitting up** (he probably won't allow you to do otherwise).
(3) Start an **IV lifeline** with D5/W.
(4) **Monitor** cardiac rhythm.

h. If you chose to withhold oxygen from this patient, or even to give it in a stingy fashion, you flunk—because the patient may die. Go back and reread the section in your textbook on COPD. **No, oxygen should *not* be withheld from this patient,** nor should it be given in very low flows. THE TREATMENT OF CHOICE FOR COPD IN DECOMPENSATION IS OXYGEN, OXYGEN, OXYGEN. That is the only drug that can save the patient's life.

i. The doctor has ordered AMINOPHYLLINE for the patient as well. We shall see in a moment whether that was a judicious choice, but meanwhile it gives us an opportunity to review the pharmacology of aminophylline.

(1) The *therapeutic effects* of aminophylline are
(a) It **stimulates the heart** to increase its rate and output.
(b) It **stimulates the central nervous system.**
(c) It **dilates the bronchi,** to decrease airway resistance.
(d) It acts as a **mild diuretic** to promote urine formation.
(2) The *dosage* of aminophylline is **0.5 mg/kg/hr** by IV infusion (sometimes preceded by a bolus of 5 mg/kg given over 20 minutes).
(3) The potential *side effects* of aminophylline include
(a) **Cardiac dysrhythmias**
(b) **Hypotension**
(c) **Nausea** and **vomiting**
(4) In fact, however, **there *is* a contraindication** to giving aminophylline to this particular patient. He has an **irregular pulse,** that is, a **cardiac dysrhythmia,** which is one of the contraindications to aminophylline administration. So what you need to do is **recheck the order with the physician** in a tactful way, for example, "Doc, I don't know if I mentioned that the patient has an irregular pulse. Do you still want us to give that aminophylline?"
(5) **Yes,** there are several drugs that are safer and more effective than aminophylline for

a patient with COPD—all of them in the general category of selective **beta-2 adrenergic drugs** (we will learn about adrenergic, or sympathomimetic, drugs in Chap. 23, when we take a closer look at drugs that affect the autonomic nervous system). Two examples are **albuterol** and **isoetharine.** They are best given by **metered-dose inhaler** with a spacer, but they can also be administered by nebulizer. The dosage is 1 to 2 puffs, which may be repeated in 15 minutes.

5. a. The massively obese patient found dozing in traffic after he drove his car into the car in front of him is most likely suffering from **pickwickian syndrome** (answer **D**). Both his weight and his somnolence point toward that conclusion.

b. His drowsiness is probably the result of **carbon dioxide retention** and hypercarbia, for carbon dioxide is, in fact, a rather potent sedative.

c. In managing this case you will have, first of all, to **persuade the patient to go to the hospital** to be checked. While it's a good bet that his drowsiness is the result of hypercarbia, you can't be completely certain that he didn't bang his head during the collision and suffer a closed head injury, so he needs to be checked out. **Monitor** his cardiac rhythm en route, and give him oxygen and assisted ventilation if he shows any cardiac dysrhythmias.

6. a. The woman with fever, cough, and pleuritic chest pain has most probably come down with **pneumonia** (answer **C**).

b. The *prehospital management* is simply to give her some of that nice **oxygen** to breathe and make her comfortable on the stretcher, probably sitting or semisitting, for the trip to the hospital.

7. a. The dyspneic college student is most likely suffering from an **acute asthmatic attack** (answer **E**). His age argues against diagnoses such as COPD or left heart failure. The fact that he has a veritable pharmacy in his pocket indicates that this isn't the first time he has ever had such an attack—so it is less likely to be, say, a spontaneous pneumothorax. And the prolonged expiratory phase of respiration is characteristic of lower airway obstruction.

b. He is indeed severely ill. The signs and symptoms pointing to that fact include the following

(1) His **pulse rate** is **over 130 per minute** (144/min).

(2) His **respiratory rate** is **over 30 per minute** (36/min).

(3) He has **more than 15 mm Hg of pulsus paradoxus** (20 mm Hg).

(4) There are **retractions of his neck muscles** on inhalation.

(5) He has a very nearly **silent chest,** which is also markedly hyperinflated.

(6) He is **sweating,** indicating activation of the sympathetic nervous system.

c. The *prehospital management* of this case should include

(1) Administer **oxygen** immediately, preferably 100% oxygen by nonrebreathing mask, but if he won't tolerate a mask, then give 6 liters per minute by nasal cannula.

(2) Start an **IV lifeline** with normal saline.

(3) Keep the patient in a **sitting position.**

(4) **Contact medical command** for orders.

d. Medical command orders you to administer TERBUTALINE, which is one of the standard medications for acute asthmatic attacks.

(1) Terbutaline is given for its **bronchodilating** effects.

(2) The correct *dosage* for an adult is **0.25 mg** (0.25 ml).

(3) It is given **subcutaneously,** usually over the lateral deltoid.

(4) The *contraindications* to giving terbutaline are

(a) **Children less than 12 years old**

(b) **Angina pectoris**

(c) **Hypertension**

(d) **Cardiac dysrhythmias** (terbutaline used with caution)

(5) The possible *side effects* of terbutaline include

(a) **Tremor** and **nervousness**

(b) **Palpitations**

(c) **Dizziness**

(d) Sometimes transient **headaches, sweating, drowsiness, nausea,** and **muscle cramps**

e. You are also instructed to help the patient take a dose from his BRONKOMETER inhaler. However, being very alert and on the ball, you realize that **there *is* a contraindication** to administering the Bronkometer, for it **should not be given together with terbutaline.** What

you have to do, therefore, is to **recheck the order with the physician**—once again with your usual tact: "Uh, Doc, we've given 0.25 mg of terbutaline sub-q. Do you really want us to give Bronkometer as well?"

8. Not everything that wheezes is an acute asthmatic attack. Other causes of wheezing include

a. **Left heart failure**

b. **Smoke inhalation** or inhalation of toxic fumes

c. **Chronic bronchitis**

d. **Foreign body obstruction** of a major airway (e.g., the patient who has a peanut lodged in a bronchus or a tumor compressing a bronchus)

9. a. The 56-year-old man with the sudden onset of dyspnea and pleuritic chest pain has most probably suffered a **pulmonary embolism** (answer **A**), to which his chronic heart disease predisposed him.

b. Prehospital *management* of the case includes the following steps:

(1) Administer **100% oxygen.**

(2) Start an **IV lifeline** with D5/W to keep a vein open.

(3) **Monitor** cardiac rhythm.

(4) **Transport** without delay.

10. a. The *first* thing you should do for the firefighter overcome by smoke is **give him oxygen** (even in the old days, long before there were paramedics, firefighters knew the importance of "getting the good gas in and the bad gas out").

b. Among the things you would like to find out in *taking the history* of this exposure are

(1) Did the firefighter **lose consciousness** during the exposure? If so, **for how long?**

(2) Was he **in a closed space** with toxic fumes?

(3) **What was burning?** Were the phonograph records, with their PVCs, on fire—meaning there is a danger of phosgene and carbon monoxide inhalation? That is important information for the emergency room staff.

(4) Does the firefighter have any significant **underlying medical problems?** A period of hypoxia during the fire, for example, could have much more serious implications for a patient with underlying heart disease than one with normal coronary arteries.

c. Warning *signs* that should alert you to the possibility *of respiratory tract injury* after a toxic inhalation include

(1) **Facial burns**
(2) **Singed eyebrows** or **nasal hairs**
(3) **Blisters** in the **mouth**
(4) **Sooty sputum**
(5) **Brassy cough**
(6) **Hoarseness**
(7) **Stridor**

d. In particular, if you hear **STRIDOR,** you should be alerted to the possibility that the airway is about to close off altogether. Stridor, therefore, is a signal to **get moving as fast as possible to the hospital.**

e. When the patient comes around and demands to return to the fray, you need, first of all, to **explain the potential seriousness of the problem** and the fact that further exposure could be fatal. If he isn't convinced, you may have to ask his superior to order him to accompany you to hospital. En route:

(1) Administer 100% **oxygen.**
(2) Start an **IV lifeline** with D5/W to keep a vein open.
(3) **Monitor** cardiac rhythm.

11. a. The steps you will take when there is a near drowning at your friend's house will depend to some extent on your own competence as a swimmer. If you are *not* a competent swimmer, do *not* go into water above your waist, and in any case **don a flotation device.** Once you are within reach of the victim, proceed as follows:

(1) **Bring him to the surface,** holding his head in neutral position.
(2) Sandwich his head and chest between your arms and step backward (into shallower water) while you **turn him onto his back,** again keeping his head and neck aligned in the neutral position.
(3) **Determine whether he is breathing.**
(4) If he is *not* breathing, **start mouth-to-mouth ventilation** even before removing the victim from the water.
(5) **Float a board beneath the victim,** and remove him from the water on the board, securing his head so that it does not roll from side to side as the board is lifted from the water.
(6) Now, **check for a pulse.** If there is no pulse, start external chest compressions.

b. Once the ambulance arrives with your colleagues from work and all their equipment, you should immediately

(1) **Administer oxygen.**
(2) **Intubate the trachea** after several minutes of preoxygenation.

c. The doctor gives you orders to administer SODIUM BICARBONATE.

(1) The *indications* for giving sodium bicarbonate include
   (a) To treat **metabolic acidosis,** which is probably the indication in this patient's case
   (b) To treat **hyperkalemia** (high serum potassium)
   (c) To **promote excretion of some types of barbiturates** when taken in overdose
   (d) To **promote excretion of myoglobin** in crush injuries and electrocution

(2) The *contraindications* to giving sodium bicarbonate include
   (a) **Hypokalemia** (low serum potassium)
   (b) Conditions in which the patient cannot tolerate additional salt, such as **congestive heart failure**

(3) The *dosage* of sodium bicarbonate is **1 mEq per kilogram** given as an intravenous bolus.

(4) The only potential *side effect* of sodium bicarbonate that is of concern in this particular case is its tendency to cause a transient **elevation in arterial PCO_2.** The way to deal with that is simply to increase the rate at which you ventilate the patient, in order to blow off the excess carbon dioxide. Other potential side effects of sodium bicarbonate, which are more likely to occur in patients with chronic heart disease and those taking diuretic medications, are salt and fluid overload and hypokalemia.

12. a. When your friend complains of a headache while climbing in the mountains, the best way to check whether he is suffering from significant mountain sickness (and not "just a headache") is to **ask him to walk heel-to-toe.** If he can't do so without losing his balance (i.e., if he shows **ataxia**), it's reasonable to assume that something serious is going on.

b. Signs and symptoms suggestive of high-altitude pulmonary edema include

(1) Severe **dyspnea**
(2) **Cheyne-Stokes respirations**
(3) **Cough** productive of pink, **frothy sputum**

(4) **Confusion** or other indications of reduced cerebral oxygenation

(5) **Cyanosis**

(6) **Tachypnea** and **tachycardia**

(7) **Crackles** (often heard first in the right middle lobe)

(8) Any signs and symptoms of **acute mountain sickness**

c. The *treatment* of choice for high-altitude pulmonary edema is to **move the patient to lower altitude** as quickly as possible. If you have oxygen immediately available, administer it as you descend, but don't delay the descent waiting for oxygen or anything else. If, however, you are unavoidably delayed (e.g., by darkness or bad weather), keep the patient warm and at rest, continue giving oxygen, and administer **dexamethasone,** 4 mg by mouth or intramuscularly.

13. Some paramedics just can't stay out of trouble, even on a Caribbean cruise.

a. The diver who lost consciousness almost immediately after surfacing probably suffered a **dysbaric air embolism.** What most likely happened was that he held his breath during ascent, causing his lungs to inflate and burst **(pulmonary overpressurization syndrome).** The enormous pressure inside his lungs, meanwhile, prevented any blood flow through the lungs during the final phase of ascent; the blood vessels were literally squeezed shut. It was only after the diver took his first breath at the surface, allowing his lungs to depressurize, that blood could flow through them again. At that point, the air from the burst alveoli bubbled straight into the pulmonary capillaries; the bubbles coalesced, and some quite big bubbles got swept into the cerebral circulation, causing the diver to black out.

b. The most important aspect of *treatment* in this case will be recompression in a **hyperbaric chamber,** so the captain should radio for some sort of assistance—probably a helicopter—to evacuate the diver to the nearest hyperbaric facility. Meanwhile:

(1) Ensure the patient's **airway.** If he is unconscious, that means **intubate the trachea.** Administer **100% oxygen.**

(2) Keep him in the **left lateral recumbent position** in about 5 to 10 degrees of head-down tilt. Avoid extreme head-down tilt, for that can increase intracerebral pressure.

(3) Start an **IV lifeline** with D5/W.

(4) If the ship has a monitor on board, by all means **monitor** the patient's cardiac rhythm.

(5) **Anticipate seizures** and have diazepam drawn up and ready.

(6) If it's available among the shipboard drugs, have a dopamine drip ready as well, to treat hypotension if it develops.

c. The second diver—the one with the backache—has no garden-variety backache. The tip-off is his comment that he is unable to urinate. That along with his back pain points to dysfunction in the lumbar spinal cord, which in turn is highly suggestive of **decompression sickness.**

d. The *treatment* of this diver will also require a **hyperbaric chamber,** so notify the facility that you'll be sending them *two* customers, not just one. Meanwhile, bring the second diver to the sick bay, where you can keep an eye on him at the same time you're monitoring his friend.

(1) Administer **100% oxygen.**

(2) Insert a **urinary catheter** if you've been trained to do so.

(3) Start an **IV** with lactated Ringer's and run it at a rate to maintain urine output around 1 to 2 ml per hour.

(4) Give **methylprednisolone, 125 mg IV.**

14. Now that you have decoded the secret message, write it in capital letters on an index card, and paste the card to the oxygen cylinder in the ambulance.

a. **asphyxia**

b. **vein**

c. **vertigo**

d. **fsw**

e. **rales**

f. **stridor**

g. **emphysema**

h. **vertex**

i. **nitrogen**

j. **ornery**

k. **nerd**

l. **nit**

Secret (??) Message: NEVER NEVER NEVER WITHHOLD OXYGEN FROM ANY PATIENT IN RESPIRATORY DISTRESS!

23
Cardiovascular Emergencies

1. Were you able to find your way around the circulatory system? Every red blood cell does so many times a day, without a map!

Aorta

Inferior vena cava

START HERE

Structures traversed en route:

Aortic _____ valve

Left ventricle _____

Mitral _____ valve

Left atrium _____

Pulmonary vein _____

Pulmonary venules _____

Pulmonary capillaries _____

Pulmonary arterioles _____

Pulmonary artery _____

Pulmonic _____ valve

Right ventricle _____

Tricuspid _____ valve

Right atrium _____

2. The structures of the heart are labelled below:

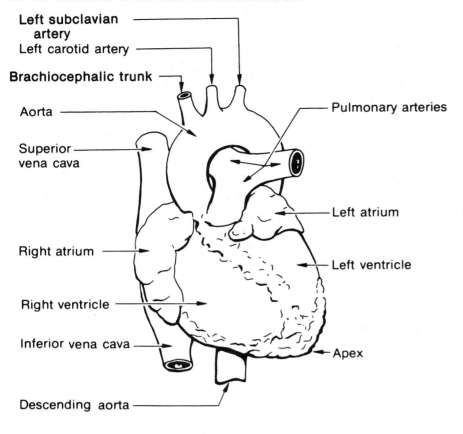

Left subclavian artery

Left carotid artery

Brachiocephalic trunk

Aorta

Superior vena cava

Right atrium

Right ventricle

Inferior vena cava

Descending aorta

Pulmonary arteries

Left atrium

Left ventricle

Apex

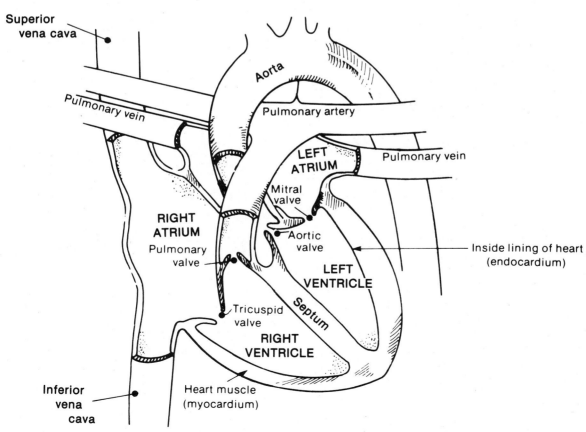

Superior vena cava

Pulmonary vein

Aorta

Pulmonary artery

Pulmonary vein

LEFT ATRIUM

Mitral valve

RIGHT ATRIUM

Pulmonary valve

Aortic valve

Inside lining of heart (endocardium)

LEFT VENTRICLE

Septum

Tricuspid valve

RIGHT VENTRICLE

Inferior vena cava

Heart muscle (myocardium)

3. When blood backs up behind the *right* side of the heart, it engorges the *systemic* circulation behind it; when blood backs up behind the *left* side of the heart, it fills the *pulmonary* circulation. The clinical symptoms and signs reflect those two different processes.

__A__ Dyspnea (**left** heart failure, with engorgement of the pulmonary vessels and extravasation of fluid into the lungs)

__B__ Jugular venous distention (**right** heart failure; blood backed up behind the right atrium engorges all the veins heading toward the heart)

__B__ Swelling of the feet (**right** heart failure, with extravasation of fluid into the peripheral tissues)

__A__ Crackles on auscultation

__B__ Hepatomegaly

__B__ Sacral edema

__A__ Pink, frothy sputum

4. The arteries that supply the heart are called the **coronary arteries.** They arise from the **aorta** and branch into (a) the **left coronary artery,** which supplies the left ventricle, and (b) the **right coronary artery,** which supplies the right atrium and right ventricle. The main *vein* of the heart crosses the heart in a groove that separates the atria and ventricles, called the **coronary sulcus,** to empty finally into the **coronary sinus,** which in turn empties into the right atrium.

5. The principal blood vessels mentioned in the question are as follows:

a.   P U L **M** O N A R Y   V E I N

b.   R **A** D I A L

c.   **J** U G U L A R S

d.   I N N **O** M I N A T E

e.   I N F E R I **O** R   V E N A   C A V A

f. S U P E R I O R   **V** E N A   C A V A

g.   T **E** M P O R A L

h.   B R A C H **I** A L

i.   U L **N** A R

j.   B A **S** I L I C

k.   A X I L L **A** R Y

l.   S A P H E **N** O U S

m.   C A R O T I **D**   A R T E R Y

n.   S U B C L **A** V I A N   V E I N

o.   A O **R** T A

p.   P O P L I **T** E A L

q.   P O S T **E** R I O R   T I B I A L

r.   P U L M O N A **R** Y   A R T E R Y

s.   D O R S A L **I** S   P E D I S

t.   F **E** M O R A L

u.   **S** U B C L A V I A N

6. a. If a person at rest has a heart rate of 72 per minute and a stroke volume of 75 ml per beat, his cardiac output is

$$\text{Cardiac output} = \text{heart rate} \times \text{stroke volume}$$
$$= 72 \text{ beats/min} \times 75 \text{ ml/beat}$$
$$= \mathbf{5,400 \text{ ml/min}}$$

b. If his heart rate then increases to 100 per minute and his stroke volume to 90 ml, his cardiac output increases accordingly:

$$\text{Cardiac output} = 100 \text{ beats/min} \times 90 \text{ ml/beat}$$
$$= \mathbf{9,000 \text{ ml/min}}$$

7. a. As implied in the previous example, one of the things that can increase ventricular *preload* is **exercise,** for muscle action "massages" the veins and causes more blood to be returned to the heart.

b. An increased preload **increases cardiac output** in several ways. The sheer volume by itself increases stroke volume. Furthermore, the increased volume returning to the heart puts greater stretch on the heart muscle, causing it to contract more forcefully (Frank-Starling effect), which again increases the stroke volume.

c. **Anything that raises the blood pressure by peripheral vasoconstriction** will increase ventricular *afterload.*

d. The effect of increasing the afterload is to **decrease cardiac output.**

e. All of the following things affect afterload:

(1) Norepinephrine **increases afterload** by causing peripheral vasoconstriction (alpha sympathetic effect).
(2) Isoproterenol **decreases afterload** by causing peripheral vasodilatation (beta sympathetic effect).
(3) Nitroglycerin **decreases afterload,** again by its vasodilatory effects.
(4) Phenylephrine, a pure alpha agent, **increases afterload** by vasoconstriction.
(5) Hypertension also **increases afterload** by the chronic state of vasoconstriction of the peripheral vessels. That long-standing increase in afterload takes its toll on the heart, which has to work much harder to pump against a greater resistance. That is why left heart failure is often seen in the late stages of hypertensive disease.

8. The two divisions of the human autonomic nervous system in general balance the effects of one another; so, for example, while the parasympathetic system slows the heart, the sympathetic system speeds it up. That balance enables very fine tuning of cardiovascular and other responses.

B   Vagus nerve (**parasympathetic**)

B   Acetylcholine (the chemical mediator of the **parasympathetic** system)

A   Tachycardia (a typical beta **sympathetic** response)

A   Propranolol (a beta **sympathetic** blocker)

A   Sweating (actually, sweating is a little of both, but a "cold sweat" under stress is the result of **sympathetic** stimulation)

B   Valsalva maneuver (The Valsalva maneuver, or a forced exhalation against a closed glottis, is a powerful vagal stimulant, hence a **parasympathetic** stimulus.)

B   Vegetative functions (**parasympathetic**)

B   Atropine (the prototypical **parasympathetic** blocker)

A   Fight/flight response (That's what the **sympathetic** nervous system was designed for!)

B   Carotid massage (has the same effect as a Valsalva maneuver, to stimulate the vagus nerve and thus activitate the **parasympathetic** system)

A   Alpha receptor (**sympathetic**)

A   Paralyzed in spinal cord injury (Spinal shock, or neurogenic shock, results from damage to the **sympathetic** nerve trunks as they emerge from the thoracolumbar spine.)

B   Bradycardia (It is the vagus nerve, the principal nerve of the **parasympathetic** system, that slows the heart.)

A   Norepinephrine (the natural chemical mediator at the nerve endings of the **sympathetic** nervous system)

A   Labetalol (a beta **sympathetic** blocker)

A   Dilated pupils (part of the **sympathetic** fight/flight response)

B   Increased salivation (That's the **parasympathetic** system preparing you to digest a meal.)

9. If you inspect a large number of ambulances, you will rapidly come to the conclusion that paramedics are the most obsessive-compulsive people in the world—people who subscribe to the motto "a place for everything, and everything in its place." That is as it should be, for the last thing you want to do in an emergency is spend a lot of time hunting for the things you need. Like all the other kits and cupboards in the ambulance, the drug box should be well-organized. How well did you sort out the cardiac and respiratory medications?

| | PARASYMPATHETIC AGENTS | SYMPATHETIC AGENTS | |
		ALPHA AGENTS	BETA AGENTS
Agonist	neostigmine	norepinephrine phenylephrine high-dose dopamine metaraminol	epinephrine isoproterenol low-dose dopamine isoetharine (beta-2) albuterol (beta-2) terbutaline (beta-2)
Blocker	atropine	chlorpromazine	propranolol labetalol

10. The depolarization of the myocardial cell occurs when the extracellular cation **sodium (Na^+)** begins to flow into the cell, changing its net charge from negative to positive.

Drugs such as verapamil and nifedipine work by blocking the uptake of **calcium (Ca^{++})**.

An excess of **potassium (K^+)** may produce a tall, pointy T wave on the ECG.

11. The normal electric conduction system of the heart is shown below.

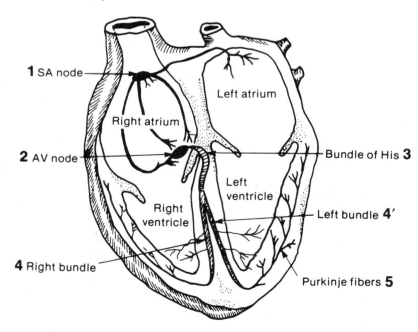

Among the structures of the electric conduction system, those that can function as a pacemaker include

Structure	Instrinsic firing rate
Sinoatrial (SA) node	60–100 per min
Atrioventricular (AV) junction	40–50 per min
Purkinje system	30–40 per min

12. The components of the ECG shown in the figure are

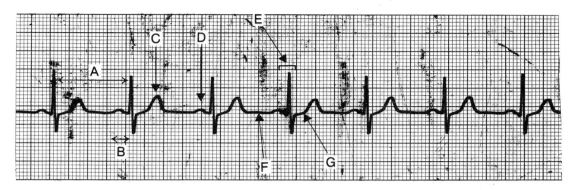

a. **R–R interval**

b. **P–R interval**

c. **T wave**

d. **P wave**

e. **QRS complex**

f. **Isoelectric line**

g. **S–T segment**

13. In evaluating patients with medical problems, such as chest pain, skills in both history taking and physical assessment are essential.

   a. In taking a history from a patient whose chief complaint is chest pain, the PQRST-A formula is a helpful reminder of what questions to ask about the pain:

   P   What **provoked** the pain? What was the patient doing when it came on? What if anything **palliates** it (makes it better)?

   Q   What is the **quality** of the pain? Sharp? Dull? Crushing?

   R   Does the pain **radiate?** From where to where?

   S   How **severe** is the pain?

   T   What was the **timing?** When did it start? What happened first?

   A   Are there **associated symptoms** (e.g., dyspnea, nausea)?

   The history should also include information about the patient's "other medical history" (medications, allergies, serious medical conditions, hospitalizations).

   b. The patient's account of his symptoms can tell you a great deal about the underlying pathophysiology.

Symptom	Suggests
Dyspnea	There is **fluid in the lungs,** a result of left heart failure.
Palpitations	The heart is beating irregularly (i.e., there is a **cardiac dysrhythmia**).
Dizziness	The circulation to the brain is inadequate, either as a result of a **dysrhythmia or pump failure.**
Sweating	Massive **sympathetic** nervous system **discharge** in response to stress.

c. The results of physical assessment can be similarly revealing.

Physical sign	Possible significance
Patient seems confused.	**Inadequate cerebral perfusion,** from either a cardiac dysrhythmia or pump failure
Skin is cold and pale.	Widespread peripheral **vasoconstriction** from massive sympathetic discharge
Pulse is very irregular.	Cardiac **dysrhythmia**
Crackles/wheezes in the chest.	Probable **left heart failure**

d. Now let's have another look at the patient's ECG strip.

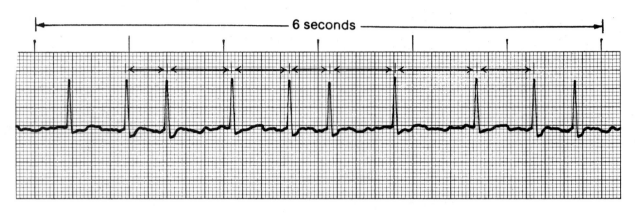

The RHYTHM is **irregularly irregular.**
The RATE is **100 per minute.**
P WAVES are **absent.**
The P–R INTERVAL is **not applicable.**
QRS complexes are **normal.**
The name of the rhythm is **atrial fibrillation.**
Treatment should be **for the underlying condition,** in this case the patient's congestive heart failure.

14. Checking out the medications on the bedside table or in the medicine cabinet is one of those opportunities for the paramedic to play Sherlock Holmes. It is also an opportunity to obtain information about the patient that might not otherwise be available to those who will take over his care in the hospital. In the case in question, even though we are dealing with an unconscious patient who can't tell us anything about his past medical history, his five medication bottles tell us a great deal:
    - He has a **history of angina,** for which he takes the nitroglycerin preparation *Isordil* and probably the calcium-channel blocker *Aldalat* (nifedipine).
    - He is under treatment for **hypertension** (*Diuril*, a thiazide diuretic, and *Aldomet*, a methyldopa preparation).
    - He is also under treatment for either **heart failure** or an **atrial dysrhythmia** or both (*Lanoxin*, a form of digoxin).

    There is one other piece of very crucial information on those medication bottles. Do you know what it is? The **name of the doctor** who prescribed the medications. By telephoning the pharmacy, the emergency room staff can probably obtain the phone number of that doctor and contact him for further information about the patient's medical history.

15. The risk factors for coronary artery disease include

   *a. **Hypertension**

   *b. **Cigarette smoking**

   c. **Diabetes**

   *d. **High serum cholesterol**

   *e. **Lack of exercise**

   f. **Obesity**

   g. **Family history** of heart disease or stroke

   h. **Male sex**

   *Denotes risk factors that can be reduced or eliminated through modifications in behavior.

16. a. Clues to the fact that this 51-year-old man has suffered a **dissecting aortic aneurysm** (answer **C**) include (1) the sudden onset of the pain, which came on with maximum intensity and stayed that way, (2) the quality of the pain ("ripping"), and (3) the discrepancy between the blood pressures measured in the two arms.

   b. The *steps of management* in dissecting aortic aneurysm are as follows:

   (1) Calm and **reassure the patient.**
   (2) Administer **oxygen.**
   (3) Start an **IV lifeline** with lactated Ringer's.
   (4) Apply **monitoring electrodes.**
   (5) If (and only if) the patient is not hypotensive, give **morphine sulfate,** 3 mg IV at a time, up to a total of 10 mg over 10 to 15 minutes.
   (6) **Transport without delay.**

   c. When the patient grows restless and begins to show signs of shock, he has probably developed **cardiac tamponade,** the most common cause of death from a dissecting aortic aneurysm. The tip-offs are the narrow pulse pressure (blood pressure = 90/80, so pulse pressure = 10 mm Hg) and distended neck veins.

   d. The action to take at that point is to **get moving without any further delay to the hospital.** If the patient is in extremis and the distance to the hospital is considerable, consult medical command regarding whether to try a pericardiocentesis in the field.

17. a. Squeezing substernal pain that comes on with exertion and goes away after a few minutes of rest is most likely to be **angina pectoris** (answer **A**).

   b. Since this apparently is the patient's first experience of angina, however, it needs to be evaluated thoroughly in the hospital. To manage this patient, all you need do is

   (1) Calm and **reassure the patient.**
   (2) Administer **oxygen** by nasal cannula.
   (3) **Monitor** cardiac rhythm.

   c. Here is the patient's rhythm strip.

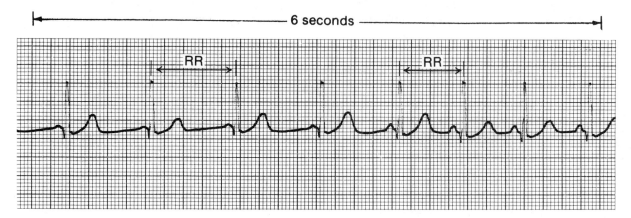

The RHYTHM is **irregular.**
The RATE is **80 per minute.**
P WAVES are **present** and precede every QRS.
The P–R INTERVAL is **0.12 second.**
QRS complexes are **normal.**

The name of the rhythm is **sinus arrhythmia.** (In fact, the changing shape of the P wave and slight variations in the P–R interval suggest there may as well be a wandering atrial pacemaker.)
No treatment is necessary.

18. a. The 35-year-old woman who had the sudden onset of pleuritic chest pain is most likely suffering from an **acute pulmonary embolism** (answer **D**). Taking oral contraceptives put her at increased risk for pulmonary embolism, and the tachypnea (respirations are 40/min) suggests some problem in oxygenation or carbon dioxide removal.

b. The *steps of management* are

   (1) Administer **oxygen.**
   (2) Start an **IV lifeline.**
   (3) **Monitor** cardiac rhythm.
   (4) **Transport** without delay.

19. a. The 48-year-old man who feels as if there's an elephant sitting on his chest has given you a classic history for an **acute myocardial infarction** (AMI) (answer **B**), and his physical findings—apprehension, sweating, elevated blood pressure—are also typical.

b. The *steps of management* in AMI are as follows:

   (1) **Put the patient at ease** physically and mentally.
   (2) Place the patient in a **semirecumbent** position.
   (3) Administer **oxygen** by nasal cannula.
   (4) **Monitor** cardiac rhythm.
   (5) Start an **IV lifeline** with D5/W to keep the vein open.
   (6) Provide **analgesia** (first a trial of nitroglycerin; if that does not relieve the patient's pain, then morphine or nitrous oxide).
   (7) Take a **12-lead ECG,** if it is local protocol to do so.
   (8) Notify medical command if the patient is a candidate for thrombolytic therapy.
   (9) Transport **without sirens** and without panic. Give aspirin (half a tablet) and a magnesium sulfate infusion en route to the hospital if they are part of your local protocol.

c. The doctor has ordered MORPHINE SULFATE. Before you carry out that order, you need to be certain it is appropriate, for even doctors can make mistakes. And if you're the person brandishing the hypodermic syringe, YOU ARE AS RESPONSIBLE AS THE DOCTOR FOR THE CONSEQUENCES OF ANY MEDICATION YOU ADMINISTER. So you need to review in your mind the pharmacology of the drug you've been asked to give.

   (1) The *contraindications* to giving morphine are
       (a) Marked **hypotension**
       (b) **Respiratory depression** (except that caused by pulmonary edema)
       (c) **Asthma** and **chronic obstructive pulmonary disease (COPD)**
       (d) Patients who have already taken **other depressant drugs**
       (e) **Head injury**
       (f) Undiagnosed **abdominal pain**
           So far, so good. The patient doesn't seem to have any contraindications.
       (g) *Inferior* wall AMI (relative contraindication).
   (2) The *dosage* of morphine is **2 to 5 mg** at a time, given **intravenously** up to a total dose of 10 mg over 15 minutes.
   (3) The potential *adverse side effects* of morphine include:
       (a) **Hypotension,** especially in volume-depleted patients
       (b) **Respiratory depression**
       (c) **Bradycardia** due to increased vagal tone

(d) **Nausea** and **vomiting**
(e) **Urinary retention,** especially if given together with a diuretic to an older man

d. Indeed, look what happened when you gave the morphine!

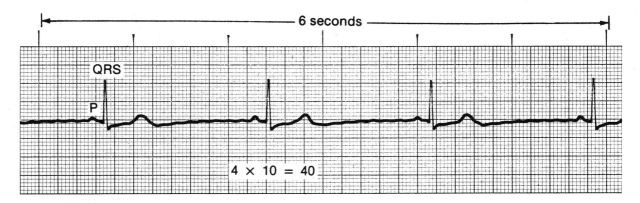

In retrospect, it is not surprising that this happened. Patients with AMI whose clinical presentation includes gastrointestinal symptoms (nausea, vomiting, belching, hiccuping) often have an infarction of the *inferior* wall of the ventricle; and patients with inferior wall AMI are apt to be more sensitive to the vagotonic effects of morphine.

The RHYTHM is **regular.**
The RATE is **40 per minute** (36/min by the box-counting method).
P WAVES are **present,** preceding every QRS.
The P–R INTERVAL is **0.16 second.**
QRS complexes are **normal.**
The name of the rhythm is **sinus bradycardia.**
Theoretically, no treatment is necessary in the field so long as the patient is hemodynamically stable.

e. Apparently the doctor at medical command is not taking any chances; he doesn't want to wait for a ventricular escape rhythm to occur. So he has instructed you to give ATROPINE, in hopes of overcoming the vagal effect of morphine and speeding up the heart rate a bit.

(1) The *contraindications* to giving atropine are
  (a) **Atrial flutter** or **atrial fibrillation** where there is a rapid ventricular response (think about why).
  (b) Patients known to have **glaucoma.**
  (c) Use with extreme caution in **acute myocardial infarction.**
    The last-mentioned caution might justify querying the physician ("Doc, the patient is well-perfused, and he's got a good story for a big-time AMI. Should we still give the atropine or just keep it handy in case he gets shocky with his bradycardia?").
(2) The *dosage* of atropine for bradycardia is **0.5 mg rapidly IV.** The dose may be repeated, if necessary, in 5 minutes and once again 5 minutes after that, to a total prehospital dosage of 1.5 mg.
(3) *Adverse side effects* of atropine include
  (a) **Blurred vision, headache,** and **pupillary dilatation**
  (b) **Dry mouth**
  (c) **Flushing**
  Explain to the patient that those are expected side effects of the drug and not a cause for concern.

20. a. The 35-year-old woman with knife-like chest pain, circumoral paresthesias, and carpopedal spasm is almost certainly suffering from **hyperventilation syndrome** (answer **E**).

    b. The treatment is simply **reassurance** and coaching her to breathe more slowly. (The old paper bag routine is too risky; if you've made a mistake in your diagnosis and the lady in fact has a pulmonary embolism, she's not going to enjoy the additional hypoxemia induced by breathing oxygen-poor exhaled air.)

    c. The patient's ECG looks like this:

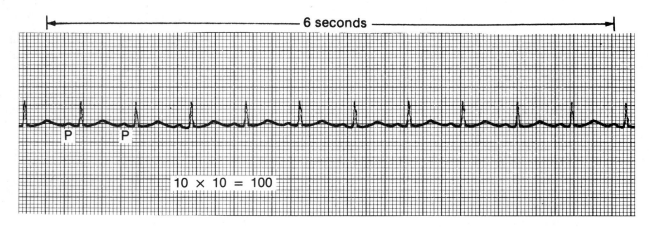

    The RHYTHM is **regular.**

    The RATE is **100 per minute** (107/min by box-counting method).

    P WAVES are **present** before every QRS.

    The P–R INTERVAL is **0.16 second.**

    QRS complexes are **normal.**

    The name of the rhythm is **sinus tachycardia.**

    The treatment is to **calm the patient down.** You can now tell her that her ECG is perfectly normal and does not show any sign of a "heart attack" (which is probably what she's worrying about).

21. a. The dyspneic man in this question has given you a fairly classic history for **left heart failure** (answer **B**)—several days of paroxysmal nocturnal dyspnea against a background of chronic hypertension. (How do we know he has chronic hypertension? Because he's taking antihypertensive medications.) The hunch is confirmed on physical examination with the finding of respiratory distress and wheezy lungs. (But for the antihypertensive medications, it would have been very difficult not to ascribe the symptoms to decompensated COPD, and that possibility still can't be ruled out altogether—the patient *is*, after all, a smoker.)

    b. The *steps of management* in left heart failure are as follows:

    (1) Administer **100% oxygen,** preferably by demand valve or with positive end-expiratory pressure (PEEP).

    (2) **Sit the patient up,** with his feet dangling.

    (3) Start an **IV lifeline** with D5/W to a keep-open rate.

    (4) **Monitor** cardiac rhythm (you'll see why in a moment!).

(5) Give **pharmacologic therapy** according to local protocol, which may include
    (a) Nitroglycerin
    (b) Morphine sulfate
    (c) Furosemide
    (d) Aminophylline
    (e) Rarely, digoxin
(6) **Transport.**

c. The physician has ordered NITROGLYCERIN.

(1) He or she did so because of nitroglycerin's effect as a **vasodilator,** in order to perform an **internal phlebotomy**—that is, to remove excess fluid from the pulmonary circulation by allowing the fluid to pool in an expanded systemic circulation.
(2) The *contraindications* to giving nitroglycerin include
    (a) **Increased intracranial pressure**
    (b) **Glaucoma**
    (c) **Hypotension**
    Caution is warranted, furthermore, in giving nitroglycerin to someone who has suffered **myocardial infarction,** especially if it involves the *inferior* wall of the heart.
(3) For acute pulmonary edema secondary to left heart failure, give up to **0.4 mg sublingually.** That dose may be repeated at 5-minute intervals, as necessary, up to a total dose of 2.4 mg.
(4) Possible *side effects* of nitroglycerin include
    (a) Throbbing **headache** (if the patient does *not* experience a transient throbbing in his head, your nitroglycerin supply may have lost its therapeutic potency)
    (b) **Hypotension**
    (c) **Dizziness**

d. The doctor has also instructed you to give FUROSEMIDE.

(1) Giving nitroglycerin was just a holding action, a way of sequestering excess fluid outside the lungs. But what the patient really needs is to get rid of that excess fluid altogether, to excrete it from the body. So furosemide is given for its **diuretic effect** in ridding the body of excess fluid. Meanwhile, however, furosemide just happens to have another effect that is very useful in congestive heart failure: It **dilates veins**—so, like nitroglycerin, it promotes the peripheral pooling of blood.
(2) The *contraindications* to giving furosemide include
    (a) **Pregnancy**
    (b) Known or suspected **hypokalemia** (Suspect hypokalemia in patients taking diuretics at home without potassium supplement.)
(3) The *dosage* of furosemide is **20 to 40 mg slowly IV.**
(4) Possible *side effects* include
    (a) **Nausea** and **vomiting**
    (b) **Hypokalemia** (with dysrhythmias as a consequence)
    (c) **Dehydration**

e. The patient's initial ECG looked like this:

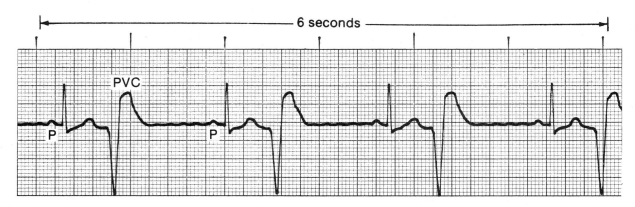

The RHYTHM is **irregular.**

The RATE is **80 per minute.**

P WAVES are **present,** but not before every QRS.

The P–R INTERVAL is **0.16 second.**

QRS complexes are both **normal** and **abnormal.**

The name of the rhythm is **normal sinus rhythm with premature ventricular contractions (PVCs)** or **normal sinus rhythm with bigeminy.**

Treatment: Chances are very good that those PVCs will diminish or disappear as soon as you improve the patient's oxygenation, so hold off any other drug therapy for a few minutes. If the PVCs continue, however, give a bolus of **lidocaine** in a dosage of **1 mg per kilogram,** and consult medical command as to whether to start a lidocaine infusion. (Lidocaine may accumulate to toxic levels in patients with heart failure, so one must be somewhat cautious about lidocaine infusions in that situation.)

22. a. The 62-year-old man with a "thousand-pound weight on his chest" and signs of inadequate perfusion (restlessness, confusion, cold and pale skin, hypotension) is most likely suffering from **cardiogenic shock** (answer **C**) secondary to a massive myocardial infarction.

   b. The *steps of management* in cardiogenic shock are as follows:

   (1) Administer 100% **oxygen.**
   (2) Place the patient **supine.**
   (3) Start an **IV lifeline** with D5/W or normal saline to a keep-open rate.
   (4) **Monitor** cardiac rhythm.
   (5) Administer **pharmacologic therapy** according to local protocol.
   (6) **Transport.**

   c. The doctor instructs you to give a DOPAMINE infusion.

   (1) The *contraindications* to giving dopamine are
   (a) Hypotension caused by **hypovolemia**
   (b) Uncorrected **tachyarrhythmias** or **ventricular fibrillation**
   (c) **Pheochromocytoma**

   (2) The correct starting *dosage* is **2 to 5 μg/kg/ min by titrated IV infusion.**
   (3) Possible *side effects* of dopamine include
   (a) **Ectopic beats, palpitations, tachycardia**
   (b) **Nausea, vomiting**
   (c) **Dyspnea**
   (d) **Angina**
   (e) **Headache**

   d. The doctor also ordered NITROUS OXIDE for analgesia.

   (1) The reason that he did *not* order morphine in this case was probably that patient's **hypotension,** which is a contraindication to morphine administration.
   (2) The *contraindications* to giving nitrous oxide are
   (a) **Head injury**
   (b) **COPD**
   (c) Acute **pulmonary edema**
   (d) **Pneumothorax** or chest injury that might involve pneumothorax
   (e) **Abdominal distention** or abdominal trauma

(f) **Facial injury**
(g) **Shock**
Since the patient under discussion is in shock, it would seem that nitrous oxide is contraindicated. Query the physician.

(3) The correct *dosage* is a **50 : 50 mixture of nitrous oxide and oxygen self-administered** by the patient. If the patient is holding the mask himself, he is unlikely to become overdosed (he'll fall asleep and the mask will drop from his face before overdose occurs).

(4) Possible *side effects* of nitrous oxide are as follows:
(a) **Drowsiness** and **light-headedness**
(b) May cause some hilarity among the ambulance crew

23. a. Here's another patient with several nights of paroxysmal nocturnal dyspnea and a story not unlike that of the patient in question 21. The tip-off in this case is the history of chronic sputum production (recently increased in volume), along with the smoking history. The patient is, therefore, most likely suffering from **acute decompensation of chronic bronchitis** (answer **D**) AND **right heart failure** (answer **A**) secondary to his long-standing lung disease (note his distended neck veins, enlarged liver, and ankle edema). Unfortunately, there is no law that says a patient may not suffer from more than one illness at the same time!

b. The *steps of management* are basically those for any other case of decompensated COPD:

(1) Keep the patient **sitting up.**
(2) Administer **oxygen** in high concentration.
(3) Encourage the patient to **cough up his secretions.**
(4) **Monitor** cardiac rhythm; if the patient is hypoxic, he is a good candidate for dysrhythmias.
(5) Start an **IV lifeline** with D5/W to a keep-open rate.

c. The doctor at medical command instructs you to administer AMINOPHYLLINE—a drug that is now considered second-line but can be given in either decompensated chronic bronchitis or acute pulmonary edema (the doctor is hedging his bets).

(1) The *contraindications* to giving aminophylline are relative, not absolute, and they include
(a) **Dysrhythmias**

(b) **Hypotension**
(c) Massive **myocardial infarction**

(2) The correct *dosage*—one that will also cover the possibility of pulmonary edema—is a **bolus of 5 mg per kilogram IV over 20 minutes** followed by an **infusion of 0.5 mg per minute.**

(3) Possible *side effects* include
(a) Myocardial irritability and **dysrhythmias**
(b) **Hypotension**
(c) **Nausea** and **vomiting**

24. a. This middle-aged black man with extremely elevated blood pressure and neurologic symptoms is most likely suffering from **hypertensive encephalopathy.**

b. Ordinarily, the *steps of management* in the prehospital phase would be as follows:

(1) Administer **oxygen** by nasal cannula. Be prepared to give definitive **airway** care (i.e., endotracheal intubation) if the patient loses consciousness.
(2) Establish an **IV lifeline** with D5/W to a keep-open rate.
(3) **Monitor** cardiac rhythm.
(4) **Transport** without delay.

c. Fate has decreed, however, that you will have to start definitive antihypertensive therapy at the scene, unless you want to carry the patient, stretcher, and all your gear down 62 flights of stairs. The doctor has therefore instructed you to administer LABETALOL.

(1) The *contraindications* to labetalol are the same as for any other beta blocker:
(a) **Bronchial asthma**
(b) **Heart failure**
(c) **Heart block**
(d) **Cardiogenic shock**
(e) **Severe bradycardia**

(2) The correct *dosage* is **2 mg per minute** by **continuous intravenous infusion** with the patient **in the supine position throughout.** The infusion is continued only **until the target blood pressure is reached.**

(3) If you've added 200 mg of labetalol (40 ml) to a 60-ml bag of D5/W, you now have 200 mg per 100 ml or **2 mg per milliliter.**

(4) If you want to deliver 2 mg per minute, you therefore have to deliver 1 ml per minute, or **60 gtt per minute.**

(5) The possible *side effects* of labetalol include
(a) **Postural hypotension** if the patient is allowed to sit up or stand up within 3 hours of the infusion

(b) **Dizziness**
(c) **Nausea**

d. In a more alert patient, the drug of choice would have been NIFEDIPINE, for it is much easier to administer in the field.

(1) The *dosage* of nifedipine for hypertensive crisis is **10 mg.**
(2) It is administered by **puncturing holes in the capsule** with a hypodermic needle and then placing the capsule under the pa-tient's tongue (**sublingual administration**).
(3) The only major *contraindication* to nifedipine is a known **allergy** to the drug.
(4) The *side effects* may include
(a) **Excessive hypotension**
(b) **Dizziness**
(c) **Flushing**
(d) **Weakness**
(e) **Nausea**

25. a. In this case of witnessed **cardiac arrest,** the initial steps of management are

(1) Open the **airway** and at the same time **check for a carotid pulse.**
(2) If the pulse is absent, quickly **move the patient to the floor** and place him supine.
(3) Bare the patient's chest.

b. At that point, your partner places the quick-look paddles from the defibrillator monitor on the patient's chest, and you see the following:

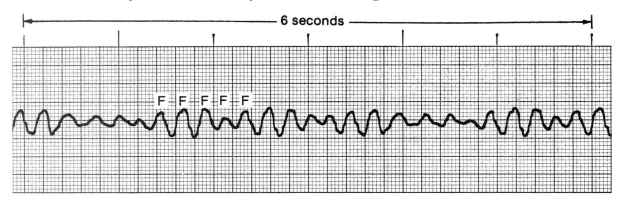

The RHYTHM is **irregular.**
The RATE is **unmeasurable.**
P WAVES are **absent.**
The P–R INTERVAL is **nonexistent.**
QRS complexes are **absent;** fibrillatory (F) waves instead.
The name of the rhythm is **ventricular fibrillation.**
Treatment consists of **immediate countershock with 200 joules.**

c. The countershock worked, restoring the patient to sinus rhythm, and medical command instructs you to give LIDOCAINE to try to stabilize that rhythm.

(1) The *contraindications* to lidocaine include
(a) **Allergy** to any drug in the lidocaine family
(b) **Second- or third-degree heart block**
(c) **Sinus bradycardia** or sinus arrest
(d) **Idioventricular rhythm**
(2) The correct *dosage* of lidocaine is **1 mg per kilogram by IV push** followed by an **intravenous infusion of 2 mg per minute.**
(3) Possible *side effects* of lidocaine include
(a) **Fall in cardiac output**
(b) **Numbness**
(c) **Drowsiness** or **confusion**
(d) **Seizures** when given in excessive doses

d. The lidocaine did not, in this case, do the trick, and the patient reverted to ventricular fibrillation. Once again, a shock brought his rhythm back to normal sinus. This time, the doctor has ordered BRETYLIUM TOSYLATE to try to stabilize the rhythm.

   (1) The *contraindications* to bretylium are
       (a) **Digitalis toxicity**
       (b) **Aortic stenosis**
   (2) The correct *dosage* for refractory ventricular fibrillation is **5 mg per kilogram by bolus IV injection.**
   (3) The possible *side effects* include
       (a) **Hypotension** (patients should be kept supine after bretylium to prevent this side effect)
       (b) **Nausea** and **vomiting**

26. Here we have an **unwitnessed cardiac arrest**—a woman who collapsed 15 minutes earlier (it is impossible to know at what point her heart stopped beating).
    a. The initial steps according to the universal algorithm are

       (1) Open the **airway.**
       (2) Check for **breathing.** If the patient is not breathing, start artificial ventilation.
       (3) Check for a **pulse.**

    b. We are told that there is no pulse, so we proceed:

       (1) Start **external chest compressions.**
       (2) Start supplemental **oxygen** as soon as possible.
       (3) Apply **monitoring electrodes** as soon as the monitor/defibrillator is available.

    c. Here is what we see on the monitor as soon as it is hooked up:

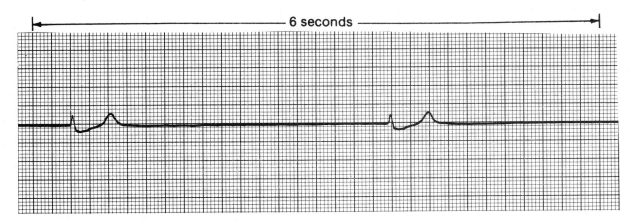

— 6 seconds —

The RHYTHM is **nonexistent.**
The RATE is **effectively zero** (those two complexes don't count for anything!).
P WAVES are **absent.**
The P–R INTERVAL is **nonexistent.**
QRS complexes are **effectively absent.**
The name of the rhythm is **asystole** or an **agonal rhythm.**
Treatment requires the whole advanced life support sequence for asystole:

   (1) **Intubate** the trachea.
   (2) Start an **IV lifeline.**
   (3) Administer pharmacologic therapy.

d. Part of the pharmacologic therapy is to give EPINEPHRINE.

    (1) The correct *dosage* is **1.0 mg** (5–10 ml of a 1 : 10,000 solution) **intravenously.**

    (2) If you haven't been able to start an IV, give the epinephrine **down the endotracheal tube.** Only as a last resort, if you also have been unable to intubate, may you use intracardiac injection (and then only if it is permitted in your EMS system).

27. a. The moral of *this* story is that it doesn't pay to stand around in an emergency room, even if there is a supply of free coffee and doughnuts. Nasty things happen in emergency rooms. That patient lying unattended in his cubicle, for instance—look what happened to him:

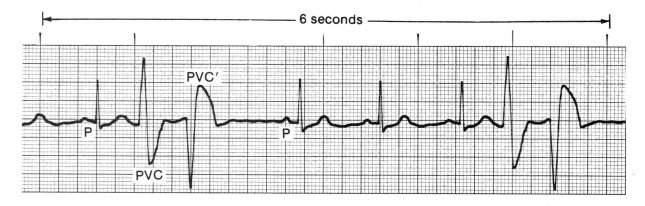

The RHYTHM is **irregular.**
The RATE is **80 per minute.**
P WAVES are **present,** but not before every QRS.
The P–R INTERVAL is **0.16 second.**
QRS complexes are both **normal** and **abnormal.**
The name of the rhythm is **normal sinus rhythm with multifocal PVCs.**
Treatment is **lidocaine,** 75 to 100 mg by IV bolus and probably followed by an infusion at a rate of 2 mg per minute.

b. Unfortunately, before you can even reach for the lidocaine, the patient's rhythm changes to this:

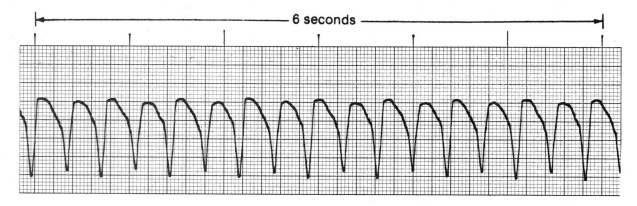

The RHYTHM is **very slightly irregular.**
The RATE is **160 per minute.**
P WAVES are **absent.**
The P–R INTERVAL is **nonexistent.**
QRS complexes are **abnormal.**
The name of the rhythm is **ventricular tachycardia.**
Treatment under the circumstances described—where all the resuscitation equipment is tied up in another room—is to give an immediate **chest thump** in an attempt to convert the rhythm back to sinus.

c. Had you had the equipment you needed, the treatment of choice *would* have been to **cardiovert** starting at an energy level of about **25 to 50 joules.**

28. a. Small wonder this lady is dizzy: There's not much time for her ventricles to fill between beats, so her cardiac output is probably quite reduced:

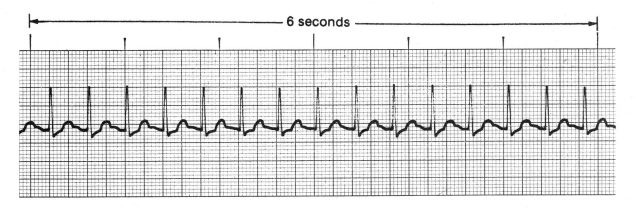

The RHYTHM is **regular.**
The RATE is **150 per minute.**
P WAVES **may be present;** it's hard to tell. If they *are* present, they are buried in the downstroke of the preceding T wave.
The P–R INTERVAL is probably 0.16 second; again, it's hard to tell.
QRS complexes are **normal.**
The name of the rhythm is **supraventricular tachycardia.**
Treatment, for a young woman like this, can safely start with a **vagal maneuver,** such as asking her to exhale against a closed glottis (Valsalva maneuver) or massaging the carotid sinus. Plunging the patient's face into a bucket of ice water is also often effective, but not always appreciated.

b. The doctor, in any case, opts for pharmacologic treatment with PROPRANOLOL.

(1) The *contraindications* to giving propranolol include
   (a) **Asthma** or **COPD**
   (b) **Hay fever** (in pollen season)
   (c) **Second- or third-degree heart block**
   (d) Congestive **heart failure**
   (e) Any state of **depressed myocardial function**
(2) The correct *dosage* of propranolol is **1 mg injected intravenously over 1 minute.**

    (3) Possible *side effects* include
        (a) **Hypotension**
        (b) **Heart failure**
        (c) **Bronchospasm**
        (d) **Nausea** and **vomiting**

c. Today, most experts favor giving ADENOSINE as a first-line drug for paroxysmal supraventricular tachycardia because of its very short half-life and low complication rate.

    (1) Adenosine is *contraindicated* in patients with **second- or third-degree heart block, sick sinus syndrome,** or known hypersensitivity to the drug.

    (2) The correct *dosage* of adenosine is **6 mg given as as rapid IV bolus over 1 to 3 seconds.** The dose should be followed by a 20-ml saline flush, to make sure the drug is circulated. If the first dose does not produce a response within 1 to 2 minutes, one may give a *second dose* of 12 mg in the same fashion.

    (3) *Side effects* are frequent with adenosine, but fortunately most of them last only 1 or 2 minutes. They include
        (a) **Flushing**
        (b) **Dyspnea**
        (c) **Chest pain**
        (d) **Headache**
        (e) **Dizziness**
        (f) **Nausea**
    Before you administer adenosine, it's a good idea to warn the patient about the side effects that may be anticipated, so that he or she will not become alarmed if those side effects occur.

d. Some doctors prefer to use VERAPAMIL to convert rapid supraventricular rhythms.

    (1) The *contraindications* to giving verapamil are
        (a) **Heart failure** or **cardiogenic shock**
        (b) **Atrioventricular (AV) blocks**
        (c) **Hypotension**
        (d) Patient already taking **beta-blocking drugs**

    (2) The correct *dosage* of verapamil is **0.1 mg per kilogram given intravenously over 1 to 2 minutes.**

    (3) Possible *side effects* of verapamil include
        (a) **Hypotension**
        (b) **Bradycardia** or **AV block**
        (c) Rarely, **cardiac arrest**

29. a. This 46-year-old man would have earned admission to the coronary care unit on the basis of his story alone—4 hours of viselike chest pain. But even if someone failed to be appropriately impressed with the patient's story, they could not fail to be impressed by his ECG:

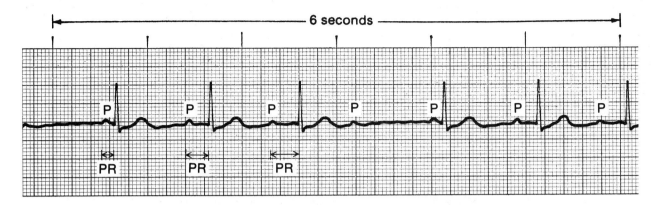

The RHYTHM is **irregular.**
The RATE is **60 per minute.**
P WAVES are **present.**
The P–R INTERVAL is **variable; it gets longer and longer.**
QRS complexes are **normal.**
The name of the rhythm is **type I (Wenckebach) second-degree AV block.**
Treatment: **None** needed at the moment, for the patient is hemodynamically stable, but the receiving hospital should be notified to have a pacemaker standing by.

   b. The patient is **not a good candidate for thrombolytic therapy** for two reasons: He is an insulin-dependent diabetic, and his blood pressure is over 180 systolic—both of which are exclusion criteria for thrombolytic treatment.

30. And well might this poor gentleman be dizzy:

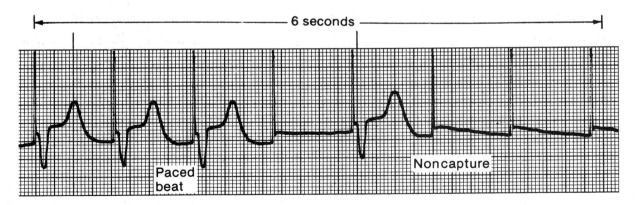

The RHYTHM is **irregular.**
The RATE is **40 per minute and declining!**
P WAVES are **absent;** there are pacemaker spikes instead.
The P–R INTERVAL is **nonexistent.**
QRS complexes are **abnormal where present at all.**
The name of the rhythm is **pacemaker rhythm with loss of capture.** At the end of the strip, we see at least 2 seconds without a single QRS complex (hence without a heart beat). That is not a healthy situation!

Treatment is to **get the patient to the hospital as quickly as possible** for an emergency transvenous pacemaker. If his own artificial pacemaker doesn't kick in to furnish him with a pulse of at least 40 to 50 per minute, you're going to have to give **external chest compressions** en route to the hospital or to try **transcutaneous cardiac pacing,** if you have the equipment and authorization to do so.

31. The 42-year-old woman with chest pain may well have long-standing rheumatic disease. Recall her ECG:

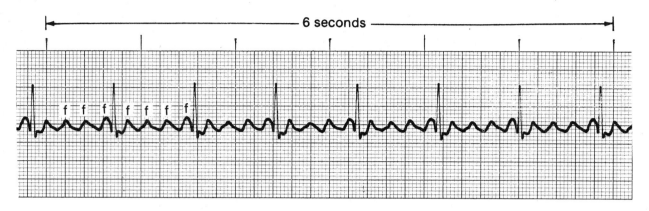

The RHYTHM is **regular.**
The RATE is **70 per minute.**
P WAVES are **absent;** there are flutter (f) waves instead.
The P–R INTERVAL is **nonexistent.**
QRS complexes are **normal.**
The name of the rhythm is **atrial flutter.**
No treatment is necessary in the field since the patient is hemodynamically stable.

32. The drug quinidine acts by slowing down conduction through the AV junction, so it's not surprising to see an ECG like this:

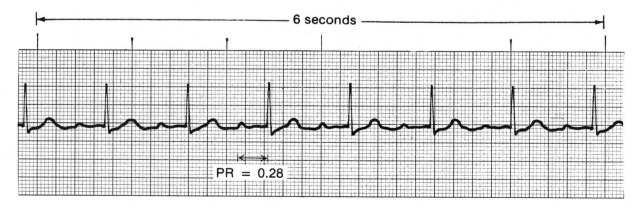

The RHYTHM is **regular.**
The RATE is **70 per minute.**
P WAVES are **present** and precede every QRS.
The P–R INTERVAL is **0.28 second.**
QRS complexes are **normal.**
The name of the rhythm is **first-degree AV block.**
No treatment is needed.

33. a. The motorcyclist is in neurogenic shock from an injury to his thoracolumbar spine. Unlike other forms of shock, neurogenic shock can produce an ECG picture such as the following:

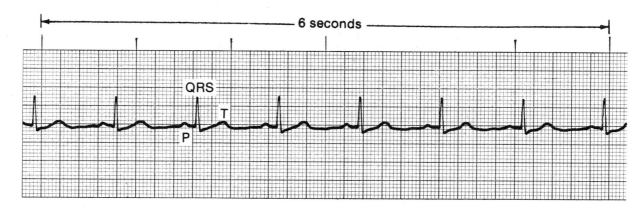

The RHYTHM is **regular.**
The RATE is **70 per minute.**
P WAVES are **present** and precede every QRS.
The P–R INTERVAL is **0.16 second.**
QRS complexes are **normal.**
The name of the rhythm is **normal sinus rhythm.**
No treatment is required for the cardiac rhythm. Treat the patient's injuries (e.g., spinal immobilization, IV fluids).

   b. The doctor decides to try to raise the patient's blood pressure with vasopressor therapy—a NOREPINEPHRINE INFUSION.

   (1) The *contraindications* to giving norepinephrine include
      (a) Patients with **hypoxia** or severe **hypercarbia**
      (b) Patients with **hypovolemia** prior to fluid therapy
      (c) Extreme caution in patients with **myocardial infarction**
   (2) The correct *dosage* of norepinephrine is **4 μg per minute by titrated intravenous infusion.**
   (3) The possible *side effects* include
      (a) Local **tissue necrosis** if the norepinephrine leaks out of the IV into the surrounding tissue.
      (b) In the case of a "runaway infusion," **headache, sweating, nausea, vomiting, hypertension,** and **ventricular dysrhythmias** may occur.

34. Here's another patient with a probable AMI and a worrisome ECG:

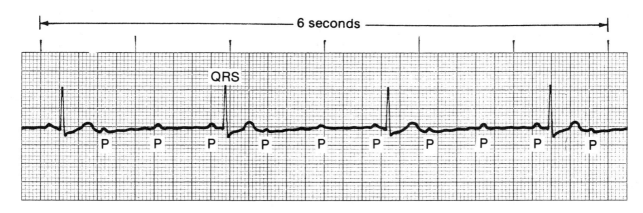

The RHYTHM is **regular.**
The RATE is **40 per minute.**
P WAVES are **present,** but **not every P wave is followed by a QRS.**
The P–R INTERVAL is **0.14 second.**
QRS complexes are **normal.**
The name of the rhythm is **type II second-degree AV block** (3 : 1 block).
Treatment: **None needed** in the field so long as the patient is hemodynamically
    stable, but the receiving hospital should be notified to have a pacemaker in
    readiness.

35. "Indigestion" and other gastrointestinal symptoms, along with the hiccups, in
    a patient who looks that sick is very likely to be an inferior wall AMI. The ECG
    strip recorded in lead II looks like this:

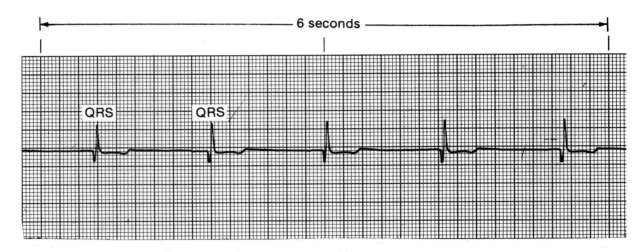

The RHYTHM is **regular.**
The RATE is **50 per minute.**
P WAVES are **absent.**
The P–R INTERVAL is **nonexistent.**
QRS complexes are **normal.**
The name of the rhythm is **junctional.**
Treatment: If the patient is hemodynamically stable, no treatment is required in
    the prehospital phase, but have **0.5 mg of atropine** drawn up and ready to
    administer should the heart rate get any slower.

36. A very slow heart rate is enough to make anyone faint, let alone an elderly
    woman. Here is her ECG:

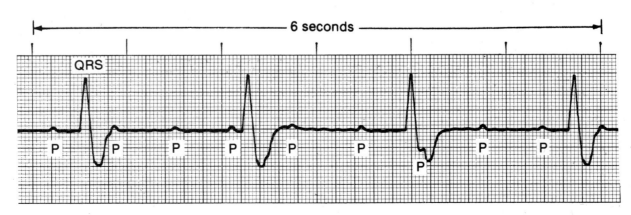

The RHYTHM is **regular.**

The RATE is **40 per minute** (36/min by box-counting method).

P WAVES are **present** but unrelated to the QRS complexes.

The P–R INTERVAL is **completely variable.**

QRS complexes are **abnormal.**

The name of the rhythm is **third-degree (complete) heart block.** Notice how the atria and ventricles are each "marching to the beat of a different drummer." The atria are being depolarized 90 times a minute, but none of the impulses are getting through, so the ventricles are plodding along at their own intrinsic rate.

Treatment: This woman's compromised mental status means inadequate cerebral perfusion, so treatment is urgent. What she needs most urgently is a **pacemaker,** and the receiving hospital must be notified to have one on standby. Meanwhile, the physician may order a **dopamine infusion** (at 5–20 μg/kg/min). Administer oxygen, and move without delay to the hospital.

37. For reasons that are not entirely clear, a lot of **myocardial infarctions** happen in the morning hours, particularly *Monday* mornings.

    a. Both analyzing a rhythm strip and looking at a 12-lead ECG require a *systematic* approach. You will find that if you simply plod through the ECG, step-by-step as outlined here, even the most complicated appearing ECG will turn out to be relatively easy to interpret.

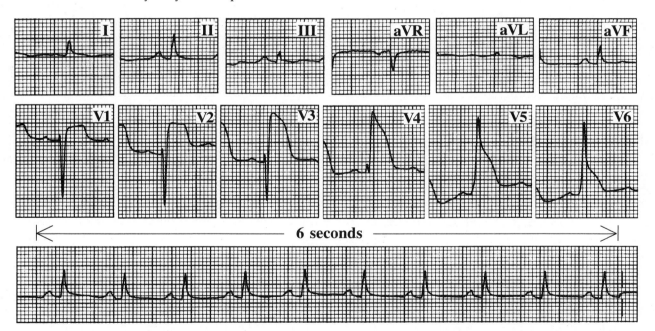

The RHYTHM is **regular.**

The RATE is **100 per minute.**

P WAVES are **present** and appear before every QRS complex except one (the fourth one in the rhythm strip).

The P–R INTERVAL is **0.16 second.**

The QRS complexes are on the borderline of **normal,** except for one grossly abnormal QRS complex (the fourth one in the rhythm strip).

The name of the rhythm is **normal sinus rhythm with a PVC.**

Q WAVES deeper than 2 mm appear only in lead aVR, where they are not considered abnormal.

S–T segments are **markedly elevated in leads V_2 through V_6.**

T WAVES are INVERTED only in lead aVL, where they are of questionable
significance.

The portions of the heart affected are the **anterior and lateral walls**.

The pathophysiologic process is acute **injury**.

b. This patient needs to be treated for an evolving ACUTE MYOCARDIAL IN-
FARCTION:

(1) Put the patient mentally and physically **at ease** (calm handling; semirecumbent position).

(2) Administer **oxygen** right away.

(3) Start an **IV lifeline** with a microdrip infusion set.

(4) Record the first set of **vital signs**.

(5) Provide **pain relief**.

(6) Once you have the results of the **12-lead ECG, notify the receiving hospital** of the patient's story, vital signs, ECG findings, and your estimated
time of arrival.

(7) **Transport expeditiously,** without sirens if possible. Administer half an
aspirin tablet and start a magnesium sulfate infusion en route to the hospital if those interventions are part of your local protocol.

c. You can pat yourself on the back looking at the patient's ECG the next morning, for your early notification of the hospital and prompt transport may
have saved a large piece of the patient's myocardium.

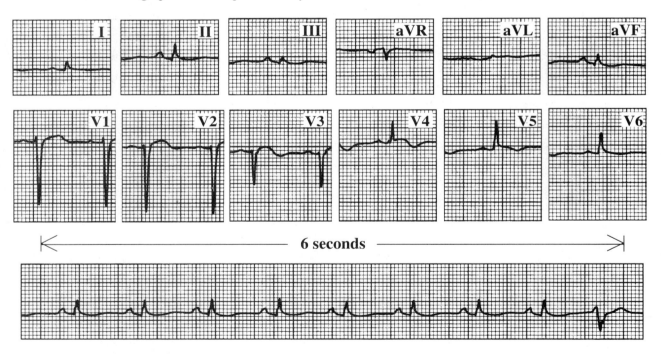

The patient's **S–T segments have returned to normal,** indicating that the
acute injury has subsided. That by itself is no reason to pop open the cham-
pagne bottles, since the ECG changes of injury will, in any case, disappear
as a myocardial infarction evolves. But what will usually take the place of
S–T elevation, if the patient goes on to suffer a full-blown AMI, are deep *Q
waves* in the same leads in which the S–T segments had been elevated. This
patient did *not* develop Q waves, so his injury did not progress to full-blown
AMI. He did, however, suffer some myocardial damage: The newly **inverted
T waves** in leads V_3 through V_6 indicate damage—but probably not nearly as
much damage as would have occurred had the patient not received early
thrombolytic therapy. When T wave inversion occurs without Q waves, it

generally indicates that only the inner half of the myocardial wall has suffered damage; we call that a **subendocardial infarction.** When the damage affects the entire myocardial wall, on the other hand, the term **transmural myocardial infarction** is used (*trans* = across; *mural* = wall), and Q waves are almost invariably present.

38. As we shall learn in more detail in Chapter 29, **AMI in the elderly** is apt to present without the typical story of chest pain. An elderly patient is just as likely to complain of weakness, as did this 74-year-old man. But his ECG tells another story:

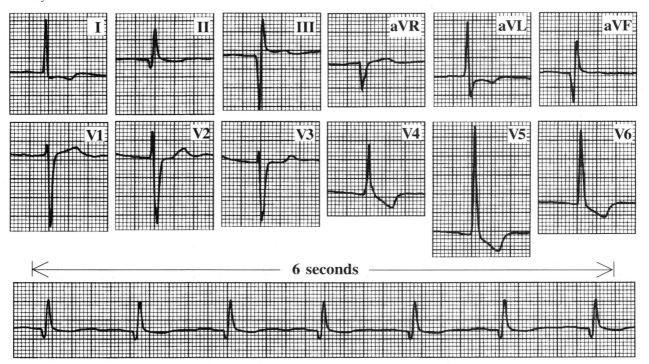

a. Once again, let's examine the rhythm strip and the ECG *systematically:*

The RHYTHM is **regular.**

The RATE is **64 per minute.**

P WAVES are **probably absent.** (There's a hint of something that *might* be a P wave in lead I, but you've got to have an eagle eye and a very good imagination to see it!)

The P–R INTERVAL is **nonexistent** if you accept the observation that P waves are absent.

QRS complexes are **normal.**

The name of the rhythm is probably **junctional rhythm.** (If you think you see a P wave, you may call it normal sinus rhythm!)

Q WAVES deeper than 2 mm are **present in leads II, III, and aVF.**

The S–T SEGMENTS are **depressed in leads I, aVL, and V$_4$ to V$_6$.** In fact, when S–T depression looks like it does here, with the end of the S–T segment pulled downward as if there is a string with a weight tied to the S–T segment, we call that a **strain pattern;** it is *not* usually associated with ischemia or injury.

The T WAVES are partially INVERTED in those leads that show a strain pattern.

The portion of the heart affected by the *acute* process (as opposed to the chronic strain) is the **inferior wall,** for that's where we see the Q waves.

The pathophysiologic process is an **infarction.** When all we can see on the ECG are Q waves, we cannot, in fact, be certain how old the infarction is.

It may have happened a few days ago, or it may have happened 10 years ago. The only way to know for sure is to compare this ECG with the patient's previous ECGs, if there are any.

b. For purposes of field management, we need to assume, however, that this is a fresh myocardial infarction. Therefore, we shall treat this patient just as we treated the previous patient, who was having severe chest pain and changes of acute injury on *his* ECG:

(1) Put the patient mentally and physically **at ease** (calm handling; semirecumbent position)
(2) Administer **oxygen** right away.
(3) Start an **IV lifeline** with a microdrip infusion set.
(4) Record the first set of **vital signs.**
(5) Provide **pain relief.**
(6) Once you have the results of the **12-lead ECG, notify the receiving hospital** of the patient's story, vital signs, ECG findings, and your estimated time of arrival.
(7) **Transport expeditiously,** without sirens if possible. Administer half an aspirin tablet and start a magnesium sulfate infusion en route to the hospital if those interventions are part of your local protocol.

39. This 64-year-old man has a good story for an **AMI**, so we would have to treat him for AMI no matter what his ECG showed. In this instance, though, the ECG gives us further support for that treatment:

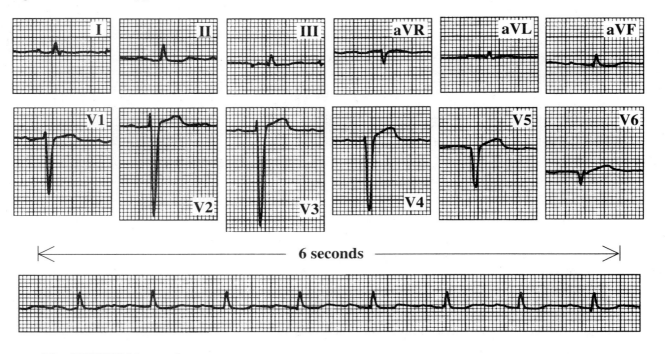

The RHYTHM is **regular.**
The RATE is **80 per minute.**
P WAVES are **present** and appear before every QRS complex.
The P–R INTERVAL is **0.21 second.**
The QRS complexes are **borderline** (they appear to be a hair wider than 0.1 second, i.e., more than 2.5 little boxes).
The name of the rhythm is **normal sinus rhythm** with **borderline first-degree AV block.**
Q WAVES deeper than 2 mm are **present in leads V₅ and V₆.**

S–T SEGMENTS are **slightly elevated in leads V₃ to V₅.** There is also some S–T depression in the inferior leads (which are the inferior leads?), which probably represents a strain pattern.

T WAVES are INVERTED only in lead aVR, where T wave inversion is not considered abnormal.

The portion of the heart affected is the **lateral wall.**

The pathophysiologic process is a transmural **infarction.**

40. There has been a lot of material to absorb in this chapter, but perhaps the most important message of all is the one you had to decode.

    a. **aneurysm**

    b. **afterload**

    c. **Wolff**

    d. **off**

    e. **on**

    f. **diaphoresis**

    g. **ischemia**

    h. **NTG**

    i. **nicotine**

    j. **attic**

    k. **td**

    Secret Message: PATIENTS WHO DIE OF ACUTE MYOCARDIAL INFARCTION OFTEN DIE OF FRIGHT.

24
Unconscious States

1. Like the words in the grid, the clues to the causes of coma or other altered states of consciousness may not be immediately obvious.

a. When a person appears to be asleep but can be roused by speaking to him, he is said to be **drowsy.** When he cannot be roused by vocal stimuli but can still be wakened by a painful stimulus, his condition is then called **stupor.** But when neither speaking nor applying painful stimuli will waken the person, then he is in **coma.**

b. Possible causes of an unconscious state include

(1) **Meningitis**	(5) **Head injury**	(9) **Heat stroke**
(2) **Hypothermia**	(6) **Overdose**	(10) **Alcohol**
(3) **Uremia**	(7) **Hypoglycemia**	(11) **Psychogenic**
(4) **Stroke**	(8) **Epilepsy**	

c. Many, if not most, of the things listed in "b" that can cause an unconscious state can also cause seizures. Another cause of seizures that occurs only during pregnancy is a condition called **eclampsia.**

d. One thing that needs to be differentiated from a seizure is a simple faint, or **syncope.**

e. A seizure may be preceded by warning sensations, called an **aura.** In a generalized motor seizure, also called a **grand mal** seizure, the patient then falls to the ground rigid and shortly thereafter begins convulsive movements. After the seizure, when the patient wakes up, he will often complain of **headache.** If the patient does *not* wake up but goes on to have another one or more seizures, the condition is called **status epilepticus.**

f. Symptoms of a stroke may include **aphasia, dysarthria,** and (rarely) **amnesia.** Stroke may be the result of thrombosis, embolism, or hemorrhage. A subarachnoid hemorrhage is one that occurs beneath the arachnoid membrane covering the brain. Recall that the other two protective layers surrounding the brain are the pia mater and the **dura** mater.

g. If the patient with a stroke (or any other patient, for that matter) does not have an intact **gag** reflex, the patient's airway is in immediate jeopardy.

h. Diabetic ketoacidosis occurs when a diabetic has taken relatively too little **insulin** for his or her needs. The symptoms of diabetic ketoacidosis include **polydipsia, polyphagia,** and **polyuria.** A patient in ketoacidosis will also often show a characteristic respiratory pattern called **Kussmaul** breathing.

2. We are faced with a 30-year-old man in coma.

   a. The dangers that threaten *any* comatose patient include

      (1) Jeopardy to the **airway,** from the tongue or secretions
      (2) Jeopardy to the **eyes** if they remain open
      (3) Jeopardy to the **limbs,** which may suffer ischemia from being kept in awkward positions

   b. Questions to ask the patient's neighbors include

      (1) When was the patient **last seen?**
      (2) Do you have **any idea of what happened** to him?
      (3) Is he **known to suffer any chronic illnesses** (e.g., diabetes, epilepsy)?
      (4) Has he been **injured recently?**
      (5) Did he **complain of any symptoms** when last seen?
      (6) Is he a known **abuser of drugs or alcohol?**

   c. Besides the neighbors, the **scene itself** may provide valuable information about what may have caused the patient's coma. Check out

      (1) The **bathroom** and **bedroom** for medicine bottles or drug paraphernalia
      (2) The **kitchen** for **insulin** in the refrigerator or other medications on the counter
      (3) The **living room** and the **kitchen trash** for empty liquor bottles.

d. The patient's physical findings can also help narrow down the possible causes of his coma:

Finding	Possible Diagnostic Significance
Cold, dry skin	**Overdose of alcohol or sedative drugs**
Pulse = 110, thready BP = 90/60	**Hypovolemia** **Hypoglycemia** **Overdose of barbiturates**
Respirations = 12 and shallow	**Overdose with sedative drugs**
Pupils dilated and do not react to light	**Cerebral anoxia** **Barbiturate overdose** **Certain eye drops**
Breath smells of alcohol	**Patient ingested alcohol**
Left arm is cold and blue	**Patient has been lying for a long time on his left arm**

e. (1) The patient is best described as **comatose.**
   (2) His Glasgow coma score is computed as follows:

   - He does not open his eyes   **1 point**
   - Arm flexion in response to pain   **3 points**
   - No verbal response   **1 point**

   TOTAL GLASGOW COMA SCORE   **5 points**

f. The steps in managing this patient are as follows:

   (1) Open the **airway** by manual methods, and insert an **oropharyngeal airway** for the time being. (If your other interventions do not succeed in rousing the patient, you will have to intubate him.)
   (2) Administer **oxygen** by **bag-valve-mask;** ventilate about 20 to 24 breaths per minute.
   (3) Establish an **IV lifeline.**
   (4) Administer **thiamine, 100 mg IV.**
   (5) Administer **50% dextrose, 50 ml slowly IV.** If no response:
   (6) Administer **naloxone, 0.8 mg slowly IV.**
   (7) If the patient is *still* comatose, **intubate** the trachea.
   (8) **Monitor** cardiac rhythm.
   (9) Keep a **flow sheet of neurologic and vital signs.**
   (10) **Splint** the patient's left arm in a position of function.
   (11) **Tape his eyes shut.**
   (12) **Transport.**

g. Dextrose 50% (D50) is often given to patients in coma of unknown cause, since it may save the life of a patient who is hypoglycemic and it will do no harm to someone who is not.

   (1) The *contraindications* to giving D50 are **intracranial hemorrhage** or any other kind of **stroke.**
   (2) The usual *dosage* of D50 is **25 gm** (50 ml of 50% dextrose) given **slowly through a free-flowing large-bore IV line.**
   (3) The potential adverse *side effects* are

(a) D50 may **precipitate Wernicke's encephalopathy** in some alcoholics if given without first administering thiamine.

(b) It may cause **local tissue necrosis** if it infiltrates out of the vein into surrounding tissues.

(4) For the reasons mentioned above, when D50 is given to a patient in coma, **thiamine** is usually given first.

(a) It is given to **prevent possible neurologic complications** (e.g., Wernicke's encephalopathy).

(b) The *dosage* is **100 mg slowly IV** (or 50 mg IV plus 50 mg IM).

3. The medications found on the unconscious patient's person or at the scene may provide valuable clues to his underlying illness(es).

 a. Luminol and Dilantin are prescribed for **seizure disorders.**

 b. Diuril is a diuretic drug, Aldomet is an antihypertensive, and Inderal is a beta blocker. If the patient has all three in his medicine cabinet, he is most probably being treated for **hypertension.**

 c. Micronase is prescribed to patients with relatively stable, adult-onset **diabetes mellitus.**

 d. Cordarone in the pocket of an unconscious patient should tell you to hook up the cardiac monitor *fast*, for it is prescribed to treat life-threatening **ventricular dysrhythmias,** such as recurrent ventricular tachycardia.

 e. Iletin is a form of insulin, prescribed to patients with juvenile-onset **diabetes mellitus** or diabetes that cannot be controlled by diet and oral hypoglycemic agents alone.

4. The patient is showing characteristic signs of **diabetic ketoacidosis.** The steps of prehospital management are aimed primarily at stabilizing vital functions and restoring fluid.

 a. Open the **airway.**

 b. Administer **oxygen** by nasal cannula.

 c. Establish an **IV** with **normal saline,** and run it wide open.

 d. **Monitor** cardiac rhythm. Be particularly alert for peaked T waves, signalling hyperkalemia.

 e. Keep a flow sheet of **neurologic and vital signs.**

 f. **Transport** in the stable side position.

5. A man in his sixties has fainted.

 a. Basically, there are only two ways that the blood supply to the brain can be diminished:

 (1) If the **heart isn't pumping enough blood out** (i.e., inadequate cardiac output)

 (2) If the **peripheral blood vessels are sequestering blood,** through vasodilatation

 b. Causes of syncope include

 (1) Severe **pain** (vasovagal)

 (2) **Fright** or seeing something shocking (vasovagal)

 (3) **Drugs** that prevent reflex vasoconstriction with postural change (e.g., antihypertensives, nitroglycerin, phenothiazines)

 (4) Severe **bradycardia** (rates less than 40/min)

 (5) Severe **tachycardia** (rates greater than 150/min)

 (6) **Vagal stimulation** (micturition syncope, cough syncope, hypersensitive carotid sinus)

 c. Questions to ask the patient and those who saw him faint include

 (1) What **position** was he in just before he fainted?

 (2) Did he have any **warning symptoms?**

 (3) Did he show any **convulsive movements** during the faint?

 (4) **How long** was he unconscious?

 (5) Does he have any **underlying illnesses?**

 (6) Does he take any **medications** regularly?

 d. The steps of treatment of a patient who has fainted are as follows:

 (1) Keep the patient **recumbent;** don't let him sit up or stand up.

(2) Ensure an open **airway,** and administer **oxygen.**
(3) **Loosen** any **tight clothing** on the patient.
(4) **Elevate** the patient's **lower extremities** for a few moments.
(5) **Monitor** cardiac rhythm.
(6) Start an **IV lifeline** with D5/W to a keep-open rate.
(7) **Treat any injuries** found during the secondary survey.

6. A young salesman has had a grand mal seizure while waiting for an appointment with his boss.

   a. The causes of seizures include

   (1) **Stroke**
   (2) **Head trauma**
   (3) **Brain tumor**
   (4) **Hypoxemia**
   (5) **Hypoglycemia**
   (6) **Toxins, drugs, or withdrawal** from drugs or alcohol
   (7) **Meningitis**
   (8) **Idiopathic** epilepsy
   (9) In a pregnant woman, **eclampsia**

   Note that this list is very nearly identical to the list of causes of coma. So if you can't remember the causes of seizures, just go through the AEIOU-TIPS roster.

   b. The steps in treating this patient are

   (1) Maintain his **airway;** suction as needed. Hold off intubating, though, until you see what D50 does for him.
   (2) Administer **oxygen.**
   (3) Start an **IV** with a **large-bore cannula in a big vein.**
   (4) Give **thiamine, 100 mg IV.**
   (5) Give **50% dextrose, 50 ml slowly IV.**

   c. Almost magically, just moments after you've given the glucose, the patient becomes fully alert and also apparently restored to his "sweet" disposition—prima facie evidence that the source of his problem was undoubtedly **hypoglycemia.** (The patient's remark about how he shouldn't have skipped breakfast suggests that he had come to the same conclusion.)

   d. The *advice* to give this patient is

   (1) Get yourself a **medical identification tag** that states you are a diabetic and wear it at all times.

   (2) Pay attention to **early warning signs of hypoglycemia,** and do something about them before the attack progresses.
   (3) Always **carry a candy bar** or other source of sugar with you, to take when you feel hypoglycemic symptoms.

7. The next seizure case you have to deal with is a lot more serious; it is a case of *status epilepticus.*

   a. When you get around to doing a secondary survey, you will want to be particularly alert for

   (1) Irregularities in the **pulse**
   (2) The combination of **bradycardia and hypotension,** which would suggest increasing intracranial pressure as a cause of the seizures
   (3) Evidence of **head trauma** as either cause or result of the seizures
   (4) **Inequality of the pupils,** again suggesting rising intracranial pressure
   (5) **Breath odors** (alcohol, ketones, poisons)
   (6) **Gingival hypertrophy,** suggesting long-term phenytoin use
   (7) **Stiff neck,** suggesting the patient has bled into the cerebrospinal fluid
   (8) Injuries, especially **posterior dislocation of the shoulder**
   (9) **Medical identification tag**
   (10) **Medication bottles** in pockets

   b. The steps in *treating* a patient in status epilepticus are

   (1) **Protect the patient from injury.**
   (2) Ensure an open **airway,** which will mean whipping in an **endotracheal tube** the first chance you get. Once the tube is in, insert an oropharyngeal airway as well, to prevent the patient from biting down on the endotracheal tube, and secure them both in place. (Patients having seizures have been known to bite an endotracheal tube in half!)
   (3) Administer **oxygen.** Remember: Deaths from seizures are hypoxic deaths.
   (4) Start an **IV** with a large-bore catheter and secure it *very* well.
   (5) Give **thiamine, 50 mg IV plus 50 mg IM** (the way this patient is moving around, there won't be any problem with his absorbing medication from an intramuscular site).
   (6) Give **50 ml of 50% dextrose slowly IV.**

c. The medication most commonly used in the field for status epilepticus is **diazepam** (Valium).

   (1) The *contraindications* to giving diazepam are in patients who are **pregnant** and those who have already taken other **sedative drugs or alcohol.**

   (2) The correct *dosage* is **2.5 mg slowly IV** given *after* you have measured a baseline blood pressure. Then wait a few minutes, recheck the blood pressure, and—if it has not fallen—give **another 2.5 mg,** and so on until the seizures stop, the blood pressure starts to fall, or a total dosage of 10 mg is reached—whichever comes first.

   (3) The possible *side effects* of intravenous diazepam include **hypotension** and even **respiratory or cardiac arrest** (those more serious complications are more likely in elderly patients).

8. The background, onset, and clinical picture of a stroke will vary depending on the underlying mechanism of the stroke:

   B Atrial fibrillation
   Clots are particularly likely to form in a fibrillating atrium, and clots that break free from the left atrium become systemic **emboli** that have a straight shot up the carotids into the brain.

   A Atherosclerosis
   Thrombus formation, on the other hand, usually occurs against a background of chronic atheromatous damage within the artery.

   C Excruciating headache
   A patient with *any* kind of stroke may have a headache, but patients who have suffered **subarachnoid hemorrhage** will report (if still conscious) that it is the worst, most excruciating headache they have ever experienced.

   B Birth control pills
   Just as oral contraceptives make a woman more vulnerable to *pulmonary* embolism, they also increase the risk of cerebral **embolism.**

   B Often presents with a seizure

   A Usually preceded by TIAs

   C Patient was on the toilet when it happened

   A Usually occurs during the night or early morning hours

   C One pupil fixed and dilated
   Intracranial pressure starts to rise within minutes of an intracerebral or subarachnoid **hemorrhage.**

   B Sickle cell disease

   A,C Patient is often a hypertensive

   C Stiff neck
   A sign that blood has entered the cerebrospinal fluid from a subarachnoid **hemorrhage** and is irritating the meninges.

   A Neurologic deficit evolves gradually over hours to days

   C Typical findings: blood pressure = 230/130; pulse = 48; respirations = 30 and deep
   These vital signs are typical of increased intracranial pressure, which is most likely to occur after intracerebral or subarachnoid **hemorrhage.**

9. For once the person calling 911 got it right: The lady with a "possible stroke" has almost certainly had a stroke.

   a. She is most likely **right-handed.** We know that the stroke involves the **left side of her brain,** since it is the right side of the body that is paralyzed. We suspect that the left side of her brain is the dominant side because the stroke has robbed her of **speech.** Most right-handed people are "left-dominant," that is, the left side of the brain is the dominant side in terms of speech and several other functions.

   b. The steps in *treating* this woman are as follows:

      (1) Protect her **airway** because she cannot (she has no gag reflex). **Suction** secretions as needed, and keep her in the **stable side position.**

      (2) Administer **oxygen** by nasal cannula.

      (3) **Monitor** cardiac rhythm, and be prepared to deal with dysrhythmias.

      (4) Start an **IV lifeline** with a microdrip infusion set and hang normal saline at a keep-open rate.

      (5) **Protect the paralyzed extremities.** The patient should be lying on her *non*paralyzed (left) side, so that she can feel if she is putting too much pressure on an arm or leg.

      (6) Maintain a running **conversation** with the patient, and provide **honest reassurance.**

10. If you assume that *every* patient in coma is either overdosed or drunk, you will be right about 70 percent of the time. That means that 30 percent of the time you will be wrong—dead wrong.

   a. **postictal**

   b. **ischemic**

   c. **thrombus**

   d. **embolus**

   e. **atherosclerosis**

   f. **atropine**

   g. **banana**

   h. **jaundice**

   i. **honest**

   j. **name**

   k. **fee**

   l. **toe**

   m. **loaf**

   n. **an**

   Secret Message: JUST BECAUSE A PATIENT'S BREATH SMELLS OF ALCOHOL DOES NOT MEAN HE CANNOT BE IN COMA FROM ANOTHER CAUSE.

25
Acute Abdomen

1. To appreciate what can go wrong inside the abdomen, one has to have some idea what is contained there.

GASTROINTESTINAL SYSTEM

bile duct
colon
duodenum
gallbladder
ileum
jejunum
liver
pancreas
rectum
stomach

URINARY SYSTEM

kidney
bladder
ureter

VASCULAR SYSTEM

mesentery
aorta
vena cava

REPRODUCTIVE SYSTEM

ovary
uterus

OTHER

spleen
peritoneum

2. The first patient with abdominal pain we had to deal with is a 42-year-old man.

   a. Poorly localized, crampy pain associated with other autonomic symptoms like nausea is called **visceral pain.**

   b. Visceral pain usually comes about because of **obstruction of a hollow organ** that causes distention and stretching of the organ wall.

   c. Visceral pain is characteristic of conditions such as **bowel obstruction, ureteral stone,** or a **stone in the bile duct.**

3. The 15-year-old girl, on the other hand, has *sharp,* well-localized pain exacerbated by coughing.

   a. Her pain is typical **somatic pain.**

   b. The mechanism of somatic pain is **peritoneal inflammation.**

   c. Examples of conditions that can produce somatic pain are **appendicitis** (which is probably what this patient has), **pancreatitis,** or a **strangulated hernia.**

4. Examples of *referred pain* include the following:

   a. In an enlarging or leaking **abdominal aortic aneurysm,** the pain is often referred to the **back, buttocks,** and **groin.**

   b. When there is a **ureteral calculus,** the pain may be referred into the **scrotum** or **labia.**

   c. Anything that produces irritation just beneath the diaphragm (e.g., a **ruptured spleen**) may produce referred pain in the **shoulder.**

5. A 49-year-old woman has called for an ambulance because of abdominal pain.

   a. In taking the *history,* one wants to learn at least the following:

      (1) What, if anything, **provoked** the pain, and what **palliates** it?
      (2) What is the **quality** of the pain?
      (3) What is the **region** (location) of the pain, and where does it **radiate?**
      (4) How **severe** is the pain?
      (5) What was the **timing** of the pain (onset, duration)?
      (6) Have there been any **associated symptoms,** such as nausea, vomiting, or changes in bowel habits?

      The patient should also be questioned about **medications** taken regularly and **previous abdominal surgery.** A woman of childbearing age should be asked the **date of her last menstrual period.**

   b. Extra-abdominal causes of abdominal pain include

      (1) **Acute myocardial infarction**
      (2) **Pneumonia**
      (3) **Pulmonary embolism**
      (4) **Diabetic ketoacidosis**
      (5) **Black widow spider bite**
      (6) **Testicular torsion**
      (7) **Lead poisoning**

6. The patient's symptoms and signs can tell you a lot.

Finding	What the Finding Tells Me
Coffee-ground vomitus	The patient is **bleeding** into his stomach, and the blood has been there for some time.
Severe bradycardia	This may be a **cardiac** and not an abdominal problem.
Melena	The patient is **bleeding** somewhere in the gastrointestinal tract.
Tenting of the skin	The patient is severely **dehydrated.**
Patient very still	The patient probably has **peritonitis.**
Pulsatile abdominal mass	Likely abdominal **aortic aneurysm.**
Rigid abdomen	Almost certainly **peritonitis.**

7. It is absolutely essential that a paramedic be able to recognize the signs of shock. That is why we keep coming back to them. Symptoms and signs of shock include

   a. **Restlessness** and **anxiety**

   b. **Thirst**

   c. **Nausea,** sometimes with **vomiting**

   d. **Cold, clammy, pale or mottled skin**

   e. **Weak, rapid pulse**

   f. **Rapid, shallow breathing**

   g. **Changes in the state of consciousness**

   h. **Fall in blood pressure**
   Notice that we put hypotension at the end of the list. Remember, if you wait for the patient to become hypotensive before you realize he's in shock, you've probably already lost the ball game.

8. The key data in recognizing that this 54-year-old patient is suffering from a **leaking abdominal aortic aneurysm** (answer **D**) are the location of his pain in the lower back, the mottling of his abdomen, and the signs of reduced circulation to the lower extremities.

9. Burning epigastric pain in a patient who regularly takes antacids is highly suggestive of **peptic ulcer disease** (answer **A**). In this case, the patient seems to be bleeding from his ulcer. Sometimes—although apparently *not* in this case—the patient will actually experience some relief of pain when the ulcer starts to bleed, for the blood in the stomach acts like any other liquid to dilute gastric acid.

10. The tip-offs in the case of this 70-year-old woman were the onset of pain after a heavy meal, the abdominal distention, and pain out of proportion to the physical findings—all hallmarks of **mesenteric ischemia** (answer **C**).

11. Any question about abdominal pain that starts off with the phrase, "On the first hot day of summer . . ." is almost a giveaway. For what happens on the first hot day of summer is that people sweat a lot more than they have been doing on previous days; furthermore, people are not yet acclimated and haven't started increasing their fluid intake to make up for the increased fluid loss. On the first hot day of summer, therefore, people become dehydrated, especially those doing manual labor outdoors. And if someone has a tendency to form kidney stones, it's dehydration that will precipitate an attack. Even if you didn't pick up on the introductory phrase, however, this patient has classic symptoms of **ureteral colic** (answer **E**)—pain in the back or side that radiates into the groin, pain so bad it reduces this construction worker to tears.

12. This question was included to determine who was still awake. The 46-year-old man with symptoms of "indigestion" and signs including diaphoresis, a scared look, and severe bradycardia is most likely suffering an *inferior wall myocardial infarction* (answer **F, none of the above**). NOT ALL CAUSES OF ABDOMINAL PAIN COME FROM THE ABDOMEN. Remember?

13. The 52-year-old woman with steady abdominal pain that started in the left lower quadrant and gradually progressed to full-blown peritonitis is most likely suffering from **diverticulitis** (answer **B**) and, indeed, seems to have perforated her bowel.

14. As to which patients are in danger, **all of them** are **except the patient with the kidney stone** in question 11. He is in no immediate danger of dying, even though he probably wishes to. All of the other patients mentioned are either in or near shock (the man with the acute myocardial infarction is in danger simply by virtue of having a myocardial infarction as well as because of his severe bradycardia).

    For the patients with acute abdomen, the steps of treatment are as follows:

    a. Ensure an adequate **airway.** Since all of these patients are likely to vomit, transport them in the **stable side position,** not supine.

    b. Administer **oxygen.**

    c. If you suspect an abdominal aortic aneurysm (patient in question 8), apply but do not inflate the MAST. Should the blood pressure start to fall, contact medical command regarding MAST inflation.

    d. Start at least one **large-bore IV** and run in lactated Ringer's full tilt (except for the 70-year-old lady in question 10—she may not be able to tolerate a fluid load, given her age and her history of cardiac disease; consult medical command for fluid orders in her case).

    e. **Monitor** cardiac rhythm.

f. **Notify** the receiving hospital of the type of case you are transporting, so that surgical staff can be alerted.

g. **Transport** without delay.

15. We scarcely ever think very much about our kidneys and how much they do for us. It is only when the kidneys are *not* working that we can begin to appreciate all the things they do when they *are* functioning. And when they aren't working, a whole lot of other things start going wrong as well. Thus patients with chronic renal failure are much more prone to

    a. **Congestive heart failure**

    b. **Malignant hypertension**

    c. **Acute myocardial infarction**

    d. **Cardiac dysrhythmias**

    e. **Cardiac tamponade**

    f. **Subdural hematoma**

    g. **Septicemia**

    h. **Bleeding disorders**

16. With more and more patients being maintained on chronic renal dialysis, paramedics will find themselves dealing more often with the problems that dialysis patients are heir to.

    a. (1) The patient who feels too weak to move and has peaked T waves on his ECG is most likely suffering from **hyperkalemia.**
       (2) The steps to take are as follows:
          (a) Continue to **monitor** his cardiac rhythm carefully.
          (b) Give **atropine, 0.5 mg rapidly IV.**
          (c) Give 10 ml of a 10% solution of **calcium chloride** IV.
          (d) Make sure the calcium chloride has infused. Then give 50 mEq of **sodium bicarbonate** IV.
          (e) **Transport** without delay, and be prepared to deal with a cardiac arrest en route.

    b. (1) The patient with paroxysmal nocturnal dyspnea has classic signs of **congestive heart failure** (CHF).
       (2) The treatment is very nearly the same as for any other patient with CHF except that some of the medications usually given in CHF will probably be useless.

    (a) Keep the patient **sitting up with legs dangling.**
    (b) Administer **oxygen with positive pressure.**
    (c) You can try giving sublingual nitroglycerin, but it is not likely to work. Don't even bother trying diuretics like furosemide—those will not work for certain.
    (d) **Transport** without delay, and **notify** the receiving facility that the patient will require emergency dialysis, which is the treatment of choice for his CHF. If the receiving hospital does not have the means to carry out an emergency dialysis, they may have to perform a **phlebotomy** of about a unit of blood as a temporizing measure until the patient *can* reach a dialysis unit.

    c. (1) The patient with a postdialysis headache and signs of increased intracranial pressure is *probably* suffering from **disequilibrium syndrome** as a consequence of the dialysis, BUT you cannot at that point rule out a subdural hematoma.
       (2) You have to assume the worst and treat him for a possible subdural:
          (a) Ensure an open **airway;** be alert for vomiting and prepared to suction.
          (b) Administer **oxygen.**
          (c) **Monitor** cardiac rhythm.
          (d) **Transport** without delay.

17. Before you sit down to memorize the 151 causes of the acute abdomen, consider the message in today's lesson.

a. **aneurysm**		i. **gastritis**
b. **colon**		j. **stone**
c. **pancreas**		k. **cation**
d. **kidney**		l. **emotion**
e. **stomach**		m. **fsw**
f. **duodenum**		n. **foe**
g. **bile**		o. **eau**
h. **teeth**		p. **hit**

    Secret Message: ONE NEED NOT DIAGNOSE THE SPECIFIC CAUSE OF AN ACUTE ABDOMEN TO KNOW THAT THE SITUATION IS SERIOUS.

26
Anaphylaxis

1. Unlike the words in the box, the signs and symptoms of anaphylaxis are rarely obscure.

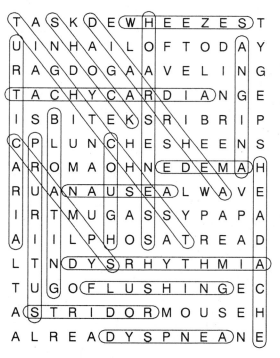

SIGNS AND SYMPTOMS	MECHANISM

CARDIOVASCULAR

angina	Decreased coronary blood flow
dysrhythmia	Myocardial ischemia from decreased coronary blood flow
shock	Leakage of fluid out of blood vessels (hypovolemic component); decreased cardiac output (cardiogenic); peripheral vasodilatation (neurogenic)
tachycardia	Reflex response to falling blood pressure

SIGNS AND SYMPTOMS	MECHANISM

RESPIRATORY

hoarseness	Laryngeal edema
stridor	Laryngeal edema
cough	Histamine itch
wheezes	Bronchospasm
dyspnea	Probably bronchospasm
tight chest	Bronchospasm

GASTROINTESTINAL

cramps	All gastrointestinal symptoms due to edema of the
bloating	gastrointestinal mucosa
nausea	
diarrhea	

CUTANEOUS

edema	Plasma leaking out of capillaries
flushing	Peripheral vasodilation
urticaria	Histamine effect
pruritus	Histamine effect

NERVOUS SYSTEM

headache	Probably vasodilatation and stress

2. Effects produced by mast-cell mediators include

 a. **Systemic vasodilatation**

 b. **Pulmonary vasoconstriction**

 c. **Increased capillary permeability**

 d. **Bronchoconstriction**

 e. **Decreased coronary blood flow**

 f. **Decreased strength and contractility of the heart**

 g. **Increased tendency to dysrhythmias**

3. a. Of the three patients described, it is the last (answer **C**) who is suffering an anaphylactic reaction. Patient A is showing classic signs of **choking,** and a shot of epinephrine will not help him a bit (except during resuscitation from the cardiac arrest he will surely suffer if you failed to diagnose his choking and act immediately). Patient B is simply experiencing a very common untoward **side effect of erythromycin,** about which he *should* have been warned by the doctor who prescribed the drug.

 b. Management of Patient C, the patient who *is* suffering an anaphylactic reaction, should include the following steps:

 (1) Ensure that his **airway** stays open. It is already in jeopardy, judging from his hoarse voice. If you are unable to whip an endotracheal tube in, then administer 4 to 10 sprays of 1 : 1,000 racemic epinephrine, and get moving at once to the hospital, administering **oxygen** throughout.

 (2) **Monitor** the ECG; cardiac dysrhythmias are likely.

 (3) Start at least one **large-bore IV** with lactated Ringer's, and run it wide open.

 (4) Unfortunately, in this particular case you probably cannot use a constricting band to isolate the injection site, since what the patient in all probability got was two shots of penicillin, one in each buttock, so there's no place to put the venous tourniquet!

 (5) You *can*, however, give **epinephrine, 0.1 mg/kg of a 1:10,000 solution** (about 5–10 ml) *slowly* IV.

 c. The physician has ordered DIPHENHYDRAMINE.

(1) The *contraindications* to diphenhydramine are
  (a) **Asthma** or **chronic obstructive pulmonary disease**
  (b) **Glaucoma**
  (c) **Prostate problems**
  (d) **Ulcer disease**
  (e) **Pregnancy**
(2) The *dosage* in this case would be **25 to 50 mg** *slowly* IV.
(3) Possible *side effects* of diphenhydramine include
  (a) **Drowsiness**
  (b) **Blurring of vision**
  (c) **Dry mouth**
  (d) **Wheezing**
  (e) **Difficulty in urinating**

d. You were also instructed to start an AMINOPHYLLINE infusion.

(1) The *therapeutic effects* of aminophylline in this situation include
  (a) An **increase in the force of cardiac contractions**
  (b) **Increased coronary blood flow**
  (c) **Stimulation of the respiratory drive**
  (d) **Bronchodilation**
(2) The *contraindications* to giving aminophylline are all relative contraindications, and they include
  (a) **Cardiac dysrhythmias**
  (b) **Hypotension**
  (c) **Acute myocardial infarction**
(3) The best *dosage* regimen is to start with a **loading dose of 5 mg per kilogram** over about 20 minutes and then an **infusion of 0.5 mg/kg/hr.**
(4) The potential *side effects* of aminophylline include
  (a) **Dysrhythmias**
  (b) **Hypotension**
  (c) **Nausea and vomiting** (very common)
  (d) **Headache**
  (e) **Excitement** or **confusion**

Before you finish with this case, be sure to have a word with your medical director—so that he or she can have a word with the people at the VD Clinic. They need to be reminded that it just won't do to give a patient a parenteral antibiotic (or any other drug) and whip him out the door! Patients should remain under observation for *at least* 30 minutes after any parenteral medication.

4. This 52-year-old man who was stung by a bee is also suffering an anaphylactic reaction, but because of his age, you have to be a little more careful in giving epinephrine.

a. The treatment is as follows:

(1) Ensure that his **airway** stays patent.
(2) Administer **oxygen.**
(3) **Monitor** the ECG throughout (keep the beep tone on).
(4) Start a **large-bore IV** with lactated Ringer's.
(5) Give **epinephrine** as follows: First, **dilute 0.1 mg (0.1 ml) of 1 : 1,000 aqueous epinephrine in 10 ml of normal saline** and inject it **over 10 minutes.** If the patient is not getting better by then, start an infusion at **1 µg per minute.**
(6) **Remove the stinger** from the patient's skin, taking care not to squeeze it. Inject 0.1 ml of 1 : 1,000 aqueous epinephrine at the site of the sting. If the site is on an extremity, put a constricting band (venous tourniquet) proximal to the sting site.
(7) Consult medical command regarding any other pharmacotherapy.

(8) **Transport** without delay.

b. EPINEPHRINE, if given in excessive dosage, may cause

(1) Extreme **hypertension**
(2) **Angina**
(3) Cardiac **dysrhythmias** and consequent **palpitations**

c. The doctor has also instructed you to give HYDROCORTISONE.

(1) There are **no contraindications** to a single dose of IV steroids in the field.
(2) The potential *side effects* of a single dose of IV steroids will be seen only if the dose is administered too fast, in which case there may be **hypotension** and even **cardiovascular collapse.**

5. Agents commonly responsible for anaphylactic reactions fall into three general categories: drugs, foods, and insect venoms.

DRUGS	**Penicillin**
	Blood products
	Horse serum products
	Vaccines
	Biologic extracts
FOODS	**Nuts**
	Seafood
	Egg whites
	Fruits
INSECT VENOMS	**Hymenoptera**
	Fire ants

6. This secret message should not have been a big
   surprise.

   a. **antibody**

   b. **antigen**

   c. **allergen**

   d. **anaphylaxis**

   e. **histamine**

   f. **wasp**

   g. **itch**

   h. **drip**

   i. **widow**

   j. **tort**

   k. **to**

   l. **gtt**

   Secret Message: A PATIENT WITH STRIDOR IS
   A PATIENT IN DANGER. DON'T ALLOW HIM
   TO ASPHYXIATE.

27
Poisons, Drugs, and Alcohol

1. It is an unfortunate fact of contemporary life that emergency medical personnel, especially those who work in the prehospital sphere, must be familiar with the nicknames and properties of illicit drugs to provide effective care. How well did you do in identifying the hidden drugs?

```
M E T S W I N I C O T I N E D
O E L L I B R I U M P I R E S
M A T E N I C E B O U G H T O
E L P H E N O B A R B I T A L
T C O C A I N E A P C O S S I
H Y D R O M O R P H O N E M P
A E R E O F P A C I F I C E E
D I R T X P A H P N F O O T Y
O H C O D E I N E E E R N H O
N E A L I M D U E T E M A A T
E L F S U N D R M E A L L D E
  S P U D H O P E I S A M A R T
  T A M A R I J U A N A D I I A
A M Y T A L S T A T E M I N K
C H L O R A L H Y D R A T E E
```

STIMULANT DRUGS

Ice: **methamphetamine**
Stardust: **cocaine**
Bambita: **methadrine**
Footballs: **Dexedrine**
Ecstasy: **MDMA**
Eve: **MDEA**
Java: **coffee**
Fag: **nicotine**

NARCOTIC DRUGS

Horse: **heroin**
Miss Emma: **morphine**
Fours: **codeine**
Dillies: **hydromorphone**
Dollies: **methadone**
Auntie: **opium**

BARBITURATES AND OTHER SEDATIVES

Red devils: secobarbital (**Seconal**)
Yellow jackets: **phenobarbital**
Bluebirds: amobarbital (**Amytal**)
Roche-tens: chlordiazepoxide (**Librium**)
Mickey: **chloral hydrate**
Rose: **wine**
Grass: **marijuana**
Hash: **hashish**

HALLUCINOGENS

Elephant: **PCP**
Acid: **LSD**
Button: **peyote**

2. When Junior, or anyone else for that matter, swallows something he shouldn't have swallowed, it's important to obtain details of the ingestion.

   a. **What** was swallowed? (Bring the container to the hospital with the patient if possible.)

   b. **When** was it swallowed?

   c. **How much** was swallowed? (Check to see how much is left in the container if there's any uncertainty—that will give you an upper limit, anyway, of the amount that could have been ingested.)

   d. **What else** was swallowed? Did Junior perhaps sample some washing powder as an hors d'oeuvre, or maybe a bit of furniture polish as a chaser?

   e. **Did he vomit?**

3. When a person is found unconscious and there is reason to suspect a toxic cause, the physical assessment should focus not only on the evaluation of the level of consciousness but also on parameters that might provide clues to a specific toxic agent. Pay particular attention, therefore, to

   a. **Unusual odors** on the breath

   b. A precise assessment of the **level of consciousness** (charted on a flow sheet)

   c. The **condition of the skin** (temperature, moisture, color)

   d. The **respirations,** for signs of respiratory depression or metabolic acidosis

   e. Abnormalities of the **pulse** and **blood pressure**

   f. Abnormalities of the **pupils** (very dilated or very constricted)

4. The trend today is not to induce vomiting in a poisoned patient unless you come upon the patient very soon after the ingestion and there are no contraindications to vomiting:

V A 3-year-old child who ingested an unknown plant about 10 minutes ago. He is awake and alert.

N A 24-year-old man who downed an unknown quantity of Liquid Plumr in a suicide attempt 15 minutes ago.
Ingestion of **corrosives** is a strong contraindication.

N A 2-year-old who took a few swigs of pretty red furniture polish before being apprehended 20 minutes ago.
Ingestion of **hydrocarbons** is also usually a contraindication to induction of vomiting, unless the patient is having toxic symptoms from the ingestion. Even then, removing the material with a nasogastric tube is probably preferable.

N A 38-year-old man experiencing "heavy" pain in his chest after popping a few amphetamine pills to "be up for a business meeting."
Symptoms of an **acute myocardial infarction** are good enough reason not to induce vomiting here.

V A 20-year-old woman who swallowed 50 Valium pills about 10 minutes earlier in a suicide attempt—then panicked and called for an ambulance.
When you're lucky enough to reach the scene so soon after an ingestion, it's worthwhile to empty the patient's stomach, for most of what she ingested is probably still within the stomach.

N A 22-year-old woman found in her apartment with empty, unmarked pill bottles on her bedside table. She is very drowsy and her speech is slurred.
A **depressed level of consciousness** rules out vomiting in this case.

N A 2-year-old child who apparently ingested the entire contents of a bottle of his mother's diet pills. He had a grand mal seizure just before your arrival.
The **seizure** activity contraindicates vomiting for this child.

__N__ A 15-year-old girl who ingested about 50 phenobarbital pills 10 minutes before your arrival. She tells you, "I didn't really want to die. I just panicked when I found out I was pregnant." Ordinarily this young lady would be a good candidate for syrup of ipecac, since she took the pills only 10 minutes ago and is still, apparently, fully awake, but her being **pregnant** is a contraindication to induction of vomiting.

__V__ A 3-year-old child apprehended in the act of polishing off a bottle containing 250 Yumyum Ninja Multivitamins.

Any manufacturer who labels a medication "yummy" or with similar devices to make it attractive to children is just asking for trouble. Medications should *not* be made attractive to children.

5. When the teenager swallows his father's antihyptertensive medications, you are advised to induce vomiting.

  a. The drug used to induce vomiting is **syrup of ipecac.**

  (1) The correct *dosage* for this teenager is the usual adult dosage of **15 to 30 ml** PO followed by a glass of water.

  (2) We have already encountered, in the previous question, most of the *contraindications* to giving syrup of ipecac:

  (a) **Depressed level of consciousness**
  (b) **Seizures**
  (c) **Pregnancy**
  (d) **Acute myocardial infarction**
  (e) Ingestion of **corrosives, hydrocarbons, strychnine,** or **iodides**

  (3) There are **no** real *side effects* of syrup of ipecac itself, but the vomiting that is syrup of ipecac's *therapeutic* effect may lead to aspiration in a patient who cannot protect his airway.

  b. Activated charcoal is given to **adsorb poisonous compounds to its surface** and thereby effectively remove them from the body.

  (1) Poisonings in which activated charcoal is *not* effective include
  (a) **Methanol**
  (b) **Acid** or **alkali** ingestion
  (c) **Organophosphate** poisoning
  (d) **Cyanide** poisoning

  (2) The usual adult *dosage* of activated charcoal is **5 to 10 tablespoons** mixed in tap water to make a slurry.

  c. The *steps in treatment* for this teenager reflect the fact that current practice now favors **giving activated charcoal as early as possible,** even before or together with syrup of ipecac:

  (1) Administer **activated charcoal,** 5 to 10 tablespoons mixed with tap water to make a slurry.
  (2) Administer **syrup of ipecac,** 1 to 2 tablespoons by mouth, followed by a glass of water.
  (3) Encourage the boy to **move around** until he feels the urge to vomit; then assist him into a position that will minimize the possibility of aspiration.
  (4) **Save a sample** of the vomitus.
  (5) **Monitor** cardiac rhythm and vital signs frequently.
  (6) **Transport** the patient to the hospital.

6. The gentleman who swallowed crystalline Drano ingested a very strong alkali that will continue burning holes in everything it touches until it is removed from the body.

  a. The objective of prehospital treatment is primarily to *dilute* the alkali:

  (1) Give 8 to 12 ounces of **milk** by mouth. Have the patient swish the first gulp around in his mouth and spit it out to try to remove the Drano crystals that are still adherent to his mucous membranes.
  (2) Start an **IV lifeline** en route to the hospital.
  (3) **Transport** without delay.

  b. You should **not induce vomiting** (it will just expose the esophagus and throat to the alkali all over again as the caustic material comes back up from the stomach).

  c. You should **not give activated charcoal** (it doesn't work, and it will just make subsequent endoscopy more difficult).

7. Down by the railway, some of the community's homeless population have congregated to console themselves with whatever they can find to drink. Sometimes, the substances chosen as cheap substitutes for ethanol can have disastrous consequences.

  a. (1) The first patient is showing classic signs of **ethylene glycol** toxicity. The pleasant taste of the substance, the gastrointestinal symptoms some hours later, and the severe respiratory distress about 24 hours later are all characteristic.

(2) The steps of management are as follows:

(a) Administer **oxygen,** as for any patient whose lungs are full of fluid.

(b) Give **activated charcoal,** 5 to 10 tablespoons mixed with tap water to make a slurry.

(c) Administer **60 ml of whiskey** by mouth. That is best done when the patient is already in the ambulance, out of view of his friends, or you may find that you have more customers for your whiskey supply than you bargained for.

(d) Start an **IV lifeline** with lactated Ringer's.

(e) Give 50 ml of **sodium bicarbonate** IV.

(f) Consult medical command regarding the administration of a **diuretic** such as furosemide or mannitol.

(g) **Notify** the receiving hospital so that arrangements for emergency hemodialysis can be started.

(h) **Transport** the patient to the hospital.

b. (1) The second patient, who appears drunk, is most likely suffering from **methyl alcohol poisoning,** probably with pancreatitis as well.

(2) The steps of management are as follows:

(a) While one would like to remove whatever methanol is remaining in the patient's stomach, it's too risky to try to induce vomiting with his depressed level of consciousness; by the time the ipecac took effect, he might be comatose altogether. It's preferable, therefore, to try to whip in a **nasogastric tube** and aspirate all you can of what's left in the stomach.

(b) Then give **1 to 2 ounces of whiskey,** again in a discreet location, such as inside your vehicle.

(c) Start an **IV lifeline.**

(d) Give 50 ml of **sodium bicarbonate** IV.

(e) **Notify** the hospital to prepare for a possible emergency hemodialysis.

(f) **Transport** without delay to the hospital.

8. a. The lady who swallowed silver polish most probably swallowed **cyanide,** as evidenced by the smell of almonds on her breath, flushing of the skin, along with tachycardia and hypotension.

b. The drug that can buy some time is **amyl nitrite,** which in effect pulls cyanide away from

the cellular enzymes it is poisoning. (Cyanide antidote kits also contain 25% sodium thiosulfate, for added effect.)

c. Amyl nitrite is given by breaking a perle into a handkerchief and having the patient **inhale** through the handkerchief **for 20 seconds,** immediately **followed by the inhalation of 100% oxygen** for 40 to 100 seconds.

d. The *side effects* of amyl nitrite include:

(1) **Hypotension**
(2) **Tachycardia**
(3) **Flushing,** especially above the clavicles
(4) A **pounding headache**

In anticipation of the hypotensive effects, keep the patient recumbent during amyl nitrite administration.

e. The steps of management, then, for this victim of cyanide poisoning are as follows:

(1) Maintain a patent **airway;** if her level of consciousness continues to deteriorate, maintaining the airway may require endotracheal intubation.

(2) Give **100% oxygen** by tight-fitting nonrebreathing mask.

(3) Administer **amyl nitrite** as just described.

(4) Start an **IV lifeline** with lactated Ringer's, and give enough **fluid to maintain the blood pressure.**

(5) **Monitor** cardiac rhythm.

(6) **Notify** the receiving hospital to ready a sodium thiosulfate infusion.

(7) **Transport** the patient without delay; amyl nitrite is only a temporizing measure, and you cannot keep it up for very long.

9. If this 2-year-old kerosene imbiber has not developed symptoms by the time you reach the scene, it is very unlikely that he will develop any symptoms at all, so there is probably little to be gained by transporting the child to the hospital. Consult with medical command, however, to clear that decision not to transport. Then spend a little time **advising the mother.** Your tone should not be accusatory ("Why did you leave that kind of stuff lying around?"), for the parent probably feels guilty enough already. Simply explain the dangers involved in storing poisonous substances in food containers or leaving *any* poisonous substances, no matter what their containers, within reach of a toddler. Give the mother one of the poison safety pamphlets that you always carry with you for cases just such as this one.

10. One doesn't have to look very far to find commonly ingested poisons. Just check out your own home.

Type of Poison	Examples
Strong acid	**Toilet bowl cleaner, battery acid, bleach disinfectant**
Strong alkali	**Drano, Clinitest tabs, Clorox, dishwasher detergent**
Volatile hydrocarbon	**Naphtha, kerosene**
Toxic plant	**Lantana, dieffenbachia, caladium, castor bean**

11. There's something called too much of a good thing, and too much insulation of a cabin heated by a wood stove is definitely in the too-much-of-a-good-thing category!

    a. In the case in question, *everyone* inside the cabin is showing signs of **carbon monoxide poisoning.**

    b. The steps to take are as follows:

       (1) As you all bundle up in your warm clothes, **open all the windows** of the cabin.
       (2) **Get everyone outdoors** as quickly as possible.
       (3) Call for an **ambulance.** Don't trust yourself or anyone else under the influence of carbon monoxide to drive.
       (4) As soon as the ambulance arrives, give **100% oxygen by tight-fitting mask** to all exposure victims, but with priority to the baby, who is clearly the most severely affected.
       (5) Keep everyone **at rest** to minimize metabolic demand for oxygen.
       (6) **Monitor** the baby's cardiac rhythm.
       (7) Ask medical command to start inquiries regarding the nearest **hyperbaric facility.**

12. a. The patient stricken with a "possible heart attack" while sitting out on the lawn is in fact the victim of his next-door neighbor's insecticide spray. While we have to take very seriously the possibility of acute myocardial infarction in any middle-aged man who complains of weakness, nausea, and a tight feeling in his chest, the hypersalivation combined with constricted pupils and severe bradycardia all point to **organophosphate poi-**

soning. And, indeed, your partner returns from his discussion with Mr. Dimbledirt carrying the offending bottle of Parathion.

    b. The drug used to treat organophosphate poisoning is the parasympathetic blocking agent, **atropine sulfate.**

    c. The *contraindications* to giving atropine sulfate are

       (1) **Atrial flutter or fibrillation** with a rapid ventricular response
       (2) **Glaucoma**

       Acute myocardial infarction is not a contraindication, but the use of atropine in that setting requires caution.

    d. Massive *doses* of atropine are often required to counteract the effects of organophosphates. We start with **2 mg IM and 1 mg IV.** Thereafter, we continue giving 1 mg IV every 5 minutes until the patient is atropinized.

    e. We can tell when we have given enough by the development of typical **signs of atropinization:**

       (1) The **pupils widen.**
       (2) The **pulse accelerates.**
       (3) The **mouth becomes dry.**

    f. The *steps of treatment* in this case, then, are as follows:

       (1) Protect the **airway.** Suction secretions as necessary.
       (2) Give **100% oxygen.**
       (3) Give the intramuscular dose of **atropine** right away.
       (4) Start **decontamination:** Get the patient into a shower and have him wash thoroughly with lots of soap and water. Stay nearby in case he feels faint or sick during the shower.
       (5) As soon as he is out of the shower, apply electrodes to **monitor** cardiac rhythm.
       (6) Start an **IV lifeline,** and administer the intravenous dose of atropine.
       (7) **Notify** the receiving hospital of the type of case you are bringing in.
       (8) **Transport** the patient to the hospital.

13. The boy who suffered a seizure after inhaling typewriter correction fluid should be treated as any other postictal patient:

    a. Protect his **airway** by positioning him on his side; suction secretions as needed.

b. Administer **oxygen** by nasal cannula.

c. **Monitor** cardiac rhythm; dysrhythmias and "sudden sniffing death" are not unheard of after inhalation of typewriter correction fluid.

d. Start an **IV lifeline** with D5/W.

e. **Transport** the patient to the hospital. Ask the nurse to notify the child's parents of your destination.

14. Like the Scouts themselves, Boy Scout troop leaders must be prepared!

a. The treatment of an uncomplicated *bee sting* is as follows:

   (1) **Scrape (don't pluck) the stinger** and its venom sac **from the wound.**
   (2) **Wash** the wound thoroughly with soap and water.
   (3) If you can find a way to rig up a **cold pack,** it will provide significant relief of pain.

b. The treatment of a *tick bite* is as follows:

   (1) Use forceps or gloved fingers to **remove the tick by its mouth parts,** without squeezing its body. The old trick of applying a match or alcohol to the tick to encourage it to release its grip doesn't always work, but you can try it if you're not wearing your instrument holster and are thus without a forceps.
   (2) **Wash** the bitten area thoroughly with soap and water.

c. (1) The boy who visited the outhouse has a somewhat more serious problem. He has suffered a **black widow spider bite.**
   (2) **Calcium gluconate** 10% can be given to relieve his pain.
   (3) The *contraindications* to calcium gluconate are not a problem in this case:
       (a) It must be given with extreme caution in patients who are taking **digitalis.**
       (b) It must not be given together with **sodium bicarbonate** in the same infusion.
   (4) The *dosage* of calcium gluconate is **5 to 10 ml** of the 10% solution *slowly* IV.
   (5) Overall, the *steps in treatment* of the boy who suffered the black widow spider bite are as follows (once the ambulance arrives):
       (a) Administer **oxygen.**
       (b) Apply a **cold pack** to the bite.

   (c) Start an **IV lifeline** with lactated Ringer's solution.
   (d) Give **calcium gluconate** as just described.
   (e) **Transport** without delay.

15. When you are called to attend the hiker who was bitten by a snake, the first thing you need to figure out is whether any venom was in fact injected into the snakebite victim.

a. Symptoms, signs, and circumstances that would suggest envenomation include

   (1) A **description of the snake** fitting that of a poisonous variety
   (2) **Fang marks** on the skin
   (3) **Burning pain** or **numbness** at the site of the bite (in viper bites)
   (4) **Ecchymoses** at the bite site (viper bites)
   (5) **Swelling** around the bite (viper bites)
   (6) **Systemic symptoms,** such as dizziness or nausea

b. The *steps of treatment* of an envenomed snakebite are as follows:

   (1) **Remove the patient from danger.**
   (2) **Calm** and **reassure** the patient.
   (3) **Remove constricting items** from the bitten extremity.
   (4) Keep the victim **at rest;** don't allow him to move about or to bear weight on the bitten extremity.
   (5) **Splint** the bitten extremity.
   (6) Begin **transport.**
   (7) En route to the hospital:
       (a) Administer **oxygen.**
       (b) **Notify** the receiving hospital of the type of snake thought to be responsible for the bite.
       (c) Start an **IV lifeline.**

16. It just doesn't pay to go to the beach. Look at all the things that can happen there. The swimmer who was pulled from the water, for example, has had an unhappy encounter with a **coelenterate,** such as a jellyfish. The steps of treatment are as follows:

a. **Rinse** his legs in seawater.

b. Pour your **gin** and tonic over the wound, unless you happen to have medical (isopropyl) alcohol handy.

c. Borrow the **meat tenderizer** from the barbecue and sprinkle it on the nematocysts.

d. Use a knife to **scrape off the nematocysts** from the skin.

e. **Rinse** the leg **again** in seawater.

f. When the ambulance arrives with its drug box, give **calcium gluconate,** 10 ml of a 10% solution slowly IV if the patient is still in pain.

17. To treat the boy injured by a sea urchin, heat some water in a bucket to about 113°F. Then **immerse both the boy's hands** in the hot water for 30 to 60 minutes.

18. The man who grazed his knuckles against someone else's teeth must be treated as any other victim of a human bite wound. That is, he needs to **wash his hands thoroughly with soap and water** and to be **evaluated in the hospital.**

19. For the man bitten by the Doberman pinscher, the treatment is as follows:

    a. Have him stop walking on the injured leg.

    b. **Clean the wound with lots of soap and water;** then **rinse with alcohol** (there goes the rest of your gin).

    c. Send someone back along the beach to **find out details about the dog** (e.g., name and address of owner), which must be reported to the local health authorities.

    d. See that the patient is **transported to the hospital** for further evaluation of his wound.

20. Evaluating the patient who has overdosed is very much like evaluating any other victim of poisoning:

    a. In *taking the history,* try to find out

       (1) **What** drug was taken.
       (2) **When** it was taken.
       (3) **How much** was taken.
       (4) Whether **any other drugs or alcohol** were also taken.
       (5) **What has been done** in attempts to help the patient.

    b. In conducting the *physical examination* of a patient who has overdosed, pay particular attention to

       (1) The **level of consciousness**
       (2) **Vital signs**
       (3) Signs of **head injury**
       (4) The size and reactivity of the **pupils**

       (5) **Odors** on the victim's breath
       (6) The presence of **needle tracks** on the arms or elsewhere
       (7) **Drug paraphernalia** in the victim's pockets or surroundings

    c. The steps in treating an unconscious patient who has overdosed on an unknown substance are as follows:

       (1) Maintain the **airway** manually (hold off intubation until you can assess the results of naloxone).
       (2) Administer **oxygen.**
       (3) Start an **IV lifeline** if possible (AIDS precautions).
       (4) Give **thiamine,** 100 mg slowly IV, followed by **50% dextrose,** 50 ml slowly IV, as for any other comatose patient.
       (5) Give **naloxone** (Narcan), 0.8 to 1.2 mg *slowly* IV. Monitor the respirations as you do so. If the naloxone improves the respirations, stop administration before the patient wakes up completely.
       (6) If the naloxone is *not* effective and the patient remains deeply comatose despite full doses of naloxone (up to 2 mg), intubate the trachea.
       (7) **Monitor** cardiac rhythm.
       (8) **Transport** the patient to the hospital.

21. When Goldilocks and the three bears lay on a big bash for their friends, things get a little out of hand.

    a. (1) GOLDILOCKS overdosed on **barbiturates.** The tip-offs are the dilated pupils that scarcely react to light and the signs of shock.
       (2) The steps in management are as follows:
          (a) Secure the **airway** with an endotracheal tube.
          (b) Administer **oxygen.**
          (c) Start an **IV lifeline** and give lactated Ringer's in volumes sufficient to maintain the blood pressure.
          (d) Consult medical command regarding whether to administer **sodium bicarbonate.**
          (e) **Monitor** cardiac rhythm.
          (f) Insert a **nasogastric tube;** aspirate and save the contents of the stomach; then lavage the stomach with saline (save the first aspirate).
          (g) **Transport** to the hospital.

b. (1) PAPA BEAR overdosed on some sort of stimulant drug, probably **crack,** in view of the crack pipe found at the scene.

(2) The steps in management are as follows:

    (a) Try to **calm him down** verbally.

    (b) If the drug was taken by mouth and not smoked, give activated charcoal.

    (c) **Monitor** cardiac rhythm; dysrhythmias are likely.

    (d) **Transport** to the hospital.

c. (1) MAMA BEAR's pinpoint pupils, slow pulse, and depressed respirations are all clues to **narcotics overdose.**

(2) The steps in treatment are as follows:

    (a) Maintain the **airway** (delay intubation).

    (b) Administer **oxygen.**

    (c) **Assist ventilations** with a bag-valve-mask.

    (d) Start an **IV lifeline.**

    (e) Give **thiamine,** 100 mg, and **50% dextrose,** 50 ml IV.

    (f) Give **naloxone,** 0.8 to 1.2 mg slowly IV.

    (g) If there is no response to the naloxone, intubate.

    (h) **Transport** to the hospital.

d. (1) BABY BEAR seems to have taken **phencyclidine (PCP),** to judge from his psychotic behavior and apparent indifference to pain.

(2) The steps in management are as follows:

    (a) Get **police assistance** to subdue the patient. He has a knife. He has already amputated one of his toes. If you get too close, he may amputate one of *your* limbs. Don't be misled by the fact that he is just a *baby* bear. Patients under the influence of PCP have astonishing strength. You will need plenty of help to subdue him.

    (b) Use very **strong restraints** to keep the patient subdued.

    (c) **Control bleeding** from the foot by pressure on the wound.

    (d) Locate the **amputated toe** and bring it with the patient to the hospital, preserved as described in a previous chapter.

    (e) **Transport** to the hospital.

e. (1) The *indications* for NALOXONE are **known narcotic overdose** or **coma suspected to be from narcotic overdose.**

(2) There are **no contraindications** to giving naloxone.

(3) The possible *side effects* of naloxone include

    (a) Very rapid administration may precipitate **vomiting** and **dysrhythmias.**

    (b) It may precipitate a **withdrawal syndrome** in addicted persons.

    (c) If given in insufficient dosage, naloxone may **wear off before the narcotic does,** in which case the patient will slip back into coma.

    (d) In rare cases, it may precipitate **pulmonary edema** or **sudden death.**

22. Always consider the possibility that drugs or alcohol is playing a role in a patient's problem, no matter how "respectable" the patient appears.

a. Findings that would support the suspicion that a patient has an alcohol problem include

(1) **"Green tongue syndrome"** from consuming chlorophyll mints to cover the odor of alcohol on the breath

(2) **Cigarette burns** on clothing

(3) **Flushed face** and **palms**

(4) **Tremor**

(5) **Odor of alcohol** on the patient's breath under inappropriate circumstances

b. Alcoholics are more vulnerable to a variety of medical problems, including

(1) **Subdural hematoma**

(2) **Gastrointestinal bleeding** (gastritis, esophageal varices)

(3) **Pancreatitis**

(4) **Hypoglycemia**

(5) **Hypothermia**

(6) **Pneumonia**

(7) **Burns**

(8) **Seizures**

(9) **Cardiac dysrhythmias**

(10) **Cancer**

c. (1) The patient's withdrawal seizure should be treated like any other seizure:

    (a) **Protect the patient** from injury.

    (b) Maintain his **airway;** suction secretions as needed.

    (c) Administer **oxygen.**

    (d) **Check for injuries** after the seizure subsides.

    (e) Start an **IV lifeline.**

    (f) Give 100 mg of **thiamine** and 50 m! of **50% dextrose** IV.

(2) If the patient has more than one seizure without waking up in between, he is by definition in status epilepticus and will

therefore require **diazepam in titrated doses,** starting with 2.5 mg IV.

23. Just because an unconscious patient smells of alcohol, there is no guarantee that his coma is not the result of something else.

   a. The easiest way to remember the causes of coma is by the mnemonic AEIOU-TIPS:

   A Alcohol (also keto**acidosis**)
   E Epilepsy or some other seizure disorder
   I **Insulin** overdose (hypoglycemia)
   O **Overdose** of depressant drugs
   U **Uremia** or other renal problem
   T **Trauma**
   I **Infection**
   P **Psychogenic**
   S **Stroke** or **space-occupying lesion** in the brain

   b. The steps in management are the same as for any other comatose patient:
   (1) Ensure a patent **airway;** suction as needed.
   (2) Administer **oxygen.**
   (3) **Assist ventilations** as necessary.
   (4) Start an **IV lifeline.**
   (5) Give 100 mg of **thiamine** plus 50 ml of **50% dextrose** IV.
   (6) If there is any question of narcotics overdose, give **naloxone,** 0.8 to 1.2 mg slowly IV.
   (7) If the patient does not waken in response to dextrose or naloxone, **intubate** his trachea.
   (8) **Monitor** cardiac rhythm.
   (9) **Transport** to the hospital.

   c. (1) THIAMINE is given to **prevent precipitating Wernicke's encephalopathy** in response to the glucose administration. The *dosage* of thiamine is **100 mg,** which may be given as 50 mg IM plus 50 mg IV, or as 100 mg slowly IV.
   (2) The possible adverse effects of 50% DEXTROSE include **necrosis at the infusion site** if it leaks out of the vein during administration.

24. a. The "man gone crazy" after 3 days in police lockup has doubtless developed **delirium tremens.**

   b. The steps in treatment are as follows:
   (1) **Talk to the patient calmly** and slowly. Assure him that you will protect him from the rats or anything else that threatens him.
   (2) **Explain everything you are doing.** Even mundane objects, like your stethoscope or sphygmomanometer may appear threatening.
   (3) Obtain **vital signs,** and maintain a flow sheet of vital and neurologic signs.
   (4) Administer **oxygen.**
   (5) If at all possible, start an **IV lifeline.** Once the line is in, secure it very well. Then give **lots of fluids.** If you use glucose-containing solutions, be sure to give thiamine first.
   (6) **Transport** the patient to the hospital. Delirium tremens has a mortality of up to 15 percent. The patient cannot be adequately monitored or treated in a jail cell.

25. Please copy the secret message below in very large letters and post it on the bulletin board of your ambulance service.

   a. **methanol**

   b. **miosis**

   c. **jaw**

   d. **hypothermia**

   e. **hydrocarbon**

   f. **huffing**

   g. **talc**

   h. **pruritus**

   i. **button**

   j. **cholesterol**

   k. **glucose**

   l. **need**

   Secret Message: THE PATIENT FOUND STUPOROUS WITH ALCOHOL ON HIS BREATH MAY BE ILL OR INJURED FROM OTHER CAUSES.

28
Communicable Diseases

1. Lady Macbeth probably would not have made a very good paramedic, for there were certain fundamental deficiencies in her character. But one thing she *did* have going for her: She washed her hands frequently!

   a. **fomite**

   b. **virus**

   c. **tuberculin**

   d. **icterus**

   e. **orchitis**

   f. **dysuria**

   g. **rash**

   h. **night sweats**

   i. **cough**

   j. **fatigue**

   k. **nausea**

   l. **cyanosis**

   m. **gag**

   n. **dilate**

   o. **banana**

   p. **DOT**

   q. **tea**

   Secret Message: THE BEST SAFEGUARD AGAINST CATCHING OR TRANSMITTING A CONTAGIOUS DISEASE IS TO WASH YOUR HANDS AFTER EVERY CALL.

2. The correct definitions are as follows:

   E — Time during which a person is capable of transmitting his disease to someone else: **communicable period**

   H — Local or systemic disease process caused by a microorganism: **infection**

   C — Inanimate object that can transmit disease microorganisms from one person to another: **fomite**

   A — Place where microorganisms live and multiply: **reservoir**

   D — Time between exposure to a microorganism and the development of symptoms: **incubation period**

   F — Relating to a hospital or other health care setting: **nosocomial**

   G — Presence of harmful microorganisms on or in a person, animal, or object: **contamination**

   B — One who harbors an infectious agent and can transmit it to others, although not himself ill: **carrier**

3. The best way to keep from catching a disease, besides staying healthy in general, is to know how a disease is spread and to take the appropriate precautions:

Disease	Mode(s) of Transmission	Protective Measures
AIDS	**Sexual contact; injection of contaminated blood products; from mother to fetus**	**Gloves, mask, extreme caution with needles and sharp objects** **Handwashing**
Hepatitis type A	**Fecal-oral, from ingesting contaminated water, shellfish, etc.**	**Handwashing**
Hepatitis type B	**Sexual contact; injection of contaminated blood products**	**Immunization** **Gloves, mask, extreme caution with needles and sharp objects** **Handwashing**
Meningitis	**Droplet spread**	**Mask** **Handwashing**
Mumps	**Saliva, droplet spread**	**Immunization, mask** **Handwashing**
Syphilis	**Sexual contact, infected saliva, semen, vaginal discharge**	**Gloves** **Handwashing**
Tuberculosis	**Droplet spread**	**Mask** **Handwashing**

4. a. The college student with fever, headache, stiff neck, vomiting, and an altered state of consciousness is showing typical signs of **meningitis,** perhaps meningococcal.

   b. The paramedic can minimize the risk of catching meningitis from a patient by **wearing a mask** and **washing hands after the call.**

5. a. The 54-year-old man with hemoptysis, night sweats, and weight loss most probably has **tuberculosis.**

   b. The paramedic can minimize the risk of contracting the infection by **wearing a mask** and **washing hands after the call.** It is also a good idea to check, about 2 months later, for evidence of new TB infection by having a **tuberculin test.**

6. a. The intravenous drug user with yellow eyes, dark urine, anorexia, and distaste for cigarettes has classic symptoms of **viral hepatitis,** most likely type B in view of his intravenous drug use.

   b. To minimize the risk of contracting hepatitis from a patient, the paramedic should employ **universal precautions,** including **barrier protection** (mask, gown, gloves) and **extreme caution with needles and IV equipment.** And oh yes, **wash your hands after the call.**

7. a. The 8-year-old with fever, sore throat, and swelling around the angles of the jaw most likely has **mumps.**

   b. The paramedic's best protection against mumps is **immunization,** either by mumps vaccine or by having had the illness as a child. The paramedic who is not immunized should **wear a mask.** And whether immune or not, **wash your hands after the call.**

8. a. The young lady with fever, conjunctivitis, and spots has **measles.**
   If *you* haven't had measles, or **immunization against measles,** you can try wearing a **mask,** but in all likelihood you will soon have measles too—just wait about 10 days. Be sure to **wash your hands after the call** though, to minimize the risks to the next patients you treat.

9. People have a lot of incorrect ideas about AIDS. It is important for paramedics to know the facts about AIDS and to help in the public education campaign on the subject.

   a. AIDS is a highly contagious communicable disease.
   FALSE. The AIDS virus is *not* a very hardy virus and is *not* easily transmitted from one person to another.

   b. Approximately 1.0 to 1.5 million Americans are infected with the AIDS virus.
   TRUE.

   c. Patients with AIDS are abnormally susceptible to many infectious diseases.
   TRUE, and that is the reason why the patient should be protected with a mask from the germs that you or your colleagues may be carrying.

   d. AIDS can be acquired through casual contact, such as shaking hands with an HIV-positive patient.
   FALSE. Even people having intimate (but nonsexual) daily contact with an AIDS patient in the same household—people sharing eating utensils, towels, and even toothbrushes (!)—have not acquired HIV, so handshaking has to be a very low risk behavior!

   e. Approximately one-quarter of AIDS patients in the United States are intravenous drug users.
   TRUE.

   f. An HIV-positive patient can transmit the AIDS virus even if he does not have clinical signs of AIDS.
   TRUE. And since we have no way of knowing whether a stranger is HIV-positive, it is safest to assume that he or she *is*—and to take the necessary precautions in handling blood or body fluids.

   g. Many health workers have acquired AIDS through contact with the blood or body fluids of AIDS patients.
   FALSE. As of the end of 1992, there have been fewer than 50 cases *throughout the world* of health workers who became HIV positive as a result of occupational exposure to AIDS.

   h. The majority of AIDS cases that have occurred in health workers as a result of occupational exposure have been among EMS personnel.
   FALSE. To date, there has been only one reported case of an EMS provider becoming HIV-positive as a result of an occupational exposure.

10. AIDS can be transmitted in only three ways:

    a. By **sexual contact** with an HIV-positive person

    b. By inoculation of **HIV-positive blood or blood products** through the skin or onto damaged skin or mucous membranes (e.g., onto an open wound)

    c. By transmission from **mother to fetus**

11. By the very nature of their work, EMS personnel are often in situations that pose a high risk of contracting hepatitis (and to a much lesser extent, AIDS). The case described in this question is typical—a lot of blood, a lot of broken glass, and therefore a lot of opportunities to sustain a cut and have it contaminated with the patient's blood.

    a. Among the precautions a paramedic can take in those circumstances are

       (1) Wear **heavy-duty rubber gloves** for extrication and all activities that do not require fine touch.
       (2) Wear **latex gloves** for all other procedures (e.g., starting IVs, intubation).
       (3) Use additional **barrier protection,** such as goggles, mask, and gown once you are in the more controlled environment of the ambulance.
       (4) Observe **extreme care in handling needles and sharp instruments.**
       (5) You guessed it: **Wash your hands** immediately if blood spills on them and again after the call.

    b. To clean the ambulance after the call:

       (1) **Strip the used linen** from the stretcher and dispose of it in the proper receptacle.
       (2) Similarly, **dispose of all disposable equipment** used during the case—again in a designated receptacle.
       (3) **Disinfect** the equipment you can't dispose of (e.g., bag-valve-mask).
       (4) **Clean the stretcher** with a germicidal/viricidal agent.
       (5) **Air out the ambulance,** with all doors and windows open, for at least 5 minutes.

    c. Once you find out that the patient has hepatitis, you need to

       (1) **Stay in touch with the hospital** to find out what type of hepatitis the patient is found to have. If it is hepatitis A, consult your medical director about getting a shot of immune globulin.

(2) **Scrub out the ambulance**—first with soap and water, then with a germicidal/viricidal disinfectant.

12. What did your personal immunization survey turn up? Are you completely covered, or do you have some deficits to make up? If your last tetanus booster was more than 10 years ago, or if you never had an immunization against hepatitis B, make sure you remedy those and any other immunization deficits *before* you take your first call.
    And be sure to wash your hands.

13. What's wrong with Figures 9-33, 9-34, 9-35, 15-3, and, indeed, several others throughout this text is that the **paramedic is not wearing gloves** to carry out a procedure involving potential contact with blood or bodily fluids. The pictures were drawn that way to show the procedures more clearly. Omitting to wear gloves is permissible in a drawing; it is *not* permissible in the field. Donning gloves before carrying out a procedure should become second nature—just as washing your hands afterward!

29
Emergencies in the Elderly

1. Among the attributes that make caring for the elderly particularly challenging are the following:

   a. Many **physiologic functions** are **diminished.**

   b. **Typical symptoms and signs** of disease **may be absent,** altered, or delayed.

   c. **Physical illness** often **presents as a mental disorder.**

   d. **Multiple problems coexist** in the same patient, producing multiple symptoms.

   e. **Adverse reactions to drugs** occur frequently.

   f. **Psychosocial factors** have an increased impact on health.

2. How many of the misconceptions about the elderly were you able to spot?

   a. The rate of aging is the same in a 35-year-old as in an 80-year-old.
   TRUE! If you're over 30, you're getting old—just as quickly as your grandmother is. It's a sobering thought.

   b. Mental deterioration and some degree of dementia are an inevitable part of the aging process.
   FALSE. There is nothing normal about dementia at any age.

   c. Elderly people are more likely than younger individuals to seek emergency care for minor, nonserious complaints.
   FALSE. To the contrary, the elderly usually delay seeking care much longer than do younger people and tend not to seek care at all for minor problems.

   d. The pain mechanism is often depressed among the elderly.
   TRUE, which makes it easy to overlook a serious problem in the elderly.

   e. Major hearing loss is universal among the elderly.
   FALSE—so don't automatically raise your voice every time you see a patient with some gray hairs.

3. Among the psychosocial stresses that accompany advancing age are

   a. **Retirement** from work, with the attendant loss of community status, sense of usefulness, and the structure that a job gives to one's daily life.

   b. **Bereavement,** as more and more friends (and often a spouse) die.

4. There are a number of changes in the body that occur as part of the normal aging process.

Organ System	Normal Age-Related Changes
CARDIOVASCULAR	**Increase in blood pressure** **Decrease in cardiac output** **Cardiac hypertrophy** **Electric conduction system atrophy**
RESPIRATORY	**Decreased vital capacity** **Increased residual volume** **Decreased air flow** **Decreased arterial PO$_2$** **Decreased cough, gag, and ciliary clearance**
RENAL	**Decreased renal blood flow** **Decreased nephron mass** **Impaired thirst mechanism** **Decreased ability to maintain salt and fluid balance**
DIGESTIVE	**Decreased sense of taste** **Decreased secretion of saliva and gastric juice** **Less efficient hepatic detoxification**
MUSCULOSKELETAL	**Decreased bone mass** **Decreased muscle mass**
NERVOUS	**Decreased visual acuity** **Loss of high-tone hearing** **Impaired proprioception**
HOMEOSTATIC	**Impaired temperature regulation** **Blunted febrile response to infection** **Impaired blood sugar control**

5. To decide whether someone is sick, one needs to know whether a given finding is normal or abnormal!

N Decreased skin turgor

D Dyspnea
Shortness of breath is a very nonspecific sign in the elderly, and it may mean anything from acute myocardial infarction to shock, but it is never normal.

D Joint pains
A bit of stiffness and some loss of agility are part of the aging process, but *pain* in the joints suggests arthritis, which is a disease process—no matter how commonly it occurs.

N Depressed gag reflex

N Cessation of menstrual periods in women

D Loss of teeth
Although common among the elderly, the loss of teeth is the result of dental and periodontal disease. Teeth that are well cared for can last a long lifetime.

D Mental confusion
Mental confusion is never normal at any age. When it occurs acutely in the elderly, it is *always* a sign of serious illness or toxicity from medications.

N Decrease in height

D Deafness
It is true that age brings loss of hearing in the high registers, but total deafness is *not* a normal consequence of aging.

D Urinary incontinence

6. Responses to illness common among the elderly include

   a. **Acute confusion** or other change in mental status

   b. **Weakness**

   c. **Dizziness**

   d. **Dyspnea**

   e. **Fatigue**

7. There are a number of problems involved in taking a history from an elderly patient, but most of those obstacles can be overcome with a little patience, tact, and ingenuity.

   a. Obstacle: The patient **has trouble hearing you.**
   What you can do about it: Sit **facing the patient,** in **good light,** and **speak slowly and clearly.**

   b. Obstacle: **Patient may not report important symptoms.**
   What you can do about it: Conduct a **review of systems** to screen the major organ systems for serious abnormality.

   c. Obstacle: The patient has **several chief complaints.**
   What you can do about it: Ask, "**What happened** *today?*" or "What is bothering you the most? How is it different from the way it was yesterday?"

   d. Obstacle: The patient is **too confused to give a history.**
   What you can do about it: Try to **obtain information from the family** or other caregivers.

8. As noted, one way to try to make sure you don't miss any important symptoms is to conduct a review of systems, which should include questions such as the following:

   a. Have you had any **pain or discomfort in your chest** (cardiovascular system)?

   b. Have you had any **palpitations** (cardiovascular system)?

   c. Have you been **short of breath** (cardiovascular/respiratory systems)?

   d. Have you been **coughing** (respiratory system)?

   e. Have you felt **dizzy** or **fainted** (cardiovascular/nervous system)?

   f. Have you had any **difficulty speaking** (cardiovascular/nervous system)?

   g. Have you had any severe **headaches** (nervous system)?

   h. Have you noticed any **funny sensations** in your arms or legs, or have you had any **difficulty walking** (nervous system)?

   i. Have you had any changes in your **appetite** or **weight** (digestive system)?

   j. Has there been any **change in your bowel movements** (digestive system)?

   k. Have you had any **pain or difficulty in urinating** (urinary system)?

9. One of the most frequent geriatric calls is for a patient who has fallen.

   a. Questions to ask in taking the history might include the following:

      (1) **How** did it happen?
      (2) Did you **feel dizzy before you fell** or have any other similar warning symptoms?
      (3) Did you **feel anything snap** before you fell?
      (4) Are you taking any **new medications?**
      (5) **Where does it hurt?**

   b. The past medical history of an elderly patient may be quite extensive, and there isn't enough time in the field to elicit all the details. The things you *need* to know in order to render appropriate emergency care are

      (1) **Major underlying illnesses** (e.g., diabetes, angina).
      (2) **Recent hospitalizations.** (Where? What doctor?)
      (3) **Allergies.**
      (4) **Current medications.** (That means *all* medications—prescribed and over-the-counter varieties. Collect them all in a bag and take them with the patient to the hospital.)

   c. In performing the physical assessment, one should look in particular for

      (1) The patient's state of **dress** and **grooming,** as an indication of her general ability to care for herself
      (2) The **level of consciousness** (AVPU or Glasgow Coma Scale)
      (3) The **position** in which the patient is found
      (4) An **elevated blood pressure,** which might signal increasing intracranial pressure, or a **decreased blood pressure,** which might suggest shock
      (5) A **very slow pulse,** suggesting either increasing intracranial pressure or the source of a syncopal episode
      (6) An **increased respiratory rate,** which may signal shock or a variety of other serious conditions

(7) **Signs of head injury** (e.g., CSF leak, Battle's sign)

(8) **Neck tenderness**

(9) Instability or **tenderness of the ribs**

(10) **Deformity in the limbs**

(11) The **state of the surroundings,** another indication of the patient's overall ability to care for herself

d. The elderly are more susceptible than younger people to

(1) **Subdural hematoma**

(2) **Compression of the cervical spinal cord**

(3) **Rib fracture**

(4) **Hip fracture**

e. Examination reveals that the patient has fractured her left hip and may be in shock (her blood pressure is quite low for someone her age). The steps in treatment should include the following:

(1) Administer **oxygen.**

(2) **Immobilize** her on a long backboard with full spine precautions. **Pad the backboard** very well.

(3) **Monitor** cardiac rhythm.

(4) Start an **IV** with lactated Ringer's, but be careful not to run it too fast. A rate of 100 ml per hour will be more than adequate until the patient reaches the hospital.

(5) **Notify** the receiving hospital.

(6) **Transport** *without* sirens.

10. Acute myocardial infarction and congestive heart failure occur commonly in the elderly, but are as likely as not to present with atypical signs and symptoms:

Condition	Possible Signs and Symptoms in the Elderly
ACUTE MYOCARDIAL INFARCTION	**Confusion, weakness, dyspnea, stroke, syncope, incontinence**
CONGESTIVE HEART FAILURE	**Sundowning** (nocturnal confusion), **fatigue,** (rarely) **blisters on the legs**

11. Conditions that may present as delirium in the elderly include

a. **Acute myocardial infarction**

b. **Congestive heart failure**

c. **Pneumonia**

d. **Dehydration**

e. **Electrolyte abnormalities** (e.g., hyponatremia)

f. **Drug toxicity**

12. In trying to assess the suicide potential of a depressed elderly person, inquire

a. What is the patient's **marital status?** Men who are unmarried, widowed, or divorced are at higher risk of suicide.

b. What are his **living arrangements?** A person living alone is at higher risk of suicide.

c. Has he ever **felt as if he'd be better off dead?** If the answer is affirmative, find out whether he has made **any concrete plans** for how he would kill himself.

13. Among the drugs used in prehospital care, those most likely to cause problems in the elderly include

a. **Lidocaine**

b. **Aminophylline**

c. **Furosemide**

d. **Morphine**

14. When you find yourself losing patience with what seems like a trivial complaint from an elderly patient, consider the thought for today:

a. **disease**

b. **falling**

c. **fever**

d. **confusion**

e. **hypertrophy**

f. widower

g. thirsty

h. shouting

i. kvetch

j. balance

k. anal

l. lean

m. male sex

n. easy

o. lane

p. neon

q. AAA

Secret Message: AN ELDERLY PATIENT NEARLY ALWAYS HAS A GOOD REASON WHEN HE CALLS AN AMBULANCE—EVEN IF IT'S NOT THE REASON HE GIVES YOU.

30
Pediatric Emergencies

1. Knowing what to expect from a child of a given age can make caring for sick or injured children a lot easier.

D	May be interested to learn about the equipment in your vehicle.
A	Can be distracted by jangling keys and cooing noises.
E	Wants to be treated as an adult.
C	Particularly fearful of cuts and mutilating injuries.
A,B	Should be examined on mother's lap.
C,D,E	Can provide at least some of the history.
B	Most likely to bite, kick, and spit.
A,B	Their physical examination should be done in toe-to-head order.
E	For this age group, a pimple may be seen as a catastrophe.
A,B	Most likely to be the victim of abuse.
A	Fontanelles not yet closed.

2. The scene of an accident where a child has been injured is probably the most stressful environment that a paramedic will enter.

   a. A child struck by a car is likely to show Waddell's triad of injuries:

      (1) **Fracture of the left femur**
      (2) **Ruptured spleen**
      (3) **Injury to the right side of the head**

   b. Perhaps hardest to deal with at an accident scene like that described will be the feelings and behavior of the child's parents.

      (1) Obviously, there is no "correct" answer to the question of how you feel when assaulted by an angry parent. If you're normal, however, you'll probably feel angry.
      (2) What you *do* with your feelings is another matter, and there *is* a correct way to handle the situation and an incorrect way. The correct way is
         (a) Mentally count to 10 before you reply to the angry father.
         (b) **Stay calm.**
         (c) Don't raise your voice.
         (d) Try to **enlist the father's help** in caring for the child; give him something constructive to do, like fetching the backboard from the ambulance or folding triangular bandages into cravats.

   c. The child's vital signs (pulse = 120, respirations = 24, and blood pressure = 90/60) are **normal for his age** (answer 3). The slight tachycardia is easily explained by the pain and excitement of the situation.

3. In order to detect signs of illness or injury in a child, one must know what is *normal*.

   a. A child who is seriously ill or injured will always be agitated and showing clear signs of distress.
   FALSE. Indeed, it's often the very quiet child you need to worry about.

   b. A sunken anterior fontanelle in an infant suggests meningitis or head injury.
   FALSE. A *sunken* fontanelle indicates dehydration. In meningitis, head injury, or any other condition that increases intracranial pressure, we would expect to see a *tense, bulging fontanelle.*

c. Neonates are nose breathers, so nasal congestion may compromise their breathing.
TRUE.

d. Infants and small children rely mainly on their abdominal muscles to breathe.
TRUE, and since the intercostal muscles are weak, they tire more quickly. So a child in respiratory failure will have an even more exaggerated pattern of abdominal breathing than usual.

e. Grunting is a sign of respiratory distress in infants.
TRUE.

4. When 2-year-old Tammy starts barking in the middle of the night, it's a great attention-getter.

a. The vital signs are **abnormal** for her age. There is **tachycardia** and **tachypnea.**

b. The most likely diagnosis is **croup.**

c. The steps of prehospital management are as follows:

(1) Give humidified **oxygen** while you set up a nebulizer.
(2) Give **racemic epinephrine,** 0.5 ml diluted in 2.5 ml of normal saline and **nebulized** into a face mask using oxygen as the carrier gas.
(3) Place the child in a **position of comfort.**
(4) **Notify** the receiving hospital of the case.
(5) **Transport** without delay.

5. Diffuse wheezing and respiratory distress in a child under a year of age are the tip-offs in this case.

a. The vital signs are **abnormal.** The baby has **tachycardia, tachypnea,** and a slight elevation in blood pressure.

b. The most likely diagnosis is **bronchiolitis.**

c. The steps of prehospital management are as follows:

(1) Give humidified **oxygen.**
(2) **Assist ventilations** gently with a bag-valve-mask.
(3) Consult medical command as to whether to give a **trial of bronchodilators.**

(4) Keep the **intubation kit handy** in case of apnea.
(5) **Monitor** cardiac rhythm.
(6) **Transport** without delay.

6. a. When little Bobby develops severe respiratory distress and signs of airway obstruction over a very short time, and he does not have a high fever, the most likely diagnosis is **foreign body obstruction of the airway,** that is, choking.

b. The steps of managing a choking baby are as follows:

(1) If he's small enough to hold comfortably upside down, flip him over and give **up to five back blows** between the shoulder blades.
(2) If the back blows do not work, turn him supine and give **up to five chest thrusts.**
(3) Open his mouth and **lift the jaw and tongue.** *If you can see a foreign body,* remove it manually. If not, repeat the back blows and chest thrusts.
(4) If the child loses consciousness, carry out **direct laryngoscopy** at once to remove the foreign body under direct vision.

c. While you are dealing with the obstructed airway, the child stops breathing. He should be given **20 breaths per minute** for artificial ventilation.

d. Check for a pulse over the **brachial artery.**

e. The correct compression point is **one fingerbreadth below the nipple line on the sternum.**

f. The compression rate is **at least 100 compressions per minute.**

g. The defibrillation dosage for a 12-kg child is **24 joules** (2 joules/kg).

h. The dosages of resuscitation drugs for a 12-kg child are

(1) Epinephrine: Initial dose is **0.12 mg** (or 1.2 ml of a 1 : 10,000 solution). Subsequent doses may be 1.2 mg each.
(2) Lidocaine: **12 mg.**
(3) Atropine: **0.24 mg.**

i. **All** of those drugs may be given via endotracheal tube.

j. **All** of those drugs may be given via intraosseous infusion.

7. A sudden, severe sore throat along with a high fever should start some warning lights blinking in your brain.

   a. The vital signs are **abnormal.** The child has both **tachycardia** and **tachypnea,** not to mention his very **high fever.**

   b. The most likely diagnosis is **epiglottitis.**

   c. The steps in prehospital management are as follows:

      (1) Approach the child **very gently** so as not to disturb him.
      (2) Give humidified **oxygen.**
      (3) Place the child in a **position of comfort.**
      (4) **Notify** the receiving hospital to have the appropriate specialists standing by.
      (5) **Transport** without delay.

   d. The special *danger* threatening this child is **complete airway obstruction** from epiglottal swelling, which may occur literally within minutes.

8. a. Sometimes hyperpnea may be the only tip-off to **salicylate overdose.** In this case, there was another clue—the white specks in the child's vomitus, which could be the remnants of tablets.

   b. The prehospital management of salicylate poisoning is as follows:

      (1) Have the mother make a **search for the source,** and bring the empty bottle with you to the emergency room.
      (2) Ensure the child's **airway.**
      (3) Administer **oxygen.**
      (4) No need to induce vomiting—the child has already done it by himself. (Save a sample of the vomitus, and bring it in a closed container to the emergency room.) So simply give **activated charcoal,** about 5 tablespoons mixed in water to make a slurry.
      (5) **Sponge the child** with tepid water to try to lower his temperature.
      (6) Start **transport.**
      (7) Establish an **IV lifeline** en route.

   (8) Consult medical command regarding whether to give **sodium bicarbonate.**

9. The little boy having an asthmatic attack during nature study is already in bad shape by the time you arrive on the scene.

   a. Five signs that suggest he is in bad shape are his

      (1) **Drowsiness** (a sign of carbon dioxide retention)
      (2) **Pulsus paradoxus** of 40 mm Hg
      (3) **Cyanosis,** indicating hypoxemia
      (4) **Hyperinflated chest,** indicating obstruction to exhalation
      (5) **Silent chest,** indicating that practically no air is moving in and out

   b. The steps in managing this case are as follows:

      (1) Give humidified **oxygen** by mask while preparing the nebulizer.
      (2) Start an **IV lifeline.**
      (3) Give a **nebulized bronchodilator,** such as albuterol, 0.5 ml in 3 ml of normal saline, with oxygen as the carrier gas.
      (4) If there is no response to the aerosolized drug, give **terbutaline,** 0.01 mg/kg SQ.
      (5) Check with medical command regarding whether to give **hydrocortisone** (7 mg/kg slowly IV) and **sodium bicarbonate** (1 mEq/kg IV) as well.
      (6) **Monitor** cardiac rhythm.
      (7) Ask your dispatcher to **notify the child's parents** and request that they meet you in the emergency room.
      (8) **Transport** the child in a **position of comfort.**

10. Most calls you receive for asthmatic attacks will be for patients already known to have asthma. Such patients will not call for help unless there is something different about this particular attack.

   a. Questions to ask in taking the history of a child having an acute asthmatic attack include

      (1) **How long** has the attack been going on?
      (2) What **medications** has the child already taken? When? In what dosage?
      (3) How much **fluid** has the child managed to take?
      (4) Does the child have any **allergies?**

(5) Has the child had any **hospitalizations** for asthma? If so, when?

b. It's easier to remember medications to give in an acute asthmatic attack if you know what you are giving them *for.*

Pathophysiologic Process	*Medication Used to Counter It*
Bronchospasm	**Epinephrine, albuterol, terbutaline, aminophylline**
Dehydration/mucous plugging	**Intravenous fluids**
Edema of bronchial walls	**Steroids** (e.g., hydrocortisone)
Hypoxemia	**Oxygen**
Acidosis	**Sodium bicarbonate**

c. When giving ALBUTEROL, you need to know:

(1) The *contraindication* in children: **diabetes**

(2) The possible *adverse side effects:* **palpitations, tremors, nervousness, dizziness, nausea**

(3) The correct pediatric *dosage:* **0.01 to 0.03 ml per kilogram** in 3 ml of normal saline given by nebulizer or 1 to 2 puffs from a metered-dose inhaler.

11. There is no easy answer to the question of how to respond in a case of sudden infant death syndrome. Each case will be a little different, and your response should be guided by local protocols and personal judgment. You need to make a quick appraisal to decide whether the mother already realizes that the baby is dead. If not, it might be worth starting CPR, so that she can feel, afterward, that everything possible was done. If you do start CPR, do it right; go through all the steps as you would for a baby you expected to survive. If, on the other hand, you feel that the mother already knows that her baby is dead, it may be better to take the more difficult option, and that is to confirm her worst fears. Should you do so, you must be prepared to spend time with the mother and to deal with her grief.

As this case illustrates, when you do confront a case of crib death, you will have to make an instant decision on the spot regarding how to proceed. If you haven't prepared yourself ahead of time for such decisions, it could be one of the longest instants of your experience.

12. Seizures in children are a lot like seizures in adults, but they tend to be considerably more upsetting to all concerned.

a. The causes of seizures in children include

(1) **Head trauma**
(2) **Meningitis**
(3) **Fever**
(4) **Hypoglycemia**
(5) **Hypoxia**
(6) **Failure** of a known epileptic **to take prescribed medications**
(7) Abuse of **drugs** (yes, in children)

b. Questions to ask in taking the history of a child who has had a seizure include

(1) Is this the child's **first seizure?**
(2) **How many seizures** has the child had today?
(3) Has the child had a **fever? Stiff neck? Headache?**
(4) Might the child have **ingested a toxic product?**
(5) Is there a **family history** of seizures?
(6) If the child is known to have seizures, **did he take his medication** today?
(7) **What did the seizure look like?**

c. In performing the physical assessment of a child who has had a seizure, look in particular for

(1) Changes in the **state of consciousness**
(2) **Skin temperature** and moisture (febrile seizure?)
(3) Evidence of **head trauma**
(4) Equality and reactivity of the **pupils**
(5) **Stiff neck**
(6) **Signs of injury** sustained during the seizure (e.g., dislocation of the shoulder)

d. From all of the information you obtain about this child, you conclude that he probably had a febrile seizure. The prehospital treatment is as follows:

(1) Maintain the **airway.**
(2) **Sponge** him with tepid water to lower his temperature.
(3) **Transport** him to the hospital.

13. The 14-year-old, unlike the previous patient, is in status epilepticus.

   a. The steps in treatment are as follows:

   (1) Place her **left side down** in a safe place (e.g., on the floor, away from furniture).
   (2) Maintain her **airway.** Be prepared for vomiting.
   (3) Administer **oxygen** by nasal cannula.
   (4) Start an **IV lifeline** as soon as feasible (i.e., after the tonic-clonic phase of the seizure has abated).
   (5) Give **50% dextrose** (D50), 1 ml per kilogram (at 14, she's old enough for an adult concentration of the drug).
   (6) If the seizures continue despite D50, check with medical control regarding the administration of **diazepam, 0.3 mg per kilogram IV** (up to a maximum of 10 mg).
   (7) **Monitor** cardiac rhythm.
   (8) Ask the school nurse or your dispatcher to **notify the parents** of your destination.
   (9) **Transport** the child to the hospital.

   b. As noted above, the drug used to terminate seizure activity is **diazepam.**

   c. The *contraindications* to giving diazepam are **pregnancy, respiratory depression, hypotension,** or previous ingestion of **alcohol or sedative drugs.**

   d. The possible *side effects* include **apnea, hypotension,** and even **cardiac arrest.**

   e. The pediatric *dosage* of diazepam is **0.3 mg per kilogram IV** (or 0.5 mg/kg rectally) up to a maximum of 10 mg.

14. Whenever you are called to deal with injury in an infant or very young child, you must always keep the possibility of child abuse in the back of your mind.

   a. What's fishy about this particular story is the claim that the 10-month-old "**stepped on a cigarette.**" At the age of 10 months, most babies are just beginning to stand up (holding on) and are not yet walking, so it's hard to imagine how a 10-month-old would manage to step on a cigarette.

   b. Clues to child abuse include

   (1) **Parental behavior:** vague, evasive, hostile, carrying the baby "like a loaf of bread"
   (2) **Discrepancies** in the history
   (3) **Delay** in seeking care
   (4) A child who looks **generally neglected** (dirty, unkempt)
   (5) A child who **does not turn to his parents for comfort**
   (6) A child who **does not cry**
   (7) The presence of **multiple bruises of multiple vintages**
   (8) Injuries in and **around the mouth**
   (9) **Suspicious burns** (as in the present case; or scald burns without splash marks)
   (10) **Fractures** in an infant less than a year old.

   c. The steps in caring for this particular child are as follows:

   (1) Put a **sterile dressing on the burn.**
   (2) **Transport** the child to the hospital.
   (3) **Notify the physician in private** of your suspicions.
   (4) Fill out whatever **legal forms** are required.
   (5) **Document everything** on your trip sheet.

   d. What if the parent refuses to permit you to transport the child? Your service should have a policy established in advance to deal with such situations. Here are some suggestions:

   (1) **Try to persuade the parent** to change his or her mind. Do so in a calm, professional manner.
   (2) If the parent still refuses, return to the vehicle for a release form. Take advantage of the privacy of the vehicle to **radio medical command** and explain the situation. See what your medical director advises.
   (3) Have the parent **sign a release form** stating that they are refusing treatment of the child against medical advice. Probably such a form has little or no legal merit, but it may give the parent pause and prompt a change of heart.
   (4) If you were unable to transport the child, immediately upon completing the call, fill out whatever **documentation** the state requires in cases of suspected child abuse, and **notify the appropriate state agency.**

(5) **Document the entire call,** including a list of whom you notified, on your trip sheet.

Remember, the abused child may be in life-threatening danger. If you fail to report a suspected case of child abuse, the next call to the same address may be for a dead child.

15. There's enough stress involved in caring for an injured child without the added stress of feeling ignorant about pediatric trauma and how to manage it. There are differences in the injuries children suffer and the details of treating pediatric injuries. Learn those differences!

  a. An infant falling from a height is most likely to sustain injury to the head.
  TRUE. The head is the heaviest part of the body, so the infant will fall head-first.

  b. The method of choice for opening the airway of a small child who has been struck by a car is head tilt–chin lift.
  FALSE! Keep the head in neutral position, and use **jaw thrust** only.

  c. To insert an oropharyngeal airway in a small child, introduce the airway tip-upward, then rotate it 180 degrees and slide it into place.
  FALSE. That method is OK for grown-ups, but in children it may dislodge teeth or injure delicate soft tissues.

  d. Because of the increased resistance to air flow of a child's tiny airways, the only means of giving effective artificial ventilation to a child is with the demand valve.
  FALSE. The demand valve should NOT be used at all in children under 12—it generates too much pressure for little lungs.

  e. A 10-kg toddler need lose only about 200 ml (less than 8 oz) of blood to be in severe shock.
  TRUE. A 10-kg toddler has a *total* blood volume of only about 900 ml, so a loss of 200 ml represents 22 percent of the infant's total blood volume.

  f. Hypotension is an early response to blood loss in infants and small children.

FALSE. Hypotension is a very *late* sign of blood loss in infants and small children because they are capable of extreme vasoconstriction to maintain blood pressure.

16. Signs of hypovolemia and shock in infants and children include

  a. **Apathy** and listlessness

  b. **Cold, pale, mottled skin**

  c. **Prolonged capillary refill** (longer than 2 seconds)

  d. **Collapsed veins**

  e. **Increasing abdominal girth**

  f. **Tachycardia** and **tachypnea**

  g. **Scanty urine output**

17. Load-and-go situations in children include

  a. **Fall from a height** of more than 6 meters (20 feet)

  b. Child involved in an **accident with fatalities**

  c. Child **ejected from a car** in a motor vehicle accident

  d. Child who was **struck by a car** while walking or biking

  e. Child in whom you are **unable to secure an airway**

  f. **Respiratory arrest**

  g. **Open pneumothorax**

  h. **Tension pneumothorax**

  i. **Cardiac arrest**

  j. **Shock**

  k. **Uncontrollable bleeding**

  l. **Coma or deteriorating level of consciousness**

  m. Signs of **increasing intracranial pressure**

18. Even in a non-load-and-go situation, you need to be able to perform the secondary survey of the injured child quickly. To do so, you need to know precisely what you are looking for at each step.

Body Area	What I Would Be Looking for in Particular
HEAD	Bulging or sunken **fontanelles** in infants **Cephalohematoma** **Battle's sign, coon's eyes**, blood or clear **fluid draining from the nose or ears** **Unequal pupils**
NECK	**Tenderness; tracheal deviation**
CHEST	Location of the **point of maximal impulse (PMI)** **Bruises, instability** **Inequality of breath sounds**
ABDOMEN	**Circumference** (assessed with tape measure) **Bruises, seat belt marks** **Distention, tenderness, rigidity**
EXTREMITIES	**Deformity, bruises** **Peripheral pulses** **Movement** and **sensation**

19. The baby who fell from the balcony has sustained a serious head injury. (Did you notice the signs of increasing intracranial pressure?!) The prehospital treatment is as follows:

a. Maintain an open **airway** (use an oropharyngeal airway if the baby becomes unconscious). **Anticipate vomiting,** and have suction at hand.

b. Administer **oxygen.**

c. **Immobilize the spine** with a baby backboard or a pediatric backboard with folded towels to elevate the baby's back slightly.

d. Start **transport.**

e. **Hyperventilate** the baby slightly with a bag-valve-mask.

f. **Notify** the receiving hospital.

20. We have two injured children in this accident.

a. The first child has an *abdominal injury* and early *shock.* He is therefore in the **load-and-go** category. His prehospital treatment is as follows:

(1) Maintain an open **airway.** Anticipate vomiting, and keep suction at hand.

(2) Administer **oxygen.**

(3) **Immobilize** the child on a backboard. Leave the tape measure in place beneath his back, so that you can make repeated measurements of abdominal girth without having to move the child.

(4) Start **transport.**

(5) **Notify** the receiving hospital.

(6) Start an **IV lifeline** en route to the hospital.

(7) Make **repeated measurements of abdominal girth** and vital signs.

(8) **Splint** the broken arm.

b. The second child has a *tension pneumothorax* (the clues were his extreme respiratory distress, tracheal deviation, and a PMI shifted to the left). He is also in the **load-and-go** category, but only after critical interventions, including decompression of the pneumothorax, have been carried out.

(1) Ensure a patent **airway.**

(2) Administer **oxygen.**

(3) **Decompress the pneumothorax** by inserting a 14-gauge Angiocath into the fourth right intercostal space in the midclavicular line.

(4) **Immobilize** the child on a backboard.

(5) Start **transport.**
(6) **Notify** the receiving hospital.
(7) **Monitor** cardiac rhythm (myocardial contusion is likely).
(8) Start an **IV lifeline** en route to the hospital.

21. a. The infant removed from the smoky house fire **should be intubated because he was unconscious in a smoky environment** and therefore at high risk for respiratory complications.

   b. Other factors that put a pediatric fire victim at high risk for airway obstruction and are therefore indications for immediate intubation include

      (1) **Stridor**
      (2) **Wheezing**
      (3) **Signs of respiratory distress**
      (4) **Facial burns**
      (5) **Singed eyebrows**
      (6) **Red, edematous mouth**
      (7) **Carbonaceous sputum**

22. When your next-door neighbor's miserable little kid jams peanuts into his ears just when you are settling down to watch a football game, the most tempting management option is to strangle the child. That is not recommended, however, nor is any procedure to try to remove the peanuts from his ears. It will require good lighting, proper instruments, and perhaps even sedation to get the peanuts out without causing damage to the ear canal or drum. Therefore **leave the child and his ears alone.** Give Johnny's mother a drink, and then graciously drive her and Johnny to the local emergency department.

23. Advanced life support procedures differ slightly in infants and children.

   a. The first step in assembling the equipment for pediatric intubation is to check the cuff on the endotracheal tube you've selected.

FALSE. For children, one uses *un*cuffed endotracheal tubes.

   b. A straight blade is preferred for pediatric intubation.
   TRUE.

   c. In intubating infants, the laryngoscope blade is slipped beneath the epiglottis, to lift it up, rather than into the vallecula.
   TRUE. If you try to lift from the vallecula, as when using a curved blade in an adult, you may simply fold the epiglottis down over the glottis and obscure your view of the vocal cords.

   d. The narrowest point in an infant's airway is the opening between the vocal cords.
   FALSE. That is true of an adult, not of an infant. In the infant, the narrowest point is at the cricoid cartilage. What that means in practice is that you're *not* home free when you've slipped the tube through the cords; it may still hang up at the cricoid cartilage. If so, you need to withdraw the tube and try a smaller one.

   e. Universal precautions are unnecessary in starting IVs on infants and children.
   FALSE! Sadly, more and more infants are being born with AIDS, and children have contracted AIDS through contaminated blood transfusions. The reason that universal precautions are called "universal" is because you use them for *every* venipuncture.

   f. A burned infant should be given about 50 ml/kg/hr of IV fluids.
   FALSE, unless you want to float him away. Give 150 ml per hour to children under 5 years old.

24. Now that you've got the drug box cleaned and straightened up, keep it that way.

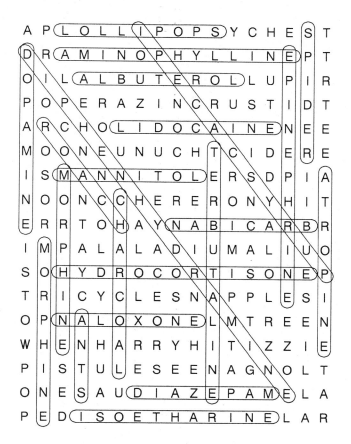

Drug	Correct Dosage
albuterol	**0.01–0.03 ml/kg** of 0.5% solution in 3 ml of normal saline given by nebulizer
aminophylline	**6 mg/kg** in 30 ml of IV fluid over 30 minutes
atropine	**0.02 mg/kg IV**
charcoal	**3–5 tablespoons in water PO**
diazepam	**0.3 mg/kg IV** (0.5 mg/kg rectally)
diphenhydramine	**1 mg/kg IV**
dopamine	**2–20 µg/kg/min**
epinephrine	**0.01 mg/kg**
hydrocortisone	**7 mg/kg slowly IV**
ipecac syrup	**5–15 ml PO**
isoetharine	**0.01 ml/kg** by inhaler
lidocaine	**1 mg/kg**
mannitol	**0.5 gm/kg**
morphine*	**0.1 mg/kg**
Na bicarb	**1 mEq/kg**
naloxone	**0.01 mg/kg**
terbutaline	**0.03 ml/kg** in 1.5 ml of saline by nebulizer

The ancillary "drugs" in the box: **lollipops.**

Things to be removed from the drug box: **ants, spider,** and **roach**—yet *another* reason for periodic inspections.

*An extra tubex of morphine turned up! Yet another reason to go through your drug boxes regularly.

25. Finally, a parting message:

    a. **hyperemia**

    b. **fontanelle**

    c. **febrile**

    d. **vagus**

    e. **scald**

    f. **toes**

    g. **asthma**

    h. **salivary**

    i. **brow**

    j. **scary**

    k. **Brillo**

    Secret Message: A VERY SMALL CHILD HAS A VERY SMALL AIRWAY. BE ALERT FOR SIGNS OF OBSTRUCTION.

Stop and Review III

1. Are all bones present and accounted for? There was at least one bone omitted from the grid. Did you notice?

a. Bones hidden in the grid:

calcaneus	ilium	sacrum
carpal	ischia	scapula
clavicle	mandible	sternum
coccyx	maxilla	tarsals
cranium	phalanx	tibia
femur	pubis	ulna
fibula	radius	zygoma
humerus	rib	

b. Bony protruberance on the ankle joint: **malleolus**

c. Socket in the shoulder bone for the humeral head: **glenoid**

d. Cup-shaped socket for the femoral head: **acetabulum**

e. Shaft of a long bone: **diaphysis**

f. Process below the femoral neck: **trochanter**

g. Highest point of the shoulder: **acromion**

2. How good a job would *you* have done as an oxygen molecule? Did you find your way?

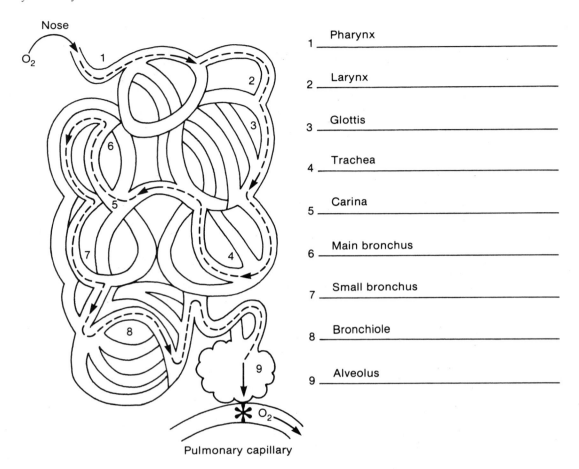

Nose

1 ___ Pharynx _____

2 ___ Larynx _____

3 ___ Glottis _____

4 ___ Trachea _____

5 ___ Carina _____

6 ___ Main bronchus _____

7 ___ Small bronchus _____

8 ___ Bronchiole _____

9 ___ Alveolus _____

Pulmonary capillary

3. While the victim of a lightning strike may look quite convincingly dead, in fact the chances of successfully resuscitating him are excellent:

   a. While awaiting the ambulance, **start basic life support:**

     (1) Quickly scan the area for **other casualties.**

     (2) Open the **airway,** with **cervical spine precautions.**

     (3) Check for **breathing;** if the patient is not breathing, start **artificial ventilation.**

     (4) Check for a **pulse;** if there is no pulse, **start external chest compressions** (yes, out there in the rain).

   b. As soon as your partner pulls up with the ambulance, there is a high priority in getting the patient into the ambulance, not simply because it's drier in there, but also because there is a continuing **hazard** outside, the ongoing thunderstorm (lightning *can* and does strike twice in the same place!). So when your partner arrives:

     (1) **Continue CPR,** now with supplemental **oxygen.**

     (2) Meanwhile your partner and anyone he can recruit to help should **slide the patient onto a backboard,** with the spine kept in a straight line.

     (3) Secure the patient to the backboard and **move him into the ambulance,** out of the rain and hazard.

(4) **Check the cardiac rhythm;** defibrillate if indicated.

(5) Continue CPR; have your partner start an **IV lifeline.**

(6) At the earliest opportunity after the patient has been well oxygenated, **intubate the trachea.**

　c. Here is the golfer's ECG:

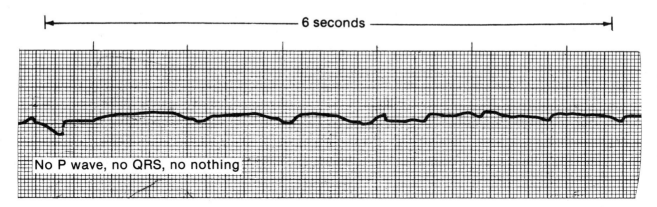

The rhythm is **nonexistent.**

There is **no rate.**

There are **no P waves,** so **no P–R interval.**

There are **no QRS complexes.**

The rhythm is **asystole.**

The treatment is **CPR.** Give **epinephrine** 1 : 10,000, 10 ml IV, every 3 to 5 minutes.

　d. While ordinarily asystole has a dismal prognosis, in the victim of a lightning strike, asystole may be entirely reversible; so it is not surprising that the pulse was restored so quickly. The patient may still, however, have some other serious injuries related to the lightning strike, such as fractures, ruptured internal organs, or muscle necrosis. Fractures should, of course, be **splinted;** ruptured viscera will probably present as shock, which should be treated as any other case of shock, with **IV fluids.** And the possibility of myonecrosis may prompt your physician to order **sodium bicarbonate,** 1–2 ampules IV, and **mannitol,** 0.5 to 1.0 gm per kilogram IV, in an attempt to prevent renal damage from the breakdown products of damaged muscle.

4. The only way to avoid aggravating the injury of a person who has sustained spinal cord trauma is to have a high index of suspicion that such trauma has occurred. That means knowing what circumstances are likely to produce injury to the spinal cord:

　a. Major **vehicular trauma**

　b. Accidents involving **diving into shallow water**

　c. Jumps or **falls from a height**

　d. **Crush injuries**

　e. **Lightning injuries**

　f. **Gunshot wound** to the head, neck, chest, or abdomen

　g. Patient who has sustained **multiple trauma**

　h. Any patient **unconscious after trauma**

　i. Any patient with **injuries above the clavicles**

5. The gentleman who drove his car into a concrete wall has a **flail chest,** which is a **load-and-go** situation. But load-and-go does *not* mean "swoop and scoop." You need to complete the primary survey and perform any critical interventions that are indicated before moving the patient:

   a. The steps of management after step B of the primary survey (the point at which we paused to describe the patient) are as follows:

      (1) Finish the primary survey with step C: **Check for external bleeding,** and control major external bleeding.
      (2) Give 100% **oxygen** via **bag-valve-mask.**
      (3) **Immobilize and extricate** the patient on a backboard.
      (4) **Stabilize the flail segment** of the chest. If he can cooperate, have the patient hug a pillow to his chest.
      (5) **Start transport,** and **notify** the receiving hospital.
      (6) **Monitor** cardiac rhythm; there is a high probability of myocardial contusion, given the mechanisms of injury.
      (7) Start an **IV** en route.
      (8) Recheck **vital signs.**

   b. It's a good thing you were clever enough to monitor the patient's cardiac rhythm, for otherwise you might have missed this:

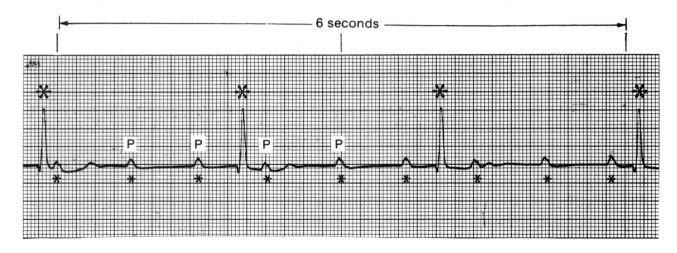

   The rhythm is **regular.**
   The rate is about **30 per minute.**
   P waves are **present,** but there is **no relationship between the P waves and the QRS complexes,** so it is impossible to speak of a P–R interval.
   The QRS complexes are **abnormal;** they are widened. In fact, they are ventricular complexes, that is, complexes that originate in the ventricles.
   The name of the rhythm is **third-degree (complete) heart block.**
   Treatment will depend on the patient's clinical status. If he is not showing signs of impaired peripheral perfusion, treatment can wait until he reaches the hospital. If perfusion is compromised, however, you need to try to speed up the heart rate with a transcutaneous pacemaker.

6. Knowing what organs are located in the abdomen, where they are located, and to what type of trauma they are most vulnerable can help you to detect otherwise subtle signs of abdominal trauma.

a. The hollow and solid organs of the abdomen are as follows:

Hollow Organs	Solid Organs
Stomach	**Liver**
Small intestine	**Spleen**
	Pancreas
Large intestine	**Kidneys**
Gallbladder	**Adrenal glands**
Ureters	
Urinary bladder	

b. The organ most likely to be injured in association with

(1) Fracture of the left ninth and tenth ribs anteriorly: **spleen**

(2) Fracture of the eleventh and twelfth ribs posteriorly: **kidney**

(3) Fracture of the pelvis: **bladder**

(4) Stab wound to the right upper quadrant: **liver**

(5) Primary blast injury: **large bowel**

7. The easiest way to remember the symptoms and signs of the compartment syndrome is according to the **six *P*s:**

a. **Pain**—the earliest and most reliable sign

b. **Pallor**—an early sign

c. **Pulselessness**—a late sign

d. **Paresthesias**—a relatively early sign

e. **Paresis,** then **paralysis**—late signs

f. **Puffiness**—a late sign

8. When minutes of the Golden Hour are ticking away, you can't take a lot of time to ponder what to do next. The sequences of trauma care must be second nature.

(1)__j__ **Move the patient to safety!** The car is on fire, for heaven's sake! At any moment you could all be blown away. Sure, we'd like to immobilize the patient properly before moving him, but the operative rule here is the first principle of triage: THE SALVAGE OF LIFE (yours included) TAKES PRECEDENCE OVER THE SALVAGE OF LIMB. So if you did not have the wit to respond to the patient with the backboard, you are simply going to have to drag him as fast as you can in whatever way you can to a spot at a safe distance from that burning vehicle.

Now to step A—AIRWAY:

(2)__l__ Open the **airway,** with cervical spine stabilization.

(3)__o__ **Suction** the mouth, and insert an **oropharyngeal airway.**

On to step B—BREATHING:

(4)__e__ Look, listen, and feel for **breathing.**

(5)__k__ **Check the chest** for open wounds, unequal breath sounds.

(6)__h__ Administer **oxygen.**

Step C—CIRCULATION:

(7)__b__ **Control** obvious external **bleeding.**

(8)__g__ Assess **pulses** and **capillary refill.**

Step D—DISABILITY:

(9)__d__ Check the **pupils.**

(10)__m__ Assess the **level of consciousness** (AVPU scale).

Step E—EXPOSE:

(11)__i__ **Cut the patient's clothing** along the seams.

LOAD-AND-GO:

(12)__f__ **Immobilize** the patient on a backboard.

(13)__a__ **Start transport.**

(14)__p__ **Notify** the receiving hospital of the patient's condition and your estimated time of arrival.

(15)__c__ **Start an IV** with lactated Ringer's solution.

(16)__n__ Conduct the **secondary survey.**

9. In a mass casualty incident, there is sometimes a need to assign evacuation priorities. Clearly those in most immediate danger are moved first.

__3__ Conscious but can't move his legs
Spinal cord injury is serious but not immediately life-threatening.

__5__ Has a sprained left ankle

__1__ Massive maxillofacial trauma
The **airway** is in jeopardy here.

__1__ Flail chest

__4__ Fractured radius/ulna

__2__ Deteriorating level of consciousness; injury unknown

__2__ Second- and third-degree burns over 27 percent of the body surface area

__3__ Eye hanging out of its socket

__1__ Very restless, with cold, clammy skin and weak, rapid pulse
Shock is a first-priority condition, no matter what the cause.

__3__ Open fracture of the tibia

__1__ Removed from burning passenger car with facial burns and stridor
Another **airway** in jeopardy.

__1__ Weak, rapid pulse; distended neck veins; equal breath sounds; muffled heart sounds
Sounds like **cardiac tamponade,** definitely priority one.

10. Uncle Bernie is apparently suffering an **acute decompensation of chronic bronchitis,** and he probably is in **right heart failure** as well, to judge from his distended neck veins and peripheral edema.

   a. The steps of management are as follows:

   (1) Administer **oxygen** in high concentration. Ideally that would mean using a nonrebreathing mask, but this patient probably isn't going to tolerate a mask; so give him 4 to 6 liters per minute by nasal cannula.
   (2) Keep him in a **sitting position.**
   (3) If the patient will allow it, start an **IV lifeline** with D5/W to keep the vein open.
   (4) If there are no contraindications, administer a **beta-2 agonist,** such as albuterol or isoetharine, by metered-dose inhaler.
   (5) **Monitor** cardiac rhythm.

   b. Here is Uncle Bernie's ECG rhythm strip:

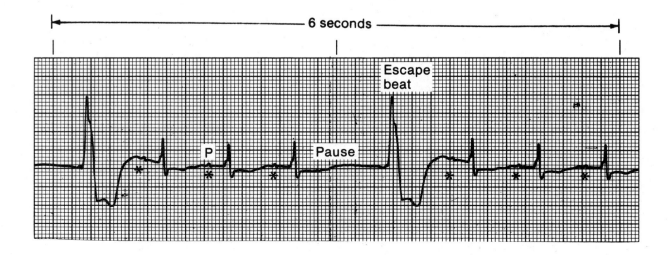

The rhythm is **mostly regular,** with an occasional interpolated extrasystole.
The rate is **80 per minute.**
P waves are **present** before every QRS, but there are two QRS complexes
   that are not preceded by a P wave and thus do not originate in the atrium.
The P–R interval is **0.20 second,** right on the borderline between normal and
   abnormal.
The QRS complexes are both **normal and abnormal.**
The easiest way to describe this rhythm is as **normal sinus rhythm with ventricular extrasystoles.** They are *not,* strictly speaking, premature ventricular contractions (PVCs), because they are not premature. They only kick in
   after a pause, when the SA node fails to fire. That suggests that there may
   be problems in the SA node, and the patient may in fact be suffering from
   what is called the **sick sinus syndrome.**
No treatment is indicated for this rhythm. Do *not* give lidocaine to treat the
   "PVCs," because they aren't PVCs—they are the body's attempt to keep
   up cardiac output despite periodic sinus node failure. If you abolish the
   escape beats, you may compromise cardiac output.

11. Here we have a classic story for acute myocardial infarction.

   a. The risk factors for coronary artery disease include

      (1) **Hypertension**
      (2) **Cigarette smoking**
      (3) **Diabetes**
      (4) **High serum cholesterol**
      (5) **Sedentary habits**
      (6) **Family history** of coronary artery disease or stroke
      (7) **Male sex**
      (8) **Obesity**

   b. As soon as you've heard this patient's description of his pain, you've heard
      enough to start treatment:

      (1) **Put the patient at ease**—physically and mentally: Place him in a **semi-
          recumbent position,** and maintain a **calm attitude.**
      (2) Administer **oxygen** by nasal cannula.
      (3) Start an **IV lifeline** with D5/W to keep a vein open.
      (4) **Monitor** cardiac rhythm.
      (5) Give something to **relieve pain**—either nitrous oxide or morphine sul-
          fate, 0.1 mg per kilogram IV.
      (6) Complete the **secondary survey.**
      (7) **Transport** without panic or haste (NO SIRENS!).

c. Here is the patient's ECG rhythm strip:

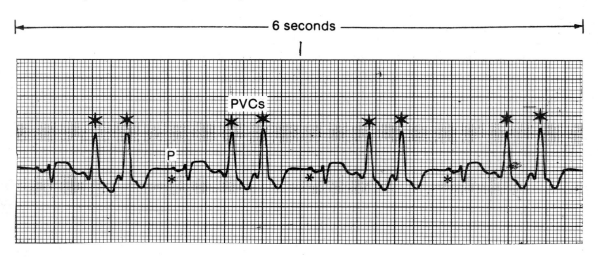

The rhythm is **irregular.**

The rate is **120 per minute.**

P waves are **present.** There is a QRS after every P wave, but not every QRS complex is preceded by a P wave.

The P–R interval is **0.12 second.**

The QRS complexes are **both normal and abnormal.**

The rhythm is **sinus rhythm with PVCs in salvos.**

These PVCs are potentially very dangerous, especially in the context of a probable acute myocardial infarction, for they may lead to ventricular tachycardia. The treatment is **lidocaine,** first an IV bolus of 1 mg per milliliter, followed by an infusion of 2 mg per minute.

12. Here we have a patient in coma of unknown cause.

   a. The easiest way to remember the possible causes of coma is through the mnemonic AEIOU-TIPS:

   A Alcohol/acidosis
   E Epilepsy/electrolyte imbalance/endocrine
   I Insulin (hypoglycemia)
   O Overdose/poisoning
   U Uremia
   T Trauma/temperature abnormalities
   I Infection
   P Psychogenic
   S Stroke/space-occupying lesion

   b. The steps in managing a patient in coma of unknown cause are as follows:

   (1) Establish an **airway** (hold off intubation, though, until you can assess the results of dextrose and naloxone).
   (2) Administer **oxygen.**
   (3) Establish an **IV lifeline** in a large vein.
   (4) Give **thiamine,** 100 mg slowly IV.
   (5) Give **50% dextrose,** 50 ml slowly IV, preferably after checking the blood glucose level.
   (6) If the patient does not waken in response to dextrose and there is reason to suspect narcotic overdose (e.g., pinpoint pupils), give **naloxone,** 0.8 mg slowly IV; if there is no response after 2 to 3 minutes, repeat the dose.

    (7) If there is no response to two doses of naloxone, **intubate** the trachea.

    (8) **Monitor** cardiac rhythm.

    (9) Keep a **flow sheet** of neurologic and vital signs.

    (10) **Protect the patient's eyes:** Tape them shut.

    (11) **Transport** the patient to the hospital.

  c. Here is the woman's ECG rhythm strip:

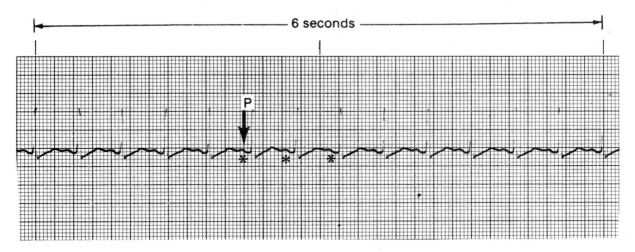

The rhythm is **regular.**

The rate is **130 per minute.**

P waves are **present.** They precede every QRS, and every P wave is followed by a QRS.

The P–R interval is **0.12 second.**

The QRS complexes are **normal.**

The rhythm is **sinus tachycardia.**

The treatment is to **treat the underlying cause.**

13. The 68-year-old woman with abdominal pain gives a story highly suggestive of **mesenteric thrombosis.** The steps in prehospital management are as follows:

  a. Place her in a **position of comfort.**

  b. Administer **oxygen.**

  c. **Notify** the receiving hospital of the type of case.

  d. Start **transport.**

  e. Start an **IV lifeline** en route.

  f. **Monitor** cardiac rhythm.

14. If you want to stay out of trouble on your night off, stay out of restaurants! The lady at the next table is suffering an **anaphylactic reaction,** apparently to something she ate. The sensation of a lump in the throat along with her squeaky voice indicate that she is in a lot of trouble. The steps in management are as follows:

  a. Give 1 : 1,000 **racemic epinephrine** by metered-dose inhaler to try to buy some time for the airway (but have your cricothyrotomy kit at hand just in case).

  b. Administer **oxygen** by nasal cannula.

  c. Start **transport.**

  d. Start an **IV lifeline** with a large-bore cannula and lactated Ringer's solution.

  e. Give **epinephrine.** Start by diluting 0.1 mg (0.1 ml) of 1 : 1,000 epinephrine in 10 ml of saline, and infuse it by Buratrol over 10 minutes. Meanwhile, prepare an infusion by adding 1 ml (1 mg) of 1 : 1,000 epinephrine to a 250-ml bag of D5/W, and piggyback it into your IV line, to run at 0.25 ml per minute as soon as your initial epinephrine dose has finished infusing.

  f. Give **diphenhydramine,** 50 mg IM.

  g. If you are a long way from the hospital, give **hydrocortisone,** 500 mg IV over 5 minutes.

15. Any patient rescued from a smoky fire must be considered to have inhaled toxic fumes until proved otherwise.

   a. When firemen tell you that carpets and mattresses were burning, you need to think about **hydrogen cyanide** inhalation, in addition to the **carbon monoxide** that nearly every fire victim inhales.

   b. Treatment of suspected cyanide poisoning is as follows:

   (1) Maintain an open **airway.**
   (2) Administer 100% **oxygen.**
   (3) **Start transport,** and **notify** the receiving hospital to prepare sodium thiosulfate.
   (4) Break one or two perles of **amyl nitrite** into a gauze pad and have the patient breathe through the gauze for 20 seconds out of every 1 to 2 minutes, followed each time by inhalation of 100% oxygen.
   (5) Start an **IV lifeline.**
   (6) **Monitor** cardiac rhythm.

16. The patient whom you are tempted to write off as "just another drunk" is in fact much more vulnerable to a whole host of injuries and medical problems than the more sober John Q. Citizen. The conditions to which alcoholics are particularly susceptible include

   a. **Subdural hematoma**

   b. **Gastrointestinal bleeding**

   c. **Pancreatitis**

   d. **Hypoglycemia**

   e. **Pneumonia**

   f. **Burns**

   g. **Hypothermia**

   h. **Seizures**

   i. **Cardiac dysrhythmias**

   j. **Cancer**

17. There's no need to be panicky about AIDS or any other communicable disease if you know something about it.

   a. There are only three ways in which AIDS can be transmitted from one person to another:

   (1) **Sexual** contact
   (2) Through **contaminated blood or blood products** (e.g., being stuck by a needle used on an HIV-positive person)
   (3) **From mother to fetus**

   b. Things one can do to minimize the risk of acquiring HIV from a patient are subsumed under the heading of "universal precautions":

   (1) Wear latex **gloves** for any contact with a patient's blood or body fluids.   .
   (2) Use **additional barrier protection** (e.g., mask, eye wear) for any procedures that may involve the splashing of blood or body fluids.
   (3) **Wash your hands** after every patient contact!
   (4) **Handle needles** and other sharp instruments **with extreme caution.** Do not recap needles. Dispose of them safely.

18. Weakness, dizziness, and shortness of breath may be the only signs that an elderly person is suffering an **acute myocardial infarction.** In this instance, the dyspnea probably signals **left heart failure** in the wake of the myocardial infarction, for there are widespread crackles in the lungs.

   a. The steps in treatment are as follows:

   (1) **Put the patient at ease,** physically and mentally.
   (2) Keep him **sitting up,** because of the congestive heart failure.
   (3) Administer **oxygen** by demand valve or nonrebreathing mask.
   (4) **Monitor** cardiac rhythm.
   (5) Start an **IV lifeline** with D5/W to a keep-open rate.
   (6) Check with medical command about specific treatment for left heart failure, such as
      (a) Nitroglycerin, 0.3 mg SL
      (b) Furosemide, 20 mg IV
      (If you are near the hospital, the doctor may prefer to delay pharmacotherapy until the patient reaches the emergency room, because of the likelihood of untoward reactions to drugs among elderly patients.)

b. Here is the patient's ECG rhythm strip:

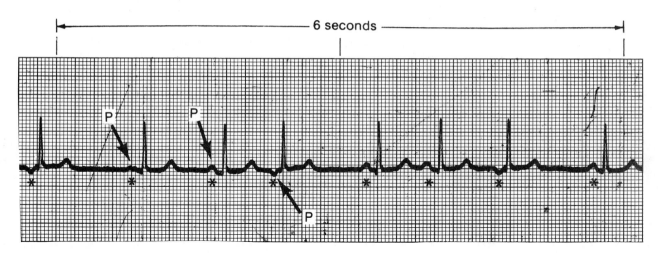

← — 6 seconds — →

The rhythm is **irregular.**
The rate is **70 per minute.**
P waves are **present** before every QRS, and every P wave is followed by a
  QRS, *but* something about the P wave is not quite right:
The P–R interval **varies from 0.11 to 0.16 second!**
QRS complexes are **normal.**
The rhythm is a **wandering atrial pacemaker;** that is what accounts for the
  variation in P-wave configuration and P–R interval.
No treatment is necessary for this rhythm.

19. Signs that should alert you to the seriousness of
    an asthmatic attack in a child include

    a. **Sleepiness**

    b. **Pulsus paradoxus**

    c. **Cyanosis**

    d. **Hyperinflation of the chest**

    e. A **silent chest**

20. Our thought for the day is an important point
    about seizures.

    a. **diazepam**   h. **cuff**

    b. **dextrose**   i. **hematemesis**

    c. **syncope**   j. **whole**

    d. **hemiparesis**   k. **OD**

    e. **dysarthria**   **Secret Message:** PATIENTS WHO DIE FROM
                                   SEIZURES DIE FROM HYPOXEMIA. SUCH
    f. **uterus**   DEATHS ARE EASILY PREVENTED.

    g. **vein**

21. Monday mornings are popular times for acute myocardial infarctions. According to one theory, some people just don't want to return to work after a nice week-end.

a. For whatever reason, this 68-year-old man has something ominous going on in his myocardium:

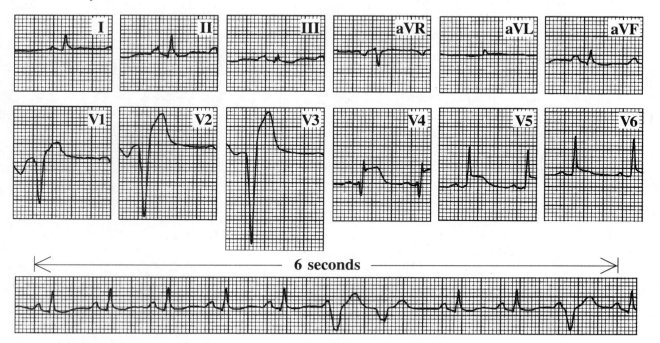

The RHYTHM is mostly **regular.**

The RATE is **100 per minute.**

P WAVES are **present** before all but three of the QRS complexes in the rhythm strip. There is a QRS complex after every P wave. (If you're a hotshot at ECGs, you may have noticed that the P waves are a bit bizarre in shape, rather large in lead III, and their axis is shifted to the right—all signs of right atrial enlargement, probably as a consequence of the patient's smoking history [and presumed chronic lung disease].)

The P–R INTERVAL is **0.18 second.**

The QRS complexes are **mostly normal** except for **three bizarre QRS complexes.**

The name of the rhythm is **normal sinus rhythm with multifocal PVCs.**

There are no Q WAVES deeper than 2 mm *yet!*

The S–T SEGMENTS are markedly **elevated in leads V₁ through V₄ or V₅.**

There are no abnormal T WAVE INVERSIONS (except after the PVCs, where one would expect to see them).

The portion of the heart affected is the **anterior wall.**

The pathophysiologic process is **injury.**

b. Even without these ECG findings, the patient would have to be treated for an acute myocardial infarction because he has a very good story. What the ECG adds to his management is some important information for the emergency room (that the patient has ECG evidence of an ischemic process) and for the specific drug management (he has salvos of multifocal PVCs, so he'll need lidocaine). His treatment, therefore, is as follows:

(1) Put the patient mentally and physically **at ease** (calm handling; semirecumbent position).

(2) Administer **oxygen** right away.

(3) Start an **IV lifeline** with a microdrip infusion set.

(4) Record the first set of **vital signs,** and start a flow sheet.

(5) Provide **pain relief** (start with a trial of nitroglycerin; if that doesn't help, give morphine, 0.1 mg/kg in titrated IV doses or nitrous oxide).

(6) Once you have the results of the 12-lead ECG, **notify the receiving hospital** of the patient's story, vital signs, ECG findings, and your estimated time of arrival.

(7) Obtain orders to give **lidocaine,** first a bolus of 1 mg per kilogram, followed by an infusion of 2 mg per minute.

(8) **Transport expeditiously,** without sirens if possible. Administer half an **aspirin** tablet and start a magnesium sulfate infusion en route to the hospital if those interventions are part of your local protocol.

22. Beware of a chief complaint of "indigestion" in a middle-aged man!

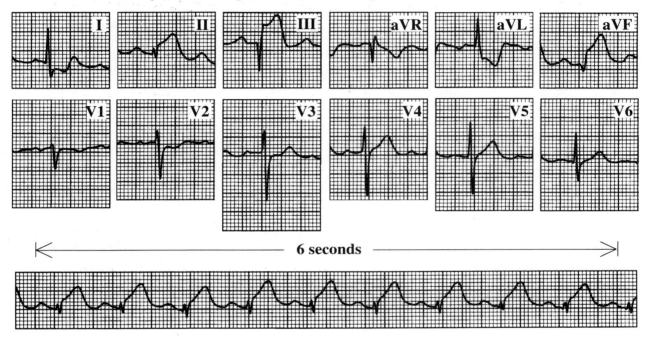

6 seconds

The RHYTHM is **regular.**

The RATE is **90 per minute.**

P WAVES are **present** before every QRS, and there is a QRS after every P wave.

The P–R INTERVAL is **0.20 second.**

The QRS COMPLEXES are **normal.**

The name of the rhythm is **normal sinus rhythm.** If you want to call it borderline first-degree AV block, you may, but it is *very* borderline!

There are no Q WAVES deeper than 2 mm. What about lead III? you ask. Recall the definition of a Q wave: It is an *initial* downward deflection of the QRS complex when there is no upward deflection preceding it. Now look *very carefully* at lead III. There is a tiny little upstroke before the downstroke of the QRS, so what you are looking at in lead III is not a deep Q wave but a deep S wave.

The S–T SEGMENTS are **elevated in leads II, III, and aVF.** (You can see the reciprocal changes of S–T depression in the leads that look at the heart from the opposite direction: I and aVL.)

There are no abnormally INVERTED T WAVES (T wave inversion is normal in lead aVR and sometimes also in V_1).

The portion of the heart affected is the **inferior wall.** That's why the patient feels as if he has "indigestion."

The pathophysiologic process is **injury.**

31
Heat Exposure

1. a. In order for the human body to maintain a nearly constant core temperature, it must balance heat loss against heat production.

Sources of Body Heat
(1) **Basal metabolism**
(2) **Exercise**
(3) **Absorption of heat**

Ways of Shedding Heat
(1) **Radiation**
(2) **Convection**
(3) **Conduction**
(4) **Evaporation of sweat**

b. The body's mechanisms for dissipating excess heat have certain limitations. All of the mechanisms, first of all, depend on **peripheral vasodilatation** to shunt blood from the core to the body surface. Three of the body's cooling mechanisms, furthermore, require a temperature gradient between the body and the outside in order to be effective. None of those three mechanisms—**radiation, convection,** or **conduction**—can work if the outside is not at least a few degrees cooler than the body core. Finally, one of the body's cooling mechanisms is dependent on the ambient humidity. When the humidity is high, that mechanism—namely **evaporation of sweat**—is ineffective in lowering the core temperature.

c. A hatless hiker standing still on a mountaintop on a windless day loses heat from his head by **radiation.** A breeze picks up. Now the hiker loses heat by **convection** as well.

d. A white-water enthusiast who capsizes his canoe in a swift-running stream loses body heat by **conduction.**

e. A soldier on maneuvers in the desert, in ambient temperatures of over 37.7°C (100°F) can shed heat only by **evaporation of sweat.**

2. Heat is a form of cardiovascular stress because the body responds to heat by vasodilatation. Increasing the diameter of the blood vessels increases their volume, so the **heart must increase its output** to prevent a fall in blood pressure. It does so by increasing both its rate and stroke volume, which inevitably means an **increase in cardiac work.**

3. A person's risk of suffering significant heat illness in response to heat stress can be increased by

a. **Exertion** or anything else that increases endogenous heat production (e.g., **fever, hyperthyroidism**)

b. **High humidity**

c. **Obesity**

d. **Diabetes**

e. **Alcoholism**

f. **Dehydration**

g. **Cardiovascular** or **cerebrovascular** disease

h. Heavy or occlusive **clothing**

i. **Drugs** such as diuretics, some tranquilizers

4. a. The fullback who is acting "crazy" after practicing on a hot, humid afternoon is most probably suffering from **exertional heat stroke.** You were fortunate to be able to record a temperature and obtain conclusive evidence. In many cases the patient will be too combative to allow you to measure the temperature, and you will have to suspect the diagnosis on the basis of his symptoms and signs alone.

b. The steps in managing exertional heat stroke in this patient are as follows:

(1) Move him to a **cooler environment,** pref-

erably your air-conditioned ambulance with the fans blowing.

(2) **Strip** off his clothing and football gear.

(3) Apply **ice packs to his flanks** while massaging his neck and torso. **Spray** the patient with tepid water, and keep a **fan** blowing in his direction.

(4) Start an **IV lifeline** with **D5/W to keep the vein open.**

(5) **Monitor** temperature and cardiac rhythm.

(6) **Be prepared for seizures.**

(7) **Transport** without delay.

5. a. The running back writhing in pain is most likely suffering from **heat cramps.**

b. The steps in treating him are as follows:

(1) Tell the coach to stop massaging the boy's legs!

(2) Move the boy to a **cooler environment.**

(3) If he is not nauseated, give him **salt-containing fluids to drink** (at least a quart).

(4) **Do not allow the boy to return to practice that day.** He should go home and rest in a cool place. Instruct him to seek medical attention if he develops headaches, dizziness, nausea, or severe fatigue.

6. a. The quarterback may indeed be coming down with mononucleosis, but it could be fatal to miss a case of **heat exhaustion.**

b. You should treat him in the field as follows:

(1) Move the boy to a **cooler environment.**

(2) Remove most of his clothing, down to his undershorts, and **sponge him** with cool water.

(3) Start an **IV with lactated Ringer's,** and run it wide open.

(4) **Monitor** cardiac rhythm and vital signs.

(5) **Transport** to the hospital.

By now, one would think Coach would have reached the conclusion that football practice in the searing heat is not healthy for a teenager. But you should in any case suggest to him that if he *must* conduct practice during the "dog days" of August, he should schedule the heavy exertion for the early morning and late afternoon hours.

7. a. The baby at the supermarket is suffering from **classic heat stroke.** The inside of an automobile that is parked in the sun in 37.7°C (100°F) tem-

peratures can very quickly reach a temperature of around 82°C (180°F)—not high enough to bake a cake, perhaps, but certainly high enough to bake a baby. This infant is in severe danger and may die.

b. Treatment is extremely urgent:

(1) Open the **airway.** Intubate as soon as you have a chance.

(2) Administer **oxygen.**

(3) **Strip** off all the baby's clothing.

(4) **Spray and fan** continuously until you reach the hospital.

(5) If you are able to do so, **start an IV** en route to the hospital with 5% dextrose in ½ normal saline, and run it at about 150 ml per hour.

(6) **Monitor** rectal temperature.

(7) **Transport** without delay.

8. a. The dog days of summer also put *you* at risk of heat illness, especially if you have to carry heat-stricken, 300-pound patients down four flights of stairs. So take some precautions to protect yourself on very hot days:

(1) Wear **light-colored, loose-fitting clothing.** If your service does not have an appropriate summer uniform, ask your union to demand one!

(2) **Stay in cool places** whenever you can.

(3) **Park the ambulance in the shade.**

(4) **Increase your fluid intake.** Carry cold drinks with you in the vehicle, and partake frequently.

(5) Wear a **cool, damp towel around your neck.**

(6) Put a **fan on the dashboard** of the ambulance.

(7) Seek medical attention at the first symptom of heat illness.

b. Of course, in order to seek attention at the first symptom of heat illness, you have to know what the symptoms *are!*

(1) **Headache**

(2) **Fatigue** or lack of energy

(3) **Dizziness**

(4) **Nausea** or vomiting

32
Cold Exposure

1. Let's hear it for all the Moms out there! They've been right all along.

   a. "Don't go out without a hat and scarf; it's freezing out there."
   Mother was right because **most heat loss from the body occurs from the head and neck.** By trapping some of that heat within insulating layers, a hat and scarf can reduce convective heat loss from above the shoulders.

   b. "Stop rolling around in the snow. You'll get a death of a chill."
   Mother was right because **snow conducts heat away from the body faster than air does.** And when the snow melts and your clothes get wet, cooling by conduction is even faster.

   c. "Get out of those wet clothes this minute."
   Mother was right because wearing wet clothing promotes **heat loss by conduction** while the clothes remain wet **and by evaporation** as the clothes dry.

   d. "Those skates are much too tight. Your toes will fall off."
   Mother was right because **anything that interferes with the circulation to the extremities predisposes to frostbite.**

   e. "Make sure you wear your windbreaker. It's blowing a gale out there."
   Mother was right because **exposure to the wind increases heat loss by convection.**

   f. "Eat. Eat. You have to have something to keep going in this weather."
   Mother was right because **metabolic heat production requires fuel,** so one needs to maintain one's caloric intake, especially in the form of carbohydrates, before anticipated exposure to cold temperatures.

2. It's important to follow Mother's advice because, by itself, the body does not have a lot of ways to defend itself against the cold. The three ways it can do so are

   a. By **peripheral vasoconstriction,** to shunt blood away from the body shell to the body core

   b. By **shivering,** to increase heat production by skeletal muscle

   c. By **increasing the basal metabolic rate,** to increase overall metabolic heat production

3. Some people are more likely to suffer cold injury than others.

   a. Factors that predispose a person to *frostbite* include:

   (1) **Tight clothing,** especially tight shoes or gloves
   (2) **Smoking**
   (3) **Hunger, fatigue,** or **dehydration**
   (4) **Hypothermia** (generalized cooling)

   b. Factors that predispose a person to suffer *hypothermia* include

   (1) **Old age**
   (2) **Infancy**
   (3) **Alcoholism**
   (4) **Chronic illness**
   (5) **Poor planning** for outdoor activity; unpreparedness

4. There are a lot of folk remedies for frostbite. Some of them are downright dangerous. Do you know the truth about frostbite?

   a. A partially frostbitten extremity is best warmed in front of a campfire or heater.

FALSE. Radiant heat is *not* a good way to warm a frostbitten extremity. Use conductive heating, such as putting a frostbitten hand into the armpit.

b. In deep frostbite, the extremity feels cold and rock hard.
TRUE. If there is any "give" when you push down on the skin, the frostbite is probably superficial.

c. If rescue circumstances require it, a patient with deep frostbite may walk on a frostbitten leg without causing major additional damage to the limb.
TRUE. Ordinarily, we don't like to have a patient walk on an injured leg. But sometimes it may be the only way to rescue someone from a remote area, and if his limb is frozen solid, he probably won't do it much more harm.

d. Antibiotic ointment should be applied gently over frostbitten areas to prevent infection.
FALSE! NEVER PUT GOO ON A BURN—from heat *or* cold.

e. A frostbitten extremity will be excruciatingly painful until it is rewarmed.
FALSE. The opposite is true! A frostbitten extremity will be numb so long as it is frozen, but will become excruciatingly painful as it is rewarmed.

f. Frost nip most often affects the tips of the ears, nose, fingers, and toes.
TRUE.

5. The slang expression "Cool it!" means to take it easy, to simmer down. And that is precisely what happens to the major systems of the body when cooled: They all slow down.

BODY SYSTEM	EFFECTS OF HYPOTHERMIA
Central nervous system	**Apathy, lethargy** **Impaired reasoning** **Dysarthria** **Ataxic gait, incoordination**
Cardiovascular system	**Contracted intravascular space** **Increased blood viscosity with sludging in the capillaries** **Edema** **Bradycardia, dysrhythmias, susceptibility to ventricular fibrillation**
Respiratory system	**Slowing of respiratory rate** **Increased tracheobronchial secretions** **Decreased cough and gag reflexes**
Muscular system	**Weakness and stiffness**
Metabolic system	**Hypoglycemia** **Ketoacidosis** **Slowed hepatic drug metabolism**

6. It only happens to paramedics—that a ski vacation turns into a search-and-rescue mission.

a. The first skier has **deep frostbite.** You don't really have the means to rewarm his leg in the field, nor can you ensure that it won't simply freeze again during transport to the ski lodge. The management therefore is as follows:

(1) **Move him to a sheltered place,** like that cabin behind the trees, until the snowmobile comes.

(2) Give him some **calories,** preferably a candy bar or some other carbohydrate source. Give him a hot, sweet drink if you're carrying a thermos.

(3) **Leave the frostbitten extremity frozen.** Don't attempt any rewarming in the field.

(4) **Pad the frostbitten leg** to prevent it from being bruised during transport.

(5) **Protect the rest of the patient's body from the cold** with insulating blankets.

b. The second skier has a more **superficial frostbite.**

   (1) **Move him to a sheltered place,** like that cabin behind the trees, until the snowmobile comes.

   (2) Give him some **calories,** preferably a candy bar or some other carbohydrate source. Give him a hot, sweet drink if you're carrying a thermos.

   (3) **Try to warm the frostbitten foot** with your hands (or by putting it in *your* armpit!).

   (4) **Pad the frostbitten leg** to prevent it from being bruised during transport.

   (5) **Protect the rest of the patient's body from the cold** with insulating blankets.

c. The third lost skier is suffering from **severe hypothermia.** Only his very occasional breathing tips you off that he's not (yet) in cardiac arrest.

   (1) In managing him:

      (a) So long as his airway is not obstructed, it's best not to touch him at all until the ambulance arrives. Send someone down to the road to intercept the ambulance, help carry equipment, and guide the paramedics to the patient.

      (b) **Move the patient VERY gently onto the stretcher,** and **carry the stretcher VERY gently** to the ambulance.

      (c) Maintain the airway manually until the patient has been well ventilated with 100% oxygen by bag-valve-mask for at least 3 minutes. Then **intubate** the trachea rapidly and smoothly.

      (d) Apply **monitoring electrodes,** and check the cardiac rhythm. If asystole should occur, start CPR, but give **basic life support (BLS) only.** If you see *ventricular fibrillation* (VF) on the monitor, you may try a series of **three defibrillatory shocks;** but if VF persists, put the defibrillator away and just continue basic life support all the way to the hospital.

      (e) If the patient's clothing is wet, GENTLY **cut away wet clothing and replace it with dry blankets.**

      (f) **Notify** the receiving hospital of the nature of the case and your estimated time of arrival (ETA).

      (g) Keep the ambulance interior around 15.5°C (60°F).

      (h) Instruct the driver to make it a **smooth ride** to the hospital.

   (2) Any number of things could trigger ventricular fibrillation in this very vulnerable patient:

      (a) Attempts to insert an **oropharyngeal airway** or **endotracheal tube**

      (b) Aggressive **artificial ventilation**

      (c) Administration of **sodium bicarbonate**

      (d) Attempts to start a **central IV line** (e.g., a subclavian)

      (e) **Rapid external warming,** for example, if the temperature inside the ambulance is very warm

      (f) **Rough handling**

7. The speedboat driver who is plunged into cold lake water is a likely candidate for **immersion hypothermia,** which can occur after relatively short exposure because of the rapidity with which water conducts heat away from the body. In managing such a case, you should observe these guidelines:

   a. Try to **prevent the victim from exerting himself.** Toss him a rope and pull him to shore, or send one of the other boats over to haul him aboard and bring him ashore. But in any case, discourage him from thrashing about in the water.

   b. As soon as you have the victim ashore, **carry him to a sheltered place,** preferably the inside of your ambulance, and **cut away his wet clothes.** Be sure to **keep him absolutely still.**

   c. **Monitor** his cardiac rhythm.

   d. **Cover him with insulating materials, and cover those with blankets.**

   e. Wrap chemical **hot packs** in towels, and place them in his **armpits** and near the **groin.**

   f. Give him a **hot, caffeine-free, sugary drink.**

   g. Keep him **recumbent.**

   h. **Transport** him to the hospital.

8. The "vagrant" in the bus station represents a classic example of the kind of case that is too often misdiagnosed.

   a. Any patient found in the circumstances described must be suspected to be suffering from

      (1) **Hypothermia**
      (2) **Hypoglycemia**
      (3) **Closed head injury**

   or all of the above until proved otherwise.

b. In view of those possibilities, the steps in management are as follows:

(1) Administer **oxygen.**
(2) Complete the **secondary survey.** Obtain vital signs, and check for injuries with particular attention to the head.
(3) Start an **IV lifeline** with D5/W.
(4) Give **thiamine,** 50 mg IM and 50 mg IV, followed by **50% dextrose,** 50 ml IV.
(5) **Monitor** cardiac rhythm.
(6) Cover the patient with warm **blankets.**
(7) **Transport** to the hospital.

9. Even our nursery rhyme companions were in danger of cold exposure:

a. When the three little kittens lost their mittens, they became most vulnerable to **frostbite** of the paws.

b. Sitting on an ice-cold tuffet, Miss Muffet was losing heat by **conduction** from her bottom to the tuffet and by **radiation,** mostly from her head and neck to the surrounding atmosphere. If there was any breeze, she was losing heat by convection as well.

c. **Jack Sprat** has a greater risk of hypothermia than his wife, for he has less natural insulation.

d. Little Jack Horner **had the right idea** eating his Christmas pie before going out into the cold, for he knew that **one needs calories to increase internal heat production** in cold weather.

e. When the wind blows, the cradle rocks, and baby **loses heat by convection.**

10. Our thought for the day affects mostly those who engage in wilderness rescue.

a. **shell**
b. **afterdrop**
c. **wind**
d. **frost nip**
e. **blister**
f. **booze**
g. **hypoglycemia**
h. **fatty**
i. **external**
j. **mittens**
k. **firm**
l. **totter**
m. **tie**
n. **I**

Secret Message: DO NOT ATTEMPT TO REWARM A FROSTBITTEN EXTREMITY IF THERE IS ANY POSSIBILITY OF REFREEZING.

33
Radiation Exposure

1. a. The three forms of ionizing radiation of concern to EMS providers are

   (1) **Alpha particles**
   (2) **Beta particles**
   (3) **Gamma rays**

   b. Of those forms of radiation, **alpha particles** can be stopped by something as thin as a piece of paper. **Beta particles** can be stopped by heavy clothing. But **gamma rays** cannot be stopped except by lead shielding, a concrete wall, or a similar heavy barrier.

   c. Although alpha and beta particles are easily blocked by clothing, they *can* **enter the body through open wounds** or by being **inhaled or swallowed,** especially when they are carried in smoke or dust.

   d. To protect oneself, therefore, from ingesting or inhaling alpha or beta particles at the site of a "dirty" radiation accident, one should

   (1) Wear a **filtration mask.**
   (2) Wear **protective clothing.**
   (3) **Refrain from smoking, eating, or drinking.**

2. Your best protection from a radioactive source can be summarized as **T-D-S:**

   a. **Time** (Keep exposure time to a minumum.)

   b. **Distance** (Get as far from the source as you can.)

   c. **Shielding** (Get behind heavy concrete barriers or the like.)

3. The patient who suffered accidental exposure to ionizing radiation at work exemplifies a "clean" radiation accident.

   a. **No special precautions are needed** in caring for this patient. There is no contamination. He is not radioactive, nor are his current surroundings.

   b. **Yes, there is evidence suggesting serious radiation injury**—the patient's complaints of **nausea.** While nausea may be simply a part of a person's response to fear and stress, in a patient who has had significant radiation exposure, nausea must be considered a serious sign until proved otherwise. The earlier nausea comes on, the more serious the situation is likely to be.

   c. If the patient was exposed to a source emitting 2,000R per hour for 15 minutes (0.25 hr), his total exposure was

   TOTAL EXPOSURE = 2,000R/hr × 0.25 hr
                  = **500R**

   d. Had the patient been working 5 feet from the radioactive source rather than only 1 foot away, his exposure would have been reduced by a factor of

   $$\frac{1}{(5)^2} = \frac{1}{25}$$

   That is, **he would have received only ¹⁄₂₅ the dose** he did receive, or 20R.

4. Transport accidents involving radioactive materials are likely to increase in frequency, so it is important to have a clear plan of action for such events and to know what you should and should not do at the scene.

   a. The ambulance should be parked upwind from the wrecked truck.
   TRUE, in order to minimize exposure to dust-borne radioactive particles.

   b. Once the fire is extinguished, the danger of radioactive contamination has passed.
   FALSE. The danger has only just begun. Smoke, dust, and the water used by the fire

fighters to extinguish the blaze may all be carrying radioactive particles.

c. The driver should be carefully examined from head to toe, then extricated from the truck cabin on short and long backboards.
FALSE. There simply isn't time to do things the way we'd ordinarily like to do them. Salvage of life takes priority over salvage of limb, and so long as the driver is sitting on top of a "hot" radioactive emitter, his life is in immediate danger.

d. If extrication will require more than a minute or two, rescuers should work in shifts.
TRUE. The object of the exercise is to limit each rescuer's exposure to the shortest time possible.

e. A dosimeter film badge should be clipped onto your protective clothing before you enter an area potentially contaminated with radioactive dust.
FALSE. Yes, a dosimeter badge should be clipped on, but it should be placed *underneath* your protective clothing, not on top of it. If the dosimeter badge is pinned *onto* your protective clothing, you'll have to pitch it into a waste container together with your protective clothes before you leave the contaminated area. In any case, what you *want* to measure is not the radiation reaching your clothing, but the radiation that potentially reached your *body*.

f. Once the patient is removed from the wreckage, first priority goes to decontaminating him.
FALSE. FIRST PRIORITY *ALWAYS* GOES TO THE ABCs. Whatever radioactive dust may or may not be contaminating the patient's skin, it does *not* pose an immediate (or even long-term) threat to life. An obstructed airway or uncontrolled bleeding does. So don't lose sight of your priorities in the panic that often surrounds radiation accidents.

5. Civil Defense personnel tell you that the emission rate 1 foot from the overturned truck is 1,000R per hour.

a. If the driver was trapped for 15 minutes (0.25 hour), he was exposed to
TOTAL EXPOSURE = 1,000R/hr × 0.25 hr
= **250R**

b. By moving him 20 feet away from the wrecked vehicle, you can reduce his exposure rate to
$$\frac{1}{(20)^2} = \frac{1}{400}$$
that is, ¼₀₀ his exposure at the source, or about **2.5R per hour.**

c. Before moving the patient from the contaminated work zone, you need to

(1) **Remove his clothes,** and stash them in a heavy-duty plastic garbage bag with a "radioactive" label.
(2) **Remove your own protective clothing,** and stash that in the same manner.
(3) **Complete the secondary survey.**
(4) Give whatever **stabilizing treatment** is necessary (e.g., cover wounds, splint fractures).
(5) Pass through the **radiation checkpoint** to make sure you are not bringing contaminated items out of the contaminated zone.

6. Our thought for the day may seem obvious when it's printed in a textbook, but it is the first thing that everyone forgets at the scene of a radiation accident!

a. **rad**
b. **beta**
c. **alpha**
d. **vomiting**
e. **ion**
f. **time**
g. **distance**
h. **upwind**
i. **Chernobyl**
j. **deface**
k. **teen**
l. **toe**
m. **cheese**
n. **Kate**

Secret Message: THE MEDICAL NEEDS OF THE PATIENT ALWAYS TAKE PRECEDENCE OVER DECONTAMINATION.

34
Hazardous Materials

1. It's a bit scary, isn't it, to realize what's inside those trucks and trains that are whizzing through your region day and night?

2. The most important step in dealing with a hazmat incident is recognizing that a hazmat situation exists in the first place. If you have to wait until you start to feel sick from your own exposure to a poisonous material before you figure out that the situation might be dangerous, you've waited too long.

H   Two-car collision downtown
If either of those cars is on fire, you may be dealing with toxic products of the combustion of automobile upholstery, including **phosgene, chlorine,** and **hydrogen chloride.**

H   Apartment-house fire
Any fire produces toxic fumes, and at the least you need to think about **carbon monoxide** and **cyanide.**

H   Three municipal workers collapsed in a sewer
When three people get sick in the same place, you have to consider an environmental source; and when the place is a sewer, consider sewer gas, or **hydrogen sulfide.**

H   Two police officers injured in a riot
The **tear gases** used to quell urban violence may have toxic effects on a large number of exposed persons.

__H__   Fire in a garden supply store warehouse
The garden store is one of the places you are likely to find stocks of **organophosphate pesticides,** which are the very same compounds that have been used in wartime as nerve gases.

__H__   Semitrailer overturned on the interstate
A semitrailer might be carrying just about **anything,** and the chances are very high that the contents are toxic.

__H__   Two "men down" on the maintenance staff of the municipal swimming pool
Most large swimming pools are chlorinated using **chlorine gas,** and the use of chlorine gas for that purpose has led to numerous mass exposures at hotels and community recreation centers.

__H__   Freight train struck car on level crossing
Like the semitrailer, the freight train has to be regarded as suspect until proved otherwise; it could be carrying **anything.**

__H__   Fire in a furniture factory
Every fire is potentially dangerous. A fire in a furniture factory is likely to involve the toxic products of combustion from upholstery and wood, including **ammonia, hydrogen cyanide, acrolein, acetaldehyde, acetic acid,** and **formic acid**—at least six good reasons to don a self-contained breathing apparatus!

All of the calls listed, then, might involve hazardous materials. That is the whole message of this chapter.

3. Three potential sources of information regarding the nature of the train's cargo are

  a. The **USDOT placard** on the side of each car

  b. The **waybill** and the **consist** carried by the conductor

  c. The **conductor** himself

4. Once you know that you are dealing with a hazardous cargo, you should take the following steps:

  a. **Radio your dispatcher** with details of the accident and **request help:**

  (1) **Hazmat team**
  (2) **Fire department** with heavy rescue gear
  (3) **Police** for crowd and traffic control
  (4) At least one **ambulance** for every two estimated casualties on the road

  b. Start setting up a **hazard zone** and getting all ambulatory persons out of the zone.

  c. **Do not enter the hazard zone yourself** unless you have EPA Level A protection, that is, chemical-resistant encapsulated clothing, gloves, and shoe covers; a self-contained breathing apparatus; and so on.

  d. Once casualties have been brought out of the hazard zone to your contaminated work zone:

  (1) Do the **ABCs.**
  (2) **Remove the casualty's clothing,** and stash it in a heavy-duty plastic bag.
  (3) **Wash** the casualty thoroughly in warm, soapy water, taking care to collect the runoff in some sort of container.
  (4) Administer **oxygen.**
  (5) Give whatever **treatment** is required according to the patient's injuries and condition.
  (6) **Notify** the receiving hospital.
  (7) **Transport.**

5. It is just as important to know what *not* to do at a hazmat incident as to know what *to* do.

  a. If there are no unusual odors at the scene of a transport accident, it is safe to assume that hazardous materials are not involved.
  FALSE. What does carbon monoxide smell like? What do beta particles smell like? Not every toxic material has a bad smell or any smell at all, for that matter.

  b. EMS personnel at a hazmat incident may become contaminated with toxic materials by touching a patient who is contaminated.
  TRUE. That's why it's necessary to wear protective clothing and to go through decontamination procedures after the call.

  c. In decontaminating a hazmat victim, one should use a brush to scrub the skin briskly with strong soap and lots of water.
  FALSE. Brisk rubbing with a brush may abrade the skin and permit the hazardous material to enter the body. Use a *mild* soap and *gentle* washing.

  d. When decontamination is carried out at the scene, it is unnecessary to notify the receiving hospital that you are bringing in a hazmat case.
  FALSE. You cannot be certain that decontamination was 100 percent complete. The hospital needs lead time to activate its own hazmat protocol before the patients arrive.

e. It is preferable that an ambulance team that was not involved in treating and decontaminating the patient be summoned to transport the patient to the hospital.

TRUE. Doing so reduces the chances of carrying contaminated materials from the scene to the hospital.

35
Obstetrics and Emergency Childbirth

1. Were you able to find all 25 words?

```
G R A A F I A N F O L L I C L E C
A I L H E A P R O V U L A T E C H
M A U M B I L I C A L C O R D R I
E R M O P E A L L R V T E G R O N
N I T N R F C L O Y A U R R O W E
A P E R I N E U M P G I L A V N S
R A R E M O N T O R I L O V E I E
C E M L I S T R U I N A V I A N X
H O M A P L A I N S A W N D O G S
E A T B A B Y I C R I E D T V U P
R I B O R B O N E S U T E R U S T
Y O U R A Y P R E P A R T U M B Y
A B O R T I O N C E I C H E E S E
```

At last! The authoritative word is out about where babies come from. Babies do not, as it turns out, come in packages delivered by the stork. Babies are the result of **sex**! In fact, our story begins at **menarche**, the time when a girl first starts having menstrual periods. Each menstrual cycle thereafter is a preparation for pregnancy.

On around the fourteenth day of the cycle, women **ovulate**, that is, a **graafian follicle** located in the left or right **ovary** ruptures, with the release of an egg, or **ovum**. If a sperm should happen along just about the time when the egg is released, fertilization may take place, usually in the **fallopian tube**, where the fertilized egg remains for about 3 days before entering the **uterus** and implanting into the endometrium. Between the third and eighth week of development, the fertilized egg is called an **embryo**. Thereafter, it is called a **fetus** until delivery. After delivery, it is officially a **baby**.

Specialized structures develop during pregnancy to support the developing baby. The baby is enclosed in a fluid-filled **amniotic sac**. It is nourished by a large, vascular organ of pregnancy called the **placenta**, which attaches to the baby via the **umbilical cord**.

At about 40 weeks after conception, the baby reaches maturity, or **term**, and is ready to make its debut in the world. (When a baby is expelled early, before the twentieth to twenty-eighth week of gestation, the woman is said to have had a miscarriage, or **abortion**.) At that point, the woman goes into **labor,** the process by which the baby is expelled from the womb, and the pregnant, or **gravid,** womb begins contracting. As it does so, the **cervix** progressively effaces and dilates until the womb becomes continuous with the birth canal, or **vagina.** The period of uterine contractions will be of shorter duration in a **primipara,** a woman who has already had a delivery in the past, than in a nullipara. Delivery is imminent when the presenting part becomes visible, that is, when **crowning** occurs. At that point, it is important to control the rate at which the baby emerges, for otherwise there may be injury to the external genitalia (**vulva**) or to the skin between the anus and the opening of the birth canal, an area called the **perineum.** All events occurring before delivery are called antepartum, or **prepartum,** while those occurring after delivery are called postpartum.

2. The functions of the placenta include

   a. **Respiratory gas exchange**

   b. **Transport of nutrients**

   c. **Excretion of wastes**

   d. **Transfer of heat**

   e. **Hormone production**

   f. **Formation of a barrier against harmful substances**

3. a. The 22-year-old who has passed blood and tissue through the vagina and is showing signs of hemorrhagic shock is most likely having an **incomplete abortion** (answer **C**). The passage of tissue indicates some sort of abortion, and the fact that she is continuing to bleed suggests that there is still tissue within the uterus.

   b. She should be **treated for shock,** for her vital signs indicate that she is already in shock:

   (1) Ensure an adequate **airway.** Anticipate vomiting, and have suction at hand.

   (2) Administer **oxygen.**

   (3) Keep the patient **recumbent.**

   (4) Start **transport.**

   (5) Start at least one **large-bore IV** en route to the hospital, and run lactated Ringer's wide open.

4. a. The 32-year-old woman has good reason to be "feeling poorly": She is carrying a dead fetus in her uterus; that is, she has a **missed abortion** (answer **D**). Her history is typical: a threatened abortion earlier in the pregnancy that seemed to get better, but failure of the pregnancy to develop normally. By 6 months,

her uterine fundus should be palpable above the umbilicus, not just barely above the pelvic brim.

   b. The prehospital management of missed abortion is simply to **transport** the patient to the hospital, where surgical evacuation of the uterus will be required.

5. a. The primigravida with painless vaginal bleeding is experiencing a **threatened abortion** (answer **A**). The absence of contractions indicates that the abortion is not yet inevitable.

   b. The prehospital treatment of threatened abortion is simply to **transport,** while providing **reassurance** to the patient that there is every chance the pregnancy will go to term.

6. a. The 16-year-old who went to the back-street abortionist has suffered one of the most common results: **septic abortion** (answer **E**). By the time you reach the scene, the girl already has signs of septic shock, and she may die.

   b. The prehospital management is to **treat for shock:**

   (1) Ensure an adequate **airway.** Anticipate vomiting, and have suction at hand.
   (2) Administer **oxygen.**
   (3) Keep the patient **recumbent.**
   (4) Start **transport.**
   (5) Start at least one **large-bore IV** en route to the hospital, and run lactated Ringer's wide open.

7. a. The 26-year-old veteran of three previous miscarriages is probably correct; she seems to be having yet another, that is, an **inevitable abortion** (answer **B**). The severe cramping and uterine contractions that accompany her

vaginal bleeding bode ill for the continuation of the pregnancy.

b. The prehospital treatment of inevitable abortion is expectant treatment for shock:

(1) Start **transport.**
(2) En route to the hospital, start a **large-bore IV** with lactated Ringer's, and run it as rapidly as necessary to maintain the blood pressure.

8. This case concerns a 36-year-old grand multip with third-trimester bleeding.

a. Three possible causes of third-trimester bleeding are

(1) **Abruptio placentae**
(2) **Placenta previa**
(3) **Uterine rupture**

b. In this particular case, the most likely diagnosis is **placenta previa.** Among the characteristic features of placenta previa manifested by this patient are the following:

(1) *Painless* vaginal bleeding. (There is severe pain with placental abruption or uterine rupture.)
(2) *Bright red* blood. (In abruption, bleeding is dark.)
(3) The *fetus remains viable.*
(4) The *abdomen* is *soft and nontender.*

c. The steps in prehospital management are

(1) Keep the patient **recumbent,** on her **left side.**
(2) Administer **oxygen.**
(3) Start **transport,** and **notify** the receiving hospital.
(4) Start **at least one large-bore IV,** and administer lactated Ringer's wide open.

9. a. The lady with the fainting spells is most probably suffering from **supine hypotensive syndrome** (answer **E**), since her pulse and blood pressure improved very quickly after she turned to her side and took the weight of her uterus off her inferior vena cava. Nonetheless, you can't take a chance on missing a concealed hemorrhage. In fact, it is women whose volume status is already marginal who are most vulnerable to the supine hypotensive syndrome. So you will have to treat the patient as someone who might develop hemorrhagic shock.

b. The prehospital management, then, is as follows:

(1) Administer **oxygen.**
(2) Keep the patient in the **left lateral recumbent position.**
(3) Start an **IV with crystalloid.**
(4) **Transport** to the hospital.

10. a. The woman who fell in a downtown department store has a chief complaint unrelated to her pregnancy—a twisted ankle. But, in fact, a careful examination reveals a very serious problem that *is* related to her pregnancy, **preeclampsia** (answer **B**), as manifested by edema and hypertension.

b. The initial prehospital treatment, therefore, is as follows:

(1) **Splint** the injured ankle.
(2) **Transport** the woman in the left lateral recumbent position **without sirens** and with interior lights dimmed.
(3) Start an **IV lifeline** en route, so that it will be there if you need it.

c. And, indeed, you did need that IV—when the woman proceeded to have a grand mal seizure and develop full-blown eclampsia. The steps to take at that point are

(1) **Protect the patient from injury** during the tonic-clonic phase of the seizure.
(2) Ensure an adequate **airway.**
(3) Administer **oxygen.**
(4) **Radio medical command** for orders. You may be asked to give either
   (a) **Diazepam,** 5 to 10 mg slowly IV, or
   (b) **Magnesium sulfate 10%,** 2 to 4 gm IV, or both.
(5) **Notify** the receiving hospital. If the woman's seizures cannot be controlled, it may be necessary to take her straight to the operating room for an emergency cesarean section.

11. When *two* pregnant woman are involved in a motor vehicle accident, it's quadruple trouble!

a. Some of the changes during pregnancy that make a woman more vulnerable to injury or that affect her response to injury include the following:

(1) **Elevation of the diaphragm,** which effectively pushes the abdominal contents into the chest, so there are more apt to be in-

juries to abdominal organs after a blow to the chest.

(2) **Forward, upward displacement of the bladder,** rendering it more vulnerable to injury.

(3) The **uterus itself** becomes more susceptible to injury as it enlarges and occupies more and more of the abdomen.

(4) **Increase in vascular volume** by as much as 50 percent, so the pregnant woman can lose a lot of blood (and the fetus can be in big trouble) before she shows signs of shock.

(5) **Relative tachycardia and hypotension** make it difficult to interpret the pregnant woman's vital signs after injury.

(6) **Redistribution of blood flow** to the pelvic area means that a pregnant woman will bleed much more profusely from injuries such as pelvic fracture.

(7) **Delayed gastric emptying** during pregnancy makes a pregnant woman more likely to vomit and aspirate after injury.

b. You find the *driver* of the car conscious, but with evidence of steering wheel trauma to the abdomen and indications of impending shock (thirst, tachycardia, slight hypotension). She must, therefore, be **treated for shock** and regarded as a **load-and-go** emergency:

(1) **Stabilize the cervical spine.**

(2) Remove the woman from the vehicle on a **long backboard,** with the usual spinal precautions.

(3) In the ambulance, keep the **backboard tilted 30 degrees to the left side.**

(4) Ensure an adequate **airway;** be prepared for vomiting.

(5) Administer **oxygen.**

(6) Start **transport,** and **notify** the receiving hospital.

(7) En route, **start at least one large-bore IV,** and run in normal saline or lactated Ringer's wide open.

c. The pregnant *passenger* does not seem to be seriously injured, although her complaints of neck pain ("whiplash") should prompt appropriate measures to stabilize the cervical spine. In any case, however, you **cannot conclude that there is no injury to the fetus.** Only careful evaluation in the hospital, and observation over several hours, can establish that fact.

12. It is helpful to know the expected duration of each stage of labor in the nulliparous and multiparous woman.

	FIRST STAGE OF LABOR	SECOND STAGE OF LABOR	THIRD STAGE OF LABOR
Begins with:	Onset of regular contractions	Descent of the fetal head into the birth canal	Delivery of the baby
Ends with:	Full cervical dilatation	Full delivery of the baby	Expulsion of the placenta and contraction of the uterus
Duration in a nullipara	8–12 hours	1–2 hours	5–60 minutes
Duration in a multipara	6–8 hours	½ hour	5–60 minutes

13. Deciding whether you have time to transport a woman in active labor to the hospital is a judgment call, and there is room for debate in some of these situations. As a general rule, you will have a lot more time with nulliparas. Multiparas can progress very rapidly through labor, so the margin for error is smaller.

D A 20-year-old woman in her first pregnancy. She says her bag of waters broke about 6 hours ago. Now her contractions are about 2 minutes apart, and she feels a need to move her bowels. You are 20 minutes from the hospital.
The urge to move the bowels indicates that the fetal head is already in the birth canal and de-

livery is imminent. The delivery may be complicated by **fetal infection,** because the amniotic sac ruptured several hours ago.

D   A 32-year-old multip (gravida 10, para 8) who has been in labor about 5 hours. Her contractions are 3 minutes apart. She says she thinks the baby's coming. You are 10 minutes from the hospital.

As a general rule, when a woman who has had eight babies tells you that the baby is coming, she knows what she's talking about! *Complications* seen more commonly in grand multips include **uterine rupture** and **postpartum hemorrhage.**

T   A 25-year-old nullipara (gravida 1, para 0) who has been in labor for 9 hours. Her contractions are 4 to 5 minutes apart. You are 20 minutes from the hospital.

In *this* case, you should have plenty of time. The woman is a beginner, and her contractions are still quite widely spaced.

D   A 30-year-old gravida 4, para 3, who has been in labor for 6 hours. She had two of her three children by cesarean section. Her contractions are 2 minutes apart, and she is crowning. You are 5 minutes from the hospital.

No doubts here: The lady is crowning! If she's had two previous cesarean sections, she is at increased risk for **uterine rupture** during labor.

T   A 28-year-old gravida 1, para 0, whose contractions started 24 hours ago. They do not come at regular intervals, and they have not gotten much more intense since they started. You are 25 minutes from the hospital.

This woman may not even be in labor at all. Her contractions sound suspiciously like **Braxton Hicks contractions.** If you sit around waiting for her to deliver, you might spend several *weeks* at the scene!

D   A 24-year-old gravida 3, para 2, who announces, as you enter her flat, "Hurry, the twins are coming any minute!" She says she has been in labor "quite a while," and you time her contractions as coming less than 2 minutes apart. You are 20 minutes from the hospital.

With the contractions coming at only 2-minute intervals in a multip, you can't afford to take a chance. The potential complications more likely in a twin birth include **cord prolapse, breech presentation,** and **postpartum hemorrhage.** The babies are also likely to be small and therefore to require the kind of special care given to premies.

14. Women have been having babies for about 4 million years, so Nature has had a chance pretty nearly to perfect the process. It doesn't always go well, of course. But as a general rule, the less one does to interfere with Nature's way of bringing babies into the world, the less one is apt to do significant harm.

    a. If you are transporting a woman in labor, and she begins crowning when you are only a minute or two from the hospital, you should instruct her to cross her legs until you reach the emergency room.
    FALSE! FALSE! FALSE! *Never* try to delay or restrain the birth of a baby!

    b. If the fetal heart rate is less than 120 per minute, the fetus is in danger.
    TRUE, and it means that you need to start moving toward the hospital and to notify the staff there of your impending arrival with a distressed fetus.

    c. A woman should be discouraged from sitting up or squatting for delivery of her baby since those positions are unphysiologic and increase the demand on the mother's energy.
    FALSE. Nature knows best.

    d. If the baby is coming fast, it is more important to control the delivery than to drape the mother with sterile towels.
    TRUE. An explosive delivery can injure both the baby and the mother.

    e. If the cut ends of the umbilical cord are oozing blood, you should unclamp them and reapply the clamps more tightly.
    FALSE. If there is oozing from a cut end of the cord, *add another clamp* proximal to the first; DON'T release the first clamp.

    f. If the placenta has not delivered within 20 minutes of the delivery of the baby, you should exert gentle traction on the umbilical cord while you vigorously massage the uterus.
    FALSE, unless you want to have to deal with some *really* dramatic postpartum hemorrhage, and perhaps an inside-out uterus for good measure.

    g. With the exception of buttocks breech, all other abnormal presentations must be delivered in the hospital.
    TRUE. Nearly every other abnormal presentation will require cesarean section or, at least, skilled obstetric intervention.

15. Science has not yet established the precise mechanism that stimulates a woman to go into labor, but any experienced EMT or paramedic can attest that one of the things that can stimulate labor is shopping! That is why paramedics not infrequently find themselves delivering babies in department stores.

    a. When the baby's face is found to be covered by the intact amniotic sac, you should **tear open the amniotic sac,** either with your fingers or a forceps, and carefully peel it away from the baby's face. Then **suction the baby's nostrils and mouth** with a bulb aspirator.

    b. When the umbilical cord is found *tightly* wound around the baby's neck, the only thing you can do is **put two clamps on the cord, 2 inches apart, and cut the cord between the clamps.**

    c. The steps to take from that point on are as follows:

       (1) Guide the baby's head downward to **allow delivery of the upper shoulder.**
       (2) Guide the baby's head upward to **allow delivery of the lower shoulder.**
       (3) Wipe the baby's mouth and nose free of blood and mucus, and **suction out the mouth and nostrils again.**
       (4) **Tell mother** and all the salesladies in the lingerie department whether it's a boy or a girl.
       (5) **Dry the baby, cover it with a blanket, and put it on the mother's abdomen.**
       (6) **Record the time** of birth and the **Apgar score,** while you await the delivery of the placenta.
       (7) When the placenta separates, instruct the mother to bear down.
       (8) *After the placenta has delivered,* **massage the uterus, put the baby to the mother's breast,** and, if your protocol so states, start an **oxytocin drip.**
       (9) Clean up, put a sanitary pad between the mother's legs, bid farewell to the ladies in the lingerie department, and **transport.**

    d. The baby's Apgar score is **9:**

Appearance	1	(Extremities are dusky.)
Pulse	2	
Grimace	2	
Activity	2	
Respiratory effort	2	
	9	

16. a. What you are dealing with there at the ski lodge is a **breech presentation.** That smooth presenting part with a crack down the middle is a buttocks, not a head!

    b. Management is as follows:

       (1) Allow the **buttocks, legs, and trunk to deliver spontaneously.**
       (2) Support and slowly **lower the baby's trunk** so that the baby is nearly hanging dependent.
       (3) *When you see the baby's hairline* at the nape of his neck, **swing his body upward,** toward the mother's abdomen, to facilitate delivery of the head.
       (4) Once the head has delivered, **suction** the baby's mouth and nostrils, and proceed as for any other delivery.

17. **Prolapsed umbilical cord** occurs in only about 1 out of every 300 deliveries, but it is more likely with a premature birth like this one. What you have to do is as follows:

    a. Position the mother **supine with her buttocks elevated** on pillows.

    b. Administer **oxygen** to the mother.

    c. With two fingers of a gloved hand, **push the baby back into the vagina** until the presenting part is no longer compressing the cord.

    d. Have your partner **cover the exposed part of the cord** with sterile gauze moistened in sterile saline.

    e. **Transport,** maintaining pressure against the presenting part.

18. a. The woman who has the sudden onset of chest pain and dyspnea immediately after delivery has probably suffered a **pulmonary embolism.**

    b. She should be managed as follows:

       (1) Administer 100% **oxygen.**
       (2) Begin **transport,** and notify the receiving hospital.
       (3) Start a **large-bore IV** en route, and give normal saline or lactated Ringer's wide open.

19. a. The *special* measures required in delivering twins, as opposed to a single birth, are simply to

       (1) **Wait for the second birth** after the first is complete. Meanwhile, keep the first baby

warm on the mother's abdomen, covered with a blanket.

(2) Treat both babies as you would premies, with scrupulous attention to their warmth, prevention of bleeding, and protection from contamination.

b. The mother's *risk factor for postpartum hemorrhage* was the very fact of her **twin pregnancy,** for the placenta covers a larger area in a twin pregnancy, and the uterine muscles become overstretched, so they contract less efficiently.

c. Other risk factors for postpartum hemorrhage include

(1) **Prolonged labor**
(2) **Retained products of conception**
(3) **Grand multiparity**
(4) **Placenta previa**
(5) A **full bladder**

d. The steps that should be taken to manage postpartum hemorrhage in the field are as follows:

(1) Continue **uterine massage.**
(2) Put either or both babies to the breast to **start nursing.**
(3) Start an **oxytocin drip** by adding 10 units of oxytocin to 1,000 ml of D5/W and running the infusion at about 20 to 30 gtt per hour.
(4) Begin **transport,** and **notify** the receiving hospital.
(5) **Start another IV with a large-bore catheter** to infuse crystalloid rapidly.

20. Vaginal bleeding is never normal in pregnancy, and when it occurs in the third trimester, it may be fatal.

a. **multigravida**
b. **eclampsia**
c. **estrogen**
d. **egg**
e. **gestation**
f. **embryo**
g. **bladder**
h. **fanny**
i. **fright**
j. **thirteen**
k. **nine**
l. **cheer**
m. **in**

Secret Message: VAGINAL BLEEDING DURING THE THIRD TRIMESTER OF PREGNANCY IS A LIFE-THREATENING EMERGENCY.

36
Neonatal Care and Transport

1. Were you able to find all the hidden words?

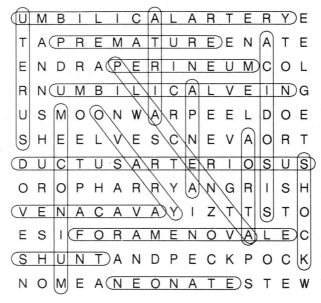

Oxygenated blood from the **placenta** enters the fetus in the **umbilical vein.** It flows through the liver into the inferior **vena cava.** Leaving that vessel, a large proportion of the oxygenated blood flows directly across the **atria** through a hole called the **foramen ovale,** thereby bypassing the lungs. When blood goes from the right side of the heart to the left side of the heart without picking up oxygen in the lungs, we call it a **shunt.** Another direct connection, the **ductus arteriosus,** links the fetal pulmonary artery to the **aorta.** Both those connections close very soon after birth. After circulating through the fetus, blood enters an **umbilical artery** to return to the placenta.

The newborn, or **neonate,** is very vulnerable to hypothermia. It is important to try to prevent hypothermia from occurring in the newborn, because hypothermia may lead to **acidosis,** which in turn may lead to **shock.** A baby born before the thirty-eighth week of pregnancy or weighing less than 2.5 kg is considered to be **premature** and is at higher risk of hypothermia.

When fetal stool, called **meconium,** is expelled into the amniotic fluid, it may find its way into the fetal airway before birth and then be aspirated deep into the airway when the baby takes its first breath. The result may be a complete failure to breathe at all, called **apnea.**

The womb: **uterus**
The organ where eggs reside: **ovary**
The region between the vagina and the anus: **perineum**

542

2. If you were expecting problems in delivering this 38-year-old multip, you were right.

   a. **Yes,** there are several indications that this may be a complicated delivery or that you may have problems with the baby afterward:

      (1) **Maternal age greater than 35 years**
      (2) **No prenatal care**
      (3) **Prolonged labor**
      (4) **Meconium staining** of the amniotic fluid
      (5) Probable **post-term baby** (It's hard to know how much to trust the mother's estimate of the gestational age.)

   b. Other risk factors for obstetric and neonatal complications include

      (1) **Maternal diabetes**
      (2) **Maternal drug or alcohol abuse**
      (3) **Antepartum hemorrhage**
      (4) **Twin pregnancy**
      (5) **Abnormal presentation**
      (6) **Prolapsed umbilical cord**
      (7) **Fetal distress**

   c. When the baby's head delivers and is found to be covered with meconium:

      (1) **Clean the mouth and nostrils** with sterile gauze.
      (2) Use a bulb aspirator to **suction the mouth and nostrils.**
      (3) Use a DeLee suction trap to **suction the oropharynx** (gently!).

   d. Once the baby is fully delivered:

      (1) Quickly **dry** the baby off.
      (2) **Clamp and cut the cord.**
      (3) Hand off the baby to your partner to **intubate and suction.**
      (4) If the baby does not breathe spontaneously, give several breaths with bag-valve-mask and oxygen.
      (5) Finish drying the baby, and **cover with warm blankets.**

3. *Return of the Spider Monster* is not recommended viewing for an impressionable woman in the third trimester of pregnancy. Look what can happen!

   a. When you find yourself holding a newborn premature infant that had the temerity to be born before you could even open your OB kit, take the following steps:

      (1) **Suction** the mouth and nostrils with a bulb syringe.
      (2) Quickly **dry the baby** with whatever you have available.

      (3) As soon as possible, wrap the baby in something warm.
      (4) When your partner brings the OB kit, **clamp and cut the cord.**

   b. In the case of a premie, it's a good idea to **wait a bit before clamping the cord,** at least until all the pulsations have stopped, **because the premie will need every drop of blood it can get.** If you clamp too early, you will deprive the baby of the last few milliliters of blood being pumped in from the placenta, and the premature baby may not be able to afford the loss of even a few milliliters.

   c. Factors likely to promote hypothermia in this baby are

      (1) Its **prematurity,** which means that it has **less insulating fat** and also **less ability to generate heat by increased metabolism.**
      (2) Staying **wet,** which will promote evaporative cooling.
      (3) Being on the **cold floor,** which will promote conductive cooling.
      (4) Being in the **cold room,** which will promote radiant cooling.
      (5) The **draft,** which will promote convective cooling.

   d. Possible adverse consequences of hypothermia include

      (1) **Acidosis,** which in turn may lead to **shock,** to **respiratory distress syndrome,** and to **increased pulmonary vascular resistance.** The last may bring about the reestablishment of a right-to-left shunt through the foramen ovale, which in turn will cause **hypoxemia.**
      (2) **Hypoglycemia.**

   e. The things you can do to try to prevent the baby from becoming hypothermic are as follows:

      (1) **Dry it thoroughly.**
      (2) **Wrap the baby in aluminum foil.**
      (3) Cover the baby with a warm **blanket.**
      (4) Place insulated **hot water bottles** alongside the baby.
      (5) Keep the baby **on the mother's body.**
      (6) In the ambulance, **turn on the heaters** full blast until the ambient temperature gets up around 35°C (95°F), even if it's summer!

   f. Besides keeping the baby warm, you need to

      (1) Take particular care to maintain a patent **airway.**

(2) Administer **oxygen** into a tent or by blow-by.

(3) Wear a surgical **mask and gown** to protect the baby from infection.

4. You think this case is exaggerated? You don't believe that teenage girls give birth on the toilet? In fact, this case is based on an actual case managed by real paramedics.

a. Immediately upon rescuing the infant from the toilet, you need to

(1) **Dry it off,** preferably with warm towels, and **cover** with a warm blanket.

(2) **Suction the mouth and nostrils.**

(3) **Stimulate** the baby to breathe.

(4) **Clamp and cut the umbilical cord.**

(5) Administer **oxygen.**

b. The indications for starting artificial ventilation are

(1) **Apnea**

(2) A **heart rate less than 100 per minute**

(3) **Persisting central cyanosis** despite 100% oxygen

c. After a minute of artificial ventilation, you find the heart rate to be 84 per minute. You should **continue artificial ventilation only.**

d. When you check again, however, the pulse rate has dropped below 60 per minute, so at that point you should **start external chest compressions** at 120 per minute.

e. The indications for epinephrine are

(1) **Asystole**

(2) A **heart rate persistently below 80 per minute** despite adequate artificial ventilation with 100% oxygen and good external chest compressions

f. The dosage of epinephrine for this 3-kg baby is **0.03 to 0.09 mg** (i.e., 0.3–0.9 ml of a 1 : 10,000 solution). It is given **via an endotracheal tube** after being diluted in 1 to 2 ml of normal saline.

5. The truth, they say, is stranger than fiction.

a. Deep pharyngeal suctioning may stimulate the vagus nerve in a newborn and cause severe bradycardia.
TRUE. The vagal response of the newborn is extremely sensitive and easily triggered by touching the back of the throat.

b. Even slight meconium staining of the amniotic fluid indicates a need to intubate the newborn immediately after delivery.
FALSE. Only if the meconium is of the pea-soup variety is it necessary to intubate and suction beyond the vocal cords. Otherwise, suctioning the mouth, nostrils, and oropharynx will suffice.

c. If the fetal heart rate is less than 120 per minute at any point during labor, you should roll the mother onto her side and give her supplemental oxygen to breathe.
TRUE. Fetal distress is usually due to hypoxemia, and fetal hypoxemia may be exacerbated by anything that reduces blood flow to the placenta (such as the uterus squeezing down on the great vessels). Turning the mother onto her side gets the weight of the uterus off the great vessels and thereby improves her perfusion. Giving her oxygen increases the oxygen saturation of the blood reaching the maternal side of the placenta.

d. Clamping and cutting of the umbilical cord should ordinarily be carried out after the cord stops pulsating.
TRUE.

e. Hypothermia in the newborn may lead to the reestablishment of right-to-left shunting and consequent hypoxemia.
TRUE.

f. Most newborns who require resuscitation will need full CPR.
FALSE. In the vast majority of cases, just giving oxygen or oxygen plus a little help with breathing is all that is required to resuscitate a newborn.

37
Gynecologic Emergencies

1. In evaluating a woman of childbearing age whose chief complaint is abdominal pain, you are going to want to know more about the pain, about associated symptoms, and about her obstetric and gynecologic history.

   a. Among the questions you should ask in taking the history, therefore, are the following:

   (1) **What provoked the pain?** Does anything make it better or worse?
   (2) **What is the pain like?** Sharp? Dull? Crampy?
   (3) **Where is the pain?** Does it radiate anywhere else?
   (4) **How severe is the pain?**
   (5) **When did the pain start?** What is the temporal relationship between the pain and other symptoms?
   (6) **What other symptoms** has the patient noticed? Has she had **vaginal bleeding?** Has she felt **dizzy or faint?**
   (7) When was her **last normal menstrual period?**
   (8) Has she noticed any **breast tenderness, urinary frequency,** or **nausea in the mornings?**
   (9) What, if any, type of **contraception** does the woman use?
   (10) Has she had any **vaginal discharge?**
   (11) How many **previous pregnancies** has she had? How many **deliveries?**
   (12) What **gynecologic problems** has she had **in the past?**
   (13) Does she have any serious **underlying illnesses?**

   b. On physical examination, what you want to look for in particular are

   (1) **Signs of hypovolemia,** such as anxiety, restlessness, cold and clammy skin, tachycardia, and postural changes in vital signs
   (2) **Signs of peritoneal irritation,** such as abdominal rigidity or pain on movement

2. a. The 20-year-old who "finally got her period" did not, in fact, get her period. She is most likely bleeding from an **inevitable abortion** (answer **B**). A missed period, crampy pain in the middle of the abdomen *followed* by bleeding, and persistence of vaginal bleeding all point to inevitable abortion.

   b. The *treatment* must be **expectant treatment for shock,** in view of the number of sanitary napkins the patient has soaked through (the increased pulse rate also suggests borderline shock).

   (1) Administer **oxygen.**
   (2) Keep the patient in the **recumbent position.**
   (3) Start a **large-bore IV** with lactated Ringer's.
   (4) **Monitor** cardiac rhythm and vital signs.
   (5) **Transport.**

3. a. The 25-year-old with fever and abdominal pain that began not long after her menstrual period is most likely suffering from **pelvic inflammatory disease** (answer **E**).

   b. The prehospital management is **gentle transport.** In view of the woman's tachycardia, fever, and history of vomiting, she is probably dehydrated, so it is a good idea as well to **start an IV** with crystalloid and run in fluids en route to the hospital.

4. a. The 24-year-old woman who thinks she has appendicitis more likely has an embryo developing in her right fallopian tube, that is, an ec-

topic pregnancy (answer **D**). Crampy, unilateral abdominal pain followed by spotting and signs of early shock are good enough evidence to start treatment.

b. Treatment is as follows:

(1) Administer **oxygen.**
(2) Keep the patient **recumbent.**
(3) Start a **large-bore IV** with lactated Ringer's, and run it wide open.
(4) Allow **nothing by mouth.**
(5) Keep the patient **warm.**
(6) **Monitor** cardiac rhythm and vital signs.
(7) **Notify** the receiving hospital.
(8) **Transport** without delay.

5. Risk factors for ectopic pregnancy include
   a. Previous **pelvic inflammatory disease**

   b. **Previous ectopic pregnancy**

   c. Using an **IUCD** for contraception

   d. Previous **pelvic surgery**

6. The classic triad of findings in ectopic pregnancy are
   a. **Abdominal pain**

   b. **Amenorrhea**

   c. **Vaginal bleeding**

7. Managing the victim of rape requires tact, sensitivity, and common sense.

   a. The paramedic should take a detailed history of the rape incident to enable the victim to ventilate her feelings about what happened.
   FALSE. If the patient *wants* to talk about it, by all means let her talk about it. But *don't* ask questions about the incident.

b. All superficial wounds and abrasions suffered by a rape victim should be carefully cleaned and covered with sterile dressings before transport to prevent infection.
FALSE. Superficial wounds and abrasions do not constitute an immediate threat to life, and cleaning them off may destroy evidence. Leave the minor abrasions, therefore, for the emergency room staff to deal with after they have collected whatever evidence needs to be collected from the wounds.

c. The patient should be discouraged from cleaning up before being examined in the emergency room.
TRUE. Cleaning up will almost certainly destroy evidence, so it is preferable that the woman go to the emergency room just as she is. If she feels strongly about it, however, don't put pressure on her. Her emotional well-being is more important than the preservation of evidence.

d. The rape victim's external genitalia should be routinely inspected for injury.
FALSE. Do not inspect or touch the victim's genital area unless there is profuse bleeding that must be controlled.

e. If the victim of rape does not wish to be examined at the hospital, she should be transported to the home of a friend or relative.
TRUE. The woman should *never* be simply left at the scene.

f. The diagnosis on your trip sheet for a victim of sexual assault should read, "Alleged rape," rather than "Rape."
TRUE. "Rape" is a legal diagnosis that the paramedic is not in a position to make. "Alleged rape" indicates that you are talking about the patient's chief complaint, without implying whether it has been substantiated or not.

38
Disturbances of Behavior

1. Whenever you find a patient behaving strangely, you need to look for the hidden causes of disturbed behavior.

2. Sometimes, one can sort out the source of a patient's disturbed behavior (organic versus psychiatric) by a careful mental status examination:

P	Obsessional thinking
P	Flat affect
O	Delirium
B	Distractibility
P	Compulsions
O	Visual hallucinations
O	Confabulation
B	Anxiety
O	Coma
P	Circumstantial thinking

3. The manner in which you approach a disturbed patient can make the difference between being part of the problem or being part of the solution!

a. The most important thing a paramedic can do to help a disturbed patient is to remain calm and steady.
   TRUE, very true. Remember, what makes a psychiatric emergency an "emergency" is often panic and confusion. A calm person taking charge of the situation can make everyone feel better.

b. There should be a maximum sense of urgency in evacuating a disturbed patient to the hospital, since there is nothing that can be done to help the patient in the field.
   FALSE. The impression you want to convey is that you have all the time in the world. Rush-

ing the patient off to the hospital will only reinforce his or her conviction that something is terribly wrong.

c. It is essential to correct a patient's misinterpretations of reality.
FALSE. You will not succeed in talking a patient out of his delusions or convincing him that his hallucinations aren't real, and you simply risk antagonizing the patient by arguing.

d. The disturbed patient should be reassured that everything will turn out all right.
FALSE. Reassure the patient, yes. But not with inane statements like, "Everything will be all right." Try something a little more realistic, such as, "Many people with problems like yours can be helped to feel better."

e. The paramedic should remain with the disturbed patient at all times until the emergency room staff takes over the patient's care.
TRUE. Once you have responded to the call, the patient's safety becomes your responsibility.

f. Police intervention is usually required to transport a disturbed patient against his or her will.
TRUE. In most jurisdictions, only the police are authorized to use force.

4. The shortest answer to this question is that **the paramedic did just about everything wrong!** Furthermore, he or she was inexcusably rude.

a. The paramedic **never identified himself** (we'll assume it was a male paramedic).

b. The paramedic used a **demeaning term to address the patient** ("dearie") instead of asking her name and addressing her with respect as Miss, Ms., or Mrs. So-and-so.

c. The paramedic **stood in front of the patient,** towering over her and also blocking her escape—a very threatening stance. He should have crouched down, so that he was at the same level as the patient, and positioned himself somewhat to the side, so that she wasn't trapped in the corner.

d. The paramedic **passed judgment on the patient's feelings** ("Big girls don't cry"). Furthermore, he **belittled the patient's problem** without even waiting to find out what the problem was! ("You're making a mountain out of a molehill.")

e. The paramedic gave **inappropriate and premature reassurance,** telling the patient in es-

sence that everything will be all right by tomorrow without even knowing what's wrong today.

f. The paramedic tried to **forestall the patient's expressions of feeling,** urging her to stop crying.

g. The paramedic **never gave the patient a chance to talk.**

h. The paramedic then turned his back on the patient and asked if someone else could tell him what was going on, **implying that the patient's version of things was of no importance.**

Needless to say, the paramedic in this story was an imposter. No *real* paramedic would ever behave like that.

5. The mental status examination helps us to organize our observations of the patient's psychologic "vital signs."

__F__ The patient cannot name three objects that you listed out loud 5 minutes earlier.

__B__ The patient is pacing up and down.

__E__ The patient smiles pleasantly as he tells you that his daughter was run over by a truck.

__A__ The patient keeps shifting his attention from you to the television or to the window.

__H__ The patient seems to be having a conversation with an invisible friend.

__G__ The patient thinks it's 1931.

__D__ The patient also thinks that he is Albert Einstein.

__C__ He tells you, "All the world is my kingdumbell and I'm the pellmellery scullop."

__D__ The patient is terrified of spiders.

__B__ He puts two fingers to his forehead in a salute every time he finishes speaking.

__E__ He complains of palpitations, nausea, tightness in his chest, and numbness around his lips.

__H__ He thinks that the sound of the wind is someone calling his name.

6. The fact that Mr. Crosby has admitted you to his apartment, even reluctantly, is a hopeful sign.

a. You might start the interview something like this: "Your neighbors have been worried about you; that's why they called us. They thought there might be some kind of problem here. **Is there any way we can help?"** If the patient then says something to the effect that there's nothing anyone can do to help, you might comment on his statement: **"You seem really discouraged."** The object is to indicate that you are a "sympathetic ear," prepared to listen to his troubles.

b. The *symptoms of depression* that this patient is showing include

    (1) A sense of **worthlessness**
    (2) **Decreased appetite**
    (3) **No apparent interest** in anything
    (4) **Lack of energy**

c. Other symptoms and signs of depression include

    (1) **Sleep disturbances**
    (2) **Difficulty concentrating**
    (3) **Psychomotor abnormalities** (retardation or agitation)
    (4) **Suicidal thoughts**

d. The *risk factors for suicide* in this patient's history include

    (1) **Male, over 55 years old**
    (2) **Widower**
    (3) **Socially isolated**
    (4) **Depressed**
    (5) Possible **alcohol problem** (empty bottles lying around)

e. Other risk factors for suicide include

    (1) **A previous suicide attempt**
    (2) A **family history** of suicide
    (3) **Suicidal thoughts,** particularly when there are **concrete plans**
    (4) **Clear warning** of intent to commit suicide
    (5) Recent **loss of a significant person**
    (6) Recent **job loss** or **financial setback**

f. Among the questions to ask in evaluating this patient's suicide risk are the following:

    (1) Have you ever felt that life wasn't worth living?
    (2) Have you thought about harming yourself?
    (3) How would you go about it—have you made any plans?

7. The young woman with a "possible heart attack" is unlikely to be suffering a heart attack (although it's not completely out of the question).

a. Her problem is most likely to be a **panic attack.**

b. The symptoms and signs that suggest that diagnosis include

    (1) **Dyspnea**
    (2) **Chest tightness**
    (3) **Feeling faint**
    (4) Her feelings of **unreality** and **impending death**
    (5) **Tachycardia**
    (6) **Sweating**
    (7) **Trembling**

c. **Yes,** there certainly are other possibilities that must be taken into account. Highest on the list is **pulmonary embolism.** One also has to consider the possibility of a **cardiac dysrhythmia,** a **reaction to a drug,** an **anaphylactic reaction,** and even an **acute myocardial infarction,** which is seen much more frequently among young people these days because of the widespread use of cocaine.

d. To manage this patient, therefore:

    (1) **Separate her from all the panicky bystanders.** Move her into a private office, or move everyone out of *her* office.
    (2) **Sit down** to talk with her.
    (3) Administer **oxygen.** Until you know that you are *not* dealing with a pulmonary embolism or cardiac event, you need to cover all bases.
    (4) Apply **monitoring electrodes,** and check the rhythm on the 'scope.
    (5) Assuming that there are no abnormal findings, **reassure** the patient that you cannot find any indication of serious illness and that the chances are she is suffering a panic attack. Tell her that to make absolutely sure, she needs to be checked out in the hospital. If it does turn out that she is having a panic attack, there are effective treatments for that condition.

8. The police officer who summoned you to the bar was on the right track, even if "psycho case" is not a very specific diagnosis.

a. The patient is probably in the **manic** phase of a bipolar disorder.

b. The evidence to suggest that diagnosis includes

    (1) His **pressure of speech.**
    (2) His **grandiose ideas** (big business deals, big spender).
    (3) His **apparently euphoric mood** that is, nonetheless, **very brittle;** his good cheer easily turns to a less pleasant affect when

he is challenged by the bartender or the police officer.

(4) His **hyperactivity,** pacing up and down.

c. In managing this patient, you will have to **try to persuade him to go voluntarily to the hospital.** If he will not be persuaded, and probably he will not, coercion will be necessary. Consult your medical director first.

9. The strangely dressed man found wandering down the middle of the street is a good example of **disorganized behavior.** Since walking in traffic is not a healthy form of activity, the patient must be assumed to be unable to care for himself and probably needs institutional care. From the description, it does not sound as if you will be able to obtain a useful history. You should simply **tell the patient gently but firmly that you are going to take him to the hospital for care.** He will probably go along without much fuss if you are non-threatening about it.

10. The karate expert is seriously ill and probably dangerous.

a. He is showing signs of **psychosis** (answer **B**)—hallucinations, persecutory delusions, loosening of associations.

b. **Yes,** there are indications that he might become violent, namely:

(1) His **body language**—sitting there like a coiled spring, gripping the armrests of the chair.

(2) The fact that he is **easily startled.**

(3) His **avoidance of eye contact.**

(4) The fact that he **views the paramedics as adversaries** (he thinks you're the FBI!).

(5) His **hearing voices that tell him to put up a fight.**

c. In managing this situation:

(1) **Observe your surroundings.** Keep yourself between the patient and the door to his room. Make note of any potential weapons.

(2) **Maintain a safe distance,** at least two arm lengths (which will keep you out of range of his foot).

(3) **Identify yourself again** as a paramedic.

(4) **Acknowledge the patient's behavior** ("You seem very worried.") and **state your willingness to help.** Don't sound too friendly.

(5) **Encourage the patient to talk** about what's bothering him.

(6) **Define your expectations** of his behavior.

(7) If talking to the patient isn't working, **back off and get help.**

(8) Explain to the patient's mother that it will be necessary to take the young man to the hospital against his will (she may be required to sign his commitment papers). Call for police backup, and consult medical command.

(9) *When you have sufficient manpower,* **apply restraints** as quickly and efficiently as you can. Once the patient is restrained, don't remove the restraints.

(10) **Maintain verbal contact** with the patient throughout transport.

11. The paramedic needs to develop a "nose for danger" and to be able to predict which situations present a high risk for violence.

a. Scenarios:

(1) Any place where **alcohol is being consumed**

(2) **Crowd incidents**

(3) **Scenes of violent injury**

b. Diagnostic groups:

(1) Patients **intoxicated with drugs or alcohol**

(2) Patients **withdrawing from drugs or alcohol**

(3) **Psychotic patients**

(4) Patients with **delirium**

12. Our thought for the day applies to all of the paramedic's work in the field, not just the care of "mental" patients. Every patient who has a functioning brain in his or her head is a "mental" patient.

a. **hallucination**

b. **delusion**

c. **perseveration**

d. **phobia**

e. **ambivalence**

f. **stereotyped**

g. **confusion**

h. **fugue state**

i. **echolalia**

j. **anxiety**

k. **restlessness**

l. **flat**

m. **thought**

n. **STD**

o. **envy**

Secret Message: THE EVALUATION OF EVERY PATIENT SHOULD INCLUDE AN ASSESSMENT OF HIS PSYCHOLOGICAL STATUS. OBSERVE AND LISTEN TO THE PATIENT CAREFULLY.

39
Communications and Dispatching

1. A lot of different people have to be able to talk to one another in an EMS communications system.

   a. **The person calling for help** needs to be able to talk with the **dispatcher.** The best technical means of establishing that link is **landline (telephone).**

   b. The **dispatcher** needs to be able to talk with the **paramedics** or other rescuers. The best technical means of establishing that link is a **two-way radio,** although a pager will suffice for dispatch.

   c. The **dispatcher** needs to be able to talk with **other agencies,** such as police, fire, utility companies, and civil defense. The best technical means of establishing that link is **landline (telephone).**

   d. The **paramedics** need to be able to talk with **medical command.** The best technical means of establishing that link is **radio or cellular telephone.**

   e. The **paramedics** need to be able to talk with the **receiving hospital.** The best technical means of establishing that link is **radio or cellular telephone.**

   f. The **area hospitals** need to be able to talk with **one another.** The best technical means of establishing that link is **landline with radio backup.**

2. Different types of radios or wavebands have different capabilities and are assigned by the FCC for different purposes.

   <u>U</u>   Best means for calling the base from skyscraper row downtown

   <u>V</u>   Best means for calling the base from a rural, wooded area

   <u>C</u>   Best means for sending a 12-lead ECG to medical command

   <u>C</u>   Best means for calling a patient's family doctor

   <u>V</u>   FCC-preferred for routine voice communications

   <u>U</u>   FCC-approved for one-lead ECG transmission

   <u>U, V, C</u>   Can be monitored by someone with a scanner

3. Most radio communications systems require a basic minimum of components.

Component	Function
Base station	Dispatch and coordination area
Mobile transceiver	Communications with ambulances
Portable transceiver	Communications with paramedics when they are out of their vehicle
Repeater	To extend the range of low-power transceivers
Remote consoles in hospitals	To allow communications with receiving hospitals
Landline/cellular backup	To extend the user network

4. Just about everything was wrong with the transmission quoted!

   a. The **unit being called should be mentioned first.** So it should have been, "County Hospital, Medic 12."

   b. It was **unnecessarily wordy,** wasting a lot of time. ("Be advised that . . ." or "Please 10-9 your message.")

   c. The **patient's name was mentioned on the air,** along with an abbreviation that a layperson could easily misunderstand. To compound the offense, the paramedic spelled out the initials of the chief complaint in **nonstandard phonetic alphabet,** using insulting words to do so.

   d. The paramedic was apparently **trying to be funny.** He may have thought the whole thing was a laugh a minute, but Maggie Jones might be forgiven if she didn't think so. Making insulting references to the patient ("well endowed with adipose tissue") or to the other party on the radio ("Are you people deaf?") is highly unprofessional and simply reflects on the immaturity of the speaker.

   e. The report of the patient's findings was **not given in any sort of standard format.** As a result, the people at County Hospital had to waste a lot of time trying to drag the important information out of the paramedics.

   f. **Words that are poorly heard by radio,** such as "yes," were used.

   g. The paramedic **did not repeat back the medication orders** to make sure he had received them correctly.

   h. The **radio was used for nonmedical communications** ("Pop a few doughnuts into the microwave.").

5. Now for our spelling lesson.

   a. THE: **TANGO-HOTEL-ECHO**

   b. QUICK: **QUEBEC-UNIFORM-INDIA-CHARLIE-KILO**

   c. BROWN: **BRAVO-ROMEO-OSCAR-WHISKEY-NOVEMBER**

   d. FOX: **FOXTROT-OSCAR-X-RAY**

   e. JUMPED: **JULIETTE-UNIFORM-MIKE-PAPA-ECHO-DELTA**

   f. OVER: **OSCAR-VICTOR-ECHO-ROMEO**

   g. LAZY: **LIMA-ALPHA-ZEBRA-YANKEE**

   h. DOG: **DELTA-OSCAR-GOLF**

6. In taking a history and carrying out a physical examination, you go to a lot of trouble to obtain important information about the patient. It would be a shame if that informaton was lost because you couldn't communicate it properly.

AGE, SEX, AND CHIEF COMPLAINT

(1) __F__   The patient is a 60-year-old woman who collapsed in the bathroom while sitting on the toilet.

HISTORY OF THE PRESENT ILLNESS

(2) __J__   She was apparently well until this morning.

(3) __D__   Her daughter says that the patient complained of a severe headache before she collapsed.

PAST MEDICAL HISTORY

(4) __B__   The patient has a history of high blood pressure. (In fact, this is really part of the history of the present illness, if you know what the patient's problem is! She seems to have had a hemorrhagic stroke, so her high blood pressure is one of the predisposing factors.)

(5) __L__   She was hospitalized 6 years ago for an AMI.

(6) __H__   The patient's medications include nitroglycerin and Aldomet.

PHYSICAL ASSESSMENT

State of Consciousness

(7) __E__   The patient was still conscious when we arrived, but she rapidly lost consciousness.

Vital Signs

(8) __A__   Pulse is 50 and regular, respirations are 36 and deep, and blood pressure is 180/126.

Head-to-Toe Survey

(9) __I__ Her left pupil is larger than the right and doesn't react to light.

(10) __K__ Her neck is somewhat stiff.

(11) __C__ The deep tendon reflexes are hyperactive.

TREATMENT GIVEN SO FAR

(12) __G__ We are administering oxygen at 4 liters per minute by nasal cannula.

7. The job of the dispatcher includes

    a. **Extracting information** from panicky callers.

    b. **Directing the right emergency vehicle to the right address.**

    c. **Giving advice** and first-aid instructions by telephone to distraught people.

    d. **Coordinating the response of different agencies** to an emergency.

    e. **Monitoring field communications** to determine if help is needed.

    f. **Keeping written records** of data such as response times.

8. The best way to find out just how difficult the dispatcher's job can be is to step into that job for a few hours. The information you need to try to obtain from the hysterical caller reporting an accident is as follows:
    • What is the **exact location** of the incident?
    • What is the **telephone number** from which the caller is phoning?
    At this point, dispatch the (first) ambulance. ("Unspecified accident at such-and-such address. Details will follow.")

    • What is the **nature of the accident** (e.g., explosion, road accident, train derailment, building collapse)?
    • **How many victims** are there?
    • Are there any **hazards** at the scene, specifically:
       (a) Traffic hazards
       (b) Fire
       (c) Spills
       (d) Downed electrical wires
    • If it is a *transport* accident (motor vehicles, train):
       (a) **How many vehicles** are involved?
       (b) Is it possible to determine what **cargoes** the vehicles are carrying?
    Contact the responding vehicle with additional information. Dispatch additional vehicles and contact other agencies as needed.

9. Radio communications, even those that take place by cellular telephone, are not private, so think before you open your mouth.

    a. **duplex**

    b. **noisy**

    c. **biotelemetry**

    d. **repeater**

    e. **hertz**

    f. **band**

    g. **ring**

    h. **ask**

    i. **November**

    j. **goofs**

    k. **main**

    l. **any**

Secret Message: BEFORE YOU START SPEAKING ON THE RADIO, REMEMBER: ANYONE MAY BE LISTENING.

40
Rescue and Extrication

1. In fact, this jumbled-up collection of rescue tools doesn't belong to a *real* paramedic, because *real* paramedics keep all their gear neat, clean, and organized.

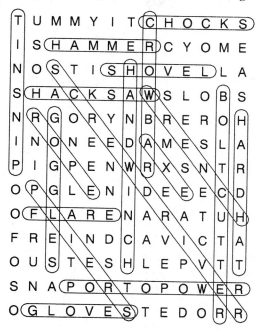

Item	Use in a Rescue Situation
flare	To demarcate a danger zone and caution oncoming traffic
wrench	Disassembly
screwdriver	Disassembly
hacksaw	Cutting through corner posts or steering wheel
pliers	Breaking away steering wheel covering
hammer	Making openings with cutting tools
axe	Cutting roof section
crowbar	Prying open a door
bolt cutter	Cutting padlocks, chains, fences
Portopower	Prying open doors, breaking seats loose
shovel	Removing debris
tin snip	Cutting seat belts
rope	Stabilizing a vehicle
hand winch	Displacing steering column, widening door opening, pulling seat back

Item	Use in a Rescue Situation
chocks	Preventing motion
hard hat	Protects rescuer's head
gloves	Protect rescuer's hands
goggles	Protect rescuer's eyes

2. You will find the hazards at an accident scene only if you know what to look for. At each accident scene, run through a mental checklist of possible hazards before you rush to help the injured.

Hazard	*Action I Would Take to Deal with It*
a. Downed electrical wire	Call for help from the electric company; meanwhile use the PA system to instruct those in the vehicle to stay inside; keep bystanders back.
b. Spilled gasoline	Call for help from the fire department; park the ambulance upstream from the spill; do not use flares in vicinity; forbid smoking.
c. Unstable vehicle	Wait for rescue crew to crib the vehicle before trying to enter it.
d. Traffic hazard	Park ambulance where warning lights will caution oncoming motorists; place reflectors on the road; assign bystanders to direct traffic until police arrive.
e. Hazardous cargo	Call for hazmat assistance; expedite disentanglement and removal of casualties to get them out of hazardous environment.
f. Bystanders	Rope off the area to keep bystanders at least 50 yards back from downed wires, several hundred yards from overturned truck.

3. A lot of extrication is common sense.

   a. The primary function of a paramedic in an extrication is to direct the disentanglement of the patient from the wreckage.
   FALSE because the primary function of the paramedic is to **provide medical care to the patient.** The details of extrication should be left to those whose primary job is extrication.

   b. The most efficient access to a patient in a badly damaged vehicle is usually through a window on the passenger side of the vehicle.
   FALSE because the most efficient access to a patient in a damaged vehicle is **through a door.** Only if it proves impossible to get in through any of the doors should one try to get in through a window.

   c. Care of the accident victim should start even before the victim is removed from the vehicle.
   TRUE.

   d. The paramedic should use a "hot stick" and wear insulated gloves to remove downed wires that are in contact with a disabled vehicle.
   FALSE because the paramedic has **no business fooling around with live electrical wires;** that is a job for experts from the power company.

   e. The best way to prevent the battery in a wrecked vehicle from shorting out and causing an explosion is to disconnect the battery wires.
   FALSE because fiddling with the battery cables is a good way to *cause* an explosion! The best way to prevent the battery from shorting out is simply to **turn off the ignition.**

   f. A disabled vehicle that is upright on four wheels still needs to be stabilized before anyone enters to reach the injured inside.
   TRUE. So long as it's on wheels, the vehicle is capable of rolling (that's what wheels are for, after all).

4. To answer this question, you need to apply a lot of the things you have learned in the past 39 chapters. How well did you do?

   a. The steps to take are as follows:
      (1) **Assess the scene** for
         (a) **Hazards.**
         (b) **Missing victims.** (Could a front-seat passenger who was not wearing a seat belt have been thrown through that shattered front windshield?)
      (2) **Call for help.** At the least, you're going to need the police, the fire department, and perhaps additional help in the extrication.

(3) Once the hazards have been dealt with, **gain access** to the patient. **Try all the doors first.**

(4) **Enter the vehicle and start care,** specifically:

   (a) Open the **airway** by lifting the head into neutral position; if possible, have one of your crew take up a position in the back seat where he or she can **apply a cervical collar** and hold the victim's head in neutral position.

   (b) Administer **oxygen.**

   (c) Quickly **check the chest** for signs of pneumothorax or sucking chest wound.

   (d) **Control external hemorrhage** by direct pressure.

   (e) **Start a large-bore IV** with lactated Ringer's.

   (f) **Cover open wounds.**

   (g) **Splint fractures.**

(5) As soon as disentanglement is complete, **remove the patient on a long backboard,** and transfer him to the ambulance.

(6) **Notify** the receiving hospital.

(7) **Transport.** This is a "load-and-go" situation.

(8) If possible, **start another IV en route.**

b. Once the patient has been transferrred to the hospital, you have to **clean up** the ambulance and all rescue equipment used in the call and **restock all kits** used.

Stop and Review IV

1. Signs of CHOKING include

   a. The victim **cannot speak or make a sound.**

   b. The victim gives the **universal distress signal for choking,** that is, clutches his neck between his thumb and index finger.

   c. The victim's skin becomes dusky or **cyanotic.**

   d. The victim makes **exaggerated, ineffective breathing movements.**

   e. If the obstruction is not immediately relieved, the victim **collapses.**

2. Indications for ENDOTRACHEAL INTUBATION in the field include

   a. **Cardiac arrest**

   b. **Deep coma** from any cause

   c. Imminent **danger of airway obstruction** (e.g., from swelling)

3. To calculate HOW MUCH OXYGEN IS REMAINING, you need to use the following equation:

$$\text{Duration of flow in minutes} = \frac{(\text{gauge pressure} - 200 \text{ psi}) \times \text{cylinder constant}}{\text{flow rate (in L/min)}}$$

$$= \frac{(800 \text{ psi} - 200 \text{ psi}) \times 0.26 \text{ L/psi}}{10 \text{ L/min}}$$

$$= \textbf{15.6 minutes}$$

4. INDICATIONS FOR ADMINISTERING OXYGEN include the following

   a. Any condition that produces *fluid in the alveoli,* such as **pulmonary edema, pneumonia,** or **near drowning**

   b. Any condition that produces *collapse of alveoli* (atelectasis), such as **airway obstruction, rib fracture, spinal cord injury, head injury, respiratory depression from overdose,** or **pneumothorax**

   c. Any situation in which *gases other than air occupy the alveoli,* such as **smoke inhalation** or **inhalation of toxic gases**

   d. **Respiratory or cardiac arrest**

   e. **Shock**

   f. **Dyspnea** or **respiratory distress**

   g. **Chest pain**

   h. **Stroke**

   There are **no contraindications** to administering oxygen.

5. How many parts of the human body were you able to locate in the box?

CARDIOVASCULAR SYSTEM

aorta
atrium
vein

NERVOUS SYSTEM

brain
ear
eye
pia mater
vagus

MUSCULOSKELETAL SYSTEM

acetabulum	orbit
atlas	pubis
carpal	rib
femur	tarsal
fibula	tibia
hip	ulna
ischium	

URINARY SYSTEM

kidney
ureter

RESPIRATORY SYSTEM

bronchus
larynx
lung
pleura
trachea

GASTROINTESTINAL SYSTEM

anus	ileum
colon	liver
duodenum	pancreas
gallbladder	stomach

FEMALE REPRODUCTIVE SYSTEM

fallopian tube	ovary
labia	uterus

6. The symptoms and signs of HYPOVOLEMIC SHOCK include

   a. **Restlessness** and **anxiety**

   b. **Thirst**

   c. **Nausea** and sometimes **vomiting**

   d. **Cold, clammy skin**

   e. **Weak, rapid pulse**

   f. **Shallow, rapid breathing**

   g. **Changes in the state of consciousness**

   h. **Fall in blood pressure**

7. The best way to remember the DRUGS THAT MAY BE GIVEN BY ENDOTRACHEAL TUBE is by the mnemonic NAVEL:

   N Narcan
   A Atropine
   V Valium
   E Epinephrine
   L Lidocaine

8. Our patient is a 52-year-old man with chest pain.

   a. There's another mnemonic for taking the HISTORY OF THE PRESENT ILLNESS when the chief complaint is *pain:* PQRST-A.

   P What **provoked** the pain? What brought it on? What makes it worse? What makes it better?
   Q What is the **quality** of the pain? What does it feel like?
   R In what **region** of the body is the pain, and where does it **radiate?**
   S How **severe** is the pain?
   T What was the **timing** of the pain, that is, the chronology of the patient's symptoms? What happened first? What happened next?
   A Are there any **associated symptoms,** such as sweating, nausea, dyspnea?

   b. Here is the patient's ECG rhythm strip:

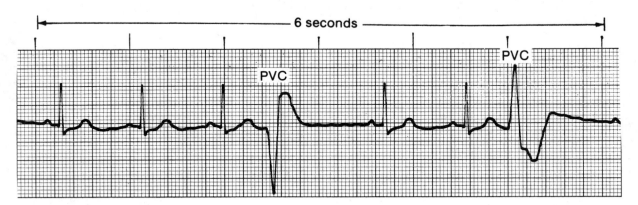

   The RHYTHM is essentially **regular.**
   The RATE is **70 per minute.**
   P WAVES are **present.** There is a QRS after every P wave, but **not every QRS is preceded by a P wave.**
   The P–R INTERVAL is **0.16 second.**
   The QRS complexes are **both normal and abnormal.**
   The name of the rhythm is **normal sinus rhythm with multifocal premature ventricular contractions (PVCs).**
   Treatment should include **oxygen** and intravenous **lidocaine,** 1 mg per kilogram bolus followed by an infusion of 2 mg per minute.

9. When dealing with the victims of trauma, the paramedic must pay close attention to mechanisms of injury. Especially when the victim is unconscious, the mechanism of injury may be the *only* clue to what injuries the patient sustained.

Vehicular Damage	*Look for These Injuries:*
Deformed steering column	**Tracheal fracture, sternal or rib fractures, flail chest, myocardial contusion, pericardial tamponade, pneumothorax, hemothorax, aortic tear**
Driver's door staved in	**Hip fracture**
Front windshield cracked	**Brain injury with increased intracranial pressure; scalp and facial cuts**
Dashboard on passenger side deformed	**Fractured patella; dislocated knee, femoral fracture, dislocated hip**

10. The methods for CONTROLLING EXTERNAL HEMORRHAGE are

   a. **Direct pressure** (the most effective method)

   b. **Elevation** of a bleeding extremity

   c. **Pressure point control** over the supplying artery

   d. **Splinting** a bleeding limb

   e. Application of a **tourniquet** (last resort)

11. Dealing with the unconscious "drunk" is the scenario in which mistakes are most frequently made both in the field and in the emergency room.

   a. The mnemonic for the CAUSES OF UNCONSCIOUSNESS is AEIOU-TIPS:

A	**Alcohol**
E	**Epilepsy**
I	**Insulin** overdose (i.e., hypoglycemia)
O	**Overdose** with depressant drugs
U	**Uremia**
*T	**Trauma** (the most likely cause in this case)
I	**Infection** (e.g., meningitis)
P	**Psychogenic**
S	**Stroke**

   b. This patient must be assumed to have suffered head trauma. He has **signs of increasing intracranial pressure** (high blood pressure, slow pulse, unequal pupils). Furthermore, he has no wallet, suggesting that he was mugged and robbed. The steps in treating a victim of head trauma are as follows:

   (1) Open the **airway** with **cervical spine precautions. Intubate** the trachea as soon as possible, since the patient is deeply unconscious and cannot protect his airway.

   (2) Administer **oxygen.** If the respiratory rate falls, assist ventilations to maintain a respiratory rate of 20 per minute.

   (3) Start an **IV to keep a vein open** in case you have to administer medications in a hurry.

   (4) So long as you are not absolutely sure of the cause of this patient's coma, give **thiamine** (100 mg) and **50% dextrose** (25 gm) IV.

   (5) **Immobilize** the patient on a backboard.

   (6) Do not allow the patient to get overheated.

   (7) **Monitor** cardiac rhythm and vital signs.

   (8) Be prepared to deal with seizures.

   (9) **Notify** the receiving hospital of a likely head injury and the possible need for neurosurgical intervention.

   (10) **Transport** to a hospital that has neurosurgical capability.

12. Some injuries frequently come in pairs, so when you find one member of the pair, you need to look for the other.

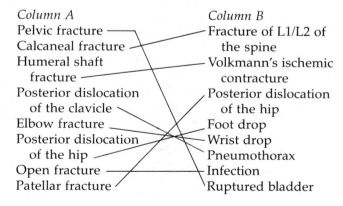

Column A	*Column B*
Pelvic fracture	Fracture of L1/L2 of the spine
Calcaneal fracture	Volkmann's ischemic contracture
Humeral shaft fracture	Posterior dislocation of the hip
Posterior dislocation of the clavicle	Foot drop
Elbow fracture	Wrist drop
Posterior dislocation of the hip	Pneumothorax
Open fracture	Infection
Patellar fracture	Ruptured bladder

13. LOAD-AND-GO SITUATIONS include the following

   a. Any case in which you are **unable to establish a secure airway**

   b. **Respiratory arrest**

   c. **Open pneumothorax**

   d. **Tension pneumothorax**

   e. **Flail chest**

   f. Full **cardiopulmonary arrest**

   g. **Shock**

   h. **Uncontrollable bleeding**

   i. **Unconsciousness after injury**

   j. **Deteriorating level of consciousness**

   k. Signs of **increasing intracranial pressure**

14. SIGNS OF RESPIRATORY DISTRESS include

   a. **Nasal flaring**

   b. **Tracheal tugging**

   c. **Retractions** of the intercostal muscles on inhalation

   d. Use of **accessory muscles** in the neck to assist breathing

   e. **Paradoxical respiratory movement** (i.e., the epigastrium is sucked in with inhalation rather than bulging out)

15. This young asthmatic is in trouble. His attack has been going on all day. Now he is showing a number of *danger signs* (Did you notice them?): tachycardia, tachypnea, pulsus paradoxus, and a nearly silent chest. For all practical purposes, then, he is in STATUS ASTHMATICUS.

   a. The steps in prehospital treatment are as follows:

     (1) Administer **oxygen.**
     (2) Start a **large-bore IV,** and run in normal saline.
     (3) Give 1 to 2 puffs of **albuterol** by metered-dose inhaler with a spacer.
     (4) If there is no response to albuterol, consult medical command as to what other drug(s) to give. You may be asked to give **terbutaline,** 0.25 mg SQ— but it would be wise to take a look at the monitor first!
     (5) **Monitor** cardiac rhythm.

   b. Here is the patient's ECG rhythm strip:

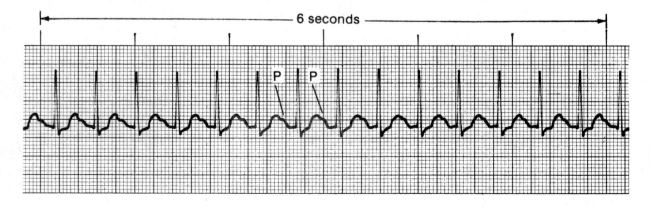

The RHYTHM is **regular.**
The RATE is **140 per minute.**
P WAVES are **present** preceding every QRS.
The P–R INTERVAL is **0.16 second.**
The QRS complexes are **normal.**
The name of the rhythm is **sinus tachycardia.**
Treatment is directed at the underlying cause, which is probably the stress of the asthmatic attack plus a near overdose of sympathomimetic drugs. It's going to be a trade-off in this patient between his asthma and his dysrhythmia, for most of the drugs we need to give for the asthmatic attack will worsen the dysrhythmia. Careful titration of medications will be required, and that is best accomplished in an intensive care unit, not in the field. Therefore, it will probably be best simply to transport this patient expeditiously, with oxygen and fluids en route.

16. The woman with shortness of breath has classic symptoms and signs of CONGESTIVE HEART FAILURE (CHF).

    a. The prehospital treatment is as follows:

       (1) Administer **oxygen by demand valve.**
       (2) Keep the patient **sitting up with legs dangling.**
       (3) Start an **IV lifeline with D5/W to keep the vein open.**
       (4) **Monitor** cardiac rhythm.
       (5) Give **nitroglycerin,** 0.4 mg SL.
       (6) Give **furosemide,** 20 mg by IV bolus.

    b. Here is the patient's ECG rhythm strip:

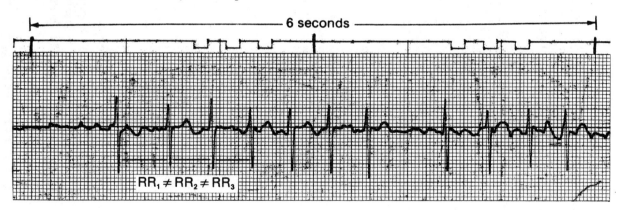

The RHYTHM is **irregularly irregular.**
The RATE is **110 per minute.**
P WAVES are **absent.**
The P–R INTERVAL is **nonexistent.**
The QRS complexes are **normal.**
The name of the rhythm is **atrial fibrillation.**
Treatment should be for the underlying cause (the patient's CHF). At the hospital, the woman will probably be given **digitalis,** both for her heart failure and to slow down the ventricular response to the atrial fibrillation.

17. This 78-year-old woman with a "possible stroke" is in fact suffering from HY-POTHERMIA. *You* may not have noticed that the house is cold because you are warmly dressed for the autumn and are exerting yourself carrying all your equipment. But the patient's cold skin and the fruity smell on her breath should have tipped you off to something amiss. The moral of the story is that a "possible stroke" may be something else altogether. DON'T TAKE ANYTHING FOR GRANTED.

   a. The steps of treatment are as follows:

     (1) Ask the patient's daughter to prepare a **warm, sweet drink,** such as hot chocolate, for her mother while you get ready to transport.

     (2) Take **hot water bottles** or chemical hot packs, wrap them in towels, and place them in the patient's armpits and over her groin.

     (3) Wrap the patient up well in **insulating materials,** then blankets.

     (4) **Monitor** cardiac rhythm.

     (5) **Transport** the patient to the hospital. (At a distance of only 10 minutes from the hospital, there is no need for you to try to rewarm the patient at the scene.)

   b. Here is the patient's ECG rhythm strip:

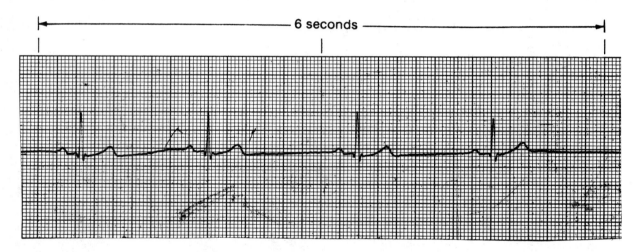

The RHYTHM is **slightly irregular.**
The RATE is **40 per minute.**
P WAVES are **present** and precede every QRS.
The P–R INTERVAL is **0.20 second.**
The QRS complexes are **normal.**
The name of the rhythm is **sinus bradycardia.**
Treatment is **atropine, 0.5 mg** IV, since she is symptomatic.

   c. The treatment of this patient's dysrhythmia required the use of **atropine,** so we need to know the pharmacology of that drug thoroughly.

     (1) The INDICATIONS for giving atropine are
       (a) **Sinus bradycardia** accompanied by PVCs or hypotension
       (b) Type I (Wenckebach) **second-degree block with bradycardia**
       (c) Third-degree heart block in the context of *inferior* AMI.
       (d) Some cases of **asystole**
       (e) **Organophosphate poisoning**
     (2) The CONTRAINDICATIONS to giving atropine are as follows:
       (a) **Atrial flutter or fibrillation** with a **rapid ventricular response.**
       (b) **Type II second-degree block.**

(c) **Complete** (third-degree) **heart block.**
(d) **Glaucoma.**
(e) Atropine should be given with extreme caution in **acute myocardial infarction.**
(3) The SIDE EFFECTS of atropine include
(a) **Blurred vision, headache, pupillary dilatation**
(b) **Dry mouth, thirst**
(c) **Flushing**
(d) **Difficulty urinating**
(4) The DOSAGE for bradycardia is **0.5 to 1.0 mg IV.** That dosage may be repeated at 5-minute intervals up to a total dosage of 2.0 mg.

18. We hold these truths to be self-evident:

a. A hypoglycemic person may appear to be drunk.
TRUE. And if he's mistaken for "just a drunk" and hauled off to police lockup to "sleep it off," he may just sleep forever.

b. A patient who has fainted should be helped into a sitting position.
FALSE! It was Nature's wisdom that sent the patient into the recumbent position, enabling the heart to perfuse the brain without having to pump uphill. Don't try to outsmart Mother Nature. *Keep* the patient recumbent.

c. If a patient with a stroke is unable to speak, he or she is also unable to understand what others are saying.
FALSE. You must assume that the patient can understand every word you say, so don't make the mistake of speaking as if the patient cannot hear you. Careless remarks can do a lot of damage.

d. The induction of vomiting is contraindicated in a patient who has swallowed a volatile hydrocarbon like lighter fluid.
TRUE. Induction of vomiting increases the danger that the volatile substance will find its way into the patient's lungs. If you *have* to get the substance out (e.g., when a patient is symptomatic from taking a large volume of something like kerosene), first intubate the trachea, then pass a nasogastric tube, and withdraw the fluid through the tube.

e. The best way to avoid contracting or spreading a communicable disease is to wash your hands after every call.
TRUE. TRUE. TRUE.

f. Elderly patients are usually hypochondriacs.
FALSE. FALSE. FALSE. To the contrary, elderly patients are more likely *not* to complain about significant symptoms than to complain about insignificant ones.

19. ALCOHOLICS ARE MORE SUSCEPTIBLE than nondrinkers to a whole variety of injuries and medical problems:

a. **Subdural hematoma** from falls

b. **Gastrointestinal bleeding**

c. **Pancreatitis**

d. **Hypoglycemia**

e. **Pneumonia**

f. **Burns**

g. **Hypothermia**

h. **Seizures**

i. **Cardiac dysrhythmias**

j. **Cancer**

20. CLUES TO CHILD ABUSE include

a. **Delays in seeking care** for an injured child

b. **Discrepancies** in the story of what happened to the child

c. **Multiple emergency room visits** for injuries to the child

d. A child who is **apathetic and doesn't cry**

e. A child who **does not turn to his parents for comfort**

f. A child who is **poorly nourished and poorly cared for**

g. A child who has **multiple bruises**

h. A child who has **old and new bruises**

i. A child with **suspicious burns** (e.g., cigarette burns, scalds to the buttocks)

j. A child with **rib fractures**

k. Any **fracture in an infant** under 1 year of age

21. RISK FACTORS FOR POSTPARTUM HEMORRHAGE include

    a. **Prolonged labor**

    b. **Retained products of conception**

    c. **Grand multiparity**

    d. **Twin pregnancy**

    e. **Placenta previa**

    f. **Full bladder**

22. The woman with abdominal pain has given a fairly typical history for RUP-TURED ECTOPIC PREGNANCY. The classic triad—amenorrhea, abdominal pain, and vaginal bleeding—is present. The woman therefore needs to be treated expectantly for shock.

    a. The steps in treatment are as follows:

       (1) Administer **oxygen.**
       (2) Keep the patient **recumbent.**
       (3) Start a **large-bore IV** with lactated Ringer's, and **run it wide open.**
       (4) **Keep the patient warm.**
       (5) **Monitor** cardiac rhythm.
       (6) **Notify** the receiving hospital of the situation.
       (7) **Transport** to a hospital with 24-hour surgical capability.
       (8) **Recheck vital signs** frequently en route.

    b. Here is the patient's ECG rhythm strip:

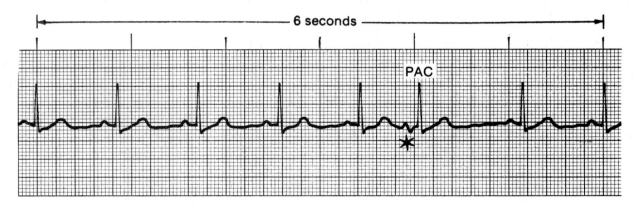

The RHYTHM is essentially **regular.**
The RATE is **70 per minute.**
P WAVES are **present** and precede every QRS.
The P–R INTERVAL is **0.16 second.**
The QRS complexes are **normal.**
The name of the rhythm is **normal sinus rhythm with a premature atrial contraction (PAC).**
Treatment is **not required.**

23. Here is the ECG rhythm strip of the 53-year-old woman who complains of "heaviness" in her chest:

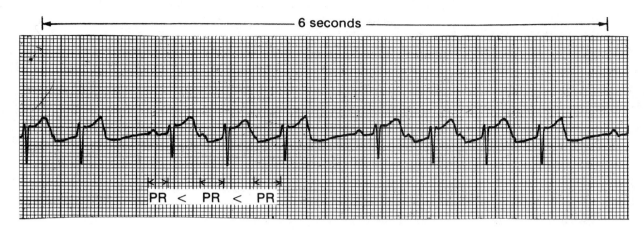

The RHYTHM is **irregular.**

The RATE is **80 per minute.**

P WAVES are **present.** There is a P wave before every QRS, but **not every P wave is followed by a QRS.**

The P–R INTERVAL is **variable;** it gets longer and longer until there is a dropped beat.

The QRS complexes are **normal.**

The name of the rhythm is **Wenckebach second-degree AV block.**

Treatment is **not required** so long as the rate is this rapid.

24. It probably isn't such a good idea for a 75-year-old with coronary artery disease to be changing the tire on his car. It may have been that exertion that precipitated this episode.

a. Here is the patient's 12-lead ECG:

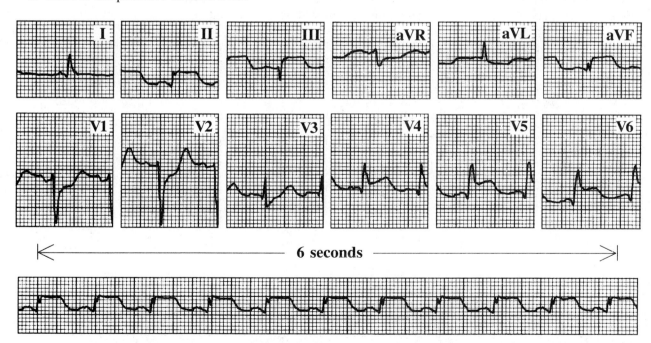

The RHYTHM is **regular.**

The RATE is **110 per minute.**

P WAVES are **present** before every QRS, and there is a QRS after every P wave.

The P–R INTERVAL is **0.13 second.**

QRS complexes are **borderline** (in V_4 through V_6, they are widened).

The rhythm is called **normal sinus rhythm.**

There are small Q WAVES in leads V_4 through V_6, which may represent a previous AMI.

The S–T SEGMENTS are **elevated in leads II, III, aVF and V_4 through V_6.** There are reciprocal changes (S–T depression) in aVR, as one would expect. There is also S–T depression in leads V_1 and V_2, which may be a reciprocal change or may reflect a process in the posterior wall of the heart.

There is no abnormal T WAVE INVERSION (inversion of T waves is normal in lead aVR, remember?).

The portions of the heart affected are the **inferior and lateral walls.**

The pathophysiologic process is **injury.**

b. This patient may well be a candidate for thrombolytic therapy—we don't have enough information about him to decide. Certainly his age should not rule out giving thrombolytic therapy; in fact, some studies suggest that the elderly are more likely to benefit from "clot-busters" than younger patients. His elevated blood pressure may simply be a reaction to his chest pain rather than a sign of chronic hypertension. So we need to ask about the medical history, medications, recent surgery, and so forth.

25. The waitress may or may not have a cardiac problem, but in this instance the ECG is not going to help you very much in making that determination.

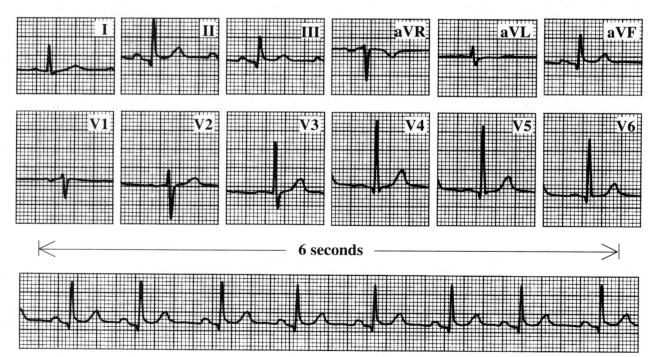

The RHYTHM is **slightly irregular.**
The RATE is **80 to 90 per minute.**
P WAVES are **present** before every QRS, and there is a QRS after every P wave.
The P–R INTERVAL is **0.17 second.**
The QRS complexes are **normal.**
The name of the rhythm is **sinus arrhythmia.**
There are no Q WAVES deeper than 2 mm.
The S–T SEGMENTS are **normal.**
There is no abnormal T WAVE INVERSION.
This is a **normal ECG.**

26. Elderly patients suffering an acute myocardial infarction may not present with the classic picture of crushing chest pain. This patient is a case in point.

    a. Here is the patient's 12-lead ECG:

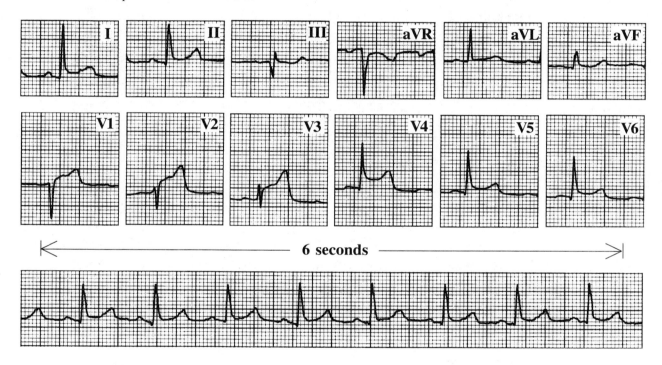

The RHYTHM is **regular.**
The RATE is **88 per minute.**
P WAVES are **present** before every QRS complex, and there is a QRS after every P wave.
The P–R INTERVAL is **0.16 second.**
QRS complexes are **normal.**
The name of the rhythm is **normal sinus rhythm.**
There are deep Q WAVES in **lead III.**
The S–T SEGMENTS are markedly **elevated in leads V_1 through V_4.**
There is **no T WAVE INVERSION.**
The portion of the heart affected by the acute process is the **anterior wall.** (The Q waves in lead III suggest there may be some old damage to the inferior wall.)
The pathophysiologic process is **injury.**

    b. The steps in treating this patient are as follows:
       (1) Put the patient mentally and physically **at ease** (calm handling; semirecumbent position).
       (2) Administer **oxygen** right away (you should have done so even before you took the 12-lead ECG!).

(3) Record a set of **vital signs,** and repeat the measurements every 5 minutes.

(4) Provide **pain relief.** There do not seem to be any contraindications in this patient to giving morphine, which is the drug of choice.

(5) Once you have the results of the 12-lead ECG, **notify the receiving hospital** of the patient's story, vital signs, ECG findings, and your estimated time of arrival.

(6) **Transport expeditiously,** without sirens if possible. Administer half an aspirin tablet and start a magnesium sulfate infusion en route to the hospital if those interventions are part of your local protocol.

27. Once again, we have an elderly patient who does not display typical signs of what may be a serious cardiac event. The moral of the story: Obtain an ECG in *every* elderly patient who seems ill, regardless of the chief complaint.

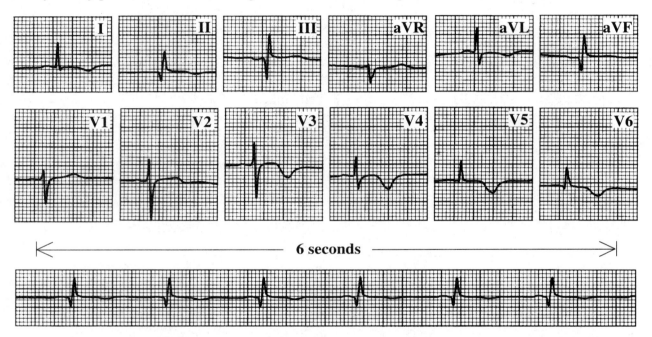

The RHYTHM is **regular.**

The RATE is **70 per minute.**

P WAVES are **present** (although hard to see in some leads) before every QRS complex, and there is a QRS after every P wave.

The P–R INTERVAL is **0.12** second.

The QRS complexes are **normal.**

The name of the rhythm is **normal sinus rhythm.**

There are Q WAVES deeper than 2 mm in **leads II, III, and aVF.**

There are marked T WAVE INVERSIONS in **leads V₃ through V₆.** The T waves are also inverted in **leads I, II, and aVL.**

The portions of the heart affected are the **inferior and anterolateral walls.** (Q waves in the inferior wall, T wave inversion in the anterolateral wall.)

The pathologic process is **infarction.** Without seeing the patient's previous ECG, it is hard to know how recent are the changes that we see in the current ECG. The inferior wall infarction might have happened this week or 10 years ago. The anterolateral wall changes are probably newer, but again, without reference to a previous ECG, it is very difficult to know for sure. The patient's physician, who *did* have access to the previous ECG, was apparently impressed enough to call for an ambulance. Try to obtain a copy of that previous ECG to take with the patient to the hospital.

28. Perhaps the most important message to take away from this book is our thought for the day.

    a. **tachypnea**

    b. **hyperemia**

    c. **kidney**

    d. **bronchus**

    e. **telemetry**

    f. **paresis**

    g. **mesentery**

    h. **otitis**

    i. **emotion**

    j. **pitter patter**

    k. **fast**

    l. **osmosis**

    m. **instant**

    n. **stat**

    Secret Message: THE MOST IMPORTANT PERSON IN ANY EMS SYSTEM IS THE PATIENT. MAKE THE PATIENT'S BEST INTERESTS YOUR FIRST PRIORITY.